THE DIDACHE

Society of Biblical Literature

Early Christianity and Its Literature

Gail R. O'Day, Editor

Warren Carter
Beverly Roberts Gaventa
David Horrell
Judith M. Lieu
Margaret Y. MacDonald

Number 14

THE DIDACHE

A MISSING PIECE OF THE PUZZLE IN EARLY CHRISTIANITY

Edited by
Jonathan A. Draper and Clayton N. Jefford

SBL Press
Atlanta

Copyright © 2015 by SBL Press

All rights reserved. No part of this work may be reproduced or transmitted in any form or by any means, electronic or mechanical, including photocopying and recording, or by means of any information storage or retrieval system, except as may be expressly permitted by the 1976 Copyright Act or in writing from the publisher. Requests for permission should be addressed in writing to the Rights and Permissions Office, SBL Press, 825 Houston Mill Road, Atlanta, GA 30329 USA.

Library of Congress Cataloging-in-Publication Data

The didache : a missing piece of the puzzle in early Christianity / edited by Jonathan A. Draper and Clayton N. Jefford.
      p. cm. — (Society of Biblical Literature early Christianity and its literature ; Number 14)
   Includes bibliographical references and index.
   ISBN ISBN 978-1-62837-048-5 (paper binding : alk. paper) — ISBN 978-1-62837-049-2 (electronic format) — ISBN 978-1-62837-050-8 (hardcover binding : alk. paper)
   1. Didache. 2. Christian ethics—History—Early church, ca. 30-600. 3. Church—History of doctrines—Early church, ca. 30–600. I. Draper, Jonathan A. II. Jefford, Clayton N.
   BS2940.T5D525 2015
   270.1—dc23   2014036281

Printed on acid-free, recycled paper conforming to
ANSI/NISO Z39.48-1992 (R1997) and ISO 9706:1994
standards for paper permanence.

Contents

Abbreviations ix

Introduction: Dynamics, Methodologies, and Progress in
　Didache Studies
　　Clayton N. Jefford 1

Part 1: Approaches to the Text as a Whole

Identity in the Didache Community
　Stephen Finlan 17

Authority and Perspective in the Didache
　Clayton N. Jefford 33

The Distress Signals of Didache Research: Quest for a Viable Future
　Aaron Milavec 59

Children and Slaves in the Community of the Didache and the
　Two Ways Tradition
　　Jonathan A. Draper 85

Reflections on the Didache and Its Community: A Response
　Andrew Gregory 123

Part 2: Leadership and Liturgy

Baptism and Holiness: Two Requirements Authorizing Participation
　in the Didache's Eucharist
　　Huub van de Sandt 139

The Lord's Prayer (Didache 8) at the Faultline of Judaism
and Christianity
    Peter J. Tomson 165

Pray "In This Way": Formalized Speech in Didache 9–10
    Jonathan Schwiebert 189

The Ritual Meal in Didache 9–10: Progress in Understanding
    John J. Clabeaux 209

Response to Essays on Leadership and Liturgy in the Didache
    Joseph G. Mueller, S.J. 231

Part 3: The Didache and Matthew

Before and after Matthew
    E. Bruce Brooks 247

The Sectio Evangelica (Didache 1.3b–2.1) and Performance
    Perttu Nikander 287

The Didache and Oral Theory
    Nancy Pardee 311

From the Sermon on the Mount to the Didache
    John W. Welch 335

The Lord Jesus and His Coming in the Didache
    Murray J. Smith 363

Matthew and the Didache: Some Comments on the Comments
    Joseph Verheyden 409

Part 4: The Didache and Other Early Christian Texts

Without Decree: Pagan Sacrificial Meat and the Early History
of the Didache
    Matti Myllykoski 429

Another Gospel: Exploring Early Christian Diversity with Paul
and the Didache
   Taras Khomych 455

The First Century Two Ways Catechesis and Hebrews 6:1–6
   Matthew Larsen and Michael Svigel 477

The Didache and Revelation
   Alan J. P. Garrow 497

The Didache as a Source for the Reconstruction of Early Christianity:
A Response
   D. Jeffrey Bingham 515

Conclusion: Missing Pieces in the Puzzle or Wild Goose Chase?
A Retrospect and Prospect
   Jonathan A. Draper 529

Bibliography...545

Contributors..589

Index of Primary Texts 595
Index of Modern Authors..625

Abbreviations

1. Ancient

1QS	Rule of the Community from Qumran, Dead Sea Scrolls
ʻAbod. Zar	Avodah Zarah
Acts Pil.	Acts of Pilate
Ag. Ap.	*Against Apion*, Josephus
A.J.	*Antiquitates judaicae*, Josephus
Apoc. Pet.	Apocalypse of Peter
Apos. Con.	Apostolic Constitutions and Canons
Apol.	*Apology*, Aristides
Apol.	*Apology*, Justin Martyr
Apol.	*Apology*, Tertullian
b.	Babylonian Talmud
Bar.	Baruch
Barn.	Epistle of Barnabas
B. Meṣ.	Baba Meṣiʻa
Bek.	Bekhorot
Ber.	Berakhot
B.J.	*Bellum judaicum*, Josephus
Cat. Luc.	*Catenae in Lucam*, Cyril of Alexandria
Cels.	*Contra Celsum*, Origen
Clem.	1–2 Clement
Comm. Matt.	*Commentarium in evangelium Matthaei*, Origen
Comp.	*De compositione verborum*, Dionysius of Halicarnassus
De aleat.	*De aleatoribus*, Pseudo-Cyprian
De or.	*De oratore*, Cicero
Dial.	*Dialogus cum Tryphone*, Justin Martyr
Did.	Didache
Doctr.	Doctrina apostolorum
ʻEd.	Eduyyot

Eloc.	*De elocutione* (*Peri hermēneias*), Demetrius
En.	Enoch
Esd	Esdras
Ep.	*Epistula*, Augustine
Ep. Aris.	Epistle of Aristides
Ep. fest.	*Epistulae festales*, Athanasius
Eph.	*Epistle to the Ephesians*, Ignatius of Antioch
Exod. Rab.	Exodus Rabbah
Gos. Eb.	Gospel of the Ebionites
Gos. Pet.	Gospel of Peter
Gos. Thom.	Gospel of Thomas
Haer.	*Adversus haereses*, Irenaeus
Hag.	Hagigah
Hist.	*General History*, Polybius
Hist. eccl.	*Historia ecclesiastica*, Eusebius of Caesarea
Hom.	*Homilies*, Pseudo-Clement
Hul.	Hullin
Inst.	*Institutio oratoria*, Quintilian
Jejun.	*De jejunio adversus psychicos*, Tertullian
Jub.	Jubilees
Kallah Rab.	Kallah Rabbati
LAB	Liber antiquitatum biblicarum, Pseudo-Philo
Let. Aris.	Letter of Aristeas
Liv. Pro. Dan.	Lives of the Prophets, Daniel
LXX	Septuagint
m.	Mishnah
Maʿaś. Š.	Maʿaśer Šeni
Magn.	*Epistle to the Magnesians*, Ignatius of Antioch
Mand.	Mandate, Shepherd of Hermas
Marc.	*Adversus Marcionem*, Tertullian
Meg.	Megillah
Mem.	*Memorabilia*, Xenophon
Miqw.	Miqwaʾot
Mon.	*De monogamia*, Tertullian
MS(S)	manuscript(s)
MT	Masoretic Text
Ned.	Nedarim
Num. Rab.	Numbers Rabbah
Oct.	*Octavius*, Minucius Felix

Odes Sol.	Odes of Solomon
OG	Old Greek
Op.	*Opera et dies*, Hesiod
Or.	*De oratione*, Origen
Paed.	*Paedagogus*, Clement of Alexandria
Pan.	*Panarion* (*Adversus haereses*), Epiphanius
PGM	Papyri graecae magicae: Die griechischen Zauberpapyri. Edited by K. Preisendanz. Berlin, 1928.
Pesah.	Pesahim
Pirqe R. El.	Pirqe Rabbi Eliezer
P.Oxy.	Oxyrhynchus papyrus
Pss. Sol.	Psalms of Solomon
Pud.	*De pudicitia*, Tertullian
Recog.	*Recognitions*, Pseudo-Clement
Rhet.	*Rhetorica*, Aristotle
Rhet. Her.	*Rhetorica ad Herennium*, Quintilian
Rom.	*Epistle to the Romans*, Ignatius of Antioch
Roš Haš.	Roš Haššanah
Sanh.	Sanhedrin
Sabb.	Shabbat
Sebu.	Shevu'ot
Sim.	Similitude, from Shepherd of Hermas
Smyrn.	*To the Smyrnaeans*, Ignatius
Spec.	*De specialibus legibus* 1–4, Philo
Spect.	*De spectaculis*, Tertullian
Strom.	*Stromata*, Clement of Alexandria
Symb.	*Commentarius in symbolum apostolorum*, Rufinus
Syntagma	Syntagma doctrinae
t.	tosefta
T. Abr.	Testament of Abraham
T. Ash.	Testament of Asher
Ta'an.	Ta'anıt
Tg.	Targum
Tem.	Temurah
Vesp.	*Vespasianus*, Suetonius
Virg.	*De virginitate*, Pseudo-Athanasius
y.	Jerusalem Talmud
Yebam.	Yebamot

2. Modern

AB	Anchor Bible
ABD	*Anchor Bible Dictionary.* Edited by David N. Freedman. 6 vols. New York: Yale University Press, 1992.
ABRL	Anchor Bible Reference Library
ACCS	Ancient Christian Commentary on Scripture
ACW	Ancient Christian Writers. 1946—
AF	The Apostolic Fathers: A Translation and Commentary
AGJU	Arbeiten zur Geschichte des antiken Judentums und des Urchristentums
AJ	*The Asbury Journal*
AJEC	Ancient Judaism and Early Christianity
AJP	*American Journal of Philosophy*
AJT	*American Journal of Theology*
AK	Arbeiten zur Kirchengeschichte
ANRW	*Aufstieg und Niedergang der römischen Welt: Geschichte und Kultur Roms im Spiegel der neueren Forschung.* Part 2, *Principat.* Edited by H. Temporini and W. Haasse. Berlin: de Gruyter, 1972–.
ATANT	Abhandlungen zur Theologie des Alten und Neuen Testaments
AThR	*Anglican Theological Review*
AYBC	The Anchor Yale Bible Commentary
BAC	The Bible in Ancient Christianity
BARIS	*Biblical Archaeology Review International Series*
BDAG	Bauer, W., F. W. Danker, W. F. Arndt, and F. W. Gingrich. *Greek-English Lexicon of the New Testament and Other Early Christian Literature.* 3rd ed. Chicago, 1999.
BDR	F. Blass, A. Debrunner, and F. Rehkopf. *Grammatik des neutestamentlichen Griechisch.* 16th ed. Göttingen, 1984.
BETL	Bibliotheca ephemeridum theologicarum lovaniensium
BHT	Beiträge zur historischen Theologie
Bib	*Biblica*
BJRL	*Bulletin of the John Rylands University Library of Manchester*
BPC	Biblical Performance Criticism
BRBS	Brill's Readers in Biblical Studies
BS	The Biblical Seminar

BSac	*Bibliotheca sacra*
BTB	*Biblical Theology Bulletin*
BTS	Biblical Tools and Studies
BVB	Beitäge zum Verstehen der Bibel
BWANT	Beiträge zur Wissenschaft vom Neuen Testament
BZNW	Beihefte zur Zeitschrift für die neutestamentliche Wissenschaft
CBET	Contributions to Biblical Exegesis and Theology
CBQ	*Catholic Biblical Quarterly*
CJA	Christianity and Judaism in Antiquity
ConBNT	Coniectanea neotestamentica (Coniectanea biblica: New Testament Series)
CQS	Companion to the Qumran Scrolls
CRINT	Compendia rerum iudaicarum ad Novum Testamentum
CT	Corpus Tannaiticum
CUASCA	The Catholic University of America Studies in Christian Antiquity
CurBS	*Currents in Research: Biblical Studies*
dGL	de Gruyter Lehrbuch
DRev	*Downside Review*
Ebib	Etudes bibliques
ECB	*Eerdmans Commentary on the Bible*. Edited by James D. G. Dunn and John W. Rogerson. Grand Rapids: Eerdmans, 2003.
ECS	Early Christian Studies
EDB	*Eerdmans Dictionary of the Bible*. Edited by David Noel Freedman. Grand Rapids: Eerdmans, 2000.
EDEJ	*Eerdmans Dictionary of Early Judaism*. Edited by John J. Collins and Daniel C. Harlow. Grand Rapids: Eerdmans, 2010.
EDNT	*Exegetical Dictionary of the New Testament*. Edited by Hortz Balz and Gerhard Schneider. ET. Grand Rapids: Eerdmans, 1990–1993.
EHPR	Etudes d'histoire et de philosophie religieuses
EKKNT	Evangelisch-katholischer Kommentar zum Neuen Testament
EuroJS	*European Journal of Sociology*
EuroJSP	*European Journal of Social Psychology*
FC	Fontes christiani

FRLANT	Forschungen zur Religion und Literatur des Alten und Neuen Testaments
GTA	Göttinger theologischer Arbeiten
HKNT	Handkommentar zum Neuen Testament
HNT	Handbuch zum Neuen Testament
HNT.E	Handbuch zum Neuen Testament. Ergänzungsband
HSCL	Harvard Studies in Comparative Literature
HTKNT	Herders theologischer Kommentar zum Neuen Testament
HTR	*Harvard Theological Review*
HTS.TS	*HTS Teologiese Studies/Theological Studies*
IB	*Interpreter's Bible*. Edited by G. A. Buttrick et al. 12 vols. New York, 1951–1957.
IBC	Interpretation: A Bible Commentary for Teaching and Preaching
ICC	International Critical Commentary
Int	*Interpretation*
JAC	Jahrbuch für Antike und Christentum
JAC.E	Jahrbuch für Antike und Christentum. Ergänzungsband
JBL	*Journal of Biblical Literature*
JCC	Jewish Culture and Contexts
JCP	Jewish and Christian Perspectives
JECS	*Journal of Early Christian Studies*
JETS	*Journal of the Evangelical Theological Society*
JHC	*Journal of Higher Criticism*
JHS	*Journal of Hellenic Studies*
JJS	*Journal of Jewish Studies*
JP	*Jerusalem Perspective*
JQR	*Jewish Quarterly Review*
JRitSt	*Journal of Ritual Studies*
JSIJ	*Jewish Studies, an Internet Journal*
JSJ	*Journal for the Study of Judaism in the Persian, Hellenistic, and Roman Periods*
JSJSup	Journal for the Study of Judaism in the Persian, Hellenistic, and Roman Periods: Supplement Series
JSNT	*Journal for the Study of the New Testament*
JSNTSup	Journal for the Study of the New Testament: Supplement Series
JTS	*Journal of Theological Studies*
KAV	Kommentar zu den Apostolischen Vätern

KEK	Kritische-exegetischer Kommentar über das Neue Testament (Meyer-Kommentar)
KSup	Kadmos Supplement
LCL	Loeb Classical Library
LEB	Lexham English Bible
LNTS	Library of New Testament Studies
LSJ	Liddell, H. G., R. Scott, and H. S. Jones. *A Greek-English Lexicon*. 9th ed. with revised supplement. Oxford: Oxford University Press, 1996.
MNTC	*Moffatt New Testament Commentary*
MSJ	*The Master's Seminary Journal*
MTSR	*Method and Theory in the Study of Religion*
NBS	Numen Book Series
NedTT	*Nederlands theologische tijdschrift*
Neot	*Neotestamentica*
NGS	New Gospel Studies
NICNT	New International Commentary on the New Testament
NIDB	*The New Interpreter's Dictionary of the Bible*. Edited by K. D. Sakenfeld. Nashville: Abingdon, 2009.
NIGTC	New International Greek Testament Commentary
NovT	*Novum Testamentum*
NovTSup	Novum Testamentum Supplements
NRTh	*La nouvelle revue théologique*
NTL	New Testament Library
NTR	New Testament Readings
NTS	*New Testament Studies*
OBO	Orbis biblicus et orientalis
OrChrAn	Orientalia christiana analecta
PFLUS	Publications de la Faculté des Lettres de l'Université de Strasbourg
PG	Patrologia graeca [= Patrologiae cursus completes: Series graeca]. Edited by J.-P. Migne. 162 vols. Paris, 1857-1886
PGL	*Patristic Greek Lexicon*. Edited by G. W. H. Lampe. Oxford: Clarendon, 1968.
PTS	Patristische Texte und Studien
QL	*Questions liturgiques*
RB	*Revue biblique*
RBL	Review of Biblical Literature (online)
ResQ	*Restoration Quarterly*

RHR	*Revue de l'histoire des religions*
RSR	*Recherches de science religieuse*
SBL	Society of Biblical Literature
SBLAB	Society of Biblical Literature Academia Biblica
SBLEJL	Society of Biblical Literature Early Judaism and Its Literature
SBLMS	Society of Biblical Literature Monograph Series
SBLSP	Society of Biblical Literature Seminar Papers
SBLSymS	Society of Biblical Literature Symposium Series
SBS	Stuttgarter Bibelstudien
SC	Sources chrétiennes, Paris: Cerf, 1943–.
SecCent	*Second Century*
SCJ	Studies in Christianity and Judaism
ScrHier	Scripta hierosolymitana
SDSSRL	Studies in the Dead Sea Scrolls and Related Literature
SEAug	Studia ephemeridis Augustinianum
SemeiaSt	Semeia Studies
SJ	Studia judaica
SJLA	Studies in Judaism in Late Antiquity
SNTSMS	Society for New Testament Studies Monograph Series
SP	Sacra pagina
SPL	Spiritualités et pensées libres
SR	*Studies in Religion*
StPatr	*Studia patristica*
StPB	Studia post-biblica
StudBib	Studia Biblica
ST	*Studia theologica*
STDJ	Studies on the Texts of the Desert of Judah
SU	Schriften des Urchristentums
SwJT	*Southwestern Journal of Theology*
TANZ	Texte und Arbeiten zum neutestamentlichen Zeitalter
TDNT	*Theological Dictionary of the New Testament*. Edited by G. Kittel and G. Friedrich. Translated by G. W. Bromiley. 10 vols. Grand Rapids: Eerdmans, 1964–1976.
TJ	*Trinity Journal*
TLOT	*Theological Lexicon of the Old Testament*. Edited by E. Jenni, with assistance from C. Westermann. Translated by M. E. Biddle. 3 vols. Peabody, MA: Hendrickson, 1997.
TLZ	*Theologische Literaturzeitung*

TS	*Theological Studies*
TSAJ	Texte und Studien zum antiken Judentum
TynBul	*Tyndale Bulletin*
TTE	*The Theological Educator*
TUGAL	Texte und Untersuchungen zur Geschichte der altchristlichen Literatur
VC	*Vigiliae christianae*
VCSup	Vigiliae Christianae Supplements
VE	*Verbum et Ecclesia*
VetChr	*Vetera christianorum*
VTSup	Supplements to Vetus Testamentum
WBC	Word Biblical Commentary
WSP	*Warring States Papers*
WTJ	*Westminster Theological Journal*
WUNT	Wissenschaftliche Untersuchungen zum Neuen Testament
ZAW	*Zeitschrift für die alttestamentlischen Wissenschaft*
ZECNT	Zondervan Exegetical Commentary on the New Testament
ZNW	*Zeitschrift für die neutestamentliche Wissenschaft und die Kunde der älteren Kirche*

Introduction: Dynamics, Methodologies, and Progress in Didache Studies

Clayton N. Jefford

1. The History

Despite its brevity of length and paucity of theological development, the text of the Didache has inspired a disproportionate degree of attention from biblical scholars and early church historians alike. Early identified as a "riddle" by F. E. Vokes and later as an "enigma" by Stanislas Giet,[1] the work remains an intriguing dilemma for those who study ancient Christian contexts and literature. It is a singular text that begs for interpretation and elucidation against the backdrop of what is otherwise known about the origin of the early church and its development prior to the standardization of ecclesiastical practices and institutional norms.

Though available for scholarly examination for less than 150 years, much has been written about the Didache in an effort to locate its origins, development, and traditions. The fruits of such efforts have often been wildly inconsistent, as is shown by scholars who wished to associate the work with an Egyptian provenance against others who preferred a Syrian locale, those who believed the materials to be remarkably ancient against those who saw the hand of later forgers at work, and those who identified the influence of diverse Jewish communities with idiosyncratic tendencies against others who believed the text to reflect the natural growth of Christian evolution as the church abandoned the roots of its Semitic heritage.[2]

---

1. So F. E. Vokes, *The Riddle of the Didache: Fact or Fiction, Heresy or Catholicism?* (London: SPCK, 1938), and Stansilas Giet, *L'énigme de la Didachè*, PFLUS 149 (Paris: Ophrys, 1970).

2. For a most useful survey of such trends, see Jonathan A. Draper, "The Didache in Modern Research: An Overview," in *The* Didache *in Modern Research*, ed. Jonathan

Among the initial scholars to give attention to the text were early church historians such as Adolf von Harnack, Paul Sabatier, Philip Schaff, Charles Taylor, and J. Rendel Harris, figures who already were well known for their vigilant research into the ancient Christian setting beyond the realm of biblical studies. Their enthusiasm created an infectious wave for their own students, many of whom continued to investigate matters associated not only with the Didache, but with the apostolic fathers in general. But with the waning of this enthusiasm early in the twentieth century, Didache studies became largely recognized as a hobby interest for only a scattered few scholars, leaving nonspecialists in the field with mostly vague notions about the text and its role within the rise of primitive Christianity.

Over the years the scholarly process of debate eventually yielded to several schools of thought that seemed to reflect the individual frameworks within which academics reconstructed their personal visions of the context and tradition behind the Didache. The best known among these perspectives are perhaps represented by three key commentaries that appeared during the last half of the twentieth century. The earliest study is found in the work of Jean-Paul Audet, whose principal volume gave consideration to the writings of the Dead Sea Scrolls.[3] Audet's publications generally offered an insightful view into the potential implications that the Scrolls, only recently discovered and still largely unpublished at the time, held for the ancient Christian context. Soon thereafter appeared a key study (followed by a subsequent update) on the Didache by Willy Rordorf and André Tuilier, a volume that appeared in the Sources chrétienne series.[4] This research focused on broad literary traditions and the status of the text within the framework of the ancient ecclesiastical setting. Finally, the contributions of Kurt Niederwimmer have found their pinnacle in his commentary late in the century, which gave focused consideration to the perspective of sources and editorial composition. Niederwimmer's

---

A. Draper, AGJU 37 (Leiden: Brill, 1996), 1–42. See also by way of introduction to the text itself, Clayton N. Jefford, *Teaching of the Twelve Apostles: Didache* (Santa Rosa, CA: Polebridge, 2013), 1–17.

3. Jean-Paul Audet, *La Didachè: Instructions des Apôtres*, Ebib (Paris: Gabalda, 1958).

4. Willy Rordorf and André Tuilier, *La doctrine des douze Apôtres (Didachè)*, SC 248 (Paris: Cerf, 1978). This was later revised in 1998 in the light of Niederwimmer's 1993 volume (see n. 5 below).

volume in many ways has come to represent the pinnacle of Didache research toward the end of the twentieth century.[5]

A glance backwards at these scholars and their fine research raises some awareness of a distinctive element concerning studies of the Didache during this period. Indeed, characteristic of such research was the relatively isolated environment in which each scholar approached the text and the vagaries of its background and evolution from within their own individual specialties. On the one hand, there is no question that such approaches have led to insightful observations about the text. It is on the shoulders of such scholars that contemporary students have offered their own observations. Yet at the same time these efforts have largely shielded any true degree of cooperative insight that may have been of use in understanding the situation of the Didache. The opportunity these scholars once had to share their individual perspectives in a collaborate sense in order to promote a greater understanding of the text and its traditions has subsequently been lost. What has now become apparent is that, while such efforts may have been herculean in their contribution to our knowledge of the topic at hand, the situation in which individual scholars have worked in isolation is perhaps better left behind in favor of a more cooperative milieu.

Thus it has become true that scholars in church history eventually recognized the need to engage others who are better trained in Scripture, that specialists in liturgical tradition have come to pursue those who focus on ecclesiastical development, that students trained in literary traditions alone recognize the nature of oral contexts and the value that such traditions held for their local cultures, and that theologians have been compelled to consult with historians. These transitions have not always been easy, and the acknowledgment that specialists in divergent fields of study have something of particular value to offer their colleagues who are trained in further disciplines has not always been recognized with grace. Nevertheless, toward the end of the twentieth century the time was clearly right to assume a more cooperative spirit. The result has been a surfeit of secondary literature now available to assist those who wish better to understand the Didache and its original setting.

---

5. Kurt Niederwimmer, *The Didache: A Commentary*, trans. Linda M. Maloney, Hermeneia (Minneapolis: Fortress, 1998); trans. of *Die Didache*, KAV 1 (Göttingen: Vandenhoeck & Ruprecht, 1993).

2. The Context

In certain respects this evolving perspective of cross-disciplinary interaction has led to a bounty of studies on the Didache that had not been witnessed previously. By way of example, recent investigations have indicated the benefit that may be gained from a more complete and detailed understanding of orality in the role that it has served as the background for much of what now appears in literary form within the text. The impetus for this insight derives from outside the discipline of church history, of course, finding its roots within a variety of social-critical studies. But an awareness of how the first generations of Christians viewed their faith from within a living, orality-based context has become an essential aspect of what scholarship now assumes in its approach to the Didache.

Together with this greater appreciation for the influence of orality in the ancient world, a greater focus has been placed on liturgical traditions and the unique place of the Didache within the development of such streams of ritual. The older belief that generally held ground prior to the work of Walter Bauer early in the twentieth century—a view that envisaged Christianity to have developed from a single kernel of mainline perspective about faith and praxis that eventually divided into multiple views and deviant streams of approach—has given way to a clearer understanding that the nascent church itself was hardly unified in perspective, even from the foundation of its roots. Thus, scholars have come to envisage that the Didache is perhaps more accurately understood as a derivative of one of these earlier approaches.

So too, the ancient concern to blend ethical instruction with ecclesiastical direction is now recognized by many scholars as a driving force among numerous early Christian communities. This has led to enhanced appreciation for the evolutionary role that the work has played within the growth of ancient Christian literature. One can no longer be satisfied with the simplistic perspective that the work is simply a "handbook" or compilation of instructions that existed without any clear purpose within the evolving history that was the social-cultural development of church instruction. Indeed! This likely was never the case at all. Some other perspective must be considered. The conclusion of the twentieth century was the time for scholarship to give flesh to such a vision.

The rise of such movements in perspective undeniably served to provide the foundation for what eventually became a specific gathering for the presentation of papers on the Didache at the annual meetings of the Society of Biblical Literature (SBL). Credit for this occasion must be allotted directly to Aaron Milavec in Ohio, who initially proposed and organized the sessions under the exploratory title of the "Didache Consultation Unit," an investigative venture by which to determine the interest of scholars within the field of early patristic studies. As chair of the sessions, Milavec included the assistance of a small, loosely assembled team of fellow researchers to help guide the process of organization and direction, including Jonathan Draper of South Africa, Nancy Pardee in Illinois, and Clayton Jefford in Indiana. Under the supervision of these individuals, papers were presented in the unit's initial phase in 2003 and continued through 2005. As a standard for these and later meetings, the unit featured two sessions of related topics on the text involving a number of researchers both in biblical studies and the apostolic fathers generally.

After the meeting in 2005, the chairmanship of the unit was handed over to Draper and renamed the "Didache in Context." Interest continued to gather among participants at the annual SBL meetings, many of whom were only secondarily engaged in the topic itself. With the departure of Milavec after the initial years, two other researchers were incorporated into the team of directors: Huub van de Sandt of the Netherlands and Alan Garrow from England. This combined team of Draper, Pardee, Jefford, van de Sandt, and Garrow continued to guide the sessions until their final meeting in 2011, thus covering a range of almost a decade during which significant papers were delivered on the text within an organized academic context of international scope.

Apart from the essential value of sharing related research work on the text of the Didache within a public setting on an annual basis, the seminar offered a sounding board for the progress of several noteworthy publications in the field. Earliest among these was the production of Milavec's own commentary, which has taken two related literary forms and clearly had significant impact on a number of scholars who have undertaken work within the discipline.[6] The influence of Milavec's work is perhaps most immediately evident in the appearance of two subsequent

---

6. He refers to these works as his "elephant" and his "mouse"; see Aaron Milavec, *The Didache: Faith, Hope, and Life of the Earliest Christian Communities, 50–70 CE* (New York: Newman, 2003), and *The Didache: Text, Translation, Analysis, and Commentary* (Collegeville, MN: Liturgical Press, 2003).

introductions to the text, specifically those authored by William Varner[7] and Thomas O'Loughlin.[8]

Additional volumes were soon forthcoming by other members of the seminar's steering committee, including two collections of essays gathered at conferences in Tilburg in the Netherlands, under the direction of van de Sandt.[9] Each of these gatherings featured papers directed specifically toward Didache studies in relationship to Scripture: in the first instance with reference to the Gospel of Matthew and in the latter in reference to Matthew and James. Most interesting with respect to these latter collections is the degree to which it had become clear to scholars of late Christian antiquity that there is a primary benefit to be gained from opportunities to share insights and research within a collaborative setting. The two conferences included roughly twenty-five scholars, each with specialties in a variety of areas of history and literature. The value of such collaboration is immediately obvious both in the essays produced and subsequent literature that has been spawned from such publications.

Yet in a more expansive context, two other related volumes have featured further collaborative efforts related to the Didache within the more generalized framework of the larger collection of the apostolic fathers. These have resulted from the centennial celebration of the Oxford Society of Historical Theology's examination of use of Scripture in the apostolic fathers that resulted over a century ago in a slim little volume from 1905.[10] In honor of that earlier collaborative effort, Andrew F. Gregory and Christopher M. Tuckett, each from Oxford University, culled together a series

---

7. *The Way of the Didache: The First Christian Handbook* (Lanham, MD: University Press of America, 2007).

8. *The Didache: A Window on the Earliest Christians* (Grand Rapids: Baker; London: SPCK, 2010).

9. These include a conference held April 7–8, 2003 (published in Huub van de Sandt, ed., *Matthew and the Didache: Two Documents from the Same Jewish-Christian Milieu?* [Assen: Van Gorcum; Minneapolis: Fortress, 2005]), and a subsequent conference held April 12–13, 2007 (published in Huub van de Sandt and Jürgen K. Zangenberg, eds., *Matthew, James and Didache: Three Related Documents in Their Jewish and Christian Settings*, SBLSymS 45 [Atlanta: Society of Biblical Literature, 2008]). Van de Sandt had previously published a volume on the Two Ways source behind the Didache, which he had coauthored with the late David Flusser: *The Didache: Its Jewish Sources and Its Place in Early Judaism and Christianity*, CRINT 3.5 (Assen: Van Gorcum; Minneapolis: Fortress, 2002).

10. *The New Testament in the Apostolic Fathers* (Oxford: Clarendon, 1905).

of contributors within the field, many of whom were able to gather at Lincoln College in April 2004 to address topics related to the apostolic fathers, principally in the specialties of their texts and contexts. The resulting papers included several pieces that investigate the Didache explicitly and have subsequently furthered our understanding of the work.[11]

Furthermore, in many ways the SBL seminar likewise proved to be a touchstone for a number of dissertations on the Didache that were published in the intervening years. The earliest of these was authored by Garrow, whose 2004 publication of his 2000 Oxford thesis under the direction of Tuckett[12] has contributed greatly to those who would place the Didache at the earliest stages of nascent Christianity's development. Together with the work of Milavec, Garrow's hypothesis has provided an avenue for scholars who prefer to see the text as a reflection of the faith's earliest foundation pillars. A second dissertation was published in 2008 from the pen of Jonathan Schwiebert,[13] whose earlier 2005 Boston University thesis reflected a specific interest in the liturgical traditions of the text. Schwiebert examines the ritual dynamics and historical impact of the eucharistic tradition preserved in Did. 9–10, furthering thought on the topic that had been featured in earlier research from the time of the work's initial rediscovery in 1873 and publication a decade later by Philotheos Bryennios. The work of Schwiebert has encouraged new considerations of the tradition within its historical context. Finally, in 2012 the latest

---

11. Andrew F. Gregory and Christopher M. Tuckett, eds., *The New Testament and the Apostolic Fathers: The Reception of the New Testament in the Apostolic Fathers*, 2 vols (Oxford: Oxford University Press, 2005). Four papers are focal for present consideration here within these two volumes; see especially John S. Kloppenborg, "*Didache* 1.1–6.1, James, Matthew, and the Torah"; Jonathan A. Draper, "First-fruits and the Support of Prophets, Teachers, and the Poor in *Didache* 13 in Relation to New Testament Parallels"; and Clayton N. Jefford, "Social Locators as a Bridge between the *Didache* and Matthew"; in *Trajectories through the New Testament and the Apostolic Fathers*, vol. 2 of *The New Testament and the Apostolic Fathers*, ed. Andrew F. Gregory and Christopher M. Tuckett (Oxford: Oxford University Press, 2005), 193–221, 223–43, and 245–64 (respectively); Christopher M. Tuckett, "The *Didache* and the Writings that later formed the New Testament," in *The Reception of the New Testament in the Apostolic Fathers*, ed. Andrew F. Gregory and Christopher M. Tuckett (Oxford: Oxford University Press, 2005), 83–127.

12. *The Gospel of Matthew's Dependence on the* Didache, JSNTSup 254 (London: T&T Clark, 2004).

13. *Knowledge and the Coming Kingdom: The Didache's Meal Ritual and Its Place in Early Christianity*, LNTS 373 (London: T&T Clark, 2008).

and most up-to-date edition of Pardee's 2002 University of Chicago dissertation has been made available in publication.[14] The underlying thesis expressed by Pardee features a concern for the comprehensive syntactical structure of the Didache that suggests the evolved history of the work versus views that envisage it as the unified expression of a single mindset. In certain respects, she has returned to the investigation of problems associated with the writing's framework that plagued a previous generation of scholars, though with a new approach featuring text-linguistic analysis.

The rise of the SBL seminar during the early 2000s, the cooperative spirit of those authors and presenters who have participated in its performance during those years, and the appearance of numerous related publications that have found a ready audience within that context (including the more broadly featured volumes of seminar participants and the numerous articles and essays not listed here)[15] have in many respects demanded some formal closing comment in the form of the collected essays of contemporary researchers who continue to work on the Didache. The present volume is an attempt to provide a capstone for the seminar and its efforts. While it does not embody all of the contributors and their literary efforts over the course of that decade, it offers a clear reflection of the type of work that was achieved and the interests that were covered during those years.

3. The Content

This volume is divided into four sections, each of which features four to five essays and a response. Scholarship from Australia, continental Europe, South Africa, the United Kingdom, and the United States is represented here, including specialists in the study of the Didache and generalists in early church history, well-established scholars in their fields and younger scholars at the beginning of their careers. In other words, these essays and responses reflect what the "Didache in Context" seminar was during the

---

14. *The Genre and Development of the Didache*, WUNT 2/339 (Tübingen: Mohr Siebeck, 2012).

15. This list should perhaps include two anticipated commentaries that remain in manuscript form. The first of these is currently under production by Jonathan Draper for publication in the new Oxford Apostolic Fathers series (several volumes are already now in print), and the second is my own book slated to appear in the Yale Anchor Bible series sometime in the next decade.

years of its existence and include a number of the papers that have not been published elsewhere.

The first section ("Approaches to the Text as a Whole") seeks to incorporate those studies that apply generally to the overall content and background of the Didache. These essays cover a broad range of ideas and approaches, and each author seeks to speak about the nature of the work as a whole and within the larger realm of its historical or theological development.

Stephen Finlan's opening essay on community identity gives special attention to the unique Christian nature of the Didache, with particular attention drawn to Jewish and Torah connections in the light of social identity theory. In many respects this effort reflects what has become a common understanding about the nature of the text with respect to its Jewish roots and foundation. This is followed by my own contribution on the nature of authority as it is viewed throughout the Didache. I understand the text to reflect at least two levels of such authority and focus primarily on how the author(s) make use of Scripture at different historical junctures, orienting my discussion around the review of an earlier study by William Varner. A contribution by Aaron Milavec appears next, identifying the many and various ways in which scholarship on the Didache, while having contributed greatly to our understanding of the text, has in his opinion made critical, mistaken assumptions in its work. He recognizes that valid studies going forward must be open to the unique voice preserved within the text itself. These essays are followed by a study from Jonathan Draper, who investigates the Didachist's use of household codes in the construction of the community's view of authority in comparison with other contemporary authors. This essay is somewhat unique within Didache studies in its effort to give this code material a particular voice within the text. Much like Finlan's essay at the beginning of the volume, Draper again provides a sound comparison with Jewish precedents, yet incorporates a larger Greco-Roman consideration as he responds to the earlier work of James C. Scott and Halvor Moxnes. In conclusion, a response to the four works is offered by Andrew Gregory, who offers an insightful analysis of these opening essays as they interrelate with respect to the question of the historical and theological development of the Didache. Gregory's initial (and perhaps primary) response is to the essay of Milavec, focusing on the importance of issues associated with a holistic reading of the text within an oral setting versus a broader consideration of the development of manuscript and literary traditions. This approach sets the tenor for his subsequent consideration of the essays of Finlan, Draper, and myself, folding the broader questions of Matthean dependence (or lack thereof), ancient views of social identity, and Jewish and Hellenistic codes into the early Christian framework of development. He is careful to offer a word of warning for those who work with ancient texts and contexts.

The second section ("Leadership and Liturgy") provides several strategies by which to understand liturgical constructions and ritual worship that are reflected in the central portion of the text. Included here once again are four essays on baptism, Eucharist, and prayer that seek to better understand how those activities presumably were witnessed within and experienced by the Didache community. The opening essay is offered by Huub van de Sandt, who addresses the topics of holiness and baptism as necessary ingredients for participation in the Eucharist as understood by the Didachist. His approach incorporates the contemporary views of Jewish sources, including special consideration for the Two Ways segment with which the Didache begins. Afterwards appears Peter Tomson's study on the Lord's Prayer as it appears within the evolving tradition of early Christian literature. His redaction-critical perspective of the text brings him to conclude that the prayer served as a boundary line between Jews and Christians during the reigns of Trajan and Hadrian. The two essays that follow are interlinked in terms of their consideration of the prayers in Did. 9–10. The first of these comes from Jonathan Schwiebert, who builds on previous arguments from his published dissertation[16] in a discussion of the formulaic nature of forms within those prayers. His analysis takes advantage of the earlier work on religious symbols reviewed by Maurice Bloch. The second of the two essays presents John Clabeaux's analysis of Schwiebert's volume on this same topic, providing a careful review of how discussion on the prayers has been advanced by this work to the benefit of Didache studies. On the one hand, he discusses the prayers themselves; yet at the same time incorporates additional insights on theology, eschatology, and the Johannine tradition. This section is concluded with a response by Joseph Mueller, S.J., who also focuses on Schwiebert's hypotheses about the prayers, offering their value in providing a focal point for the honing perspectives of van de Sandt and Tomson. It will undoubtedly become clear to the careful reader that contemporary views concerning

---

16. See n. 13 above.

ritual and *praxis* within the Didache tradition have been greatly impacted by such careful analysis of liturgical materials and their performance within the community. In this respect, this particular collection of essays holds together well.

The third section of the volume ("The Didache and Matthew") turns specifically to the relationship between the Didache and Scripture, particularly with respect to the Gospel of Matthew. The first of these studies is offered by Bruce Brooks, who provides a broadly outlined view of how the Didache represents some of the earliest views of nascent Christianity in comparison with other better known New Testament materials. He envisages the work as a growth text with a liturgical orientation that was typical of what he defines as "Alpha Christianity," a movement among the earliest Christians that is further illustrated by such works as James, the hymn embedded in Phil 2, and the earlier layers of the Gospel of Mark. The two essays that follow are linked in certain respects, much like those of Schwiebert and Clabeaux in the second section. The first of these features a study of the Two Ways tradition by Perttu Nikander, who gives particular consideration to the oral nature of that material and the various ways in which it likely was performed within the community of the Didache. He focuses on the nature of "sound mapping" and aural structure as studied previously by Margaret Ellen Lee and Bernard Brandon Scott. Nancy Pardee's essay concludes these two studies, working off a previous paper offered by Nikander at an SBL session in November 2010. Pardee offers a developing perspective on oral theory and the Didache as presented in that earlier study, proposing a renewed call to give particular attention to the issues of genre, literary composition, and "recontextualization" as elements that undoubtedly lie behind the evolution of the textual tradition. Thereafter, John Welch provides a later edition to his earlier studies on the literary connections between the Didache and Matthew's Sermon on the Mount. He offers his belief that the Didache, as well as other early Christian literature, has made extensive use of the Sermon both in its literary construction and theological perspective. This argument takes advantage of "inverted parallel" analysis as identified and explored in the earlier work of Moshe Seidel. The final essay in this section is given by Murray Smith, who brings the unit to full completion with a consideration of the eschatological perspective of the Didachist. Smith argues against those who believe that the reference to κύριος ("Lord") in the text intends the appearance of God, preferring the reading that this is an intentional reference to the return of Christ by the author. He provides extensive literary parallels from elsewhere within the tradition to make his case. The closing response is an analysis of these five contributions by Joseph Verheyden, offering a careful review of each author's arguments and views with respect to the Didachist's knowledge and employment of Scripture. Verheyden is less in sympathy with opinions that do not envisage the evolution of the Gospel of Matthew prior to that of the Didache and thus is vigilant to focus on each author's position in terms of its logic and assumptions. This is the kind of review that indicates the value of divergent opinions and critical analysis in academic research.

The final section ("The Didache and Other Early Christian Texts") is oriented toward the issue of how the Didache relates to subsidiary first-century literature. These studies are drawn primarily with insights taken from biblical works, some of which are readily identified in the New Testament (so Hebrews and Revelation). But the remaining essays address less obvious texts in terms of literature and authors more broadly employed by contemporary traditions. The first of these essays is by Matti Myllykoski, who addresses the topic of the Apostolic Decree (known from Acts 15) as it relates to the Didache, focusing on the way in which the Two Ways (as a treatise) came to be incorporated into the contexts of the Didachist and author of Matthew. Myllykoski's essay takes stock of ancient Jewish-Christian concerns as the community of the Didache reacted against both Pauline antilegalism and strict observance of the law at the same historical moment. Thereafter appears the contribution of Taras Khomych, who turns his attention to the circumstances of Paul and whether the apostle worked with another separate "gospel" and evangelical tradition. A focus of this study envisions the contrasting images of Christology at work in the mind of the Didachist and Paul. Khomych finds both similarities and striking differences in this comparison, thus indicating a more refracting vision of theology and perspective among our earliest Christian sources. The next study is that of Matthew Larsen and Michael Svigel, who explore the likelihood of a commonly circulating Two Ways tradition that was known not only by the Didachist, but also by the author of Hebrews. They argue that the mindset behind Heb 6:1–6 is specifically driven toward the individual Christian's growth in faith and understanding, assuming knowledge of a Two Ways catechetical pattern that was already available to the author's readership. Alan Garrow next explores the common relationship between the book of Revelation and the Didache in terms of their shared eschatological concerns and eucharistic traditions. Employing the earlier work of David Barr on the enactment of oral materials within

Revelation, Garrow concludes that the Didache provides the actual foundational patterns for the "creative fountainhead" from which the text of Revelation derived. The final essay in this section features a response by Jeffrey Bingham. Bingham offers a broad review of the various contributions of the authors. Bingham offers a broad review of the works, classifying the discussion into the four categories of unity and diversity, Jewish heritage, liturgy, and hermeneutics. In conclusion, he acknowledges that contemporary explorations of the Didache and its traditions offer another perspective by which to understanding the foundational pillars of early Christianity. In many respects, this serves as a summary understanding that stands behind the rationale for the volume as a whole.

The concluding essay for the volume is offered by Draper, who notes a number of important features of the Didache that are now generally accepted by scholars. Among these is the recognition that the Didachist incorporated various early sources, not having written simply from contemporary perspective. In addition, there is greater awareness of the Jewish context within which the text was produced and especially of the significant role that Jewish and Christian mysticism may hold for better understanding the work. To this one may add a renewed focus on the tradition of the Gospel of Matthew, as well as some further concern for the role of the apostle Paul and Johannine tradition, including the text of Revelation. Closing with a call for further exploration into the practice of early Christian initiation rituals and practices, he concludes that the challenge of the text continues for contemporary scholars in their quest to better understand Christian origins and literature.

We trust that readers will find the essays contained in this volume to be useful tools in their own pursuits of such questions for the origins and development of earliest Christianity. The call of the Didache still resounds, encouraging a persistent response from biblical scholars and specialists of late Christian antiquity alike. The answer to the "riddle" of the Didache waits to be found. The tradition continues to summon those who would respond.

Part 1
Approaches to the Text as a Whole

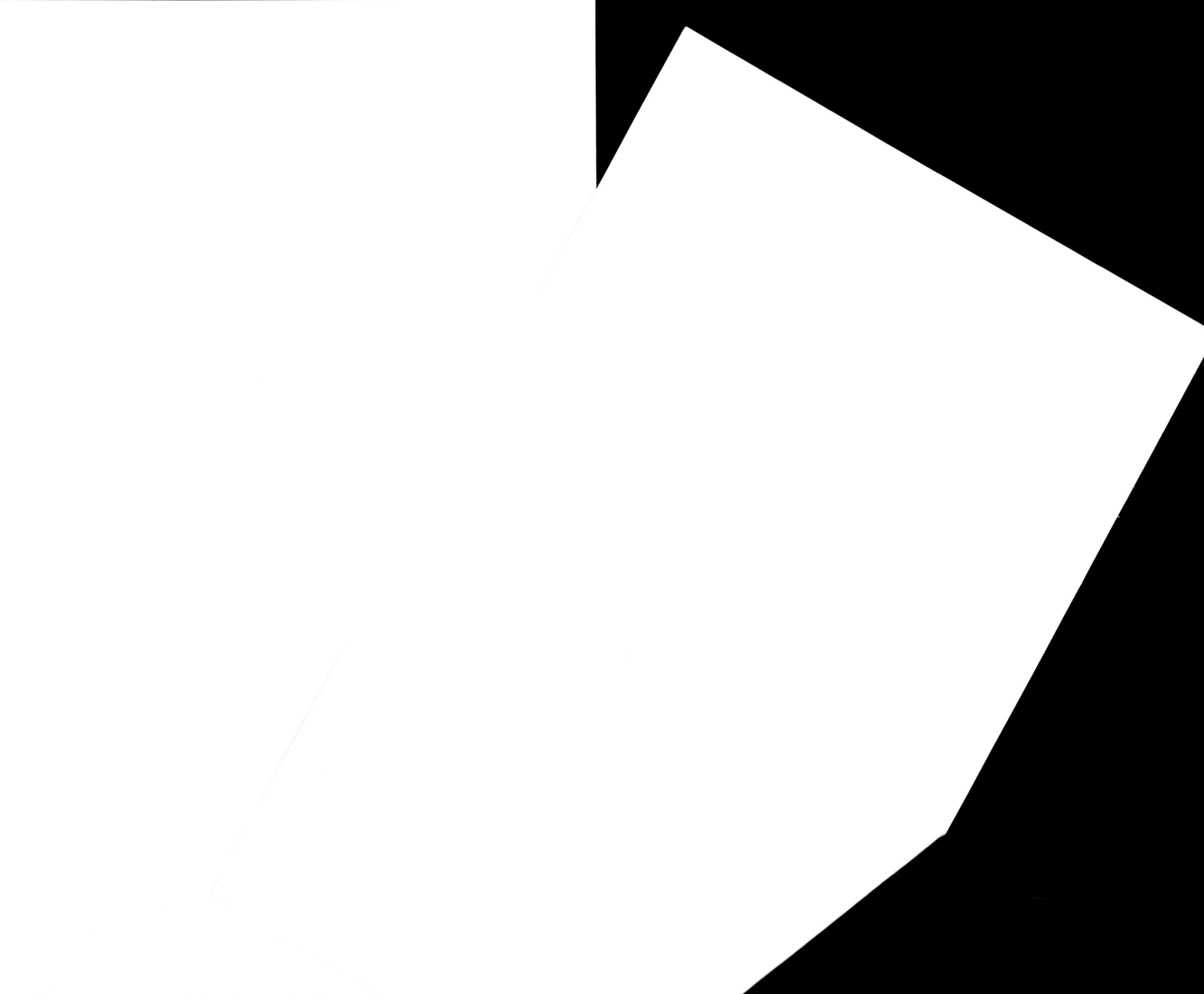

Identity in the Didache Community

Stephen Finlan

The question of identity in the Didache author's implied community is intertwined with the question of the desirability of Torah observance by gentiles. The more closely any community is tied to observance of the Torah, the more confidently can its identity be called a *kind* of Jewish identity. But this shows how broad is the range of Jewish identities, when it can include gentiles. Simple labels such as "Jewish" or "Jewish-Christian" do not suffice for this topic. I will attempt to uncover the processes of identity formation, rather than simply to assign labels.

1. Law and Perfection

Perfection occurs in several key verses that have relevance to group identity. The first instance is in a text that closely resembles Matt 5: "pray for your enemies ... if anyone should strike you on the right cheek, turn to him/her also the other, and you will be perfect" (Did. 1.3–4;[1] see also Matt 5:39, 44, 48). Matthew 5 and Did. 1 share this exhortation to go beyond the mere letter of the law to its *spirit*.[2] Jonathan Draper says perfection means "to keep the Torah better than other groups in Israel."[3]

But I must ask: Can the group literally be "in Israel," since it may be predominantly gentile? The work self-identifies as being "for the gentiles

---

1. The translation used for Didache quotes is Aaron Milavec, *The Didache: Text, Translation, Analysis, and Commentary* (Collegeville, MN: Liturgical Press, 2003). I drop the underscoring, umlauts, and other graphic coding that Milavec uses.

2. It is not necessary to settle the dispute about whether Matthew and the Didache emanate from the same community at different stages of development (Jonathan A. Draper, "Do the Didache and Matthew Reflect an 'Irrevocable Parting of the Ways' with Judaism?" in *Matthew and the Didache: Two Documents from the Same Jewish-Christian Milieu?* ed. Huub van de Sandt [Minneapolis: Fortress, 2005], 217–41 [219,

[τοῖς ἔθνεσιν]."[4] Analyzing the social group addressed by the Didache is complicated, since it "contained a membership of Gentile Christians on various levels of Jewish perfection."[5] I will turn to a current sociological approach, Social Identity Theory (SIT), to shed some light on the social side of "perfection."

1.1. Social Identity Theory

According to SIT, it is crucial to group identity to have a group prototype, a concept of an ideal or perfect member, "a representation of a person that embodies the identity of the group ... an ideal image."[6] The exhortation to "bear the whole yoke of Lord" (6.2) then says something about what is expected of the ideal member of the group. In fact, the whole Two Ways section (Did. 1–6) consists of "the rules [ἐντολὰς] of the Lord" (4.13) that a member of the group is expected to keep. The Two Ways section bears a strong resemblance to other ancient Jewish texts used for "initiation of newcomers to particular groups within Judaism."[7] In a way, this makes the specifically Christian material even more important, since it is what distinguishes this group from other groups with Jewish beliefs.

SIT tells us that "the need for social differentiation" leads to a heightening of differences between the perceived in-group and particular outgroups.[8] The group may have recently split from another group, which

---

239]) or whether they are unaware of each other (Aaron Milavec, "When, Why, and for Whom Was the *Didache* Created? Insights into the Social and Historical Setting of the *Didache* Communities," in van de Sandt, *Matthew and the Didache*, 80–81).

3. Draper, "Didache and Matthew," 226; see also 230.

4. In the superscript (Milavec, *Didache: Text*, 3, 40). See Jonathan A. Draper, "The Holy Vine of David Made Known to the Gentiles through God's Servant Jesus: 'Christian Judaism' in the *Didache*," in *Jewish Christianity Reconsidered: Rethinking Ancient Groups and Texts*, ed. Matt Jackson-McCabe (Minneapolis: Fortress, 2007), 257.

5. David Flusser, "Paul's Jewish-Christian Opponents in the *Didache*," in *The Didache in Modern Research*, ed. Jonathan A. Draper, AGJU 37 (Leiden: Brill, 1996), 211.

6. Coleman A. Baker, "Social Identity Theory and Biblical Interpretation," *BTB* 42 (2012): 129–38 (132).

7. Jonathan A. Draper, "The Two Ways and Eschatological Hope: A Contested Terrain in Galatians 5 and the *Didache*," *Neot* 45 (2011): 221–51 (223).

8. Raimo Hakola, "Social Identities and Group Phenomena in Second Temple Judaism," in *Explaining Christian Origins and Early Judaism: Contributions from Cog-*

would now become an out-group and which now may be vilified as "the hypocrites" are in Did. 8: "Do not pray as the hypocrites but as the Lord ordered in his good news. Pray thus: Our Father" (Did. 8.2, with wording very close to that of Matt 6:9–13). The implication may be that we are not like the "hypocrites" from whom we have just separated. Group identity formation seems to require "social comparison and accompanying competition,"[9] which can lead to hostility toward out-groups, manifested in stereotyping and name-calling.

At first glance, then, SIT does not settle the question of whether the Didache community is "in Israel" or not. It seems to be "in Israel" in its concept of what the ideal member is expected to do, but it is sharply differentiating itself from some "hypocrites" who do not pray the Lord's (Jesus's) Prayer. I will draw on SIT as I strive to discern possible group identity behind the Didache, but will not be dogmatic in my use of SIT.

1.2. Bearing the Yoke

Reflection on the identity of the group addressed by the Didache has often focused on 6.2–3. The passage reads: "For, on the one hand, if you are able to bear the whole yoke of the Lord, you will be perfect; but if, on the one hand, you are not able, that which you are able, do this. And concerning eating, bear that which you are able. From the food, on the other hand, sacrificed to idols, very much keep away, for it is worship of dead gods" (Did. 6.2–3). The demand to avoid food sacrificed to idols is considerably stricter than Paul's principle that it may be eaten unless someone at the meal raises an objection (1 Cor 10:25–29).

Draper argues that the "yoke of the Lord" signifies "obedient observance of the Torah"[10] and sees Did. 6.2 as "an incentive for Gentiles to move towards full acceptance of the Torah."[11] Actually, it is hard to tell whether the "yoke of the Lord" in the Didache signifies obedience to the

---

nitive and Social Science, ed. Petri Luomanen, Ilkka Pyysiäinen, and Risto Uro (Leiden: Brill, 2007), 259–76 (262).

9. Susann Liubinskas, "Identification by Spirit Alone: Community-Identity Construction in Galatians 3:19–4:7," *AJ* 67 (2012): 27–55 (30).

10. Draper, "Holy Vine," 261.

11. Jonathan A. Draper, "Eschatology in the *Didache*," in *Eschatology of the New Testament and Some Related Documents*, ed. Jan G. van der Watt, WUNT 2/315 (Tübingen: Mohr Siebeck, 2011), 575.

whole Torah or only to that *distillation* of Torah found in the Two Ways section (which would make the Didache's "yoke" entirely different from the "yoke" in rabbinic sources). Whichever yoke is intended, the gentiles are free to bear as much as they are able (6.3), except that abstaining from idol food is mandatory.

Treating Torah as nonmandatory or as recommended only in truncated form makes Torah obedience more an act of imagination than a concrete expectation. Torah then has mainly an *imaginal* function as part of the mental exercise of conceptualizing group identity, but is no longer mandatory in its entirety.

Draper has a different angle on this. He says that the Didache, while not commanding Torah adherence for gentiles as it does for Jews, yet *imagines* gentile Christians becoming obedient to the Torah in the end times (16.2).[12] The conscious "continuity with God's covenant with Israel … as opposed to the enumerated ethical failures of their previous Gentile identity" is an essential part of the group's identity.[13] This sets up a system where "Torah observant Jews are the perfect; Gentiles are less than perfect but can rise in the status hierarchy according to the extent of the[ir] Torah observance."[14] I would question this, however, since the things actually commanded in the Two Ways section are not Torah-specific but are morality, kindness, fairness, and honesty and echo the Sermon on the Mount more than any other source.

Draper sees circumcision as recommended but not required. Gentiles are accepted "provided that they adopt the minimum of cultic purity" and follow the "Noachic" laws, but they are *encouraged* to take on "the whole yoke of the Lord," including circumcision.[15] Circumcision is not mentioned one way or the other in the Didache. Rather than debate circumcision, I prefer to consider the purity question. Circumcision can be considered a subcategory of purity after all. I think it is potentially misleading to speak of the Didache requiring "cultic purity." The Didache community has no temple, no priesthood, and no systematized rule comparable to

---

12. Draper, "Two Ways," 234.
13. Jonathan A. Draper, "Mission, Ethics and Identity in the *Didache*," in *Sensitivity towards Outsiders: Exploring the Dynamic Relationship between Mission and Ethos in the New Testament and Early Christianity*, ed. Jacobus Kok, Tobias Nicklas, Dieter T. Roth, and Christine Hays (Tübingen: Mohr Siebeck, forthcoming), 7 (manuscript).
14. Draper, "Mission, Ethics and Identity," 10 (manuscript).
15. Draper, "Didache and Matthew," 240.

Leviticus, which is what "cultic purity" would tend to imply. The demand to shun food sacrificed to idols (6.3) and the need for flowing water (7.2–3) are purity concerns, but not enough to apply the label "cultic purity" without qualification.

We need to notice that sacrifice and purity in the Didache are used in a metaphorical way to signify moral or spiritual rectitude. Confession should accompany the Eucharist, "so that your sacrifice may be pure.... [Be] reconciled, in order that your sacrifice may not be defiled" (14.1–2). These are metaphorical usages. Similarly, "ransom" is given an ethical meaning. Unselfish giving is equated to a ransoming (λύτρωσις) of sins (Did. 4.6). Ransom is fundamentally an economic/social term, not necessarily connected with sacrifice. I only bring it up because ransom is part of Christian atonement thinking in Rom 3:24–25 and 1 Cor 7:23. The Didache gives ransom the same abstract and ethical meaning it gives to "sacrifice."

In the Didache, purity no longer has a *national* or a *temple* dimension, which makes it profoundly different from both Pharisaic and Sadducean thinking. Purity in the Didache has no connection with temple cult or priestly rules. Therefore, to my mind, it is misleading to speak of "cultic purity," which usually implies cultic purification rites and a sharp separation between Jew and gentile. "Purity" is far more abstract in the Didache than it is in a community where gentiles are considered impure. Similarly, "law" is more abstract and metaphorical than it would be in a community that followed the temple cult.

2. The *Imaginal* Function of the Moral Torah

The Didache reflects a Christian culture and identity. Unlike Paul, the Didache actually does use the word "Christian" (12.4). Adherence to Torah is optional ("that which you are able," 6.3). I would agree with Huub van de Sandt, that the leniency "represents a tuning to the perspective of Gentile believers.... An observant Jew does not have the choice mentioned here."[16] For this reason I think it at least incomplete, if not actually misleading, to say that gentiles are encouraged to take on "the full culture and identity of

---

16. Huub van de Sandt, "The Didache Redefining Its Jewish Identity in View of Gentiles Joining the Community," in *Empsychoi Logoi: Religious Innovations in Antiquity*, ed. Alberdina Houtman, Albert de Jong, and Magda Misset-van de Weg, AJEC 73 (Leiden: Brill, 2008), 252.

Israel."[17] The Jewish elements are transformed and universalized; therefore they are not "fully" (*nationally*) within the Israel orbit.

Only in a symbolic sense can believers be said to be taking on an "Israel" identity. In another article Draper rightly argues that lawlessness in Did. 16.4 "refers to those who refuse to abide by the ethical provisions of Torah."[18] But when only the moral law (really a *portion* of it) and not the ritual law is enjoined, we should carefully qualify any remark that the group is Torah-following. If purity is symbolic and not cultic and if membership is largely gentile, then one can speak only of a kind of *symbolic* or *ancestral* Jewish identity.

The Two Ways chapters are full of Torah commandments, but the language of Israel is absent from the group's self-identification. Who are the faithful members of the community? Those who "giv[e] according to the rule" (1.5), who do not murder or commit abortion (2.2), are "not greedy" (2.6), do not hate (2.7), who are not angry or envious (3.2), who are "merciful and harmless" (3.8), "those whom the Spirit has made ready" (4.10). Notice how little ritual and how much morality there is here. The author wants to preserve Jewish *ethics*.

Clayton Jefford says the "materials ... are both Jewish in nature and beyond Jewish in scope."[19] The ethnic composition of the Didache community is also "beyond Jewish." Does this mean that the community can at least be called "symbolically Jewish"? Aaron Milavec would say no, the gentiles were included "without requiring them to become Jews"; they were saved *as gentiles*.[20] I think, however, that we can concede that the group had a *kind* of Jewish identity, while also having a Christian identity.

2.1. Differences and Self-Definition

To do justice to the Didache, we need to make statements that account for the two poles of the community's identity. Jürgen Zangenberg does this by saying "the didachist might have considered his group as still being 'Jewish,'" yet its rules made "practical cohabitation with unbaptized nonbelievers ... increasingly problematic," and he calls this an "awkward rela-

---

17. Draper, "Didache and Matthew," 240.
18. Draper, "Eschatology in the *Didache*," 576.
19. Clayton N. Jefford, "The Milieu of Matthew, the Didache, and Ignatius of Antioch: Agreements and Differences," in van de Sandt, *Matthew and the Didache*, 41.
20. Milavec, "When, Why, and for Whom," 75.

tion between separation and continuity."[21] Indeed, it seems that social pressures will force such a group to "pick sides." The group was hoping to draw Jews into the community, but it was nevertheless a Christian community. It may have understood itself as *truly* Jewish, but Jewish groups that rejected the messiahship of Jesus would have disputed that.

The Didache's eucharistic wording utilizes the Hebrew table grace or *Birkat Hamazon*.[22] But it is the *differences* that are most revealing, such as the replacement of "the 'land' by the Name (10.2)."[23] The Jewish prayer was centered around hopes for the restoration of Zion, altar, and temple, but these are conspicuously absent from the Didache, which bespeaks a "community which has lost this sense of group identity within a Jewish matrix," according to van de Sandt.[24] But this is overstated, since the group clearly is holding on to a *kind* of Jewish identity. Its Christian identity is more *determinative*, however. Nationality has been abandoned.

What is more significant? Is it the extensive similarity between the Didache's Eucharist and the text of the Jewish meal prayer, or is it the Christian alterations? One can choose to emphasize the continuity or the discontinuity. If we are observing two groups diverging from a common social matrix, then the discontinuity is more revealing. When Christianity and rabbinic Judaism diverge from their original common matrix, each group will increasingly emphasize its differences from the other group. There may be more similarities than differences between the Didache and the *Birkat*, but the differences are hugely significant, signaling the trajectory of change. Distinctively Christian ideas will be essential in the group's self-definition and self-understanding. SIT confirms that it is the differences, not the common ground, that shape the identity and self-expression of diverging groups. The groups will consciously heighten their differences.[25] Group beliefs "unify group members and ... differentiate them from outgroups."[26]

---

21. Jürgen K. Zangenberg, "Reconstructing the Social and Religious Milieu of the Didache: Observations and Possible Results," in *Matthew, James, and Didache: Three Related Documents in Their Jewish and Christian Settings*, ed. Huub van de Sandt and Jürgen K. Zangenberg, SBLSymS 45 (Atlanta: Society of Biblical Literature, 2008), 65.

22. Huub van de Sandt and David Flusser, *The Didache: Its Jewish Sources and Its Place in Early Judaism and Christianity*, CRINT 3.5 (Assen: Van Gorcum; Minneapolis: Fortress, 2002), 322–23.

23. Van de Sandt, "Didache Redefining its Jewish Identity," 255.

24. Ibid., 257–58.

25. Hakola, "Social Identities," 262, 272.

26. Daniel Bar-Tal, "Group Beliefs as an Expression of Social Identity," in *Social*

The Didache is trying to articulate a Jewish identity *and* a Christ-believing identity, but the Jewish identity has become symbolic and not concrete (national) as gentiles continue to join the group. The assertion of Jesus as Messiah and world Savior will have the social effect of alienating the group from rabbinic Judaism, even though the group imagines itself as still following "the rules of the Lord" (4.13). In the Didache, Torah is no longer the possession of an ethnic group.

2.2. Distinction from "Hypocrites" and "Dogs"

In Did. 8 we see some key comments for differentiating and defining the group. Didache 8.1 tells the community to fast on Wednesday and Friday, not on Monday and Thursday as "the hypocrites" do. Didache 8.2 tells the community to "pray thus" (οὕτως προσεύχεσθε, just as in Matt 6:9) and not "as the hypocrites" pray.[27]

Draper may be right to argue that it is anachronistic to see "hypocrites" as a "blanket condemnation" of Jews, since there is no "definitive or normative form" of Judaism. Rather, they are being distinguished from a *particular* Jewish community. "The opponents are Pharisees or nascent Rabbinism," whose sources *do* refer to fasting on Mondays and Thursdays.[28] Van de Sandt disagrees, arguing that Mondays and Thursdays were not unique to the Pharisees but were the normal Jewish fast days.[29] Van de Sandt argues that the instruction to fast for one or two days before baptism (7.4) is another indication of the Didachist's distance from Judaism if baptisms were performed on Sunday (14.1). Since a good meal was commanded for Sabbath, this would constitute a Sabbath violation, and so "the *Didache* has dropped—at least in this respect—the observance of

---

Identity: International Perspectives, ed. Stephen Worchel et al. (London: Sage, 1998), 93–113 (95).

27. On differences from and similarities to Matthew here, see Peter J. Tomson, "The Halakhic Evidence of *Didache* 8 and Matthew 6 and the *Didache* Community's Relationship to Judaism," in van de Sandt, *Matthew and the Didache*, 137.

28. Draper, "Didache and Matthew," 231, citing m. Meg. 3:6; 4:1; m. Taʿan. 4:2; b. Taʿan. 12a; and also, from a later time, Tertullian, *Jejun.* 16. See also his "Christian Self-Definition against the 'Hypocrites' in *Didache* VIII," in *The* Didache *in Modern Research*, ed. Jonathan A. Draper, AGJU 37 (Leiden: Brill, 1996), 223–43 (233). Anti-Pharisaic passages may indicate that "at this stage Didache and Matthew represented one and the same community" (Tomson, "Halakhic Evidence," 140).

29. Van de Sandt, "Didache Redefining its Jewish Identity," 261.

the Jewish Sabbath."[30] Given the community's transition "to an increasingly gentile" context, van de Sandt argues that it makes more sense to see "hypocrites" as polemic use "against Jews in general." The author is "strengthening the community's social identity" in distinction from the Jewish community.[31]

I think it likely that van de Sandt and Draper are correct about different aspects of the community's self-definition, that van de Sandt is correct in seeing the community as engaging in Christian self-definition, while Draper is correct in seeing the "hypocrites" as a particular Jewish group (a close "relative") from which the Didachist is making a distinction. On balance it seems that van de Sandt is acute in discerning Christian self-definition, while Draper is attuned to the Jewish self-definition. Both kinds of self-definition are going on, but I think we need to notice that the group's Jewishness is increasingly symbolic and ancestral.

Draper expands upon the clues to the Jewish ancestry of the Didache community. He argues that, before the addition of chapter 8 to the Didache, "the original community of the *Didache* saw no need to differentiate itself from the Jewish community. They differentiated themselves not from Jews but from pagans." Someone who joined "would see her/himself joining a particular … faithful, Torah-observant Jewish community."[32] At first the group was "defining itself primarily against the Gentiles" but lacked a "clear differentiation from other Jewish groups." Chapter 8 does show such differentiation, "nor are the possibilities of reconciliation left open."[33] But surely the Christology is more fundamental than the choice of fasting days. Calendrical debates are evidence of deeper ideological divergences. It is Christology (however embryonic) that signals the Didache community's separation from its ancestral Jewish group.

Numerous passages signal this separation: the surprising looseness about Torah (6.3), affirmation of the messiahship of Jesus (9.3–4; 10.3), the instruction to "eucharistize" (εὐχαριστήσατε; 9.1; 10.1),[34] and baptizing in the names of the persons of the Trinity (7.1, 3). These would surely

---

30. Ibid., 263.
31. Ibid., 264–65.
32. Draper, "Christian Self-Definition," 230.
33. Ibid., 243.
34. Even though some forms of grace in Hellenistic Judaism may have begun with the verb εὐχαριστεῖν (van de Sandt and Flusser, *Didache*, 322), its usage in the Didache is Christian.

distinguish the community from any Jewish group that did not identify Jesus as the Messiah.

Another sharp social distinction is made using the pejorative "dogs." The community is told not to allow any unbaptized people to participate in the eucharistic meal, "for the Lord has likewise said concerning this: 'Do not give what is holy to the dogs'" (9.5). "Dogs" was a common Jewish put-down for gentiles. The phrase is used in rabbinic literature, as in m. Tem. 6:5 and Pirqe R. El. 29.[35] A similar concept of separation at meals may be seen in the Pseudo-Clementine instruction against eating "common meals with the unbaptized (Hom. 1.22; 8.22 ... Recog. 1.19, 22).... Such a rule in the Didache shows both a very Jewish concern with ritual purity and also a sectarian concern to exclude non-members."[36] It is more "sectarian" than "Jewish" in my view, since the exclusion has no ethnic implication.

The term "ritual purity" needs to be nuanced. It is true that "the holy" (τὸ ἅγιον) is the term for cultic holiness in the LXX,[37] but we need to recognize that the meaning has been spiritualized in the Didache. It no longer has anything to do with the temple, priesthood, purity of the nation, or Levitical rituals. It is now the Christ-believing community and its Eucharist that are holy. Inasmuch as the Eucharist is a ritual, one can speak of "ritual purity," but this needs to be distinguished from Levitical purity. Just as the Christ-believing identity of the group forever distinguishes it from all groups that do not believe in Christ, so its usage of ritual terms is to be distinguished from the use of the same terms in Levitical or rabbinic texts.

"Dogs" is extremist language, but it is not (in the Didache) directed against gentiles but against unbaptized persons. It is an example of an extremist position in the service of self-definition, which SIT calls "group polarization.... Groups make judgments which are more extreme than the average initial positions of the group members."[38] Draper is well aware of SIT and mentions the "*stereotyping* not only of others from out-groups but of *ourselves* as members of our in-group."[39]

---

35. Draper, "Didache and Matthew," 236, and "Christian Self-Definition," 239–40.
36. Draper, "Christian Self-Definition," 241.
37. Ibid., 239.
38. Michael A. Hogg and Craig McGarty, "Self-categorization and Social Identity," in *Social Identity Theory: Constructive and Critical Advances*, ed. Dominic Abrams and Michael A. Hogg (New York: Springer, 1990), 15.
39. Draper, "Mission, Ethics and Identity," 3 (manuscript).

Draper discerns that the Didache stands at a certain stage "in the process of alienation from Israel" and argues "that the Didache stands at the beginning of a process and Matthew further down the line!"[40] Thus I envision the same trajectory as Draper does, but I would emphasize the significant progress along the line of alienation or separation that the Didache group has made, while Draper stresses the group's Jewish roots. Of course, any theory on the likely path of development of the Didache group must take note of the many Jewish usages and concepts that Draper has uncovered, but we must note how the Christian beliefs have caused the Jewish terms to take on a transformed meaning.

2.3. Ingathering of Gentiles

Whenever Israel-specific images are used in the Didache, they are universalized. Therefore, it is potentially misleading to say that the Didache has a "royal Davidic kingdom eschatology"[41] and aims at "the restoration of Israel, the kingdom of David, through Jesus the new David,"[42] if these remarks are understood in a nationalistic way. Draper claims that "the holy vine of your servant David" now made known to the gentiles (9.2) signifies Jesus as "the one who revives [David's] kingdom," indicating that gentiles "become members of Israel by adoption through Jesus as the heir of David ... Jesus as the heir of David and restorer of the Kingdom of Israel."[43]

Of course the vine of David is indeed the *Jewish* messiah, and the vine is an old symbol for Israel itself (possibly based on Num 13:23),[44] but here the messiah functions for "your church" (9.4; 10.5) rather than for Israel, and prayer is to "our Father" (9.2–3) rather than to the God of Israel. The prophecy has been internationalized. The Didachist draws upon prophetic language for the gathering of Jewish exiles[45] to picture the ingathering of the church, a denationalized image that includes gentile believers. It is

---

40. Draper, "Didache and Matthew," 239.
41. Draper, "Two Ways," 241.
42. Draper, "Eschatology in the *Didache*," 569; see also his "Didache and Matthew," 239.
43. Draper, "Didache and Matthew," 238–39.
44. But van de Sandt and Flusser cite Ps 80:8–12, 15; Jer 2:21; Ezek 15:1–5; Hos 10:1 (*Didache*, 324).
45. Isa 11:12; 27:13; 43:6; 49:22; 66:20; Jer 23:8; 31:8–12; Zech 10:10.

"your church," not Israel that is "gathered together from the ends of the earth" (9.4) and "the four winds" (10.5).

That the author is thinking of a universal community incorporating gentiles is signaled by the repeated use of the terms for the earth or the world (γῆ or κόσμος). The gentile will inherit the *earth* (3.7); God's kingdom will come "upon earth" (8.2); the evil one is a *world* deceiver (κοσμοπλανὴς), which tends to imply a *world* savior (16.4); and "the world will see the Lord coming" (16.8).

Further, the author uses nonnational terms for believers. It is *people* ("the false prophets and the corrupters"; 16.3), not nations, who are judged in the time of testing. It is ἄνθρωποι ("humans"), those who have "remained firm in their faith," who are being saved in 16.5. Obviously the "symbolic universe"[46] of Judaism is everywhere in the Didache, but the gentiles are now included, and that changes everything.

The national cult of sacrifice is mentioned, but it is spiritualized: "let none who has a quarrel with his fellow join in your meeting until they be reconciled, that your sacrifice be not defiled" (14.2; Lake, LCL). The next verse has a royal theme, but it is internationalized: "'In every place and time, offer to me a pure sacrifice. Because a great king am I,' says [the] Lord, 'and my name [is] wondrous among the gentiles'" (quoting Mal 1:11, 14). Socially speaking, the emphasis is on "every place and time" and on "gentiles." The "king" has no *national* connection here. A temple image does occur, but it is spiritualized: "We give thanks, holy Father, for your holy name, which you tabernacle in our hearts" (10.2).

If something as basic to Jewish practice as sacrifice and temple can be reconceived in a wholly metaphorical manner, it should caution us against taking "king" or "David" in a nationalistic sense. We see similar symbolic or spiritualized usages of Israel-specific terms in the New Testament, as in "the Israel of God" (Gal 6:16), "temple of the living God" (2 Cor 6:16), "his kingdom" (Luke 1:33), and "a chosen race, a royal priesthood, a holy nation" (1 Pet 2:9), all of which lack any *national* meaning.[47] Jesus is a literal descendant of David in Rom 1:3 and Rev 5:5, but we would not speak of Christ as "restorer of the kingdom of Israel" in Paul or the Revelator.

---

46. Magnus Zetterholm, *The Formation of Christianity in Antioch: A Social-Scientific Approach to the Separation of Judaism and Christianity* (London: Routledge, 2003), 6.

47. Unless otherwise stated, translations from the Bible follow the NRSV.

2.4. Difference from Pauline Theology

Since some might infer that I am pushing the Didache too close to the universalizing theology of Paul, it is necessary to make some distinctions. Paul's soteriology is based upon sacrificial and redemption metaphors for the death of Christ and a judicial metaphor (justification) for the beneficial result. Paul even places the messiah's death at the center of individual experience (believers are "united with him in a death like his"; Rom 6:5). The Didache does not refer to the death of Jesus at all, much less make it soteriologically central.

In the Didache's lengthy liturgy spoken over the bread and cup, there is no mention of a body broken or of blood poured out. Instead, the cup signifies "the holy vine of your servant David," and the bread bespeaks the church "gathered together from the ends of the earth" like the grains were gathered from hillsides to form the bread (Did. 9.2, 4). The author is making a messianic point (David's vine) and an ecclesiastical point (church gathered from everywhere). What is relevant about Jesus in this ritual is not his death, but the revelation of God through him: "the life and knowledge which you revealed to us through your servant Jesus" (9.3); "the knowledge and faith and immortality which you revealed to us through your servant Jesus" (10.2). "Servant" (παῖς) surely echoes the Servant Songs of Isaiah, but universality is stressed in the same passages: "ends of the earth ... created all things" (9.4; 10.3). Universality was also a theme of Second Isaiah, of course.

In the Didache Jesus is the Messiah, revealer, life-giver, embodiment of glory (9.4), and imparter of knowledge, showing the way of *gnosis* and *pistis*, which are not set against each other. Of course the knowledge of God found in 9.3 and 10.2 looks back to דעת אלהים or דעת יהוה ("knowledge of God"), an important theme in biblical spirituality (Prov 2:5; Isa 11:9; Jer 9:24; Hos 4:1; Hab 2:14), but knowledge of God is now *christologized*. Many of these messianic and revelatory themes can also be found in Paul, but there they are secondary to the need for the reconciliation that comes through the messiah's death and resurrection (Rom 5:8–11). Clearly Paul's soteriology was not the default position for all early Christ-believers.[48]

---

48. I need not settle the dispute over whether the Didache is unaware of Paul (Milavec, "When, Why, and for Whom," 74 n. 2) or whether it actually attacks Paul in 11.2 (see Jonathan A. Draper, "Torah and Troublesome Apostles in the Didache Community," *NovT* 33 [1991]: 347–72 [350–56]).

The absence of any atonement teaching in the Didache becomes even more significant if the document is pre-Pauline, as some have argued (a minority opinion, but not an absurd one). The Palestinian setting, the primitive baptism rituals and church organization, the absence of any connection with a theology of the cross, all bespeak an early date,[49] maybe "a mid-first century dating."[50] The Didache seems to give us a glimpse of Christian beliefs before Pauline and deutero-Pauline atonement thinking became dominant. Atonement theology is not essential to being "Christian." Christology need not imply substitutionary atonement. The Didache's Christology involves Christ as life-giver, teacher, and revealer, but not as sacrificial victim.

It seems that Draper focuses on passages that endeavor to move the community in a Torah-observing direction. He may be discerning the viewpoint of *one* of the Didache's authors or redactors. The intriguing mixture of law and liberality, toleration in the present and hope for more strictness in the future, may suggest that one of the redactors is more conservative than his community. It seems likely that the community being addressed has a substantial gentile population and has been moving toward increasingly metaphorical and liberal interpretation of Torah, a trend being resisted by this particular redactor, who warns not to "wander from this way of training" (6.1), not to listen to "another teaching" (11.2), and to beware of "lawlessness" (16.4). The author or redactor seems to realize that it is not possible to swing the community wholly over, so Torah obedience in the present is not strictly demanded, but *hope* for the future is expressed: "the whole time of your faith will not be of use to you if in the end time you should not have been perfected" (16.2).[51] Another possibility, however, is that the author is not exhorting obedience to Torah but to the commands in the Didache itself. The author would be resisting any tendency toward looseness about the code of behavior in the Two Ways section.

The document may give indications of different layers of composition, though that is not certain. In any case, I do not think that a conserva-

---

49. Joan Hazelden Walker, "A Pre-Marcan Dating for the Didache: Further Thoughts of a Liturgist," *StudBib* 3 (1978): 405–8.

50. Milavec, "When, Why, and for Whom," 63. Draper seems to allow the possibility of a date between 50 and 70 CE ("Holy Vine," 281).

51. Focusing on 16.2–3, Draper says concerning the danger of false prophets that "the threat comes from inside the community" ("Eschatology in the *Didache*," 575).

tive voice overwhelms the universalizing voice of 2.7, 3.8, 6.2, 9.4, 10.3–5, and 14.3 or the absence (throughout) of any pitting of Israel against the nations. The Didache has a universalizing direction. The community is not "Israel" but the "church" (4.14; 9.4; 10.5; 11.11).

3. Christian Identity

The Didachist may be struggling for adequate language to describe how the Jewish messiah became the world messiah and how God's people became internationalized, fulfilling the prophecy that "many nations shall join themselves to the Lord" (Zech 2:11).

The Didache asserts a Christian identity, even while it holds on to an increasingly abstract and symbolic Jewish identity. But then Christian identity has always involved a kind of symbolic conversion to Judaism, an adoption as children of Abraham (Gal 3:7; 4:5), an identity as "a holy nation" (1 Pet 2:9). In this regard there is a similarity between Pauline, Petrine, and Didachist versions of Christianity, even though they differ greatly in the amount of Torah observance they recommend or allow.

Converts to the Didache community are converting first of all to *belief in Christ*, not to membership in Israel. It is Jesus the Christ who brings knowledge of God (9.3; 10.2). The Didachist denationalizes the prophetic language for the gathering of Jewish exiles and applies it to the church. Ethics derive from the Sermon on the Mount, converts are baptized in the names of the persons of the Trinity (7.1, 3) without any mention of the standard procedures for proselyte-conversion to Judaism,[52] and the Lord's Prayer is recited three times a day (8.2–3). The eschatological hope is for a gathering of the church, not for a "restoration of Israel and Jerusalem."[53] In the matter of Christian identity then, there is no gap between the Didache and the community to which it is addressed. But on the issue of Torah observance, and therefore on some aspects of

---

52. "The initiatory rite ... comprised three parts: circumcision, immersion in water (baptism), and the presentation of an offering in the temple" (citing Sipre Num. 108; George Foot Moore, *Judaism in the First Centuries of the Christian Era*, 3 vols. [Cambridge: Harvard University Press, 1927–1930], 1:331).

53. Huub van de Sandt, "The Gathering of the Church in the Kingdom: The Self-Understanding of the *Didache* Community in the Eucharistic Prayers," in *Society of Biblical Literature 2003 Seminar Papers*, SBLSP 42 (Atlanta: Society of Biblical Literature, 2003), 75.

"identity," there may be a small gap between the community and a particular redactor who is distressed by the community's increasing distance from Torah.

The Didache is far more attached to Jewish identity than Paul is, and Paul would reject its imposition of even a limited Torah observance. But we should recognize this as intra-Christian polemic. The Didache is as Christian as Paul is. The only kind of "conversion to Judaism" of which we can speak is a symbolic or *imaginal* conversion to a *Christianized* and *symbolic* Judaism.

Christianity can be described as a kind of transmogrified or universalized Judaism, as long as it is not *reduced* to that. Conversion, in either Paul's or the Didache's community may be a kind of symbolic conversion to Judaism, but it is an *actual* conversion to a Christ-community that is clearly distinct from both temple-based and rabbinic Judaism.

Authority and Perspective in the Didache

Clayton N. Jefford

1. Introduction

Scholars have long recognized the difficulties that arise from comparisons of Scripture with the text of the Didache. Early researchers settled on the basic assumption that the Didachist must have had a variety of written scriptures available at the time of writing, with Matthew as the primary gospel on which much of the text was based. With respect to Old Testament texts and traditions, such assumptions are undoubtedly true. But with respect to New Testament writings, such presuppositions are easily challenged, and more recent studies have indicated either the presence of independent oral traditions,[1] parallel textual developments,[2] or even the possibility that certain New Testament authors may have made use of the Didache itself.[3]

Even a cursory reading of the Didache spawns immediate recognition of biblical texts and themes well known to most readers. The opening call to recognize the Two Ways of existence (that is, life and death; 1.1) leads to instructions about love of God and neighbor, followed by the negative expression of the so-called golden rule (1.2). Prohibitions against sins listed in the Decalogue (murder, adultery, theft, etc.) appear thereafter (2.2–3.6; 5.1), followed by the comforting words "my child" drawn

---

1. Already evident in the work of Helmut Koester, *Synoptische Überlieferung bei den apostolischen Vätern*, TUGAL 65/5.10 (Berlin: Akademie, 1957), 159–241.

2. This is an underlying assumption for Kurt Niederwimmer, *The Didache: A Commentary*, trans. Linda M. Maloney, Hermeneia (Minneapolis: Fortress, 1998), 52; see especially his "Der Didachist und seine Quellen," in *The Didache in Context*, ed. Clayton N. Jefford, NovTSup 77 (Leiden: Brill, 1995), 15–36.

3. Most recently, Alan J. P. Garrow, *The Gospel of Matthew's Dependence on the Didache*, JSNTSup 254 (London: T&T Clark, 2004).

from wisdom literature (3.1–6; 4.1) and a brief household code (4.9–11). Subsequent instructions to baptize in the name of the Trinity (7.1, 3) are followed by the so-called Lord's Prayer (8.2), counsel not to give holy items to dogs (9.5), and concluding warnings about the end times (16.1–8). Such clear equivalents prod most readers to question the sort of literary relationship that must have existed between the Didache and Scripture.[4]

The history of research into this question has produced a variety of studies related to the topic of the Didachist's use of biblical sources. The most recent, and perhaps most complete, of these was published by William Varner in 2005.[5] Varner's concerns are typically what scholars might otherwise consider, that is, the form of scripture employed and the manner in which it is used.[6] His study is a careful analysis of these two elements, focusing on the nature of the quotations and allusions in the Didache, the basic manuscript traditions behind the sources that were employed, and the purposes for which those materials were incorporated. Included here are not only canonical materials, but similarly relevant noncanonical sources.

---

4. This was true already from the beginning of such research; see Philip Schaff, *The Oldest Church Manual Called the Teaching of the Twelve Apostles (ΔΙΔΑΧΗ ΤΩΝ ΔΩΔΕΚΑ ΑΠΟΣΤΟΛΩΝ)* (London: T&T Clark; New York: Funk & Wagnalls, 1885), 78–95; Adolf von Harnack, *Die Apostellehre und die jüdischen Beiden Wege* (Leipzig: Heinrichs, 1886); Gustav Wohlenberg, *Die Lehre der zwölf Apostel in ihrem Verhältnis zum neutestamentlichen Schrifttum: Eine Untersuchung* (Erlangen: Deichert, 1888). More recently, one might consider Jean-Paul Audet, *La Didachè: Instructions des Apôtres*, Ebib (Paris: Gabalda, 1958), 166–86; Willy Rordorf and André Tuilier, *La doctrine des douze Apôtres (Didachè)*, SC 248 bis (Paris: Cerf, 1998), 83–91; Niederwimmer, *Didache*, 42–52; Kari Syreeni, "The Sermon on the Mount and the Two Ways Teaching of the Didache," in *Matthew and the Didache: Two Documents from the Same Jewish-Christian Milieu?* ed. Huub van de Sandt (Assen: Van Gorcum; Minneapolis: Fortress, 2005), 87–103; and Christopher M. Tuckett, "The *Didache* and the Writings that Later Formed the New Testament," in *The Reception of the New Testament in the Apostolic Fathers*, vol. 1 in *The New Testament and the Apostolic Fathers*, ed. Andrew F. Gregory and Christopher M. Tuckett (Oxford: Oxford University Press, 2005), 83–127.

5. William Varner, "The Didache's Use of the Old and New Testaments," *MSJ* 16 (2005): 127–51. Parallel materials appear in his subsequent volume, *The Way of the Didache: The First Christian Handbook* (Lanham, MD: University Press of America, 2007), 41–54.

6. Or as he indicates, the linguistic and hermeneutical questions; so Varner, "Didache's Use," 128.

In the final analysis, Varner comes to five basic conclusions about the scriptural sources behind the text.[7] These are important guideposts by which to measure the intention of the Didachist, both with respect to the author's understanding of the nature of authority and with reference to the matter of perspective on tradition. His five conclusions are as follows: (1) the Didachist saw authority in Scripture; (2) the Didachist made considerable use of the Gospel of Matthew; (3) the Didachist incorporated segments of the Torah and the Prophets drawn from the LXX; (4) the Didachist did *not* make use of allegory as a mode of interpretation; and (5) the Didachist employed Scripture in the same way as the New Testament authors.

Such conclusions are worth consideration to the extent that two other elements are included. The first of these relates to what Robert Kraft once identified as the essential nature of both the Didache and Barnabas, that is, "evolved literature."[8] The text of the Didache is known primarily from a single manuscript tradition in Greek,[9] but even here are numerous problems that suggest the tradition may have evolved through more than one editorial hand. For example, the section of materials from 1.3b–2.1 known as the "ecclesiastical section" (the *Sectio Evangelica*) features several so-called Q texts, a source that is otherwise little featured throughout the work.[10] Most scholars now recognize this segment as secondary to the text, an insertion from a later hand. At the same time, there is some question about whether the Greek manuscript contains the final verses of the original text or whether that wording has been lost.[11] If the latter, it is impossible to know how such an omission may have occurred over the course

---

7. See Varner, "Didache's Use," 141–42; *Way of the Didache*, 53–54.

8. Robert A. Kraft, *Barnabas and the Didache*, AF 3 (Toronto: Nelson, 1965), 1–3.

9. Codex Hierosolymitanus 54.

10. See Richard Glover, "The Didache's Quotations and the Synoptic Gospels," *NTS* 5 (1958): 12–29; Bentley Layton, "The Sources, Date and Transmission of *Didache* 1.3b–2.1," *HTR* 61 (1968): 343–83; Michael Mees, "Die Bedeutung der Sentenzen und ihrer auxesis für den Formung der Jesusworte nach Didache 1,3b–2,1," *VetChr* 8 (1971): 55–76; John S. Kloppenborg, "The Use of the Synoptics or Q in *Did.* 1:3b–2:1," in van de Sandt, *Matthew and the Didache*, 105–29; Christopher M. Tuckett, "Synoptic Tradition in the Didache," in *The* Didache *in Modern Research*, ed. Jonathan A. Draper, AGJU 37 (Leiden: Brill, 1996), 110–28.

11. See Aaron Milavec, "The Saving Efficacy of the Burning Process in *Didache* 16.5," in *The* Didache *in Context: Essays on Its Text, History and Transmission*, ed. Clayton N. Jefford, NovTSup 77 (Leiden: Brill, 1995), 151–54; Robert E. Aldridge,

of the manuscript's transmission, but nevertheless the present Greek text would thus be defective. Finally, numerous words and phrases that now appear in the manuscript are missing from the fourth-century Apostolic Constitutions and Canons, a text that preserves a majority of the Didache with substantial elaboration.[12] This suggests the Greek manuscript, dating much later to sometime in the early eleventh century, has acquired various alterations not originally associated with the *Vorlage* and thus may not reflect the perspective of the Didachist. Efforts to distinguish between original text and additions are difficult, though perhaps not impossible to some extent. The evolution of the text must certainly be considered in any permissible discussion of the appearance of Scripture within the Didache.

A second element to consider relates to the first, coming in the form of what James Sanders has identified as the question of "canonical criticism,"[13] a consideration of what any particular author views as authoritative canon with respect to texts and traditions. An author thus chooses among sources considered to be respected in support of the argument at hand. The use of such sources presumably reflects both the perspective of the author and the audience. In the case of the Didachist, one assumes that the biblical sources included in the text reflect those traditions held in highest esteem within the immediate community context.

A consideration of canonical elements is not unexpected but is made more complex when one imagines that the Didache is possibly a compilation by diverse authors and editors. Unless these contributors derive from the same community setting and are de facto in agreement with respect to canonical authority, their assorted contexts must be established in order to understand how individual sources have been put into use. Each author necessarily represents a tradition, which itself works with recognized literary authorities. One must thus recognize how each tradition interprets

---

"The Lost Ending of the *Didache*," VC 53 (1999): 1–15; Garrow, *Gospel of Matthew's Dependence*, 38–66.

12. Much of this alteration is likely due to the author's desire to accommodate the Didache as a source to the needs of the readership, which often includes the addition of numerous passages from Scripture by way of illustration.

13. James A. Sanders, *Torah and Canon* (Philadelphia: Fortress, 1972). Sanders applies this specifically to use of the Old Testament in the New Testament, but the same may be said about the authors and writings of late Christian antiquity.

its authorities in order to identify the literary convention within which scriptural sources are used for each passage.[14]

It is assumed here that such distinctions cannot be made with certainty in the case of the Didache, particularly since scholars disagree concerning the background and composition of the text. At the same time, however, one may perhaps separate different scriptural references and the manner by which those sources are used to help establish possible layers of development that have accrued over time. This will be the goal of the present essay, taking advantage of Varner's work in the process.

2. Clear Citations of Scripture

A reasonable place to begin is those instances in the Didache where the author has acknowledged use of authoritative sources. Several of these are scattered throughout the text.

The first appears at Did. 1.5. Here the Didachist (= Did¹) appears to quote from either Matt 5:42 or Luke 6:30.[15] There is little question that the author views this as a "citation" of authoritative teaching (either oral or written), since the text continues with the line "fortunate is the one who gives according to [this] instruction." The term "instruction" (ἐντολή) suggests both conscious reference and authoritative source. The text itself reads as follows:[16]

> Did. 1.5a: Give to each one who asks of you and do not be anxious.
> παντὶ τῷ αἰτοῦντί σε δίδου καὶ μὴ ἀπαίτει
> Matt 5:42: τῷ αἰτοῦντί σε δός ... μὴ ἀποστραφῆς
> Luke 6:30: παντὶ αἰτοῦντί σε δίδου ... μὴ ἀπαίτει

---

14. This is not to assume that the authorities in question are necessarily written in the case of the Didache; see, e.g., Ian H. Henderson, "Didache and Orality in Synoptic Comparison," *JBL* 111 (1992): 283–306; see also his related essay on *style-switching* throughout the text in "Style-Switching in the *Didache*: Fingerprint or Argument?" in Jefford, Didache *in Context*, 177–209.

15. Stanislas Giet, *L'énigme de la Didachè*, PFLUS 149 (Paris: Ophrys, 1970), 190; Rordorf and Tuilier, *Doctrine des douze Apôtres*, 85–86; Niederwimmer, *Didache*, 81–83, notes further the parallel with Herm. Mand. 2.6.

16. All translations of the Didache are my own.

A quick scan of the wording suggests closer similarity to Luke than Matthew, and even Varner, who otherwise is focused on the Didachist's primary concern for Matthew, admits Lukan influence here.[17]

But one must not forget that scholars typically view this verse as part of the larger secondary insertion of 1.3b–2.1 and thus not original to the text. If the reference in 1.5 is indeed a citation of Luke as an authoritative source (as it well appears to be), it is thus not necessarily reflective of the Didachist's perspective but that of a secondary editor (= Did²). This later contributor to the text appears to hold a certain respect for Luke not otherwise obvious elsewhere in the Didache. And so one must attribute this viewpoint not to the Didachist but to what was likely an early redactor of the text.[18]

One should also observe that, by the same argument, Did² held the Decalogue as an authoritative source, since that material is likewise introduced as a "second instruction [ἐντολή] of the teaching" in 2.1, which one assumes are also the words of this editor. This is hardly surprising, but is worth note in an effort to associate sources of authority with this particular redactor.[19] One thus may attribute at least two sources of authority to

---

17. Varner, "Didache's Use," 132: "Though such a variation may prohibit blind dogmatism about the Didache's sole usage of Matthew, its rarity of occurrence illustrates the point that the Didachist used Matthew almost exclusively." See also Tuckett, "Synoptic Tradition in the Didache," 125–28, who finds evidence of Lukan redactional activity behind the saying here (126). Kloppenborg, "Synoptics or Q," observes in support of Tuckett's position that "agreement with Luke's παντί and δίδου, both normally attributed to Lukan redaction, seems to signal the Didache's knowledge of Luke." Though against Tuckett's presupposition of written sources, see Aaron Milavec, "Synoptic Tradition in the *Didache* Revisited," *JECS* 11 (2003): 443–80.

18. Such designations as Did¹ and Did² are not to be confused with Audet's own D1 and D2 labels (Audet, *Didachè*, 110–15). Though Audet used similar terminology, his scope was limited to the immediate editing of the early textual tradition and did not take into consideration the later emendation of the Greek manuscript itself, which is my own concern here.

19. This begs the question of other usages of "instruction" (ἐντολή) within the Didache of which there are five total. Apart from the two mentioned in 1.5 and 2.1, the term appears in 4.13, as well as 13.5 and 7. There is some question about whether the latter two references are original to the *Vorlage*, since neither is preserved by the Apostolic Constitutions and Canons and the former is likewise missing from the Georgian version of the Didache, which otherwise tends to read similarly to the Greek text of Codex Hierosolymitanus 54. Whether these usages may be attributed to Did² is debatable, but neither reflects a known text of Scripture and thus the matter stands

the secondary editor Did² and quite likely three: Torah, Lukan tradition, and dominical sayings.

A second citation appears at 8.2, where the listener is told not to pray like the hypocrites, but "as the Lord instructed in his gospel, pray as follows" prior to the introduction of the so-called Lord's Prayer.[20] The form of the prayer is very close to that of Matt 6:9–13 rather than Luke 11:2–4, preserving both the terminology and structure of Matthean tradition. Varner seems to agree with Udo Schnelle here that the reference to "in his gospel" (ἐν τῷ εὐαγγελίῳ) is a clear indication that the Didachist knew a written form of Matthew at this point.[21] As further support for his argument, he gives explanation for the doxological conclusion "for yours are the power and the glory forever" found at the end of Did. 8.2, which appears only secondarily in certain later manuscripts that preserve the Matthean version of the prayer. Varner observes:

> Though this addition to the prayer in the Didache initially may appear to encourage Byzantine text advocates since it could support an early date for this ending, the truth is just the opposite. The doxological ascrip-

---

moot for present purposes. With respect to 4.13, the warning here that one accept the "Lord's commandments … neither adding nor subtracting" recalls Deut 4:2, 12:32, or Prov 30:6 (if one considers the "Lord" to be God) or perhaps vaguely of Rev 22:18 (if one considers the "Lord" to be Christ). Both the Apostolic Constitutions and Canons and Apostolic Church Order preserve this verse, thus suggesting that it is original to the text. In either case, as with 13.5 and 7 above, there is no specific scriptural source at reference here and thus little to be gained by pursing the matter further for present discussion.

20. Literature on this passage is expansive with primary focus on the nature of "hypocrites." See, e.g., Édouard Massaux, *The Apologists and the Didache*, vol. 3 of *The Influence of the Gospel of Saint Matthew on the Christian Literature before Saint Irenaeus*, trans. Norman J. Belval and Suzanne Hecht; NGS 5.2; Macon, GA: Mercer University Press, 1993), 154–55; Jonathan A. Draper, "Christian Self-Definition against the 'Hypocrites' in *Didache* 8," in *The Didache in Modern Research*, ed. Jonathan A. Draper, AGJU 37 (Leiden: Brill, 1996), 223–43; Marcello Del Verme, *Didache and Judaism: Jewish Roots of an Ancient Christian-Jewish Work* (London: T&T Clark, 2004) 144–88; and most recently, Stephen E. Young, *Jesus Tradition in the Apostolic [Fathers]: Appeals to the Words of Jesus in Light of Orality Studies*, WUNT [...] Siebeck, 2011), 218–24. Tuckett ("Synoptic Tradition in the [...] this reference.

[...]idache's Use," 132, in reference to Udo Schnelle, *The History [of the New] Testament Writings*, trans. M. Eugene Boring (Minneapolis:

tion appears later in the Didache in almost the exact same form and is appended to the Eucharistic prayers in 9:2, 3, 4 and 10:2, 4, 5. It is very similar to a common ending to prayers in the Jewish liturgy which exist even today. A better explanation of the manuscript tradition is that the Didache is an early witness to the tendency of scribes to add doxological ascriptions, which increased in Byzantine times when doxological ascription crystallized and, in the Middle Ages, became part of the received text—at least in the Byzantine section of the church.

This connection with parallel prayers in Did. 9–10 via similar conclusions is well taken. But as the context suggests, the Didachist seems familiar with the Lord's Prayer largely within the context of other messianic Jewish prayers, all appearing in the Didache within the framework of chapters 8–10. This is no comment on the origins of any of these prayers, but the introductory formula "in his gospel" in 8.2 suggests that at least this opening prayer belongs to a tradition of teachings that stands apart from the prayers of chapters 9–10.[22]

There is little reason to doubt that the introductory formula here is original to Did¹, though use of the same or similar wording elsewhere is not as certain. The Didache provides some form of this phrase four times (8.2; 11.3; 15.3, 4), with only the first appearance preserved in the witness of the Apostolic Constitutions and Canons, a text one might expect to welcome such a useful reflection of literary tradition. Where the phrase is preserved at 8.2, the wording reads with a slight alteration. The form in both the Apostolic Constitutions and Canons and Ethiopic versions reads simply "in *the* gospel," while the Didache adds "of him" (αὐτοῦ). The former reading surely understands the reference to be a known textual convention, while the latter is not so clear, perhaps reflecting oral tradition.[23] In the final analysis, the text at 8.2 suggests that the Didachist gave significant authority to the teachings (= gospel?) of Jesus, preserved at least in this case according to the terminology and structure known from Matthean tradition.

A third citation appears at 9.5 where a reference is introduced with the words "for the Lord has also spoken about this." That reference is the

---

22. Draper argues that the whole of chapter 8 may be secondary to the text, so Draper, "Christian Self-Definition." See too in this volume, the essay of Peter J. Tomson ("The Lord's Prayer [Didache 8] at the Faultline of Judaism and Christianity"), specifically under "3. Comparing Contexts."

23. See Koester, *Synoptische Überlieferung*, 203–9.

dominical saying "Do not give what is holy to dogs," known elsewhere only from Matt 7:6. While the two references are virtually identical in Greek,[24] the contexts diverge: Matthew's reference is related to the judgment of others; that of the Didache is a warning against participation by the unbaptized in the Eucharist. Varner believes, however, that the context is in fact not so different, the Matthean setting having placed the saying at the conclusion of materials about judging generally (7:1–5 to 7:6) and the location of the Didache usage being associated with the "moral and spiritual responsibility" of the assembly's leadership to make such judgments with respect to participation in the Eucharist.[25] Such an astute observation readily displaces the more specific concerns that commentators often brought to the matter of context in a broad sense. Yet there is another element that should be considered as well.

The only clear textual parallel to this section is preserved once again in the Apostolic Constitutions and Canons (7.25.5–7). Here too one might expect this editor to have eagerly incorporated such a reference to a commandment by the Lord, as well as such clear affirmation of a dominical saying in the process. But instead, the text reads as follows:

> Let no one eat of things who is uninitiated, but only those who are baptized into the Lord's death [εἰς τὸν τοῦ κυρίου θάνατον]. But if any of the uninitiated should keep it hidden and take a share, they eat eternal judgment, because not being of the faith of Christ.[26]

The rationale behind the logic of the Apostolic Constitutions and Canons is clear then, since the author is undoubtedly concerned with refusal of the unbaptized from the ritual of the Eucharist within a later setting. It is within this context that one observes the warnings against hiding one's status in order to join the assembly. Yet a reader might suspect that, since this author is constantly incorporating scriptural references into the bulk of the writing elsewhere, this moment would yet again have been a welcome dominical condemnation of such persons as drawn explicitly from

---

24. The only discrepancy is that the final word in Matthew (κυσίν) carries a moveable ν that is otherwise absent in the Didache. For more on this text, see Huub van de Sandt, "'Do Not Give What Is Holy to the Dogs' (Did 9:5d and Matt 7:6a): The Eucharistic Food of the Didache in Its Jewish Purity Setting," *VC* 56 (2002): 223–46.

25. Varner, "Didache's Use," 135–36.

26. All translations of the Apostolic Constitutions and Canons are my own.

Scripture. Instead, the reference to the saying itself and the introductory words "for the Lord has also spoken about this" are both missing.

It is suggested here that, contrary to Varner's generous analysis of the passage, the entire phrase that now appears in Did. 9.5b ("for the Lord has also spoken about this: 'Do not give what is holy to dogs'") has been secondarily added into the text at this point by a later hand and was never actually known to the author of the Apostolic Constitutions and Canons as part of the Didache source. Whether one should attribute this apparent addition to Did² remains uncertain. Yet the fact that Did² has appealed to dominical sayings previously (see 1.5a) certainly puts the present material within a realm of possibilities for this editor. In either case, with the absence of a true secondary witness by the Apostolic Constitutions and Canons here, one is tempted to believe that both the introduction and the saying itself are the addition of a later perspective.

The next reference to Scripture as authoritative source is the well-known usage in Did. 14.3. The certain foundation for this quotation is Mal 1:11, 14, as is readily observed in a comparison of parallels:

Did. 14.3
    (a) For this is that about which the Lord said:
        αὕτη γάρ ἐστιν ἡ ῥηθεῖσα ὑπὸ κυρίου
    (b) In every place and time offer me a pure sacrifice,
        ἐν παντὶ τόπῳ καὶ χρόνῳ προσφέρειν μοι θυσίαν καθαράν
    (c) because I am a great king, says the Lord,
        ὅτι βασιλεὺς μέγας εἰμί λέγει κύριος
    (d) and my name is marvelous among the nations.
        καὶ τὸ ὄνομά μου θαυμαστὸν ἐν τοῖς ἔθνεσι

Mal 1:11, 14 (LXX)
    (b) καὶ ἐν παντὶ τόπῳ θυμίαμα προσάγεται τῷ ὀνόματί μου καὶ θυσία καθαρά (1:11b)
    (c) διότι βασιλεὺς μέγας ἐγώ εἰμί λέγει κύριος παντοκράτωρ (1:14c)
    (d) καὶ τὸ ὄνομά μου ἐπιφανὲς ἐν τοῖς ἔθνεσιν (1:14d)

Mal 1:11, 14 (MT)
    (b) ובכל־מקום מקטר מגש לשמי ומנחה טהורה (1:11b)
    (c) כי מלך גדול אני אמר יהוה צבאות (1:14c)
    (d) ושמי נורא בגוים (1:14d)

Varner correctly observes the minor differences among parallels here, with the Didachist omitting "Almighty" (צבאות, παντοκράτωρ) from Mal 1:14c (or Mal 1:11, as he sees it), and the insertion of the "functionally equivalent word" of "marvelous" (θαυμαστὸν; see נורא, ἐπιφανὲς in Mal 1:14c) shortly thereafter.[27] Though as Varner observes, the more important issue is why Malachi has been employed here at all. The likely reason is because of the reference to "the nations" (τοῖς ἔθνεσι) in this passage, a natural link to the longer title of the Didache and the prophecy of a pure sacrifice by non-Jews when "Malachi's Jewish people were offering defiled sacrifices (see Mal 1:6–10)." This implies a reversal that Malachi already recognized and the Didachist saw fulfilled "as spiritual" in the eucharistic rituals of the messianic community, "commemorating the one great sacrifice for Christians through Jesus."[28]

This may indeed be the case. Yet as Robert Gordon has suggested, the focus of such rituals for Christians and rabbinic Judaism became the element of prayer.[29] This is a primary concern for the Didachist in the same place where Varner points to the significance of eucharistic ritual (see Did. 8–10). Whether one should see these prayers as linked to the eucharistic tradition of the New Testament is not at issue here. A more vital observation is that the prayers and ritual event that they claim are likely associated with this particular use of Scripture from Mal 1:11, 14 and thus are inherently authentic to the structure of the *Vorlage* as envisioned by the Didachist.

Though there is much in terms of detail that may be said about the use of this text by the Didachist, in result it is apparently safe to associate the prophetic source of Malachi with the original vision of Did¹, a perception that held the early community of believers as the (intended?) focus of the ancient prophet himself. This is hardly unexpected, since the motif of prophetic fulfillment otherwise permeates New Testament thought. Yet at

---

27. Varner, "Didache's Use," 139. Apostolic Constitutions and Canons (7.30.2) follows Malachi more closely here, reincorporating the term παντοκράτωρ (which appears elsewhere in the Didache at 10.3 only) to its original location. This author introduces the citation with a more ecclesiastical consciousness, however, using the words "to God, who said concerning his universal church" (θεῷ τῷ εἰπόντι περὶ τῆς οἰκουμενικῆς αὐτοῦ ἐκκλησίας).

28. Varner, "Didache's Use," 139–40.

29. Robert P. Gordon, "Targumic Parallels to Acts XIII 18 and Didache XIV 3," *NovT* 16 (1974): 285–89. My thanks to Jonathan Draper for bringing this brief article to my attention.

least here one may thus identify the writings of the prophets as one of the more important (if not *the* most significant) sources for Did¹, much as that of Torah, Lukan tradition, and dominical sayings may be linked with Did².

The last citation of Scripture appears in Did. 16.7, where the words "as it has been said" (ὡς ἐρρέθη) are used to introduce a clear citation. The connection with Zech 14:5 is without question:[30]

Did. 16.7
  (a) The Lord will come, and all the holy ones with him
      ἥξει ὁ κύριος καὶ πάντες οἱ ἅγιοι μετ' αὐτοῦ

Zech 14:5 (LXX)
  (b) καὶ ἥξει κύριος ὁ θεός μου καὶ πάντες οἱ ἅγιοι μετ' αὐτοῦ

Zech 14:5 (MT)
  (b) ובא יהוה אלהי כל־קדשים עמך

One observes that there are few differences among these texts. The Didachist does not include the words "my God" (אלהי; ὁ θεός μου) and agrees with the LXX in the reading "after him" (μετ' αὐτοῦ) against the Hebrew "after you" (עמך). It is possible that this is either a loose citation or simply is drawn from oral tradition.

With respect to the author's perspective, Varner observes that the Didachist does not view this event as a "'general' resurrection, but one that consists of believers only" based on the opening phrase "but not of all" (οὐ πάντων δέ). He argues that the text sees the "holy ones" (οἱ ἅγιοι) as believers, reflecting Paul's words in 1 Thess 3:13, and not as angels.[31] At the same time, he admits that angels accompany the Lord elsewhere in the New Testament, as in Matt 25:31.[32]

---

30. Koester (*Synoptische Überlieferung*, 187) likewise agrees that this text derives from Zechariah and not Matt 25:31. Neither does Massaux (*Apologists and the Didache*, 167–73) include it within his otherwise extensive listing of Matthean parallels to Did. 16.

31. Contra Niederwimmer, *Didache*, 225, and Milavec, *The Didache: Faith, Hope, and Life of the Earliest Christian Communities, 50–70 CE* (New York: Newman, 2003), 655.

32. Varner, "Didache's Use," 140, given in the text as 25:30. The word used in Matthew is specifically "angels" (ἄγγελοι), however.

One is struck by several elements in this consideration. The first is that the Didachist is often opaque about whether references to "the Lord" are intended as allusions to God the Father or, instead, to the Messiah. The prophet clearly infers the former in Zech 14:5, which the Didachist may indeed have shifted to the latter figure here, as most commentators assume.[33] At the same time, however, this is a reading molded by the vision of Paul, whose words are not otherwise prevalent throughout the Didache. Furthermore, it is not at all clear that the Didache envisioned a limited resurrection here at all. It is true that such is indicated by the text as it now stands, but the Apostolic Constitutions and Canons (7.32.4) omits the wording "but not of all; rather, as it has been said" in favor of a simple "and then" (καὶ τότε). This is surprising, since such terminology would seem typical of what might otherwise be expected from that author's fourth century perspective. One is led to suspect that, once again, both these phrases "but not of all" and "as it has been said" are secondary to the text of the Didache and thus were unknown as part of that source as used in the Apostolic Constitutions and Canons.

Regardless of how one views the original intention of the text, it seems reasonable to attribute the citation to the Didachist again, once more reflecting the author's concern for the teaching of the prophets and its significance for the early messianic community.[34] The Didachist then is clearly anxious to include the following elements: Torah (based on the inclusion of the Two Ways materials), prophets (seen with the use of Malachi and Zechariah), and teachings of Jesus (at least within their narrower Jewish context).

3. Allusions and Echoes of Scripture

The remainder of the Didache features numerous echoes and allusions to Scripture. Varner divides such references into three basic classifications: parallels with the Gospel of Matthew, noncanonical materials (whose use

---

33. So Klaus Wengst, *Didache (Apostellehre), Barnabasbrief, Zweiter Klemensbrief, Schrift an Diognet*, SU 2 (Darmstadt: Wissenschaftliche Buchgesellschaft, 1984), 31; Niederwimmer, *Didache*, 225 n. 30. Though against the supposition that the Didachist has the Messiah in view here, see Milavec, "Saving Efficacy," 151 n. 47.

34. Though some commentators do not consider this verse to be original to the text. Niederwimmer (*Didache*, 225 n. 27), e.g., considers it to be "a gloss by the Didachist."

Varner primarily rejects),[35] and Old Testament passages (devoted primarily to the use of Malachi and Zechariah, as observed above). Whether this should be considered a complete listing of potential parallels with Scripture may be debated, but following the guidelines of Varner's own work, it is useful to work with these categories here.[36]

Varner begins his focus with the obvious reflection of the Gospel of Matthew that appears in the Didache, or one might at least say those materials that are linked with Matthean tradition.[37] He lists thirty-four potential parallels (including the title), which are scattered throughout the course of the writing. Such a list is determined by how one counts relevant items, and some scholars have seen considerably more parallels in the process.[38] Regardless of the count, though, it is clear that a heavy emphasis on materials from the Matthean tradition is to be found.

From the outset some of these may be eliminated as not directly relevant to the views of Did[1]. One finds, for example, that five of Varner's parallels (all drawn from Matt 5) appear within Did. 1.3b–2.1. As observed

---

35. Varner acknowledges the exception of Sir 12:1 (which he considers as non-canonical) behind Did. 1.6 following the short study of Patrick W. Skehan ("*Didache* 1,6 and Sirach 12,1," *Bib* 44 [1963]: 533–36), though even here he argues that the Didachist does not make use of this source in a straightforward manner as a consideration of scriptural authority. In fact, it seems quite likely that both Matthew and the Didache are highly dependent on Sirach when compared with other authors among the New Testament and Apostolic Fathers; see my "'The Wisdom of Sirach and the Glue of the Matthew-*Didache* Tradition,'" in *Intertextuality in the Second Century*, ed. D. Jeffrey Bingham and Clayton N. Jefford, BAC (Leiden: Brill, forthcoming).

36. E.g., one might consider whether there are other potential New Testament parallels with the Didache as follows: 1.2 (Gal 5:14; Jas 2:8); 1.3 (1 Cor 5:5); 1.4 (1 Pet 2:11); 1.5 (Acts 20:35; 2 Thess 3:10); 3.6 (Phil 2:14); 4.8 (Acts 2:44–45; 4:32); 4.10 (Eph 6:9; Col 4:1); 4.11 (Eph 6:5–8; Col 3:22–25); 4.14 (Jas 5:16; 1 John 1:9); 6.3 (Acts 15:29); 10.2 (John 17:11); 10.3 (Rev 4:11); 10.5 (John 17:23; 1 John 4:12); 10.6 (1 Cor 16:22); 11.2 (2 John 10); 12.1 (Rom 12:13); 12.4 (2 Thess 3:7–12); 13.1 (1 Cor 9:13–14; 1 Tim 5:18); 15.3 (1 Cor 5:11); 16.4 (1 John 2:18, 22; 4:3; 2 John 7); 16.5 (1 Cor 3:13; 1 Pet 1:7); 16.6 (1 Cor 15:52; 1 Thess 4:16); and 16.7 (1 Thess 3:13). This listing does not even include possible parallels with either Luke or Mark, whose materials should be considered alongside of those from Matthew in many cases.

37. Varner, "Didache's Use," 130–36.

38. John W. Welch, e.g., has identified over seventy such connections in his "Law, Ethics, Ritual, and Eschatology from the Sermon on the Mount to the Post-Temple *Didache*" (paper presented at the annual meeting of the Society of Biblical Literature, Boston, November 25, 2008); see the current form of that paper provided elsewhere in this volume as "From the Sermon on the Mount to the Didache."

above, this section of the Didache is not usually accepted as original to the *Vorlage* and thus, as secondary, must likely be associated with the hand of a later redactor (Did²?) and not directly with the Didachist (Did¹).

A similar situation arises in the case of Did. 7.1, where Varner follows traditional assumptions that the trinitarian formula used for baptism (both here and at 7.3) reflects the well-known wording of Matt 28:19. Whether this formula was originally part of the Matthean narrative may be debated, but its certain absence from the Apostolic Constitutions and Canons once again suggests that its presence in Codex Hierosolymitanus is an editorial addition and thus likely more accurately associated with a later editor and not with the Didachist. This element of ecclesiastical detail should thus be linked with Did² as reflective of a later context.

Similar instances are likewise in doubt for various reasons. For example, the reference to "hypocrites" in Did. 8.2 is listed by Varner as parallel to similar occurrences in Matt 6:2, 5, and 16. This is most likely true, though a reader is pressed to explain why each author indisputably has a different antecedent in mind for "hypocrite": Matthew undoubtedly thinking fraudulent Jews (though the introduction to the Lord's Prayer in Matt 6:7 specifies the "nations" [οἱ ἐθνικοί]), with the Didachist more likely envisioning either all Jews[39] or some particular Jewish group.[40] One might again question whether such an emphasis in the Didache does not suggest a later hand a work. The same might be said about the reference to giving holy things to dogs in Did. 9.5b (par. Matt 7:6), which has been mentioned above as a possible secondary addition to the text. Both here and at the beginning of 8.2, where the Lord's Prayer is introduced, references to "the Lord" are offered as intended reflections of the teachings of Jesus. One can hardly question that the authority of Jesus as Messiah was respected by the earliest of Christians, but the text seems to assume authoritative status behind the teachings associated with the *person* of Jesus as opposed to his association with scriptural norms or traditional teachings. Some ques-

---

39. So Huub van de Sandt, "The Didache Redefining Its Jewish Identity in View of Gentiles Joining the Community," in *Empsychoi Logoi: Religious Innovations in Antiquity*, ed. Alberdina Houtman et al., AJEC 73 (Leiden: Brill, 2008), 261–65.

40. For the latter view in one perspective or another, see esp. Draper, "Christian Self-Definition," and "Do the Didache and Matthew Reflect an 'Irrevocable Parting of the Ways' with Judaism?" in van de Sandt, *Matthew and the Didache*, 217–41; Clayton N. Jefford, "Conflict at Antioch: Ignatius and the *Didache* at Odds," StPatr 36 (2001): 262–69; and Del Verme, Didache *and Judaism*, 143–88.

tion remains about the historical setting in which such a perspective might have arisen in the case of these particular teachings.

So, too, the observation in Did. 14.2 about the need to reconcile a quarrel before offering sacrifice, which clearly reflects the teaching of Matt 5:23–24,[41] is omitted entirely at this juncture by the Apostolic Constitutions and Canons. Upon closer observation it is evident that the text of the Didache (as it stands in the Greek) reads smoothly even without this comment, as thus:

> (14.1) When you come together on the Lord's day and after having acknowledged your offenses so that your sacrifice may be pure [καθαρός], break bread and give thanks.... (14.3) For this is that about which the Lord said, "In every place and time offer me a pure [καθαρός] sacrifice." (citation of Mal 1:11, 14)

The catchword between these verses is the adjective "pure" (καθαρός), while the term used in 14.2 is the verb "defile" (κοινόω), which is certainly related but most assuredly different. Should one assume that the Didachist has introduced an acknowledged citation of Scripture in the form of Malachi by means of materials from Matthew that has otherwise gone undesignated? This is certainly possible, of course. But because of the absence of these words from the Apostolic Constitutions and Canons, one might be tempted once more to suggest that they were not originally part of the text fashioned by Did[1] but belong to the editorial hand of Did[2]. There is an element of speculation here, but the unnecessary repetition of thought in the Didache makes the suggestion quite possible if not likely.

Other parallels that Varner raises do indeed seem at home within the text and should be associated with Did[1]. Varner offers Matt 5:17–20 on instruction about Torah as an apt parallel to Did. 11.1–2, which itself is a warning against those who offer a different "teaching" (διδαχή) from that of the Didachist. This may truly be the case, though here the specifics of the Matthean teaching have been omitted in the Didache. References to abolishment of the Torah, relaxing of related commandments, and righteousness that exceeds that of the scribes and Pharisees have all gone missing in the process. The Didachist is focused on *divergent teaching*

---

41. For an intriguing argument in support of the antiquity of the wording in 14.2 and 16.1 based on syntax, see Brian J. Wright, "Greek Syntax as a Criterion of Authenticity: A New Discussion and Proposal," *CBQ* 74 (2012): 84–100 (96–97).

and seems hardly bothered by Jewish hypocrisy, much like the situation of Did. 8 (par. Matt 6:2, 5, 16) above.

Varner next indicates that the counsel of Did. 11.7 against testing prophets is a likely parallel to Matt 12:31 ("Therefore I tell you, people will be forgiven for every sin and blasphemy, but blasphemy against the Spirit will not be forgiven" [NRSV]). The Matthean text is likely based on Mark 3:30, another potential parallel. But since both the Didache and Matthew contain the word "sin" (ἁμαρτία) here, which Mark omits, the Matthean reference is indeed the more probable parallel. Varner is surely correct to attribute this connection to the Didachist, particularly since the Coptic, Ethiopic, and Georgian parallels all include this reading as well. One wonders why he did not then turn to Matt 7:15–23 with respect to the fruit of a tree and the nature of deception as probable parallels to the following verse in the Didache (11.8). Though the reference is much broader in scope, it too is supported by the Coptic, Ethiopic, and Georgian parallels and likely should be included as well.

Additional parallels between the Didache and Matthew are likewise to be attributed to the vision of Did¹, as Varner indicates. The observation about prophets being worthy of their food (Did. 13.1; Matt 10:10) is widely supported by literary parallels. Yet it may be worth observation that the following verse about a true *teacher* being worthy of food (Did. 13.2) is *not* found either in the Apostolic Constitutions and Canons or the Ethiopic tradition, indicating that the *Vorlage* behind the Greek text has conceivably been edited here. This saying was widely known by early Christian authors (see Luke 10:7; 1 Cor 9:13–14; 1 Tim 5:18), though admittedly the Didachist's use of "food" (τροφή) agrees with Matthew as opposed to these other parallels, which read "pay" (μισθός).

Finally, Varner indicates numerous connections between Matt 24 and Did. 16 that are often argued by other scholars.[42] These include the

---

42. The history of interpretation for comparison of Matthean parallels with Did. 16 is long and arduously argued. See, e.g., George Eldon Ladd, "The Eschatology of the Didache" (Ph.D. diss., Harvard University, 1949), 19–28; John S. Kloppenborg, "Didache 16: 6–8 and Special Matthean Tradition," *ZNW* 70 (1970): 54–67; Milavec, "Saving Efficacy"; Vicky Balabanski, *Eschatology in the Making: Mark, Matthew and the Didache*, SNTSMS 97 (Cambridge: Cambridge University Press, 1997); Tuckett, "Synoptic Tradition in the Didache," 95–104; Joseph Verheyden, "Eschatology in the Didache and the Gospel of Matthew," in van de Sandt, *Matthew and the Didache*, 193–215; and now most recently, William Varner, "The Didache 'Apocalypse' and Matthew 24," *BSac* 165 (2008): 309–22.

following: Did. 16.1 (see Matt 24:42; 25:13); 16.3 (24:11–12); 16.4 (24:10, 12); 16.5 (24:10); 16.6 (24:30–31); and 16.8 (24:30). This final chapter of the Didache is something of a muddle with respect to subsequent manuscript traditions. It is clear that the author of the Apostolic Constitutions and Canons, for example, has greatly reshaped Did. 16.1 around the sentiment of Matt 24:50 and Luke 12:35–37, 46 rather than the tradition of Matthew and thereby reveals a concern for the priority of Scripture over against the words of the Didachist. With reference to 16.4–5, the Apostolic Constitutions and Canons diverges from the Didache in favor of the wording of 2 Thess 2:8–9. The Didache reads as follows:

> (16.4) And then the deceiver of the world will appear as a son of God and perform signs and wonders, and the earth will be handed over into his hands, and he will do such atrocities as have never existed before. (16.5) Then all humanity will come to the fire of testing, and many will fall away.

The Apostolic Constitutions and Canons offers alternatively:

> And then the deceiver of the world will appear—the enemy of truth, the prince of lies, "whom the Lord Jesus will destroy by the spirit of his mouth," who destroys the ungodly with his lips—and many will fall away.

It is unclear why the imagery of 2 Thessalonians (offered in quotation marks here) was selected for inclusion at this point, though it is possible that the author either no longer understood the focus of the Didachist's argument or wished to approach the topic from another perspective.

The conclusion of the Didache (16.6–8) provides yet another problem, the question of whether the Didachist has paid special attention to Matthean tradition at this juncture or Did² has manipulated the text in favor of Gospel readings. Varner is certainly correct to observe the sudden turn toward Matthean materials in terms of theme and phraseology here. While one might expect such parallels with respect to similar ideas elsewhere in the text, the focused nature of such equivalences makes these closing verses very intriguing. Whether one may assume that this passage originally served as the end of the text by Did¹ remains for debate, but a comparison with the Apostolic Constitutions and Canons does not suggest as much. We have already seen the presence of Zech 14:5 in Did. 16.7, which bears other parallels to Matt 25:31 and 1 Thess 3:13. Varner does not include this Matthean parallel, preferring to focus on chapter 14, but it is clearly present in the mind of the author. The Apostolic Constitutions and Canons, however, adds additional Matthean parallels, namely, Matt 16:27 and 25:46, as well as an allusion to 1 Cor 2:9. And at Did. 16.8 alternative extensions to the text are supported by a variety of witnesses, including the Apostolic Constitutions and Canons and *De abrenuntiatione in baptismate* of Boniface.[43] A good case may be made from these optional conclusions that the Didache itself once possessed some wording that no longer exists in Codex Hierosolymitanus.[44] Yet the difficulties inherent in any attempt to postulate what the ending envisioned by Did^1 may have been is difficult to assess. For present purposes, it is perhaps safe to say simply that the entire scope of Did. 16 is problematic in terms of which portions should be attributed to Did^1 and which reflect the editorial activity of Did^2. In either case, it is clear that Matthean tradition was important to both writers.

Other potential parallels with Matthew as identified by Varner are mitigated by additional scriptural options, leaving them only secondarily related to the Matthean tradition. One must assume that this is the case with the Two Ways teaching in Did. 1.1, which Varner associates with Matt 7:13–14 but is perhaps more directly dependent on any number of Old Testament equivalents, especially that of Deut 30:15.[45] Similarly, it may be that the Didachist does *not* rely on Matt 22:38–39 and 7:12 as the basis for the teachings behind Did. 1.2, but instead on Deut 6:5, Lev 19:18, and Tob 4:15, texts which are themselves the basis of the Matthean parallels. An even more likely scenario is seen in the use of the Decalogue at Did. 2.2–3.8, which Varner associates with parallel elements in Matt 5 and 19:18, but which may as easily derive either from Exod 20:13–17 or Deut 5:17–21, not to mention a variety of lesser Old Testament parallels. One is thus left with some confusion about the extent to which the Didache (1) opts for use of the Old Testament as an authority, which Matthean tradition has likewise employed; (2) uses Old Testament texts *because* Matthean tradition has considered them important as well; (3) relies on Matthean texts that simply happen to have used Old Testament texts and traditions themselves (ala Varner); or (4) reflects the use of Old Testament texts as authoritative at the level of Did^1 but employs them *because*

---

43. Aldridge, "Lost Ending," 1–15.

44. Audet, *Didachè*, 73–74; Wengst, *Didache (Apostellehre)*, 20; Garrow, *Gospel of Matthew's Dependence*, 44–66.

45. Otherwise, one might consider Prov 12:28, Jer 21:8, Job 33:14, and even Sir 15:17.

they are associated with Matthean tradition at the level of Did². This final option is certainly conceivable based on the subsequent manuscript traditions and should not be dismissed without further consideration.

4. Use of the Materials

The Didache thus employs Scripture in several different ways on at least two different levels. The original approach of the Didachist (Did¹) is to incorporate materials of Torah, Prophets, and teachings of Jesus as they relate to the Torah and the Prophets. This is clearly evident in the Two Ways segment, for example, as seen here without the interpolation of 1.3b–2.1:

1.1	Deut 30:15; Prov 12:28; Jer 21:8; Job 33:14; Sir 15:17; Matt 7:13–14
1.2	Deut 6:5; Sir 7:30; Matt 22:37; Mark 12:30; Luke 10:27a // Lev 19:18; Matt 22:39; Mark 12:31; Luke 10:27b; Gal 5:14; Jas 2:8 // Tob 4:15; Matt 7:12; Luke 6:31
2.2	Exod 20:13–15; Deut 5:17–19; Matt 19:18; Mark 10:19; Luke 18:20 // Deut 18:10 // Exod 20:17; Deut 5:21
2.3	Zech 5:3; Matt 5:33 // Exod 20:16; Deut 5:20; Matt 19:18; Mark 10:19; Luke 18:20 // Exod 21:17; Matt 15:4 // Prov 12:28; Zech 7:10; 8:17
2.4	Sir 5:14; 6:1; 28:13 // Prov 21:6
2.7	Lev 19:17–28; Matt 18:15–17; Jude 22–23
3.1	1 Thess 5:22
3.2–6	Exod 20:13–17; Deut 5:17–21; Matt 5:21–37
3.4	Lev 19:26, 31; Deut 18:10–11
3.6	Wis 1:11; Phil 2:14
3.7	Ps 36:11 (LXX); Matt 5:5
3.8	Isa 66:2
3.10	Sir 2:4
4.1	Sir 7:29–31; Heb 13:7 // Matt 10:40; 18:20
4.2	Sir 6:28; 51:26–27; Matt 11:28–29 // Sir 6:34–36
4.3	Lev 19:15; Deut 1:16–17; Sir 4:9
4.5	Sir 4:31; Deut 15:7–8; Acts 20:35
4.6	Tob 4:8–10
4.7	Prov 19:17
4.8	Sir 4:5a // Acts 2:44–45; 4:32

4.10	Sir 4:30 // Eph 6:9; Col 4:1 // Luke 1:17
4.11	Eph 6:5–8; Col 3:22–25
4.13	Deut 4:2; 13:1 (LXX); Prov 30:6
4.14	Jas 5:16; 1 John 1:9
5.1	Matt 15:19
6.1	Lev 15:13

Viewing only this small section of the Didache, it is clear that numerous themes in the text find parallel in a variety of scriptural sources that do not make Varner's list, as seen for example with the situation of Proverbs, Tobit, Acts, James, and 1 John. This listing is much open to debate, and its parallels are oftentimes simply suggestive and not likely true foundations for the text. To that end, unless the Didache can be shown to *emphasize* a particular source, the coincidence of a parallel is mostly inconsequential. What is left from this sampling is some recognition that the text is highly dependent on materials from Exodus, Leviticus, and Deuteronomy that have likewise found parallel in Matthew.[46] In other words, the Didache (whether one speaks of Did[1] or Did[2] in this case) reveals special interest in Torah materials associated with the teachings of Jesus, particularly as preserved in the Matthean form.[47]

From Did. 6.2 to 16.8, the situation is quite similar, though the foundation of Torah is no longer evident. One might at the most look toward the prophets as a substitute for this Old Testament layer of support as follows:

6.2	Sir 51:26–27; Matt 11:29–30
6.3	Acts 15:29
7.1, 3	Matt 28:19
8.1	Matt 6:16
8.2	Matt 6:5 // Matt 6:9–13; Luke 11:2–4
9.4	Neh 1:9
9.5	Matt 7:6
10.2	John 17:11 // Luke 1:49; Matt 6:9; Luke 11:2
10.3	Wis 1:14; Sir 18:1; 3 Macc 2:9; Rev 4:11
10.5	Matt 6:13 // John 17:23; 1 John 4:12 // Matt 24:31; Zech 2:10

---

46. One observes here yet again that a high preponderance of parallels to Sirach is evident throughout. See n. 35.

47. In many cases these materials find parallel in Mark and Luke, but without consistency and typically without distinctions among readings.

10.6	Matt 21:9, 15 // 1 Cor 16:22
11.2	2 John 10
11.7	Matt 12:31
11.8	Matt 7:15–23
12.1	Ps 117:26 (LXX); Matt 21:9; Rom 12:13
12.4	2 Thess 3:7–12
13.1	Matt 10:10; Luke 10:7; 1 Cor 9:13–14; 1 Tim 5:18
13.3	Sir 7:29–31; Matt 10:10
14.2	Matt 5:23–24
14.3	Mal 1:11, 14
14.5	Num 15:20–21
15.3	Matt 18:15 // 1 Cor 5:11
15.4	Matt 6:1–18
16.1	Matt 24:42, 44; 25:13; Mark 13:35, 37, 33; Luke 12:35, 40
16.3	Matt 20:10–12; Mark 13:13 // Matt 7:15; Mark 13:22
16.4	1 John 2:18, 22; 4:3; 2 John 7 // Matt 24:10 // Matt 24:24 // Joel 2:2
16.5	1 Cor 3:13; 1 Pet 1:17 // Zech 13:8–9 // Matt 24:10 // Matt 10:22; 24:13; Mark 13:13
16.6	Matt 24:30–31; 1 Cor 15:52; 1 Thess 4:16
16.7	Zech 14:5; Matt 25:31; 1 Thess 3:13
16.8	Dan 7:13; Matt 16:27; 24:30; 26:64; Mark 13:26; Luke 21:27

Here one continues to see the presence of Matthean parallels, as Varner has observed, and no longer the focus on Torah provided as the framework for the Two Ways segment. There is more presence of the Prophets, illustrated above in the discussion of Malachi and Zechariah. One might argue for the presence of additional Pauline parallels and Johannine phrases throughout, though these are scattered and in no sense focal to the Didachist's argument. Much of this material appears either in the eucharistic prayer and discussion on accepting teachers in 10.1–11.2 or in the eschatological section of chapter 16, materials that find ready parallel elsewhere in Paul's writings and Johannine literature.

Most importantly, what is *not* here are appeals to the teachings of Jesus based simply on the *authority* of the figure of Jesus Christ. It is true that there are scattered references to teachings as found in the *Gospels* but, as has been argued above, the great majority of these likely belong to the hand of Did² and not to the Didachist. Thus the authority of the gospel as text (or at least as textual tradition) must be ascribed to a later perspective that appreciates literary convention in an evolved understanding of ecclesiastical authority, a view of Matthew not shared by the original author of the Didache, who is identified here as the Didachist or Did¹. It would seem that while the Matthean tradition was an important lens for scriptural interpretation in the view of Did¹, it was the Gospel text itself that likely served that same role for Did².

5. Summary and Conclusions

Reviewing Varner's observations about use of Scripture in the Didache, what can one say in response? Let us review these remarks in order:

(1) The Didachist saw authority in Scripture. This comment is offered under the assumption that the Didache is a single perspective and thus a reflection of only one view of canon. This seems *not* necessarily to be the case, since the text likely preserves an original vision (= Did¹) and at least one editorial layer (= Did²). As for the former, the Torah and the Prophets hold primary concern. With respect to the Prophets, this is easily envisioned by the way in which the Didachist specifically cites passages from Malachi and Zechariah as authoritative sources. With respect to the Torah, this is necessarily true, because it is the tradition on which the Two Ways is constructed. The Didachist likely has simply incorporated a Jewish Two Ways source here as a valid foundation of community authority.⁴⁸ The editor (Did²) must have been in agreement with this view by logical deduction, having maintained the Two Ways as the opening of the text, though there is nothing to indicate that this tradition held any *special* importance in this respect. More important for Did² is the Gospel of Matthew, whose *text* as opposed to its *tradition* seems to hold primacy of place, indicating a mindset that appreciated the evolved authority of gospel development.

(2) The Didachist made considerable use of the Gospel of Matthew. This observation seems true both for the Didachist and the secondary editor. As for the latter, it is evident that the *Gospel* of Matthew (either in literary or oral form) was valued in its own right. The question of whether the Didachist (Did¹) knew any such source remains a matter of how one assigns a date to the two works and their relationship to one another.

---

48. So the assumption of van de Sandt and Flusser (among others), which I too accept here; see Huub van de Sandt and David Flusser, *The Didache: Its Jewish Sources and Its Place in Early Judaism and Christianity*, CRINT 3.5 (Assen: Van Gorcum; Minneapolis: Fortress, 2002).

Regardless, there is no reason to doubt that at least the community *tradition* in which Matthew developed held primary importance for the author of the *Vorlage* itself.

(3) The Didachist incorporated segments of the Torah and the Prophets drawn from the LXX. This is particularly difficult to substantiate either with respect to the Didachist or the editor. It is true that certain passages drawn from Scripture indicate a clear dependence on the LXX,[49] but many source texts are similar in both the MT and LXX forms. Nevertheless, there is no single instance in the Didache where the author clearly has preferred a Hebrew text or tradition over that of the Greek, and thus Varner's observation may indeed be seen as a reasonable assumption.

(4) The Didachist did *not* make use of allegory as a mode of interpretation. This is patently true, but it is not evident how this observation is particularly useful apart from corollary observations. One might note that the Didachist (as well as the editor) did approach Scripture metaphorically, as is sometimes the practice of Paul (see Gal 4:21–31) or is presumably true for certain parables of Jesus (so Matt 13:3–24, 37–43). But the author of James likewise uses no allegory. Does this mean that the Didachist (as well as the editor presumably) is more Jewish in some sense? This is widely assumed by most authors, but not based on this particular category, since even the rabbis employed allegory. At the same time this comment does differentiate the Didache from texts like Barnabas with its rampant allegorical language, but not from other authors who run the ideological gamut from Clement of Rome to Ignatius of Antioch. It is especially hard to know the extent to which the Didachist (or the editor) read the eschatological texts behind chapter 16 as literal or allegorical, since no subsequent interpretation is offered. Varner's observation ultimately seems reasonable here again, though its value remains uncertain.

(5) The Didachist employed Scripture in the same way as the New Testament authors. This final observation is indeed curious, especially since Varner offers no similar analysis of how Scripture was employed by the authors of the New Testament, and they did not use Scripture in the same way among themselves. For example, New Testament authors use Scripture literally at times, typologically at others, allegorically and metaphorically elsewhere. This varies according to author and topic. The Didachist

---

49. See the scattered usages of Sirach, Tobit in 1.2, Exodus and Proverbs in 2.3, Psalms in 3.7 and 12.1, Deuteronomy in 4.13, and the prohibitions of the Decalogue scattered throughout chapters 2–5.

(as well as the editor) seems on the surface to have employed Scripture in a simple literal fashion, shaped on the one hand by the plain value of the direct teaching of the text and, on the other, occasionally by the prophetic dimension of fulfillment, as Varner argues for the author's use of Mal 1:11 and 14 in Did. 14.3.

What seems evident with respect to the use of Scripture in the Didache is as follows. There are at least two different perspectives concerning Scripture at work here. The first, and presumably original, perspective (Did[1]) revered the Torah (seen in the Two Ways), Prophets (seen with Malachi and Zechariah), and teachings of Jesus (within a distinctly Jewish context). There is discernible sympathy for Matthean tradition here, though it is difficult to know whether the gospel text itself was available for consultation. One observes that with this limited canon in hand (to use the terminology of Sanders), there is nothing to identify the Didachist as anything other than a messianic Jew. The author of the *Vorlage* fits reasonably well into the historical moment in which Paul and his contemporaries found themselves in the first century.[50]

The second and later perspective at work within the Didache (Did[2]) preserves the same respect for the Torah and the Prophets, as well as a sayings tradition behind the teachings of Jesus (perhaps Q?). Beyond this, however, it appears that the literary form of Matthew's Gospel has gained prominence of place for the subsequent editor (Did[2]) of the text, intermingled to some limited extent with Lukan tradition. This evolution of perspective suggests a later situation (late second century?) in which the concept of canon has been expanded and, at least to some extent, certified as authoritative for the tradition. One might easily envision that the influence of Irenaeus is already at work for Did[2], having shaped a perspective that reads Old Testament texts and traditions through a specifically Christian lens. This editor is now a "Christian" in the full institutional sense of the word; this writer respects the authority of a new tradition that had not yet been settled for the Didachist.

Ultimately, the Didachist and the later editor both work within a similar tradition of interpretation. But while the perspective of the former is limited to the Torah, Prophets, and teachings of Jesus, the latter further includes a limited Lukan perspective and dominical sayings associ-

---

50. There is thus ample reason to see great antiquity behind the traditions that underlie the Didache and perhaps even to assign the Didachist to a pre-Matthean trajectory; so the view of Garrow, *Gospel of Matthew's Dependence*.

ated specifically with the *text* of Matthew as an authoritative source. Thus the sources behind the Didache derive from within a single trajectory of vision, but with a clear evolution of perspectives and development of literary authority.

The Distress Signals of Didache Research: Quest for a Viable Future

Aaron Milavec

During the hundred years following its discovery, Adolf von Harnack and, after him, his successors succeeded in giving a determined direction to Didache research. In so doing, the Didache took on a discernible identity and was valued as contributing to the pressing academic discussions of the day. During the last forty years Harnack and his successors have been largely marginalized. As a result, the field of Didache studies has been caught up in a confusing diversity of scholarly opinions. There is no single origination hypothesis, no single methodology, and no single research program to guide our way. The field of Didache scholarship is thus in disarray and unable to substantially contribute to the academic questions of our day.

In this essay I want to sketch out how research programs from the past have contributed to the current crisis. I also want to sketch out how recent approaches to Didache studies offer some promise to resolve this crisis. My comments will be grouped under three headings: (1) Mistaken Identity of the Didache as a "Church Order"; (2) Problematic Reliance on the Synoptics; (3) Failure to Recognize that "the Lord" Who Is Coming Is the Father and Not Jesus.

1. The Mistaken Identity of the Didache as a "Church Order"

A unified reading of the Didache has been impossible until very recently, because the prevailing assumption has been that the Didache is "the oldest church order" created in stages with the compiler splicing together pre-existing documents with only a minimum of editing.[1] In practice, source

---

1. Joseph G. Mueller, "The Ancient Church Order Literature: Genre or Tradition?" *JECS* 15 (2007): 337–80.

and redaction criticism expend so much energy in hypothesizing, on the basis of shifts in the logic and rhetoric of the text, where one source ends and another begins that any unity gets entirely obscured in the analysis. Furthermore, since the hypothesized sources in the form that the compiler knew them cannot be independently known and verified (e.g., as in the case of the Synoptics), scholarly debates have been unable to arrive at any working consensus, since every major author relies upon his or her own "reconstruction" of the original sources. Georg Schöllgen, accordingly, accurately summarized the academic disarray as follows:

> It is significant that there is neither a consensus nor even only a limited number of types of solution between these extraordinarily complex theories of origin. Nearly every attempt to solve the problem stands by itself, and forms its own criteria for the supposed division of sources. So one cannot avoid the impression of arbitrariness, especially if even the smallest stylistic differences must serve as signs of a change of author.[2]

Against this background, it is not surprising that three recent German commentaries offer three divergent "theories of origin" for our text:

(1) According to Klaus Wengst,[3] the author of the Didache set down in the initial ten chapters the existing traditions of his community and then created 11–15 by way of offering rules to protect those traditions.

(2) According to Kurt Niederwimmer, the compiler of the Didache was most probably "a respected and influential bishop" who "quotes existing, sometimes archaic rules and seeks both to preserve what has been inherited and at the same time to accommodate that heritage to his own time [the turn of the first century]."[4]

(3) According to Georg Schöllgen, it is impossible to find any persuasive ordering principle in the Didache; rather, for him, the author "simply provides an authoritative regulation on controversial points,"[5] which he

---

2. Georg Schöllgen, "The Didache as a Church Order: An Examination of the Purpose for the Composition of the Didache and Its Consequences for Its Interpretation," in *The Didache in Modern Research*, ed. Jonathan A. Draper, AGJU 37 (Leiden: Brill, 1996), 65.

3. Klaus Wengst, *Didache (Apostellehre), Barnabasbrief, Zweiter Klemensbrief, Schrift an Diognet*, SU 2 (Darmstadt: Wissenschaftliche Buchgesellschaft, 1984).

4. Kurt Niederwimmer, *The Didache: A Commentary*, trans. Linda M. Maloney (Minneapolis: Fortress, 1998), 228.

5. Schöllgen, "Didache as a Church Order," 63.

sets out at random. Schöllgen consequently identifies breaks in the text as signalling the transition from one controversial point to the next and *not* as indicators of multiple authors/editors.

While the origination hypothesis of each of the three German scholars is manifestly different, they all agree on two important points. (1) The Didache was produced by an author bent upon reporting or regulating the affairs of an existing community within which they functioned. Gone is the notion of a scribe or scribes sewing together blocks of preexisting materials by adding editorial stitches at the boundaries. While all three German scholars disagree as to what precisely were the traditional materials being used by the author, they all agree that the author was selecting and editing and ordering practices known to his community in such as way as to faithfully address urgent community needs. (2) The Didache as a consequence was composed by a single author producing a unified text for use within an existing community. All three German scholars have abandoned the notion of Stanaslas Giet and Willy Rordorf calling for two distinct stages of composition by different persons at different times.[6] With even greater force, they reject Jean-Paul Audet and Clayton Jefford who identified three temporally separated stages of composition.[7]

In brief, one can notice here how the traditional notion of a "church order" and its associated notion of authorship as being limited to minor editing has being abandoned when it comes to examining the Didache. In its place, one can detect how recent German scholarship has paved the way for a responsive and true authorship functioning within the constraints of a living community. In this way the disarray created by a rigid emphasis on source and redaction criticism has been partially overcome and the way was open to examining the Didache as a unified document regulating the affairs of a functioning community.

A Note in Defense of Orality

While each of the three German commentators revived the notion of a single author of the Didache, none of them has seriously taken into account the possibility that the Didache was created in "a culture of high

---

6. Ibid., 67–70.
7. Niederwimmer, *Didache*, 42–43.

residual orality"⁸ wherein "oral sources" (attached to respected persons) were routinely given greater weight and were immeasurably more serviceable than "written sources."⁹ In such a society no one practiced silent reading. Every act of reading was tantamount to winding up the gramophone so that one could "hear" again the "oral source" that initially created the grammata (the silent string of notations without spaces transcribed on the parchment). The character and meaning of a text, consequently, was only available due to the recognition that comes from "hearing" it being recited. Furthermore, in societies where there is only a marginal access to and reliance upon written materials, "oral sources" offered a measure of socially maintained and person-centered stability without ever supposing that one needed or relied upon the frozen rigidity of a written text.[10]

Each of the German scholars considered above suffers from the bias toward textuality and the ignorance of orality when it comes to examining the Didache. A more fruitful point of departure consequently would be to begin by noting that the Didache has clues throughout pointing to the primacy of "oral recitation." Here are a few instances of this:

(1) The novice being trained in the way of life is told to honor "the one *speaking* to you the *word* of God" (Did. 4.1), thereby signalling that oral rather than written transmission of the training was presupposed. Moreover, the novice trembles "at the *words* that you have *heard*" (Did. 3.8).[11]

(2) In every instance where the Didache cites specific mandates from the Hebrew Scriptures, meanwhile, the oral aspect (as opposed to the written) is highlighted: "It has been *said*" (Did. 1.6); "The Lord has likewise *said*" (Did. 9.5); "This is the thing having been *said* by the Lord" (Did. 14.3); "As it has been *said*" (Did. 16.7).

---

8. Paul J. Achtemeier, "*Omne verbum sonat*: The New Testament and the Oral Environment of Late Western Antiquity," *JBL* 109 (1990): 3–27 (3).

9. Ibid., 9–11. Also Walter J. Ong, *The Presence of the Word: Some Prolegomena for Cultural and Religious History* (Minneapolis: University of Minnesota Press, 1967), 52–53.

10. Achtemeier, "Omne verbum sonat," 27. See further Ong, *Presence of the Word*, 231–34.

11. The translation of the Didache is my own and can be found in its entirety in my two Didache volumes (see n. 23). Unless otherwise stated, translations of the Bible follow the NRSV.

(3) The Didache gives repeated attention to speaking rightly (Did. 1.3b; 2.3, 5; 4.8b, 14; 15.3b) and entirely neglects to mention false or empty writing.
(4) At the baptism, the novice is immersed in water "having *said* all these things beforehand" (Did. 7.1).
(5) The same holds true when later in the Didache the baptized are warned only to receive teachers who "should train you in all the things *said* beforehand" (Did. 11.1). This indicates that both true and false teachers were being heard. No mention is made of either true or false writings.

As soon as one explores the dominant role of orality within traditional communities, one has to abandon the notion of a single authoritative text produced by a single author. Studies in the Synoptics, for example, have moved to seeing living communities as being both the repositories and the shapers of their oral narratives.[12] These narratives in the course of time get transcribed on parchment, but the authority of that parchment depends upon the fact that what is transcribed can be read out loud by a trained reader and that listeners immediately discover an "echo" of what was currently being narrated and lived by the leading teachers and elders within that community.[13]

Three consequences suggest themselves. (1) Phrases such as "the author of the Didache" might better be replaced by phrases such as "the narrators of the Didache" in order to focus on the oral transmission and the aural reception surrounding the use of the Didache. (2) Aural reception of the Didache is associated with the phenomenology of "trembling" (Did. 3.8). Having been set upon the path of life by "the God who made

---

12. James D. G. Dunn, *Jesus Remembered*, vol. 1 of *Christianity in the Making* (Grand Rapids: Eerdmans, 2003), 191–200. Fully developed by Werner Kelber, "The Oral-Scribal-Memorial Arts of Communication in Early Christianity," in *Jesus, the Voice, and the Text: Beyond the Oral and the Written Gospel*, ed. Tom Thatcher (Waco, TX: Baylor University Press, 2008), 235–62.

13. John L. McKenzie, "The Social Character of Inspiration," *CBQ* 24 (1962): 115–25. Already fifty years ago, McKenzie argued that it was impossible to adequately describe or to verify the interior states of those writing under the influence of divine inspiration. As a social phenomenon, however, one could readily understand and verify the situation that prevails when a single author, as a service to the community, transcribed the oral transmission of the authoritative and guiding narratives that animated the community.

you" (Did. 1.2), the novice trembled with excited anticipation and reverential fear. This was the phenomenology exhibited when Israel originally experienced the word of the Lord from Mount Sinai (Exod 19:16) and when the prophets encountered God's word (e.g., Ezra 9:4; Isa 66:2; Hab 3:16). Among the rabbis it was a commonplace to remember that every master taught his disciples "with awe and fear, with trembling and trepidation" (b. Ber. 22a). Reading seldom has this effect.[14] (3) When the way of life is acknowledged as an oral recitation, it follows that the ordering of the training might meticulously follow a very sophisticated schema from beginning to end. It was through my own oral recitation of the Didache that I myself progressively discovered this schema.[15] This effectively undercuts Schöllgen's pessimistic affirmation that it is impossible to find any persuasive ordering principle in the Didache.

Seeing the trend in the last thirty years, my expectation is that future Didache scholars[16] will increasingly use studies of orality to appreciate the nature, character, and use of the Didache within its community setting.

2. Problematic Reliance on the Synoptics

The dating of the Didache has been heavily dominated by presuppositions[17] regarding the sources used in its composition. Harnack wrote in his influential 1884 commentary: "One must say without hesitation that it is the author of the Didache who used the *Epistle of Barnabas* and not the reverse."[18] Harnack accordingly dated the Didache between 135 and

---

14. Jonathan Draper provides additional testimonies to this phenomenon in his essay included in this volume.

15. For details, see Aaron Milavec, *The Didache: Faith, Hope, and Life of the Earliest Christian Communities, 50–70 CE* (New York: Newman, 2003), xxxii–xxxiii.

16. Perttu Nikander provides an illustrative study of orality in his article included in this volume.

17. Presuppositions regarding the character of the early church also interfered with an early dating. See, for example, Thomas O'Loughlin, "Reactions to the *Didache* in Early Twentieth-Century Britain: A Dispute over the Relationship of History and Doctrine?" in *Religion, Identity and Conflict in Britain: From the Restoration to the Twentieth Century. Festschrift for Prof. Keith Robbins*, ed. Stewart J. Brown et al. (Farnham, Surrey, UK: Ashgate, 2013), 177–94.

18. Adolf von Harnack, *Die Lehre der zwölf Apostel nebst Untersuchungenzuraltesten Geschichte der Kirchenverfassung und des Kirchenrechts*, TUGAL 2.1, 2 (Leipzig: Hinrichs, 1884; repr. Berlin: Akademmie, 1991), 82.

165 and fixed the place of origin as Egypt, since Barnabas was conjectured to have been composed there. It was not until 1945 that Edgar J. Goodspeed, aided by the Latin versions of Barnabas that had no two way section, finally put to rest the assumption that the Didache had to depend upon Barnabas.[19]

Once the Epistle of Barnabas was no longer considered as the source for the Didache, an earlier dating for the Didache could be entertained and a fresh impetus was given to the question as to whether the framers of the Didache used one or more of the canonical Gospels. It is telling that as late as 1958 Audet devoted forty-two pages to the Barnabas dependence issue and only twenty pages to the gospel dependence issue.[20] Audet concluded that, when examined closely, even the so-called "evangelical addition" of Did. 1.3b–5 could not be explained as coming directly either from Matthew or from Luke.[21] Accordingly, in the end Audet contributed more than any other scholar by showing, text by text, how securely the Didache was anchored in a Jewish horizon of understanding. Thus, Audet concluded that this pointed to a completion date prior to 70 in a milieu (Antioch) that did not yet have a written gospel.[22]

Recent scholars have been willing to call into question direct dependency upon any written gospel. Jonathan Draper, John Kloppenborg, Aaron Milavec, Niederwimmer, Rordorf, and Huub van de Sandt argue in favor of this position.[23] Opposition voices, however, are still heard.

---

19. Edgar J. Goodspeed, "The *Didache*, Barnabas and the Doctrina," *AThR* 27 (1945): 228–47.

20. Jean-Paul Audet, *La Didachè: Instructions des Apôtres*, Ebib (Paris: Gabalda, 1958), 121–63, 166–86.

21. Ibid., 186.

22. Ibid., 192, 210.

23. Jonathan A. Draper, "The Jesus Tradition in the *Didache*," in Draper, *The Didache in Modern Research*, 72–91; John S. Kloppenborg, "*Didache* 16:6–8 and Special Matthaean Tradition," *ZNW* 70 (1979): 54–67; Aaron Milavec, *Didache: Faith, Hope, and Life*, 693–740; a summary statement was also included in the final three pages of the student edition: *The Didache: Text, Translation, Analysis, and Commentary* (Collegeville, MN: Liturgical Press, 2003); Niederwimmer, *Didache*, 48–51; Willy Rordorf and André Tuilier, *La doctrine des douze Apôtres (Didachè)*, SC 248 bis (Paris: Cerf, 1978), 91, and more emphatically in the 1991 expanded edition (p. 232); see also Willy Rordorf, "Does the Didache Contain Jesus Tradition Independently of the Synoptic Gospels?" in *Jesus and the Oral Synoptic Tradition*, ed. Henry Wansbrough (Sheffield: Sheffield Academic, 1991), 394–423; Huub van de Sandt and David Flusser,

Christopher Tuckett of Oxford University, for example, reexamined all the evidence and came to the conclusion that the Didache "presupposes the finished gospel of Matthew (and perhaps Luke)."[24] If Tuckett is correct, then the earliest possible dating of the Didache would be the late 80s, the date when most scholars suppose that these gospels were finalized.

My early work with Rordorf led me to realize that the nearly universal agreement that the Didache made use of Matthew stood on very weak grounds. In my 2003 essay "Synoptic Tradition in the *Didache* Revisited,"[25] I made a strong case for showing that the received text of the Didache does not exhibit familiarity with Matthew's Gospel, otherwise the framers of the Didache would have made use of the "words of Jesus" to support community practices such as the confession of failings prior to the Eucharist and not be forced to stretch the Hebrew prophets to perform that service. Moreover, I showed that the framers of the Didache displayed verbal usages, community discipline, and a theological orientation that set it apart from the community orientation and practices of those following the Matthean tradition.

The academic community has much to gain from a free and open exchange between two opponents. Following the publication of my essay "Synoptic Tradition in the Didache Revisited," therefore, I was pleased that Tuckett took an interest in refocusing his own position while correcting various ways in which I may have "misunderstand and/or misread"[26] his position. In my rejoinder that was also published in the *Journal of Early Christian Studies*, I begin by setting forth two methodological points where Tuckett and I find substantial agreement:[27] (1) the framers of the Didache were not "citing from an open gospel set out before them" nor does the fourfold use of "good news/gospel" (εὐαγγέλιον, 8.2; 11.3; 15.3,

---

The Didache: Its Jewish Sources and Its Place in Early Judaism and Christianity, CRINT 3.5 (Assen: Van Gorcum; Minneapolis: Fortress, 2002), 48–52.

24. For the sake of brevity, citations will be largely limited to the text of Tuckett's refutation of my position in "The Didache and the Synoptics Once More: A Response to Aaron Milavec." *JECS* 13 (2005): 509–18.

25. Aaron Milavec, "Synoptic Tradition in the *Didache* Revisited," *JECS* 11 (2003): 443–80. This article is an updated and shortened version of material from my book, *Didache: Faith, Hope, and Love*, 693–740.

26. Tuckett, "Didache and the Synoptics Once More," 510.

27. Aaron Milavec, "A Rejoinder [to Tuckett]," *JECS* 13 (2005): 519–521. Given my severe space limitations, I forego the temptation to explain and to nuance these statements from our respective sides.

4) necessarily refer to a written source; (2) even in instances where the Didache manifests an exact or nearly exact verbal agreement with Matthew, this does not in and of itself establish familiarity and borrowing of one from the other. This is so because both could, in these instances, be making use of oral/written traditions independently available.

Jefford, in his book-length treatment of this issue, repeatedly comes across this impasse, namely, how to differentiate between the Didache making use of Matthew's Gospel and the Didache having access to a shared (oral) tradition from which both the author of the Didache and the author of Matthew are able to freely borrow.[28] Tuckett, in response to this question, endeavors to frame a criterion that "could be applied with a degree of objectivity,"[29] namely: "If material which owes its origin to the redactional activity of a synoptic evangelist reappears in another work, then the latter presupposes the finished work of that evangelist."[30] Tuckett uses this principle to demonstrate that Did. 16 shows borrowing from Matt 24. Time does not permit me to unravel the particulars of this demonstration. What I can say, however, is that I had sincerely hoped that Tuckett might have changed my mind in 1996 when I first encountered his work. He failed to do so. I appreciate his redoubled efforts to convince me yet again in 2005 after I had published my two volumes on the Didache. Every time I reenter into his framework of thinking, however, I confess that I find only fleeting intellectual satisfaction. Tuckett, needless to say, remains firmly convinced that Did. 16 made use of the redactional work found within Matt 24. He is further convinced that this borrowing took place precisely because the author of the Didache regarded the Matthean tradition (even if it was an oral transmission) as an "authoritative source." But here is the stumbling stone: If the Matthean tradition was indeed the "authoritative source" that Tuckett assumes, how can he explain why the author of the Didache would have taken over only a mere 2 percent of Matt 24 while seemingly ignoring and/or rejecting the other 98 percent? A response to this question has not been forthcoming.

Slowly the tide is turning. At the international specialist conference on "The *Didache* and Matthew"[31] held at Tilburg in 2003, I publicly polled

---

28. Clayton N. Jefford, *The Sayings of Jesus in the Teaching of the Twelve Apostles*, VCSup 11 (Leiden: Brill, 1989).

29. Tuckett, "Didache and the Synoptics Once More," 517.

30. Ibid., 517.

31. Papers from the conference have been subsequently edited and published;

the twenty-three participants at the end of the conference. Six judged that the Didache made use of Matthew; one person judged that Matthew made use of the Didache; but the overwhelming majority (sixteen) held that the Didache was created without any reliance upon Matthew. As more Didache scholars come to accept this emerging consensus, the way will open up for dating and for interpreting the Didache independent of the influence of Matthean studies.[32] I, for one, welcome this prospect and believe that the future of Didache studies securely lies in walking along these lines.

3. Failure to Recognize that "the Lord" Who Is Coming Is the Father and Not Jesus

My decision to accept an early dating for the Didache never was based exclusively on my conclusions regarding textual independence. Nearly eighteen years ago, for example, I noticed that the Didache focuses upon orthopraxis in much the same way as does the Manual of Discipline and the Mishnah. In this regard, reading Jacob Neusner's *Why No Gospels in Talmudic Judaism?* and Werner Kelber's *The Oral and the Written Gospel* were influential, for they both, following entirely different lines of reasoning, demonstrate that the gospel genre would have been quite foreign to the Galilean disciples of Jesus. Combined with this, Audet's masterful thesis showing how every part of the language and logic of the Didache finds its meaning within a Jewish horizon of understanding supported in my mind the possibility that the Didache might represent a Jewish form of Christianity that predated the formation of the Gospels.

Somewhat later I was able to notice that the Didache focuses on God the Father as the expected savior coming to gather his elect into the kingdom. In Paul's Epistles and in the sermons of Acts, this focus gets decidedly altered. The one who heralded the kingdom is now being celebrated as the savior who has been raised from the dead, taken up into heaven, and is sitting at the right hand of God awaiting the time for his triumphant return when he will raise the dead to life, judge the nations, and establish

---

see Huub van de Sandt, ed., *Matthew and the Didache: Two Documents from the Same Jewish-Christian Milieu?* (Assen: Van Gorcum; Minneapolis: Fortress, 2005).

32. The case of the Didache is thus comparable to that of Hebrews. As soon as it was accepted that Paul was not the author, then it was likewise required that Hebrews could be interpreted based upon its own internal logic and rhetoric quite independent of the theology of the authentic Pauline Epistles.

God's kingdom. The Didache, interestingly enough, focuses exclusively on what God the Father will do—much in the same way that it would appear that Jesus did when he proclaimed the kingdom of God in his tours of the villages of Galilee. Thus, quite clearly the Didache must have originated within a community wherein the faith of Jesus (rather than faith in Jesus) was still running strong.[33]

In his book *The Birth of Christianity*, John Dominic Crossan (following Helmut Koester and Kloppenborg) identifies two primary but markedly different Jesus traditions propagated in earliest Christianity: (1) the tradition which placed central emphasis upon Jesus's sayings and life as a divinely approved guide for living, a tradition Crossan labels as "the Life Tradition"; and (2) the tradition which placed central emphasis on Jesus's death and resurrection, a tradition found in the Epistles of Paul and the sermons of Acts which Crossan labels as "the Death Tradition"[34] The Didache, along with the Gospel of Thomas and the Q Gospel, in contrast to this, follow the "Life Tradition" and retain a form of Eucharist wherein the Father is the honored guest and thanks are given for what he has already done and what he will bring to pass in the future. In this Eucharist, it is understandable why there is no memorial of the saving death of Jesus and no expectation of the return of Jesus as Lord in the end times.

What is striking in Crossan's exposition is that he puts forward a hermeneutical principal advising scholars investigating these two early and very distinct forms within earliest Christianity to "not privilege one over the other":

> We should not privilege ... the death and resurrection over the sayings, as [was done] in past theology, nor the sayings over the death and resurrection, as in present reaction.... Furthermore, whatever descriptive term is used for one, be it proclamation or kerygma, tradition, or gospel, the same term should be used for the other. Finally my own preferred terminology is the Life Tradition and the Death Tradition.[35]

---

33. This comes forward in my writings, beginning with "The *Didache*: A Window on Gentile Christianity before the Written Gospels," *The Fourth R* 18 (2005): 7–11, 15–16.

34. John Dominic Crossan, *The Birth of Christianity: Discovering What Happened in the Years Immediately after the Execution of Jesus* (San Francisco: HarperSanFrancisco, 1998), 407, 415, 420, 501–4, 521, 550, 572–73.

35. Ibid., 415.

Crossan's insights offer a very fruitful point of departure for exploring the unique character of the Didache in the context of alternative forms of early Christianity. His hermeneutical principle serves to safeguard a climate that is both impartial and ecumenical.

3.1. An Examination of the Use of κύριος in the Didache

The Didache makes use of κύριος ("lord") twenty-four times. In each instance the context can be explored in order to discern whether the "Lord God" or the "Lord Jesus" is meant. The purpose of this exercise is to open up the hidden spirituality of the Didache and to provide a sure starting point for exploring its inner workings.

Within the eucharistic prayers, Jesus is portrayed four times as παῖς ("the servant") who reveals the life and understanding of the Father (Did. 9.3). This accords well with the understanding of the Christian Scriptures that Jesus proclaimed "the good news of God" (Mark 1:4; Rom 1:1; 2 Cor 2:7; 1 Thess 2:2, 9; 1 Pet 4:17)—never the "good news of Jesus." Thus, in the four places within the Didache wherein "good news" (εὐαγγέλιον) is found (Did. 8.2; 11.3; 15.3, 4), it must be supposed that this refers to an oral source[36] and that it comprises the "good news of our Lord God" (Did. 15.4) transmitted by his servant, Jesus.

For the reasons just mentioned, it must also be supposed that when it comes to baptizing and receiving visitors "in the name of the Lord" (Did. 9.5; 12.1), this means first and foremost, doing these things "in the name of the Father" (Did. 7.1). The members of the Didache were singularly preoccupied with his "name" (Did. 8.2; 10.2) and mute when it came to the "name of Jesus." More especially, the daily prayers petition that "your [the Father's] name be made holy" (Did. 8.2), and the weekly Eucharist speaks of "your [the Father's] holy name, which you tabernacle in our hearts" (Did. 10.2). Within the prayer life of this community, consequently, the presence of the Father is singularly and consistently evoked. The presence of Jesus is not dwelt upon.[37]

---

36. Historically speaking, the term εὐαγγέλιον referred to an oral production, and only in the latter third of the second century were books recording the "good news" first designated by this name. Helmut Koester, *Ancient Christian Gospels: Their History and Development* (London: SCM; Philadelphia: Trinity, 1990), 1–54.

37. This does not mean that David and Jesus are not specifically honored as the Lord's "servants" within the eucharistic prayers. Rather, my purpose here is to high-

On four occasions the Didache makes reference to persons being honored or received "as the Lord" (Did. 4.1; 11.2, 4; 12.1). The most elaborate of these is the following:

[A] My child, the one speaking to you the word of God,
   [1] you will remember night and day,
   [2] and you will honor him/her as the Lord,
      for where the dominion of the Lord is spoken of,
      there the Lord is (Did. 4.1).

Here the novice was being shown the appropriate posture to take toward his or her personal trainer from whom he or she receives the way of life: (1) remembering and reflecting at night and during the day on his/her life and words; and (2) honoring him or her "as the Lord." In this instance, the novice honors his or her mentor "as the Lord God," for it is "the word of God" and the way of life revealed by the Father that was being transmitted.[38] This parallels what R. Eleazar ben Shammua said: "The reverence

---

light that prayers are addressed directly to the Father and that there is no need to add at any point "from him, with him, and through him [Jesus]." Thus, the Lord God is boldly and familiarly addressed as "our Father," and the eucharistic meal honors him as the unseen host who is praised throughout the meal for his work in guiding, liberating, and sanctifying his children. In contrast, the Pauline memorial of the Last Supper shifts this focus toward Jesus. Now the guiding, liberating, and sanctifying functions are either shared or entirely taken over by Christ Jesus. The development of eucharistic theology, meanwhile, has been singularly preoccupied with explaining the manifold ways that Christ is present. Christian denominations vie with one another in inventing new ways to evoke the presence of Christ. Hence, even though most or all of the traditional canonical prayers are still addressed to the Father, the minds and the hearts of today's worshippers are predisposed toward encountering Jesus. This is the direct result of the "Death Tradition."

I mention these things here because the very fabric of our current eucharistic spirituality blocks us from rightly appreciating and rightly entering into the spirituality of the Didache. Even dedicated scholars and pastors are prone to read into the Didache what they want to find there and to discover therein what they imagine ought to be there if it is to be credited and harmonized with what we now know about early Christianity. The clues of the Didache are thus bent into all sorts of fantastical directions that have few checks and balances, and, as a result, the authentic voice of the Didache is muffled.

38. Niederwimmer judges that "the Lord God" would have been intended in its original Jewish context but that here it refers to the "Lord Jesus" (*Didache*, 105).

owing to your master [mentor] should be like the awe owing to Heaven [= God]" (m. 'Abot 4:12; Kallah Rab. 52b).[39]

3.2. The Lord's Prayer

The Didache declares that members should pray three times a day "as the Lord ordered in his good news" (8.2). The "Lord" in this case could possibly refer to Jesus, but this would yield to a Matthean bias that might be misplaced in the context of the Didache. The focus in the Didache is quite clearly cantered upon "how does the Lord God want us to pray?" at the three ordinary times each day.[40] Given the fact that the Lord's Prayer in the

---

This demonstrates that even seasoned scholars can unknowingly transport into the Didache their bias in favor of identifying Jesus as Lord. They acquire this bias in studying Paul and in participating in Christian piety. It is difficult for them, accordingly, to imagine how the Didache can be true to Jesus while absolutely being centered upon the presence, the purposes, and the saving grace of the Father. Niederwimmer refers to the "original Jewish context" without even for a moment reflecting that Jesus himself and the movement he left behind were solidly rooted within a Jewish context. Thus, even in the Synoptics we find Jesus saying to his disciples: "Whoever welcomes me welcomes the one who sent me" (Matt 10:40; Luke 9:48). And even Paul, who was consumed with promoting the messianic identity of Jesus, finds no difficulty in referencing the final consummation of history as taking place when "the Lord will become king over all the earth; the Lord will be one and his name one" (Zech 14:9) as requiring that "when all things are subjected to him [Christ-Jesus], then the Son himself will also be subjected to the one who put all things in subjection under him, so that God may be all in all" (1 Cor 15:28).

39. Jonathan Draper adds more references supporting this when he notes that "speaking the Name or Word or Torah mediates the presence of God is widespread in Jewish thinking"; see in this volume, the essay of Jonathan A. Draper ("Children and Slaves in the Community of the Didache and the Two Ways Tradition").

40. The framers of the Didache specify: "Three times within the day präy thus" (Did. 8.3) [for use of the umlaut, see n. 48 below]. At the same time, the framers found no necessity to define those times during the day when these prayers take place, nor do they specify the posture of prayer. The silence of the Didache on these points suggests that everyone was familiar with those times due to the practice of the community, which, in its turn, was shaped by the practice of the synagogue. Following Paul F. Bradshaw, "the times were traditional and unchanged, and so need no explicit mention" (*The Search for the Origins of Christian Worship* [New York: Oxford University Press, 1992], 26). Taras Khomych follows this line of thinking when he contrasts εὐαγγέλιον as found in Paul and in the Didache: "As opposed to Paul, the Didache is notably not centered on Christology. This document presents Jesus as

Gospel of Matthew (6:9–13) differs markedly from what one finds in the Gospel of Luke (11:2–4), and given the distinct possibility that Jesus (like most of his contemporaries) prayed extemporaneously, and, finally, given the absence of any tradition that Jesus routinely acted as prayer leader for his disciples, one has to be cautious in assuming that the Didache knows anything of Matthew's account of the origin of this prayer.[41]

Furthermore, the Didache does not stop with saying "as the Lord ordered," but continues with "in his good news." The good news, of course, is God's good news of his plans to establish a kingdom on earth as it is already established in heaven. The framers of the Didache consequently presuppose that the oral tradition for the Lord's Prayer was already established and in use within their community life. The Didache sanctions this usage as what "the Lord ordered in his good news" and insures that this prayer template had the authority (1) to override the use of the Eighteen Benedictions (m. Ber. 4:3, m. Ta'an. 2:2), which guided synagogue Jews in their prayers three times a day, and (2) to reign in the enthusiasm of Christians who might be expected to promote the second coming of Jesus in their daily prayers.[42]

God's servant [παῖς], who revealed the will of the Lord"; see in this volume, the essay of Taras Khomych ("Another Gospel: Exploring Early Christian Diversity with Paul and the Didache").

41. The scholars of the Jesus Seminar, meeting in Atlanta in 1988, said that certain lines of the prayer appeared to be most authentic, namely, "hallowed be thy name," "thy kingdom come," "give us this day our daily bread," and "forgive us our debts." But they said that these were likely to have been paraphrases of earlier statements and that it was unlikely Jesus ever strung these lines together in a single prayer. For a detailed analysis, see Milavec, *Didache: Faith, Hope, and Life*, 300–50.

42. Suffice it to say here that the phrase "dö not pray as the hypocrites" (Did. 8.2) [for use of the umlaut, see n. 48 below] signals that there was some contention within the Didache communities regarding what prayer template was to be used for the threefold daily prayers. Keep in mind that such prayers were regularly prayed in small groups (in households and in workshops). In this case a gifted prayer leader would improvise and expand within the progression given by the prayer template, and "because yours is the power and the glory forever" would be used as the expected refrain (as also in the weekly Eucharist). Given the restricted eschatological horizon of the Didache, one can imagine that someone who misused the daily prayers to promote Jesus as the Messiah coming upon the clouds of heaven would be as objectionable as someone who promoted defense of the Jerusalem temple as part of God's final showdown with the gentiles. The framers of the Didache had the pastoral genius of know-

3.3. The Eucharistic Meal

In connection with the Eucharist, we find the following instruction:

> (And) lët[43] no one eat or drink from ÿour eucharist except those baptized in the name of [the] Lord, for the Lord has likewise said concerning this: "Do not give what is holy to the dogs." (Did. 9.5)

Within the context of the Didache's Eucharist, "Lord" is reserved for "Lord God" and prayers are addressed entirely to the Father. Given the identification of Jesus as παῖς ("the servant") of the Father (Did. 9.2–3; 10.2–3), one would not be astonished that Did. 9.5 retains the notion that baptism was practiced "in the name of the Lord God."[44] On the other hand, within the "Death Tradition," baptism was performed "in the name of Jesus Christ" (Acts 2:38; 8:16; 10:48; 19:5; 1 Cor 1:13; Gal 3:27), but we would not expect that to be the case here.

---

ing where to be lenient and to honor diversity and where to draw the line and enforce a necessary unity. The community that prays together stays together.

43. In my two Didache volumes, I adapted the practice of using an umlaut by way of signaling that the verb is plural. I retain this practice in this essay.

44. Scholars generally agree that Did. 9.5 represents an earlier tradition that was gradually replaced by the trinity of names. See James D. G. Dunn, *Unity and Diversity in the New Testament* (Philadelphia: Westminster, 1977), 155–56. The tradition of acting "in the name of the Father, the Son, and the Holy Spirit" (Did. 7.1, 3) should not be thought of as reflecting early evidence of the doctrine of the Trinity. Christianity took over from Judaism an instinct for monotheism that made it impossible for Jews to imagine any physical person being confounded with the invisible and all-powerful Lord of the universe. For an in-depth story, I would recommend the historical grounding and the exegetical lucidity of James D. G. Dunn, *The Partings of the Ways between Christianity and Judaism and Their Significance for the Character of Christianity* (London: SCM; Philadelphia: Trinity, 1991), 163–229. A key passage in his work appears on page 190, as follows: "Paul in fact calls Jesus 'Lord' as much as a means of distinguishing Jesus from God as of identifying him with God. We have already cited 1 Cor 8:6 more than once: 'For us there is one God, the Father … and one Lord, Jesus Christ.' Evidently Paul could confess Jesus as Lord, while *at the same time* confessing that God is one; the two claims were not seen to be in any kind of competition. Paul could acknowledge the lordship of Christ, without apparently diminishing his commitment to Jewish monotheism.… We should also note a phrase which recurs quite often in the Pauline corpus, 'the God and Father of our Lord Jesus Christ' [Rom 15:6, 2 Cor 1:3, 11:31; Eph 1:3, 17; Col 1:3; also 1 Pet 1:3]. Even Jesus as Lord has God as his God."

In the entire New Testament, Matthew alone has the trinity of names associated with baptism, "in the name of the Father and of the Son and of the Holy Spirit" (28:19). Arthur Vööbus points out, however, that Eusebius cites the great commission of Matthew more than two dozen times as "teach all nations in my name."[45] It is quite probably, consequently, that Eusebius's text of Matthew's Gospel did not have a trinitarian formula and that this was later edited into copies of Matthew's Gospel. Accordingly, the retention of the simple formula "baptized in the name of the Lord" (Did. 9.5) may also be a remnant of how 7.1b and 7.3 were expressed in earlier recitations of the Didache. Hence, some weight must be given to the possibility that the trinitarian formula was introduced into the Didache in much the same way that an early copyist emended Matt 28:19 to conform to the liturgical practice of his day.[46]

Many scholars immediately jump to the conclusion that the second use of "the Lord" clearly refers to Jesus, since a word for word repetition of "Do not give what is holy to dogs" is found on the lips of Jesus in Matt 7:6.[47] This conclusion is doubtful for three reasons: (1) to begin with, the Didache up to this point has not used "Lord" by way of referring to Jesus; (2) when a similar formula is used in Did. 14.3, the citation in this case is from Mal 1:11, and consequently the appeal to what was "said by [the] Lord" clearly and unambiguously refers to the Lord God;[48] (3) finally, the

---

45. Arthur Vööbus, *Liturgical Traditions in the Didache* (Stockholm: ETSE, 1968), 37–39.

46. Ibid., 37–39; Jonathan A. Draper, "A Commentary on the Didache in the Light of the Dead Sea Scrolls and Related Documents" (Ph.D. diss., Cambridge University, 1983), 146–47.

47. Niederwimmer, *Didache*, 153.

48. Niederwimmer at this point allows that "κύριος here probably does not refer to Jesus" (*Didache*, 198). This is an understatement. Niederwimmer is deliberately tentative here, because he was hoping to show that all of the references to "the Lord" in the Didache might have referred to the Lord Jesus. For the moment, however, one can judge from the implied Christology of the Didache that it would have been blatantly blasphemous for members of the Didache communities to even imagine that Jesus might somehow adopt Mal 1:11 as referring to himself and, accordingly, direct that the gentiles should offer pure sacrifices to him. Even as late as the early third century, Christian communities were still struggling with whether it was fitting to offer prayers to Jesus (e.g., Origen, *On Prayer*). Thus, it would be ludicrous to imagine that the Didache, given its Jewish horizon of understanding, would have entertained anything but a strict monotheism. The words of Mal 1:11 thus could *only* be understood as "having been said by the Lord God" (Did. 14.3).

context of the saying about "holy things" in Matthew clearly pertains to Jesus's teaching and has no oblique reference to the Eucharist.

The saying itself, when read within the context of the Didache, clearly associates the eucharistic bread and wine as "holy"[49] (see also Did. 10.3) and as a "sacrifice" (Did. 14.2–3) and, therefore, not to be given to "the dogs." The reference to "dogs" was pejorative, since in the experience of the first-century hearer, the dog here was not a beloved household pet but "the annoying and despised eastern dog of the streets"[50] who is essentially a wormy, uncared-for, scavenger "commonly consuming flesh not acceptable for humans, such as animal carcasses and even human bodies."[51] Moreover, in the Christian Scriptures, the term "dogs" is used on multiple occasions as a metaphor to designate the gap between "the children of God" and the gentiles (Matt 15:26–27; Mark 7:26–27; Phil 3:2; 2 Pet 2:22).

Within the rabbinic literature, however, "it is the flesh of [temple] sacrifice that the much quoted saying refers: 'what is holy is not to be released to be eaten by dogs' (b. Bekhorot 15a interpreting Deut 12:15; m. Temurah 6:5; b. Temurah 117a and 130b [actually 17a and 30b]; b. Shebiit 11b and b. Pesahim 29a)."[52] In pagan temples, given the absence of refrigeration, those periods when there was an excessive number of flesh sacrifices resulted in transporting some of the meat offered to a god to be sold in the local meat market. Among the rabbis, therefore, the saying of Did. 9.5 seemed to say that meats offered to the Lord were "holy" and therefore ought not to be fed to dogs (literally) or sold off to "dogs" (metaphori-

---

49. The wine and bread were "consecrated" (Latin: *con* [intensive] + *sacrare* [to make sacred]). They were entirely set aside from ordinary wine and bread by the prayer of thanksgiving that consecrated them. This point has been hotly contested because the Eucharist of the Didache is not a memorial of the Last Supper nor do the words, "This is my body.... This is my blood" appear. Edward J. Kilmartin makes the observation that prayers of thankful praise must be considered the apostolic forms of "consecration" as framed within the "Life Tradition" ("Sacrificium Laudis: Content and Function of Early Eucharistic Prayers," *TS* 35 [1974]: 268–87 [273]). Enrico Mazza also makes the point that "the problem of the validity of the consecration is a problem which does not exist in the Jewish concept of the ritual meal" ("Elements of a Eucharistic Interpretation," in Draper, Didache *in Modern Research*, 287). For further details, see Milavec, *Didache: Faith, Hope, and Life*, 357–421.

50. Otto Michel, "κύνω, κυνάριον," *TDNT* 3:1101.

51. Frederick J. Simoons, *Eat Not This Flesh: Food Avoidances from Prehistory to the Present* (Madison: University of Wisconsin Press, 1994), 247.

52. Michel, "κύνω, κυνάριον," 3:1102.

cally, the gentiles). The framers of the Didache, consequently, had only to redraw the lines between insiders and outsiders, between the children and the dogs, in order to discover that such a saying of the Lord God applied to their Eucharist. In order to do so, however, the Eucharist had to be seen as the equivalent to a temple sacrifice. And this is exactly what happens in Did 14.1–3 wherein the framers of the Didache used Mal 1:11 to affirm that the Lord God regarded the eucharistic meal as a sacrifice. This in turn invited the use of another saying of the Lord God ("Do not give what is holy to dogs") as an ironclad directive against inviting the nonbaptized to partake of this Eucharist.

3.4. Living on the Threshold of the Lord's Coming

Just as the message of the Didache continued the message of Jesus of Nazareth, so too, the Eucharist of the Didache perpetuated the proleptic anticipation of the kingdom that marked the table fellowship of Jesus. Fed on the Eucharist, therefore, those who shared the way of life of the Father were nourished in their altered social reality. The consecrated cup evoked the holy vine of David; the consecrated broken loaf evoked the life and knowledge of the Father. The former indicated that the Father had elected Israel and established a kingdom of promise through David, his servant. Drinking the cup of the holy vine, therefore, allowed newly baptized gentiles to join in fellowship with Israel and to share her eschatological expectations.

Above all, the Eucharist of the Didache was profoundly forward looking: those whose lives were nourished on the broken loaf were set aside for the final ingathering—for just as the fragments that form the loaf were once "scattered over the hills" (Did. 9.4) and only later kneaded and baked in one loaf, so too those who ate of fragments of this consecrated loaf knew that the Father would one day harvest them "from the ends of the earth" so as to gather them into a kingdom on earth. Those who ate, therefore, tasted the future and collective promise that the "one loaf" signified.

Participants at the eucharistic meal would have had little inclination to speculate regarding some form of bodily or sacramental presence of Jesus. Their focus was elsewhere. For them, *the Father was the unseen but very much present host at every eucharistic meal.* The drink and food served were provided by him (Did. 10.3; 1.5). His "holy name" was dwelling within their "hearts" (Did. 10.2). The prayers addressed to this "holy Father" (Did. 10.2) were directly and immediately received by him. But, above all, he was the "almighty Master" (Did. 10.3) who was poised "to save ... to protect ... and to gather" his entire church into "the kingdom ... prepared for her" (Did. 10.5). In their way of experiencing things, consequently, members of the Didache communities looked to the Father for their redemption—just as his "servant Jesus" (Did. 9.3; 10.3) had done before them.

The following refrains bring the official Eucharist to its close:

Come, grace [of the kingdom]!
And pass away, [Oh] this world! Hosanna to the God of David!
If anyone is holy, come! If anyone is not, convert!
Come Lord [*Marana tha*]! Amen! (Did. 10.6)

The Didache is not intent upon the coming of the Son of Man (Matt 10:23; 16:27–28; 25:31–46; 26:64) or the return of Jesus (1 Thess 4:16–17; 1 Cor 1:7–8; Acts 1:11; Rev 1:7) but awaits the coming of "the God of David" (Did. 10.6) who after all the failures of fleshly kings will finally come to rule the world himself. This is the eschatology of the prophet Zechariah. The Lord God is finished using intermediaries. For his final coming, the Lord God will come himself personally.[53] The closing lines of the Didache

---

53. Most Christians, and many scholars among them, will have great difficulty with suggesting that God himself is expected to usher in the final kingdom. To begin with, Christian sources and homilies seldom if ever probe this line of thinking. When one reads the prophetic books of the Bible, this is the reoccurring theme. Yet Christians are in the habit of reading the prophets by way of confirming the mission of Christ. Yet in Genesis one finds God rolling up his sleeves and planting a garden in Eden (Gen 2:8). This would be a good place to begin to show how anthropomorphic images of God fit easily into the Jewish tradition. Jacob Neusner, in his excellent volume *The Incarnation of God: The Character of Divinity in Formative Judaism* (Philadelphia: Fortress, 1988), provides a wide assortment of such illustrations. So we can now turn our attention from the first pages to the last pages of the Christian Bible. The book of Revelation has a wide assortment of end time scenarios. The favorite by far of most Christians is the scene wherein the Lord God is seated on his throne in the new Jerusalem that has come down from heaven and a voice says: "'See, the home of God is among mortals. He will dwell with them as their God; they will be his peoples, and God himself will be with them; he will wipe every tear from their eyes [see Isa 25:8]. Death will be no more; mourning and crying and pain will be no more, for the first things have passed away.' And the one who was seated on the throne said, 'See, I am making all things new'" (21:3–5). In the book of Revelation, Jesus has the form of a lamb "that was slaughtered" (Rev 5:9, 12). In the final apocalyptic vision in this book, however, it is the Lord God who is at the center of the healing action. But God and the lamb together provide light for the city and a beacon for the nations: God's glory

return to this expectation when they cite Zechariah in support of the selective resurrection of the just, saying:

> "The Lord will come and all the holy ones with him." Then the world will see the Lord coming atop the clouds of heaven (Did. 16.7–8)

Within the "Life Tradition" it has become quite clear that the one who was to come to establish his kingdom was "the God of David" (Did. 10.6) and not "the Son of David" as found in Matt 21:15. Under the influence of Matthew, it is not surprising that the fourth century Apostolic Constitutions and Canons altered the closing words of Did. 10.6 to read, "Come Lord! Hosanna to the Son of David" (7.26.5)[54]. Thus, as the "Death Tradition" took hold, the prayers of the Didache were revised to make room for the "second coming" of the Lord Jesus.[55] "Come Lord [*Marana tha*]" remains, but in the Apostolic Constitutions and Canons the Son of David is expected and not the God of David. The Didache, on the other hand, forces us to go back to an older belief where the focus was set upon the "God of David" (Did. 10.6) who is both "the Father" and "the Lord" who will gather the elect into *his* kingdom (Did. 9.4; 10.5).[56]

---

replaces the sunlight/moonlight and the Lamb provides an oil lamp. The contrast is evident: "And the city has no need of sun or moon to shine on it, for the glory of God is its light, and its lamp is the Lamb. The nations will walk by its [i.e., by the city's] light, and the kings of the earth will bring their glory into it [the city] (21:23–25). Thus, right within the New Testament canon, one has a vision of an apocalyptic future very much centered upon the arrival and the saving activity of the Lord God.

54. Knowing this, it becomes clear how impossible it would be to rely upon the fourth-century Apostolic Constitutions and Canons to reconstruct the so-called "lost ending" of the first-century Didache. Unfortunately, even scholars such as Niederwimmer come to the conclusion that a "lost ending" is "obvious from the structure of the Didache apocalypse (16:3–8), as well as from the paraphrasing conclusions of this section in the *Apostolic Constitutions*" (Niederwimmer, *Didache*, 20). For a detailed examination, see Milavec, *Didache: Faith, Hope, and Life*, 828–36.

55. John A. T. Robinson, *Jesus and His Coming*, 2nd ed. (London: SCM; Philadelphia: Westminster, 1979) observes with T. S. Glasson that the parousia does not derive from messianic passages within the Hebrew Scriptures but from end time visions of the Lord God coming to his people, with the "single adjustment that the Lord was the Lord Jesus" (140).

56. Some scholars have asked me why the Didache makes no room for the messianic claims on behalf of Jesus that are promoted by the "Death Tradition." I respond to this very excellent question as follows:

If Acts gives us anything near an accurate picture of Paul's impact upon the synagogues in Asia Minor that he visited, then one can gain a certain sympathy for those who wanted Paul silenced and were willing to take action against him as "a disturber of the peace" (Acts 24:5). From the point of view of Paul's opponents, Paul appeared as an irresponsible and irrepressible fanatic who dominated the open forums in the synagogue every Sabbath and used the Hebrew Scriptures by way of demonstrating that everyone had to champion Jesus of Nazareth, because God had raised him from the dead and thereby singled him out as the one who would return in the final days to usher in the messianic age. When Paul did get silenced, he then withdrew from that synagogue those Jews and "Godfearers" who accepted the renewal of faith and hope that came with his apocalyptic visions. In so doing, however, it can also be imagined that such actions often broke up families and introduced factionalism into the very heart of the local synagogue.

This is perhaps the sort of apocalyptic factionalism that the framers of the Didache were trying to prevent. How so? First, by codifying the way of life, the liturgical templates, the treatment of visiting prophets, and the end times scenario. Second, by insisting that these are boilerplate protections for all concerned: "You will not at all leave behind the rules of the Lord, but you will guard the things that you have received, neither adding nor taking [anything] away" (Did. 4.13; 6.1; 11.1–2; 15.4). Third, visiting apostles and prophets are honored "as the Lord," but then their stay is deliberately limited and their conduct carefully supervised (Did. 11.1–13.4). After the official Eucharist is finished, the prophets are allowed to give thanks "as much as they wish" (Did. 10.7) and as they wish. Thus, a Christian prophet could paraphrase 1 Thess 4 in its entirety. Another prophet could recite a "secret of the Most High" as found in 2 Esd 12:31–36. And still another could glorify King Hezekiah or even name his own "master" as the future messiah (b. San. 98a). From the vantage point of the Didache, all such apocalyptic visions regarding the identity and the role of the messiah were left "open and unresolved" in the face of the certainty that the Lord God was coming to gather his elect into his kingdom. What remained certain, consequently, is that *lex orandi, lex credenda* ("the rule of praying is the rule of believing"). Fourthly, the terms "Christian" (Did. 12.4) and "Christ-merchant" (Did. 12.5) appear in the Didache not as unqualified endorsements, but by way of giving cautions regarding unfortunate tendencies found among these outsiders (Did. 12.3). Fifthly, it must be observed that the Didache also leaves "open and unresolved" another troublesome source of factionalism, namely, whether Jerusalem or the temple will have any role to play in God's future kingdom.

In sum, the rule "You will not cause dissention, and you will reconcile those fighting" (Did. 4.3) applies to all of this as well. And no amount of apocalyptic speculation can override the final call for "watchfulness … for the whole time of your faith will not be of use to you if in the end time you should not have been perfected" (Did. 16.1–2). Finally, the fact that the end times opens with havoc in the heart of the Jesus movement (Did. 16.3–4) is most probably a sign that such bitter havoc has already been tasted by the framers of the Didache relative to the endless varieties of

Conclusion

In the end I return to the crisis facing Didache scholarship. We have been at a standstill for a long time. During a thirty-year period when the number of participants and the number of papers increased three-fold during the annual meetings of the SBL, the number of persons addressing the Didache has still remained at a comparatively low level. This is because the legacy of source and redaction criticism and the influence of Harnack has hopelessly fragmented the text and reduced it to a second-century church order. The thrust of my essay has been to show that this orientation is being progressively abandoned. "The decision to reject one paradigm," Thomas Kuhn rightly notes, "is always simultaneously the decision to undertake another."[57]

First, the voice of the Didache was muted by the supposition that it was spliced together like a church order. In truth, however, it exhibits a finely tuned oral integrity from beginning to end. Next, the voice of the Didache was distorted because it was interpreted in the shadow cast by the Gospel of Matthew. Freed of the Christology and ecclesiology of Matthew, the Didache demonstrates a highly sophisticated community of householders bound to the way of life in anticipation of the final ingathering into the kingdom of God. Finally, in the third section the voice of the Didache was freed from the high Christology that even scholars with the stature of Niederwimmer have mistakenly tried to overlay the document. Thus, the hermeneutical caution of Crossan helps us to safeguard the "Life Tradition" within the Didache and to enable it to stand up for itself without being overwhelmed by the "Death Tradition."

Not all examinations of the Didache are created equal. Some force us to notice more about the text. Some examinations break through the surface of text and weave together the clues offered by the text into tantalizing visions of the communitarian way of life that stood behind the text. Superior theories have a greater fruitfulness—they are "fraught with further intimations of an indeterminate range"[58] that reveal themselves from time to time in "as yet undisclosed, perhaps as yet unthinkable,

---

apocalyptic variations that visitors bring with them into the heart of the Didache communities.

57. Thomas S. Kuhn, *The Structure of Scientific Revolutions* (Chicago: University Press, 1962), 77.

58. Michael Polanyi, *Tacit Dimension* (Garden City, NY: Doubleday, 1966), 23.

consequences."[59] Such theories also provide a greater intellectual satisfaction—they say more about what are the hidden depths of meaning within the text. As part of their greater fruitfulness and greater intellectual satisfaction, however, they also often carry with them a concomitant vulnerability to being falsified.

As someone who spent many sleepless nights puzzling over the Didache, I still believe that I have much to learn from those who are coming after me and will inevitably dismantle and reconstruct much of what I have done. Among all my reviewers, however, I am especially indebted to Robert J. Daly, professor emeritus of patristic studies at Boston College. In his review of my thousand-page volume, he makes some very perceptive and timely observations that serve to define how in the present moment a new direction in Didache studies is emerging not only within my own scholarship, but also among the small group of pioneering scholars who have embraced proposals that find common ground with the position that I have set out above. I find it fitting, therefore, to give Daly the last word when it come to defining a "viable future" for Didache studies:

> Building on, but also fundamentally correcting more than a hundred years of research and interpretation, Milavec's basic thesis, convincingly demonstrated in magnificent detail, is that the *Didache* is neither a church order in the ordinary sense of the word, nor a text sometimes awkwardly patched together by several hands from several sources, nor a document that is dependent on any of the gospels (it's actually prior to them) or on other Christian texts, but an orally transmitted guide for mentors given the responsibility of progressively introducing adult pagans into this new Christian way of life.
>
> It is also a book that could not have been written even as recently as one or two decades ago. To list some of the reasons for this: (1) the relative maturation of nonpolemical approaches to matters of Christian origins—no longer is interpretation driven by a specifically Catholic or Protestant confessional need to prove this or that; (2) the maturation and broad acceptance of sociological analyses of the New Testament and early Christianity; (3) the general availability of an explosion of knowledge about postbiblical Judaism and about late antiquity in general; and (4) a methodological shift away from the relative dominance of textuality over orality—that is, one no longer assumes that the first question is how

---

59. Ibid., 23.

this document developed as a written text, but is ready to ask first about the life situation that can explain the text as received. In other words, the fundamental principle of interpretation that Milavec consistently follows to good effect is not to look for exogenous reasons for interpreting the text, but to go the extra mile in allowing the text, as received, and from its own context, to explain itself.

Following this method of interpretation, Milavec shows that the *Didache* is not only not dependent on any of the gospels, but is most likely prior to them and, in any case, theologically very different. What it reveals is a, so-to-speak, pre-Christological stage of Christianity. There is no mention of Christic sacrificial atonement; no mention even of the passion and death of Christ. Instead Jesus is spoken of as the "Servant"; nor is it Jesus, but the Father, who is spoken of as the Lord, the one who will come in the Last Days.[60]

---

60. Robert J. Daly, Review of *The Didache: Faith, Hope, and Life of the Earliest Christian Communities, 50–70 CE*, by Aaron Milavec, *Catholic Books Review* (2004). Online: http://catholicbooksreview.org/2004/milavec.htm.http://catholicbooksreview.org/2004/milavec.htm

Children and Slaves in the Community of the Didache and the Two Ways Tradition

Jonathan A. Draper

This paper explores the *Haustafel* (= HT) in Did. 4.9–11 and parallel versions of the Two Ways against the background of the "moral economy" as defined by James C. Scott and Halvor Moxnes. These texts insist on "generalised reciprocity" and reject the "balanced reciprocity" practised by the elite in the Greco-Roman context and the "negative reciprocity" they mete out to the underclasses. For this reason the intrusion of the patriarchal ethic of the HT, with its uncompromising one-way instruction concerning children and its support for the institution of slavery, are surprising, as is the absence of instructions concerning husbands and wives. Less surprising perhaps is the absence of instructions concerning the emperor. The background and implications of the instructions are examined to try and reconstruct the social situation in households in the Didache community. The paper concludes that the HT is firmly situated in the social location of *koinonia* or community of goods in the earliest Christian Jewish communities, which challenges traditional mores but also occasions the specific limitations to *koinonia* that undermine the egalitarianism of the community. The evidence of the Didache reveals both the social dynamics of the HT and its enduring influence on emerging Christianity.

1. Introduction

In recent years biblical scholars have shown a renewed interest in the HT genre of literature in the New Testament, driven by both a feminist critique since the ground-breaking work of Elizabeth Schüssler Fiorenza's *In Memory of Her* and also a renewed interest in socioeconomic location of texts in the ancient world.[1] There has been a shift in the scholarly consensus from viewing these texts against the background of Stoic philosophy or Hellenistic Judaism toward understanding them as a topos of "household management."[2] The evolution and status of the debate has been astutely set out and critiqued in a recent paper by Margaret Y. MacDonald[3] so that there is no need to repeat it here. Her insistence that what appears in texts is always only partly a reflection of what goes on in reality (that it stands in dialogical tension with reality so that the discussion needs to be more nuanced) is welcome. My own study in this paper has been formed by the work of Carolyn Osiek, MacDonald, and Moxnes, though they are not to blame for what I say. In particular, Moxnes's careful economic analysis of the embedded economic relations reflected by Luke's Gospel in *The Economy of the Kingdom*[4] has raised questions that prompted me to undertake a "moral economy" analysis of the whole text of the Didache as an integral reflection of an attempt to construct an alternative economy to the surrounding Greco-Roman economic relations based on patron-client relations, an alternative economy that was only partially successful.[5] My economic analysis viewed the HT table in Did. 4 as having subverted and ultimately undermined this egalitarian economy, something I wish to pursue in more depth in this paper, particularly since the HT in the Two Ways tradition has been largely ignored in the discussions of New Testament scholars.

A quick flip through the recent literature on the HT shows that these authors either do not refer at all to the Two Ways found in Did. 1–6 and

---

1. Elisabeth Schüssler Fiorenza, *In Memory of Her: A Feminist Theological Reconstruction of Christian Origins* (London: SCM; New York: Crossroads, 1983).

2. James D. G. Dunn, *The Epistles to Colossians and to Philemon*, NIGTC (Grand Rapids: Eerdmans, 1996), 243.

3. Margaret Y. MacDonald, "Beyond Identification of the Topos of Household Management: Reading the Household Codes in Light of Recent Methodologies and Theoretical Perspectives in the Study of the New Testament," *NTS* 57 (2011): 65–90. She insists that "there is a need for greater nuance with respect to the function of the codes in community life to allow for more complexity and even contradiction based on the variety of actors and perspectives that shaped [New Testament] communities and texts" (72).

4. Halvor Moxnes, *The Economy of the Kingdom: Social Conflict and Economic Relations in Luke's Gospel* (Philadelphia: Fortress, 1988).

5. Jonathan A. Draper, "The Moral Economy of the *Didache*," *HTS.TS* 67 (2011), Art. #907. DOI:10.4102/hts.v67il.907.

Barn. 18–29 (and other early Christian extracanonical texts in the Two Ways tradition) or only occasionally refer to the Apostolic Fathers in parenthesis. The general assumption is that, if material is not in the New Testament, it is late and does not need to be taken into consideration. But from 1883 a range of scholars have considered the Two Ways (usually represented by the Doctrina apostolorum) to be a pre-Christian Jewish proselyte tract incorporated into a Christian document or as presenting one of the very earliest Christian catechetical patterns.[6] Alfred Seeberg's overelaborate claims for the existence of such a Jewish-Christian Ur-text behind most of the New Testament Epistles led to the theory being discounted (see the recent helpful paper of Benjamin Edsall[7]). This perspective has continued to be argued extensively in recent years, however, as for example in my own doctoral thesis.[8] Huub van de Sandt and David Flusser have even gone as far as to provide us with a critical text of their hypothesized pre-Christian, Jewish, Greek Two Ways.[9] Aaron Milavec,[10] on the other hand, argues that the whole of the Didache dates to the middle of the first century CE and represents the earliest Christian life, something

---

6. E.g., Charles Taylor, *The Teaching of the Twelve Apostles, with Illustrations from the Talmud* (Cambridge: Deighton Bell, 1886); Alfred Seeberg, *Der Katechismus der Urchristenheit* (Leipzig: Deichert, 1903); *Die beiden Wege und das Aposteldekre* (Leipzig: Deichert, 1906); *Die Didache des Judentums und der Urchristenheit* (Leipzig: Deichert, 1908); Gunther Klein, *Der älteste christliche Katechismus und die jüdische Propaganda-Literatur* (Berlin: Reimer, 1909).

7. Benjamin Edsall, "*Kerygma*, Catechesis and Other Things We Used to Find: Twentieth-Century Research on Early Christian Teaching Since Alfred Seeberg (1903)," *CurBS* 10 (2012): 410–41.

8. Jonathan A. Draper, "A Commentary on the Didache in the Light of the Dead Sea Scrolls and Related Documents" (Ph.D. diss., Cambridge University, 1983); see also "Ritual Process and Ritual Symbol in Didache 7–10," *VC* 54 (2000): 1–38; "A Continuing Enigma: The 'Yoke of the Lord in *Didache* 6:2–3 and Early Jewish-Christian Relations," in *The Image of Judaeo-Christians in Ancient Jewish and Christian Christian Literature*, ed. Peter J. Tomson and D. Lambers-Petry, WUNT 158 (Tübingen: Mohr Siebeck, 2003), 106–23; Huub van de Sandt and David Flusser, *The Didache: Its Jewish Sources and Its Place in Early Judaism and Christianity*, CRINT 3.5; (Assen; Van Gorcum; Minneapolis: Fortress, 2002); Aaron Milavec, *The Didache: Faith, Hope, and Life of the Earliest Christian Communities, 50–70 CE* (New York: Newman, 2003).

9. Van de Sandt and Flusser, *Didache*, 122–30. They even go so far as to suggest that "Jesus in formulating his instruction used traditional materials transmitted both in the Sermon on the Mount and in the Greek Two Ways" (193).

10. Milavec, *Didache: Faith, Hope, and Life.*

supported also lately by Thomas O'Loughlin.[11] Much of this discussion seems to have escaped New Testament scholars and social historians of early Christianity. But if it is correct that this material provides a window on first century Jewish communities or the earliest Christian communities or, as I would argue, the early Christian Jewish communities in a tension with the early Pauline communities, then it would be essential that it is factored into the discussion of the HT tradition and the burgeoning discussion on early Christian households and families. I would argue that this is particularly important because the HT in the Two Ways tradition is set in an explicit and coherent socioeconomic context in the text itself, though this has not been recognized.[12] Previous studies of the HT material have been misled by the assumption that paraenesis is a random collection of ethical instruction with no *Tendenz*, which arises from the form critical approach of Martin Dibelius in his *Commentary on the Epistle of James* (1976)[13] and was adopted by Pierre Prigent,[14] Robert Kraft,[15] and Klaus Wengst[16] in their analyses of the Two Ways material in Barnabas. I have modified the position I took in my doctoral dissertation in that, while I still believe that the Two Ways tradition in the Didache, Barnabas, Doctrina apostolorum, Ecclesiastical Canons, and Epitome apostolorum can be shown to continue the topos and outlines of the Jewish *Derek Eretz* tradition, I do not think that this tradition is necessarily pre-Christian Jewish

---

11. Thomas O'Loughlin, *The Didache: A Window on the Earliest Christians* (Grand Rapids: Baker; London: SPCK, 2010).

12. I raised this question in the discussion of the HT material in my doctoral thesis (1983) when the Stoic hypothesis prevailed and was given its classic presentation by James E. Crouch, *The Origin and Intention of the Colossian Haustafel*, FRLANT 109 (Göttingen: Vandenhoeck & Ruprecht, 1972).

13. Martin Dibelius, *James: A Commentary on the Epistle of James*, rev. H. Greeven; trans. M. A. Williams, Hermeneia (Philadelphia: Fortress, 1976).

14. Pierre Prigent, *Les testimonia dans le christianiasme primitive: L'épître de Barnabé I–XVI* (Paris: Gabalda, 1961); Pierre Prigent and Robert A. Kraft, *Epître de Barnabé*, SC 172 (Paris: Cerf, 1971).

15. Robert A. Kraft, *Barnabas and the Didache*, AF 3 (Toronto: Nelson, 1965).

16. The suggestion that Barnabas represents a collection of Jewish legal interpretations had already been made by Leslie W. Barnard ("The Epistle of Barnabas and the Tannaitic Catechism," *AThR* 41 [1959]: 177–90) and has been renewed more recently by Martin B. Shukster and Peter Richardson ("Temple and Bet Ha-midrash in the Epistle of Barnabas," in *Separation and Polemic*, vol. 2 of *Anti-Judaism in Early Christianity*, ed. Stephen G. Wilson, SCJ 2 [Waterloo, ON: Wilfrid Laurier University Press, 1986], 17–31).

as it stands, as argued by van de Sandt and Flusser. It was developed within the early Christian Jewish communities under the pressure of the need for the catechesis and socialization of gentiles. We have no evidence for its use in its current form in Jewish communities, but widespread evidence of early Christian usage.

The heart of a moral economic analysis lies in the premise that the economy of premodern societies was/is embedded in their ethical system, the social universe that conveys meaning. The accumulation of capital was not an end in itself but rather related to honor and shame, patterns of patron-client relationships stretching up to the ruler himself and down to the lowest human being. Land and the control of its produce, control of the fertility of women, and control of the product of the labor of human beings was represented by the gods and their laws. Conversely, ethical and social rules are always simultaneously representations of economic relations. They receive ideal elaborations in the texts of the elite, but these texts usually represent the "official transcript" except where the marginalized insert their "hidden transcript" into the discourse of the powerful.[17] Here religion plays a key part in modelling the alternative social universe of the poor, powerless, and marginalized. Hence the emergence of a "Christian" literature as the final product of a largely illiterate movement of Galilean peasants may provide a glimpse of their alternative social universe, the way they began to embody it in communal life before it was, in turn, taken up into the modified discourse of a new Christian elite.

2. The Variants of the Christian Two Ways Text as Socially Meaningful

Those who have written on the first six chapters of the Didache, with the notable exception of Milavec, have usually been more interested in tracing the "original text" of the Two Ways and settling the question of whether the Didache or Barnabas is more original. If David C. Parker[18] is correct, however, there is no original text in a society that is primarily oral in its communications, and instead we have multiple representations of a tradition that is fluid and continually subject to change, to respond

---

17. The terminology comes from James C. Scott, *Domination and the Arts of Resistance* (New Haven: Yale University Press, 1990).

18. David C. Parker, *The Living Text of the Gospels* (Cambridge: Cambridge University Press, 1997).

to, and to reflect the social situation of the scribes, since text and oral performance are continually interacting and reshaping each other. Looked at in this way, the variants in the representation of the HT of the Two Ways take on new meaning as reflecting social and economic development. Most scholars accept that the structure of the Two Ways tradition is best represented by that of the Didache and Doctrina apostolorum (e.g. van de Sandt and Flusser prefer the Doctrina apostolorum for the structure but the Didache for the text) rather than Barnabas.[19] Beyond that it is often argued that the text of Barnabas represents earlier traditions closer to Jewish origins. Since that writer is frequently polemical, though, this needs to be interrogated. Beyond the Doctrina apostolorum, there are also two related fourth century representatives of the tradition that do not have the way of death, namely, the Ecclesiastical Canons and Epitome apostolorum, though its representation of the tradition is sketchy to say the least. The fifth century Arabic Life of Shenudi represents a Coptic Egyptian text that is also reasonably faithful to the tradition, in my opinion, though its exact Greek basis is often difficult to reconstruct, since it is a Coptic text that survived only in Arabic. The Apostolic Constitutions and Canons contains the whole text of the Didache rather than the separately existing Two Ways, again reasonably faithfully but with added commentary and obvious redactions. Then two later Greek texts follow something of the structure and some of the text, paraphrased at times as the basis for an ascetic monastic lifestyle in Fides Nicanae and Syntagma doctrinae, somehow associated with Athanasius, which ultimately influences the composition of the late fourth century *Rule of St. Augustine* and the *Rule of Benedict*.

---

19. Besides van de Sandt and Flusser, *Didache*, see the classic discussions of the Two Ways in Jean-Paul Audet, "Literary and Doctrinal Affinities of the 'Manual of Discipline,'" in *The* Didache *in Modern Research*, ed. Jonathan A. Draper, AGJU 37 (Leiden: Brill, 1996), 129–47; trans. of "Affinités Littéraires et Doctrinales du 'Manuel de Discipline,'" *RB* 59 (1952): 219–38; Willi Rordorf, "An Aspect of the Judeo-Christian Ethic: The Two Ways," in *The* Didache *in Modern Research*, ed. Jonathan A. Draper, AGJU 37 (Leiden: Brill, 1996), 148–64; trans. of "Une chapitre d'éthique judéo-chrétienne: les deux voies," *RSR* 60 (1972): 109–28.

3. The *Haustafel* in the Didache and Its Economic Logic in the Moral Economy

In my article "The Moral Economy of the Didache,"[20] I have argued that there is a consistent socioeconomic pattern of generalized redistribution in the Didache, which is consistent with the creation of the kind of alternative economy of the weak and marginalized in the Roman Empire as described by Scott.[21] It is a rejection of the unequal power relations epitomized by a patron-client system radiating out from the emperor and percolating down to the lowest level of the empire, including its conquered peoples. Central to this resistance is insistence on generalized reciprocity, the insistence that labour, goods, and wealth are given to people by God with the express purpose of giving to others so that all benefit. For this reason, inside the community no one is allowed to turn away a needy person, or refuse to give, or even to call their property their own. There is a balanced reciprocity in that goods given to those in need are really given to God, who will reward the giver and remove their sins in exchange. In addition, although they are sharing perishable material goods with the poor, they are also receiving imperishable spiritual gifts from them in return. So the Hellenistic principle of *isotes* among friends is not abandoned entirely: it is deconstructed and reconstructed in a radical fashion. Moreover, there is a serious and implementable sanction against abuse of the system of generalized redistribution, namely, that those taking without need are subject to judgment and punishment by the community "until they have repaid the last farthing." Most probably this would involve exclusion from the community until they repaid in the fashion of 1 Cor 5–6. Συνοχῇ (Did. 1.5) does not mean "prison" primarily but "pressure" or "distress." Paul forbids members to go to pagan courts but to exercise judgment themselves. Didache 4 takes the same line, as we shall see.

In "The Moral Economy," I note that the generalized reciprocity and egalitarian alternative economic system developed within this early Christian community should not be romanticized (as I believe it is by Milavec and O'Loughlin), but that its limitations and problems should be explored also. Chief among these internal contradictions in the system is the presence of the HT insisting on the subjection of children and slaves in chapter 4, and the recognition of the importance of patronage of the

---

20. Draper, "Moral Economy."
21. Scott, *Domination and the Arts of Resistance*.

wealthy alongside the (probably impoverished) spiritual leadership in chapter 15. The former limits the liberatory potential of the movement for the weakest and most exploited members of the community. The latter reintroduces the web of imperial connections embedded in patron-client relationships by the back door and ensures that, in the long run, the empire strikes back. In this paper I will only be exploring the relationship of the HT in chapter 4 to the moral economy that I have described in the previous paper. First, I set out the material schematically and use the section numbering from the Didache as the basis for the discussion of Barnabas and other forms of the Two Ways in schematic 1. Items found only in the Didache are italicized.[22]

Schematic 1: Didache 4

1. The Teacher/Prophet

A   4.1 Remember night and day
       the one who speaks to you the word of God,
          and honor him [male?] as the Lord [τιμήσεις ... ὡς κύριον].
    For where the things concerning the Lord are spoken,
       there is the Lord.

2. Regular Communal Assemblies for Judgment

B   2. And you shall seek out the presence [ἐκζητήσεις ... τὰ πρόσωπα] of the saints daily [καθ' ἡμέραν],
       so that you can find rest in their words
    3. You shall not make a schism,
       but you shall reconcile the warring factions.
   You shall judge justly;
       you shall not show favouritism [οὐ λήψῃ πρόσωπον] leading to transgression;
    4. you shall not doubt [διψυχήσεις] whether it should be or not

3. Requirement for Generalized Reciprocity

C   5. Do not be one who stretches out your hands to receive,
       but one who shuts them up when it comes to giving.
    6. If you have [earned anything] through [the work of] your hands,
       you shall give a ransom for your sins.
    7. You shall not doubt [διστάσεις] whether to give,
       and you shall not grumble when you give,

---

22. Translations of the Didache are my own unless otherwise indicated.

for you shall know who is the good giver of the reward.
D 8. *You shall not turn away the needy person [male?],*
   but you [sg.] shall share all things with your brother [and sister?],
   and you shall not say they are your own.
   For if you [pl.] are sharers in what is immortal,
   how much more in perishable things?
4. Household Management
E1 9. You [sg.] shall not hold back your hand
   from your son or from your daughter,
   but from their youth you shall teach the fear of God [τὸν φόβον τοῦ θεοῦ].
F1 10. You [sg.] shall not reprove in your anger your male slave or your female slave,
   who hope in the same God,
   lest they should no longer fear [φοβηθήσονται] the God who is over you both.
   For he has not come to call with respect of persons [κατὰ πρόσωπον],
   but those whom the Spirit has prepared.
F2 11. And you [pl. male?] slaves shall be subject [ὑποταγήσεσθε] to your [pl. male?] masters,
   as to an image of God [ὡς τύπῳ θεοῦ], in shame and fear.
12. You [sg.] shall hate all hypocrisy [ὑπόκρισιν],
   and everything which is not pleasing to the Lord.
5. Conclusion of the Way of Life: Binding Nature of Its Teaching
G 13. You [sg.] shall not abandon any commandments of the Lord,
   but you shall keep what you have received,
   neither adding nor subtracting.
H 14. You shall confess your transgressions [*vl.* in church],
   and you shall not come to your prayer with an evil conscience.
   This is the way of life.

In my schematic arrangement I am suggesting five blocks of progressively ordered and related catechetical teaching that constitute the final instructions in the way of life and set out a kind of constitution of the community into which the catechumens are being initiated. Whereas much of the previous teaching has been paraenetic, generalized lists of ethical behaviour and prohibited behaviour, this chapter sets out concrete social relations in the community. It is consistent with the rest of the Didache but forms an integrated and well-structured unit. Block 5 constitutes the conclusion of the way of life set out in chapters 1–4 and emphasizes the binding and unchanging nature of these social relations as commandments of the Lord. I suggest that, although the instruction forbidding hypocrisy (G) may well belong with block 4 and not block 5, it fits equally well with the general conclusion, since double mindedness is consistently rejected in the whole of the Two Ways. Its rhetorical function here in terms of its position in the text, however, may relate rather to the behaviour of slaves than to the general conclusion.

In block 1, which concerns the relationship of community members to teachers and/or prophets, we need to note the use of the language of patronage, though the advantages being brokered are spiritual ones. She or he is to receive the τιμή, which would usually be reserved for God, because she or he speaks the words of God and hence mediates God's presence. The principle that speaking the Name or Word or Torah mediates the presence of God is widespread in Jewish thought, as in the well-known m. 'Abot 3:3:

> But if two sit together and words of the Law [are spoken] between them, the Divine Presence rests between them, as it is written, *Then they that feared the Lord spake one with another: and the Lord hearkened, and heard, and a book of remembrance was written before him, for them that feared the Lord, and that thought upon his name* [Mal 3:16]. Scripture speaks here of "two"; whence [do we learn] that if even one sits and occupies himself in the Law, the Holy One, blessed is he, appoints him a reward? Because it is written, *Let him sit alone and keep silence, because he hath laid it upon him* [Lam 3:28].[23]

It is taken up in the famous saying of Jesus in Matt 18:20: "For where two or three are gathered together in my name I am there amongst them."[24] There are signs that this way of honoring a superior in the community as if they were the Lord (τιμήσεις ... ὡς κύριον) links to questions of patriarchal hierarchy, since the concept recurs in the instruction to the slaves at the bottom of the chain of patron-client relations that they should obey their owners/ masters as if they were a "type" of God (ὡς τύπῳ θεοῦ). In block 1 of chapter 4, however, the text provides the basis for the honor due to the teacher/prophet as patron, even though these figures were financially

---

23. All references to rabbinic texts are taken from *The Soncino Classics Collection: The Soncino Talmud, the Soncino Midrash Rabbah, the Soncino Zohar, the Bible, in Hebrew and English*, Judaic Classics Library (New York: Davka), electronic text.

24. Celia Deutsch, *Hidden Wisdom and the Easy Yoke: Wisdom, Torah and Discipleship in Matthew 11.25–30*, JSNTSup 18 (Sheffield: JSOT, 1987).

in need of support from the community, as the reservations in Did. 11 show and as the monetary and material resources made available to them in Did. 13 clearly show they were. Instead of giving material resources to the community as patrons should, they receive resources. Later versions of the Two Ways make this explicit, as we shall see. This is the cause of the conflict in Did. 15, in my opinion, since it undermines the patron-client basis on which bishops and deacons are appointed: honor in exchange for resources. In this respect, 4.1 sets out alternative economic relations in which honor is not given on the basis of material resources and patronage but on spiritual resources of God's word. But this coheres with the thought in block 3 that material resources and spiritual resources should be equally weighted and with the insistence of chapter 15 that prophets and teachers receive equal honor with bishops and deacons.

Block 2 provides for regular meetings of the assembled community for judgment. The "rest" that people seek to find in the assembly is, in this case, the settlement of legal disputes. The proximity of block 3 suggests that the majority of questions to be addressed by the community assembled for judgment would be socioeconomic, though no doubt questions concerning the testing of visitors (chs. 11–12) and unresolved quarrels between members (chs. 14 and 15) would also feature. The instructions here are based on Lev 19:17–18, as also in Did. 2.6–7 and 15.3.[25] The block shows signs of internal and external coherence: The saying on judgment begins with coming together to seek the communal (τὰ πρόσωπα, v. 2) assembly and ends with a prohibition of showing favoritism toward the individual (οὐ λήψῃ πρόσωπον, v. 3), something repeated in verse 10 (κατὰ πρόσωπον) in the instructions to slave-masters. Judgment must not be done double-mindedly (οὐ διψυχήσεις, v. 4), something repeated in the instructions on giving (οὐ διστάσεις, v. 7) and again in the instruction to slaves in that ὑπόκρισις appears in tandem with other words suggesting double dealing/thinking/acting in 5.1 (ψευδομαρτυρίαι, ὑποκρίσεις, διπλοκαρδία, δόλος).

Block 3 is the central and principle statement around which the whole series of instruction coheres. It is also central in the structuring of this

---

25. Jonathan A. Draper, "Pure Sacrifice in Didache 14 as Jewish Christian Exegesis," *Neot* 42 (2008): 223–52; see also Huub van de Sandt, "Two Windows on a Developing Jewish-Christian Reproof Practice: Matt 18:15–17 and *Did.* 15:3," in *Matthew and the Didache: Two Documents from the Same Jewish-Christian Milieu?* ed. Huub van de Sandt (Assen: Van Gorcum; Minneapolis: Fortress, 2005), 173–92.

material. Giving of one's material resources is not an option but a requirement, because it is actually giving to God and a prerequisite for a "ransom for your sins" (v. 6). Doubting (διστάσεις) and grumbling (γογγύσεις) are excluded by recognizing that God is the one who gives and also rewards the giver (v. 7). More radically, however, community members are prohibited from refusing to help the needy person, because they must share everything with other members of the community. They can call nothing their own:

> συγκοινωνήσεις δὲ πάντα τῷ ἀδελφῷ σοῦ καὶ οὐκ ἐρεῖς ἴδια εἶναι
> εἰ γὰρ ἐν τῷ ἀθανάτῳ κοινωνοί ἐστε, πόσῳ μᾶλλον ἐν τοῖς θνητοῖς (v. 8)

The argument is based "from light to heavy," a fundamental Jewish exegetical technique (*qal wahomer*): since the community members already share in imperishable goods, how much more are they sharers in the much less important perishable goods. Indeed, their catechetical instruction in the way of life already has put them in debt spiritually to "the one who has spoken the things of the Lord" to them. In any case, since these goods are given to human beings by God for the express purpose of giving to all from God's own gifts, one is obligated to give to all who ask (1.5). Possessions do not belong to individuals. This radical demand is not simply an ideal, but backed up by the judicial system of the community as set out in block 2:

> Anyone who exploits the community by taking without being in need will give an account [to the community assembled in judgment] concerning what she or he took and why, and being in distress [ἐν συνοχῇ] [as a result of exclusion from the community] will be examined concerning what she or he has done and will not be released from there [by readmission to the community] until she or he has paid back every farthing. (1.5)

As I have already indicated, debtor's prison would most likely be beyond the community's ability to impose. Nevertheless, it is hard to imagine a more express implementation of a system of generalized reciprocity in terms of the moral economy theory than the requirement that one should call nothing one's own but share everything in common with fellow members of the community. In any case, the rules of block 3 would have severe consequences if applied rigorously in a Christian Jewish community. The first and foremost consequence of renouncing ownership of one's property would be the disinheritance of one's children and the manumission of any slaves one owned. This leads naturally to block 4. Kurt Niederwimmer[26] is quite wrong, in my opinion, in supposing that the problems occasioned by this instruction to practice community of goods are ignored in what follows: "Hereafter the Didachist gives no further attention to the problem of private property in his own remarks."

Block 4 is connected with the preceding blocks because of the insistence on equality before God and community of goods between community members. This has important intracommunal implications for parents and slave-owners and their subordinates. Interestingly, husband-wife relations are not mentioned here or anywhere in the document, leaving only arguments from silence. Either the problem was too big to allow it to be raised at all, or it was no issue in the community, or it was a complex mix of both. The last option seems most likely to me: it was too big in that there were Christian Jewish and Christian gentile wives, concubines, and slave women under the control of unbelieving gentiles who could use such an instruction to wives to submit as ammunition to withdraw them from the community. It was too small in that Jewish patriarchy was far stronger and more established than the rather fluid gentile situation where elite Greek and Roman women might enjoy a considerable amount of freedom. If both circumstances obtained simultaneously, then it would be both unwise and impractical to lay down a ruling. Most important, in my estimation, is that the document is directed toward gentiles wishing to join a Christian Jewish community. Marriage between gentile and Jewish Christians would have been unthinkable unless a gentile became "perfect" (got circumcised, ate *kashrut*, and kept ritual purity). Therefore, different legal situations might apply to gentile and Jewish Christian married women. In any case, the rules concerning giving over one's property to the community clearly did not extend to releasing free women from their husbands and fathers in the way it might have implied release of slaves by their masters. Slave women would have been in the same situation in terms of the legal implications as their male counterparts and are thus covered by the same instructions.

The teaching in E1 counters the objection of children to the alienation of their inheritance, drawing on the wisdom tradition: spare the rod and

---

26. Kurt Niederwimmer, *The Didache: A Commentary* (Hermeneia; Minneapolis: Fortress, 1998), 109.

spoil the child. It must be remembered that progeny remained under the authority of their male parent until the patriarch died. This was true both for Jews and for gentiles in the Greco-Roman world, where the right of the father to put his child to death was an accepted principle. (Male) community members were expected to exercise their rights as patriarchs to enforce on children the adoption of the new faith of their parents, including their submission to the alternative economic system. Acceptance of the system of generalized reciprocity advocated here would make these children dependent on the community and force them to participate in it and integrate. At one level this promoted the principles of an alternative economic system in embryo. At another level it undermined it fundamentally by reaffirming and enshrining in it the patriarchal authority of the male head of household. Moreover, the invocation of patriarchal authority is legitimated by the "fear of God" (τὸν φόβον τοῦ θεοῦ). It is noteworthy that there is no limitation on this authority (such as, for example, "fathers do not provoke your children"!) nor is there any reciprocal instruction to children (for example, "children obey your parents"), possibly because some of the members of the community still had living patriarchs who might seek to exercise their authority to remove their adult child from the community. The instruction would then become counterproductive in the life of the community. In any case, the inclusion of this patriarchal instruction right after the blueprint for an egalitarian "economic safety net"[27] as set out introduced a radical contradiction into the heart of the ideal that ensured its ultimate failure as a genuine alternative economy, in my opinion. Block 5 turns to the issue of slaves, an issue that would have presented itself immediately to any elite person who joined this community, who would have been expected to be a patron of the community by becoming a bishop or deacon, making their house, resources, and influence available to the community. Gentile slaves purchased by Jews were required to be circumcised (if a man) or immersed (if a woman) and to keep the Torah to the same extent as women and immature children. They became a part of Israel, but with limited rights and responsibilities.[28] This was necessary to preserve the ritual purity of the household (something that would have concerned the Didache community also), given their dedication to ritual purity (7.1–4). The principle as stated by Rab Huna (d. 297 CE [A2])[29] but

---

27. Milavec, *Didache: Faith, Hope, and Life*, 173–227.
28. See van de Sandt and Flusser, *Didache*, 137.
29. Citations following Herman L. Strack, *Introduction to the Talmud and Midrash*

seemingly everywhere applicable is, "Every precept that is obligatory on a woman is obligatory on a slave; every precept that is not obligatory on a woman is not obligatory on a slave" (b. Ḥag. 4a). According to the Mishnah, while women, slaves, and minors are exempt from reciting the Shema and putting on the *tefillin*, they are required to perform the *tefillah*, *mezuzah*, and *berakot* after meals. So on this basis God hears the prayers of slaves as well as the prayers of a woman and a child: R. Judah b. Shalom [A5 342–443] said in the name of R. Eleazar, "Before God, however, all are equal, women, slaves, poor and rich" (Exod. Rab. 21:4). God's blessings pronounced over Israel by the priests apply also to proselytes, women, and slaves (Num. Rab. 11:8). Their cries can reach the ears of God who is over both master and slave, and this places limits on the behaviour of Jewish slave owners!

A particularly germane background to the passage and the problems that the instruction that "You shall call nothing your own" would have posed to slave owners is provided by a halakah in the name of R. Simeon of Mizpah (T1, alive while the temple was still standing), found both in m. Pe'ah 3:8 and also in t. Pe'ah 1:13, in which form I cite it here:

> A. One who consigns [all of] his property to his slave—[the slave] becomes a free-person [because the slave as part of the estate, now owns himself]. If [in his consignment of the property the owner] had retained any land at all—the slave does not become a free person, [for we assume that the property retained includes the slave].
> B. R. Simeon says [T1, while temple was still standing], "Lo, he who says, 'Lo all of my possessions are given to so-and-so, my slave, except for one ten-thousandths part of them' [m. Pe'ah 3:8] has said nothing [of binding force],
> C. Unless he specifies [the property in] such-and-such a city or [in] such-and-such a field.
> D. And even if he owns [only] that very field and that very city, [so that, in effect, he wishes to give the slave nothing at all], the slave acquires the property and may buy his freedom."
> E. And when they said these words in front of R. Yosé, he said, "He who gives a right answer smacks his lips" [Prov 24:26].[30]

(New York: Atheneum, 1931. English translation of the German 5th edition prepared by the author.

30. Jacob Neusner and Richard S. Sarason, trans., *The Tosefta: Translated from the Hebrew, with a New Introduction* (Peabody, MA: Hendrickson, 2002).

If a Jewish person gave away all or part of his possessions to his slave (the masculine is used following the intention of the halakah, though it would probably apply in some circumstances to women and their maidservants, as in the case of Queen Berenice of Adiabene, according to the tractate Gerim), his slave would be regarded as manumitted. In the case of common ownership of property, in which the slave was regarded as owner in common of all the wealth and property of the community, he could legitimately argue that he was now freed. The social consequences of the alternative socioeconomic arrangements of this early Christian Jewish community were thus as serious for the question of masters and slaves as for fathers and children (patriarch/kyriarchs and their subordinates) and calls for a special instruction. The instruction provided, however, also undermines the egalitarian and liberatory potential of the movement deriving from Jesus. The fundamental principles of the community are: the Spirit falls on patriarchs and subordinates alike; there is no favouritism with God and therefore there can be none in the community; all things must be shared. The solution of the community is to reassert the patriarchal control of slave-masters but limit their power with a strong warning.

As with the instructions on parents and children, the instructions on masters and slaves begin with a directive to the patriarch/kyriarch, but in this case it affirms the authority of the slave-master and hence the institution of slavery itself, only indirectly protecting the slaves by limiting their power to punish their property without restraint "in their bitterness" (ἐν πικρίᾳ σου). The word πικρία is a metaphorical application from a word meaning "bitter taste" to "bitter feelings" or "harshness" or "violent temper."[31] In other words, harsh and arbitrary treatment of slaves is prohibited, the kind of treatment that often left a slave with lasting physical damage or even ended in death. It is noteworthy that both male and female slaves are specifically mentioned, since female slaves were doubly at risk as objects of sexual exploitation by their owners.[32] Their inclusion sends an important signal, especially in the context of the prohibition in the Didache's reformulation of the ethic of the second half of the Decalogue not only of anger as leading to murder but also of desire (ἐπιθυμία), because it leads to fornication (πορνεία) and ultimately to adultery (μοιχεία, 3.2-3). The behaviour of the slave-owner might lead a

---

31. LSJ 1403b–1404a.
32. Carolyn Osiek and Margaret Y. MacDonald, with Janet H. Tulloch, *A Woman's Place: House Churches in Earliest Christianity* (Minneapolis: Fortress, 2006), 95–117.

slave to cease to "fear" (φοβηθήσονται) the God who is over both of them. Two observations follow here: the slaves had no choice but to convert with their owner, in line with Jewish practices for slave owning. Second, the "fear of God" in verse 10 is rhetorically equated with "fear of the Master" in verse 11, so that the alternative socioeconomic community practice is given with one hand and taken away with the other.

The basis for this instruction to the slave owner (no gender is specified, so it must be held to refer to both male and female slave owners) is fundamental to the community's ethos, as we have seen: the same God is the hope of both parties and God has no favourites but gives the Spirit to both. The whole passage is difficult syntactically and semantically,[33] perhaps reflecting the complexity of the issue for the community. In the first place, the exact reference of οὐ γὰρ ἔρχεται ... καλέσαι is not clear: the present tense here could refer to the coming of God in judgment or to the first or second coming of Jesus, though his name is not mentioned; the calling could refer to the call to all human beings inherent in the gospel, but could also refer forward to the coming judgment. To my mind it does seem to include a certain note of eschatological warning to back up an otherwise unenforceable instruction, since although the judgment of the community against violent behaviour might result in expulsion from the community for the slave owner, this would remove one of its patrons. The expression ἐφ' οὓς τὸ πνεῦμα ἡτοίμασεν is also difficult: it may indicate that the process of preparation and acceptance of the slave into God's covenant through the preparation of the Spirit is complete (aorist tense), but it could also mean that God or Jesus came to prepare his people to receive the Spirit as a gift, even the slave ("upon whom" the Spirit has come) and so confers on all community members equal status before God as those who possess the Spirit. This is the interpretation I prefer, given the importance of the Spirit in this community evidenced in chapter 11 (though the Spirit seems always to be the Spirit of prophecy in the Didache). The same word πρόσωπον is used here as in the requirement to judge justly in block 2, rhetorically reinforcing the instruction concerning the equality of all members of the community. So, although the instruction affirms the institution of slavery and the rights of slave owners, these rights are in theory strictly circumscribed by a requirement to respect the equal humanity of a slave, which is supported by a raft of religious taboos since it is unenforceable any other way.

---

33. See Niederwimmer, *Didache*, 110–11 for a discussion.

The instruction to slaves appears to apply to both male and female slaves, although no differentiation is provided this time, perhaps because it is rhetorically unnecessary. Nevertheless, the inclusion of slaves in an anonymous plural group reduces their humanity. It requires them as a group to submit to their κυρίοις. The plural could be taken as inclusive of both male and female owners, but may have only the male patriarch in mind, since the owner is to be a type of God, and one wonders whether the gender neutrality of God was even on the horizon. Clearly the reciprocal instruction to the slave is necessary because their equal humanity before God and equal right to share in the community of goods of the community would undermine the right of the slave owner to continue to own them and to command them to obey. This would then result in elite members of the community ceasing to be able to function as patrons offering their status and their resources to protect and promote the community's interests with the outside world. The sanction the instruction receives is severe: the slave owner (male?) is a "type" or image of God, like the image of the emperor struck on an imperial coin. While slaves and women, for that matter, are instructed to respect and submit to their patriarchs as "to the Lord" elsewhere (Col 3:22–23; Eph 6:5), the language here could be regarded as more extreme. The slave owner is to be the image of God to the slave, and as such, the "fear" that is due to God by both slave-owner and slave, since God is over them both, is now due to the slave-owner by the slave (ἐν αἰσχύνῃ καὶ φόβῳ), since he stands as the image of God. This instruction to slave-owners and slaves is reinforced by an instruction appealing to a general principle that community members should "hate all hypocrisy and all that is not pleasing to the Lord" (v. 12), which I read as the conclusion to the instructions to slave owners and slaves. Against this is the fact that the preceding instruction is in the second person plural, since slaves are addressed as a group, which certainly is not suggestive of equal status. The instructions as a whole are couched in the second person singular, however, and the return to a key ethical understanding of the community would require a return to the generalized pattern. A repeated refrain in the Didache is a prohibition of "double-mindedness" in various forms and expressions. Hypocrisy is set alongside these expressions of "double-mindedness" and so reinforces the command to slave-owners not to oppress or ill-treat their slaves and to slaves to submit to slave owners without reservation or their own kind of bitterness, so standing parallel to the prohibition of "bitterness" in the conduct of their masters. They should do everything that is pleasing to the Lord, which would coincide with doing what is pleasing to the slave owner, since he stands as a "type" of God. This is an uneasy compromise to be sure, but it is directed in my opinion toward keeping the ideal of generalized reciprocity in place.

Block 5 provides a conclusion to the way of life as a whole. It presents the instructions of the way of life as "commandments of the Lord" (v. 3), which must not be tampered with either by adding or subtracting, a common device in writing to reenforce its authority (see, for example, Rev 22:18–19). These instructions would be particularly poignant to children, however, and more particularly to slaves, who might spend much time "confessing their transgressions" of "hypocrisy" in their attitudes to cruel slave-owners.

4. The HT in the Doctrina apostolorum

The Latin Doctrina apostolorum follows Did. 1–6 very closely, so much so that there has long been a debate over whether it is an extract from it or a source for it. Besides smaller variations, the main difference is the absence from the Doctrina apostolorum of the "Q" tradition in Did. 1.3–6 and a different ending in the Doctr. 6.2–3. This has led to speculation as to whether it represents a pre-Christian Jewish source for an originally Jewish Two Ways teaching. Therefore, the differences between the texts, though small, may often be highly significant. Set out in the same structured way as we have noted for the Didache, it appears as follows (dotted line indicates omissions, while italics represent additions or variations).[34]

Schematic 2: Doctrina apostolorum

1. The Teacher/Prophet
A   4.1. Qui loquitur tibi uerbum domini dei
       memineris die ac nocte
          reuereberis enim quasi dominum
   unde enim dominica procedunt
      ibi et dominus est.
2. Regular Communal Assemblies for Judgment
B   2. Require autem facies sanctorum …

---

34. The text of the Doctrina apostolorum is taken from Willy Rordorf and André Tuilier, *La doctrine des douze apôtres (Didachè)*, SC 248 bis (Paris: Cerf, 1998), 208–9.

ute te reficias uerbis illorum.
3. Non facies dissensions
... pacifica litigantes
iudica iuste
sciens quod tu iudicaberis.
Non deprimes quemquam in casu suo ...
4. Nec dubitabis *uerum [cj. *utrum*] erit ac non erit.

3. Requirement for General Reciprocity

C 5. Noli esse ad accipiendum extendens manum
et ad reddendum subtrahens.
6. Si habes per manus tuas ... redemptionem peccatorum.
7. Non dubitabis dare
nec dans murmuraueris
sciens quis sit huius mercedis bonus redditor.

D 8. Non auertes te ab egente
communicabis autem omnia cum fratribus tuis
nec dices tua esse
si enim [...] mortalibus socii sumus
quanto magis hinc initiantes esse debemus?
Omnibus enim dominus dare uult de donis suis. [cf. Did. 1.5]

4. Household Management

E 9. Non tolles manum tuam a filiis ...
sed a iuuentute docebis eos timorem *domini.*

F1 10. Seruo tuo uel ancillae
qui in eundem sperant dominum
in ira tua non imperabis
timeat utrumque dominum et te;
non enim uenit ut personas inuitaret
sed *in* quibus spiritum *inuenit.*

F2 11. Vos autem serui subiecti dominis uestris estote
tamquam formae dei
cum pudore et *tremore.*
12. Oderis omnem affectationem
et quod deo non placet *non facies.*

5. Conclusion of the Way of Life: Binding Nature of Its Teaching

G 13. ... Custodi ergo, *fili,* quae *audisti*
neque appones *illis contraria* neque diminues
14. ... Non accedas ad orationem cum consientia mala.

Haec est uia uitae.

For the most part, the Doctrina apostolorum follows the text of the Did. 4.1–8 with little variation, but the variations are significant. In the first place, καθ' ἡμέραν is omitted, as in the Epitome apostolorum, so that it is unlikely that a daily "church meeting" was ever in mind in the earliest tradition. Second, and more important, a note of eschatological warning is introduced into the requirement to judge justly and avoid favoritism, thus strengthening its urgency: "You shall judge justly, knowing that you will be judged. You shall not oppress anyone in his case." Third, in the requirement "to give the fruit of your labor for the redemption of your sins," the word "give" appears to have been accidentally omitted so that it reads literally, "If you have through your hands redemption of sins" (v. 6) and then runs on "you shall not doubt to give [etc.]" (v. 7). Fourth, there is another seeming omission in verse 8, so that it would read, "If we are sharers *in mortal things*, how much more ought we to do this being initiated?" (leipography from *si en[imim]mortalibus*). The textual variant could make reasonable sense in that the Two Ways teaching was intended as preparation for initiation (see Did. 7.1), so that the ordinary sharing of all human beings in mortal things is contrasted with the sharing in imperishable things of those who have been initiated into the community. That wording does, however, weaken the sense of material sharing being a natural consequence of sharing in immortality. Fifth, the Doctrina apostolorum adds here the saying found in the Jesus tradition section in Did. 1.5b: "Indeed the Lord wishes to give to all from his gifts." This in return strengthens the emphasis on community of goods still further, since the material goods belonging to members are in any case God's gifts and remain God's own property to dispense to others in the community through its members. One wonders whether the insertion of this material from 1.5 here in the Latin text was made later to compensate for the leipography above.

In block 4 of the HT:

E2 You shall not hold back your hand from *your sons*, but from their youth you shall teach them the fear of *the Lord*.
F1 You shall not command your male slave or your female slave, who hope in the same *Lord*, in your anger. *Let him or her fear both the Lord and you.* For he did not come to invite according to person but *those in whom he has found the Spirit* [v.l. *a humble spirit*].

F2 And you slaves be subject to your masters as types of God with shame *and trembling*. You shall hate all hypocrisy, and you shall not do what does not please God.

It is noteworthy in E1 that the Doctrina apostolorum has the plural *filiis* and lacks the express inclusion of daughters, even if they could be understood to be included within the masculine plural. This difference is significant in terms of the "invisibility" of women, their inclusion within the male, and their treatment as property to be disposed of in patriarchal society. Second, θεός is often represented by κύριος in the Doctrina apostolorum, a signal that the Lord Jesus may be in mind, at least in the later redactions, since in the same places the tradition is divided. The Doctrina apostolorum is often regarded as the earliest form of the Two Ways, but even if it is, its wording may in places be later. In the New Testament HT, ἐν κυρίῳ is an important aspect of the rhetoric, but not in the Two Ways, except in the Doctrina apostolorum.

In the instructions on slaves and masters, there is a noteworthy variant contained in "let him or her fear both the Lord and you" after "lest he or she should no longer fear the Lord who is over you both." The inclusion of this reduces the strength of the injunction to the slave-owner by placing the fear of the Lord alongside that of the slave-owner, thus revealing an elite perspective rather than that of the embryonic alternative socio-economic community we are exploring here. It shows itself to be a later development. Finally, the text has a variant reading in the difficult passage, concerning whom the Lord has come to call: the Doctrina apostolorum has "those in whom he has found the Spirit." The idea that God's Holy Spirit indwells slaves who fear God is a radical one: so radical that a variant reading is inserted above the line of the Latin manuscript replacing "Holy Spirit" with "humble spirit" (*humilum*)! There are a few variations in the conclusion at block H, but these have no bearing on the HT tradition and can be ignored here.

5. Other Versions of the Independent Two Ways Tradition Following the Order in the Didache

In addition to the Doctrina apostolorum's close parallel to the Didache, there is a range of other versions of the independent Two Ways tradition. They highlight the role of the teacher in chapter 4 so that it intrudes from block A into block B. Here we follow the Ecclesiastical Canons and the Epitome apostolorum.[35]

SCHEMATIC 3: ECCLESIASTICAL CANONS AND EPITOME APOSTOLORUM

1. The Teacher/Prophet
A 4.1 *Thomas said,*
     the one who speaks to you the word of God,
     And who is the cause of your life
     And who gives you the seal in the Lord
        You shall love him [male?] as the apple of your eye
     Remember him [male?] night and day
        and honour him [male?] as the Lord.
  For where the things concerning the Lord are spoken,
     there is the Lord.

2. Regular Communal Assemblies for Judgment
B 2. And you shall seek out *his* presence daily
     and that of the rest of the saints,
     so that you can find rest in their words.
  3. *Cephas said,* You shall not make a schism,
     but you shall reconcile the warring factions.
  You shall judge justly;
     you shall not show favouritism leading to transgression;
  4. *In your prayer* you shall not doubt whether it should be or not.

3. Requirement for Generalized Reciprocity
C 5. [Do not be one who stretches out your hands to receive,
     but one who shuts them up when it comes to giving. EC; EP *omit.*]
  6. If you have [earned anything] through [the work of] your hands,
     you shall give a ransom for [the forgiveness of ἄφεσιν; EP] your sins.
  7. [You shall not doubt whether to give,
     and you shall not grumble when you give,
        for you shall know who is the good giver of the reward. EC; EP *omit.*]
D 8. You shall not turn away the needy person [male?],

---

35. The English translation is my own. A critical text can be found in Alistair Stewart-Sykes, *The Apostolic Church Order: The Greek Text with Introduction, Translation and Annotation*, ECS 10 (Strathfield, AU: St. Paul's, 2006). EC refers to the Ecclesiastical Canons; EP refers to the Epitome apostolorum.

but you shall *share* [συγκοινωνήσεις; EP] all things with your brother [and sister?],
    and you shall not say they are your own.
For if you are sharers in [death, θανάτῳ, EP] what is immortal,
    how much more in perishable things [mortal things, θνητοῖς, EP]?

4. Household Management

E1 9. [You shall not hold back your hand
    from your son or from your daughter,
        but from their youth you shall teach the fear of God. EP; EC omit]
    12. [You shall hate all hypocrisy
        and everything which is not pleasing (ἀρέσκει) to the Lord. EP: EC *omit*.]

5. Conclusion of the Way of Life: Binding Nature of Its Teaching

[H 14a. You shall confess your transgressions,
G   13a. You shall not abandon any commandments of the Lord,
H   14b. and you shall not come to your prayer with an evil conscience.
G   13b. You shall keep what you have received
    neither adding nor taking away [ὑφαιρῶν; EP]
        This is the way of life. EP: EC *omit*.]

This version of the material is followed closely in the teaching of the famous Coptic monk, Bishop Shenudi, though with many additions. The text is found in Arabic, so some of the variants may be attributed to that.[36]

Schematic 4: The *Vita Shenudi* (Fifth Century)

1. The Teacher/Prophet

A   4.1 *O my son*, remember night and day the word of God *in your heart*
    For the Lord is present where *his Name* is spoken,
        and he is eternally worthy of honour and praise.

2. Regular Community Assemblies for Judgment

B   2. *O my son, walk on the way of purity* at each moment:
    you will become strong and powerful in the best way

---

36. The English translation is my own from the French translation in Émile Amélineau, *Monuments pour servir à l'histoire de l'Égypte chrétienne aux IVe, Ve, VIe, et VII siècles*, vol. 4 of *Mémoires publiés par les membres de la Mission archéologique française au Caire, 1885–1886* (Paris: Leroux, 1888), 289–97. My translation was checked against the Arabic text by Gerhard van Gelder at St. John's College, Oxford. I am grateful for his suggestions and advice.

so that you can *rejoice* in their *sweet* words *and their delightful sayings*
3. *O my son*, do not seek to quarrel with your brothers
but rather strive to reconcile the warring factions
Then you shall judge justly
and you shall not *be ashamed of reprimanding the offender for his offence*
or the sinner for his sin.

3. Requirement for Generalized Reciprocity

C 5. *O my son*, do not stretch out your hand to receive,
but shut it when it comes to giving
Beware of acting thus.
6. *As far as you are able*, you shall give *to the poor*
in order to cover your *many* sins;
7. but you shall not doubt *in your gifts* whether to give
moreover, you shall not be sad when you give
and you shall not regret it if you act mercifully:
you know well who recompenses one *honestly and faithfully*
it is Jesus the Messiah who pardons sins.
D 8. *O my son,* you shall not turn away the poor
but give *according to your ability*
sharing with everyone who is troubled
and everyone who is in need *of you*
for if *we* share *with those who do not have anything* in perishable things,
we share with them in imperishable *and lasting* things.

5. Conclusion of the Way of Life: Binding nature of the Its Teaching

G 13a. And if *we* keep these commandments
H 14b *we* walk on the way of life
in the path blessed for eternity
which is to the unique king, the Lord Jesus the Messiah,
who gives life to those who love him.

All of the HT is omitted from the Ecclesiastical Canons and the *Vita Shenudi*, probably signaling the monastic orientation of those documents and its use in initiation into the ascetic religious life, so that neither children nor slaves were a concern. Certainly the explicit narrative of the *Vita Shenudi* is an oral performance of the Two Ways to the neophytes and monks by the much venerated Coptic ascetic Bishop Shenudi. The Epitome apostolorum, however, does indicate knowledge of the HT material in this independent Two Ways tradition also, since it has the instruction on children: "Bartholomew said, 'You shall not hold back your hand from your son or from your daughter but from their youth you shall teach them the fear of the Lord'" (11). Perhaps this signals that children remained an issue for some ascetics, even if they had renounced their slaves along with the rest of their property. It is an important indication of such a vestigial interest in the HT that the later Two Ways tradition found in Egypt, the Syntagma doctrinae and Fides Nicanae, which are really versions of the same text, contain a prohibition on striking anyone except in order to discipline a small child and even then with a strong reserve:

> γίνου ταπεινὸς καὶ ἥσυχος τρέμων διὰ παντὸς τὰ λόγια κυρίου μὴ γίνου μάχιμος μὴ τύπτε ἄνθρωπον [ἤ.] εἰ μὴ μόνον παιδίον σου μικρὸν πρὸς παιδείας καὶ αὐτὸ παρατετηρημένως σκόπει μὴ πως διὰ σου φόνος γίνηται πολλαὶ γὰρ εἰσιν αἱ ἀφορμαὶ. τοῦ θανάτου. (Syntagma VIII [4.1–2]; Fides Nicanae)
> 4.1 Be humble and quiet fearing always the words of the Lord. 4.2 Do not be aggressive. Do not strike anyone, except only *your small child* for instruction, but observing it closely, watching carefully, lest through you murder is born, for many are the means of death.

The wording shows clearly that this instruction comes from the Two Ways tradition, with its reminiscence of Did. 3.1–6 as well as 4.9–10. Incidentally, these texts also provides evidence that "not holding back one's hand" from disciplining one's child might lead to injury or death and that commanding one's slave in one's anger might have the same consequences. In any case, this version of the saying clearly limits it to small children, so it would not apply to adult progeny under the authority of the family patriarch, which could be the case in the Didache.

6. The HT Tradition in the Epistle of Barnabas

While the HT in the independent Two Ways tradition, whether it is earlier or later than the Didache, follows substantially the same pattern, Barnabas in this as in other material follows a different logic. Indeed, some have argued that it has no logic.[37] This was still following Dibelius's *Traditionsgeschichlich* approach to the Pastoral Epistles in which he described

---

37. So, Prigent, *Testimonia*, and Kraft, *Barnabas and the Didache*.

paraenesis as a form that had no central thrust or *Tendenz* but was a loose and incoherent collection of traditional material. As I have argued elsewhere,[38] this cannot be said of Barnabas, which expressly changes the social location of the Two Ways material from catechesis for initiation into the community (Did. 7.1) into a secondary *gnosis*. In the first place, it is expressly *written* (whereas the Two Ways in the Didache, existing in writing as it does, represents the outline for an oral performance of catechesis)[39] and by an *individual* ("I have written to you," Barn. 17.2; "I hasten to write," 4.9), whereas the Didache nowhere signals the contribution of an individual, utilizing the imperative of communal decisions. It is written in the form of an *epistle*, whereas the Two Ways in the Didache provides generalized "teaching of the twelve apostles to the gentiles." In other words, without making any claims about its author, it has adopted the Pauline epistolary mode in order to issue directions to one or more communities. It adopts the same polemical tone as Paul against doctrinal positions it considers wrong, whereas the Didache is concerned with wrong praxis ("keep the commandments that you have received neither adding nor subtracting") or *anomia*, failure to observe the Torah according to its understanding, when it polemicizes against false teaching. This switch in Barnabas is neither accidental nor innocent. In chapter 17 the author explains that in what precedes the text has "not omitted anything of the matters relating to salvation," while in 18.1 this version of Two Ways begins with, "But now let us pass on to another *gnosis* and teaching." It is possible, but not probable, that the author simply came across new material and inserted it without reflecting on the matter. Whether I am right in my argument that this is part of his attack on Christian Judaism, it is certainly a deliberate and conscious "editorial decision" with consequences. I would argue that the author's seemingly haphazard arrangement of the units of material from the Two Ways tradition is equally a deliberate and conscious deconstruction in much the same way that I would argue that the Gospel of Thomas is a deliberate deconstruction of

---

38. Jonathan A. Draper, "Barnabas and the Riddle of the Didache Revisited," *JSNT* 58 (1995): 89-113.

39. Jonathan A. Draper, "Vice Catalogues as Oral-Mnemonic Cues: A Comparative Study of the Two Ways Tradition in the Didache and Parallels from the Perspective of Oral Tradition," in *Jesus, the Voice, and the Text: Beyond the Oral and the Written Gospel*, ed. Tom Thatcher (Waco, TX: Baylor University Press, 2008), 111-35.

the "Q" tradition and for the same reasons, namely, to defamiliarize and resocialize the initiand.

Even a cursory read through of Barnabas shows a clear *Tendenz* running through it, which affects the presentation of the HT also. First, there is a problem with the office of "teacher," since the title is rejected by the author in 1.8 and 4.9 ("not as a teacher"), even as "teaching" is being given. Second, the author makes a radical rejection of the Torah and denies the status of covenant people to the Jews, seeing his task as being to prevent Christians becoming "proselytes to their law" and thereby getting "shipwrecked" (3.6; 4.6). Third, the Hebrew Scriptures are taken allegorically and eschatologically, so that the ritual provisions of the Torah are either turned into ethics for Christians or into signs of the imminent arrival of the parousia. In the case of the block of rules governing community life in Did. 4, certain patterns do also emerge. It will be our contention that these are not accidental due to a faulty memory or a faulty source, but represent an attempt to "spike" the Two Ways teaching at points where Barnabas disagrees with its teaching. We shall focus on this block, set out in below.

Schematic 5: Barnabas 19.4–12

Block 2 Material Moved to Block 3 and Interpolated from Chapters 2–3
    <u>You shall not commit fornication</u>. 2.2
    <u>You shall not commit adultery</u>. 2.2
    <u>You shall not corrupt children</u>. 2.2
    <u>The word of God shall not go out from you in impurity of any others</u>. 2.3
B You shall not show favoritism to reprove any leading to transgression. 4.3
    <u>You shall be meek</u>. 3.7
    <u>You shall be quiet</u>. 3.8
    <u>You shall be trembling at the words which you hear</u>. 3.8
    <u>You shall not remember evil against your brother</u>. 2.3
B You shall not doubt whether a thing shall be or not. 4.4
    You shall not take the name of the Lord in vain (cf. "bear false witness" 2.3).
    <u>You shall love</u> *your neighbor* <u>more than your own soul</u>. 2.7
Block 4 Inverted and Interpolated with Material from Outside the HT
    <u>You shall not kill a child in the womb;</u> 2.2
        <u>and moreover you shall not put to death what has been born</u>. 2.2
E You shall not hold back your hand from your son or from your daughter, 4.9
        but from their infancy you shall teach them the fear of the Lord. 4.9
    <u>You shall not covet your neighbor's goods</u>. 2.2

    You shall not be avaricious. 3.5
      You shall not be joined in soul with the haughty, 3.9
          but you shall conduct yourself with the righteous and lowly. 3.9
      You shall receive as good things the things which happen to you. 3.10
      You shall not be double-minded or double-tongued, 2.4
          for a double tongue is a snare of death. 2.4
F2 You shall be subject *to masters* [κυρίοις] 4.11
      as the image of God, with shame and fear. 4.11
F1 You shall not command with bitterness your male slave or your female slave, 4.10
      who hope in the same God, 4.10
          lest they cease to fear the God who is over both of you; 4.10
      For he did not come to call men according to their outward appearance, 4.10

Block 3 Inverted and Interpolated with Material from Blocks 1 and 2
D You shall share in all things with your neighbor; 4.8
      You shall not call anything your own; 4.8
    for if you are sharers of things which are incorruptible, 4.8
        how much more should you be of those things which are corruptible! 4.8
  You shall not be double-minded or double-tongued, 2.4
      [for the double tongue is a snare of death. v. l.] 2.4
        As far as possible, you shall be pure in your soul.
C1 Do not be ready to stretch forth your hands to take, 4.5
      whilst you hold them back to give. 4.5
A *You shall love, as the apple of your eye,* 4.1
      every one that speaks to you the word of the Lord. 4.1
         remember *the day of judgment* night and day. 4.1
B And you shall seek out daily the presence of the saints, 4.2
      either laboring in word and going out to encourage,
      and endeavoring to save a soul by the word,
C2 or with your hands working for a ransom for your sins. 4.6
C3 You shall not hesitate to give, 4.7
      Nor shall you grumble when giving, 4.7
         but you shall yet come to know who is the good paymaster of the reward. 4.7

Block 5 with Part of Block 2
G You shall guard what you have received, 4.13
      neither adding nor subtracting anything. 4.13
         You shall *hate* the evil one completely. Cf. 4.12

B You shall judge righteously. 4.3
    You shall not cause division, 4.3
        but shall make peace between those who quarrel 4.3
           by bringing them together.
H You shall confess your sins. 4.14
    You shall not come to prayer with an evil conscience. 4.14
        This is the way of *light*. 4.14

The clear and logical structure found in Didache and Doctr. 4 has been severely compromised in this rendering of the same material. Little of it is absent outright, but its restructuring changes the meaning and impact. First, as one would expect, given Barnabas's aversion to teachers (probably reflecting the emerging domination of the rabbinate under Roman rule), block 1 is removed and neutralized by redaction and inserted into material concerning giving in block 3, which is restructured to contain all the financial material on giving. The teacher is no longer honored as mediating the Lord's presence, but instead is "loved as the apple of your eye" and placed under the threat of judgment: "remember the day of judgment day and night."

Second, the material on sharing financial resources and calling nothing one's own from block 3 is placed *after* the teaching on the submission of children and slaves from block 4. The rhetorical and probably legal force of this would be that patriarchal authority and legal jurisdiction over children and slaves is affirmed as preceding and overruling the sharing of material things with the community. The rules for the admission of proselytes in the rabbinic tractate Gerim specify that everything depends on the order in which people are circumcised and baptised: if the slave goes first, they are regarded as manumitted; if the slave-owner goes first and then holds his hand on the head of his slaves as they are baptized, then they remain his slaves. Thus, in Barnabas sharing is limited and bounded by the prior obligation to unconditional obedience to social superiors. This suspicion is confirmed by the insertion of a block of material drawn from Did. 2 and 3 concerning envy, covetousness, greed, seeking to rise above one's station, acceptance of one's fate as God's will, and duplicity. This disarms in advance the suggestion of equality and manumission, in case slaves might expect it.

Third, it is interesting also that the instruction to discipline one's son or daughter is linked to instruction against abortion and exposure of children. This has a double effect: first to suggest that the children in question are small children and not adults; second to warn the parent against violence toward their children, since there are many ways to put a male or female child to death besides exposure, and it would be permitted in Roman law in certain circumstances. The effect might be to minimize the right of (unbelieving) parents to control their (adult) children and prevent them from joining the community.

Fourth, slaves are no longer directly addressed at all. Instead, the instruction to submit to slave owners and the instruction to slave owners not to mistreat their slaves are inverted. What had been an instruction to slaves to submit to slave owners now begins the couplet and becomes a general instruction to the individual to submit to their "lords/masters" as types of God in shame and fear. Addressing slaves directly would already make them social equals in a certain sense. In other words, the same "you" (singular) is addressed in both instructions: submit to your superiors in the patriarchal hierarchy as types of God and do not mistreat your slaves in case they cease to hope in God.

7. The Apostolic Constitutions 7.9–17

The Apos. Con. 7 contains the whole of the Didache, but edited in a distinctive way that mostly respects the underlying text but tends to add supporting and illustrative material to it from the Hebrew Scriptures. It also removes material with which it flatly disagrees (for example, the injunction to keep as much of the food law as possible and the prohibition on eating meat offered to idols in Did. 6.2–3). It clearly continues to regard the Didache as an ancient and authoritative source for Christian living, which it places alongside other such sources in its collection. Its version of the HT is therefore of considerable interest, since it indicates how it was understood in the third or fourth century (no exact date is possible). In the schematic below it can be seen that it preserves the structure and most of the material intact, but with varying emphases.[40]

Schematic 6: Apostolic Constitutions 7.9–17

1. The Teacher/Prophet
A   You shall *glorify* the one who speaks the word of God to you,

---

40. My translation. A critical text may be found in P. A. de Lagarde, *Constitutiones apostolorum* (London: Williams & Norgate; Leipzig: Teubner, 1862).

and you shall remember him [male?] day and night
and you shall honor him [male?] *not as the cause of your birth
but as the one who has become a good patron to you*
[ὡς τοῦ εὖ εἶναί σοι πρόξενον γινόμενον].
For where the *teaching* [διδασκαλία] concerning *God is
there God is.*

2. Regular Communal Assemblies for Judgment

B   You shall seek out daily the face of the saints
In order that you may rest in their words.
You shall not make schisms *among the saints*
You shall remember the Koraites
You shall make peace among those who are fighting
As Moses reconciling them to become friends.
You shall judge justly
"For judgment is the Lord's" [Deut 1:17].
You shall not show favouritism *to reprove* leading to transgressions
as Elijah and Micaiah did to Ahab
and Ebedmelech the Ethiopian to Zedekiah
and Nathan to David
and John to Herod.
You shall not be double-minded *in your prayer* whether it shall be or not.
For the Lord said to Peter upon the sea:
"O you of little faith, why are you doubting?" [Matt 4:31].

3. Requirement for Generalized Reciprocity

C   Do not be one who stretches out the hand to receive
but shuts it up when it comes to give.
If you have anything through the work of your hands give
in order that you have work for the redemption of your sins.
For "by alms and acts of faith sins are purged away" [Prov 15:27; 16:6]
You shall not be in two minds to give *to the poor*
and you shall not grumble when you give
for you shall know who is the repayer of your wage/reward.
For he says, "He that has mercy on the poor man lends to the Lord;
according to his gift so shall it be repaid to him again" [Prov 19:17].

D   You shall not turn away the needy
For he says, "He that stops his ears,
so that he does not hear the cry of the needy
himself shall also call

and there shall be no one to hear him" [Prov 21:13].
You shall share in all things with your brother
and you shall not say anything to be your own
for sharing in common has been provided by God for all human beings
[κοινὴ γὰρ ἡ μετάληψις παρὰ θεοῦ πᾶσιν ἀνθρώποις παρεσκευάσθη].

4. Household Management

E1 You shall not hold back [οὐκ ἀρεῖς] your hand from your son or from your daughter
but you shall teach them the fear of God from their youth;
For he says, "Correct your son,
so that he shall afterwards be a source of hope for you" [Prov 19:18].

F1 You shall not command [οὐκ ἐπιτάξεις] your male slave or your female slave
who *trust* [πεποίθουσιν] in the same God in bitterness *of soul,*
in case *they may groan against you*
and wrath will come upon you from God.

F2 And you, slaves, be subject [ὑποτάγητε] to your masters as images [τύποις] of God
with *attention* [προσοχῇ] and fear,
as to the Lord and not to men [cf. Eph 6:7].
You shall hate all hypocrisy;
and whatever is ... pleasing to the Lord, *you shall do.*

5. Conclusions of the Way of Life: Binding Nature of the Teaching and HT Additions

G Do not at all depart from the commandments of the Lord,
but you shall keep the things which you have received *from Him,*
neither adding *to them* nor taking away *from them.*
"For you shall not add to his words, in case he convicts you,
and you become a liar" [Prov 30:6].

H You shall confess your sins *to the Lord your God*
And you shall not add to them,
so that it will go well for you with the Lord your God,
who does not desire the death of a sinner, but his repentance.

[E+] You shall care for [θεραπεύσεις] your father and mother as causes of your birth,
"in order that you may live long on the earth which the Lord your God gives you" [Exod 20:12].
Do not despise your brothers or your kinsfolk;
because *"you shall not overlook the household of your seed"* [Isa 58:7].

[F+] *You shall fear the king* [τὸν βασιλέα],

> *knowing that his election is of the Lord.*
> *You shall honor his rulers* [τοὺς ἄρχοντας] *as ministers of God,*
> *for they are judges of all unrighteousness,*
> *to whom pay taxes, tribute and every obligation with a willing mind.*
> H You shall not proceed to your prayer *in the day of your wickedness,*
> *before you have released your bitterness* [πρὶν ἃ λύσῃς τὴν πικρίαν σου].
> This is the way of life
> *In which may you be found through Jesus Christ our Lord.*

In the first place, the Apostolic Constitutions and Canons emphasizes the importance of the teacher, not merely as the one who mediates the word of God and so facilitates the new birth of a person as a Christian, but as having a continuing role in a patron-client relationship (*proxenon*). In other words, the intrusion of Greco-Roman patriarchy is now advanced. Block 2 remains largely intact with added reenforcement of examples and texts from the Hebrew Bible in Greek, which does not always follow the Septuagint. Double-mindedness, however, is now referred to prayer to God, rather than judgment in community assemblies, and is given the example of the Lord's command to Peter to walk on the water. Block 3 likewise heightens the importance of giving to the needy with four quotations from Proverbs (15:27; 16:6; 19:17; 21:13) and an unidentified saying at the conclusion, which is not unlike the addition given by drawn by Doctrina apostolorum from Did. 1.5: "For sharing in common has been provided by God for all human beings." The HT in block 4 again remains largely unchanged with the addition of supporting material at the end of each of its three sections: from Proverbs (19:18), an allusion to the groaning of the people of Israel in Egypt and an insistence that the respect is "to the Lord and not to men," similar in tone to Eph 6:7, moving it toward the "in Christ" terminology of the HT in the New Testament.

Most interesting is the way in which the Apostolic Constitutions and Canons inserts additional HT material in block 5. In the first place is the second half of the parent-child reciprocal instruction that is missing in Didache: "Care for your father and mother" based on the Decalogue in Exod 20:12 and also Isa 58:7; in the second place is the requirement to fear and honor the king as "elected by God" and other rulers who are "ministers of God." No supporting texts are provided here. The instruction not to proceed to prayer "with an evil conscience" in Didache, however, refers instead to "in the day of your wickedness, before you have released your bitterness [τὴν πικρίαν σου]," which refers back to the bitterness of the slave-master, broadened now to the bitterness displayed by and reflected back toward all one's social and political superiors, one's κυρίοις. Thus it echoes in a certain respect the concern of Barnabas, which turns a requirement to obey the slave-master to a requirement to obey the government or indeed any higher authority, in my opinion. Finally, the Apostolic Constitutions and Canons subordinates the whole Two Ways teaching to Jesus Christ our Lord, something found also in the conclusion to the *Vita Shenudi* (is this a surviving trace of recognition of a Jewish or Jewish Christian origin of the Two Ways material and a need to "baptize it"?).

8. Conclusion

The first thing to emerge from this preliminary study is the consistent and indeed largely verbatim continuity in the central block of teaching concerning the community's socioeconomic relations: the obligation to share all material things with the community, to call nothing one's own, and to give especially freely to the poor and needy. This remains true from the earliest layers of the text in the Didache, Barnabas, and the Doctrina apostolorum to the latest layers of the text in the Apostolic Constitutions and Canons, *Vita Shenudi*, Ecclesiastical Canons, and Epitome apostolorum, as well as the later monastic rules.

Second, the structural analysis suggests that this insistence on calling nothing one's own and sharing all things in common is directly linked to the instruction concerning children and slaves. Children stood to lose their patrimony, while slaves might anticipate manumission. The instructions on socioeconomic relations directly and unequivocally reassert patriarchal authority and control in this context.

Third, there is no moderation or counter to the absolute authority of a parent over a child nor any explicit requirement of a reciprocal relationship beyond what would be required of all members in the general love command (for example, 1.2). It is a one-way command to parents to enforce membership of the community on their children by physical punishment if necessary. Slaves and slave-owners, on the other hand, clearly were more problematic, since as property, slaves posed a contradiction to the idea of common ownership of all things and calling nothing one's own. Moreover, some halakic interpretations of property law might regard slaves as legally free if their masters renounce their property or put it into common ownership in a community of which slaves were also members. This calls forth extensive argumentation in the earliest representatives of the tradition (Didache and Doctrina apostolorum). God views all human beings without favouritism; God calls all human beings to fear, and gives the Holy Spirit to those who do respond to this call. This imposes an obligation on the slave-owner to recognize their equality before God and to treat them appropriately, without bitterness at this social reversal. On the other hand, their slaves remain slaves and are required to be subject to their masters as a type of God. They are not even allowed to dissemble hypocritically and give only lip service to their masters.

Fourth, the absence of an instruction concerning moderation in the exercise of parental discipline is partially addressed by Barnabas by attaching it to material drawn from elsewhere in the Two Ways: "You shall not kill a child in the womb and moreover you shall not put to death what has been born." In this case, not only infanticide might be implied but also the patriarchal head of the family's right to harm or kill his child. This is certainly suggested by the interpretation of the way of life given in Syntagma 4.2: "Do not be aggressive. Do not strike anyone, except your small child for instruction, but observing it closely, watching lest through you murder is born, for many are the means of death."

Fifth, this difficult and even contradictory position with regard to slaves has impacted the transmission of the tradition. Barnabas takes great pains in reorganizing the tradition on socioeconomic relations so as to remove what seems to have been a continuing cause of tension. First, the Two Ways in chapters 18–20 is an advanced *gnosis* following on from what appears in chapters 1–17, concerning which the author says: "To the extent that it is possible clearly to explain these things to you, I hope, in accordance with my desire, that I have not omitted anything of the matters pertaining to salvation" (17.1). The author relocates the instructions concerning community of goods and calling nothing one's own until after the instructions concerning children and slaves. Further, the author removes the reciprocality of master-slave instructions, since the instruction to slaves is transposed to appear before instructions to slave owners and transformed into an instruction to obey one's superiors in general so that slaves are not addressed at all. Instead, the same person is addressed by implication in both sections of the HT: "Submit to your superiors and don't abuse your slaves." This rearranged block is prefaced with material from elsewhere in the Two Ways enjoining obedience in general and warning against coveting: "You must not covet your neighbour's possessions; you must not become greedy. Do not be intimately associated with the lofty, but live with the humble and righteous. Accept as good the things that happen to you, knowing that nothing transpires apart from God. You shall not be double-minded or double-tongued. Be submissive to masters" (19.6–7). Slaves become objects and not subjects again, silent and not the addressees of the instruction.

Sixth, the absence of husband-wife instruction altogether is noteworthy and puzzling in a general instruction concerning social and economic relations in the community. Perhaps it can be explained on the basis of the rabbinical principle mentioned above, that everything that applies to women and children applies to slaves and vice versa. So the continued subjection of the women and children to their male patriarch was implied in the instruction on the continued subjection of slaves.

Finally, I suggest that the HT in the Two Ways tradition should not be passed over as quickly and silently as it has been in previous discussions of the HT tradition in the New Testament. Indeed it may provide valuable missing pieces of the puzzle. This is because it comes with its own socioeconomic relations, namely, community of goods, and because the tradition as it develops provides clear evidence of initial tension and then evolution from being the fundamental rule for all who joined the community to become an advanced *gnosis* for ascetics that is not required of all Christians. Despite this, or perhaps even because of this, the instruction to practice *koinonia* of goods and to call nothing one's own survived as a continuing provocation and inspiration in the life of the church, as it has done until today.

Reflections on the Didache and Its Community: A Response

Andrew Gregory

There is widespread agreement about scholars that many critical questions about the Didache remain unresolved,[1] even if enormous progress has been made in appreciating what its text might mean for our understanding of the history of at least part of the early Jesus movement. Among the questions that remain unresolved are not only when the Didache reached something like the form in which our only surviving complete Greek text was copied in 1056 and later published in 1883 in the first modern edition, but also where it was likely written, for what purpose, and for and by whom its contents were first preserved in writing and then transmitted to others. Paradoxically, despite this uncertainty, wider developments in the study of early Christianity may mean that it matters less when and where we might place its origin as a written text, for there is now widespread recognition that the beliefs and practices of early followers of Jesus developed in different ways and at different rates in different places. Thus it may matter less to pin down the particular circumstances of its composition to a specific date and a specific place than to pay careful attention to its text as a written witness that tells us something about at least some of the concerns of the people among and to whom it was transmitted and possibly even among and for whom it was first written down. Just as there is a widespread conviction that much or all of the Didache reflects a very Jewish way of following Jesus, albeit in a form open to gentiles,[2] so too

---

1. Georg Schöllgen, "The Didache as a Church Order: An Examination of the Purpose for the Composition of the Didache and Its Consequences for Its Interpretation" in *The Didache in Modern Research*, ed. Jonathan A. Draper, AGJU 37 (Leiden: Brill, 1996), 43; Robert A. Kraft, "Didache," *ABD* 2:197–98.

2. See especially Jonathan Draper, "The Holy Vine of David Made Known to the

there is widespread recognition that there continued to be Jewish followers of Jesus throughout the second century CE and beyond who continued to follow Jewish law and whose practices and beliefs may have been quite different from those of other followers of Jesus.[3] Thus it matters less precisely when or where the Didache was located, because there should be little difficulty in positing a Jewish-Christian community made up of the ideal readers that its text would appear to imply *at some location* in the eastern Mediterranean world (whether it be Egypt, Asia Minor, Palestine, or Syria) *at some point* between the middle of the first and the end of the second or even the beginning of the third century CE.

Much of the progress that scholars have made in their understanding of what we might reasonably conclude from the text of the Didache as we now have it or as we might seek to reconstruct its earlier forms has come about through patient engagement with its text and content, especially at those points where there is disagreement.[4] Such conclusions as we might draw are always provisional and contingent not only on the questions that we ask and how we ask them, but also on the evidence that is available at any one time; just as the rediscovery of the Didache in 1873 led to changes in our understanding of the early Jesus movement, so too the discovery of the Dead Sea Scrolls in 1947 led to changes in the way in which many scholars have understood the Didache and the context in which it is read. Such development in our understanding of an ancient text and the aspects of the ancient realities that it might reflect will sometimes feel like progress when new insight becomes possible, but progress can take the shape either of confirming a particular hypothesis or of demonstrating why it is false and ought to be abandoned. This is only what historians should expect, so

---

Gentiles through God's Servant Jesus: 'Christian Judaism' in the *Didache*," in *Jewish Christianity Reconsidered: Rethinking Ancient Groups and Texts*, ed. Matt Jackson-McCabe (Minneapolis: Fortress, 2007), 257–83.

3. For a very useful introduction to the study of Jewish Christianity, see James Carleton-Paget, "Jewish-Christianity," in *The Early Roman Period*, vol. 3 of *The Cambridge History of Judaism*, ed. William Horbury, et al. (Cambridge: Cambridge University Press 1999), 731–75. Fuller treatments include Edwin Broadhead, *Jewish Ways of Following Jesus*, WUNT 1/266 (Tübingen: Mohr Siebeck, 2010) and the range of authors included in Jackson-McCabe, *Jewish Christianity Reconsidered* and in Oskar Skarsaune and Reidar Hvlavik, *Jewish Believers in Jesus: The Early Centuries* (Peabody, MA: Hendrickson, 2007).

4. For a history of research up to the mid 1990s, see Jonathan Draper, "*Didache* in Modern Research: An Overview," in Draper, Didache *in Modern Research*, 1–42.

it seems surprising that Aaron Milavec suggests that the fact that different scholars approach the Didache in different ways and draw different conclusions means both that the field of Didache studies is "caught up in a confusing diversity of scholarly opinions" and that it is "in disarray and unable to substantially contribute to the academic questions of our day."[5] Yet just the opposite seems to be true. Even if there are important issues on which there is a diversity of scholarly opinion (although, in my judgement, it is sometimes less marked than Milavec would imply), the result of that diversity is not confusion but a continuing process in which ancient evidence and modern understandings and arguments are tested and proposals are either refined or rejected. Thus disagreements are helpful, for they lead to further discussion in a way that allows judgments to be made about which hypotheses or conclusions seem more plausible in the light of the evidence that we have, even if that evidence is often more partial (in both senses) than historians might wish.

Milavec's essay is characteristically provocative and wide-ranging, although readers may wish to refer to his lengthy commentary on the Didache[6] for a more detailed analysis or exposition of the basis for some of the claims that he makes in his contribution to this book. There he explains his view that "a unified reading of the Didache has been impossible because the prevailing assumption has been that the Didache was created in stages, with the compiler splicing together preexisting documents

---

5. See in the present volume Aaron Milavec, "The Distress Signals of Didache Research: Quest for a Viable Future," above 59–83, quotations on 59.

6. Aaron Milavec, *The Didache: Faith, Hope and Life of the Earliest Christian Communities, 50–70 CE* (New York: Newman, 2003). Many of its conclusions are set out more briefly in Milavec, *The Didache: Text, Translation, Analysis, and Commentary* (Collegeville, MN: Liturgical Press, 2003). Milavec quotes from one reviewer, Robert Daly, in his essay in the present volume, above 82–83. Other reviews of either or both of his books include those by Mark Bredin (review of *Faith, Hope, and Life of the Earliest Christian Communities, 50–70 CE*, RBL 6 [2005]; online: http://www.bookreviews.org/pdf/4439_4472.pdf); Jonathan A. Draper (review of *The Didache: Text, Translation, Analysis and Commentary*, Neot 39 [2005]: 203–7); Stuart G. Hall (review of *The Didache: Text, Translation, Analysis, and Commentary*, JTS 55 [2004]: 704–6); Clayton Jefford (review of *The Didache: Faith, Hope, and Life of the Earliest Christian Communities, 50–70 CE*, CBQ 66 [2004] 662–64); Joseph Mueller (review of *The Didache: Faith, Hope, and Life of the Earliest Christian Communities, 50–70 CE* and *The Didache: Text, Translation, Analysis, and Commentary*, TS 66 [2005]: 890–91); and Nancy Pardee (review of *The Didache: Text, Translation, Analysis, and Commentary*, JECS 13 [2005]: 525–36).

with only a minimum of editing." This is why, he claims, other scholars have failed to notice "that the Didache has a marvellous unity from beginning to end," because it has blinded them to the "holistic unity" that becomes clear when the Didache is heard "as a whole" in the light of the way in which it was structured for oral recitation.[7] This is the "hidden key" that explains why Milavec thinks that the identification of the Didache as a church order (which seems not so far in many respects from his own characterisation of it as a training manual for baptismal candidates[8]) is so important. It is because Milavec thinks not merely that this understanding of its genre is mistaken, but because he argues that this misunderstanding has led scholars to believe that the Didache was a composite work rather than a unified text that captured in written form the instructions delivered orally by mentors training novices who wished to be "assured of following the progressive, ordered and comprehensive path that master trainers in the community had effectively culled from their own successful practice in apprenticing novices."[9]

This is an important point, for it means that Milavec interprets each section of the Didache in the light of other sections, and it requires him to find internal consistency where others see tension and therefore postulate that different sources have been brought together. Yet few scholars have been persuaded by the way in which Milavec explains the apparent tensions and duplications in the text, and most scholars continue to see them as evidence to suggest that it now includes material from what were once different sources.[10] It will not do for Milavec simply to note that different scholars give different accounts of how these sources may have been compiled and to claim that these differences necessarily undermine their efforts, for the fact that most scholars are persuaded of the need to adopt this approach might be judged more significant than the differences in how they do so. Furthermore, there is in fact a large degree of support for the division of the Didache into four main sections,[11] each of which may

---

7. *Didache: Faith, Hope and Life*, xii.

8. Ibid., xxv.

9. Ibid., xvii, see also viii.

10. For an extensive critique of Milavec's approach see, in the present volume, below, Nancy Pardee, "The Didache and Oral Theory," 311–33.

11. See, for example, Kurt Niederwimmer, *The Didache: A Commentary*, trans. Linda M. Maloney, Hermeneia (Minneapolis: Fortress, 1988); translation of *Die Didache*, KAV 1 (Göttingen: Vandenhoeck & Ruprecht, 1993), 1; Jonathan A. Draper, "Didache" in *The Apostolic Fathers: An Introduction*, ed. Wilhelm Pratscher (Waco, TX: University of Baylor Press, 2010), 1.

reflect a particular source or sources, but Milavec appears to underplay the force of this consensus. There is more disagreement among scholars about how the Didache may have been edited into something like the form in which it was found in the eleventh century manuscript that Byrennios found in Istanbul than about whether it was edited or if it evolved over time, but Milavec's argument obscures this significant distinction. Milavec's insistence that scholars should seek to make sense of the Didache in the form in which it has been transmitted is of course important, but this should not exclude the possibility that precisely such an engagement with the text as it stands may lead readers to identify tensions within the text even if they agree with Milavec that it is "not simply an arbitrary collection of traditions."[12] It is possible to recognize evidence that points to the use of different sources and to development over time without concluding that the text is the result of a "compiler splicing together preexisting documents with only a minimum of editing."[13]

It may be ironic that Milavec's wish to read the text in the way that the Byrennios manuscript might invite results in just as ecclesiastically focused a reading as that of scholars whom Milavec criticizes because of their dogmatically driven presuppositions. However, for the purpose of seeking to understand the Didache historically as an ancient text, it is more important to observe that Milavec's commitment to reading it as a fully integrated and unified whole necessarily leaves no scope for finding any evidence of development over time in the different sections of the text. According to Milavec, the text reflects the practice and belief of one particular community at one particular time and has been shaped by that community alone. Other scholars, however, find evidence for different views in different parts of the text, because they see the Didache in its current form as a text that includes different sources that may reflect different outlooks, either from one community as it developed, or from different communities.

This observation has a bearing on the two other areas that Milavec identifies as contributing to what he describes as "the current crisis"[14] in Didache research. The first is the question of the relationship between certain material in the Didache and certain material found also in synoptic double tradition, that is, traditions that are found in both Matthew and

---

12. Draper, "Holy Vine," 259; see also Draper, "*Didache*," 8 n. 8.
13. Milavec, "Distress Signals," 59.
14. Ibid., 59.

Luke but not in Mark, and might consequently be attributed to the postulated sayings source, Q. According to Milavec, one of the factors that impede progress in a proper understanding of the Didache is the continuing belief that the Didache shows literary dependence on Matthew. This view, he argues, should be rejected as was the older belief that the Didache was dependent on the Epistle of Barnabas. The only scholar whom Milavec cites as representing the view that the Didache shows the literary influence of Matthew is Christopher Tuckett, and the published dialogue between them nicely illustrates many of the issues that are at stake.[15]

Clayton Jefford's essay in the present volume also considers the relationship between the Didache and Matthew, and it throws into sharp relief how questions about the unity of the Didache and its relationship to synoptic tradition and other possible sources have a very significant bearing on each other.[16] For Milavec, as noted above, the Didache is to be read as a unified text. In addition, as he explains briefly in the present volume, he denies that the Didache shows any familiarity with Matthew's Gospel or with Matthean tradition. Tellingly, however, he both begins and concludes his discussion of this point by appealing to what the Didache does not do, which means that he relies on an argument from silence: Milavec notes points at which the Didache could have appealed to relevant material in Matthew, yet did not, and places a great deal of weight on these silences or omissions.[17] Jefford's approach is different, for he engages not with what might have been included in the text of the Didache, given certain conditions or presuppositions, but with what is actually there. As may be seen from his patient discussion, which reflects and draws on a wide range of previous work, there are in fact only quite limited sections of the Didache where any literary dependence on Matthew (and possibly also on Luke) may be found, and these may be from sections of the text that were added to the Didache some time after the main part of the text was written. Far from reading the Didache in a shadow overcast by Matthew as a canonical text, or being otherwise driven by theological or ecclesiastical presuppositions, Jefford's discussion exemplifies careful and patient attention to detail

---

15. Aaron Milavec, "Synoptic Tradition in the *Didache* Revisited," *JECS* 11 (2003): 443–80, Christopher Tuckett, "The Didache and the Synoptics Once More: A Response to Aaron Milavec." *JECS* 13 (2005): 509–18, Aaron Milavec, "A Rejoinder [to Tuckett]," *JECS* 13 (2005): 519–23.

16. Clayton Jefford, "Authority and Perspective in the Didache," above 33–58.

17. Milavec, "Distress Signals," 66, 75.

and proceeds from an analysis of each piece of evidence to an analysis of the text as a whole. Thus he concludes not only that as originally written the Didache was quite independent of Matthew, even if it drew on teachings of Jesus in a way that shows "discernible sympathy for Matthean tradition" (so agreeing with Milavec that "the Didache was created without any reliance upon Matthew"[18]), but also that at a later stage material dependent upon Matthew (and possibly Luke) was inserted into its text.

Through his analysis, Jefford demonstrates not only how the case for the Didache, having been edited and expanded at some point after its original inscription as a written text, emerges from careful engagement with its content, but also why the issues of literary integrity and relationship to other texts and traditions are interlinked. Furthermore, he succeeds in showing how, despite the influence of Matthew (and possibly Luke) on this later form of the Didache, there remains good reason to believe that other parts of its text might originate at an earlier date and reveal perspectives that are not only independent of canonical texts but possibly earlier than and independent of the traditions that they contain. More importantly, perhaps, Jefford shows in addition not only how the Didache shows an increasingly "Christian" perspective as it moves from using an earlier form of Jesus tradition to a later form that reflects one or two gospels that would come to be recognized as canonical but also how the respect for Torah and prophets exhibited in the earlier layer of the Didache remains important even as other authoritative texts are added. Thus Jefford shares with Milavec the view that "the sources behind the Didache derive from within a single trajectory of vision," although the latter would prefer to speak of oral traditions and tradents rather than sources. However, he disagrees in that he sees within this single trajectory of vision not different but complementary oral performances of the same tradition but rather evidence of "a clear evolution of perspectives and development of literary authority."[19] Even as its community develops or evolves in ways that might be increasingly easy to label as "Christian," it continues to be shaped by what may still be thought of as—but no longer limited to—"Jewish" practice and belief.

Closely linked to Milavec's claims that scholars have approached the Didache through the blinkers of undue interest in canonical versions of

---

18. Ibid., 68.
19. "Authority and Perspective," 58.

Jesus tradition is his further claim that they have also approached the text with theological or christological assumptions that lead them to interpret it as referring to Jesus where in fact it refers to God. The latter claim raises similar methodological issues as the former with regard to the integrity or unity of the Didache when it was first written and also with regard to the transmission of its text. If it is a composite text in the form in which it has been transmitted in the Byrennios manuscript then there is a distinct possibility that the word "Lord" might be used in different ways to refer either to Jesus (seen as Lord in the Pauline or "high" sense) or to God and that different uses might reflect the different times or places of origin of different sources now included in the text. If its text has been changed over time, there is also a good chance that the word Lord might have been added at some point with precisely the purpose of heightening the Christology of the text, so that it referred to Jesus in a way that seemed closer to what later Christians would expect or so that it could be taken to refer to Jesus where in an earlier version it had referred to God. The latter would appear to be the case if the use of "God" at Apos. Con. 7.30.2 may be take as evidence that the Didache originally read "God" and not Lord at Did. 14.3.[20]

Milavec's point that the particular reference to the coming of the Lord at Did. 16.7–8 should be taken to refer not to Jesus but to the coming of God the Father demonstrates how the text may be read in different ways, as does his claim that every other use of the word Lord should also refer to God (not Jesus), regardless of whether his preferred interpretation is correct. Yet he is far from alone in making the point that we cannot simply assume that any use of the word Lord implies a reference to Jesus. Milavec cites Kurt Niederwimmer as an example of someone who tends to give too much christological significance to the use of the word κύριος, reading it in a Pauline way to mean not only Jesus but Jesus in an exalted christological sense, but he makes no mention of other scholars writing on the Didache who would readily support his view that Lord may be best understood always or mostly to refer not to Jesus but to God (whose servant Jesus is).[21] Further, he does not acknowledge that, at the point at which he

---

20. I owe this reference to Jonathan Draper, "*Didache*" in Pratscher, *Apostolic Fathers*, 15.

21. Draper, for example, in his description of the theology of the Didache, treats the term "Lord" in his discussion of God the Father, not under the heading of Christology. As he observes, "It is not clear where, if ever, the word 'Lord' refers to Jesus as opposed to the Father, but there is no evidence that it refers to Jesus." Further, as

criticizes Niederwimmer, the latter sees evidence of later Christian redaction in the Didache and argues that this passage is evidence of a Christian editor changing the way in which the Didachist had expected his readers to understand his use of κύριος.[22] Yet Milavec's point remains, which is that scholars may obscure the Didache's theology if they assume references to Jesus where no such references should be found, even in passages that are similar to synoptic tradition. If (as seems all but certain) the Didache is a witness to a form of Torah-observant Jewish Christianity that was later eclipsed by the dominance of an increasingly gentile and non Torah-observant Christianity, then it is imperative that scholars do their utmost to let its own distinctive voice be heard.

The question of what sort of Jewish or Christian or even Jewish-Christian identity might characterize the community implied by the Didache is the subject of Stephen Finlan's essay in the present collection.[23] He does not focus on either the theology or Christology of the text, but does claim that the text is trying to articulate an identity that is not only Jewish but also "Christ-believing."[24] Thus he appears to place significant weight upon the one point at which the Didache may refer to Jesus as Christ (Did. 9.4)[25] and to a second point where it refers to the believer either living as a Christian or trading on Christ (Did. 12.4–5), although he does not reflect on what it means to refer to its community as "Christ-believing." Certainly the fact that the Didache refers to the person who comes in the name of the Lord as a Christian suggests that at some point in the history of its

---

Draper also observes, there is reason to believe that at least one use of "Lord" might have originally been a reference to "God." See Draper, "*Didache*," in Pratscher, *Apostolic Fathers*, 15. Jefford also notes the difficulty in deciding whether "Lord" is intended to refer to God the Father, to Jesus as a human teacher, or to Jesus Christ as the Son of God: Jefford, *The Apostolic Fathers: An Essential Guide* (Nashville: Abingdon, 2005), 73, and Jefford: *Reading the Apostolic Fathers: An Introduction* (Grand Rapids: Baker, 2012), 43–44.

22. Niederwimmer, *Didache*, 105, esp. n.14 and n.18.
23. Stephen Finlan, "Identity in the Didache Community," above, 17–32.
24. Ibid., 26.
25. The reading of the end of the thanksgiving prayer at 9.4 is uncertain, for although the Byrennios manuscript and other ancient parallels do contain the words "through Jesus Christ," these words are absent from the parallel text in the Apostolic Constitutions and Canons, and they are not included in the corresponding section of the thanksgiving prayer at Did. 10.4. For a defense of the reading, see Niederwimmer, *Didache*, 150–51.

community their relationship to the one whom they identify as the Christ came to play a significant role in their identity, but this need not mean that they necessarily believed in Christ as more than a prophetic figure who spoke God's word to them and made God present among them, which would be consistent with the rest of the text and the possibility that most or all of its references to Lord refer not to Jesus but to God. Thus although Finlan uses Social Identity Theory to assert that the identity of the group behind the Didache may be seen more clearly in where it differs from rabbinic Judaism (with whom he seeks to contrast it), Finlan does not pause to ask why the text's apparently limited references to Jesus as Christ must differentiate its community more sharply from rabbinic Judaism (who did not refer at all to Jesus in this way) than it would from Pauline communities (who referred very frequently to Jesus in this way). Finlan claims that the Didache is "as Christian as Paul is,"[26] but it is difficult to know what this might mean or how it might differ from saying that the Didache is "as Jewish as Paul is." Does either statement advance our understanding or simply restate the problem?

Much recent scholarship on Paul would affirm the view that Paul's critique of non-Christian Judaism was that it had no place for Christ at its centre, but it is difficult to claim the same of the Didache when it refers so infrequently to Jesus as Christ and may hardly refer to Jesus at all except in a way that is consistent with its explicit references to him as servant of God. Finlan's claim that in the Didache "knowledge of God is now *christologized*" (emphasis original)[27] is a very bold claim that might easily be thought the result of reading its references to Christ or cognate terms in the light of Paul's much more frequent use of Christ to refer to the crucified and risen Jesus than to the Didache's predominant presentation of Jesus as a teacher whose words are to be followed. Finlan's failure to read the Didache's use of this language within the context of how often and in what way it refers elsewhere to Jesus makes it difficult to accept the weight that he seeks to put upon it.

Further, his passing remark earlier in his essay that, in reference to how the community understood itself, "surely the Christology is more fundamental than the choice of fasting days"[28] strongly suggests that his reading of the text depends much less on what it says than on what he

---

26. Finlan, "Identity," 32.
27. Ibid., 29.
28. Ibid., 25.

thinks it should say. Just because Paul would argue that observing certain days might be to miss the point of following Jesus (Gal 4:10) or at best a matter of indifference, useful only in so far as it might be helpful in following the Lord (Rom 14:5–6), it need not follow that such observance could not have been considered much more important within the community implied by the Didache, for whom this was clearly a matter of concern (Did. 8.1). In fact, the difference that it suggests between Paul's perspective and that of the Didachist might suggest that the difference between them was as great if not greater than the difference between the Didachist and that of many rabbinic or Second Temple Jews. Finlan may be correct when he suggests that labels like Jewish or Jewish-Christian do not suffice to explain the different kinds of Jewish identity that a particular community might have. However, although he expresses the desire to move away from a simple model of Jewish or Christian with Jewish-Christian somewhere in the middle, he appears nevertheless to assume that communities who have some place for Jesus will necessarily have more in common with each other than with communities that do not in some way acknowledge Jesus, even if there are many other ways in which they appear to be alike or to have a great deal else in common. Thus Finlan's presuppositions about the relative importance of Christology appear to influence his entire approach to the text.

If the other essays in this section have in common a desire to locate the Didache and its community somewhere on a spectrum of Jewish, Christian, or Jewish-Christian identity, Jonathan Draper's essay seeks rather to locate the Didache and its community in the wider Graeco-Roman world.[29] He analyzes the Household Code found in Did. 4.9–11 and in parallel versions of the Two Ways tradition in the light of what he has elsewhere described as "The Moral Economy of the Didache," which he characterizes as an insistence on generalized reciprocity, which requires members of its community to share their goods with each other so that all may benefit from them.[30] Here he notes some of the practical limits to that vision or aspiration, when the concrete realities of social relationships in the community and the economic demands that they entail overcome abstract ideals. Thus, argues Draper, the teaching in the Two Ways tradition about children and about slaves limits restricts the impact of its teaching elsewhere about the

---

29. Jonathan A. Draper, "Children and Slaves in the Community of the Didache and the Two Ways Tradition," above, 85–121.

30. Jonathan A. Draper, "The Moral Economy of the Didache," *HTS.TS* 67 (2011).

need for members of the community to redistribute wealth among themselves, recognizing that anything they give to others they also give to God. In situations where children might lose their inheritance, or slaves might be manumitted, ideals are quickly relativized in order to ensure that patriarchal authority (which Draper finds to be more influential in a Jewish rather than in a gentile context[31]) is not challenged.

Three general points that emerge from Draper's discussion may be noted. The first, which follows directly from his analysis of the impact of the Household Code and its requirement for children and slaves to remain subject to parents and to masters, is a reminder of the need for scholars to pay careful attention to detail when reading their sources. Broad generalizations must be subject to careful analysis, and the latter will often problematize or call into question the former, however attractive they might seem before they are interrogated in this way. Second, by reading the Didache synchronically—in this case in relation to Pauline texts, since he sees it as a window on early Jewish Christian communities in tension with early Pauline communities[32]—Draper remind us of the importance of the sort of comparative study that allows different texts to illuminate each other and opens the question of whether or how the teaching of the Didache on reciprocity might relate to Paul's concern for his collection for the saints in Jerusalem, which Paul presents as an example of what the reciprocal relations between Jewish and gentile followers of Christ might entail.[33] Third, by reading the Two Ways tradition diachronically and noting the different ways in which it has been transmitted in the different witnesses to its text, Draper reminds us not only that the Didachist likely drew on at least this one earlier source when committing his words to writing, nor even only of the difficulties that there are today in seeking to reconstruct the form that the Didachist's written text might have taken, but also that the very notion of original text is subject to challenge. As Draper observes, appealing to David Parker, "there is no original text in a society that is primarily oral in its communications, and instead we have multiple representations of a tradition that is fluid and continually subject to change, to respond to, and to reflect the social situation of the scribes, since text and oral performance are continually interacting and reshaping each other."[34]

---

31. Ibid., 89.
32. Ibid., 88.
33. See Rom 15:27; 2 Cor 8:8–15; 9:6–15.
34. Draper, "Children and Slaves," 89.

Thus we return to two of the points that Milavec identified as of central importance in determining how the Didache should be read, but which appear to point in a different direction than Milavec would have us believe. The first point concerns our access to the text of the Didache and the question of how we might move from that text to any historical community that might stand behind it and the ideal readers that it implies. For Milavec, the ancient text of the Didache is understood as more or less equivalent to the form in which it was copied in 1056 and published by Byrennios in 1883.[35] Yet, as Draper and Jefford have shown in their essays, there are other ancient witnesses to parts of the Didache that preserve readings that differ from those in the Byrennios manuscript and are likely at least sometimes to witness to readings that are older than some of the text that it transmits.[36] Since some of those witnesses suggest that the Two Ways tradition was older than the Didache, it follows too that the Didachist may have drawn on at least this one source, and possibly others as well, and that his use of sources may be the most satisfactory reason for some of the apparent tensions within the text. This cannot be proven beyond doubt, but scholars who have explored this hypothesis have certainly been able to use it to make good sense of the text as it has been transmitted to us and as ancient witnesses suggest that it may have been transmitted to, and by, the scribes who copied them.

Closely related to questions about how we might today access the form or forms in which the Didache was written and circulated before the Byrennios manuscript was copied in 1056 are questions about how we approach any text that was written in a world in which orality was much more important than it is in the modern West. Milavec is, of course, correct to insist that modern readers accustomed to working with a literary mindset (or "suffer[ing] from the bias toward textuality," as Milavec puts it[37]) need to work hard to appreciate the importance of oral recitation in a society still oriented primarily towards the spoken word and to grasp what oral communication actually entailed. Yet it remains the case that we have

---

35. Milavec, *Didache: Faith, Hope and Life*, 5–9, where he explains why he has decided to follow the Byrennios manuscript, to which he refers as "the original."

36. For examples, see above Jefford, "Authority and Perspective," and Draper, "Children and Slaves," *passim*. For a fuller discussion of the problems in seeking to reconstruct the earliest possible text of the Didache, see also Draper, "*Didache* in Modern Research," 1–4, Niederwimmer, *Didache*, 19–29.

37. Milavec, "Distress Signals," 62.

access to the text of the Didache only in the form that it was inscribed at particular times, and as it has since been transmitted in writing. Any oral performance, recitation, or other form of communication or transmission that might stand behind some or all of the written text is accessible to us only through that medium, so scholars need to be sensitive to the complex ways in which oral and written texts may interact with each other and to issues of secondary as well as primary orality.[38] Certainly we need to be aware of the limitations and distorting effect of the predominantly or exclusively literary approaches for which Milavec critiques earlier generations of scholars, but we need also to recognize the way in which scholars working on orality now emphasize the interplay between written texts and oral performances, which makes it difficult to see any manuscript simply as the transcription of one particular recital at one particular time in the way that Milavec appears to characterize the text of the Didache as he presents it. Milavec is almost certainly correct in his expectation that "future Didache scholars will increasingly use studies of orality to appreciate the nature, character, and use of the Didache within its community setting,"[39] and he has made an important contribution to this process, but it is vital that such work on the Didache is conducted in dialogue with scholars working on other aspects of what Werner Kelber has called "The Oral-Scribal-Memorial Arts of Communication in Early Christianity."[40]

---

38. On the interfacial relationship between orality and writing, see Alan Kirk, "Memory, Scribal Media and the Synoptic Problem," in *New Studies in the Synoptic Problem*, ed. Paul Foster et al., BETL 239 (Leuven: Peeters, 2011), 459–466 (461), and Kirk, "Manuscript Tradition as a *Tertium Quid*: Orality and Memory in Scribal Practices," in *Jesus, the Voice, and the Text: Beyond The Oral and the Written Gospel*, ed. Tom Thatcher (Waco, TX: Baylor University Press, 2008), 215–34.

39. Milavec, "Distress Studies," 64. For two examples of recent work on the oral nature of the Didache, each with further bibliography, see below Nancy Pardee, "The Didache and Oral Theory," which includes a substantial critique of Milavec's account of the oral nature of the Didache, and Pertuu Nikander, "Orality and Writing in the Context of the Two Ways Teaching and the *Didache*."

40. This is the title of Werner Kelber's chapter in Thatcher, *Jesus, the Voice, and the Text*, 245–62, in which he responds to a variety of perspectives on his groundbreaking work, *The Oral and Written Gospel: The Hermeneutics of Speaking and Writing in the Synoptic Tradition, Mark, Paul and Q* (Philadelphia: Fortress, 1983; repr. Bloomington, IN: Indiana University Press, 1997).

Part 2
Leadership and Liturgy

Baptism and Holiness:
Two Requirements Authorizing Participation in the Didache's Eucharist

Huub van de Sandt

While the first segment of the Didache (chs. 1-10) contains an ethical Two Ways teaching and a series of wide-ranging directives concerning the ritual of baptism, the Lord's Prayer, and the eucharistic celebration,[1] the additional regulations in the second division (chs. 11-15) give us a glimpse of the local church or churches for which the Didache was written. A variety of disciplinary measures is presented, designed particularly to correct abuses in the lives of the members of the Didache community. Chapters 11-13 are concerned with the attitude of the local Didache community towards outsiders who visit the community; chapters 14-15 focus on the circumstances within the community itself.

The chapters in the middle of all these instructions contain prayers for what the Didache describes as *eucharistia*. The eucharistic prayers in

---

1. Didache 8 may be an insertion "from a different context," according to Jonathan A. Draper, "Christian Self-Definition against the 'Hypocrites' in Didache 8," in *The Didache in Modern Research*, ed. Jonathan A. Draper, AGJU 37 (Leiden: Brill, 1996), 223-43 (227). Kurt Niederwimmer (*The Didache: A Commentary*, trans. Linda M. Maloney, Hermeneia [Minneapolis: Fortress, 1998] views Did 8.1-3 as "an addition" (131), while Willy Rordorf and André Tuilier (*La doctrine des douze Apôtres* [Didachè], SC 248 bis [Paris: Cerf, 1978) take the section as interrupting "la suite logique de la partie liturgique, qui comprend essentiellement le baptême d'une part (ch. 7) et les prières eucharistiques (ch. 9-10) d'autre part" (36). See also Clayton N. Jefford, *The Sayings of Jesus in the Teaching of the Twelve Apostles*, VCSup 11 (Leiden: Brill, 1989), 105; Peter J. Tomson, "The Halakhic Evidence of Didache 8 and Matthew 6 and the Didache Community's Relationship to Judaism," in *Matthew and the Didache: Two Documents from the Same Jewish-Christian Milieu?* ed. Huub van de Sandt (Assen: Van Gorcum; Minneapolis: Fortress, 2005), 131-41.

9.2–4 and 10.2–5 encircle a real meal.[2] They begin with an expression of thanksgiving addressed to God in nearly identical wording, and when we read these prayers side by side throughout, the resemblances in phraseology and content will become quite obvious. Because their similarity is not restricted to a casual analogy but appears to pervade the whole pattern of the two prayers, certain phrases that at first sight do not seem to share similar content may nevertheless clarify one another. This is of importance when it comes to the conditions for admission to the Eucharist given in 9.5 and 10.6b.

In the following our interest will be focused on the requirements for participation in Didache's Eucharist. Before going into the subject, it is important to emphasize that early Christian communities, including the Didache group, generally understood themselves as being part of a wider community of Judaism. Anybody who takes a closer look at the Didache text will notice that it is profoundly Jewish. The traditions embodied in the Didache text for the major part originate from Jewish Christian circles (that is, from Jews who believed in Jesus) and were seen as ingredients of the Jewish community. Instead of looking at the Didache as an independent unit belonging to patristic studies only, we will find that the manual fits in a wider context of Jewish religious and cultural history.

Central to this study are the phrases in Did. 9.5 (baptism) and 10.6b (holiness), which appear to set the acceptable limits of table fellowship. The questions to be discussed regard the character of these passages and their mutual connection. Neither of the two directives was articulated by the celebrant. Each has to be considered as being a rubrical instruction at the end of a prayer, offering a warning against unworthy attendance. But why was it that baptism and holiness were deemed absolute prerequisites for admission to the Eucharist? What is the link between being baptized and seeking holiness in one's everyday life on the one hand and the communal meal on the other? In order to understand their nature and relationship, it is necessary to examine the verses within their Didache context and in the setting of first-century CE Palestine, where the holiness of the

---

2. See Klaus Wengst, *Didache (Apostellehre), Barnabasbrief, Zweiter Klemensbrief, Schrift an Diognet*, SU 2 (Darmstadt: Wissenschaftliche Buchgesellschaft, 1984), 43–48; Enrico Mazza, *The Origins of the Eucharistic Prayer*, trans. Ronald E. Lane (Collegeville, MN: Liturgical Press, 1995), 16–30; Bernd Kollmann, *Ursprung und Gestalten der frühchristlichen Mahlfeier*, GTA 43 (Göttingen: Vandenhoeck & Ruprecht, 1990), 91–98.

temple extended outward and—particularly in Qumran—physical, ritual impurity was believed to be connected to moral, inner impurity.

The present contribution is divided into two parts, dealing with baptism and holiness respectively. With regard to baptism, we will start by concentrating on what is said in Did. 9.5. After the instructions for blessing the wine (9.2) and blessing the bread (9.3–4), the verse reads as follows:

> Let no one eat or drink of your Eucharist [εὐχαριστίας] save those who have been baptized [βαπτισθέντες] in the name of the Lord, since the Lord has said, "Do not give to dogs what is holy" [μὴ δῶτε τὸ ἅγιον τοῖς κυσί] (Did. 9.5).[3]

The verse emphasizes that only those who have been baptized are allowed to take part in the Eucharist. The use of the word "baptized" is remarkable here. What does it mean exactly? Outside of 9.5, the Didache only speaks of baptism in chapter 7. But Did. 7 does not give an explanation of baptism either, not of what the rite was thought to mean nor about that which was expected from the act of baptizing. In fact, the section in Did. 7 does not even seem consistent with the general drift of Did. 9.5. In the traditional scholarly view, the rite portrayed in chapter 7 is the initiatory ceremony new members of the Didache community are to undergo. The act of being immersed results in transforming an individual from outsider to insider.[4] It has the character of an initiatory rite, of an absolute prerequisite for admission to the community. How does the custom of baptizing new converts concur with the phenomenon of a baptism authorizing participation in the communal meal in Did. 9.5? And for whom was the requirement in 9.5 meant? Was it intended for the neophytes or for those already belonging to the community? This study attempts to answer these questions.

The first part (§1. Baptism) will examine the function and meaning of baptism in Did. 9.5. The steps that will be taken in this process are the following. Didache 9.5 prohibits nonbaptized people from taking part in the Eucharist. We will see that the tenor of the clause supporting this exclusion (9.5d) is particularly close to that of the temple purity terminology (§1.1). It will be demonstrated next that the ultimate roots of Christian baptism

---

3. For this translation, see Aelred Cody, "The Didache: An English Translation," in *The Didache in Context*, ed. Clayton N. Jefford, NovTSup 77 (Leiden: Brill, 1995), 3–14.

4. See also Aaron Milavec, *The Didache: Faith, Hope, and Life of the Earliest Christian Communities, 50–70 CE* (New York: Newman, 2003), 268.

in Did. 7.1–3 lay in the Jewish immersion ceremony carried out whenever one was preparing to visit the temple. But, at the same time, baptism in Did. 7 appears to embody concessions with regard to a formerly strict practice (§1.2). The fading interest in a stringent performance of this purity ritual can be explained by reference to the increasing emphasis on the ethical dimension of baptism by the prefix of the Two Ways in Did. 1–6 (§1.3). Finally, an attempt will be made to explain the sequence of the Two Ways and baptism in Did. 1–7 by providing a well-defined trend within contemporary Judaism. In addition to a ritual aspect, there was a moral side to (im)purity as well (§1.4).

The second part (§2. Holiness) deals with two clauses of 10.6b. Didache 10.6 is characterized by a sudden shift in diction and phraseology, because this verse, as an abrupt chain of short and apparently loosely connected sentences, does not fit into the context stylistically and thus probably constitutes an intrusion. The verse is the sequel to the prayer of thanksgiving (10.2–5) after a satiating meal (see 10.1). Like the statement in 9.5, the clauses in 10.6b articulate a rubrical comment of invitation and caution:

If anyone is holy, let him come.
If anyone is not, let him repent.

The celebrant bids the participants to leave their seats in order to take part in the communal meal and, at the same time, warns against unworthy attendance. But what does the clause "if anyone is holy" mean? Is it an implicit reference to baptism in Did. 9.5? Does it merely reiterate that it is only the baptized that may eat from the Eucharist? Is the "holy" one of Did. 10.6b identical to the baptized person of Did. 9.5? Or does 10.6b have an ethical connotation in the sense that community members should strive for moral sanctification? And if so, how is the latter view to be related to the communal meal and the shared food?

The problems regarding Did. 10.6b might be solved by reference to the confession and reconciliation mentioned in Did. 14 (and 15.3), where ethical conditions for the purity of a sacrifice are formulated (§2.1). This to a certain extent links up with the point made in the first part (1. Baptism) as terms like "sacrifice" and "pure" in Did. 14 suggest a temple ritual. And here again, it is one's moral attitude that is central. The purity required to take part in the Eucharist is no longer attained primarily through the performance of ablutions, but has been transferred to a state of moral blamelessness with regard to the confession of sins and mutual reconciliation (§2.2).

1. Baptism

After the first table prayer, a rubrical comment follows in Did. 9.5, emphasizing that no one but those baptized is allowed to eat and drink of the Eucharist. The only place in the Didache outside 9.5 that mentions baptism (βαπτίζω, βάπτισμα) is Did. 7. In Did. 7.1c–3a, various types of water are mentioned, which shows a paramount interest in ritual purity as it reflects the central concern that one should use the most appropriate water available for baptism.

1.1. Baptism as Authorizing Admission to Special Food in Did. 9.5

The saying in Did. 9.5d ("Do not give to dogs what is holy") underscores the preceding cautioning expressed in 9.5a–c. The maxim is undoubtedly quoted as an authoritative word of the Lord to emphasize that all those who have not been baptized are excluded from the Eucharist. The wording "what is holy" (τὸ ἅγιον) in Did. 9.5d probably refers to sacrificial food, a meaning suggested by its usage in LXX Exod 29:33; Lev 2:3; 22:6, 7, 10–16;[5] Num 18:8–19; Ezra 2:63; and par. Neh 7:65. The term "holy things" (קדשים) refers to the animal meat or agricultural produce designated for sacrifice in the temple. Since the expression in Did. 9.5d deals with "what is holy" (τὸ ἅγιον), it has a cultic ring to it and suggests a customary Jewish sacrificial temple ritual.

As a rule, holy food was eaten inside the temple itself. The food was to be eaten in a state of purity, meaning that the priest must not recently have been in contact with processes and substances considered to be defiling, which included childbirth (Lev 15:1–32; 12:1–8), animal carcasses (Lev 11:24–28), menstrual and seminal emissions (Lev 15:1–32), skin disease (Lev 13–14), and a human corpse (Num 19:11–19).[6] God's

---

5. Particularly relevant to our investigation is the passage in LXX Lev 22:6–7, 10: "he shall not eat of the holy things [οὐκ ἔδεται ἀπὸ τῶν ἁγίων] unless he has bathed his body in water. When the sun is down he shall be clean [καθαρός]; and then shall he eat of the holy things [καὶ τότε φάγεται τῶν ἁγίων], for they are his bread.... And no stranger shall eat the holy things [οὐ φάγεται ἅγια]: a sojourner of the priest's or a hired servant shall not eat the holy things."

6. Shmuel Safrai, "Religion in Everyday Life," in *The Jewish People in the First Century: Historical Geography, Political History, Social, Cultural and Religious Life and Institutions*, ed. Shmuel Safrai and Menahem Stern, vol. 2, CRINT 1.2 (Assen: Van Gorcum, 1976), 793–833 (828–30); Emil Schürer, *The History of the Jewish People in*

continued presence in the temple depended to a certain extent on the continual service of the priests who performed their duty in perfect purity (Lev 21:17–23). The officiating priests and the people present had to be ritually pure, and purity could be achieved through the prescribed ablution, that is, by a simple immersion of the whole body into a specially constructed pool (*mikveh*).

But how is this temple-oriented view of holiness related to the Eucharist in the Didache? The stereotypical form of expression in Did. 9.5d[7] suggests that the Didache community probably represented a part of a broader trend in ancient Jewish piety that continued beyond the destruction of the temple. In Second Temple Judaism, a practice developed expanding the concepts of holiness beyond the altar and temple in Jerusalem[8] to the synagogue,[9] to study and prayer,[10] and to the communal meal outside the orbit of the Jerusalem sanctuary and its officials.[11] This

---

the Age of Jesus Christ (175 B.C.–A.D. 135), ed. Geza Vermes et al. (Edinburgh: T&T Clark, 1973–1987), 2:475–76.

7. The phrase "Do not give to dogs what is holy" is paralleled word for word in the first part of a more extensive Jesus saying in Matt 7:6. The use of the saying in the Didache, however, seems to argue against its having been borrowed from Matthew. See Huub van de Sandt, "'Do Not Give What Is Holy to the Dogs' (Did 9:5d and Matt 7:6a): The Eucharistic Food of the Didache in Its Jewish Purity Setting," *VC* 56 (2002): 223–46.

8. See, also for the following, Huub van de Sandt, "Why does the Didache Conceive of the Eucharist as a Holy Meal?" *VC* 65 (2011): 1–20 (6–15).

9. Late antique synagogues came to be viewed as holy places; see Shaye J. D. Cohen, "The Temple and the Synagogue," in *The Early Roman Period*, vol. 3 of *Cambridge History of Judaism*, ed. W. Horbury et al. (Cambridge: Cambridge University Press, 1999), 298–325 (320). See also Arnold Goldberg, "Service of the Heart: Liturgical Aspects of Synagogue Worship," in *Standing before God: Studies on Prayer in Scriptures and in Tradition*, ed. A. Finkel and L. Frizzell (New York: KTAV, 1981), 195–211; Steven Fine, *This Holy Place: On the Sanctity of the Synagogue during the Greco-Roman Period*, CJA 11 (Notre Dame: University of Notre Dame Press, 1997), 41–59. Rich evidence (including images of the menorah, shofar, lulav, and etrog) is also found in the mosaics embellishing the synagogue floors; see Martha Himmelfarb, *A Kingdom of Priests: Ancestry and Merit in Ancient Judaism*, JCC (Philadelphia: University of Pennsylvania Press, 2006), 170–71.

10. As early as Dan 6:11 a prayer was directed thrice daily toward Jerusalem. Study acquired this characteristic as well; see Fine, *This Holy Place*, 51.

11. See Jonathan Klawans, *Purity, Sacrifice, and the Temple: Symbolism and Supersessionism in the Study of Ancient Judaism* (Oxford: Oxford University Press, 2006), 175–22.

also had consequences for the rules of purity. In addition to maintaining the purity of priestly food, there was strong concern regarding the eating of ordinary food in purity outside the temple as well.[12] The absence of impurity[13] was increasingly considered to be an appropriate prerequisite for aspects of daily life such as prayer and eating. This trend of copying aspects of the temple service by performing cultic practices beyond the temple site are perceptible in the collective meals of the Dead Sea Scrolls community. Members of the Qumran community bathed before eating communal food (1QS V, 13; 4Q514 1 I, 5–7; 11QT^a XLIX, 20–21; see also Josephus, *B.J.* 2.129).[14] Like the Qumran group, the Pharisees, and many others as well, applied temple purity rules to prayer, Torah study or meal practices.[15] Impure Jews could be purified through a purification ritual,

---

12. See John C. Poirier, "Purity beyond the Temple in the Second Temple Era," *JBL* 122 (2003): 247–65 (256–59); Eyal Regev, "Non-Priestly Purity and Its Religious Aspects According to Historical Sources and Archaeological Findings," in *Purity and Holiness: The Heritage of Leviticus*, ed. Marcel J. H. M. Poorthuis and Joshua Schwartz, JCP 2 (Leiden: Brill, 2000), 223–44 (225–29), and Regev, "Pure Individualism: The Idea of Non-priestly Purity in Ancient Judaism," *JSJ* 31 (2000): 176–202 (177–78).

13. "Purity is the absence of impurity;" see (also for the concepts of "holy," "pure," and "impure" in general) Jacob Milgrom, "The Dynamics of Purity in the Priestly System," in Poorthuis and Schwartz, *Purity and Holiness*, 29–32 (29), and Milgrom, *Leviticus 1–16: A New Translation with Introduction and Commentary*, AB 3 (New York: Doubleday, 1991), 730–32.

14. For this practice, see Lawrence H. Schiffman, *The Eschatological Community of the Dead Sea Scrolls: A Study of the Rule of the Congregation*, SBLMS 38 (Atlanta: Scholars Press, 1989), 62. For instances demonstrating the shift of the scrolls from priestly to general washing, see Jonathan D. Lawrence, *Washing in Water: Trajectories of Ritual Bathing in the Hebrew Bible and Second Temple Literature*, SBLAB 23 (Atlanta: Society of Biblical Literature, 2006), 88–97, 113–14. There are also references to the Essene practice of bathing prior to communal meals in Josephus, *B.J.* 2.129–131; see also Todd S. Beall, *Josephus' Description of the Essenes Illustrated by the Dead Sea Scrolls* (Cambridge: Cambridge University Press, 1988), 17.

15. New Testament evidence testifies to the fact that the Pharisees, predecessors of the rabbis and other groups within Jewish society, observed nonpriestly purity rules; see Luke 11:38, demonstrating that it was Pharisaic practice to bathe completely (ἐβαπτίσθη) before eating; Mark 7:1–23, where Jesus's disciples are criticized for eating with defiled hands, see also Matt 15:1–20. See also Gedalyahu Alon, who found that "in the days of the Tannaim the eating of unconsecrated food in purity was a widespread custom"; see his "The Bounds of the Laws of Levitical Cleanness," in *Jews, Judaism and the Classical World: Studies in Jewish History in the Times of the Second Temple and Talmud*, trans. I. Abrahams (Jerusalem: Magnes Press, 1977), 190–234 (207); and

and many took part in such rituals, regardless of whether they lived near Jerusalem and irrespective of whether trips to the temple were in their immediate plans. Archaeological finds of stone baths and stone vessels prove that forms of extra-temple, nonpriestly purity were unquestionably a widespread facet of religious life in ancient Judaism.[16]

Didache 9.5d shows that the original temple-centered means of expressing piety is maintained in a new way. The use of "what is holy" (τὸ ἅγιον) in Did. 9.5 suggests a channeling of temple sanctity to the community meal in the Didache. The temple's sanctity and significance is directed to a new context. The status of being explicitly sacrificial, originally restricted to the temple service, is conferred on what in essence is not sacrificial (a meal).

What about the "dogs" in Did. 9.5d? Examples stemming from the Tannaitic period (first and second centuries CE) make it clear that a dedicated animal, although blemished, has a lasting status of belonging to the divine sphere (Sipre Num. 18:15;[17] m. Tem. 6:5). It does not lose

---

compare also Hannah K. Harrington, "Did the Pharisees Eat Ordinary Food in a State of Ritual Purity?," *JSJ* 26 (1995): 42–54, who concludes: "What is evident is a conscious effort to make an extension of the laws for priestly food to the private home" (54). See in addition, Himmelfarb, *Kingdom of Priests*, 85–87; Regev, "Non-Priestly Purity," 225-37; Regev, "Pure Individualism," 177–85; Poirier, "Purity beyond the Temple," 247–65. The Tosefta testifies to this development as follows: "Come and see how far purity has broken out in Israel" (t. Sabb. 1:14; see also b. Sabb. 13a). Observing ritual purity outside the temple area for early Jews remained first and foremost the precondition for encountering the sacred.

16. See Roland Deines, *Jüdische Steingefässe und pharisäische Frömmigkeit: Ein archäologisch-historischer Beitrag zum Verständnis von Joh 2,6 und der jüdischen Reinheitshalacha zur Zeit Jesu*, WUNT 2/52 (Tübingen: Mohr 1993), *passim*; Thomas Kazen, *Jesus and Purity Halakhah: Was Jesus Indifferent to Impurity?* ConBNT 38 (Winona Lake, IN: Eisenbrauns, 2010), 53–54, 74–76, 185, etc. The existence of immersion pools in remote areas, such as Galilee in the Second Temple period, suggests that people would also immerse themselves on occasions other than visits to the temple. According to Lawrence: "*miqva'ot* were found in both Judea and the Galilee" (*Washing in Water*, 182). Nearly all *mikva'ot* of the period ending with the destruction of the temple in 70 CE, however, are located in Jerusalem and Judea: "There are a few in other regions such as Samaria, Galilee, and the Golan" (159). See also figure 1 "*Miqva'ot* in the Second Temple period" (204).

17. Pisqa 118; see also Haym S. Horovitz, ed., *Siphre d'be Rab I: Siphre ad Numeros adjecto Siphre zutta*, CT 3/3.1 (Leipzig: 1917; corr. repr. Jerusalem: Wahrmann, 1966), 138.

its holiness, as it still is God's property. The release of holy things from divine ownership (by paying redemption money so that they could be used in other ways) is forbidden. Indeed, redeeming them was equivalent to feeding them to the dogs. The feeding of holy things to dogs was evidently so appalling and scandalous that it underlies the denial of one's right to have sacrificial meat at one's disposal.

The idea of dogs devouring dedicated food was felt to be particularly horrifying in the Second Temple period.[18] The concept motivating the expression in Did. 9.5d is attested by witnesses in rabbinic literature, the Qumran scrolls,[19] the story about Joseph and Aseneth (probably composed for Jews between the first century BCE and the second century CE),[20] and in Pseudo-Philo's Liber antiquitatum biblicarum (Biblical Antiquities).[21] It is not unlikely that the fixed rabbinic formula itself, "Holy things [dedicated sacrifices] are not to be redeemed to feed them to dogs" אין פודין את הקדשין להאכילן לכלבים)), was also widespread as early as the first century CE.[22] In these cases the wording seems merely to confirm an understanding that did not necessitate any further elaboration.

---

18. See also for the following, van de Sandt, "Do Not Give What Is Holy to the Dogs," 230-31, 236-39.

19. In a halakah found in 4QMMT 58-62, it is ruled that dogs should not be brought into Jerusalem, since they defile sacred food.

20. "And Aseneth took her royal dinner and the fatlings and the fish and the meats and all the sacrifices of her gods and the vessels of their wine of libation and threw everything through the window as food for the dogs" (καὶ ἔρριψεν πάντα διὰ τῆς θυρίδος τοῖς κυσὶ βοράν) (10.14). For the conjecture βοράν instead of βρῶμα in the reading of MS A (τοῖς κυσὶ βρῶμα) or βορρά in MS B (τοῖς κυσὶ εἰς βορρά), see Marc Philonenko, *Joseph et Aséneth: Introduction, texte critique, traduction et notes* (Leiden: Brill, 1968).

21. Our text concerns the rage of God against Jephthah's rash and careless vow in Judg 11:30-31, since his sacrifice might also have consisted of something unclean like a dog (LAB 39.11): "And God was very angry and said, Behold Jephthah has vowed that he will offer to me whatever meets him first on the way; and now if a dog should meet Jephthah first, will the dog be offered to me?" (*Et nunc si canis primum obviaverit Iepte, numquid canis offeretur mihi?*). For the Latin text, see Daniel J. Harrington and Jacques Cazeaux, eds., *Pseudo-Philon: Les antiquités bibliques*, 2 vols., SC 229 (Paris: Cerf, 1976), 1.278, lines 82-84; for the translation, see Daniel J. Harrington, "Pseudo-Philo," in vol. 2 of *The Old Testament Pseudepigrapha*, ed. James H. Charlesworth (New York: Doubleday, 1985), 297-377 (353).

22. See, e.g., m. Tem. 6:5; t. Tem. 4:11; b. Tem. 17a; 31a; 33a-b; b. Bek. 15a; b. Šebu. 11b; y. Ma'aś. Š. 2:5, 53c.

In Did. 9.5 baptism is indeed referred to as the general prerequisite authorizing participation in the Eucharist and preventing pagans from sharing the meal. The particular antonymy of the holy thing(s) on the one hand and dogs on the other provides the Eucharist with distinct features of a sacrificial offering in the sanctuary.[23] The established proverb is used here in a metaphorical sense, as it is meant to enforce and justify the exclusion of the unbaptized—characterized here as (scavenging) dogs—from the eucharistic food. Feeding the dogs has become a metaphor for admitting nonbaptized people, that is, pagans, to the pure meal of the pure community. The dogs represented the gentiles in their impure state.[24] Communal meals were not open to nonbaptized people. The saying particularly close to the context of the temple-offering shows the application of the cultic terminology to an extra-temple domain and to figurative dogs.[25]

The above argument is also corroborated by the use of the term "Eucharist" (εὐχαριστία) in Did. 9.5. In this verse the word εὐχαριστία not only refers to the utterance of the blessings like the one in 9.1, but also to the eucharistic food over which the blessing is spoken: "Let no one eat or drink of your Eucharist." Since the prayer does not give any explanation for this nomenclature, one may assume that the term "Eucharist" was used in the Christian milieu of the Didache in this technical sense.[26] The meal

---

23. It is important to recall at this stage that the stereotyped form of expression is found in both Talmuds, echoing materials far into the fourth and fifth centuries and always in discussions relating to the cult.

24. It is quite possible, however, that the "dogs" in the expression in Did. 9.5d were already associated with "gentiles" prior to the composition of the Didache. Jonathan Draper refers to Lev 22:10 LXX: "where it is gentiles who are prohibited from τὸ ἅγιον: καὶ πᾶς ἀλλογενὴς οὐ φάγεται ἅγια;" see his "Do the Didache and Matthew Reflect an 'Irrevocable Parting of the Ways' with Judaism?" in van de Sandt, *Matthew and the Didache*, 217–41 (236).

25. The purifications and communal meals did not ultimately replace temple worship as a preferred means of honoring God. On the contrary, even the Qumran sectarians expected to go back to the temple system of offerings once these were carried out in line with their own beliefs and ideas; see Ian C. Werrett, *Ritual Purity and the Dead Sea Scrolls*, STDJ 72 (Leiden: Brill, 2007), 7–8. Certain passages of the Dead Sea Scrolls (like 1QM II, 5–6; CD VI, 11–16; and XI, 16–21) place the physical temple and sacrifices at the center of their preoccupations.

26. See Robert A. Kraft, *Barnabas and the Didache*, AF 3 (Toronto: Nelson, 1965), 167; Hans Conzelmann, "εὐχαριστέω, εὐχαριστία, εὐχάριστος," *TDNT* 9:407–15 (414–15); Wengst, *Didache (Apostellehre)*, 44.

as well as the food consumed is not understood as an ordinary meal but as something special.

1.2. The Rite of Baptism in Did. 7.1–3

Didache 7 is the earliest surviving description of the administration of baptism.[27] The discussion in Did. 7.1c–3a of the various types of water alludes to Jewish ablutions for ritual purification, and the directives in Did. 7 seem to have their parallels in Jewish halakhic instructions about water for ritual washings. It was a principal issue to determine what sort of water was needed for the purificatory washing. In rabbinic sources, six types of water supply are distinguished in an ascending order of value beginning with the lower qualities of water and proceeding to the higher ones (m. Miqw. 1:1–8). "Living" or running water has long been highly valued in Israel (see Lev 14:5, 50, 52; Num 19:17) and in the Hellenistic Roman world.[28] In Did. 7.1–3 it says:

> As for the baptism [βαπτίσματος], baptize [βαπτίσατε] this way. Having said all this beforehand baptize [βαπτίσατε] in the name of the Father and of the Son and of the Holy Spirit in running water [ἐν ὕδατι ζῶντι]. If you do not have running water, however, baptize [βάπτισον] in another kind of water; if you cannot [do so] in cold [water], then [do so] in warm [water]. But if you have neither, pour water on the head thrice in the name of Father and Son and Holy Spirit.

The interest in ritual purity is still paramount in Did. 7 as it reflects the concern that one should use the most appropriate water available for baptism. In the Hebrew Bible, purification was necessary before participating in temple worship, and this remained for ancient Jews, first and foremost, the prerequisite for encountering the sacred. Ritual impurity bars a person from God's presence, and it is a biblical principle that it forms a barrier that must be removed (Num 19:20).

---

27. Everett Ferguson, *Baptism in the Early Church: History, Theology, and Liturgy in the First Five Centuries* (Grand Rapids: Eerdmans, 2009), 202.

28. Theodor Klauser, "Taufet in Lebendigem Wasser! Zum religions- und kulturgeschichtlichen Verständnis von Didache 7,1–3," in *Gesammelte Arbeiten zur Liturgiegeschichte, Kirchengeschichte und Christlichen Archäologie*, ed. E. Dassmann, JAC.E 3 (Münster: Aschendorff, 1974), 177–83 (177, 180–82).

Ritual purity was thus considered a prerequisite not only for animals destined for sacrifice, but also for the priests who regularly presided at sacrifices and for those who came to the temple to offer sacrifices.[29] Those people who were ritually defiled and those animals which, when dead, were considered ritually defiling were banned from the sanctuary. The קדשים (the parts of the sacrifices eaten by the priests) called for prior purification rituals. Because God resided in Israel, it was essential (according to Lev 15:31) for all Israelites to observe certain ritual purity laws when they wished to enter the sanctuary.

The text in Did. 7.1c–3a itself, however, may reflect a development that abandoned an originally strict ritual practice. At an earlier stage it just might have been the "living water" (מים חיים) exclusively that was called for as necessary for the performance of Christian baptism.[30] The directives in our passage, however, seem to differ. On the one hand, the purity required to approach God is still attained through the performance of ablutions or immersions. On the other hand, the text does not reflect a continuous, strong adherence to Jewish halakah governing ritual purity. The regulations give the impression that the importance of the baptismal instruction with regard to correct practice is diminishing.[31] They embody concessions toward a formerly strict practice. Should circumstances so demand, they permit performance of the rite of baptism "in another kind of water" (Did. 7.2a). And if there is neither cold nor warm water, one was allowed to pour water onto the person's head instead of immersing them

---

29. Jonathan Klawans, "Pure Violence: Sacrifice and Defilement in Ancient Israel," *HTR* 94 (2001): 135–57 (134).

30. John the Baptist baptized in the Jordan (Matt 3:6; Mark 1:5). The earliest form of baptism seems to have been performed on the banks of a river, at a well, or on the seashore (Acts 8:36; 16:13).

31. Ferguson, for example, considers the "allowance of pouring instead of immersion" as an "anomaly" and "a break with Jewish practice" (*Baptism in the Early Church*, 206). This need not necessarily constitute a break with its Jewish environment, however. We will notice below that the highlighting of "moral purity," common in early Christian literature, was also widespread in the Qumran scrolls (and in Philonic texts; see Jonathan Klawans, *Impurity and Sin in Ancient Judaism* [Oxford: Oxford University Press, 2000], 64–66). One may thus view this change in emphasis as an internal Jewish phenomenon. See also Huub van de Sandt and David Flusser, *The Didache: Its Jewish Sources and Its Place in Early Judaism and Christianity*, CRINT 3.5 (Assen: Van Gorcum; Minneapolis: Fortress, 2002), 283 and n. 39.

in it. Why were the rules governing ritual purity losing their significance in Did. 7, while the interest in ritual purity remained as strong as ever?

1.3. The Prebaptismal Moral Catechesis in Did. 1–6

The opening line of the Didache ("There are two ways, one of life, the other of death") introduces the subject treated in these chapters. The way of life (Did. 1–4) contains moral instruction that is expounded at greater length than the way of death, which comes down to a mere list of warnings (Did. 5). Then, after the warning in 6.1 to maintain and observe the aforesaid prescriptions, the subsequent verses (6.2-3) present a reduction of the previous standards for those who are unable to "bear the entire yoke of the Lord." The transition to baptism in Did. 7.1b by means of the phrase "having said all this beforehand, baptize in the name of the Father" shows that the Two Ways teaching in Did. 1–6 in some form served as a prebaptismal instruction within the community.[32] It might well be that the diminished attention paid to the ritual level of purity in baptism in Did. 7.1c–3a is related to the emphasis on ethics in the preceding Two Ways teaching.

Our first concern, however, is to briefly portray the Two Ways as an independent tradition. It is important to realize that the Two Ways instruction ranges across a variety of Christian documents from the first five centuries. The close resemblances between the most important versions of the Two Ways (including Did. 1–6; Barn. 18–20, and the Doctrina apostolorum)[33] are generally explained in modern research by their— direct or indirect—dependence on an earlier Jewish Two Ways document that is no longer known to us. Each of these writings represents an independent witness to the ancient Two Ways tradition in which the basic pattern is essentially the same, particularly the contrasting of two ways, one

---

32. See André Benoit, *Le baptême chrétien au second siècle: La théologie des Pères*, ÉHPR 43 (Paris: Presses Universitaires de France, 1953), 6–7; Nathan Mitchell, "Baptism in the *Didache*," in *The Didache in Context*, ed. Clayton N. Jefford, NovTSup 77 (Leiden: Brill, 1995), 226–55 (236–37); Rordorf and Tuilier, *Doctrine des douze Apôtres*, 30--2.

33. The others are represented by the Apostolic Church Order; the Epitome of the Canons of the Holy Apostles; the Arabic Vita Shenudi; Pseudo-Athanasius, *Syntagma Doctrinae*; and *Fides CCCXVIII Patrum*; see van de Sandt and Flusser, *Didache*, 59–70.

of life and one of death, each of which is followed by a distinct catalogue of virtues and vices respectively.

The ancient Greek Two Ways, freed from the present Didache context, was constructed, preserved, and handed on within pious Hassidic circles that maintained highly refined ethical standards. The text shows an undeniable relationship with a particular type of rabbinic literature called *Derek Eretz*.[34] Both the Greek Two Ways and the rabbinic *Derek Eretz* tractates reveal a specific trend in early Jewish thought that calls on a newly refined moral sensitivity. We note here that oral tracts with subjects concerning *Derek Eretz* existed as early as the second century CE and that part of these writings reflect the teachings of pious Jewish circles in the first and second centuries CE on moral behavior.[35] These men constituted concrete groups within the society of the rabbis, practicing charities, performing deeds of loving kindness, and possessing virtues of dedication to humility and modesty. Thus, the tradition of the Two Ways was transmitted and kept alive within virtuous Jewish factions but also developed into a prebaptismal catechesis for gentiles[36] in the Didache community and prob-

---

34. Van de Sandt and Flusser, *Didache*, 172–80.

35. Myron B. Lerner, "The External Tractates," in *The Literature of the Sages*, ed. Shmuel Safrai, CRINT 2.3 (Assen: Van Gorcum; Philadelphia: Fortress, 1987), 367–404 (380); Shmuel Safrai, "Teaching of Pietists in Mishnaic Literature," *JJS* 16 (1965): 15–33 (25–28); "Hasidim we-Anshei Maase," *Zion* 50 (1984–1985): 133–54; "Jesus and the Hasidim," *JP* 42–44 (1994): 3–22; "Jesus and the Hasidic Movement," in *The Jews in the Hellenistic-Roman World: Studies in Memory of Menahem Stern*, ed. Isaiah M. Gafni, A'haron Oppenheimer, and Daneil R. Schwartz (Jerusalem: The Zalman Shazar Center for Jewish History; The Historical Society of Israel, 1996), 413–36 (Hebrew).

36. As a result of their education, Jews generally would have grasped what God required of them. The Two Ways section would therefore appear to be an admonition to outsiders, to gentiles rather than to Jews, to bring their behaviour up to the community's standard. For non-Jews the line of former beliefs and previous conduct had to be changed. The Two Ways dichotomy served as a framework for understanding the radical alteration in behaviour and commitments that the gentile convert was expected to make. She or he is exhorted to leave behind households in which pagan gods and customary gentile criteria of morality abounded and instead to embrace a higher model of behaviour. The Two Ways' new function of providing instruction for gentiles brought about some changes in its form. The alterations are reflected first in the doctrine's supplementary long title ("Doctrine of the Lord [brought] to the Nations by the Twelve Apostles") prefacing the Didache after its short title ("Doctrine of the Twelve Apostles").

ably in other first-century Christian communities as well.[37] The prefacing of the baptismal ceremony in Did. 7 with the original Jewish instruction of the Two Ways in Did. 1–6 resulted in an "ethicization" of the baptism ritual. This brings up the question of how this phenomenon is to be understood. For what reason was the rite of baptism introduced with the ethical approach of the Two Ways in the Didache at a specific moment in history?

1.4. Baptism and Morality in Their Jewish Setting

Mastery of the Two Ways teaching became a prerequisite for baptism. The attachment of the moral instruction as a prefix to the rite of baptism in Did. 7 fits with purity practices in the late Second Temple period. In order to look at things in a proper perspective, the publication by Jonathan Klawans dealing with the general role of purity in early Judaism is particularly relevant. One of his most important points is the distinction between "ritual" and "moral" impurity.[38] Whereas the sources of *ritual* impurity are mostly confined to natural phenomena (including childbirth, the carcasses of animals, menstrual and seminal emissions, skin disease, or a human corpse), *moral* impurity results from immoral acts such as sexual sins (Lev 18:24–30), idolatry (Lev 19:31; 20:1–3), and bloodshed (Num

---

37. Recently a reconstruction of the original Greek Two Ways teaching was published (van de Sandt and Flusser, *Didache*, 112–39) and, since this (hypothetical) text of the Two Ways has become available, it is now possible to detect traces of the Two Ways in Jewish and Christian first-century documents. This opens up a whole new area of research that awaits further fruitful exploration with respect to New Testament literature and allows us insight into the situation of the writer and hearers that otherwise might be missed. Since both the writer and addressees of the Gospels and New Testament letters were baptized, they may have been familiar with the Two Ways teaching. The tradition might have been just as fixed and its influence on the faith and action of the first readers and writers just as strong as the influence of popular hymns is on people today. If familiarity with the Two Ways' catechesis preceding the rite of baptism was indeed widespread among first-century Christian communities, this would give us deeper insight into the preconceptions (*Vorverständnis*) of early Christians, which in turn would help us to arrive at a better understanding of their documents. The identification of preliterary traditions in literary texts allows insight into the situation of the writer and hearers that otherwise might be overlooked. It is not the wide diffusion of the Two Ways that is central to this paper, however, as it would take up too much space to enter into details here.

38. Klawans, *Impurity and Sin in Ancient Judaism*, 21–31.

35:33-34).[39] As noted above, ritual impurity is unavoidable in the normal course of everyday life. It is impermanent and not sinful,[40] whereas moral impurity is the direct consequence of a deliberate, grave sin that leads to long-lasting regression and the degeneration of the sinner. Unlike some forms of ritual impurity, moral impurity is not associated with contact-contagion and does not affect the ritual status of the individual.[41]

The line between "outer" (ritual) and "inner" (moral) impurity is reasonably distinct in the Hebrew Bible and views on the matter are quite different in rabbinic literature. In fact, the rabbis were strongly opposed to the idea that ritual impurity is connected to moral impurity. They were unreceptive to the thought of fusing together the two types of impurity. Interestingly, in the Dead Sea Scrolls moral purity is not isolated from ritual purity, and we often find the two completely intertwined there. Texts that are undoubtedly sectarian in origin, such as 1QS, 1QpHab, 1QH, and 4Q512, integrate the two concepts into one single notion of impurity. The Rule of the Community states that new members are cleansed by their humble repentance as well as the sprinkling of cleansing waters:

> For it is through the spirit of the true counsel of God that are atoned the ways of man, all his iniquities, so that he may look at the light of life. And it is through a holy spirit of the community, in its truth, that he is purified of all his iniquities. And through a spirit of uprightness and of humility his sin is atoned. And through the compliance of his soul with all the laws of God his flesh is purified by being sprinkled with cleansing waters and made holy with the waters of repentance (III, 6-9).[42]

Every member of the sect was in need of purification, but an immersion would only be effective in the case of a person's meek submission to all

---

39. Klawans, "Pure Violence," 154-55, and *Impurity and Sin in Ancient Judaism*, 26-31.

40. Klawans, *Impurity and Sin in Ancient Judaism*, 22-26. See also Jonathan A. Draper, "Pure Sacrifice in Didache 14 as Jewish Christian Exegesis," *Neot* 42 (2008): 223-52 (226-28), and John Clabeaux, "Purity Regulations in the Didache" (paper presented at the Annual Meeting of the Society of Biblical Literature, San Antonio, TX, 19 November 2006).

41. Klawans, *Impurity and Sin in Ancient Judaism*, 26-31.

42. This rendering is based on the translation of Florentino García Martínez and Eibert J. C. Tigchelaar, *The Dead Sea Scrolls: Study Edition* (Leiden: Brill; Grand Rapids: Eerdmans, 1997), 1:75.

of God's precepts. Conversely, purifying waters are inaccessible to the unrepentant and "perverse" (1QS III, 4–5 and V, 13–14). Admission to the regular ablutions and the subsequent meal was restricted to those who were pure and free of sin.[43] Ritual purification by means of ablutions was not a mechanical process, but was made possible only by God's grace. The purificatory rites were thought to have no effect unless they were accompanied by the appropriate inner disposition.[44] Without repentance and right behavior, immersion was meaningless.

The laws of ritual impurity offered in the Dead Sea Scrolls lend substantial weight to our understanding of the practice in Did. 1–7. We have established earlier that the rendering of the baptismal ceremony in Did. 7 does not reflect a continuous, strong adherence to Jewish halakhot governing ritual purity. We also noticed that in the Qumran scrolls the line between ritual and moral impurity is frequently blurred. The Qumran community members believed that wholehearted repentance combined with deeds of righteousness caused their lustrations to be effective. A similar view may well underlie the presentation of baptism in the Did. 7. Because baptism is not limited here to a mere cultic action but has taken on an ethical shape as a result of being preceded by the original Jewish Two Ways instruction,[45] its precise ritual details become less relevant. What is

---

43. See Lawrence H. Schiffman, *Reclaiming the Dead Sea Scrolls* (Philadelphia: Jewish Publication Society of America, 1994), 102–3. Eyal Regev emphasizes that the basic notion of sin producing impurity was very common in ancient Greek religion as well; see his "Moral Impurity and the Temple in Early Christianity in Light of Ancient Greek Practice and Qumranic Ideology," *HTR* 97 (2004): 383–411 (393–94). For New Testament passages in which the concepts of moral impurity appear to co-exist with those of ritual impurity, see e.g. Klawans, *Impurity and Sin in Ancient Judaism*, 148–56, and Regev, "Moral Impurity and the Temple," 390–92.

44. Klawans, *Impurity and Sin in Ancient Judaism*, passim; "The Impurity of Immorality in Ancient Judaism," *JJS* 48 (1997): 1–16; Jacob Neusner, *The Idea of Purity in Ancient Judaism: The Haskell Lectures 1972–1973*, SJLA (Leiden: Brill, 1973), 78, 87, 119; Regev, "Moral Impurity and the Temple."

45. On the other hand, the Two Ways may well have spread as a result of its being directly or indirectly linked to Christian baptism. The commonalities of perspective with regard to the law in the Gospel of Matthew and the letter of James are probably the result of their sharing a section of the Jewish Two Ways. The Two Ways materials in Matthew and James are linked to a prebaptismal teaching. Alistair Stewart-Sykes recently showed that James's exhortations were meant "as a means of restoring the hearers to their baptismal resolve"; see "Ἀποκύησις λόγῳ ἀληθείας: Paraenesis and Baptism in Matthew, James, and the Didache," in *Matthew, James and Didache: Three*

important is that baptism in Did. 7 carried with it a commitment to right conduct (Did. 1–6). The Didache does articulate an interest in issues relating to ritual impurity, but probably prioritized the maintenance of moral impurity over the preservation of ritual impurity.

2. Holiness

Like the phrase in Did. 9.5, the clauses in 10.6b offer a rubrical comment and reveal a comparable cautioning against contemptible attendance. They constitute a general admonition to the readers of the manual reminding them to repent and be prepared. In Did. 10.6 access to the Eucharist is under discussion again, and this issue is repeated in Did. 14. Just as moral purity prepared the members of the Qumran community for the communal meal, so too did the same type of purity make ready the believers of the Didache community for the Eucharist (Did. 10.6 and Did. 14).

2.1. Holiness in a Moral Sense: Did. 10.6 and Did. 14

Similar to the cautioning of Did. 9.5 is the warning against unworthy attendance in 10.6b:

> If anyone is holy [ἅγιος], let him come.
> If anyone is not, let him repent.

Related Documents in their Jewish and Christian Settings, ed. Huub van de Sandt and Jürgen K. Zangenberg, SBLSymS 45 (Atlanta: Society of Biblical Literature, 2008), 341–59 (347). Compare in addition Wiard Popkes, *Adressaten, Situation und Form des Jakobusbriefes*, SBS 125–126 (Stuttgart: Katholisches Bibelwerk, 1986), 125–56. Also the supposed real-life setting (*Sitz im Leben*) of the Two Ways tradition used by Matthew—that is, the setting of the Two Ways before it was introduced into the present context of the gospel—might have been a catechetical situation, perhaps even an instruction for neophytes; see Georg Braumann, "Zum Traditionsgeschichtlichen Problem der Seligpreisungen MT V 3–12," *NovT* 4 (1960): 253–60 (259–60); Wiard Popkes, "Die Gerechtigkeitstradition im Matthäus-Evangelium," *ZNW* 80 (1989): 1–23 (17). For the Two Ways in the letter of James, compare Huub van de Sandt, "James 4,1–4 in the Light of the Jewish Two Ways Tradition 3,1–6," *Bib* 88 (2007): 38–63, and "Law and Ethics in Matthew's Antitheses and James's Letter: A Reorientation of Halakah in Line with the Jewish Two Ways 3:1–6," in van de Sandt, *Matthew, James and Didache*, 315–38. Furthermore, see Darian R. Lockett, "Structure or Communicative Strategy? The 'Two Ways' Motif in James' Theological Instruction," *Neot* 42 (2008): 269–87.

In an argument analogous to the purity discussion in Did. 14.2–3,[46] the author says that only a "holy" one may participate in the celebration. Those who are called "holy" in 10.6 are probably not those who have been baptized in 9.5. Rather than referring to the neophytes of Did. 9.5, the term ἅγιος ("holy") is likely to denote the experienced members of the community, meaning that not every baptized person is automatically holy.[47] The demand for holiness seems to be an additional condition quite apart from the baptism mentioned in Did. 9.5.[48] It is not ritual purity but moral purity that is involved. The text appeals to those already baptized to come as ἅγιοι to the communal meal.

Didache 14 repeats and substantiates the argument already made in Did. 10.6 about the restrictions concerning access to the Eucharist.[49] If one loses the prerequisite qualification of holiness, one must restore it through repentance. Anyone who neglected to confess their transgressions prior to the Eucharist could not be considered as offering the "pure sacrifice" that the Lord required. The text in Did. 14 does not teach that the Eucharist is a sacrifice (θυσία) but seems to take this idea for granted.[50] It is used as an

---

46. Didache 14 deals with the assemblies on the day of the Lord and requires of the community that they "break bread and give thanks" (κλάσατε ἄρτον καὶ εὐχαριστήσατε), expressions that exactly correspond to the wordings κλάσμα in 9.3–4 and εὐχαριστεῖν in Did. 9.1–3 and 10.1–4. The two expressions appear accordingly to represent a hendiadys, denoting a single rite of "breaking the bread with thanksgiving." Didache 14 therefore refers to the same reality as that described in Did. 9–10.

47. Jonathan A. Draper, "Ritual Process and Ritual Symbol in Didache 7–10," *VC* 54 (2000): 121–58 (141–42).

48. See Rordorf and Tuilier, *Doctrine des douze Apôtres*, 69 n. 2.

49. See also Boris Repschinski, "Purity in Matthew, James and the Didache," in van de Sandt, *Matthew, James and Didache*, 370–95 (394).

50. Another possibility might be that the term θυσία embodies the eucharistic prayers of the community. Rather than being tied to the elements of bread and wine, the term "sacrifice" would be connected to the preceding εὐχαριστήσατε, that is, to the meal prayers recited over the eucharistic elements; see Draper, "Pure Sacrifice," 241; Jonathan Schwiebert, *Knowledge and the Coming Kingdom: The Didache's Meal Ritual and Its Place in Early Christianity*, LNTS 373 (London: T&T Clark, 2008), 166–67; Matthias Klinghardt, *Gemeinschaftsmahl und Mahlgemeinschaft: Soziologie und Liturgie frühchristlicher Mahlfeiern*, TANZ 13 (Tübingen: Francke Verlag, 1996), 403–4, 479; Niederwimmer, *Didache*, 197 and n. 23; Rordorf and Tuilier, *Doctrine des douze Apôtres*, 70–71; Wengst, *Didache (Apostellehre)*, 54–55.

This theory is unconvincing, however. It would mean that only the eucharistic prayers would bear the character of a sacrifice. Nevertheless, the text of Did. 14 seems

argument for maintaining that Christians should participate in this sacrifice only with an unpolluted conscience.

According to Did. 14.1, the confession purifies those participating in the Eucharist and constitutes the precondition for the ritual purity of the meal. The subsequent verse corroborates this idea by the summons to resolve interpersonal conflicts and to exclude quarrelling brethren "lest your sacrifice be defiled." Fights, quibbles, and controversies within the community are regarded as moral impurities defiling the Eucharist so that fellow Christians in conflict must be excluded from celebration of the Eucharist until they reconcile. The purity required to approach God is not primarily attained through the performance of ablutions or immersions, but has been shifted to a state of moral innocence pertaining to the confession and reconciliation. Finally, this concern is legitimated in Did. 14.3 by "a saying of the Lord." If one loses this condition, purity must be restored through repentance.

After the digression in 15.1–2, naming the qualities and capacities required for the offices of bishops and deacons, the text proceeds in 15.3 to the theme that to a certain extent was already dealt with in 14.1–3:[51] the

---

to assume the idea that the term "sacrifice" implies more than just the prayers formulated in Did. 9–10. Since the essential act of a meal ("break bread and give thanks") is the consumption of food (see also n. 46 above), the eucharistic meal can only be called a sacrifice when the act of eating and the food itself is involved; see Helmut Moll, *Die Lehre von der Eucharistie als Opfer: Eine dogmengeschichtliche Untersuchung vom Neuen Testament bis Irenäus von Lyon*, Theophaneia 26 (Köln: Hanstein, 1975), 115. See also Jonathan Schwiebert, who states: "Typical Greek, Roman and Jewish 'sacrifices' (θυσίαι) involved a meal as the culminating event of the ritual. The animal or item to be sacrificed was variable, from ritual to ritual, but the *meal* tended to be prominent and non-negotiable. Greek even used a separate term for animals or produce 'slaughtered' without a meal involved (σφάγια, typically offered to the chthonic deities). These were not *thysiai*. A proper *thysia* involved a meal, preceded by a ritual (i.e., sacrifice) that dedicated the food to the god(s)"; see *Knowledge and the Coming Kingdom*, 167. See in addition, Georg Schöllgen, "The Didache as a Church Order: An Examination of the Purpose for the Composition of the Didache and Its Consequences for Its Interpretation," in Draper, *The Didache in Modern Research*, 43–71 (59); Robert J. Daly, *Christian Sacrifice: The Judaeo-Christian Background before Origen*, CUASCA 18 (Washington, DC: Catholic University of America Press, 1978), 312–13, 502–3. Consult also Alistair C. Stewart, "Didache 14: Eucharistic?" QL 93 (2012) 3–16, who however sees Did. 14 as referring to an agape meal.

51. See the quotation in Pseudo-Cyprian with a reference to the Doctrinae apostolorum (Teachings of the Apostles) that combines Did. 14.2 and 15.3 in chapter 4

correctio fraterna, implying a friendly confrontation of someone with the error s/he has committed:[52]

> Correct one another not in anger but in peace, as you have it [written] in the gospel; and let no one speak to anyone who wrongs another—let him not hear [a word] from you[53]—until he has repented.

If the errant brother or sister, despite this correction, persists in sin, the members of the community are prohibited to further relate to them until the moment of repentance (15.3).

The passages in 9.5 and 10.6b tell us plainly that the absence of ritual (9.5) as well as moral (10.6) impurities are essential conditions for the celebration at the table of the Lord. In 10.6 the purity of the Eucharist is not mentioned, although purity concerns would seem to be at the back of the argument here as well. Not only ritual purity was a prerequisite for partaking in the ceremony of eating sacred food within the Didache community but so was holiness, that is, repentance and reconciliation.

2.2. Moral Holiness and Special Food in Its Jewish Setting

The Dead Sea Scrolls, and the Rule of the Community (1QS) in particular, provide us with the most appropriate context for our passage in Did. 10.6 and 14.1-3 as they detail a rigorous concern for the purity of the food. In the Rule of the Community, sinful outsiders were taken to be ritually defiling (1QS V, 13-15). The idea that the deeds and the body of the outsider are impure is found in 1QS III, 4-6, where we find that an unrepentant outsider can never attain ritual purity. Even novices to the community

---

of his *De Aleatoribus* ("About Dice-players"). Compare also Jean-Paul Audet, *La Didachè: Instructions des Apôtres*, Ebib (Paris: Gabalda, 1958), 79-81, and Niederwimmer, *Didache*, 9.

52. See also Huub van de Sandt, "Two Windows on a Developing Jewish-Christian Reproof Practice: Matt 18:15-17 and *Did.* 15:3," in van de Sandt, *Matthew and the Didache*, 173-92.

53. Because the shift in subject makes this translation somewhat problematic, the rendering of Stanislas Giet may be correct: "ni de votre part ne lui prête l'oreille," that is, "let no one on your part listen to him;" see *L'énigme de la Didachè*, PFLUS 149 (Paris: Ophrys, 1970), 244. Giet does not take the ἀστοχῶν ("offender") but the μηδείς ("no one"), which is also the subject of λαλείτω ("speak"), to be the subject of ἀκουέτω ("hear"). See Rordorf and Tuilier, *Doctrine des douze Apôtres*, 79 n. 2

who had not yet completed their initiation were not permitted to touch the "purities of (the) many" (1QS V, 13–14; VI, 16–17). They were prohibited from joining others at the communal table or even to touch pure food until a year had passed and their spirit and deeds had been examined (1QS VI, 13–23).[54]

Other passages in the Rule of the Community, however, deny the communal meals specifically to disobedient community members as well. Individuals already belonging to the community who violated community rules were excluded from the table.[55] These include those who knowingly lie about the amount of their personal possessions:

> If one is found among them who lies knowingly about wealth, he shall be excluded from the midst of the pure food of the many [מתוך טהרת רבים] for one year, and be fined one fourth of his bread. (1QS VI, 24–25)

They also included those who have spoken in anger against one of the priests:

> And if he has spoken angrily against one of the priests registered in the book, he shall be punished for one year and excluded, under the sentence of death, from the pure food of the many [מן טהרת רבים]. (1QS VII, 2–3)

A third example concerns those slandering:

> And the man who goes about slandering his fellow shall be excluded from the pure food of the many [מטהרת הרבים] for one year and shall be punished; but the man who goes about slandering the many shall be expelled from them and will never return. (1QS VII, 15–17)

A final illustration probably has a more general drift as it may include all those members of the community who sin, regardless of the nature of their trespasses:

> No man among the men of the community, the covenant of the community, who insolently strays from anyone of the commands shall touch the pure food of the men of holiness [אל יגע בטהרת אנשי הקודש]. (1QS VIII, 16–17; see also lines 22–24)

---

54. Neusner, *Idea of Purity in Ancient Judaism*, 52–53.
55. See Hannah K. Harrington, *The Purity Texts*, CQS 5 (London: T&T Clark, 2004), 23–24.

Participation in the communal meal depended on each community member's level of purity. The ritually defiling force of sin causes those within the community who commit sins to be ritually defiled like the outsiders and excludes them from the community's pure food. In a word, moral failure causes ritual impurity. The unconsecrated foods and drinks (i.e., the food and drinks not related to the cult or the temple) consumed at the communal meal were considered almost as holy as the sacrifices offered in the temple.[56] This meal, ordinary food referred to as "purity" (the טהרה),[57] is shared only by those who are clean (1QS V, 13; VI, 25; VII, 16, 19). It was eaten in a state of purity; that is, all members had to bathe before eating it,[58] because food could be contaminated if a transgressor ate of it. Immersion without repentance was pointless.

The communal meal was thus fundamental to the sectarian concept of purity. This also holds good for the relation between the life of the Didache community and the Eucharist: just as disputes, quarrels, and strife, in short moral impurity, desecrate the "sacrifice," so does the purity of the participating community make it pure. The Jewish requirement of being in a state of ritual and moral purity was still the precondition for partaking in the ceremony of eating holy food within the community of the Didache. Of course, baptism also marks an important step in the process by which an individual is welcomed into a religious group. Rather than becoming a member of the community through the water (as suggested in Did. 7),

---

56. Jodi Magness, *The Archaeology of Qumran and the Dead Sea Scrolls*, SDSSRL (Grand Rapids: Eerdmans, 2002), 119; Yair Furstenberg, "Defilement Penetrating the Body: A New Understanding of Contamination in Mark 7.15," *NTS* 54 (2008): 176–200, esp. 187.

57. For the expression "purities of (the) many," טהרת רבים as referring to the "pure food," that is, the common meal eaten by the full members of Qumran, see Jacob Licht, *The Rule Scroll: A Scroll from the Wilderness of Judaea: 1QS-1QSa-1QSb* (Jerusalem: Bialik Institute, 1965), 294–303 (Hebrew); Lawrence H. Schiffman, *Sectarian Law in the Dead Sea Scrolls: Courts, Testimony and the Penal Code* (Chico, CA: Scholars Press, 1983), 161–68, esp. 162–63. See also Friedrich Avemarie, "'Tohorat ha-Rabbim' and 'Mashqeh ha-Rabbim': Jacob Licht Reconsidered," in *Legal Texts and Legal Issues: Proceedings of the Second Meeting of the International Organization for Qumran Studies, Cambridge 1995*, ed. M. Bernstein, Florentino García Martínez, and J. Kampen, STDJ 23 (Leiden: Brill, 1997), 215–29; Harrington, *Purity Texts*, 23–25; and Russell C. D. Arnold, *The Social Role of Liturgy in the Religion of the Qumran Community*, STDJ 60 (Leiden: Brill, 2006), 90–92.

58. See n. 14 above.

however, it is not initiation as such that has priority in the Didache's baptism but the ritual of the eucharistic meal.⁵⁹

3. Concluding Remarks

The ritual of baptism in the Didache is framed between the Two Ways (Did. 1–6) and the Eucharist (Did. 9–10). This has consequences for its meaning and function. The practice of baptism includes primarily a strong commitment to right conduct (Did. 1–6) in which, not so much the initiation of the individual into the community predominates (Did. 7.1c–3a), but rather the preparation for the community's holy food. In Did. 9.5 the nonbaptized, the gentiles, were prohibited from taking part in the Eucharist, "since the Lord has said, 'Do not give to dogs what is holy.'" In light of the Qumran sources, it is reasonable to assume that it is not only the nonbaptized in general who are excluded from participation in the Eucharist but also the catechumens,⁶⁰ that is, those candidates for community membership being in the process of receiving instructions before baptism.

---

59. It corroborates the assumption that the baptismal ritual is likely to have taken place on the same day (Sunday? see Did. 14) immediately before the sacred meal. Evidence in Christian communities supporting this supposition is found in Justin Martyr, *Apol.* 1.65–66. Hans-Ulrich Weidemann believes this Eucharist to be a "*Taufeucharistie*" at variance with the "Sonntagseucharistie": "Justins Schilderung der Taufeucharistie macht deutlich, dass die Initiation eines zu Glauben Gekommenen auf die eucharistische Gemeinschaft mit der ganzen Gemeinde hinzielt und in ihr ihre Vollendung findet. Daher schildert Justin auch anlässlich der *Taufeucharistie* den entscheidenden Vollzug und das Verständnis der Eucharistie (Kap. 66), und nicht anlässlich der Sonntagseucharistie;" see Weidemann's, "Taufe und Taufeucharistie: Die postbaptismale Mahlgemeinschaft in Quellen des 2. und 3. Jahrhunderts," in *Ablution, Initiation, and Baptism: Late Antiquity, Early Judaism, and Early Christianity*, ed. David Hellholm et al., BZNW 176 (Berlin: de Gruyter, 2011), 2:1483–1530 (1486–87). In addition to the testimony of Justin, other evidence is found in the Apostolic Tradition 21, where initiation is followed by "prayers of the faithful" (25), the "kiss of peace" (26), and the Eucharist (28–37); see Paul Bradshaw, Maxwell E. Johnson, and L. Edward Phillips, *The Apostolic Tradition: A Commentary*, Hermeneia (Minneapolis: Fortress, 2002), 120–22. Compare also Draper, "Ritual Process and Ritual Symbol," 127–28; Willy Rordorf, *Der Sonntag: Geschichte des Ruhe- und Gottesdiensttages im ältesten Christentum*, ATANT 43 (Zürich: Zwingli-Verlag, 1962), 257–68; Milavec, *Didache: Faith, Hope, and Life*, 239.

60. See above. Interesting in this case is also the observation "Catecuminus in cena dominica non concumbat" in the Latin collection of the Apostolic Tradition

At Qumran, one's impure status was by no means permanent and by performing certain purification rituals involving immersion in water the individual could become pure over and over again. The Didache, however, appears to be referring to baptism as a one-time event and not a repeated rite. On account of the choice for the way of life and the rejection of the way of death tied to the baptismal ritual, a radical restraint from evil expressed in a once-for-all baptism was required. After baptism, the Didache community members were supposed not to lapse back into immoral acts again.

The separation of the sinner from the Didache community in Did. 15.3 is probably best understood in light of the respect for and careful handling of pure food. Food could be contaminated if a sinner ate from it. In the Didache pure food must be kept from falling into the hands of those who are impure, either because they are gentiles and not baptized or because they are impenitent sinners from within the community. Impurity was the biggest threat to the group's holiness and hence to its access to God. The exclusion in Did. 15.3 might thus have functioned less as a punishment of the sinner than as a means of preserving the purity of the community. The imposed separation of the sinner from the Didache community in 15.3 reflects the community's rigorous concern for the admission procedure in Did. 9.5. In the respective cases, exclusion of the offender and the nonbaptized from the community ensures that they will not spread their defilement. In this context it is important to note that the regulations in the third section of the Didache (11–15) discuss questions of internal community life and comprise guidelines for good order and church discipline. Not only the presence of a gentile outsider (Did. 9.5 and Did. 7) but also a backsliding insider (Did. 10.6 and Did. 14) pollutes the holy food.

The warning to practice table fellowship with those baptized only (9.5) and to become holy (10.6) shows new boundaries being drawn between "in" and "out." Like the Rule of the Community, the Didache strongly associates participation in the community's food with membership of the community. In Did. 9.5 "what is holy" probably refers to sacrificial food and the very term "sacrifice" in Did. 14 is used to describe ordinary food as special. Because contagion of "what was holy" is not allowed, not only are unclean

---

27.1; compare Bradshaw, Johnson, and Phillips, *Apostolic Tradition*, 144; for the Latin text, see Wilhelm Geerlings in Georg Schöllgen and Wilhelm Geerlings, eds., *Didache: Zwölf-Apostle-Lehre; Traditio Apostolica: Apostolische Überlieferung*, FC 1 (Freiburg im Breisgau: Herder, 1991), 280.

outsiders to be excluded, but also insiders who have not properly repented and become reconciled with their brothers or sisters. Exclusion from the meal simply means exclusion from the community, and full membership is achieved when the candidate is allowed to share in the food. The intense communion meal strengthened the group's self-awareness. Like other early Christian communities—and unlike, for example, the Pharisees who ate most of their meals at home—the Didache group gathered for communal meals and made them the climax of their group life.

The Lord's Prayer (Didache 8) at the Faultline of Judaism and Christianity

Peter J. Tomson

By its wording and form, the prayer Jesus taught his disciples is a typically Jewish prayer well comparable to the category of "short prayers" cited in rabbinic literature. Both Jews and Christians, however, would readily define it as the central prayer typical of Christianity. This seeming contradiction is not coincidental. The following paper studies the versions of the Lord's Prayer preserved in the Didache and the Gospels in their respective literary and historical contexts and in comparison with rabbinic traditions, all from a redaction-critical perspective. The analysis involves recent discussion of the development of organized early Jewish prayer. The conclusion will be that from being one among many Jewish prayers, the Lord's Prayer became a Christian boundary marker at the rupture that occurred between Jews and Christians under Trajan and Hadrian and that the institution of the rabbinic daily prayer of Eighteen Benedictions played a crucial role in this development. A range of conclusions follow for the relationship of Jews and Christians.

1. Three Versions

Since antiquity, the Lord's Prayer was known as preserved in two versions: the well-known Matthean version canonized in Christian liturgy and the barely known shorter one in Luke. Its occurrence in the Didache was discovered in the nineteenth century and has been studied mainly by scholars. It has the potential to revolutionize our understanding of how this ancient Jewish prayer could evolve into a kernel of Christian liturgy.[1]

---

1. For the Didache and its Jewish background, see esp. Huub van de Sandt and

The versions of the prayer in Matthew and the Didache are almost identical and can practically be treated as one. They constitute the major point of resemblance between the closely related documents of Matthew and the Didache.[2] The context in both documents is also similar, but it contains characteristic differences. In particular, the Didache context features some details of singular historical significance. Luke, in double contrast, not only brings the prayer in a shorter and actually quite different version, but also in a distinctly different context. In fact the unique historical importance of the Lukan version in its particular context is brought out best when compared both with the Didache and with Matthew.

For understanding the genesis of the prayer and its subsequent history, it is important to study both the three versions and their respective contexts in a historical perspective. We begin by reviewing them in synopsis.[3]

David Flusser, *The Didache: Its Jewish Sources and Its Place in Early Judaism and Christianity*, CRINT 3.5 (Assen: Van Gorcum, 2002); also Marcello Del Verme, *Didache and Judaism: Jewish Roots of an Ancient Christian-Jewish Work* (London: T&T Clark, 2004). See further Jean-Paul Audet, *La Didachè: Instructions des Apôtres*, Ebib (Paris: Gabalda, 1958); Willy Rordorf and André Tuilier, *La doctrine des douze Apôtres (Didachè)*, SC 248 bis (Paris: Cerf, 1978); Klaus Wengst, *Didache (Apostellehre), Barnabasbrief, Zweiter Klemensbrief, Schrift an Diognet*, SU 2 (Darmstadt: Wissenschaftliche Buchgesellschaft, 1984); Kurt Niederwimmer, *Die Didache: A Commentary*, KAV 1 (Göttingen: Vandenhoeck & Ruprecht, 1993); Jonathan A. Draper, ed., *The Didache in Modern Research*, AGJU 37 (Leiden: Brill, 1996). See also next footnote.

2. For studies on Matthew and the Didache see Huub van de Sandt, ed., *Matthew and the Didache: Two Documents from the Same Jewish-Christian Milieu?* (Assen: Van Gorcum, 2005). See also Peter J. Tomson, "The Halakhic Evidence of *Didache* 8 and Matthew 6 and the *Didache* Community's Relationship to Judaism," in van de Sandt, *Matthew and the Didache*, 131–41. For studies on Matthew, the Didache, and James, see Huub van de Sandt and Jürgen Zangenberg, eds., *Matthew, James and Didache: Three Related Documents in Their Jewish and Christian Settings*, SBLSymS 45 (Atlanta: Society of Biblical Literature, 2008).

3. From the extensive literature on the Gospels, I shall mainly refer to the superb commentaries of Ulrich Luz, *Das Evangelium nach Matthäus*, 5th ed., vol. 1, EKKNT 1 (Zürich: Benzinger; Neukirchen: Neukirchener, 2002); and Joseph Fitzmyer, *The Gospel according to Luke*, AB 28–28A (Garden City, NY: Doubleday, 1981–1985). In what follows, the translation of the Lukan and Matthaean versions largely follows NRSV; the Didache version is my own translation assimilated to NRSV's Matthew.

Luke 11:1-5	Matt 6:1-18	Did. 8.1-2
He was praying in a certain place, and after he had finished, one of his disciples said to him, Lord, teach us to pray, as John taught his disciples. He said to them:	Beware of practicing your piety before others.... So whenever you give alms, do not sound a trumpet before you, as the hypocrites [ὑποκριταί] do in the synagogues and in the streets....	Let your fastings not coincide with that of the hypocrites, for they fast on the second and fifth (weekday), but you should fast on the fourth day and Preparation Day.
	And whenever you pray, do not be like the hypocrites; for they love to stand and pray in the synagogues and at the street corners....	And do not pray as the hypocrites do, but pray as the Lord has commanded in his gospel.
When you pray,	When you are praying, do not heap up empty phrases as the gentiles [ἐθνικοί]ᵃ do....	
say:	Pray then in this way:	Pray in this way:
Father,	*Our Father in heaven* [ἐν τοῖς οὐρανοῖς],ᵇ	*Our Father in heaven* [ἐν τῷ οὐρανῷ],ᵇ
Hallowed be your name.	*Hallowed be your name.*	*Hallowed be your name.*
Your kingdom come [ἐλθάτω].	*Your kingdom come.*ᶜ	*Your kingdom come* [ἐλθέτω].
	Your will be done, on earth as it is in heaven.	
Give us each day our daily bread [ἐπιούσιον].ᵈ	*Give us this day our daily bread.*	*Give us this day our daily bread.*
And forgive us our sins, for we ourselves forgive [ἀφίεμεν] *everyone indebted to us.*	*And forgive us our debts* [τὰ ὀφειλήματα], *as we also forgive* [ἀφήκαμεν]ᵉ *our debtors.*	*And forgive us our debt* [τὴν ὀφειλήν], *as we also forgive* [ἀφίεμεν] *our debtors.*
And do not bring us to the time of trial.	*And do not bring us to the time of trial, but rescue us from the evil one.*ᶠ	*And do not bring us to the time of trial, but rescue us from the evil one.*

		For yours is the power and the glory in the ages.
And he said to them, Suppose one of you has a friend…. So I say to you, Ask, and it will be given you.	For if you forgive others their trespasses, your heavenly Father will also forgive you….	Three times daily pray in this way.
	And whenever you fast, do not look dismal, like the hypocrites.	

Notes

a. ὑποκριταί: MSS B, etc.

b. Matthew = plural; Didache = singular.

c. Matthew: ἐλθάτω as in Luke (not mentioned in NA27). MSS B, Koine text, etc. and Didache: ἐλθέτω.

d. An inimitable *hapax legomenon*, found in all versions and notoriously difficult to translate.

e. So MSS ℵ, B, etc.; ἀφίεμεν: MSS ¹ℵ, Koine text, etc.; ἀφίομεν: MSS D, W, etc., see also Luke and Didache. ἀφήκαμεν is an aorist not a perfect; it is forced to translate "have forgiven." See the reservations of Luz, *Evangelium nach Matthäus*, 453; *pace* Fitzmyer, *Gospel According to Luke*, 897.

f. The personal "evil one" is one option of the ambiguous Greek (and Semitic), which also allows an impersonal "evil."

2. Comparing Texts

Let us now study the text of the three versions in comparison, in a series of brief comments.

(1) The versions of the Didache and Matthew are identical except for three small grammatical differences (indicated in the notes to the texts).

(2) The Lukan version is remarkably shorter: the sentences about "your will" and "the evil one" are lacking. It seems to be a more authentic version, even if the phrase "forgive us our *sins*" could be a concession to Greek readers who would misunderstand "our debts."[4]

(3) The address in Luke is a mere "Father." Comparison with other gospels shows this more personal address to be typical of Jesus, especially in the Aramaic form אבא (= ἀββα), which was also used in Pauline churches

---

4. See Fitzmyer, *Gospel according to Luke*, 897.

(e.g., Matt 11:25 = Luke 10:21; Matt 26:39, 42; John 11:41; 17:1; see esp. Mark 14:36, ἀββα ὁ πατήρ, and see also Rom 8:16; Gal 4:6). In rabbinic literature, a similar form of address is associated with the ancient Hasidim, holy men and miracle workers. Also, many prayers cited in a later rabbinic work that shows affinity to these Hasidim feature the address אבי שבשמים ("My Father in heaven"). This shows that the address "Father" was rare but not unique in ancient Judaism.⁵

(4) The collective form "*our* Father in heaven" in Matthew and the Didache is equivalent to more normal rabbinic usage, אבינו שבשמים, with Matthean ἐν τοῖς οὐρανοῖς reflecting the Semitic plural "heavens."⁶

(5) The question of the "original" language of Jesus's prayer, though not essential to this inquiry, is hard to decide. With very few Aramaic exceptions, all rabbinic prayers are in Hebrew. It seems certain that Jesus read Hebrew and likely that he spoke it. He could have taught the prayer in either language, for Aramaic אבא/ἀββα is also used in mishnaic Hebrew.⁷

---

5. In m. Ta'an. 3:8, the Hasid "Honi the Circledrawer" in his prayer for rain says the people see him as "an intimate son before you" (כבן בית לפניך), and afterwards he is ironically called "a spoiled son before his father." אבי שבשמים is found in Seder Eliahu Rabba (M. Friedmann, ed., *Seder Eliahu Rabba and Eliahu Zuta and Nispachim le-Seder Eliahu Zuta* [Vienna: 1904; repr., Jerusalem: Wahrmann, 1969], 51), plus another eighteen mentions, against seven of אבינו שבשמים (search CD ROM Bar Ilan Responsa Project). See esp. Shmuel Safrai, "Yeshu veha-tenua he-hasidit," in *The Jews in the Hellenistic-Roman World*, ed. Isaiah M. Gafni, A'haron Oppenheimer, and Daniel R. Schwartz (Jerusalem: The Zalman Shazar Center; The Historical Society of Israel, 1996), 413–36 (417–20). Joachim Jeremias thought the word "Abba" to be unique of Jesus; see his *Die Verkündigung Jesu*, vol. 1 of *Neutestamentliche Theologie* (Gütersloh: Gütersloher Verlagshaus, 1973), 67–73; see the reply by James Barr, "Abbā Isn't 'Daddy,'" *JTS* 39 (1988): 28–47. See also Fitzmyer, *Gospel according to Luke*, 902–3, and differently Luz, *Evangelium nach Matthäus*, 442. See Elke Tönges, *Unser Vater im Himmel: Die Bezeichnung Gottes als Vater in der tannaitischen Literatur*, BWANT 8/7 (Stuttgart: Kohlhammer, 2003), 12–23, survey of scholarship; 257–62, remarks on New Testament usage.

6. Πατὴρ ... ἐν τοῖς οὐρανοῖς: thirteen times in Matthew, once in Mark 11:25; ὁ πατήρ ... ὁ οὐράνιος: seven times in Matthew; see BDR 141.4. אבינו/אביהם שבשמים: three times in the Mishnah, once in the Tosefta, six times in halakic midrashim. See Luz, *Evangelium nach Matthäus*, 444.

7. Edward Yechezkel Kutscher, *Words and Their History* (Jerusalem: Kiryath-Sepher, 1974), 1–2 (Hebrew); Barr, "Abba Isn't 'Daddy.'" See differently Luz, *Evangelium nach Matthäus*, 437–38; Fitzmyer, *Gospel according to Luke*, 900–901 with an Aramaic reconstruction of the Lukan version; as also in Jeremias, *Verkündigung Jesu*, 191.

(6) The two-membered doxology in the Didache differs from the doxology that became habitual in Christian liturgy. A doxology is lacking in Luke and in the major manuscripts of Matthew;[8] in the other manuscripts of Matthew, it appears in widely divergent versions. This reflects the infinite variety of an *ad libitum* conclusion.

(7) Patristic writings and New Testament manuscripts show that the version of Matthew and the Didache quickly became dominant.[9] Even Origen, one of the few church fathers to pay attention to the Lukan version,[10] in his commentary on the prayer switches to the Matthean version as soon as possible.

(8) Origen interestingly comments that it concerns two different prayer versions that Jesus taught in specific circumstances: a personal version intended for the disciple who asked the question about Jesus's prayer, as in Luke, and a community prayer taught by Jesus to his disciples gathered on top of the mountain, as in Matthew (Origen, *Or.* 18).[11] Origen does not elaborate, however, on literary and historical features typifying the Gospels of Matthew and Luke.

(9) A singular, isolated verse in Mark makes it likely that a primitive form of the Matthean version or a part of it found early acceptance: "Whenever you stand praying, forgive, if you have anything against anyone; so that your Father in heaven may also forgive you your trespasses" (Mark 11:25). Significantly, the phrase "stand praying" (στήκετε προσευχόμενοι) is elsewhere used only in Matthew, of the Pharisees (Matt 6:5, ἑστῶτες προσεύχεσθαι), and it also agrees with rabbinic usage (e.g., m. Ber. 5:1).[12] Likewise the phrase "Father in heaven" surprises, as otherwise it is special to Matthew and rabbinic literature.[13] Furthermore, there is a striking similarity in content with the passage about forgiveness in Matt 6:12–15. These

---

8. MSS ℵ, B, D, etc.

9. See Kenneth W. Stevenson, *The Lord's Prayer: A Text in Tradition* (Londen: SCM, 2004), 28: "Nothing is known of any liturgical use of the Lucan version in antiquity."

10. Another example (with more "Matthean prejudice" than Origen) is Cyril, *Cat. Luc.*, see PG 72.685, 688, 692.

11. See Luz, *Evangelium nach Matthäus*, 436 n. 15.

12. See Herman L. Strack and Paul Billerbeck, *Kommentar zum Neuen Testament aus Talmud und Midrasch* (Munich: Beck, 1922–1974), 2:28. See also the name Amidah for the Jewish main prayer below. Interestingly Origen, *Or.* 31 finds the upright *orans* attitude most fitting for prayer.

13. See n. 6 above.

three elements give the verse in Mark an authentic character and seem to betray knowledge of the Lord's Prayer in a primitive form related to the one in Matthew and the Didache.[14]

(10) Nothing in the two versions of the Lord's Prayer defines it as a Christian text. This becomes abundantly clear from the contrast with the Trinitarian doxology found in one of the manuscripts.[15] By form and vocabulary, the Lord's Prayer is altogether Jewish.[16]

3. Comparing Contexts

We shall now compare the three contexts, paying ample attention (*pace* Origen in his day) to literary specifics in a perspective of historical development, or in other words, in a redaction-critical approach. In doing so the similarities between Matthew and the Didache will strike us all the more, especially as contrasted with the very different situation in Luke.

The Lukan context has two remarkable features: there is a narrative introduction, and in it, there is no polemics. The introduction narrates how Jesus himself had been praying and, when asked by one of his disciples, he taught him the prayer text. Jesus's own prayer practice does appear in other gospels (Mark 1:35; 6:46; Matt 14:23), but it is especially conspicuous in Luke (Luke 5:16; 6:12; 9:12, 28). Furthermore, the prayer Jesus teaches is not contrasted with that of others. On the contrary, the disciple asks Jesus to teach them to pray "as John taught his disciples." This is typical of Luke, whose narrative displays a recurring dynamic of communication, confrontation, and renewed communication between Jesus and the Pharisees.[17] In Acts, the other Lukan text, we find specific differences in the attitude of the Pharisees and of the Sadducees toward Jesus's disciples. Luke's distinct characterization of both groups is confirmed by Josephus's descriptions.[18] Seen in that light, it is significant that Luke juxtaposes the

---

14. Similarly Luz, *Evangelium nach Matthäus*, 436 n. 11.
15. MS 1253.
16. Extensive material in Strack and Billerbeck, *Kommentar*. See also the summary by Luz, *Evangelium nach Matthäus*, 455–57.
17. See Peter J. Tomson, *"If This Be from Heaven": Jesus and the New Testament Authors in Their Relationship to Judaism*, trans. Janet Dyk, BS 76 (Sheffield: Sheffield Academic, 2001), ch. 5.
18. See Steve Mason, "Chief Priests, Sadducees, Pharisees and Sanhedrin in Acts," in *The Book of Acts in its Palestinian Setting*, vol .4 of *The Book of Acts in Its First Century Setting*, ed. Richard Bauckham (Grand Rapids: Eerdmans; Carlisle: Paternos-

prayer of Jesus with that of John the Baptist. Implicitly, it is also put on a par with the prayer of other Jewish teachers.

Both in the Didache and Matthew, we find a demarcation over against the "hypocrites," though this has a different place in both documents. In the Didache the phrase is used only in chapter 8, a remarkable chapter also in other respects. The Didache, an ancient text highly respected in the early church, gives rules for Christian liturgy and community life, on the whole serenely and without polemics. Didache 8, however, not only features this exceptional polemical demarcation, but also differs by form and content. First, unlike Did. 7.1 and 9.1, which each start a new subject, Did. 8.1 does not begin with the transition formula περὶ δέ ("now about"). Second, Did. 8.1 is about weekly fast days, which is a sidetrack in relation to 7.4, which mentions fasting before baptism. Hence Did. 8, with its double feature of fasting and praying unlike the "hypocrites," seems to reflect a later stage of redaction.

Two elements in Did. 8 merit further study in comparison with Jewish sources: the specific fast days and the prayer thrice daily. The restriction of communal and personal fast days to Mondays and Thursdays is the explicit object of rabbinic rulings (m. Ta'an. 1:6; 2:9; 3:1; see also m. Meg. 1:3; 3:6; 4:1; Epiphanius, *Pan.* 1.16).[19] It follows that the Didache's "hypocrites" are rabbis, or their predecessors, Pharisees. While contesting the ruling of the "hypocrites," the Didache's own preference for Wednesdays and Fridays as fast days accords with the alternative calendar current in ancient Judaism that was first identified in the book of Jubilees (6:23–38) and is reflected also in a number of Qumran writings.[20] Hence, this should not be read as expressing an anti-Jewish motivation but rather an *alternative Jewish tradition*. The Didache's type of Christianity seems rooted in a non-Pharisaic strand of ancient Judaism.

---

ter, 1995), 115–77; Peter J. Tomson, "Gamaliel's Counsel and the Apologetic Strategy of Luke-Acts," in *The Unity of Luke-Acts*, ed. Joseph Verheyden, BETL 142 (Leuven: Leuven University Press; Peeters, 1999), 585–604.

19. The Didache appears to be the earliest written source for this piece of information.

20. See Annie Jaubert, *La date de la Cène: Calendrier biblique et liturgie chrétienne* (Paris: Gabalda, 1957); James C. VanderKam, *Calendars in the Dead Sea Scrolls: Measuring Time* (London: Routledge, 1998). See now Stéphane Saulnier, *Calendrical Variations in Second Temple Judaism: New Perspectives on the "Date of the Last Supper" Debate*, JSJSup 159 (Leiden: Brill, 2012).

The custom of praying three times a day is already mentioned in the Old Testament (Dan 6:11; Ps 55:18) and is self-understood in early rabbinic tradition (m. Ber. 4:1; t. Ber. 3:1–3), where the three times of prayer are taken to coincide with the times of the daily sacrifices in the temple. Therefore this represents a point of departure shared by the Didache authors with the Pharisees and rabbis. The Didache's protest concerns *the particular prayer* to be said thrice daily: not that of the "hypocrites," but the Lord's Prayer.

We observed that the expression "hypocrites" found twice in Did. 8 is not otherwise used in the Didache. By contrast, it is typical of Matthew, especially in the polemical phrase, "Woe to you, scribes and Pharisees, hypocrites" (Matt 23:13, 15, 23, 25, 27, 29).[21] As compared with the other gospels and the Didache, Matthew is dominated by polemics with the Pharisees.[22] This is most remarkable in the two large characteristic sections seemingly interpolated in the basic order of Mark otherwise followed in Matthew: the Sermon on the Mount and the discourse against "scribes and Pharisees." Both discourses, located in the opening and closing parts of the gospel's main body (Matt 5–7 and 23), depict Jesus's teaching in sharp distinction from the Pharisees.

Two elements from the anti-Pharisaic polemics of these sections are relevant here. In the first place, this concerns the threefold demarcation over against religious practice of the "hypocrites" in Matt 6:1–18. Almsgiving, praying, and fasting should not be done in public but "in secret" (ἐν τῷ κρυπτῷ). It is plausible that this emphasis accords with the tradition of Jesus.[23] Some literary analysis is apposite. The three items of almsgiving, praying, and fasting are phrased in a uniform style with recurring expressions. In this framework the section with the Lord's Prayer stands off by style and content (Matt 6:7–15).[24] Moreover its first two verses (6:7–8) are set off against "the gentiles" (ἐθνικοί), which is another contrast with the threefold framework and its polemics against the "hypocrites"

---

21. ὑποκριτής appears another seven times in Matthew and furthermore in Mark 7:6 and Luke 6:42; 12:56; and 13:15.

22. See Tomson, *"If This Be from Heaven,"* 267–76.

23. Luz, *Evangelium nach Matthäus*, 420–21. The phrase is used also in Rom 2:29, and there may well represent an adaptation of Jesus tradition to the specific rhetorical purpose of Romans.

24. See the similarities in content between Matt 6:14–15 and Mark 11:25.

(ὑποκριταί).²⁵ It follows that an editor has inserted verses 7–15 at some stage of the gospel's history.²⁶ While his aim seems to have been to oppose the religious practice of the Pharisees, he left the antigentile orientation of 6:7 in place, with the neglect of coherence characteristic of gospel redactors. Taken as a whole, the similarity in content and terminology of Matt 6:1–18 with Did. 8 is striking.

The other element of anti-Pharisaic polemics consists in the prohibition ascribed to Jesus not to have oneself called "rabbi," as is done by the scribes and Pharisees: "for you have one teacher." Nor should one be called "father" or "instructor": "for you have one Father, the heavenly one" (ὁ οὐράνιος) and "one instructor, the Messiah" (Matt 23:7–10). Again the phrase "heavenly Father" is typical of Matthew. Furthermore, the mention of the "Messiah" (χριστός) definitely signals a late redactional stage. The same appears from the selective use of "rabbi" in Matthew as compared with other gospels. In Mark and John, both Jesus and the Baptist are innocently called "rabbi" or "rabbouni."²⁷ Luke avoids the Hebrew rabbi altogether and replaces it with the very Greek ἐπιστάτα ("master"; Luke 5:5; 8:24 [twice]; 9:33 [cf. Mark 9:5]; 9:49; 17:13). But Matthew, characteristically, replaces rabbi with "Lord" when Peter is speaking (Matt 17:4, cf. Mark 9:5)—incidentally, a title curiously uncriticized in Matt 23:7–10—but leaves it in place twice when it concerns "Judas who betrayed him" (Matt 26:25, 49). Hence "rabbi" is used in Matthew, but only by Jesus's enemies, Judas and the Pharisees. It follows that in the extant late redactional stage, the Gospel turns against the title of "rabbi" used by the Pharisees, since it is perceived as a new extraneous phenomenon. Seen in a larger perspective, this corresponds with the consistent use in rabbinic literature of "rabbi" as a formalized title for teachers working *after the destruction of the temple*. It seems Matthew is confronted with the novel phenomenon of "rabbinic" Judaism, and by implication, the same is true of the Didache.²⁸

---

25. For ἐθνικοί, see also Matt 5:47 and 18:17. See also the "correction" ὑποκριταί in Matt 6:7 in MS B, etc.

26. For the whole passage see Luz, *Evangelium nach Matthäus*, 418–21.

27. ῥαββί: the Baptist: John 1:38; 3:26; Jesus: Mark 9:5; 11:21; 14:45; John 1:49; 3:2; 4:31; 6:25; 9:2; 11:8. ῥαββουνί: Jesus: Mark 10:51; John 20:16.

28. The argument is more developed in Peter J. Tomson, "The Didache, Matthew, and Barnabas as Sources for Jewish and Christian History," in *Jews and Christians in the First and Second Centuries: How to Write Their History*, ed. Peter J. Tomson and Joshua Schwartz, CRINT 13 (Leiden: Brill, 204), 348–82.

This will do for an analysis of the early Christian sources about the Lord's Prayer. We now turn to the rabbinic sources about early Jewish prayer. This is a strange maneuver only as long as we presume that Jesus's prayer was conceived and transmitted in a different world than that of other Jews. If we accept Jesus was a Jew, we must study his prayer as part of multiform ancient Jewish prayer.

4. The Development of Early Jewish Prayer

The beginnings of organized Jewish prayer are difficult to assess. The main sources here are in rabbinic literature, a body of more or less loosely edited collections of disparate traditions originally transmitted orally, hard to date and evaluate historically. Recent decades have seen renewed discussion on the origins of ancient Jewish prayer. We are especially interested in the rabbinic main prayer designated the "Eighteen Benedictions" in view of its content (although in actual practice, derived from Babylonian Jewry, it has nineteen). In Hebrew it is also referred to as Tefillah ("the Prayer") or Amidah ("the Standing"), a name strikingly reminiscent of the singular verse in Mark 11:25 reviewed above.

For a long time the view of Ismar Elbogen, originally published in 1913, has been dominant.[29] Elbogen concluded that, although the Eighteen Benedictions was established in its actual form by Gamaliel the Younger by the end of the first century CE, its origins were much more ancient.[30] Gamaliel's contribution must have consisted only in providing the "arrangement" of the eighteen benedictions, which each had their own longer or shorter prehistory. In one case he found a direct motive in contemporaneous events: the Birkat Haminim (or "Benediction about the Heretics") by which he meant to separate Christians from Judaism.[31] Both elements of Elbogen's theory (the gradual growth of the Eighteen Benedictions and Gamaliel's authorship of the "Benediction about the Heretics") have drawn criticism more recently. We deal with the former first.

---

29. Ismar Elbogen, *Der jüdische Gottesdienst in seiner geschichtlichen Entwicklung* (1913; repr. Hildesheim: Olms, 1962), esp. 27–41. Elbogen's theory was further refined by Joseph Heinemann, *Prayer in the Talmud: Forms and Patterns*, SJ 9 (Berlin: de Gruyter, 1977). See also Gedalyahu Alon, *The Jews in Their Land in the Talmudic Age* (Jerusalem: Magnes, 1980–1984), 1:266–72.

30. Elbogen, *Jüdische Gottesdienst*, 30.

31. Ibid., 36.

In large part basing himself on nonrabbinic sources, Ezra Fleischer, in a long article published in 1989, set out to destroy the foundation of Elbogen's theory. His point of departure was that nowhere in the pre-70 sources do we find evidence of a statutory daily prayer. The synagogue was an "assembly" for scripture reading and teaching, not praying.[32] Prayers were said on an individual basis, at any place but preferably in the temple, as also seen among Jesus's disciples (Acts 2:44; 3:1). Jesus was opposed to praying in public places (Matt 6:5-6) and liked to pray "in a deserted place" or "on a mountain."[33] Only the Qumran scrolls mention fixed daily community prayers, and the reason why is revealing. The sectarians denied the validity of the temple service in Jerusalem and formed a "human sanctuary," replacing the sacrificial cult with their "spiritual" worship service. The institution of obligatory daily prayer by Gamaliel the Younger was an analogous maneuver, necessitated by the destruction of the temple and the loss of its daily service as the frame of reference for the liturgy.

Fleischer's thesis found basic support but was criticized for its schematic approach.[34] Certainly the daily temple service was the referential center for Jewish prayers, and its discontinuation occasioned many innovations. In addition, however, the sources indicate that already before the destruction many kinds of communal and personal prayers were said outside the temple on the Sabbath, festivals, and fast days, as also basic forms of daily prayer. So much appears from discussions about pertinent details

---

32. Ezra Fleischer, "On the Beginnings of Obligatory Jewish Prayer" (1990), in *Statutory Jewish Prayers*, ed. Shulamit Elizur and Tova Beeri (Jerusalem: Magnes, 2012), 1:3–47 (Hebrew).

33. See Luz, *Evangelium nach Matthäus*, 37, and see n. 31 above. A desire for intimate devotion is felt in the "cleansing of the temple" with the argument that it must be "a house of prayer for all the nations": Mark 11:17; Matt 21:13.

34. Stefan C. Reif, "The Development of Ancient Jewish Prayer," *Tarbiz* 60 (1990–1991): 677–81 (Hebrew); see also Stefan C. Reif, *Judaism and Hebrew Prayer: New Perspectives on Jewish Liturgical History*. (Cambridge: Cambridge University Press, 1995), 84, 90, 353–54; M. Z. Fuchs, "Teshuvot li-shenei mehapkhanim," *Sinai* 114 (1994–1995): 162–70; R. Langer, "Revisiting Early Rabbinic Liturgy: The Recent Contributions of Ezra Fleischer," *Prooftexts* 19 (1999): 179–94. Fleischer published a response to Reif, which was republished in Fleischer, *Statutory Jewish Prayers*, 49–54, along with an answer to Langer in the same volume, 55–58. Reuven Kimelman, "Rabbinic Prayer in Late Antiquity," in *The Late Roman-Rabbinic Period*, vol. 4 of *The Cambridge History of Judaism*, ed. Steven Katz (Cambridge: Cambridge University Press, 2006), 573–611, basically describes the Amoraic period and takes no position on this issue.

between the schools of Shammai and Hillel, which by and large predate the destruction of the temple. By consequence, Gamaliel's intervention cannot have been a complete innovation (t. Roš Haš. 2:17; Ber. 3:12).[35] The evasive nature of the rabbinic sources makes it difficult to decide here and to determine exactly what happened. A safe conclusion seems that Gamaliel's measure consisted in prescribing a personal and communal daily prayer consisting of (about) eighteen benedictions and that basic elements of these may have been extant already.[36]

We shall study the discussion about the institution of the Eighteen Benedictions in a moment. First it is necessary to pay attention to the genre of "short prayers" mentioned in the course of the dispute. Let us review two related passages, one from the Mishnah, the central rabbinic collection of formulated laws, and the other from the Tosefta:

> Rabbi Yoshua says: "One who is underway at a dangerous place (at the hour of prayer), says a short prayer.[37] (And) he says: 'Save, O Lord, your people[38] Israel. At every passage of crossing let their needs be before you.[39] Blessed are you, Lord, who hears prayers.'" (m. Ber. 4:4)[40]

> *One who is underway at a dangerous place*—with robbers—*(at the hour of prayer), says a short prayer.* What is a short prayer? Rabbi Eliezer says: "Your will be done in heaven above, and grant repose to those who fear

---

35. See Shmuel Safrai, "Gathering in the Synagogues on Festivals, Sabbaths and Weekdays," *BARIS* 499 (1989): 7–15; Shmuel Safrai and Zeev Safrai, *Mishnat Eretz Israel: Tractate Brachot* (Jerusalem: Liphshitz, 2010), 164–76 (Hebrew).

36. See also the important observations by Naomi Cohen, "The Nature of Shim'on Hapekuli's Act," *Tarbiz* 52 (1982–1983): 547–55 (Hebrew); "Ma hideish Shmuel Hakatan ba-virkat ha-minim?" *Sinai* 94 (1984–1985): 57–70.

37. The added phrase עשרה שמנה מעין in MS Kaufmann, otherwise the prime manuscript, does not appear in a number of other important manuscripts and must be rejected as a harmonization with m. Ber. 4:3.

38. שארית is lacking in MS Kaufmann and the Yerushalmi.

39. MS Kaufmann first hand מלפניך צורכיהם העבר הצבור פרשת בכל. Safrai and Safrai, *Mishnat Eretz Israel*, 174–76, agreeing with a study by David Henshke, accept this reading as authentic, פרשת הצבור being equivalent to פורשים מן הצבור ("those who part from the community'"). This renders the meaning "All those parting from the community, let their needs be hidden before you," thus representing a primitive form of the Birkat Haminim.

40. Translations from rabbinic literature here and in the following are mine.

you, and do what is good in your eyes. Blessed be He who hears prayers." (t. Ber. 3:7)

The Tosefta is a companion text to the Mishnah,[41] and we have here a nice example of how it can quote, supplement, and comment on the Mishnah. In this case the Tosefta supplements an alternative example of a "short prayer," more precisely, one delivered by R. Eliezer, the habitual partner in discussion of R. Yoshua. Both rabbis were contemporaries of Gamaliel the Younger, which would date the prayer texts they are attributed with to the later first century CE.

Significantly, Eliezer's "short prayer" shows some striking similarities with the Lord's Prayer in its Matthean form, especially the sentence, "Your will be done on earth as it is in heaven."[42] By its form and size, Yoshua's prayer text is also comparable, and the same goes for other "short prayers" quoted in related sources. Correctly therefore, Jesus's prayer has been recognized as belonging in the category of "short prayers."[43]

This sheds a revealing light on the narrative introduction in Luke 12:1–5, where one of the disciples asks Jesus to teach them a prayer "as also John taught his disciples." The passages from Mishnah and Tosefta just reviewed and the Lukan narrative converge in informing us of the existence of short "model prayers" taught by various Jewish teachers including Jesus.

The phenomenon of "short prayers" did not mean one would always be brief in praying. Variance in length and wording was always understood. It is told of R. Akiva, a younger contemporary of Eliezer and Yoshua, that his

---

41. Abraham Goldberg, "The Tosefta: Companion to the Mishna," in *Oral Tora, Halakha, Mishna, Tosefta, Talmud, External Tractates*, vol. 1 of *The Literature of the Sages*, ed. Shmuel Safrai, CRINT 2.3a, (Assen: Van Gorcum; Philadelphia: Fortress, 1987), 283–98.

42. Interestingly, Eliezer is attributed with other opinions reminiscent of the teachings of Jesus: (1) Torah is more important than subsistence (Jacob Nachum Epstein and Ezra Zion Melamed, eds., *Mekhilta d'Rabbi Šimon b. Jochai* [Jerusalem: Mekize Nirdamim, 1955], 106; in H. S. Horovitz and I. A. Rabin, eds., *Mechilta d'Rabbi Ismael* [Jerusalem: Wahrmann, 1930, repr., 1970], 161, the author is R. Elazar from Modiin); see also Matt 6:25–34; Luke 21:22–32; (2) circumcision overrules Sabbath; t. Šabb. 15:16 and John 7:23; (3) obligations to parents overrule vows; m. Ned. 9:1 and Mark 7:9–13 = Matt 15:3–6; (4) prayer must be personal supplication: see below.

43. Samuel Tobias Lachs, *A Rabbinic Commentary on the New Testament: The Gospels of Matthew, Mark, and Luke* (Hoboken, NJ: Ktav, 1987), 118–19. Other short prayers: t. Ber. 4:4 (8b); b. Ber. 29b, with all traditions put together.

prayer would be short when serving as prayer leader, but extremely long when saying his private prayer (t. Ber. 3:5). By the same token, Luke tells us not only that Jesus taught his disciples a short prayer, but also that by himself he would pray through the night (Luke 6:12).

Indirectly this reveals that Luke does not want to tell us, as Origen thought (*Or.* 2.4–5),[44] that Jesus taught his disciples the type of "spiritual prayers" he said himself. He did not teach them a long, spirit-driven prayer, but a "short prayer" of the type the Baptist and other teachers were known also to have taught, obviously in order to provide their disciples with an example on which to model and develop their own prayers. The Lord's Prayer, much like other "short prayers," was meant as a minimum, a ration for times when words are scarce.

5. The Institution of the Eighteen Benedictions

We now turn to the institution of the Eighteen Benedictions by Gamaliel the Younger as reported in rabbinic literature. He appears here as *Rabban Gamliel*, "Gamliel our Master," the strong leader of a regime of rabbis that resided in Yavneh, a small town West of Jerusalem, one generation after the destruction of the temple. He is attributed with a series of administrative decrees seemingly aimed at lending new structure and coherence to Jewish worship after the demise of the temple ritual.[45] In recent decades the actual power of his regime has become the object of serious doubt.[46] Two elements deserving of more attention in the discussion than is usual are the rabbinic indications (esp. m. 'Ed. 7:7) of the support Gamaliel

---

44. His wish to stress the difference with synagogue prayers is frustrated by the parallel with John the Baptist.

45. Standard summary in Alon, *Jews in Their Land*, 206–87.

46. The evolving work of Jacob Neusner led the way. It is interesting to compare the first edition of his *A Life of Rabban Yohanan ben Zakkai c. 1–80 CE*, StPB 6 (Leiden: Brill, 1962) with the "completely revised edition" of 1970. See also Peter Schäfer, "Die sogenannte Synode von Jabne; Zur Trennung von Juden und Christen im ersten/zweiten Jh. n. Chr." *Judaica* 31 (1975): 54–64, 116–24; Peter Schäfer, *Der Bar Kochba-Aufstand: Studien zum zweiten jüdischen Krieg gegen Rom* (Tübingen: Mohr Siebeck, 1981). More recently, see Seth Schwartz, *Imperialism and Jewish Society, 200 BCE to 640 CE* (Princeton: Princeton University Press, 2001). For discussion, see Peter J. Tomson, "Transformations in Post-70 Judaism: Scholarly Reconstructions and Their Implications for our Perception of Matthew, Didache, and James," in van de Sandt, *Matthew, James and Didache*, 91–121.

might have had from the Roman administration (which some think indicates a relative power base for his regime)[47] and, in this connection, the sympathy that the Rome-based Josephus shows for the "Pharisees" in the later works around 100 CE, that is, the time when Gamaliel is estimated to have risen to power (see Josephus, *Life* 428–429).[48] The present paper is tangentially connected with this discussion and in that respect emphasizes a third element: the import of the evidence contained in early Christian sources.[49] The sources about the Lord's Prayer are a case in point.

Gamaliel's initiative is preserved in the Mishnah. This document is to be seen as a redacted selection from multiple strands of oral tradition, aiming at formulating rabbinic law concerning all domains of life. Its style is characteristically concise and often consists of a listing of opinions. In these a succession of layers representing subsequent generations of teachers is often discernible. The thickest layer is the one corresponding to the generation of Usha, ca. 150 CE, Usha being the rabbinical centre during that period. From a redaction-historical point of view, the question always is what intention the final editor of the Mishnah (according to tradition R. Yehuda the Prince, ca. 200 CE) may have had in arranging (or omitting) the various opinions.[50] We cite the relevant part from the tractate Berakhot, "Benedictions," up till the words of R. Yoshua about "short prayers" we already reviewed:

> (The hour of) morning prayer is till midday; Rabbi Yehuda says, "Till the fourth hour. Afternoon prayer is till evening;" Rabbi Yehuda says, "… Evening prayer has no set time;" Rabbi Yehuda says… (…)

---

47. See Alon, *Jews in Their Land*, 119–31; Shmuel Safrai, "Bikkureihem shel hakhamei Yavne be-Roma," in *In Times of Temple and Mishnah*, ed. Shmuel Safrai (Jerusalem: Magnes, 1996), 365–81. There are serious doubts about this interpretation, however.

48. For this argument, see Shaye J. D. Cohen, "The Significance of Yavneh: Pharisees, Rabbis, and the End of Jewish Sectarianism," in *The Significance of Yavneh and Other Essays in Jewish Hellenism*, TSAJ 136 (Tübingen, Mohr Siebeck, 2010), 44–70, 55.

49. See the forthcoming article mentioned above n. 23. The point was made in relation to the Birkat Haminim by William Horbury, see below n. 60.

50. For this analytical method, see Goldberg, "Tosefta," 211–44. For discussion of the material, see G. Stemberger, *Einleitung in Talmud und Midrasch*, 8th ed. (Munich: Beck, 1992), 113–52; see 47–54 on oral transmission.

> Rabbi Nehonya ben Hakana used to say a short prayer when entering and leaving the House of Study. They asked him: "What is the place (sense) of this prayer?" He said to them (…)
> Rabban Gamliel says: "Every day, a person is to say eighteen benedictions."
> Rabbi Yoshua says: "(Only) a summary of the eighteen."
> Rabbi Akiva says: "If the prayer is fluent in his mouth, he prays eighteen, if not, a summary of the eighteen."
> Rabbi Eliezer says: "He who makes his prayer fixed, it is no supplication."
> Rabbi Yoshua says: "One who is underway at a dangerous place (at the hour of prayer), says a short prayer." (m. Ber. 4:1–4)

The introductory sentence gives diverging specifications of the hours of prayer; the repeated mention of R. Yehuda's name ascribes this discussion to his generation, the one of Usha. The principle of three prayers a day itself is not disputed. Hence this represents the consensus of the preceding Yavneh generation of Gamaliel and colleagues. We saw that the principle is also shared by the Didache, presumably around the same time, ca. 100. In the continuation Gamaliel's ruling with ensuing discussion is sandwiched between two passages on "short prayers." A narrative introduction tells of the short prayer said by Nehonya, an older contemporary. Gamaliel's clause seems to be formulated in reaction, lapidarily. It provokes three objections, and finally Yoshua's short prayer follows.

The intention of the final editor with this seemingly undecided discussion may be read from the disposition of opinions.[51] Eliezer rejects the ruling on principle. He is against the whole idea of a form of prayer fixed for all: prayer needs to be personal ("his prayer"), and it must be "supplication" and include variation. Incidentally, this emphasis brings him close to what is told of Jesus (see Matt 6:6; Mark 11:22–24; Luke 18:1).[52] His opinion, however, is preceded by the ones of Yoshua and Akiva. Yoshua objects to the rule prescribing eighteen benedictions three times daily for all: he wants to go no further than a "summary," a short prayer inspired by the eighteen. Akiva, the younger contemporary and former disciple of Yoshua and Eliezer, intermediates and adds a conces-

---

51. Fleischer, "Beginnings of Obligatory Jewish Prayer," 426–28 simply supposes Yehuda the Prince reckoned with persisting resistance.

52. See n. 42 above. The same opinion is ascribed to another earlier contemporary, Shimon ben Nataneel, m. Avot 2:13.

sion: when someone's prayer is fluent, the eighteen are to be said, but if not, only a summary. The discussion ends with Yoshua's opinion, already quoted, that in times of distress only a "short prayer" is to be said. This is open to the assumption that, in normal circumstances, the Eighteen Benedictions are the rule.

Thus analyzed, the course of the discussion subtly suggests a gradual softening of the initial protest against Gamaliel's initiative. Yoshua's fundamental objection is accommodated by Akiva in his habitual role of mediator. The radical rejection by Eliezer stands isolated, and the resulting implicit understanding is that, barring exceptional circumstances, the Eighteen Benedictions are the rule. This is confirmed by later discussions in the Talmud that take the Eighteen Benedictions for granted. In spite of initial resistance,[53] Gamaliel's initiative has won out. The Talmud summarizes the process succinctly: "Shimon ha-Pekoli arranged the Eighteen Benedictions in their proper place before Rabban Gamliel at Yavneh."[54]

If we now combine these results with our findings about the early Christian sources, a conclusion of great importance follows. Gamaliel's institution of the Eighteen Benedictions seems to have met with considerable resistance both in his own rabbinic circle and in the community of the Didache and Matthew. This conclusion may be spelled out in seven steps.

(1) Matthew's polemics, on prayer among other things, is aimed at the "hypocrites" or Pharisees who recently had begun calling themselves "rabbi."

(2) The Didache, closely related to Matthew, turns against the "hypocrites" who have the second and fifth weekday for fast days instead of the fourth and sixth ones and who pray another prayer than the Lord's Prayer.

(3) Fasting on the second and fifth days, Monday and Thursday, is the rule in rabbinic tradition, while the preference for Wednesday and Friday is associated with an alternative Jewish calendar the Didache-Matthew community seems to have supported.

(4) The similarities of Matthew's polemics against the Pharisaic rabbis and the Didache's resistance against Pharisaic-rabbinic fast days suggest that both texts also militate against the prayer text propagated by the Pharisees-rabbis.

(5) The objection in the Didache and Matthew to this rabbinic daily prayer parallels the initial protest registered in the Mishnah against the

---

53. See the memory of the violent discussion between Yoshua and Gamaliel about the status of the daily evening prayer, b. Ber. 27b–28a.

54. See b. Ber. 28b; b. Meg. 17b. For the sequel, see below.

institution of the Eighteen Benedictions. As regards Gamaliel's rule of eighteen, the three rabbis cited reject it altogether or propose a "short prayer" as a "summary of the eighteen" instead, while the editors of the Didache and Matthew simply stick to Jesus's short prayer in its Matthean form.

(6) The rule to pray thrice daily presupposed by the Didache shows that a similar custom did exist in pre-70 Judaism. In addition, Mark 11:25 makes the pre-70 existence of some form of the Matthean "ecclesial" version of the Lord's Prayer likely and by implication also the pre-70 existence in whatever form of Pharisaic daily synagogue prayers.

(7) All of this underscores the historical plausibility of the rabbinic reports of Gamaliel's institution of the Eighteen Benedictions as a daily prayer for all.

6. The Confrontation of Judaism and Christianity

The above results on the matter of prayer have important implications for the communities involved. On a closer look the three named rabbis and the authors of the Didache and Matthew not only share their protest against the Eighteen Benedictions in common. There is also a significant difference between them. Eliezer, Yoshua, and Akiva remained members of the rabbinic community.[55] But the anti-Pharisaic, antirabbinic polemics of Matthew and the Didache makes it abundantly clear that their churches were not a part of this community. Nevertheless, Matthew shows many similarities with rabbinic vocabulary and terminology. We have noted some examples in passing. The implication is that the close ties that had existed between the Didache-Matthew churches and the Pharisaic-rabbinic community were now broken.

More precisely, the community we may see reflected in Matthew and the Didache now feels cornered by the apparent imposition of the Eighteen Benedictions as a daily prayer and by the rule that fasting must be done on Mondays and Thursdays.[56] The novel rabbinic movement led by Gamaliel the Younger, which Matthew and later church fathers keep indicating as "Pharisees," seems to have had had the means to impose its rulings on the nascent Christian community and to encroach on their independence. Put

---

55. The banning of R. Eliëzer is not connected to this; see b. B. Meṣ. 59b.

56. Concerning this item, we have no tradition of a novel rabbinic rule. Fast days were the subject of early rabbinic discussion, however, see Vered Noam, *Megillat Ta'anit: Versions, Interpretation, History* (Jerusalem: Yad Ben-Zvi, 2003) (Hebrew).

differently, the Didache and Matthew register the impact of the rabbinic regime headed by Gamaliel.

As we have stated, recent discussion has included severe doubts about the real power of this regime. Particular attention was given to the Birkat Haminim, the "Benediction about the Heretics." This concerns the second criticized element of Elbogen's theory that we must now discuss. We quote once again the relative Talmudic tradition about the institution of the Eighteen Benedictions, this time with the sequel:

> Shimon ha-Pekoli arranged the eighteen benedictions in their proper place before Rabban Gamliel at Yavne. Said Rabban Gamliel to the sages: "Is there anyone who could put the benediction about the heretics in order?" Shmuel the Smaller rose and put it in order.[57] (b. Ber. 29b; see also b. Meg. 17b; y. Ber. 4:3 [8a])

Elbogen took this tradition simply to mean that indeed Shmuel the Smaller added the benediction at Gamaliel's behest. While *minim* can indicate any kind of heretics, the implication would be "that this prayer actually referred to Christians, and that it was one of the means to achieve full separation of both religions." In support, Elbogen referred to patristic reports about deprecations of Christians in synagogues and to rabbinic traditions showing how Jewish Christians would be damning themselves while pronouncing the Birkat Haminim.[58] In recent decades, this part of Elbogen's description has been rejected on the grounds that explicit mentions of "Christians" occur only in textual witnesses of rabbinic prayers beginning in the fourth century.[59] On the other hand, other

---

57. According to the Yerushalmi, Shmuel the Smaller's Birkat Haminim complemented the number of benedictions to become eighteen; according to the Bavli, he made them nineteen. Cohen, "Nature of Shim'on," 551–53 suggestively proposes eighteen was seen as a round figure, not an exact number.

58. Elbogen, *Jüdische Gottesdienst*, 36–39. See the more explicit presentation in Alon, *Jews in Their Land*, 288–307.

59. Schäfer, "Sogenannte Synode"; G. Stemberger, "Die sogenannte 'Synode von Jabne' und das frühe Christentum," *Kairos* 19 (1977): 14–21; Reuven Kimelman, "Birkat Ha-minim and the Lack of Evidence for an Anti-Christian Prayer in Late Antiquity," in *Aspects of Judaism in the Graeco-Roman World*, vol 2. of *Jewish and Christian Self-Definition*, ed. E. P. Sanders (London: SCM, 1981), 22–44; Pieter W. van der Horst, "The Birkat Ha-minim in Recent Research," in *Hellenism, Judaism, Christianity: Essays on Their Interaction* (Leuven: Peeters, 1998), 113–24.

studies have upheld Elbogen's thesis specifically on the basis of the early Christian evidence.[60]

For our purposes, we merely need to establish that the Birkat Haminim plays no visible role in the conflict with the "Pharisees" or rabbis reflected by Matthew and the Didache. Nevertheless, those documents testify to a painful conflict. Apparently the Pharisees-rabbis already wielded sufficient power without such an adaptation of the Eighteen Benedictions.

Rabbinic and Christian sources indicate that around the turn of the first century the incipient rabbinic movement took other measures, ostracizing "heretics" *including Christians*. Rabbinic rules effectively excommunicating *minim* appear to have been adapted or put in place, and by this time their applicability to Christians must have become explicit.[61] Of prime importance for dating this development is again the Christian source material, especially the repeated communication in John that "the Jews" or "the Pharisees" had "already decided" (συνετέθειντο) to make Christians ἀποσυνάγωγοι (John 9:22; 12:42; see also 16:2), which must be translated "put out of the community."[62] This source must be dated to around 110 CE.[63]

---

60. See esp. William Horbury, "The Benediction of the *Minim* and Early Jewish-Christian Controversy," in *Jews and Christians in Contact and Controversy* (Edinburgh: T&T Clark, 1998), 67–110, and the introduction, 3–14.

61. The central rabbinic passage is t. Ḥul. 2:19–24. See Adiel Schremer, *Brothers Estranged: Heresy, Christianity, and Jewish Identity in Late Antiquity* (Oxford: Oxford University Press, 2010); Joshua Schwartz and Peter J. Tomson, "When Rabbi Eliezer was Arrested for Heresy," *JSIJ* 10 (2012): 1–37, http://www.biu.ac.il/JS/JSIJ/10-2012/SchwartzandTomson.pdf.

62. For this meaning of ἀποσυνάγωγος, see Shaye J. D. Cohen, "Were Pharisees and Rabbis the Leaders of Communal Prayer and Torah Study in Antiquity? The Evidence of the New Testament, Josephus, and the Early Church Fathers," in Cohen, *Significance of Yavneh*, 266–81 (esp. 275–76); Peter J. Tomson, "The Wars against Rome, the Rise of Rabbinic Judaism and of Apostolic Gentile Christianity, and the Judaeo-Christians: Elements for a Synthesis," in *The Image of the Judaeo-Christians in Early Jewish and Christian Christian Literature*, ed. Peter J. Tomson and Doris Lambers-Petry, WUNT 158 (Tübingen: Mohr Siebeck, 2003), 14–18, although there incorrectly restricted to the Birkat Haminim.

63. On internal literary-historical grounds, this dating is made by Raymond E. Brown, *An Introduction to the New Testament*, ABRL (New York: Doubleday, 1997), 376.

7. Historical and Theological Conclusions

Let us sum up in some general conclusions, first on the level of history. The classic form of the "short prayer" taught by Jesus is extant in Matthew and the Didache. These documents were finalized when the "rabbinic" regime of Gamaliel the Younger took shape, and they signal resistance to the rules it issued concerning prayer and fasting. Initial resistance involving prayer was also registered in the Mishnah. The influence of this regime that is here reflected proves its power, the doubts of modern scholars notwithstanding. The question of the sources of this power is beyond the purview of the present study.[64]

Matthew and the Didache do not contain echoes of a "Benediction about the Heretics" being applied to Christians, nor do they even show signs of the excommunication of Christians evidenced in early rabbinic traditions and the Gospel of John. These developments must have occurred not long after the final redaction of Matthew and the Didache.

Without any polemics, Luke relates how Jesus taught his disciples a brief prayer, just as John the Baptist and other Jewish teachers did. We saw the potential authenticity of this report confirmed in rabbinic traditions about short prayers. Also, the short version of the Lord's Prayer that Luke copied from an unknown source sounds more authentic and more typical of Jesus. The Matthean text sounds more "rabbinic" and seems to have been taking shape within the community, a process that may have begun before the redaction of Mark. It must have been the subsequent supremacy of Matthew that made the Lukan version fall into disuse, although we could also speculate that the "ecclesial" features of the Matthean version correspond with the Christian positioning in the emerging conflict with rabbinic Judaism.

We should not miss the opportunity also to draw some theological conclusions. First, theologically, there is no fundamental difference between the two versions of the Lord's Prayer. By content and wording, both texts are closely related to the various Jewish prayers from the period. Decisive differences are found only in the context. In both preserved versions, Jesus's short prayer is a Jewish prayer.

Second, in Matthew and the Didache, this Jewish prayer is framed in a setting reflecting conflict with the Jewish leaders called Pharisees or

---

64. See above in nn. 47–48.

"rabbis." Here a theological dissonance is felt between the Jewish prayer text and the anti-rabbinic and ultimately anti-Jewish context in which it is mounted.[65] By contrast, Luke's framing of the short prayer of Jesus makes his own voice heard among those of other Jewish teachers. There is no dissonance between the Jewish text of his prayer and its context in Luke.

A third theological conclusion concerns present-day readers even more directly. In the framework of the New Testament canon, Christianity's break with Judaism is not an inherent necessity but is contingent on particular circumstances. Theologically, the continuity of Judaism and Christianity depicted by Luke carries as much weight as the rupture reflected by Matthew. Judging by the way the prayer of Jesus is transmitted in the New Testament, the relationship of Jews and Christians remains an undecided issue. It is the extracanonical text of the Didache that helps us realize this.

---

65. On Matthew's eventual anti-Judaism, see Peter J. Tomson, "Das Matthäusevangelium im Wandel der Horizonte: Vom 'Hause Israels' (10,6) zu 'allen Völkern' (28,19)," in *Judaistik und neutestamentliche Wissenschaft: Feschrift*, ed. Lutz Doering, Hans-Günther Waubke, and Florian Wilk, FRLANT 226 (Göttingen, Vandenhoeck & Ruprecht, 2008, 313–33; and, "*If This Be from Heaven*," ch. 6.

Pray "In This Way": Formalized Speech in Didache 9–10

Jonathan Schwiebert

There is widespread agreement that certain phrases in the Didache's meal prayers are fixed or formulaic. A short list by any measure would include the phrase "through Jesus your servant" and the doxologies that conclude each prayer unit. But a cursory glance at the following chart will reveal that, at least in three of the six prayer units, more than these two expressions are formulaic.[1]

Did. 9.2	Did. 9.3	Did. 10.2
We thank you, our Father, for the holy vine of David your servant,	We thank you, our Father, for the life and knowledge,	We thank you, holy Father, for your holy name, which you made to reside in our hearts, and for the knowledge and faith and immortality
which you made known to us through Jesus your servant. To you be glory forever. [Amen.]	which you made known to us through Jesus your servant. To you be glory forever. [Amen.]	which you made known to us through Jesus your servant. To you be glory forever. [Amen.][1]

I have pointed out elsewhere that these fixed expressions tend to cluster toward the beginning and ending of these prayer units, leaving a central variable phrase (or two).[2] A similar phenomenon can be seen in two other

---

1. Translations of the Didache are my own.
2. Jonathan Schwiebert, *Knowledge and the Coming Kingdom: The Didache's Meal*

prayer units, which (in the extant text of the Didache) conclude the pre- and postdinner prayers:

Did. 9.4	**Did. 10.5**
Just as this bread fragment was scattered upon the hills and, gathered, became one, so let <u>your assembly</u> be <u>gathered</u> <u>from the</u> corners of the earth <u>into your kingdom</u>.	Remember, Lord, <u>your assembly</u>, to rescue it from all evil, and to complete it in your love, and to <u>gather</u> it <u>from the</u> four winds, [after it is made holy][a] <u>into your kingdom</u>, which you prepared for it.
Because yours is the power and the glory forever.[b]	Because yours is the power and the glory forever.
[Amen.]	[Amen]

Notes

a. The words are lacking in the Coptic and may therefore be a secondary addition. See Kurt Niederwimmer, *The Didache: A Commentary*, translated by Linda M. Maloney, Hermeneia (Minneapolis: Fortress, 1998), 161.

b. I have emended the text of the doxology. See Schwiebert, *Knowledge and the Coming Kingdom*, 64–66.

Although these two prayer units are verbally distinct, they do share key vocabulary and also conclude on a strikingly similar note—and with the same doxology (distinct, however, from the shorter doxology above). As I have pointed out elsewhere, if this longer doxology is a congregational response, then the final words of these two prayers ("into your kingdom") is not open to change: it is formulaic, or fixed. The doxology, at any rate, is fixed.[3]

Finally, even in the outlier (the only prayer unit not yet cited), we encounter the formulaic phrase "through Jesus your servant" (*without*, however, the phrase "which you made known to us") and the (shorter) doxology that always follows it in Did. 9–10:

Ritual and Its Place in Early Christianity, LNTS 373 (New York: T&T Clark, 2008), 88–91.

3. See Schwiebert, *Knowledge and the Coming Kingdom*, 68–69. Ironically, the doxology is not "fixed" in the textual tradition, but then different doxologies are in usage in the New Testament and other liturgical texts, one of which likely affected the manuscript tradition here.

You, Almighty Master, created all things for the sake of your name, and have given nourishment and drink to all humanity, for their enjoyment, so that they would thank you. But us you have favored with spiritual nourishment and drink, and eternal life though Jesus your servant. For all things we thank you, because you are powerful.[4] To you be glory forever. [Amen.] (Did. 10.3-4)

I take it as uncontroversial that formulaic speech exists in these prayers, then: certain phrases that are fixed in advance of the liturgy's enactment through word and gesture and action. The degree of formulaic speech is disputed, but its presence, almost never.[5]

The more difficult question concerns how to interpret such fixed expressions. And here critics divide at best into observable tendencies. On the one side, and relatively few in number, stand critics who read the text of the prayers almost as if they were a theological treatise to be exegeted by standard hermeneutical methods. Representative here are Willy Rordorf and André Tuilier. Observe that two fixed expressions in the first set of prayers above employ (1) παῖς ("child/servant") and (2) γνωρίζω ("make known"). Rordorf and Tuilier argue that the juxtaposition of these two terms is intended to mean that Jesus "revealed the profound significance" (2) of the Jewish notion of the messiah (1). Moreover, since both Jesus and David are called παῖς in the text of the prayers, Jesus is clearly a *Davidic* messiah, and the community's prayers are themselves "Davidic."[6] In their hands the phrase "vine of David" (9.2), which Adolf von Harnack famously found impervious to interpretation, further shows that the church is "essentially founded on the messianic vocation of Israel."[7] For

---

4. The text is somewhat suspect here; see Schwiebert, *Knowledge and the Coming Kingdom*, 70–71.

5. The parallelism is so extensive that it has given rise to the suggestion that we have two versions of one liturgy, one in chapter 9 and the other in chapter 10. See Maurice Goguel, *L'Eucharistie: Des origins à Justin Martyr* (Paris: Fischbacher, 1910), 237, 241–42; Alan J. P. Garrow, *The Gospel of Matthew's Dependence on the* Didache, JSNTSup 254 (London: T&T Clark, 2004), 27. More plausible to me is a prayer pattern that the community follows in its meal prayers that bracket the meal.

6. Willy Rordorf and André Tuilier, *La doctrine des douze Apôtres (Didachè)*, SC 29 (Paris: Cerf, 1998), 43–44. Note that to make this claim, Rordorf and Tuilier must directly link the wording of a formula used in several prayer units to the wording of a phrase that appears only once.

7. Ibid., 45.

them the prayers "proclaim" the parousia of the resurrected Christ "not only proper to the end of time, but that it is already realized in the Eucharistic synaxis."[8]

Observe the procedure: authorial word choice, syntactical arrangement, and repetition of key terms are used by the interpreter to disclose the intention of the text, its meaning, or interpretation. This is essentially the manner in which exegetes traditionally tackle a Pauline epistle, for example. Put another way: *what the reader should understand* from the text is gleaned from grammatical-linguistic observations. Needless to say, most interpreters of the Didache's prayers have been highly trained in such analysis, and the desire to employ their considerable powers of observation is entirely understandable.

It is on the face of it somewhat puzzling then that this exegetical approach is relatively rare: on another side stands the more common tendency merely to assert the formulaic nature of these phrases and assume that as such they are impervious to interpretation. So, for instance, Martin Dibelius in his classic source-critical study does not venture beyond a claim that the phrase "which you made known" means that Jesus reveals salvation.[9] Regarding the doxologies of Did. 9, he states that each "has so little connection with the [preceding] request, that it is best understood as a stereotyped response."[10]

Yet Dibelius does not entirely neglect exegetical tactics. Consider his treatment of "the holy vine of David." For him, if not for us, this is an opaque symbol whose meaning had become well known to those who used these prayers. He traces a tradition-historical lineage through Jer 2:21; Ps 79(80):9, 15; 4 Ezra 5:23, and a (postulated) Hellenistic synagogue prayer tradition. In light of this history, as a symbol the phrase can in effect be translated into another word: "salvation."[11] The meaning or intention of the text's author then remains important, or at least relevant, to a proper interpretation of certain phrases within the prayers.

Kurt Niederwimmer's approach is in general along the same lines. He calls the choice of the verb εὐχαριστέω only "formal," "without theologi-

---

8. Ibid., 101.

9. Martin Dibelius, "Die Mahl-Gebete der Didache," in *Zum Urchristentum und zur hellenistischen Religionsgeschichte*, vol. 2 of *Botschaft und Geschichte*, ed. Heinz Kraft and Günther Bornkamm; Tübingen: Mohr Siebeck, 1956), 117–27.

10. Ibid., 122.

11. Ibid., 119–20.

cal significance."[12] Even briefer is his treatment of the concluding doxologies: "The community gathered for the meal responds to this prayer by saying...."[13] Yet he also occasionally shades into treating the language of the prayers as theological speech:

> In place of the [traditional Jewish] address "Lord our God, Ruler of the universe," we read, "our Father.".... This predication certainly expresses the self-concept of the group, who understand themselves as the table company of children who receive the goods of time and eternity from the hand of the heavenly Father.[14]

For Niederwimmer, a self-concept is expressed in the choice of the word "Father" over the choice of some other phrase ("Lord our God"). Here at least the verbiage rises above "formulaic." His reading of the phrase "holy vine of David" is even more in the vein of an exegetical treatment:

> I understand this to mean that in the presence of the cup and the wine, which are earthly gifts, the thoughts of the community are directed farther, to the *heavenly* good, which God has given to God's own and which can be understood through the metaphor of the "holy vine." The concepts are thus transparent: the subject of revelation is God, and its object is the "holy vine," that is, salvation, and more specifically eschatological salvation, which was once promised but has now been given.[15]

Interestingly, Niederwimmer once again derives (or at least defends) this interpretation from the juxtaposition of this phrase with the formulaic expression "which you revealed through Jesus your servant." Arrangement of phrases reveals meaning; word choice plays a secondary role in Niederwimmer's reading.

A few more recent interpreters, paying closer attention to the ritual and oral-performative features of the text, have strained against these two options. Aaron Milavec, reading the prayers through an oral performative lens, sees symbolic reservoirs in the puzzling expressions of the prayers, which are to be tapped and verbally expounded by a prayer leader. Even so, he ends by rendering these phrases into other, fuller ones meant to

---

12. Niederwimmer, *Didache*, 145.
13. Ibid., 152.
14. Ibid., 145.
15. Ibid., 146.

capture and bring out their deeper "meaning."[16] In that sense, though not in others, his procedure still resembles Niederwimmer's.

Jonathan Draper, attuned to the ritual setting of these prayers, offers a somewhat analogous avenue of interpretation via Victor Turner's symbolic approach. For instance, Draper takes the "vine of David" as a symbol (indeed a primary symbol) of the liturgy and finds that as symbol it alludes to "a rich symbolic tradition in the culture of Israel." This tradition is shared for Draper in the fifteenth benediction of the Shemoneh Esreh, Isa 11:1–12, and various other texts within the Jewish Scriptures and the Dead Sea Scrolls. The tradition reveals that the strange phrase "vine of David," taken as equivalent to "sprout of David," "has both dynastic-messianic significance and also communal covenant dimensions."[17] In developing this interpretation, however, Draper too resorts to an exposition of the fixed expression, "which you revealed through Jesus your servant," taking it to mean (in this connection) that Jesus "reveals the vine to those initiated into the community as king of the renewed kingdom."[18]

Under the heading of symbolism, then, we seem to move back into the domain of exegesis. Ritual formulas are parsed as units of language, however dense, and become again carriers of meaning not far different from the way in which normal language operates.

If it is possible to extrapolate from these few examples, scholars appear to differ on the question of whether the fixed expressions in these prayers can bear meaning as words. The reigning approach is apparently to acknowledge the essentially uncommunicative nature of formulaic speech. But wherever an opening seems to present itself, interpreters are in the habit of looking for (and finding) thoughts and ideas expressed in the language of the prayers. The terminological decisions, the grammatical constructions, and the juxtapositions of phrases remain exegetical keys by which we might grasp after the denotative meaning of the prayers' language. As language, the assumption goes that we can translate

---

16. E.g., his treatment of the "holy vine"; see Aaron Milavec, *The Didache: Faith, Hope, and Life of the Earliest Christian Communities, 50–70 CE* (New York: Newman, 2003), 361–64.

17. Jonathan A. Draper, "Ritual Process and Ritual Symbol in Didache 7–10," *VC* 54 (2000): 121–58 (150).

18. Ibid., 148. Like Rordorf and Tuilier, then, Draper's interpretation requires a direct link between phrases that occur repeatedly and a phrase found only once.

the prayers into other equivalent verbal forms, thereby accessing a fuller sense of their meaning.

I would suggest that these two tendencies exist in unexamined tension within the literature. If, on the one hand, formulaic speech is impervious to interpretation, then its juxtaposition with nonformulaic speech (or simply, puzzling expressions) cannot disclose some deeper meaning in those expressions. Put another way, a verbal object that people use but do not think of as "words" cannot become "words" in the hands of the interpreter who needs them to be "words." And this procedure is all the more problematic when the same interpreters treats the expressions as objects (and not "words") elsewhere in their treatment.

Let me illustrate the two tendencies with a trivial example: In my culture, the expression "goodbye" is used mostly (I gather) as a kind of verbal object. Suppose someone said something nasty to me on the telephone and then concluded the conversation with "goodbye." Would it be legitimate to take the "good" from "goodbye" and use it to soften the nasty comment? Could I drag out the ancient origins of the phrase in "God be with ye" and argue that the nasty comment was a joke and the person's true intentions were positive? Failing these, could I at least claim that by using the polite term "goodbye" the speaker meant to maintain a relationship, despite the nasty remark? In fact, none of these interpretations of "goodbye" would be valid or at all plausible. What then is a more useful approach to fixed formulas like "goodbye"? Do they mean nothing at all? This conclusion would also be unwarranted, I think. Yet these are the two tendencies that a closer attention to the uses and properties of formulaic speech can help us move beyond.

In what follows I have selected one scholar of ritual and, in particular, ritual speech whose account seems to me both persuasive and capable of clarifying central issues at stake. Others could be chosen. This is my choice and is not put forward as the last (but rather the almost first) word on the subject.[19]

---

19. One thing in the above account I find both plausible and useful: the idea that certain turns of phrase have a prior history in the Scriptures and traditions of Judaism and early Christianity. But what use we must make of these tradition-historical observations is not yet clear until we know how such formulas function.

1. The Limitations of Formalized Language

Maurice Bloch has argued with respect to religious rituals that symbols, songs, and dance embody an extreme form of tradition. Choreography and script reveal a tradition so fixed that the ritual participant must accept that tradition in advance or abandon the performance prior to beginning it. But in agreeing to a preformulated script, he argued that language undergoes severe limitation.[20]

The Didache's meal prayers contain not only formulaic speech, but arguably a kind of script. The fixed phrases identified above, which conclude each of the six prayer units, are in every case followed by predictable doxologies. Critics disagree whether the community would respond to the prayer units with the doxology itself or with an "amen" (found only in the Coptic). Either solution advances the main claim: the wording of the prayers is signaling a verbal exchange between the participants. The language is fixed. It is even conceivable that these prayers are entirely fixed, that they were meant to be performed verbatim. Such a conclusion seems unwarranted, however, precisely because they vary in predictable places.[21]

When we encounter a script, we are immediately confronted with the notion of "choice," so important for exegetical treatments of texts. Bloch points out several categories of choice that a speaker has in "everyday speech acts." These include loudness, intonation, choice of vocabulary, flexibility in the sequence of utterances, and a full range of stylistic variation. In formalized speech acts, on the other hand, each of these categories can be curtailed and often is. For instance, only certain tones of voice may be appropriate, only a partial vocabulary may be available, and importantly, the sequence of speech acts may be fixed in advance.[22]

Bloch further points out that this surrendering of choices has "a geometrical effect on the restriction of forms of speech":

> If we think of the sentence "the cat sat on the mat" and assume that there are three alternative nouns for each noun locus we find that there are nine possible sentences. If we say that the verb can be in one of three

---

20. Maurice Bloch, "Symbols, Songs, Dance and Feature of Articulation: Is Religion an Extreme Form of Traditional Authority?" *EuroJS* 5 (1974): 55–81.
21. See my discussion in *Knowledge and the Coming Kingdom*, 66–71, 78–83, 88–89, and sources cited there.
22. Bloch, "Symbols, Songs, Dance," 60.

tenses there are then twenty-seven possible sentences and then that these sentences can be said in one of three intonations, there are then eighty-one possible sentences. Now if we look at this backwards *we see that by just specifying one restriction*, say intonation, saying that only one intonation is suitable, *the number of possible sentences drops* from eighty-one to twenty-seven. *If, however, we bring in two restrictions occurring at the same time*, say that with a certain intonation only certain nouns are acceptable, *the effect on the choice of sentences is dramatic*. In fact it falls from eighty-one possible sentences to three.[23]

Given our exegetical predilections, it is important to linger here a moment. Remember that we humans use all of these choices (intonation, word choice, verb tense) to convey our *meaning* to one another. Not surprisingly, therefore, when we come to interpret what someone has said or written, we are prone to weigh the writer's or speaker's choices to interpret their meaning insofar as we can. In the case of texts, we have no access to intonation (a sad loss, but largely unavoidable), and therefore we tend to put additional emphasis (in our interpretations) on the word choices and syntactical arrangement and verb tenses we find.[24]

Meanwhile, there is another kind of restriction to observe: sequential communication. Bloch writes: "The first and the most obvious of the implications of abandoning linguistic choice is that an utterance instead of being potentially followed by an infinity of others can be followed by only a few or possibly only one."[25] An almost infinite number of responses can follow an everyday speech act, but in situations where only a few responses are appropriate: "with increased formalisation *A* predicts to an ever greater extent *B*." He sums up:

> In terms of the experience of an individual it means that as he uses formalized language *he very largely implies his last words by his first*, since once he is speaking in the right way there is only one predetermined line along which he can proceed.[26]

In fact, one speaker's words can (within the accepted code) predict the next speaker's words, including the appropriate tone, the choice of vocabulary,

---

23. Ibid., 61 (emphasis mine).
24. A glance at a standard biblical commentary will illustrate my point admirably.
25. Bloch, "Symbols, Songs, Dance," 62–63.
26. Ibid., 63 (emphasis mine).

and so on. In these situations, the language's communicative power is radically reduced. The speaker's ability to "intend" and "express" (precisely what we normally exegete) is lost.

Put another way, what may appear to be a conversation between two parties becomes in a formalized context completely unlike an actual conversation. In everyday speech acts, speakers are communicating information and other things, like emotional states and relational connections ("How are you?"—"Not all that well, honestly."—"Really, what's wrong?"). In formalized speech acts, this kind of exchange is ruled out by the "rules," by the obligation of the second speaker to say a certain thing and not something else. That loss of true conversation, with its lost freight of new information, ought to impact how we interpret a formalized exchange.

Take, for instance, a conversation in which "How are you?" can only (politely) be answered with "Fine. How are you?" There the conversation says nothing about the actual state of either speaker and only communicates acceptance of a polite code, an acknowledgement of the other's existence within that code, or some such thing. The "meaning" of the words has nothing to do with the "content" of the words.

As this illustration demonstrates, among the things "lost" in a formalized exchange is the expectation of a neat fit between language and particular situations or circumstances. Two routine functions of language, Bloch contends, "disappear" in formalized speech: "the ability of language to communicate messages concerning particular events and its ability to convey specific messages leading to particular action." But formalized speech excels in another arena, namely, asserting unity. As words and utterances lose their flexibility, their capacity to adjust to the particular needs of the moment, they gain the ability to make "all events ... appear as though they were all alike." Put another way, words are uttered in a given context that are appropriate to that context. They do not express by any necessity the actual state of affairs but rather the polite or accepted utterance befitting the current occasion. They assert, for whatever reason, that this is how it ought to be and consequently say nothing about how it actually is.[27]

---

27. Ibid., 62. Examples from political rhetoric abound, including for instance expressions of praise heaped upon one politician by another, which are unreliable predictors of actual esteem or respect. Bloch uses his observations also to think about political speech acts and traditional utterances and their occasions before turning to the matter of ritual utterances, which is our present concern.

For these reasons and others, Bloch affirms that "to look for 'meaning' in a fixed utterance without qualification is clearly misleading." Consider the differences between a script and an argument. In an argument, a statement B that follows a statement A is (1) open-ended and (2) open to contradiction. Neither of these properties holds in formalized contexts: we have already seen that, there, statement B is not open-ended, but predicted in advance by statement A. The second point follows from the first: you cannot contradict statement A if your answer is a predetermined statement B and one of agreement (like an "amen"). "Formalised language is therefore non logical and any attempt to represent it as such, whether by a paraphrase into ordinary language which implies 'explanation' or by the use of tabular representation containing a logical form, is misleading."[28]

Given Bloch's argument (and if it is sound, as I think it is, at least in its leading points), we must acknowledge that a large number of efforts to interpret the vocal utterances of ritual speech, including at points the texts of the prayers in Did. 9–10, are incompatible with the observation that these are "fixed utterances" wherein the speaker (whether the prayer leader or the one who responds to the prayer leader) has little or no choice about such "everyday speech" elements as selection of vocabulary, tense of verbs, syntactical structure, juxtaposition of phrases, and (probably) intonation. In other words, if Bloch is correct, the patterns that almost all students of these prayers acknowledge, discussed briefly above, rule out recourse to a grammatical-linguistic interpretation. The person who prays "in this way" accepts a code, and the person who responds in kind either with the doxology or the "amen" also accepts that code.

Does this mean that we cannot interpret the prayers at all, that the phrases are meaningless? In fact, it happens that Bloch's observations also challenge the other tendency in the literature, to which we now turn.

2. Interpreting the Prayers through Their Context

Part of what interests Bloch is the question of how formalized language "communicates without explanation," especially since language in ritual has often been taken to "explain" some aspect of reality. His argument challenges us to consider that the expressions in our prayers are not trying to

---

28. Ibid., 66.

explain anything. As he puts it, in formalized speech "communication has stopped being a dialectic and has become a matter of repeating correctly."[29]

This little quote is a nice clue to the drift of his argument. "Repeating correctly" is about compliance, not communication. For Bloch, the "force" of formalized language is "traditional authority, but disguised in that it has been accepted unconsciously before the event by the acceptance of the proper, of the polite, or the appropriate way of behaving."[30] One accepts not the "truth" of the thing being said, but the authority behind its formalization. Drawing from J. L. Austin, Bloch refers to this authority as "illocutionary force," "not to report facts but to influence people."[31] How, then, do we interpret it? Or can we interpret it at all?

A useful place to begin is with Bloch's remark that "the experience of the ritual is an experience fused with its context and therefore only an attempt to explain what this event as a whole is for is an explanation of the content."[32] Here we encounter several insightful leads, each worth exploring. The first is that ritual is something one experiences only in a particular context. Our first task when we come to interpret any particular ritual object or verbal formula is to clearly define (insofar as possible) where and when and by whom it is used. Bloch's remark offers also a second lead, a complement to the first: a ritual's purpose, its "context," is already an explanation for the ritual's *content*. Bloch does not clarify whether this is an all-encompassing explanation, ruling out other modes of interpretation, but he does lead us to suppose that context deserves pride of place. Moreover, he adds, we must consider not a particular moment in isolation but rather the whole ritual within which this particular moment occurs. Here alone will we find the "context" that provides a privileged insight into the ritual speech we aim to understand.

Turning to the Didache's prayers with this advice in hand, we discover that a fair amount of information is available to us regarding this ritual's larger context.[33] We can infer, for instance, that this formulaic speech

---

29. Ibid., 72.
30. Ibid., 66–67.
31. Ibid., 67 (citing Austin, *How to Do Things with Words*, 234).
32. Bloch, "Symbols, Songs, Dance," 77. He goes on: "because the units of meaning are changed so that they can serve purposes only for religious events, and since they are inseparable from the context, there can be no explanation without an explanation of what the event or the context is."
33. For the purposes of this present analysis, I forego any discussion of redactional

comes immediately before and after a meal, and one in which people are expected to eat until their appetite is sated (10.1). Peeking outward into the rest of the Didache, we know (or can infer) that this meal alternates with a cycle of fasting: regular twice-weekly fasting and occasional additional fasting with novitiates (7.4–8.1). We know that (at least ideally) everyone eating the meal has received a minimum of instruction in the way of life, followed by immersion in water or pouring from a cup (7.1–3). We know too that diners can expect to encounter spirit-inspired speech at their meal (11.7–12). And last of all, we know that the meal is called a "thanksgiving" and is considered "holy" (9.1, 5).

When we come to interpret the content of the meal prayers, then, we can (and should) bring to bear this whole network of associations of context. At the level of abstraction that Bloch seems to recommend, the ritualized, authoritative speech we encounter in these prayers is about the community and its gathering. By embarking on the thanksgiving with its prayers and responses, the community celebrates and reaffirms its gathering. It, so to speak, asserts the reality of its existence as a meaningful group in the midst of an environment that must surely entail rival allegiances: to family, to city, to empire, and so on. Fasting from food "out there" contrasts to partaking fully "in here," making the meal around which these acceptable words are said into a "thanksgiving" for a kind of community that is not obvious or given.

The extent of tension with alternate allegiances, which can here only be suggested, may shed interesting light on how freighted this particular fasting-eating alternative is for these ritual participants. For instance, fasting from meals implies (does it not?) abstinence from family or other group gatherings. But this is only partial. The fasting occurs only on two days of the week. It is possibly tied to the preparatory rite for inclusion in the community. At least the instructions lay side-by-side. So then, the meal partly displaces family membership or identity, but not completely. Meanwhile, fasting on days that do not coincide with "the hypocrites" (that is, other Jews) seems to entail a more radical kind of dissociation. The cycle of fasting completely disagrees with these others' cycle of fasting

---

layers in the text. What I say here applies best (and perhaps only) to the final form of the text. Earlier layers (for which we must subtract this or that detail) might require adjustments to the "context" and hence the interpretation I provide. My own effort to relegate each relevant detail to a particular redactional phase can be seen in *Knowledge and the Coming Kingdom*, 148–82.

(both occur only on two days, but these two days are entirely distinct). There is no overlap except in the idea that it must be done.[34]

We can add another layer of context by picking up the observation from above that the formulas used in the prayers are often (though not always) drawn from Jewish tradition. It might be possible to say that Jewish tradition is the silent authority that has been accepted by those who gather at this meal were it not for the intrusion of phrases that cannot be ascribed to that tradition. The most obvious of these is "through Jesus your servant," which obviously does not arise from mainstream Judaism. We are thus left with a community with Jewish traditions that is not coterminous with the Jewish community, that practices a Jewish sort of fasting discipline but on different days, and that views these other Jews as "hypocrites." The traditional language of the prayers seems to reinforce this community's Jewish identity, even while it disrupts it by asserting a difference, a peculiarity, reinforced by the language of "holiness" and the other rites associated with this one.

We can go further. Philo of Alexandria claims that "(it would be irreverent) ... and equally unlawful to enjoy and partake of any form of food for which thanks had not been offered [εὐχαριστήσαντας] in the proper and rightful manner" (Philo, *Spec.* 2.175).[35] This remark suggests that the idea of offering verbal thanksgiving for a meal is a peculiarly Jewish instance of "the appropriate" and "polite" thing to do. The prayers in this context mean something like "we too are pious."

But again Bloch presses us to answer the question of what this entire ritual is for. Only then will we understand its content. When we say "entire ritual," in this case I think we must include the cycle of fasting, instruction, and immersion or pouring: the preparatory rites, if you will. We must also bring in the ecstatic speech, the sense of holiness, the hedging about of the meal: its immediate rites and usages. Next, we must not forget that the ritualized speech in this case is prayer, speech addressed to God (not

---

34. Would agreement that it should be done have been seen by members of either community as a point of commonality? It is difficult to say. Jews, Muslims, and Christians agree that God should be worshiped in community one day a week, though again on different days. Do they see this point of agreement as meaningful, binding them into one community?

35. Cited in Huub van de Sandt and David Flusser, *The Didache: Its Jewish Sources and Its Place in Early Judaism and Christianity*, CRINT 3.5 (Assen: Van Gorcum; Minneapolis: Fortress, 2002), 321. This was evidently a customary term for meal prayers (so Jean LaPorte, *Eucharistia in Philo* [New York: Mellen, 1983], 53–55; Paul in Rom 14:6; and the Eighteenth Benediction of the Amidah).

the people) and not in the persona of an elder or some ancestral figure but rather in the voice of the whole assembly: a "we." Someone (we do not know who) speaks for the whole assembly, and the assembly permits this, because this is at least a part of what the gathering means: they are there, among other reasons, to speak as one to God. Finally, there is the food. The prayers justify the sharing of the meal and make it something more than the obvious: a holy, quasisacrificial feast (9.5; 14).

I have already addressed the fasting. The content of the instruction is also relevant: it consists almost entirely of ethical rulings, guidelines for a way of life that stands in sharp contrast to a way of death. This instructional content evidently culminates in ritual washing, after which the meal is open: the washing acts as a sentinel on the ritual of the meal. Being immersed (or poured over) "in the name of the Lord" suggests within a Jewish cultural context an association with that Lord characterized by belonging, perhaps an allegiance or maybe discipleship.[36] Interestingly, the washing is apparently also the gateway to ecstatic speech, which can (and cannot) be critiqued by the community (11.7–12). Apparently the one-time recipient of instruction can become by possession of the spirit a purveyor of knowledge and insight. But the Didache says very little about "spirit" or its possessors, the "prophets." The danger associated with spirit-talk is above all that it might lead people to do things that contradict the surer teaching received from the tradition. But even the ritual formulas used at the meal setting can be supplemented by prophets (10.7).

The larger context then has begun to come into view. The ritual speech under investigation takes place at a regular communal meal. As such it asserts the (Jewish or traditional) piety of the group, its adherence to what is "proper." At the same time the meal is uncommon ("holy"), reserved for those who have undergone a period of instruction that clarifies for them in what ways they are (however fictitiously) distinct from outsiders. This instruction has a clear terminus, marked ritually by a water rite that involves fasting. Fasting reappears also in the weekly cycle of behavior that binds the community in a common calendar (an experience of time) and contrasts in a concrete way with the eating that takes place at the meal. The community that fasts together also eats together. They are "together" in time and then again literally together at the meal. The ritual speech

---

36. Paul (himself a Jewish man, of course) uses the phrase "baptized into Moses" in a similar way (1 Cor 10:2).

we are looking at is not so sacrosanct that it should rule out spirit-talk. This is a community that holds a role for spirit-people ("prophets"), but all spirit-talk must be held to the standard of the tradition, however tolerant of spirit-people one may be. Finally, the whole ritual serves (among other things) to reassert the existence of the community that gathers for the meal and the legitimacy of the meal itself as something more than a common, everyday meal. All that the community is, is bound up with it: yoked to the Lord Jesus (and his teachings), partially distinct from the surrounding world and other allegiances, more radically distinct from certain Jews, on the path to life, open to spirit.

All this we learn, not from an examination of the "meaning" or "syntax" of the prayers themselves, nor by translating them into an exposition. All this rather comes from the "context" that the ritual inhabits within the Didache as it now stands and within the world from which it was written. Its assertion of the essential existence, the meaningful unity and identity of the group, is simply that: an assertion. We have no way of knowing whether "on the ground" community members "believed" or felt invested in this identity above all others. But in some important ways (though bets are hedged here, interestingly) the community's existence and unity asserted by virtue of the prayers taking place are made primary, a reference point for all of life: ethical, ritual, and eschatological.

Perhaps some readers may wonder if this is enough, or if we have traded away too much of the "meaning" of the words in this kind of contextual interpretation. For on this reading, why say these words and not some other words? Why the insistence on particular formulas, if their denotative meaning is lost? Here then I think we must come back to a question left unanswered above: whether the context of the ritual is coterminous with its interpretation or whether there remains a role for words to communicate in something more like the manner of normal speech. In other words, we must critique Bloch's theory.

3. The Role of Tradition or Possible Limits to Bloch's Theory

For Bloch, "the interesting question is the *disconnection* between the religious statement and the real world, a disconnection which is produced by the mode of communication of ritual." He goes further: ritual speech, for him, "serves to hide the actual situation and preserve authority."[37] Here

---

37. Bloch, "Symbols, Songs, Dance," 77 (emphasis mine).

that would mean the assertion (fiction?) that this is more than a meal and, in fact, somehow embodies an extraordinarily meaningful community. In coming to terms with his theory, we must meet this final question, then, and decide whether ritual speech is ultimately an extreme form of control or "authority." Bloch ascribes just such a potent force to "tradition."

Let me sketch out two possible directions we may take going forward. On the one hand, with Bloch we might conclude that what is happening in the Didache's ritual choreography is an assertion *from above*, from tradition, of the existence and purity of a community that does not exist in any essential sense. The ritual formulas serve to hide the multiple identities and mixed allegiances of the participants as well as the material aspects of the food. They do so at the loss of flexibility in language, in other words, at the loss of actual give-and-take and negotiation that may result in more conditioned but realistic agreement among the participants. For Bloch the Didache's ritual can succeed in asserting this kind of unified identity and allegiance, so long as the participants perform their roles, saying the lines scripted for them in advance. And in many cases they will do this, having no choice.

But (continuing with the first alternative) insofar as this kind of ritualized, formalized speech is practiced, it cannot help being a top-down assertion or, if you prefer, control from without. It entails a loss of freedom, not only of expression, but of self-definition, self-assertion, and defiance of tradition. Bloch's interpretation then is a fairly dismal view of ritualized speech and its capacity for human fulfillment. It seems in some sense to make ritual into control or power and on some level to exist outside of the individual who participates in the ritual. It might perhaps even make the ritual participant into a colluder, one who participates in their own restriction, self-limitation, and even individual annihilation.

In seeking refuge from such a dismal view, we might look to the example of marriage. Here too scripted lines are found that once begun must inevitably lead to the end (for example, "I now pronounce you"). In a traditional wedding each line would be carefully prescribed. The things spoken, the objects used, all may be dictated from without, from tradition. This all might well be described as a fiction, a cultural imposition, and a form of self-limitation. But the individual participant is likely to feel quite differently about the ritual. For instance, the ritual speech may well come after a lengthy period of prior negotiation between two equal parties. It might be accompanied by intense emotional investment, and as a result it might reflect the "true feelings," the deepest aspirations and hopes of the ritual participants. Thus, even though countless generations before me have uttered the words "to have and to hold from this day forward, for better for worse, for richer for poorer," I might well feel a profound investment in precisely these words that I utter to my beloved. I might believe them to be true, hope that they will prove true. I might invest myself fully in the ritual utterances as though they were words that I chose from an infinite number of possible choices to express my particular love for and commitment to this particular person.

In other words, ritual participants might well so invest in or agree with the "context" of a particular ritual occasion that they (from their own resources) fill the ritual speech used within that context with a meaning that is more akin to "everyday speech acts." But there is one difference in that case: the speech acts take from tradition an added weight of authority. One becomes in such an instance infused with the context, the setting, the "polite" or "appropriate" in such a way that words here can mean more (not less) than words can mean in any other place. So it may be for the true believer, at least sometimes, if not always.

The ritual does not prescribe such an emotional state, but where the stakes are high (as often in marriage), it does invite such an investment. And where it occurs, I am not convinced that the critic, standing outside the liturgy and looking on from an analytical perspective, can rightfully dismiss such an investment as collusion in oppressive authoritative structures. For perhaps ritual participants really do experience the best form of themselves in the saying of these words, which carry more meaning here than words can possibly carry in the rough-and-tumble mundane world. In any case, insofar as members of the community *mean* what they say in these prayers, they will be asked to invest in the fragile community that gathers here, as nowhere else, and that speaks these like no other words. To some readers, this may perhaps be a subtler form of control. But to those who believe, it may instead unleash the freedom to hope for a better world to come.

In other words, and by way of conclusion, the choice to embark upon the ritual is not trivial, and the choice of which ritual to embark upon is likewise not trivial. The choice of this ritual script over some other possible ritual script, whether from Jewish tradition or the emerging Christian movement, can indeed tell us something significant about the community that prays "in this way." The choice of words, the juxtaposition of particular phrases, the verb tenses, cannot perhaps be translated into other words like those of a homily or an argument, but they have meaning in that they embody traditional, if fixed and scripted, hopes and aspirations of the community. The formulas may not act exactly as symbols pregnant with meaning, at least not in a clear or obvious sense, but the participants in the ritual would have been free to invest something of their identity in the words themselves as if they were choosing just what to say at just this moment. No doubt that choice could at other times have amounted to nothing more than a verbal object, the polite, proper, accepted thing to say before and after partaking of food, a way of pretending the meal meant more than the ingestion of food. But whether out of politeness or with genuine investment, those who chose to embark on this ritual thereby asserted the meal to be a gathering of unusual significance, a place where "we" are set apart and "our" coming together is about something more than the obvious food on the plate.

The Ritual Meal in Didache 9–10: Progress in Understanding

John J. Clabeaux

The meal rituals presented in Did. 9–10 and referred to in Did. 14 have long eluded consensus as to how the meal was celebrated and what exactly it involved. It has given rise to speculative reconstructions that are presented as *the true understanding* of the ritual. In the last two decades a greater possibility of consensus is emerging, which is informed by liturgical studies such as those of Paul Bradshaw and the applications of ritual studies by Jonathan Draper and Jonathan Schwiebert. Schwiebert's *Knowledge and the Coming Kingdom*[1] represents a significant advance in comprehending not only what the prayers in Did. 9–10 meant, but how they fit within the development of early Christian liturgical practice. In the "Afterword" of his classic commentary on the Didache, Kurt Niederwimmer mused:

> It is not easy to locate the Didache within the whole sweep of the history of early Christianity. Still, one can form a more or less complete picture of this document, and from that alone is it possible to give a rather accurate estimate of the place occupied by the Didache.[2]

I believe Schwiebert to have succeeded in this, and I focus on his work for three additional reasons: It is one of the most sustained and detailed treatments of Did. 9–10. Second, Schwiebert has been an active participant in the "Didache in Context" group of the Society of Biblical Literature. He

---

1. Jonathan Schwiebert, *Knowledge and the Coming Kingdom: The Didache's Meal Ritual and Its Place in Early Christianity*, LNTS 373 (London: T&T Clark, 2008).
2. Kurt Niederwimmer, *The Didache: A Commentary*, trans. Linda M. Mahoney, Hermeneia (Minneapolis: Fortress, 1998), 228.

built well on foundations laid by Draper[3] and with direct support from Helmut Koester (Harvard University), a New Testament scholar and early church historian who spent the greater part of his career in the study of the sayings of Jesus traditions. The help Schwiebert received from Jewish scholars Paula Frederickson (Boston University) and Jonathan Klawans (Boston University) enabled him to avoid the mistakes often made in Didache research involving Jewish prayers and customs. Finally, in this book Schwiebert has significantly clarified that the central focus of the thanksgiving prayers and ritual are the *knowledge* communicated in the tradition of the sayings of Jesus and the *immanent onset of the eschaton*. He accomplishes this by careful textual analysis, with attention to oral features of ritual development and ritual dynamics, and then by a study of the trajectory of the Didache meal prayers in later Christian literature. He brings this off well, showing restraint and nuance in demonstrating that: (1) the Didache meal ritual does not invoke the Last Supper or deal directly with the death and resurrection of Jesus, as is often assumed until relatively recently in discussions; (2) the sayings material in the Didache relates most closely, but not perfectly, to the sayings traditions in Q more than to the Gospel of Thomas or to the Gospel of John; (3) the meanings of the Didache meal prayers were sometimes absorbed by compromise but in the end were misunderstood and overridden both in orthodox works such as the Apostolic Constitutions and Canons and equally badly by ascetic and gnostic Egyptian texts, resulting in what Schwiebert calls "a dead end that has two faces"[4] for the Didache meal prayer tradition.

The story of the use of the Didache meal prayers in different, even conflicting, traditions is the subject of the last three chapters of the book.[5] It is one of the most instructive sections of the book and demonstrates that the later use of a text is not a reliable indicator of the original meaning of the text. The meaning of the Didache eluded both the orthodox appropriation, with their explicit Last Supper and passion connections, and the Valentinians, among others, who made of it what they would. In the end the meaning of the Didache's prayers must be interpreted from what is said in Did. 9 and 10. We simply do not yet have sufficient insight into what the Didache community was actually like to be confident of the accuracy

---

3.[3] Jonathan Draper, "Ritual Process and Ritual Symbol in Didache 7–10," *VC* 54 (2000): 121–58.

4. Schwiebert, *Knowledge and the Coming Kingdom*, 239.

5. Ibid., 183–250.

of our readings of these prayers. But thanks to Schwiebert and those on whom he depends, we are getting closer.

In this essay, I will address these three demonstrations by Schwiebert in greater detail and highlight matters of special significance for the advancement of Didache studies. I conclude by commenting on theological implications of the results under discussion for those who wish to understand Christian meal prayers today.

1. The Didache Prayers Themselves

In his first four chapters Schwiebert provides a detailed "state of the question" on the challenges Did. 9–10 presents to understanding how it relates to what was to develop as Christian eucharistic prayers. The first chapter ("Ritual History of an Idiosyncratic Tradition") makes a cogent plea to consider it likely that, in the earliest days of the Jesus movement, there could be markedly different understandings of what the community meal involved and communicated. For years research was taken up with the discussion of whether this was a Eucharist or an agape, presuming a perfect agreement on what exactly those two terms described, where or whether there were "words of institution" (there are none), at what point the bread and wine were changed into the body and blood (neither body nor blood are mentioned in Did. 9–10), and whether the Didache Eucharist involved an actual "filling" meal or only the "eucharistic elements." It is made clear in the chapters of Schwiebert's book that follow (chs. 2–4) that the actual meal came after the prayers of Did. 9, and the meal was then followed by the blessings of Did. 10. This is not like present mainstream Christian practices, but it is what a plain reading of Did. 10.1 requires when it says, "Then after you are full, give thanks like this."[6]

One thing has been and remains for many people not a question, namely, that the prayers of Did. 9–10 were based on Jewish meal prayers. This assumption almost always specifies the Birkat Hamazon with which the Didache prayers have only a few words in common. I have yet to speak to a Jew familiar by experience with the Birkat Hamazon who sees any significant similar content. But year after year, this is passed on as what

---

6. Much as people would like to see the liturgical dialogue in Did. 10.6 ("If anyone is holy, let him come") as some sort of invitation to come forward to receive, the plain meaning of 10.1 rules out the possibility. Translations of the Didache are from Schwiebert, *Knowledge and the Coming Kingdom*, 63 (10.1) and 72 (10.6).

Schwiebert describes "tongue in cheek" as "a 'golden link' between Jewish meal prayers and the Christian Eucharistic anaphoras."[7] There are more terms and concepts in parallel with the prayers of Did. 9–10 in the Lord's Prayer as it appears in Did. 8 than there are to any Jewish meal prayers we can actually establish as in use in this period. To this we will shortly return.

In chapter 2 ("The Last Supper Tradition"), Schwiebert presents the requisite parallel column displays of the Markan, Matthean, Lukan, and Pauline (1 Cor 11) eucharistic prayers and then their later interpretation in Ignatius of Antioch, John 6, and Justin Martyr. This is familiar ground, but the way that Schwiebert presents it is very effective in that it sets a baseline by which one can see that almost everything in Did. 9–10 is different from the canonical Last Supper tradition. In the four eucharistic texts from the Gospels and Epistles, and in all three of the later church fathers, one sees "body and blood" and connection to the passion narrative, neither of which is mentioned in Did. 9–10. The assumption that it must be implied in Did. 9–10 is undone by Schwiebert's thorough ritual analysis in chapter 3 ("The Logic of the Didache's Meal Ritual"). This is an important chapter. I am not convinced about certain details of his argument, but on the whole I find it quite convincing. I noted after reading it how much he owed to Draper's "Ritual Process and Ritual Symbol in Didache 7–10."[8] In that essay, Draper showed how Victor Turner's three stages of initiation rites ("separation, liminality, and aggregation") are modeled in Did. 1–10. It is a highly satisfying explanation not only of the logic of Did. 7–10, but actually of Did. 1–10 in that the teaching of the Two Ways will separate the gentiles seeking to enter into the community. They are in a liminal state just prior to baptism in Did. 7, for which they and those carrying out the rite with them must fast. Then in Did. 8 they are given the prayer that, in their praying it three times a day from that day on, will remind them of that rite of *liminality*, instantiate their *separation* from other gentiles and the community's prerabbinic competitors that the author calls "the hypocrites," and *aggregate* them with their fellows who also pray it three times a day. The meal ritual is the consummate means of enacting and remembering their aggregation. I will return to this. Schwiebert's interpretation is affected by Draper's, but rather than repeat Draper's arguments, Schwiebert provides further evidence from

---

7. Schwiebert, *Knowledge and the Coming Kingdom*, 10. He is no more convinced of this "golden link" than I.

8. Draper, "Ritual Process and Ritual Symbol."

his analysis of the "fixed elements" that appear in the prayers in Did. 9–10, namely, (1) the "we thank you Father," which occurs exactly three times (9.2, 3; and 10.2), (2) the "which you made known" clauses, which also occur three times in the same verses (9.2, 3; and 10.2), (3) the "gather into your kingdom" petition, which appears at the end of each set of prayers (9.4 and 10.5), and (4) the doxologies throughout the prayers, four short (9.2, 3; 10.2; and 10.4) and two long (9.4 and 10.5).[9] Schwiebert indicates the ritual effects of each of these. The "we thank you" prayers provide "a formal realization that gratitude is being required by some specific situation—for example eating." But the last one "*constructs* a relationship of dependence between the speaker(s) and the deity … namely as children to a father. This relationship of dependence is not communicated or explained by these words, but *assumed* or *inculcated* by them."[10]

In the three "which you made known" clauses, "the ritual participants are being scripted in the role of a group who has received knowledge from God."[11] The "gather into your kingdom" petitions "take for granted the existence (if only in the future) of a 'kingdom' belonging uniquely to God and defining the fate of the community."[12] And then in the doxologies, "the community signals its acceptance of each prayer spoken by the leader."[13] All of this comes to a climax in the dramatic liturgical dialogue of 10.6.[14] This reading of the ritual cues substantiates Schwiebert's argument that the prayers are primarily focused on "knowledge and the coming kingdom" as opposed to the body and blood of Christ or the saving death and resurrection.

My only serious reservations about Schwiebert's arguments in this chapter involve his emendation of the doxology in Did. 9.4. He agrees with Klaus Wengst that "through Jesus Christ" is a later addition, as that title appears nowhere else in the Didache. But Schwiebert adds that there was also a corruption of the "power and glory" from 8.2 to the reversed order of "glory and power" in 9.4. He bases this argument in part on the fact that, without the "through Jesus Christ" clause in 9.4, both 9.4 and 10.5 have

---

9. Schwiebert, *Knowledge and the Coming Kingdom*, 78.
10. Ibid., 79 (emphasis original).
11. Ibid., 80.
12. Ibid., 81.
13. Ibid., 81.
14. Ibid., 82.

exactly twice as many syllables as the shorter doxologies.[15] My objection is that text criticism must be carried on with great caution in the Didache, given the limited number of manuscripts. The Coptic fragment does not include Did. 9. Schwiebert's argument from syllable count and scansion is trumped by a pattern of reversals that Draper noted in these prayers. Draper's discussion of the structure of Did. 9–10 is more elegant and does not need to resort to textual emendation. Draper sees a clean structure of three units before the eating of the meal (two blessings and one petition) and three units after the meal (again two blessings and a petition), all of which is concluded with the liturgical dialogue in 10.6.[16] The short and long doxologies mark off the parallelisms in this two-fold structure and some of these parallelisms are chiastic; that is, they involve reversals of order. In Did. 9 we encounter cup (9.2) and bread (as fragment, 9.3), but in Did. 10.3 we see the order "food and drink" and "spiritual food and drink," reversing the order of Did. 9. Draper further points out that in 9.3 we see "life and knowledge" and then in 10.2 "knowledge and faith and immortality," which, if we take *immortality* as equivalent to *life*, reverses the order of "life and knowledge" that appeared in 9.3. This is important, because it can be seen again in the pattern of the long doxologies in 8.2, 9.4, and 10.5. "Power and glory" appears in 8.2, "glory and power" in 9.4, and "power and glory" in 10.5. Given the other reversals mentioned by Draper, the reversal of order in 9.4 does not require textual emendation, and this eliminates Schwiebert's supporting argument for dropping the "through Jesus Christ" in 9.4.[17]

The pattern of the doxologies in Did. 8–10 brings us back to Draper's arguments about structure in Did. 7–10.[18] In "Ritual Process and Ritual Symbol in Didache 7–10," Draper provided a helpful three-parallel-column presentation of the text of Did. 7–8, then 9, and then 10. Draper followed up on Niederwimmer's suggestion that the eucharistic prayers of Did. 9–10 may have been the *Sitz im Leben* for the development of the doxology in the Lord's Prayer in Did. 8.2, commenting that "most of the

---

15. Ibid., 65.
16. Draper, "Ritual Process and Ritual Symbol," 139–40.
17. Niederwimmer, *Didache*, 138, presents an important chart of the short and long doxologies in Did. 8, 9, and 10. I recall showing it to Reuven Kimelman in a discussion on the Didache prayers. He immediately noted the change of word order in 9.4 and remarked "that helps establish an *inclusio* from 8.2 to 10.5."
18. Draper, "Ritual Process and Ritual Symbol," 139–40.

ritual symbols of the Eucharist Prayers are found also in the Lord's Prayer" and that the Lord's Prayer is integral to the structure of the Didache, and in fact that the Lord's Prayer in Did. 8 may have been formulated the way it was precisely for the purpose of the initiation process.[19] I wish to follow up on this by revising his parallel column presentation of Did. 7–10 by restricting it to the prayers in Did. 8–10 to see what it reveals about the relationship of the Lord's Prayer to the eucharistic prayers.

Did. 8	Did. 9	Did. 10
	First about the cup:	
	<u>We give thanks to you,</u>	<u>We give thanks to you,</u>
<u>Our Father,</u>	<u>Our Father,</u>	<u>Holy Father,</u>
who are in heaven		
<u>hallowed be your name.</u> **Your kingdom come,** Your will be done on earth as in heaven.	for the <u>holy</u> vine of David your servant,	<u>for your holy name,</u> which you caused to dwell in our hearts, and for the knowledge and faith and immortality,
	<u>which you have made known to us through Jesus your servant.</u>	<u>which you have made known to us through Jesus your Servant.</u>
	<u>To you be glory into the ages.</u>	<u>To you be glory into the ages.</u>
		You, Almighty Master, have created all things on account of your name,
<u>Give us today our daily bread</u> and forgive us our debt, as we forgive our debtors.	Then, about <u>the fragment</u>: We give thanks to you, <u>Our Father</u> for the life and knowledge, which you have made known to us <u>through Jesus your servant.</u>	<u>food and drink you have given to the sons of men</u> for refreshment. But to us you have graciously given spiritual food and drink and eternal life <u>through Jesus your servant.</u>

---

19. Ibid., 137–38. The earlier article was "Christian Self-Definition against the 'Hypocrites' in *Didache* 8," in *The Didache in Modern Research*, ed. Jonathan A. Draper, AGJU 37 (Leiden: Brill, 1996), 223–43.

			For[a] (or before) all things we give thanks to you because you are mighty.
		To you be glory into the ages.	To you be glory into the ages.
	And lead us not into testing but deliver us from the evil one,	Just as this fragment was scattered over the mountains and, when gathered, became one, so let your church be gathered from the ends of the earth **into your kingdom**.	Remember, Lord, your church, by delivering it from every evil and making it complete in your love, and gather it from the four winds **into your kingdom**, which your prepared for her.
	For yours is the power and the glory into the ages.	For yours is the glory and the power through Jesus Christ into the ages.	For yours is the power and the glory into the ages.

Note

a. MS H reads πρό for a translation of "before." It is an easy misreading of the more sensible ὑπέρ (*Lectio difficilior preferendum est, sed non sine sensu*).

When the prayers are aligned in this way, many parallels and reversals "pop out." The underlines on the chart indicate the strongest direct parallels in vocabulary or concepts. Note particularly the very last lines of each column: the long doxology appears in all three, but chapter 9 has "power and glory" reversed and may have had the special name indicated by διὰ Ἰησοῦ Χριστοῦ. This could have been added later, but there is no manuscript evidence for the text without it, and its presence is attested (admittedly weakly) by Apos. Con. 7.25.4 by διὰ αὐτοῦ. Then notice the very first lines: only chapters 9 and 10 have the "we thank you" formula, but all three have "Father" followed by something being "hallowed." Only chapter 10 has the unusual "Holy Father," which appears elsewhere only in John 17:11. Both 8 and 10 have the "holy name," but 9 has the unusual "holy vine of David." The greater extent of word for word repetition in 9 and 10 is due, I think, to the predominance of formulaic language in the meal prayers, as in the "we thank you" prayers, the "which you have made known" clauses, and the short and long doxologies. Schwiebert refers to these as the "fixed elements" of the Didache prayers and makes a powerful argument for their importance in stressing the significance of the coming kingdom in these prayers.[20]

The bold-face type indicates a *long-range, reverse parallel*. The "kingdom" occurs in the first element of chapter 8 but in the last of both 9 and 10. This may seem like *reaching* on my part, but it may suggest a deliberate progression in the movement from the Lord's Prayer to the end of the meal prayers. That progression may also be attested by the way in which the simple "daily bread" (or "bread of tomorrow" or "bread of the age to come") in the central unit of 8 is paralleled in the other center units by "fragment" in 9.3 and then doubly paralleled by "food and drink" and "spiritual food and drink" in 10.3.[21]

The petition of the third element of the Lord's Prayer in Did. 8 ("and lead us not … but deliver us from evil") is strongly paralleled in 10, which even picks up the word "evil." The word "evil" does not appear in Did. 9, but perhaps this is to indicate that the *evil* to be feared is the scattering of the "assembly" or whatever the author means by ἐκκλησία.

---

20. Schwiebert, *Knowledge and the Coming Kingdom*, 78–82.

21. "Bread of tomorrow" and "bread of the age to come" are alternative translations for ἐπιούσιος, traditionally rendered as "daily." They are mentioned here because they correspond with the intensely eschatological tone of Did. 9–10. Hans Dieter Betz, *Sermon on the Mount: A Commentary on the Sermon on the Mount, including the Sermon on the Plain (Matthew 5:3–7:27 and Luke 6:20–49)*, Hermeneia (Minneapolis: Fortress, 1995), 397–400. Betz discusses the possibilities in detail, noting at the outset "The problem of the meaning of the term ἐπιούσιος has been debated since antiquity." He is least impressed by the arguments from semitic roots and the arguments from the versions that render it by the more mystical "*supersubstantialem* (Vulgate) or *perpetuum* (Curetonian Syriac). He gives serious consideration to meanings derived from ἐπιέναι (such as, "for the following day") and those derived from ἐπι ουσία, such as "what is necessary for existence (398). Frederick Danker (BDAG, 376–77) pushes in the direction of a translation that emphasizes eschatology, but it takes time to discover this. He lists in order four major meanings: (1) "necessary for existence"; (2) "for the current day"; (3) "for the following day"; and (4) "for the future," which is subdivided into five "sub-meanings." He cites thirteen articles later than 1500 for the first meaning, six for the second, and eighteen for the third. In support of the fourth meaning, he cites thirty-one articles later than 1500, with twenty-five of these articles supporting the last of the five "sub-meanings": "referring to the coming kingdom and its feast." *Also sprach Danker!* He seems to be pushing the argument toward a translation that is very favorable to Schwiebert's argument that "the coming kingdom" is a primary matter of importance to the Didache prayers.

It is difficult to determine whether the meal prayers were the source of the Lord's Prayer in Did. 8 or the other way around. If the Lord's Prayer were constructed from the meal prayers, it is difficult to understand why the "we thank you" formula and the creational references are missing from the Lord's Prayer. But if the Lord's Prayer were the source of the meal prayers, it is hard to understand why forgiveness of sin is absent from the meal prayers. Still, the single closing doxology of the Lord's Prayer could have served as the model for both the short and long doxologies in the meal prayers, but the reverse is also possible.

The web of connections between the prayer in Did. 8, which is placed directly after the baptismal instruction and just before the meal prayers, supports Draper's conclusions about the interconnectedness of 7–10 as leading to an experience of aggregation. The rather high percentage of formulaic words supports Schwiebert's conclusions about the significance of the fixed parts of the prayers signaling the primary importance of the experience of the community members being placed in a situation of dependence on the Father for supplying the knowledge and life and not only awaiting but nearly "living into" the coming kingdom.

2. The Relationship of the Didache Meal Ritual to Other Early Christian Texts

Schwiebert's fifth chapter ("The Original Milieu of Didache 9–10") begins with a well nuanced expression of the Jewish background of Didache, indicating that it was a community of a Greek-speaking background with a strong desire to bring in gentiles. He does not take particular rabbinic prayers and argue that they affected the Didache prayers. His discussion of the possible effect of Q on the Didache is quite compelling. One might hesitate to accept a relationship between the Didache and Q, since the Didache shares so many features and expressions with Matthew that the use of Q would seem unnecessary. More importantly, positing a relationship between the Didache and Q is bedeviled by the many unresolved questions about both. We know precious little about the actual community that produced the Didache, when it existed, where it existed, and over how much time its text was used or ignored. There are also many questions difficult to resolve that surround the exact makeup of Q. What was the full extent of Q? Are the roughly 6,500 words in an English translation that we now possess about 90 percent of Q, or merely 20–50 percent? The higher percentage is reasonable, since that is about the percentage of Mark that

Matthew and Luke manifest. But I have no way of knowing for certain that Q was not two to four times as long as our recovered 6,500 words or even if the extent of Q could vary in every performance of it. There could well have been many things in Q that Matthew and Luke did not feel were necessary or helpful.

Also problematic is the likelihood that Q, like the Didache, is subject to questions about stages of composition (early Q, Q^1, Q^2, etc.). This seriously complicates developing a convincing theory, since every proportional possibility must be multiplied by all other proportional possibilities in the argument. Yet what I found compelling about Schwiebert's chapter is that he demonstrates a number of solid parallel passages in the Didache and early Q, but he does not from this conclude that Did. 9–10 is the Q meal ritual. What he concludes is that from among the set (Q, Gospel of Thomas, and Gospel of John) the best parallels are with Q. That is no small finding in that it presents us with two first century witnesses (Q and the Didache) for Jesus groups for whom the word "gospel" means the sayings of Jesus rather than the kerygma, as it did in the Pauline Epistles and other early Christian literature.[22] The importance of this for our interpretation of the Didache meal ritual is that we must not read it presuming direct reference to the Last Supper and the paschal mystery as in canonical New Testament texts. But I am equally impressed by the fact that Schwiebert does not spell out more exactly the relationship between the Didache and Q. A number of important features of Q are entirely missing from the Didache, for instance the title "Son of Man," the figure of John the Baptist, and the theme of "being opposed to this generation." But it is true that the Two Ways teaching in the Didache does reflect Q's *Deuteronomic* theme, and the Didache's emphasis on active prophecy also supports this connection. But in my examination of Q, I found many passages closer to Matthew than to reconstructed Q. The baptismal formula in Did. 7.1, which is repeated in 7.2, is like Matt 28:19 and so according to some ought to be eliminated from the Didache as a later addition that was meant to conform it to canonical formulae.[23] The Didache Lord's Prayer is closest to

---

22. Niederwimmer, *Didache*, 50. He cites Helmut Koester, *Synoptische Überlieferung bei den apostolischen Vätern*, TUGAL 65/5.10 (Berlin: Akademie, 1957), 10.

23. I am reluctant to dispatch these Trinitarian formulae in Did. 7.1 and 7.2 to a much later revision of Didache as Schwiebert does (*Knowledge and the Coming Kingdom*, 152 n. 8). Schwiebert sees these formulae in Did. 7.1–2 as contradicting Did. 9.5 "baptism in the name of the Lord." He cites Arthur Vööbus, Huub van de Sandt and

Matthew's; Did. 8 has parallels to Matt 6:1–18 (fasting and praying not as "the hypocrites" do); Did. 16 has been well argued as possibly dependent on an apocalypse very like that of Mark 13 (possibly a source of Mark 13) and Matt 24.[24]

Particular phrases from Matthew appear:

- Matt 5:41: the command to go a second mile with one who forces you, though not in Luke, appears in Did. 1.4.
- Matt 5:39: the specification of the "right cheek" is in Did. 1.4 but not in Luke 6:29.
- Matt 5:48: "be perfect" seems to be reflected in Did. 1.4 immediately after the command not to strike back.
- Matt 5:26: "the last penny" appears in Did. 1.5d, but "penny" is missing in Q.
- Matt 19:18 and 5:33: prohibitions appear in Did. 2.2–4 but not in Q.
- Matt 24:31: "gather from the four winds" appears in Did. 10.5b but not in Q.

Sadly, the exact wording of Q is even more elusive than the exact wording of the Didache. Also, just as the Didache is known to have likely endured "updating" similar to what is obvious in manuscripts of 1QS, so it seems that Q, reconstructed in the first place from two different gospels, developed in stages. Dieter Lührmann's observation that "the community from which Matthew obtained Q had already reworked Q" would explain some

---

David Flusser, and Alan Garrow as being in agreement. But is there any evidence from the period that formulae of baptism were so restricted or that Paul, who generally uses the language of "baptized into Christ" (Gal 3:27), would object to the Trinitarian formula? It may be that both 7.1 and 7.2 were glossed, but is there any evidence beyond a requirement of consistency in sacramental formulae? A similar tendency is in evidence in the removal of "through Jesus Christ" in Did. 9.4. Should we also remove "Holy Father" from 10.2, since it appears nowhere else in the Didache, and may have been added by a scribe familiar with the Gospel of John?

24. Alan J. P. Garrow, *The Gospel of Matthew's Dependence on the* Didache, JSNT-Sup 254 (London: T&T Clark, 2004), 190–215. I do not find his emended ending of the Didache (29–66) convincing. Schwiebert points out in a note (*Knowledge and the Coming Kingdom*, 121 n. 35) that Koester long ago (*Synoptische Überlieferung*, 190) argued against the availability of any of the Synoptic Gospels to the composer of the Didache.

of these special connections between the Didache and Q by providing a Q particular to the Matthean community. But it is a hypothesis. The point of these remarks is to express agreement with the caution Schwiebert shows by saying Didache is closer to Q than any other source. We are not entirely clear on what texts or oral traditions were available to the Didache community. Yet Q, or a sayings source related to it, was certainly among them.

3. Schwiebert's Analysis of the Didache Meal Ritual Trajectories: Theological Implications

A warning from Niederwimmer: The Didache is "written without theological claims and entirely focused on praxis and the order of community life.... A reconstruction of the "theology of the *Didache*" would therefore be a foolish enterprise."[25] Without a doubt, the Didache is not systematic theology; it is better described as halakah. But there can be theology implicit in halakah. Thomas O'Laughlin notes that from the time of its discovery the Didache triggered outrage both from *ultra-montane* Catholics and from "extreme Protestants," because it calls into question fixed theological positions about how the Eucharist ought to be conducted, but also demanded fixed times of prayer and fasting, thus annoying people on both ends of the spectrum.[26] Yet a significant dedication to the study of the Didache perdures. In fact, some joke that the Didache does not merely attract readers, it takes prisoners. It is important to examine this *appeal* of the Didache. Consider that the Didache is deceptively familiar to those who know the early Christian canon, but is often even more outspoken than the canonical works that it resembles. It has robust even strident apocalyptic expectation, as in the Pauline Epistles and the book of Revelation, but also radical moral commands like in the Synoptic Gospels. It uses the title ὁ παῖς σύ (with Davidic associations) as in the early chapters of Acts, but also contains the Johannine emphasis on the mystical indwelling of the holy name, and in Did. 9.1 the elusive "holy vine of David" may be related to John 15:1–11. Then there is the liturgical dialogue in Did. 10.6 that compares well with 1 Cor 16:22 and Rev 22:17–20. Finally, there is the elusive relationship to the Gospel of Matthew. It lacks direct reference to the Last Supper and passion/resurrection tradition that we see in

---

25. Niederwimmer, *Didache*, 228.
26. Thomas O'Laughlin, *The Didache: A Window on the Earliest Christians* (Grand Rapids: Baker; London: SPCK, 2010), 8–10.

Matthew, but it has the teaching of the Two Ways that appears in a different form in Matt 7:13–27, the demands for forgiveness of Matt 5:23–26 and 6:14–15, and rules for community order as in Matt 18:15–35 (but again in a very different form). Because of references to εὐαγγέλλιον in the Didache, it was long presumed that the Didache postdated that gospel. Alan Garrow argues persuasively that the Didache was a source for Matthew.[27] But it must be admitted that, in spite of all of these similarities to canonical traditions, "knowledge and the coming kingdom" are forcefully proclaimed in the Didache without direct reference to the Last Supper or the passion and resurrection of Jesus, which are presumed in all the canonical references cited above. To be fair, there is no indication that the Didache community did not believe in the passion and resurrection, but there is no assurance that the community did. People bothered by the fact that the same holds true for Q can deal with the problem by saying that, since we do not have the entire text of Q, we cannot make firm assertions about what precisely was or was not held by that community. But the Didache is nearly complete, a written text, with echoes and resonances in other traditions and texts. These echoes and resonances are examined by Schwiebert in his last three chapters. He describes possible relationships between the language and ritual logic of the Didache and the meal rituals of other groups of Christians from the second to fourth centuries. Schwiebert has engaged the Didache with sensitivity and openness to its uniqueness. His monograph is a tribute to what is amazing about this text, but it will not let those of us who would understand this text rest, satisfied that we comprehend it.

In chapter 7 ("Didache's Meal Ritual and Early Prayer Traditions in Rome and Asia Minor"),[28] he begins with a marvelous description of the development of liturgy in the first four centuries of the Christian movements. He shows that the "great liturgical compromises" that we see in evidence in the fourth century were already happening in the second and

---

27. Garrow, *Gospel of Matthew's Dependence*. Not every argument and reconstruction by Garrow needs to be accepted for him to have succeeded in shifting the basic presumption of Matthean priority to the Didache. As seen in n. 21 above, Koester demonstrated the likelihood of that long ago in (*Synoptische Überlieferung*, 190). The Didache is a community rule in many ways more primitive and less refined than the Gospel of Matthew. Matthew may have fused some of its traditions with the passion/resurrection material of the other Synoptic Gospels.

28. Schwiebert, *Knowledge and the Coming Kingdom*, 186–90.

third. Traditions initially different from and even competing with positions that came to be orthodox were incorporated, even if it meant their subordination to the emerging orthodox position. Schwiebert shows us Luke connecting Jesus as servant, the teacher/revealer of Q and the Didache, to Jesus who suffered, died, and rose from the dead, as in Mark.[29] Then Schwiebert shows that the παῖς title in combination with the doxology so frequent in the Didache appears in 1 Clement, Martyrdom of Polycarp, and the Apostolic Tradition associated with Hippolytus. The Apostolic Tradition is especially notable for its use of similar prayer language to that of Did. 10.[30] Justin Martyr seems to have fewer clear and distinct echoes of the Didache, but even in Justin we see

> praise and thanksgiving for creation, perhaps in great detail; thanksgiving and petition for preservation from evil, including expectancy for the coming kingdom; and thanksgiving for being made worthy of the eucharistic gifts given by Christ (his flesh and blood) which call to mind his sufferings.[31]

Here we see quite clearly the combination of the Didache features with the eventually prevailing association with the passion.

Schwiebert describes a similar situation in chapter 8 ("The Influence of the Didache's Ritual Logic in Egypt"), but the texts he cites are far less familiar. In the Sacramentary of Serapion of Thumis (fourth century) and the papyrus from *Dêr Balizeh* (third–fourth centuries), we see the image of the church as grain once scattered and now gathered. But instead of "into the kingdom" as in the Didache, it is "into the one Catholic church." But each of these texts presupposes an institution narrative and Last Supper connections. In the papyrus from *Dêr Balizeh*, not only is grain used as a symbol of ingathering, but also water and wine. It is gathered now rather than in the future as in the Didache. Cyprian further to the west reflects this image of gathering in the wine.[32]

Schwiebert cites the ascetic meal prayer in the Pseudo-Athanasian, *Virg.* 13, which resembles Did. 9.4:

---

29. Ibid., 186–90.
30. Ibid., 190–201.
31. Ibid., 206.
32. Ibid., 209–11.

> When you recline at table and begin to break bread, sealing (it) three times, in this way give thanks and say,
>> "We thank you, our Father, for your holy resurrection, for through Jesus your servant you have made it known to us. And just as this bread was scattered, which is upon this table, and being gathered became one, so let your assembly be gathered from the corners of the earth into your kingdom. Because yours is the power and the glory forever and ever. Amen."[33]

There can be no question regarding the influence, if not of the Didache text itself, of an orally transmitted tradition of its meal ritual. Unlike the echoes from Rome and Asia Minor, we see here "gathering from the four corners into the kingdom" rather than "into the church." In the very next section (*Virg.* 14), we see elements of Did. 10 with giving thanks, doxology, reference to creation, the "name above every name," "fleshly nourishments" contrasted with "heavenly food," and "through your beloved servant our Lord Jesus Christ, with whom to you be glory, honor, dominion, forever and ever, amen."[34] Once again the echoes of the Didache are clear, but so are the touches of the Last Supper/passion tradition with the reference to resurrection and the fact that these prayers are to be prayed according to a schedule of the third hour, sixth hour, and ninth hour that seems to have been set by the passion narrative.

Next Schwiebert discusses traces of the Didache in Barnabas, which are more thoroughly connected to the passion and then echoes the Epistle to Diognetus, which refers to the "servant" figure, but also shows possible influence from Paul's letter to the Romans and the Sermon on the Mount.[35]

A Valentinian prayer from the Tripartite Tractate (late 200's) exhibits clear gnosticizing tendencies, yet a source of the prayer seems to be Did. 9-10, as elements of its ritual logic are present.[36] The Tripartite Tractate parallels are rather faint, but some Valentinian Expositions (XI 43, 20-38 and 44, 1-37) show striking parallels with the Didache prayers, but also introduce gnostic features.

In Clement of Alexandria's *Stromata*, Schwiebert shows echoes of the Didache's ritual logic. In *Strom.* 7.6.31.7-8, Jesus is "him through whom

---

33. Ibid., 213.
34. Ibid., 214.
35. Ibid., 217-22.
36. Ibid., 222-28.

we receive our knowledge," and it moves immediately to prayers of glorification and petition. He shows several other passages that express the combination of "glorification and knowledge." But Schwiebert further points out that the actual eucharistic prayers in these texts do not look like Did. 9–10 except for the use of doxologies. But unlike the Didache, these prayers make direct reference to the saving death of Jesus.[37]

His discussion of *Strasbourg Papyrus* 254 (fourth–fifth centuries) is the most striking. The prayer begins with reference to creation "through your wisdom," which turns out to be "the light of your true Son." We see prayers of "giving thanks," described as "sacrifice" (but the language is that of Rom 12), multiple references to "the holy name," and then "remember your holy and only Catholic church." There follows an open ended petitionary prayer, and it ends with "through our Lord and Savior, through whom be glory to you through the ages." Schwiebert wisely concludes that here we see both "kinship and distance." Yet he is able to conclude the chapter with the well-grounded assertion that "the phrases and formulae, as well as the ritual logic of the Didache are better attested in Egypt than elsewhere."[38]

Less needs to be said of Schwiebert's last chapter ("The End of a Trajectory"), since the texts and arguments of Ignatius of Antioch, Irenaeus, and the Apostolic Constitutions and Canons are more familiar and widely known. Clearly in this period, battle lines were drawn and firm efforts made to assert the Last Supper-related meal prayers (with unambiguous and repeated reference to the body and blood) and with almost every possible reference to the distinctive features of Did. 9–10 prayers being altered or removed. This is most clearly displayed in Apos. Con. 7.25–26 in which:

- the cup prayer is removed
- thanks is offered for "life" but not "knowledge"
- "knowledge, faith and immortality ... made known" is replaced with "knowledge and faith and love and immortality that you gave"
- some doxologies are removed
- reference to "the fragment" is removed

---

37. Ibid., 229–34.
38. Ibid., 235–37.

- thanks for "the precious blood of Christ and the precious body is added"
- the liturgical dialogue of Did. 10.6 calling for the coming of the Lord and this world passing away is replaced "with an invitation by the priest to the congregation to 'come forward' and partake of the elements."[39]

Schwiebert's arguments are presented in detail because the story of the trajectory and final near extinguishing of the voice of the Didache that it evidences is an important story. The Didache, which survives in full in only one manuscript, goes back to a very early time and affected North Africa, the Eastern Mediterranean, and Rome, but was eventually nearly eliminated. It is worthwhile to deal with the potential theological or at least ecclesiological implications of this process.

The Didache meal that Schwiebert describes was a ritual in which (1) the initiates along with the community expressed gratitude for knowledge that came from a loving Father, "mediated by his Servant, Jesus"; (2) the gathered community "was scripted in the role of an eschatological potentiality" (i.e., the coming kingdom, which was incredibly important to them); and (3) "this religious and social posture was achieved above all by the periodic repetition of the fixed formulae of the community's meal ritual; and it also must have been fostered by (and helped to foster) the type of instruction transmitted in these circles."[40] If Schwiebert is correct in this description of the distinctive features of this ritual, I am not so surprised that, even though other Christian groups had meal rituals with direct links to the Last Supper and passion, the features peculiar to the Didache remained valuable, honored, and celebrated in as many different times and places as they were.

What can be disturbing to a person steeped in a eucharistic tradition is to imagine how a meal prayer that did not relate directly to the Last Supper and passion could have perdured. More importantly, it raises another question: Was anything lost in the eventual elimination of such a ritual as we see in Did. 9–10?

It is questionable how serious a role apocalyptic eschatology plays in the consciousness of the average participant in many forms of present day

---

39. Ibid., 246.
40. Ibid., 248.

Christian liturgical worship. In the popular imagination, "heaven" is far more often the language of that for which one hopes, as opposed to the age to come, the transformation of a universe (and a people) being freed from its slavery to corruption. The more prevalent view of the afterlife as "heaven" seems to diminish any serious importance to the coming kingdom as described in the Didache, the Pauline Epistles, and other apocalyptic sections of the New Testament. "Heaven" is readily sentimentalized and individualized. The community that prayed the Didache seemed to cry out in its own time as though the age to come was nearly in reach and that, just as glorification took place in the pronouncement of the doxologies, so was the kingdom nearer and the people more united in sober expectation as it cried out "Come!"

Further, as an educator I am concerned with the dearth of serious religious education for adults in mainline congregations and parishes. In its simplicity, Did. 9–10 (although really 1–10) expresses the absolute character of and the need for the nurture and development of the "gift of knowledge." It calls for continuous rather than occasional prayer (even fasting) and a far more integrated and pervasive engagement in instruction. Was the general success of the liturgical tradition that emphasized the elements (bread and wine) and their association with "body and blood" given for the forgiveness of sins accomplished at the expense of a robust understanding of the presence of God in the Word?

The strong case that Schwiebert made for relationship with Q and the basic agreement with that tradition in its lack of direct connection to the Last Supper, death, and resurrection tradition invites one final comment on theological implications. What is clear is that, while the Didache makes no direct reference to the death and resurrection, neither does it expressly deny them. The rather consistent pattern of authors later than the Didache merging its ritual logic with clear passion and resurrection traditions suggests that they did not view the Didache's theology as directly opposed to their own. This may not entirely be a matter of misunderstanding. "Resurrection" is never mentioned in the Didache, but some sort of concept of the resurrection fits with the Didache's references to the gift of "life" in 9.4 and "immortality" in 10.6. This is not evidence that the framers of the Didache proclaimed the resurrection, but it should be noted that the "life" that they did proclaim has many possible referents. In the Gospel of John, "life" is connected to the role of Jesus as restoring "life" by his passion and resurrection. In addition to this interest in the gift of "life," John shares with the Didache a mysticism of the indwelling of the "name." Besides the reference to "baptism in the name" in Did. 9.5, we see that expression in 10.2: "for your holy name, which you caused to dwell in our hearts, and for knowledge, and faith, and immortality, which you made known through Jesus your Servant." The mystical workings of "word" (and "the words") and "the name" in John's theology appear in John 17:6–8:

> I have made your name known to those whom you gave me from the world. They were yours, and you gave them to me, and they have kept your *word*. Now they know that everything given me is from you, for the *words* that you gave to me I have given to them, and they have received them and know in truth that I came from you.

and more dramatically in 17:11b:

> Holy Father, protect them *in your name* that you have given me, so that they may be one as we are one.

In 17:12 this *name*, which protects them, keeps them from being "lost." Here we have the convergence of *the giving of knowledge, the giving and retaining of the word*, and the *protection by the name*. This is related to John 15:1–11 on the "true vine." In John 15:1–11 we also see the *word* as active in "cleansing" and contributing to the "remaining on the vine" (15:4–5) rather than being "cast into the fire" (15:6). These expressions may bear no direct relation to the Didache prayers, but what we do not know about the location and origin of the Didache community should make us hesitate to deny any relationship to the Johannine tradition.

The connection between the Didache and the Gospel of John as demonstrated by Johannes Betz[41] may shed light on how the Didache's ritual logic is likely to have influenced later canonical Christian writings. Betz's arguments are especially relevant to the point being made in this part of my essay, because they deal precisely with a "Lord's Supper theology" of the Didache, which he sees as related to that of the Gospel of John.[42] Betz sees the following themes in both works: (1) Jesus as a revealer, (2) the

---

41. Johannes Betz, "The Eucharist in the *Didache*," in Draper, *Didache in Modern Research*, 244–75. Betz's argument (274) that Did. 9–10 is not an agape and a Eucharist but a Eucharist based on an agape text does not need to be accepted in order to appreciate the strength of his analysis of the verbal and material relationship between the Didache and the Gospel of John.

42. Betz, "Eucharist in the *Didache*," 255.

image of the vine associated directly with Jesus, (3) the association of the bread with life and immortality, and (4) prayer for sanctification and gathering.[43] He presents a chart with nineteen different terms in Did. 9–10, which appear in seven chapters of the Gospel of John. With support from Rudolf Schnackenburg, Betz concludes that "the fourth Gospel knew and used the Eucharistic prayers and formulations of the Didache tradition, even if it was from the oral stream of tradition."[44] Betz argues persuasively that the Didache was not dependent on John and also that it is doubtful that the author of the Fourth Gospel "had Didache as a literary entity before him." Finally, he acknowledges that "what the Didache says preliminarily and briefly, is amplified and clarified, and more strongly Christologized in the Fourth Gospel."[45]

Betz also notes the connection between the Didache and John on the issue of "the vine." Starting with the use of the image of vineyard in Isa 5 as Israel, Betz sees the vine in Did. 9.2 as Christ and all Christians, as in 1 Cor 10:17. He states that in that passage "'holy vine of David' refers primarily to the person of Jesus as the Davidic Messiah, but secondarily to the meal fellowship constituted and actualized by him: so we come in fact close to the Johannine understanding of the vine."[46]

These points of contact between John and the Didache tradition are quite important in terms of understanding the relationship of the Didache to canonical New Testament works. In its relation to John, the Didache seems to be part of a stream of tradition that was taken seriously by the author of the Fourth Gospel, but it represents important steps in an earlier stage in the development of eucharistic theology on which the Gospel of John was to build. The Fourth Gospel has increased the theological complexity, but it seems that important contributions were made by the early Syrian meal tradition, which, while it did not proclaim the death and resurrection, still spoke of the significance of the meal in ways that were formative for the later Christological development of the author of the Fourth Gospel, who could be very suspicious of unsympathetic views. What we *do* see in the Gospel of John, which is much later than the Didache, is a concentration of certain language and images that for John do not exist "over

---

43. Ibid., 255.
44. Ibid., 256. Rudolf Schnackenburg, *The Gospel According to St. John*, 3 vols. (London: Burns & Oates, 1968), 1:152.
45. Betz, "Eucharist in the *Didache*," 256.
46. Ibid., 267.

against" a death and resurrection emphasis. As was seen in the second to fourth centuries, both sets of ideas can be brought together and not always with the violence that was done to the Didache in Apos. Con. 7.25–26.

As a final expression of gratitude for Schwiebert's *Knowledge and the Coming Kingdom*, it should be said that the readiness of so many traditions to bring the ritual logic of the Didache into their streams of theology and ritual traditions suggests that these traditions saw something valuable in the Didache. In spite of the Didache's final suppression, can we not yet see a value in it for Christianity today? If we can, then by studying the early centuries of Christian liturgy, and this very early work in particular, we might yet be like "the householder who brings out of his or her storehouse new things, but also old things" (Matt 13:52c).

Response to Essays on Leadership and Liturgy in the Didache

Joseph G. Mueller, S.J.

The four chapters to which I have the privilege of responding present us with rich perspectives on ritual and prayer in the central portion of the Didache, chapters 7–10. Of these four essays, Jonathan Schwiebert's asks the most basic question about the interpretation of this passage. He challenges us to think deeply about how the ritual character of these chapters should determine the way readers interpret them. It is for this reason that in what follows I will respond first to Schwiebert's essay. His contribution has helped direct my thinking about Huub van de Sandt's contribution on prerequisites for participation in the Eucharist of the Didache and about Peter Tomson's reflections on the place of the Lord's Prayer in this document. I give over the last part of my response to John Clabeaux's review of Schwiebert's marvelous book on the meal ritual of the Didache.

Chapters 3–6 of that book, *Knowledge and the Coming Kingdom: The Didache's Meal Ritual and Its Place in Early Christianity*, drew inspiration from Maurice Bloch's theory of ritual in order to build an interpretation of this ancient Eucharist. Schwiebert's contribution in this present volume begins by helpfully summarizing the main findings of those chapters, but he goes on to examine more explicitly than he did in his book the way Bloch's theory can help and hinder interpretation of the meal ritual presented in Did. 9–10. In the beginning of his essay, Schwiebert rightly takes as settled the notion that these prayer texts transmit to us formulaic speech, phrases fixed in advance of the liturgy's enactment. He judiciously points out that figuring out how to interpret this ritual, with its fixed and variable elements, provides more of a challenge than determining which of its elements are fixed or variable.

He calls on Bloch's theory of ritual to invite the students of the Didache to change the ways they usually have interpreted the fixed formulae of chapters 9 and 10. Schwiebert tells us that most seem at least to imply that these expressions do not mean much of anything, but when they can, scholars find ideas and thoughts expressed in these formulae by comparing them to other ancient texts, sometimes nonritual ones. Supposed authorial decisions on the terms, grammatical constructions, and word order in these fixed formulae guide the search for this sort of meaning in them, a search that aims at displaying their meaning by translating the fixed lines of the ritual into equivalent expressions.

Bloch's theory tells us that this way of finding meaning in a ritual text like Did. 9–10 cannot reveal the relationship people have to the words of the rite while they are practicing it, for no one makes decisions about the terms, grammar, and phrasing of fixed formulae of a ritual while they are executing that ritual with other people in a communal assembly. Indeed, while they are engaged in this Eucharist itself, the leader and the rest of the assembly make no decision even about the order in which they take their respective turns to pronounce the various fixed formulae. Thus, no participant's decisions on grammar, vocabulary, and textual structure can provide a foundation for an interpretation of what the leader and the assembly mean while they are performing this ritual. It is precisely by seeing things from the point of view of an individual actually using formalized language that Bloch can tell us that such a person's activity of meaning or explaining something by his or her words tends to shrink to the vanishing point. The participants in a ritual do use the fixed formulae of the rite to assert both the unity of the assembly's members and the notion that, at least, during the performance of the ritual, things are going as they should for the assembly.

Schwiebert deftly uses this last insight into the performative force of ritual formulae to found a number of perceptive observations on the purpose and meaning of the Didache meal ritual. In the process, he wisely follows Bloch's counsel to interpret a rite by attending to where, when, and why the ritual words are used, as well as by whom and in the context of which other rites and activities. Attention to this ritual context allows him to see in the meal ritual an expression of the assembly's relationships with family, other Jews, non-Christian gentiles, Jesus, and God, as well as an assertion of the assembly's divinely given health and unity founded on the meal ritual itself. Space limitations kept Schwiebert from mentioning two elements of the ritual context of the Didache Eucharist that have their importance. First, chapter 14 shows us that reconciliation defines, in part, the type of holiness that Schwiebert rightly notes characterizes the meal ritual. I will say more about this part of the eucharistic context of the Didache when I respond below to Huub van de Sandt's essay. Second, the Didache Eucharist takes place on the Lord's Day (14.1), whatever that is.[1]

Schwiebert asserts that his interpretation of the Didache Eucharist comes entirely from examining the ritual context of that meal and "not from an examination of the 'meaning' or 'syntax' of the prayers themselves, nor by translating them into an exposition."[2] But does he not somewhat overdraw this contrast? At one point in his interpretation of the meal ritual, Schwiebert does well to note,

> We must not forget that the ritualized speech in this case is prayer, speech addressed to God (not the people) and not in the persona of an elder or some ancestral figure but rather in the voice of the whole assembly: a "we." Someone (we do not know who) speaks for the whole assembly, and the assembly permits this, because this is at least a part of what the gathering means: they are there, among other reasons, to speak as one to God.... The prayers justify the sharing of the meal.[3]

The word "God" does not occur in Did. 9–10. How, then, do we know these prayers are addressed to God? The meaning of the words "Father" and "Lord" tells us that these prayers are directed to God.[4] Thus, his interpretation does seem to come, at least in part, from the meaning of the

---

1. See Jonathan Schwiebert, *Knowledge and the Coming Kingdom: The Didache's Meal Ritual and Its Place in Early Christianity*, LNTS 373 (London: T&T Clark, 2008), 165 n. 49 and 176. See also Ignatius, *Magn.* 9.1; Justin, *Dial.* 41; *Apol.* 1.67. Ignatius links life and Jesus's role as giver of knowledge, themes of the Didache Eucharist, to a reference to the κυριακήν, seen precisely as the occasion of Jesus's resurrection from death. For Justin, Jesus's death and resurrection connect the Sunday Eucharist to Jesus's function of conveying saving knowledge through teaching. Is the Lord's Day Didache meal ritual, then, as distant from a tradition of eucharistic commemoration of the Jesus's death and resurrection as Schwiebert and others believe? Or does Did. 14.1 refer to the Day of Atonement? See Jonathan A. Draper, "Pure Sacrifice in Didache 14 as Jewish Christian Exegesis," *Neot* 42 (2008): 228–29.

2. See in the present volume, Jonathan Schwiebert, "Pray 'In This Way': Formalized Speech in Didache 9–10," above 189–207 (204).

3. Ibid., 203.

4. In Did. 4.11, we learn that slaves are to see in their "lords" types of God, but never is the word "God" explicitly linked to the word "father" in the Didache. Knowledge of ancient Jewish prayer forms and of their use—among others, the Lord's Prayer

prayers, that is, from the meaning of their words. One indication of this fact is that he quite naturally translates some of the terms of the prayer, "Father" and "Lord," into the equivalent expression "God." Furthermore, the block quote above shows Schwiebert deriving his interpretation from the syntax of the prayers. The syntactical fact that the prayers use throughout the first person plural pronoun leads him to conclude that these are prayers of an entire assembly. Finally, Schwiebert's interpretation notes that the prayers of Did. 9–10 justify something, namely, the sharing of a meal. Since justifying is a form of explanation, his interpretation attributes an explanatory function to the prayers, even though Bloch's theory criticizes such an interpretation. Indeed, Schwiebert tells us that Bloch "challenges us to consider that the expressions in our prayers are not trying to explain anything."[5] My point here is not to criticize any of Schwiebert's interpretations of the Didache Eucharist that I have quoted here; indeed, they seem astute to me. I merely wish to indicate that his interpretation differs less than he seems to think from those accounts of Did. 9–10 that he tells us Bloch's theory would rule out. It makes total sense, then, that Schwiebert ends his essay with a critique of Bloch's theory.

This critique notes that ritual participants can so commit themselves to a particular ritual occasion that they fill the rite's verbal formulae with a meaning much like that of everyday speech, characterized as it is by individual expressive choices about terms, syntax, phrasing, and conversational distribution of speech roles. In fact, he notes, the investment in the tradition conveyed by the ritual can make what the ritual has us say mean even more to us than do our everyday communicative speech acts. The ritual invites, even it if does not prescribe, such investment in its words and in the act by which we mean what they say. Schwiebert points out that this investment in the act of meaning what the ritual says opens us to invest in the community performing the ritual. This investment in the community is, to use Schwiebert's apt expression, "the choice to embark upon the ritual," and it "is not trivial."[6] It is in considering this investment and this choice that Schwiebert's own interpretation is itself justified in not following all of Bloch's strictures, for he understands more expansively and accurately than Bloch does the meaning act people can accomplish by

---

in Matt 6 and Did. 8—help us to see that the Didache meal ritual is calling God "Father" and "Lord."

5. Schwiebert, "Pray 'In This Way,'" 199.
6. Ibid., 206.

enacting the words, syntax, phrasing, and alternation of speaking roles in a ritual.

Schwiebert goes on to note that "the choice of which ritual to embark upon is likewise not trivial. The choice of this ritual script over some other possible ritual script ... can indeed tell us something significant about the community that prays 'in this way.'"[7] I take this comment as the most helpful element in his critique of Bloch's theory. While Schwiebert uses this theory to study fruitfully the ritual words of Did. 9–10 from the point of view of those who use these formulae in their ritual context, one can also legitimately interpret those words in the context in which we find them in the Didache, that is to say, as objects of rubrical instruction. Indeed, the immediate context of these formulae in the Didache is that of the objects of the specification of what a group should say or do on a certain ritual occasion:

> Now concerning the Eucharist, give thanks in this way.... Let no one eat or drink from your Eucharist, except those baptized.... Now after you have been filled, give thanks in this way.... Now let the prophets give thanks as much as they wish. (9.1, 5; 10.1, 7)[8]

Thus, it is totally legitimate to interpret these prayers as the object of a decision recorded in the Didache, a decision about who will say what and when. This is not the decision made by a person as he or she is repeating the fixed formulae during the performance of the rite, nor is it the act of meaning that results from some person's or group's particularly strong investment in a particular performance of the rite. The decision in question is, rather, made by those who determine (or the one who determines) what the rite will look like, or, at least, what form of the rite should be written down. One can fruitfully and reasonably interpret the rite from the point of view of these persons or this person and therefore take into account all of the linguistic choices that ritual performance can lead people not to make, for the fixing or recording of a rite is not the same action as participating in it.

Understanding the fixing or recording of a rite will look different, then, from understanding that rite's performance. Therefore, the type of interpretation that Schwiebert criticizes earlier in his essay—one that sees

---

7. Ibid., 206.
8. All translations are my own.

the rite as the object of choices about words, syntax, phrasing, and scripting—can be a totally legitimate understanding of the rite, if it sees the rite as something chosen by the tradition or the individual recording the rite. A scholar legitimately considers the theology expressed by the choice of one ritual script over another, even if, when performing either script, one would not intend the theological meaning of the script in the way one does when choosing which script is the better. Schwiebert's approach has the merit of helping us to distinguish clearly these two interpretive points of view, while allowing us to conclude to the legitimacy of both in our interpretation of the Didache meal prayers or of any other ritual text.

Schwiebert's attention to ritual context and to points of view from which ritual texts can be interpreted can help us to clarify the way in which van de Sandt's chapter in this volume treats the textual units at the base of his interpretation of the Didache community's limitations on who could participate in its Eucharist:

> Now let no one eat or drink of your Eucharist but those baptized into the name of the Lord, for the Lord has said concerning this, "Do not give what is holy to the dogs." (9.5)

> If someone is holy, let that person come. If someone is not, let that person convert. (10.6)

Van de Sandt sees both of these texts as "directives" and bits of "rubrical instruction."[9] These qualifications fit well with 9.5, but less so with 10.6. The former verse comes right after a doxology ending the thanksgiving prayers that are performed before people are filled with a meal (10.1). The second word of 9.5 (δέ) often functions in the Didache to introduce a new unit of the text and so fits well with the transition from prayer text to rubric. Yes, in its only nonrubrical appearance in Did. 9–10 (in 10.3), this Greek word clearly has the adversative function of indicating a contrast between food and drink from the almighty Master for people's enjoyment, on one hand, and spiritual food and drink and eternal life through Jesus for the community's "us," on the other hand. But apart from 10.6, which is in question here, no ritual rubric in the Didache goes without δέ at the

---

9. See in the present volume, Huub van de Sandt, "Baptism and Holiness: Two Requirements Authorizing Participation in the Didache's Eucharist," above 139–64 (140).

front. For rubrics on permitted and forbidden foods, see 6.3; on baptism see 7.1, 2, 3, 4 (prebaptismal fast); on fast days see 8.1; on daily prayer see 8.2; on when and how to begin the Eucharist, see 14.1 and 2.

Didache 10.6 begins and ends with formulaic acclamations of prayer: "Let grace come, and let this world depart. Hosanna to the God [or house, or Son] of David.... Maranatha. Amen." In between them, van de Sandt would locate a rubric about the eucharistic participation of the holy and the conversion of the unholy, a rubric that has nothing much to do with the prayer formulae immediately before and after it. Every other rubric adjoining a text of prayer in the Didache tells people to say the prayer in question or to let certain people pray it and others not. From all of this, I conclude that 10.6 contains no rubrics and that the verse is composed of two sets of prayer acclamations,[10] each one beginning with two sentences with a third-person singular imperative verb and ending with an acclamation using Hebrew or Aramaic. The whole prayer unit ends with the Amen.

(a) Let grace come, and let this world depart. Hosanna to the God [or house, or Son] of David.
(b) If someone is holy, let that person come. If someone is not, let that person convert. Maranatha.
(c) Amen.

If these conclusions are correct, another difficulty in van de Sandt's interpretation of Did. 10.6 is removed. His essay tells us that, with the words "If anyone is holy, let him come," the "celebrant bids the participants to leave their seats in order to take part in the communal meal."[11] However, 10.1 presupposes that those present at the celebration have already eaten their fill: "Now after you have been filled, give thanks in this way." Is van de Sandt distinguishing here between a satiating meal eaten before the prayer in 10.1–5 and a communal meal taken after this prayer? If not, why invite the assembly to a meal after it has taken place? The oddness of inviting people to a meal after they have just had one disappears when 10.6 is read as a series of acclamations and when all the imperatives are seen, not

---

10. I thus agree on this point with Jonathan Schwiebert's and John Clabeaux's essays in this volume, as well as with Jonathan Draper's interpretation of Did. 10.6. See his "Ritual Process and Ritual Symbol in Didache 7–10," *VC* 54 (2000): 121–58 (130–31, 141–42); see also Schwiebert, *Knowledge and the Coming Kingdom*, 72–79.
11. Van de Sandt, "Baptism and Holiness," 142.

as directions for a holy person or this world to do something or other, but as expressions of desire for, or agreement with, the way things are or soon will be.

Finally, in the spirit of Schwiebert's essay, I point out that the fact that 10.6 contains no rubrics, but only acclamations, shows that the "argument" van de Sandt wants to see in the acclamation on eucharistic participation for the holy and conversion for the unholy is no argument at all. Acclamation and argument constitute two distinct activities. Whether from the point of view of those who say this acclamation during a performance of the Didache Eucharist, from the angle of those choosing to put this acclamation at this place in the rite or from the outlook of those who choose to engage in this rite rather than to do something else, we should not see this acclamation as an argument. It does express convictions, however, and van de Sandt's essay illuminates those convictions admirably by pointing out their connection to the arguments in Did. 9.5 and in 14.1–3, both of which passages contain rubrics the justifying arguments for which are signaled by the use of γάρ to introduce a quotation of the Lord's words.

Van de Sandt presents a very plausible interpretation of the limitation of the Didache Eucharist to the baptized in 9.5. His argument moves from that limitation to the explanatory dominical logion that follows: what is holy is for not dogs. He establishes that what is holy here is food for sacrifice like that in the temple, in accord with LXX and other Jewish sources. On that basis he interprets baptism in the Didache as a presacrificial purification rite. The incorporation of the Two Ways treatise into baptismal purification shows that that purification is ethical as well as ritual. This fact explains the less than punctilious attitude in Did. 7 about the type of water used for baptism. The prescriptions of this chapter are interpreted in terms of the Mishnah treatise on baths (m. Miqw. 1:1–8). Van de Sandt thus artfully reads the restriction of Eucharist to the baptized in its context within the Didache, as well as in a wider Jewish context.

His argument for these broad lines of his interpretation convinces me, but some of the details of his discussion leave me with questions. First, he emphasizes rightly that the rubric in 9.5 has the effect of excluding gentiles from the Eucharist, but would it not also exclude Jews who were not baptized into the name of Father, Son, and Holy Spirit (7.1)? Second, van de Sandt's comparison between Did. 7 and m. Miqw. 1:1–8 leads him to conclude that the Didache here represents a lessening concern for the details of which sorts of water are apt for ritual cleansing. But is this really what is going on here?

This mishnaic passage is unlike Did. 7 in various ways. No word for "pure," "impure," "clean," or "unclean" occurs in Did. 7, while these words occur frequently in this part of the Mishnah. In m. Miqw. 1:1–4a, what differentiates the different types of water is contact with something unclean or impure, but this issue never comes up in Did. 7. In the rest of m. Miqw. 1:4, what differentiates the different types of water is whether they are near places frequented by people, but this question never surfaces in Did. 7. There is a preference for flowing water over contained water in m. Miqw. 1:5–6, as we see in Did. 7, but while the mishnaic text reports different views on how such water is purified, Did. 7 never mentions purification of water as an issue. Perhaps the most interesting parallels with Did. 7 are in m. Miqw. 1:7–8, verses that allow living water, spring water, and a pool of standing water all to be used in purification and in that order of preference. The Mishnah text is later than the Didache. Simeon bar Yochai, mentioned in m. Miqw. 1:3 and 1:5, lived in the mid-second century; the houses of Shammai and Hillel, both of which were functioning in the first century, are mentioned in m. Miqw. 1:5, but this passage mentions them in connection with the issue of how water is purified, a concern never mentioned in Did. 7. For all of these reasons, it is unclear to me that m. Miqw. 1:1–8 allows us to conclude that Did. 7 represents a slacker ritual observance than what we see elsewhere. I therefore cannot be so sure as van de Sandt is that Did. 7 shows a lessening of concern for ritual purity, in favor of an increased concern for ethical purity as a prerequisite for eucharistic participation. While the text itself in Did. 7.1c–3a might "reflect a development that abandoned an originally strict ritual practice,"[12] it might not. It might just represent a compendium of different contemporaneous practices, all of which the Didache community had always thought valid.

All of that said, I find myself admiring van de Sandt's clear exposition of Did. 10.6 and 14.1–3. He shows well that confession and reconciliation form part of the holiness required for the purity of the Didache Eucharist. The parallels he shows between these parts of the Didache and the Qumran documents indicate persuasively a certain priority of the ethical over the ritual in the purity concerns of the Didache community. However, I am not sure that I would agree when he seems to affirm that baptism in the Didache has more to do with introducing someone to eucharistic participation than it does with initiating that person into the community itself. In view of the meaning of that meal as an affirmation of the community's

---

12. Ibid., 150.

unity, identity, and defining belief and expectation—so ably portrayed by Schwiebert's essay—van de Sandt's contrast between initiation into the community and initiation into the Eucharist is hard to understand. Van de Sandt hits the right note when he lets go of this contrast near the end of his essay: "Exclusion from the meal simply means exclusion from the community, and full membership is achieved when the candidate is allowed to share in the food."[13]

In the Didache, baptism is mentioned in connection with the Eucharist only once (9.5). The noun or verb for baptism occurs eight times in Did. 7, and none of these occurrences is part of a link between baptism and Eucharist. A number of these occurrences are related to fasting. The contrast between the fasting of the hypocrites and that of the Didache community provides the opening for the mention made of the Lord's Prayer in this document. Tomson's essay in this volume situates this prayer with respect to its context in the Didache, to the versions of Matthew and Luke in their respective literary contexts, and to the larger historical context for all of these documents.

He notes that the patristic and New Testament manuscript record indicates that the Matthew-Didache version of the prayer came early on to predominate over the Lukan version. I agree with him that even Mark 11:25 does seem to show traces of the former's use. While Luke places the prayer easily next to a mention of the prayer instruction of another Jewish teacher, John the Baptist, Matthew, and the Didache set it off in opposition to prayer practices of the hypocrites. Showing that the opposition in Did. 8.1 to the hypocrites on the matter of fast days is a Jewish position against a Pharisaic or early rabbinic practice attested in the Mishnah, Tomson sensibly reads the option of this document for the Lord's Prayer as a similar, Jewish move against the same opponents. He adduces passages from the Mishnah and Tosefta that do converge enough with the Lukan narrative about Jesus teaching the Lord's Prayer (12:1–5) to warrant the conclusion that that prayer, like those taught by other Jewish teachers of the time, was a short model prayer of variable length and wording to be used when brevity was called for. Tomson shows clearly from m. Ber. 4:1–4, that the Didache shares the thrice-daily rhythm of prayer with the customs inculcated by a number of first-century rabbis.

---

13. Ibid., 164.

Tomson rightly asserts that the Didache preference for fasting on Wednesdays and Fridays agrees with the ancient Jewish calendar attested in Jub. 6:23–28 and other Qumran documents. But there is nothing in this passage of Jubilees about which days of the week are proper for which activities. Jubilees 50:13 does forbid fasting on the Sabbath, but this issue never arises in Did. 8. Thus, while the fast days of the Didache do fit with the calendar of Jubilees, so do the fast days the Didache identifies as those of the hypocrites. Tomson could, therefore, have explained further how the Jubilees calendar clarifies the relationship between the Didache community and the hypocrites. More precisely, it is unclear how the relationship between Did. 8.1 and Jub. 6 helps to show, as Tomson thinks it does, that the Didache community opposes Gamaliel's institution of the Eighteen Benedictions. Yet I would grant, in agreement with Tomson, that it makes sense that the rabbinic option for the Eighteen Benedictions represents at least part of what the Didache opposes by proposing the text of the Lord's Prayer for daily use.

However, I am not convinced, as Tomson is, that objections in Did. 8 and Matt 6 to the prayer of the hypocrites parallels the protest registered in the m. Ber. 4:1–4 against the institution of the Eighteen Benedictions. In fact, the only thing we know that the Didache does not like in hypocrite prayer is that it does not use the Lord's Prayer. Yes, the Lord's Prayer is a short prayer, like those proposed in m. Ber. 4 as alternatives to the Eighteen Benedictions, but if the Didache would think of all the rabbis mentioned there as hypocrites, its rule to use the Lord's Prayer could be critiquing Gamaliel together with his rabbinic opponents. The only opposition to the hypocrites over prayer in Matt 6 is the preference for private over public prayer, while this matter is an issue in neither the Didache nor in m. Ber. 4. Meanwhile, Matt 6 does not contrast the text of the Lord's Prayer with hypocrite prayer, as the Didache does, but with prolix gentile usage. I conclude that Tomson might not have found as much evidence in Did. 8 and Matthew as he would like for the historicity of the accounts in rabbinic literature of Gamaliel's establishment of the Eighteen Benedictions as a universal daily Jewish prayer. Still, Tomson makes a firm case for the Jewish contextualization of the thrice-daily use of the Lord's Prayer taught in Did. 8.2–3.

Because Clabeaux has contributed to this volume a reflective review of Jonathan Schwiebert's *Knowledge and the Coming Kingdom*, I will spare the reader a review of that review. Those who want to evaluate Clabeaux's solid essay would best begin by reading Schwiebert's impressive book. Here I will respond to Clabeaux's closing reflections on the potential theological or ecclesiological implications of the influence the Didache's Eucharist had on the history of Christian prayer, as Schwiebert presented that influence in the last chapters of *Knowledge and the Coming Kingdom*.

Having asked what might have been lost as the Didache's eucharistic ritual fell into desuetude, Clabeaux notes first the absence from today's Christian liturgy of an obviously strong emphasis on eschatological expectation of God's coming kingdom. Of course, the sidelining of the Didache Eucharist is only one factor among very many that account for our time's muted Christian hope for the perfection of God's assembly at the end of the world. Throughout Christian history, the tensed muscles of an imminent eschatological expectation have very often accompanied deep disaffection with the status quo viewed with the wide-angle lens that takes in whole empires and world systems. Thus, where Christians evidence a slackened interest in the final perfection of the world-historical process through God's transcendent initiative, their implicit or explicit judgment or enthusiasm about the most basic cultural frameworks of daily life might be in need of deep revision, if not reversal. The study of an ancient text like the Didache is available perhaps mostly to those too comfortable with the way of the world. Those of us who need it should try to benefit from the tonic of studying its eucharistic ritual.

Clabeaux points out that when the Didache meal ritual ceased to be practiced, Christians lost one expression of gratitude for the knowledge brought to us from God by Jesus, for example, in the form of catechetical moral instruction and the sayings of Christ. He then asks whether the dominant emphasis on associating the bread and wine with Jesus's body and blood given over for the forgiveness of sin cost Christians "a robust understanding of the presence of God in the Word."[14] My reading of Christian history leads me to answer in the negative. Yes, over the centuries at various times and places and to varying degrees, Christians have needed the reform that brings them back to God's word. But the New Testament gives ample witness to the need for such reform even in the days when some Christians still practiced the Didache meal ritual. The Didache itself shows us that its community knew that Christians kept a tenuous hold on the instruction on which their life depended (6.1; 11.2, 10; 16.2–5). On the other hand, I agree with the great French Jesuit teacher Édouard

---

14. See in the present volume, John J. Clabeaux, "The Ritual Meal in Didache 9–10: Progress in Understanding," above 209–30 (227).

Pousset (1929–1999), who liked to repeat that, throughout Christian history, the gospel returns in a fresh way where it is needed. Sometimes we might think that we have to wait too long for that return. Perhaps a lively eschatological expectation like that nourished by the Didache meal ritual can help to make us hunger so much for the gospel that we become instruments of its return in our own time and place.

At the end of his essay, Clabeaux presents arguments for the idea that the Gospel of John concentrates, likely much after the Didache is written, language and images related to a number of themes in the Didache Eucharist, without seeing these images and language as opposed to an emphasis on Jesus's death and resurrection, a thematic complex absent from that Eucharist. He adds this point to the evidence that Schwiebert's book collects of aspects of the Didache meal ritual explicitly linked in other ancient Christian sources to Jesus's death and resurrection. Leaving to others more qualified than I the task of evaluating his case for the Didache-John connection, I underline that Clabeaux's point here is more historical than theological. He tries to show that a number of ancient sources bring into unproblematic coexistence two thematic complexes: on one hand, knowledge through Jesus and the coming kingdom; on the other hand, Jesus's death and resurrection. But Clabeaux does not ask what, if anything, about the theologies respectively implied by these thematic complexes allowed for this coexistence in a single ritual or a single gospel. That is a precisely theological question, one that takes us to a point of view different from the history or sociology of religious texts and movements.

I can only adumbrate a response to this question at the close of this response to four stimulating studies. Our Father gives us knowledge through Jesus his servant, he gives us spiritual food and drink and eternal life through the same Jesus, and it is again through Jesus that glory and power will belong to our Father for his gathering of the church in perfect love at the end of the world. God gives us knowledge through Jesus's teachings, as well as through that servant's mighty deeds, the greatest of which is his death and resurrection, after which he instructed his followers with a new efficacy. Jesus's death and resurrection confirm that his teachings and servanthood had God as their origin and goal. His death and resurrection confirm this fact in part because it is through them that God gives spiritual food and drink and eternal life to Christians. After having preached eternal life, after having performed marvelous signs of it through healings and exorcisms, God's servant showed himself to be the very heaven-sent nourishment of this life by dying and rising from the dead. Because this life is perfected in love for God and neighbor, the nourishment of this life must be shared with thanksgiving at the center of a community living the way of life. Knowing that God's servant, their teacher, has come to perfection in immortal risen life, the community awaits the consummation of its loving unity in the eternal life that comes through its spiritual food and drink. This waiting is active and so requires following the way of life and continual reconciliation as the preludes to sharing in the meal that concretizes the community's defining expectation. These few statements do not outline the theology of the Didache. They sketch a theology that can be fed by the Didache, the record of a first-century Christian Jewish community eager to set itself off from nascent rabbinical currents in its adhesion to the teaching of a servant whose name and prayer proclaim that Israel's God saves.

Part 3
The Didache and Matthew

Before and after Matthew

E. Bruce Brooks

In this paper I will argue that the Didache is a growth text, that it makes contact with Matthew only at the end of its formation period, and that its core is best understood if it is related to the period *before* Matthew and Luke: the time of Mark and of other texts that seem to reflect a preresurrection form of belief and practice that I have elsewhere called Alpha Christianity. Since at several points my exposition departs from current scholarship on the Didache, it may assist readers (and avoid many separate and complicated footnotes later on) if I begin by briefly introducing some of the considerations that lie behind those departures.

1. Prolegomena

This is a set of mutually consistent solutions to problems otherwise solved by many, bearing upon the existence and nature of a Christianity arising before Paul and persisting during his lifetime and afterward.

1.1. Growth Texts

Not all texts are written at one sitting, and authority texts in particular are likely to extend themselves over time in order to remain valid under changing conditions. One physically obvious example is the Gortyn law code from early Crete, literally cut in the stones comprising the walls of the room in which law cases were heard, but with two extensions at the end, the second of which is in a different "hand" than the preceding text.[1] The Gospels, which evidently aspire to tell the truth about Jesus in

---

1. For a complete description, see Ronald F. Willetts, *The Law Code of Gortyn*, KSup 1 (Berlin: de Gruyter, 1967); for the addendum, especially 4, 27, and 78.

narrative form, are in their nature authority texts, and for John in particular a three-stage composition process has recently been proposed by Urban C. von Wahlde.[2] These and like extensions are not corruptions in the usual scribal sense, and they are not forgeries. They are an integral if later part of the text and reflect continued management of that text by its original author (or if we envision a school or municipal text, by its original proprietor or his successors). I propose in this paper to consider the evidence for the Didache as a growth text.

1.2. Mark

That Mark is a growth text[3] is readily shown by considering its interpolations, many of them signaled by the fact that they interrupt the context, that when they are removed the context closes up to make a perfectly consecutive text, and that the interpolations themselves can be combined on the basis of similar content to make plausible accretion layers. Mark 14:28 and 16:7 are of this type.[4] In each case the verse following ignores the verse in question and addresses a comment or responds to a situation in the verse preceding. The two passages are related (the second refers back to the first) and thus form a layer of their own. What they add to the previous story is not the forthcoming appearance of Jesus to the disciples in Galilee, which was already implicit in the narrative, but Jesus's *foreknowledge* of that appearance. I take this as an instance of the progressive divinization of Jesus, a process easily seen in the four Gospels taken together,[5] but

---

2. *The Gospel and Letters of John* (Grand Rapids: Eerdmans, 2010).

3. A complete if tentative reconstruction was presented in E. Bruce Brooks, "Structural Evolution in Mark" (paper presented at the New England regional meeting of the Society of Biblical Literature, 21 April 2006); see now "The Resurrection of Jesus in Mark," *WSP* 3 (forthcoming).

4. Noticed by Heinrich J. Holtzmann, *Die Synoptiker*, HCNT 1/1 (Tübingen: Mohr, 1901), 174; Ernst Lohmeyer, *Das Evangelium des Markus*, KEK 1.2 (Göttingen: Vandenhoeck & Ruprecht, 1937), 312; Frederick C. Grant, "The Gospel According to St. Mark," IB 7:627–917 (879); more guardedly by Vincent Taylor, *The Gospel According to St. Mark* (London: Macmillan, 1959), 549. The insecurity of these interruptive passages in context passes without comment in many recent commentaries. This I attribute to the *Zeitgeist* (the same is true of all canonical New Testament texts) and not to any defect in the evidence.

5. For a brief account, see E. Bruce Brooks, "Gospel Trajectories," *WSP* 1 (2010): 171–72.

which, as these interpolations show, is also in progress *within Mark itself.* The characteristic of earliest Christianity is that it lies at the beginning of this trajectory, and divinized Jesus not at all.

Other passages in Mark that have been convincingly analyzed as layered include the Markan apocalypse (by Vincent Taylor)[6] and the Markan passion narrative (by Adela Yarbro Collins).[7] The latter reconstruction ends at Mark 15:38 and thus does not include the resurrection.[8] Notice also that the atonement doctrine (the salvific value of Jesus's death) is later in Mark than the resurrection doctrine. Whereas the resurrection has been thoroughly worked into the text, the atonement doctrine is exiguous: it appears in only two passages: Mark 10:45 and 14:24b, both of which may be removed without detriment (in the latter case, arguably with benefit) to the context. Stratified Mark thus contains a sort of archaeological history of the evolution of early Christian thought.[9]

---

6. See Taylor, *Gospel According to St. Mark*, 636–41; E. Bruce Brooks, "Mark's Apocalyptic Discourse," *WSP* 3 (forthcoming).

7. I should add that Yarbro Collins prefers to call the earlier form the pre-Markan passion narrative, whereas I consider it to be an early state in a continuous process of additions to Mark and thus *within* the Markan formation process.

8. Adela Yarbro Collins, *Mark: A Commentary*, Hermeneia (Minneapolis: Fortress, 2007), 819 and preceding commentary. For an independent argument that the resurrection is not original in Mark, see Peter Kirby, "The Case against the Empty Tomb," *JHC* 9 (2002): 175–202. The resurrection predictions in Mark evidently stand or fall together, and the second of them (Mark 9:30–32) is in conflict with Mark 9:33 as to whether Jesus talked with his disciples on the way, or did not do so and had to ask afterward what they had been saying. Of the two, it is the latter that makes better sense in the immediate context. It follows that 9:30–32, and with it the other resurrection predictions, are late in Mark.

9. A common response to evidence for interpolation in Mark is the Edwards "sandwich" thesis. The prize example of this supposed authorial structure is the Woman with the Flow of Blood (Mark 5:24b–34) interrupting the Jairus's daughter narrative (Mark 5:22–24a and 5:35–43). Of this and all the "sandwiches," Edwards observes, "Almost always the insertion is the standard by which the flanking material is measured, the key to the interpretation of the whole"; see James R. Edwards, "Markan Sandwiches," in *The Composition of Mark's Gospel*, ed. David E. Orton, BRBS 3 (Leiden: Brill, 1999), 215. A similar and stronger statement could be made of an interpolation, whose purpose is to update the "flanking material." The point of the Jairus story was the power of *Jesus* to heal. The point of the inserted Woman story is quite different: it is the power of *faith in Jesus* to heal, even without the personal intervention of the historical Jesus (Mark 5:34: "And he said to her, daughter, *your faith has made you well*" [unless otherwise noted, biblical citations follow the ASV]). By

Mark is usually dated to after 70 by interpreting Mark 13:14 as a reference to the destruction of Jerusalem by the army of Titus. But desecration is not destruction, and this passage (with its clear reference to Dan 11:31 and thus to the desecration of the temple by Antiochus Epiphanes)[10] is more plausibly taken as referring to the threatened desecration of the temple by Caligula in the summer of 40.[11] When a gospel writer wishes to portray the army of Titus besieging Jerusalem, the result is likely to read more like Luke 21:20, which in that gospel replaces the parallel Mark 13:14. The latest firm *terminus post quem* in Mark is the reference to the execution of James Zebedee by Herod Agrippa I, probably in 44, which is predicted in Mark 10:39. There is no reason *in the text* to date any of Mark after around 45, and the majority of Mark would then have been earlier. As a whole then, Mark belongs to the early, not the middle, period of early Christianity. Given the evident similarity between certain Didache passages and Matthew, scholarship on the Didache has naturally focused on Matthew, sometimes to the extent of excluding Mark and other seemingly early texts from consideration. I propose in this paper to bring Mark (and the also early Epistle of James) back into the picture.

1.3. Luke

This text is also stratified, as is most easily seen in the passages that occupy different positions in the narrative from their counterparts in Mark and create inconcinnities in their new positions. These can only have been relocated at a later point during the formation of the text.[12] One of the most

---

inserting this story, Mark updates what had been merely a story of Jesus and directly addresses the concerns of the churches of his own time.

10. The reference to Daniel is made explicit in the Matthean version of this passage; see Matt 24:15.

11. This has often been pointed out. It may be the basis of the Paschal Chronicle's assigning to Mark the date 40 and the early tradition, expressed at the end of several uncial manuscripts, that Mark was written in the tenth year after the ascension, which on some views about the chronology of Jesus would again give 40. Among more recent treatments, see for example James G. Crossley, *The Date of Mark's Gospel: Insight from the Law in Earliest Christianity*, LNTS (London: Clark, 2004), 29–30. The threat was removed by the death of Caligula in January 41, so that Mark 13:14 can only have been written in 40. This is one of two passages in Mark for which an absolute *terminus post quem* can be determined. For the other, Mark 10:39, see below.

12. See E. Bruce Brooks, "Prolegomena to Proto-Luke" (paper presented at the

obvious is the Nazareth episode (Luke 4:16–30) in which Jesus's hearers demand that he do wonders such as he had done at Capernaum. But at this point in the present Lukan narrative, Jesus *has not yet been* to Capernaum.

In his Gospel and also in the Acts, Luke takes a highly revisionist view of Paul. Paul's most characteristic doctrine is probably the atonement, asserted with typical vehemence in Paul's last letter, Rom 3:20–24 and (with the example of Abraham) in 4:1–3. Luke in his Gospel suppresses the two Markan passages in which this doctrine occurs, and in Acts he never shows Paul as preaching that doctrine.[13] It was apparently Luke's intention to transmit both Jesus tradition and later Christian history in a form that would be more suitable for the future than the actual facts. Among the more upsetting of those facts was the bitter exchange between Paul in Romans and the last addition to James,[14] which in 2:20 holds Paul's doctrine of faith (in the atonement) up to scorn ("Do you want to be shown, you foolish fellow, that faith apart from works is barren?") and in 2:21–24 goes on to refute Paul's example of Abraham, arguing that Abraham was an instance of deeds, not merely of faith ("Was not Abraham our father justified by works, when he offered his son Isaac upon the altar?"). These disputes among Christians were probably divisive, and Luke may have felt that some sort of peace needed to be achieved within Christianity so as to save energy for the conflicts that it was experiencing from outside. I propose in this paper to bring this conflict between Paul and earlier Christianity into sharper perspective.

1.4. Matthew

Matthew 24:15 repeats without modification Mark 13:14, with its Caligula desecration prediction.[15] The text thus does not appear to be aware of

---

Annual Meeting of the Society of Biblical Literature, San Diego, CA, 17 November 2007) and "Acts-Luke," *Alpha* (forthcoming). The latter argues for a three-stage composition process for Luke, the second and third of which correspond to a two-stage formation process for Acts.

13. It is mentioned only in Acts 21:28 as part of Paul's farewell to the Ephesians, but as a personal idea of Paul's, not as something that Luke represents him as preaching to the churches.

14. For this stratification, see E. Bruce Brooks, "The Epistle of James," *Alpha* (forthcoming).

15. It may be asked, if the Caligula prediction did not come off, why was it retained in Mark (and repeated in Matthew)? I reply that authority texts in their

the Titus destruction of 70 (which *is* unmistakably reflected in the parallel of Luke 21:20). The final state of Matthew is thus most plausibly dated *before* 70 and the final state of Luke *after* 70. The impetus for composing both may well have been the deaths of the major apostles Paul (probably in 60, since the two years of virtual freedom in Rome mentioned in Acts 28:30–31 may be an instance of the consistently pro-Roman stance of Acts)[16] and Peter (probably in 64, the first year of the Neronian persecution). These, not to mention the other turmoil of the time, could have suggested the need for a new account of Jesus and his legacy. The available time window is small and seems to require something like:

Luke A (ca. 66) > Matthew (ca. 68) > Luke B (after 70)

This would have been during the Jewish War, making a Palestinian place of composition problematic. But Luke has been persistently associated with Antioch, and since the two gospels are obviously closely related, Syria may be a reasonable hypothesis for Matthew also.[17] The difference between Luke (who consistently speaks for the poor) and Matthew (who is comfortable with large numbers, and, as in Matt 23:2 and many like passages, is somewhat in reaction against Jesus's abridging of the traditional laws) is as likely to be social as geographical.

1.5. Q

This is a conjectural source, supposed to be earlier than Matthew and Luke and used by both. "Q" is thought to account for much of the material common to Matthew and Luke but absent in Mark. Perhaps the strongest evidence for such a source is: (1) the apparent bidirectionality (often called "alternating primitivity") displayed by the common material and (2) the

---

nature do not subtract; subtraction is an admission of error in a text already to some degree public. What usually happens instead is that the seeming difficulty is made good by reinterpretation.

16. The final imprisonment of Paul is imagined very differently by whoever wrote 2 Tim 4:6–18. That this describes a second imprisonment has been shown to be untenable; see John Macpherson, "Was There a Second Imprisonment of Paul in Rome?" *AJT* 4 (1900): 23–48.

17. See the careful discussion in W. D. Davies and Dale C. Allison, *A Critical and Exegetical Commentary on the Gospel according to Saint Matthew*, 3 vols., ICC (Edinburgh: T&T Clark, 1988–1997), 1:138–47; in the end they opt for Antioch.

assumption that both Matthew and Luke are integral texts, written at a single date. The latter assumption seems to hold for Matthew (I see no philological warrant for a stratification analysis and do not believe that one has ever been proposed), but as argued above, not for Luke. Michael Goulder sought to undermine the Q hypothesis by demonstrating Matthew > Luke directionality for all the common material. This works for the parable of the talents (Matt 25:14–30 || Luke 19:11–27), which involves a narratively superfluous king in the Lukan version, and thus suggests the directionality Matthew > Luke.[18] But it founders on the parable of the feast (Matt 22:1–14 || Luke 14:16–24), which involves a narratively superfluous king in the *Matthean* version, and thus equally implies the directionality Luke > Matthew. But if the earliest stage of Luke were earlier than Matthew and the second stage of Luke were later than Matthew and aware of Matthew, the above and other facts can be accommodated. A further advantage of that model is that the minor agreements (not addressed in the Q hypothesis) can also be accommodated. So can such elements as the respective birth narratives, which cannot be derived by the usual redaction scenario from a common ancestor (they have almost no details in common), but have a clear Matthew > Luke directionality (in Luke, but not in Matthew, the birth story overrides a perfectly satisfactory beginning in the historical synchronisms of Luke 3:1–2).[19] The conjectural "Q" will thus play no part in the following argument.

1.6. Paul

The strongest argument for an early Christianity is that Paul began by persecuting it. The second strongest is that he sometimes quotes what have been recognized as pre-Pauline formulas.

Paul was a vehement personality and was just as zealous to assert his apostolic credentials (against those of the "superlative apostles," 1 Cor

---

18. It also involves other absurdities; see his delightful account in Michael Goulder, *Luke: A New Paradigm*, 2 vols., JSNTSup 10 (Sheffield: JSOT, 1989), 2:680–83.

19. The effect of the transition has often been noticed, e.g.: "At this point, the narrative emerges into the clearer light of day, and joins the main stream of the older evangelical tradition which began not with the birth but with the baptism of Jesus" (William Manson, *The Gospel of Luke*, MNTC [London: Hodder & Stoughton, 1930], 24). For the divinization trajectory that is implied in the divine birth narratives of both Matthew and Luke, see again Brooks, "Gospel Trajectories."

11:5 and 12:11) as he had earlier been to exterminate the Christians in his vicinity (Gal 1:13–14). Paul is an author to read with care, not least because, in addressing Christians whose beliefs differed from his, he was prone to adopt their way of speaking initially as a first step in converting them to his own quite different point of view. An extreme example is Rom 1:2, where he speaks of the Davidic descent of Jesus, seemingly to ingratiate himself with those he imagines himself as addressing, at least some of whom evidently took the old Davidic messiah tradition of Jesus seriously. Paul had no interest in the Davidic or any other descent of Jesus, or in any other aspect of Jesus during his lifetime (see 2 Cor 5:16, where that knowledge is superseded by a higher knowledge of Jesus). It was exclusively Jesus *as resurrected* that interested Paul (emphasized as late as 1 Cor 15:14: "If Christ has not been raised, then our preaching is in vain, and your faith is in vain"). The joke is that the author of the deutero-Pauline text of 2 Timothy took this passage as genuine rather than rhetorical and included it accordingly (in 2:8) as Paul's own belief and indeed his teaching, doubtless thinking to strengthen thereby the perceived Pauline character of his work.

For present purposes, there are three major points requiring to be explained about Paul: (1) his persecution of the early Christians, (2) his conversion to Christianity, and (3) his adoption of the atonement interpretation of the resurrection. For the second, biographies of Paul usually find it sufficient to refer to the experience on the Damascus road, though this is a Lukan fiction not greatly resembling what is probably Paul's own account of the same experience in 2 Cor 12:2–5. In any case, what inner breakthrough prepared, or was expressed by, that experience? The first two questions are perhaps both best answered by Paul himself, with a guarded assist from Luke. Immediately after recalling that he "persecuted the church of God violently," Paul in Gal 1:14 describes himself as "extremely zealous ... for the traditions of my fathers" (the zeal and the persecution are even more closely linked in Phil 3:6: "as to zeal a persecutor of the church"). These traditions would have included not only the written commandments, with the Decalogue at their center, but the oral elaborations developed and prized by the Pharisees. Jesus in Mark is frequently at odds with the Pharisees over such traditions as food purity and such Decalogue prescriptions as the one enjoining observance of the Sabbath. Further, and more specifically, in Mark 10:19 Jesus gives an abridged version of the Decalogue. This is sometimes characterized as the "second table of the Decalogue," but this is not precisely correct. The actual inventory (with its sequence numbers in the Decalogue at Deut 4:7–21, which is also that of Exod 20:1–17) is murder (#6), adultery (#7), theft (#8), false witness (#9), fraud (not in the Decalogue),[20] and respect for parents (#5). This abridgement, plus the Markan Jesus's frequent and conspicuous offenses against the Sabbath commandment and several Pharisaic purity rules, would be well calculated to infuriate the Pharisee Paul.

As to Paul's motive for converting to Christianity, I think the likeliest possibility is that the Christianity to which Paul converted was not the same as the Christianity that he had previously persecuted. If at some point there had arisen within the Christianity of the time a new theory that emphasized the resurrection of Jesus, this might easily have resonated with Paul's Pharisaic belief in the resurrection of the dead and produced the sort of about-turning—the sudden recognition—that Paul's conversion seems to exhibit.[21] That this idea was a *development* in Christianity and not original doctrine (Jesus can hardly have taught it to the crowds during his lifetime, and no gospel depicts him as doing so) has been argued above. In support of the centrality of the resurrection in Paul's conversion, we may notice the emphasis that Paul, to the end of his writings, places on the resurrection (1 Cor 15:14, above cited), and his early visit to Jerusalem to confer with Peter, who had been the first to receive a vision of the risen Christ (this gospel tradition is repeated by Paul at 1 Cor 15:5: "and that he appeared to Cephas, then to the Twelve"). Luke in Acts also makes the resurrection the distinguishing point for Paul, saying that he "preached Jesus and the resurrection" (Acts 17:18b) and later in Jerusalem defended

---

20. But compare Mal 3:5, which also mentions other Jesus commandments. The prohibition of fraud is a signature of certain early Christian traditions. Besides Mark 10:19, it also occurs at Jas 5:4 (with a probable echo in 1 Cor 6:8) and Luke 19:8. There are similar prohibitions in the Two Ways vice list.

21. A point in favor of the two-Christianity view suggested here is that Paul as a Christian continued to oppose those who did not share his theological views, in particular those who did not place equal emphasis on the death of Jesus. See his curse in the afterthought at the end of 1 Corinthians ("If anyone has no love for the Lord, let him be accursed [anathema]. Our Lord, Come!"). The latter translates the Aramaic prayer Maranatha, given in its original form in Did 10.6. Paul's meaning is, "Let the Lord indeed come, and condemn these heretics." At this and similar moments, I suggest that we are seeing an example of the general pattern to which attention was called by Walter Bauer in 1934 (see his *Rechtgläubigkeit und Ketzerei im ältesten Christentum*, BHT 10 [Tübingen: Mohr Siebeck, 1934]): an original belief becoming heretical in terms of a later belief. Paul here represents the later belief.

himself by saying that he was being persecuted by other Jews who, unlike himself, did not believe in a resurrection (Acts 23:6; so also before Felix, Acts 24:21).

The atonement doctrine is our third difficulty. Rudolf Bultmann, following Wilhelm Bousset, suggested that Paul himself invented it, but the available facts do not seem to support this. We have firsthand testimony for Paul's theology only during seven years from late in his life: from 1 Thessalonians (ca. 51) to Romans (ca. 57). But even in that short span some development may be observed, and it seems that the atonement, which is so vigorously stressed in Romans, is not yet present in 1 Thessalonians.[22] It is present, but as a seemingly late addition, in Mark. Given a latest *terminus post quem* of circa 45 for Mark, it is probable that the atonement doctrine had been acknowledged by that text not long before, perhaps circa 43. This is eight years before the date usually assigned to 1 Thessalonians. It thus seems that Paul got the atonement doctrine from somewhere else, perhaps most likely from theoreticians at Jerusalem, the zone of John, Mark's primary acquaintance, and as the site of the temple, also the place where sacrifice-based concepts like the atonement might naturally have arisen.

1.7. Torah

The term "law" in our texts does not invariably invoke the whole of the Torah, whether written or oral. We have seen that Jesus in Mark preaches a reduced Torah (as it happens, precisely those parts of it that do not involve a specifically Jewish form of piety). In this paper, I will not be equating the term "law" with the full Torah. I will also not be using the term "Jewish Christian," which implies that the only significant difference within early Christianity is the contrast between Jewish and gentile origin. Though this polarity existed and was consequential, I find that *doctrinal* differences among Christians of whatever origin were also significant.

---

22. See, for example, Herman N. Ridderbos, "The Earliest Confession of the Atonement in Paul" in *Reconciliation and Hope: New Testament Essays on Atonement and Eschatology Presented to L. L. Morris on His 60th Birthday*, ed. Robert L. Banks (Carlisle: Paternoster, 1974), 76–89; and compare Karl Paul Donfried, *Paul, Thessalonica, and Early Christianity* (London: T&T Clark, 2002), 81–83.

1.8. Alpha Christianity

There are several extant texts which have in common that (1) they seem to portray a relatively early form of Christianity, and (2) they do not mention the resurrection. These include James, the hymn embedded in Phil 2^{23} (which features an exalted and even preexistent Christ but not one whose death is said to have salvific significance), and from the preceding argument, the early layers of Mark. Among later texts, it is conspicuous that Peter in the Pseudo-Clementine Recognitions preaches endlessly, but never mentions the resurrection or any doctrine connected with the resurrection. This seems to represent a vigorous survival (despite what was by then its heretical status) of Alpha doctrine.[24] In this paper, I will attempt to show the affinity of the Didache with this Alpha Christianity, whose ritual prescriptions I believe it preserves.

---

23. As reconstructed by Lohmeyer, it includes an intrusive half-verse added by Paul in quoting it and introducing, if not the resurrection in an explicit form, an allusion to the *theologia crucis*. See Archibald Macbride Hunter, *Paul and His Predecessors*, 2nd ed. (London: SCM, 1961), 41; Joseph A. Fitzmyer, "The Ascension of Christ in Pentecost," in *To Advance the Gospel: New Testament Studies*, 2nd ed. (Grand Rapids: Eerdmans, 1998), 267.

24. I do not wish to imply that preresurrection Christianity, here called Alpha, was itself uniform. There were undoubtedly many local variants and varieties. For example, a fairly coherent group, the Ebionites (seemingly a Christian counterpart of the Essenes), shared many of the traits here mentioned, including the focus on the poor (whence the name) that is developed in Luke, but they also had some distinctive beliefs and used their own texts, including a gospel based on Matthew (Jean Daniélou, *The Theology of Jewish Christianity*, trans. and ed. John A. Baker [Chicago: Henry Regnery, 1964], 55–64). That they used Matthew rather than Mark need occasion no surprise. Beginning at some point not long after the destruction of Jerusalem, everybody, including Luke, was increasingly using Matthew; for its prominence, see Édouard Massaux, *The Influence of the Gospel of Saint Matthew on the Christian Literature before Saint Irenaeus*, trans. Norman J. Belval and Suzanne Hecht, 3 vols., NGS 5.2 (Macon, GA: Mercer University Press, 1993), 3:183–89. For another focus, see Ray A. Pritz, *Nazarene Jewish Christianity Jewish Christianity: From the End of the New Testament Period Until Its Disappearance in the Fourth Century*, StPB 37 (Leiden: Brill; Jerusalem: *Magnes, 1988*).

2. The Didache[25]

The Didache has been an object of interest since the discovery of an almost complete text by Bishop Bryennios in 1873 (first published 1883), but opinions about its place in the scheme of things still differ. One focus of attention is the text's gospel parallels, the strongest resemblances being chiefly to Matthew.[26] The question is whether these are intrinsic, in which case

---

25. Like nearly all titles of ancient texts, the ones attached to the Bryennios manuscript were most likely labels meant to distinguish the text from others and are thus not original. Of them, "The Teaching [ΔΙΔΑΧΗ] of the Twelve Apostles" is physically emphasized in the Bryennios manuscript (see the facsimile in J. Rendel Harris, *The Teaching of the Apostles* [London: C. J. Clay; Baltimore: Johns Hopkins University Press, 1887], plate I) and is probably earlier; after it, and in the manuscript run together with the text proper, is "The Teaching of the Twelve Apostles to the Gentiles." This may come from a later time and reflect a later perception. I find nothing in the Didache itself that unambiguously suggests a limitation to gentile converts or churches.

26. Authorities differ as between reliance on common tradition and the unequivocal use of Matthew. In the end, one must use one's own judgment. I have consulted chiefly Oxford Society of Historical Theology, *The New Testament in the Apostolic Fathers* (Oxford: Clarendon, 1905); Massaux, *Influence of the Gospel*, 1950; Robert A. Kraft, *Barnabas and the Didache*, AF 3 (Toronto: Nelson, 1965); Wolf-Dietrich Köhler, *Die Rezeption des Matthäusevangeliums in der Zeit vor Irenaeus*, WUNT 2/24 (Tübingen: Mohr Siebeck, 1985) as appended to Massaux, *Influence of the Gospel*; and William Varner, *The Way of the Didache: The First Christian Handbook* (Lanham, MD: University Press of America, 2007). Discussion still continues, and the century update of the Oxford Committee study (Andrew Gregory and Christopher M. Tuckett, eds., *The New Testament and the Apostolic Fathers: The Reception of the New Testament in the Apostolic Fathers*, 2 vols. [Oxford: Oxford University Press, 2005]) still offers room for it. For a survey, with whose conclusion I cannot agree, see Christopher M. Tuckett, "Synoptic Tradition in the Didache," in *The Didache in Modern Research*, ed. Jonathan A. Draper, AGJU 37 (Leiden: Brill, 1996), 92–128. I consider two instances to be unequivocal. Didache 8.2, "And do not pray like the hypocrites, but like the Lord commanded in his gospel. Pray this way." There follows the Lord's Prayer in its Matthean, not its Lukan, version (see also Jonathan A. Draper, "The Jesus Tradition in the *Didache*," in *The Jesus Tradition Outside the Gospels*, vol. 5 of *Gospel Perspectives*, ed. David Wenham [Sheffield: JSOT, 1985], 279). Didache 15.4, "And do your prayers and alms and all your actions, as you have it in the Gospel of our Lord" (cf. Matt 6:1–4, 5–15) confirms that the author of these passages regarded the Gospel of Matthew (not some more indefinite "gospel" teaching) as authoritative for the Jesus tradition. Then these verses of the Didache are unambiguously aware of Matthew in its Gospel form, not in some preliminary version. That Matthew might have used the earlier Didache, or something having the same tendency, is not out of the question; see further below.

the Didache is post-Matthean and thus late, or interpolative, in which case the Didache or its earliest textual state is pre-Matthean and thus early.[27] I here seek to show, with special attention to the formal evidence, that the Matthean (and Lukan) elements are interpolative, and that the original Didache attests the earlier form of Christian belief and practice which I have above called Alpha, in contradistinction to the Beta or resurrection Christianity preached by Paul.

The principal witness is the Bryennios manuscript, written in 1056. Other significant witnesses are the P.Oxy. 1782 fragments (late fourth century) and a fifth century Coptic fragment (Br. Mus. Or. 9271) containing Did. 10.3b–12.2a, probably an extract rather than part of a copy.[28] A version of the Two Ways portion also appears at the end of the Epistle of Barnabas, and the entire Didache is included in a comprehensive fourth century Beta document, the Apostolic Constitutions and Canons.

The Didache consists of three readily distinguishable parts. The first is the Two Ways document, Did. 1.1–6.2, originally a separate tract,[29] of

---

Didache 1.5, "To everyone asking you for anything, give it and do not ask for it back." Here the text is closer to Luke 6:30 than to the parallel Matt 5:41, 40 (Varner, *Way of the Didache*, 20). Then the Didache was aware of Luke as well as Matthew (the source for Did. 1.4, immediately preceding) and thus aware of both the second-tier gospels, though regarding Matthew more highly. A claim of contact with the Gospel of John (at Did. 9.4) has been refuted by Arthur Vööbus, "Regarding the Background of the Liturgical Traditions in the Didache," *VC* 23 (1969): 81–87. With respect to the Gospels, the Didache as we have it seems to occupy a position not unlike that of the Gospel of Thomas: some echoes of Mark (organic; see below), contact with Matthew and/or Luke, but none with John. The Luke > Thomas directionality has been convincingly argued most recently by Mark Goodacre, *Thomas and the Gospels: The Case for Thomas's Familiarity with the Gospels* (Grand Rapids: Eerdmans, 2012). The directionality of the Didache/Matthew parallels, and whether some form of the Didache existed before those contacts were made, is precisely the question explored in the present paper.

27. With the third-text option I have dealt in the "Q" section of §1 5, above, by suggesting an alternative to "Q."

28. For details, see Kurt Niederwimmer, *The Didache: A Commentary*, trans. Linda M. Maloney, Hermeneia (Minneapolis: Fortress, 1998), 19–26. Some other relevant manuscripts will be mentioned below.

29. The instructional part of the Two Ways seems to end with the list of evil deeds in 5.2, which concludes "May you be delivered, children, from all of these!" (trans. Varner, *Way of the Didache*). Didache 6.1, "See to it that no one leads you astray from this way of teaching, since he is teaching you apart from God," refers instead to the whole of the Two Ways teaching and, with 6.2, is probably a transition to the following church order section of the Didache. Compare the introductory phrase in Barn. 18.1,

which a version is included in Barn. 18–20. There are partial parallels in the vice lists of Rom 1:19–2:29 and Gal 5:13–6:10, both of which have been challenged as interpolated in the respective Pauline Epistles.[30] The Two Ways tract functions as the ethical section of the Didache; it is addressed to ordinary believers: members rather than leaders of local churches. Comparison of the Bryennios and Barnabas versions permits recovery of their archetype: the passages common to both.

Next comes Did. 6.3–12.1, with instructions for administering the sacraments and receiving apostolic visitors. This is the church order or liturgical section of the Didache; it is addressed to church leaders. Attention to the structural use of the itemization formula περὶ δέ helps to distinguish an original core from later supplements.[31]

Last is the apocalypse, Did. 16, the doctrinal section. Like the Two Ways, it is addressed to ordinary believers and thus contrasts with the preceding material. Didache 16 itself appears to be an integral production.

The Didache is incorporated whole into Apos. Con. 7, but with "orthodoxizing" changes that introduce the resurrection doctrine and thus compromise its original Alpha character.[32] Apostolic Constitutions 7.32.5 continues beyond the defective end of the Bryennios manuscript and seems to

---

"Let us now pass on to another kind of knowledge and instruction," which seems to link the Two Ways tract to a text that had ended satisfactorily at Barn. 17.2, "For if I should write you concerning things present or yet to come, you would not grasp them, because they are as yet hidden in parables. Let this, then, be enough" (trans. James A. Kleist, *The Didache; the Epistle of Barnabas; the Epistles and the Martyrdom of St. Polycarp; the Fragments of Papias; the Epistle to Diognetus*, ACW 6 [Westminster, MD: Newman, 1948]). The implication of these bridging passages is that a Two Ways tract was appended to an already complete Epistle of Barnabas and separately prefixed to the preexisting liturgical portion of the Didache.

30. For Rom 1:18–2:29, see William O. Walker Jr., *Interpolations in the Pauline Letters* (London: Sheffield, 2001), 166–89; for Gal 5:13–6:10, see John Cochrane O'Neill, *The Recovery of Paul's Letter to the Galatians* (London: SPCK, 1972), 65–71. I consider these arguments to be definitive.

31. For details of this argument, see §2.2.1 below.

32. The lack of the resurrection and associated doctrines in the Didache has been noticed. The concept of Jesus as redeeming others through his suffering can be connected to the Didache only by its use of the Greek word πᾶς, considered as evoking the "suffering servant" of Isa 59:2–4 (Varner, *Way of the Didache*, 94). There is no direct warrant *in the text* for that linkage.

preserve the material lost from that manuscript. These last verses I number as Did. 16.8–11.[33]

This is the Didache text with which I will work. I now take up the three sections in turn, for closer examination, paying particular attention to possible interpolations.

2.1. The Two Ways: Did. 1.1–6.2

This is at bottom a list of good and evil deeds, plus the statement that the path of good deeds leads to life and the path of bad deeds leads to death. It is clearly not the "faith" scenario preached by Paul in Romans. It is instead in the same category as the "works" scenario argued by an Alpha document, the Epistle of James.[34]

---

33. I follow Robert E. Aldridge, "The Lost Ending of the *Didache*," VC 53 (1999): 1–15, except that with support from Boniface, which lacks it, and from Aldridge himself (p. 10), who suspects that it "may be a later addition," I regard the next verse, his Did. 16.12, "And they shall rejoice in the Kingdom of God, *which is in Christ Jesus*" (p. 15), as a Beta addition in the Apostolic Constitutions and Canons. The preceding Did. 16.11, "to inherit those things which eye hath not seen, nor ear heard, nor have entered into the heart of man, such things as God hath prepared for them that love him," can be seen as drawing on 1 Cor 2:9, but that passage is itself an explicit quote whose exact original is not to be found in the Septuagint. Opinions about its source vary. James Moffatt, agreeing with Jerome, suggests a free rendition of Isa 64:4. Fitzmyer points to further possibilities, including an Apocryphon of Elijah (so Origen). It suffices for our purpose to say that Paul was quoting *some* text then current, whether freely or precisely, which may also have been available to the writer of this part of the Didache. It is not proved (but see n. 100 below) that the Didache is here derivative from 1 Corinthians. With Aldridge, then, but with the above qualification, the Didache originally ended in this way (Alpha tenets *emphasized*): "Then the world will see the Lord coming upon the clouds of Heaven, with the angels of his power, in the throne of his Kingdom, to condemn the Devil, the deceiver of the world, and to render to every one *according to his deeds*. Then shall the wicked go away into everlasting punishment, but *the righteous shall enter eternal life*, to inherit those things which eye hath not seen, nor ear heard, nor have entered into the heart of man, such things as God has prepared for them that love him" (16.6–11, trans. Aldridge, "Lost Ending of the *Didache*"). This would seem to be a fittingly sonorous conclusion to the entire document, in its final form.

34. For the sharp interchange between these two texts, see under "Luke" in §1.3 above.

2.1.1. Barnabas

The Oxford Committee finds that Barnabas quotes or echoes Jewish Scriptures, including noncanonical ones,[35] inexactly and sometimes in combination; the same applies to its use of canonical New Testament texts. On that understanding, Barnabas has sometimes striking resemblances to Romans among the genuine Pauline Epistles, and of the deutero-Pauline Epistles, to Ephesians, Hebrews, and the Pastorals. The case for knowledge of 1 Peter is considerable, but not for 2 Peter. There are possible links to Matthew among the Gospels.[36] This tends to locate Barnabas before 1 Clement (ca. 96) and to identify it as aware of several deutero-Pauline writings. Then authorship by Paul's associate, Mark's cousin Barnabas, is chronologically improbable, and Barnabas must instead be thought to be borrowing the established name of Barnabas.

Barnabas ends naturally at Barn. 17 ("Let this, then, be enough"). The text is in effect reopened to include the Two Ways at 18.1 ("Let us now pass on to another kind of knowledge and instruction"). The seventeen-chapter text is attested in a ninth century Latin manuscript at St. Petersburg;[37] the Two Ways addendum is in place in both Sinaiticus (fourth century) and the Bryennios manuscript (copied in 1056). It seems clear that the Two Ways portion was added to an original seventeen-chapter Barnabas. The authorial stance of Barnabas should then be assessed from those seventeen chapters.

Barnabas is structured like a Pauline church letter and certainly has that model in mind. But despite its profession of warm regard, it has no discernible address and was apparently intended as a general letter. The issue for Barnabas is the status of Jewish tradition and its appropriation by the Christians, and to this message it gives systematic attention. Whereas Hebrews as it were seeks to symbolically reinhabit Jewish sacrificial tradition from the inside, Barnabas rejects and interiorizes sacrifices (ch. 2) and fasts (ch. 3). It claims the covenant for the Christians (ch. 4), explains the atonement (chs. 5–8), and interiorizes circumcision (ch. 9) and food laws (ch. 10). It cites scriptural predictions of baptism and explains the

---

35. Kraft (*Barnabas and the Didache*, 182–84) also notes many Barnabas quotes from now unidentifiable Jewish writings.

36. Kraft (*Barnabas and the Didache*, 181–85) sees a quotation (?) of Matt 22:14 in Barn. 4.14b and a "strong allusion" to Matt 26:31 paralleled in Barn. 5.12b.

37. Kirsopp Lake, trans., *The Apostolic Fathers*, 2 vols, LCL 24–25 (Cambridge: Harvard University Press, 1912), 1:338.

cross (chs. 11–12) and again claims the covenant, this time specifically for the gentiles (ch. 13). It allegorizes the Sabbath (ch. 14) and rejects other month and day observances (ch. 15). It enjoins the building of a spiritual temple for the Lord (ch. 16)[38] and concludes with a brief passage (ch. 17) saying that nothing has been omitted that is "necessary for salvation." It is thus a complete presentation of the teachings that a gospel might include, but not structured as a life of Jesus. The same might be said of Romans, the only genuine Pauline letter of which Barnabas is unquestionably aware. Doctrinally, Barnabas is a Beta document. Its allegorical style of argument, like that of Hebrews, is Alexandrian.

2.1.2. The Barnabas Two Ways

The version of the Two Ways that appears as Barn. 18–20 includes one reference to the atonement (19.2, "glorify him who ransomed you in death," no parallel in the Didache version), presumably to adjust the Alpha stance of the Two Ways to the Beta position of the rest of Barnabas.[39] Its list of good and bad deeds is very different in sequence from that of the Didache Two Ways. Which is earlier?

Here are the two versions, with sequence numbers in each appended to the other:

Didache Two Ways 5.1	Barnabas Two Ways 20a–d
1. murders (φόνοι) (7)	1. idolatry (εἰδωλολατρεία) (6)
2. adulteries (μοιχεῖαι) (6)	2. audacity (θρασύτης) (20)

---

38. Barnabas 16.4–5 "owing to the war it [the temple] was destroyed by the enemy" makes plain that Barnabas is post-70, which agrees with the evidence for relative date above cited. On the strength of 16.4b "at present even the servants of the enemy will build it up again" is taken by some to refer to the period under Hadrian (ca 120) when the possibility of actually rebuilding the Jerusalem temple under Roman auspices seemed to exist; Joseph B. Lightfoot (*The Apostolic Fathers: Revised Texts with Short Introductions and English Translations*, ed. J. R. Harmer [London: MacMillan, 1912], 241) argues otherwise. The present tense of the text is probably signaled by the Dan 7:7–8 prophecy about ten kings subdued by one king (Barn. 4.4). One opinion sees the tenth king as Vespasian (ruled 69–79). Prophecy is perhaps by nature dark, to be made clear only in the event, and too much should not be built on these numbers or possible numbers.

39. A similar conclusion is reached in Jonathan A. Draper, "Barnabas and the Riddle of the Didache Revisited," *JSNT* 58 (1995): 89–113.

3. lusts (ἐπιθυμίαι)
4. fornications (πορνεῖαι)
5. thefts (κλοπαί)
6. idolatries (εἰδωλολατρίαι) (1)
7. feats of magic (μαγεῖαι) (15)
8. sorceries (φαρμακίαι) (14)
9. robberies (ἁρπαγαί) (8)
10. perjuries (ψευδομαρτυρίαι)
11. hypocrisies (ὑποκρίσεις) (4)
12. double-heartedness (διπλοκαρδία) (5)
13. fraud (δόλος) (11)
14. haughtiness (ὑπερηφανία) (9)
15. malice (κακία) (12)
16. willfulness (αὐθάδεια) (13)
17. covetousness (πλεονεξία) (16)
18. foul speech (αἰσχρολογία)
19. jealousy (ζηλοτυπία)
20. audacity (θρασύτης) (2)
21. pride (ὕψος) (~ 3)
22. boastfulness (ἀλαζονεία)

3. pride of power (ὕψος δυνάμεως) (~ 21)
4. hypocrisy (ὑπόκρισις) (11)
5. double-heartedness (διπλοκαρδία) (12)
6. adultery (μοιχεία) (2)
7. murder (φόνος) (1)
8. robbery (ἁρπαγή) (9)
9. haughtiness (ὑπερηφανία) (14)
10. transgression (παράβασις)[a]
11. fraud (δόλος) (13)
12. malice (κακία) (15)

13. willfulness (αὐθάδεια) (16)
14. sorcery (φαρμακεία) (8)
15. magic (μαγεία) (7)
16. covetousness (πλεονεξία) (17)
17. lack of the fear of God (αφοβία θεοῦ)

Note
a. The term is Pauline (Gal 3:19; Rom 2:23, 4:15, 5:14) and Deutero-Pauline (1 Tim 2:14; Heb 9:15), which agrees with the Pauline focus of Barnabas noted above.

The Barnabas list is evidently a simplification, rationalization, and revision of the Didache list:

- The three sexual offenses (Did. #2–4) are subsumed under one (Barn. #6)
- Thefts and robberies (Did. #5, 9) are combined as one (Barn. #8)
- Perjuries and fraud (Did. #10, 13) are combined as one (Barn. #11)
- Covetousness and jealousy (Did. #17, 19) are combined as one (Barn. #16)

- Foul talk and boastfulness (Did. #18, 22) are omitted or subsumed as transgression (Barn. #10)

These statements are in the order of both the Didache and Barnabas lists. In addition:

- Idolatry (Did. #6) is put first (Barn. #1) and framed by the symmetrical want of fear of God (Barn. #17, last)

These rearrangements in Barnabas have their logic: the combination of items in the list makes for tidiness, and the framing of the list with "idolatry" and "want of fear of God" gives a nice effect. On the other side, Rendel Harris has shown that the Didache version is based on a Jewish list of faults to be avoided or atoned (the Vidui prayer), twenty-two in number, each fault beginning with a different letter of the Hebrew alphabet.[40] This abecedarius form (found also in the Psalms and suggesting an origin in Jewish practice), which is lost in Barnabas, is undoubtedly the earlier. The directionality then seems to be Didache > Barnabas.[41]

The Didache version is also earlier than the Barnabas version in content. It is rooted, as is not consistently true of Barnabas, in law observance as the key to eternal life. This is what Mark, the earliest gospel, reports Jesus as saying in Mark 10:19, when asked about "inheriting eternal life: "Thou knowest the commandments."[42] Jesus in Mark does not preach *himself*; he points to *the law*, albeit in a simplified version, minus Pharisaic complications, and with the characteristic addition of "fraud." It is characteristic of what I have above called Alpha Christianity. I see Barnabas as adapting an Alpha document to a Beta context.

2.1.3. The Archetype

If we compare the Didache and Barnabas versions as wholes, we find that certain parts of each version have no counterpart in the other. Rearrangement of material in Barnabas, as exemplified above, extends to mixing of

---

40. Harris, *Teaching of the Apostles*, 82–83.
41. Here as elsewhere in this paper, I consider the preceding argument to be definitive and have chosen not to weary the reader by citing scholarship that, sometimes at book length, has reached a different conclusion.
42. For details of the Jesus commandments, see under "Paul" in 1.6, above.

material from one chapter to another, so that a full two-column comparison becomes hard to read.[43] The major sections of the Didache Two Ways that have no counterpart in Barnabas are the following:

- Did. 1.2b-6. The so-called *Sectio Evangelica*, drawn almost entirely from Matthew and Luke, with verses also from Sirach and other texts.[44]
- Did. 3.1-6, the "fence" passage,[45] warns of actions that, though not themselves sinful, may be the occasion of sin. It represents a Jewish development rather than a Synoptic extension of the original Two Ways.
- Did. 6.1-2. This ending to the Didache Two Ways is not found in Barnabas, which has its own conclusion in Barn. 21.1-9.[46]

Certain passages in Barnabas, most conspicuously the Beta improvement in Barn. 19.2a (2), "Glorify him who redeemed you from death," are not in the Didache version, which is consistently Alpha in its theology.[47]

2.1.4. Translation

I conclude this section with a translation of the Didache Two Ways,[48] eliminating the passages identified above as not attested by Barnabas and

---

43. For a specimen, see Kraft, *Barnabas and the Didache*, 134–62.

44. This section is also lacking in the Doctrina Apostolorum version. That it appears in the fourth-century P.Oxy. fragments merely shows that the fragments are later than the first-century formation period of the Didache, and in the specific textual tradition of the Didache version of the Two Ways.

45. Kraft (*Barnabas and the Didache*, 146) quotes m. 'Abot 1:1: "Make a fence around the Torah."

46. Didache 6.3 is sometimes included in this section. For reasons to be explained below, I regard it as the opening of the second main section of the Didache, none of which finds a place in Barnabas.

47. "Ransom/redeem" appears in the Didache only at 4.6, where it refers to the individual's good deeds counterweighting or paying the price of evil deeds (for that process, see Jas 5:20, "cover a multitude of sins"). As the Didache Eucharist prayers show (Did. 9.2 "revealed"; 9.3 "knowledge revealed"; 10.2 "knowledge revealed"), Jesus only gives *knowledge*, shows the *way* of salvation (Mark 12:14, "Way of God"). Consistently, Mark 10:19 shows Jesus in the very act of "showing the way."

48. Translation and some notes are drawn from Varner, *Way of the Didache*, revised as seems useful in light of the present discussion. The reader may wish to

indenting and italicizing one further passage that appears, like the above, to be a later Matthean improvement. Occasional comparison is made to Alpha texts such as James or the seemingly earlier strata of Mark, which share sufficient doctrinal and organizational features to be considered witnesses to the same kind of Christianity.

1.1 There are Two Ways, one of life and one of death, and there is a great difference between the two ways.
1.2a On the one hand, then, the way of life is this: First, you love the God who made you.
2.1 And the second command of the teaching:
2.2 You will not murder, you will not commit adultery, you will not corrupt children, you will not have illicit sex, you will not steal, you will not practice magic, you will not practice sorcery, you will not murder a child by means of abortion, nor kill one that has been born; you will not desire the things of your neighbor, [2.3] You will not swear falsely, you will not bear false witness, you will not speak evil of anyone, you will not hold grudges. [2.4] You will not be double-minded or double-tongued, for being double-tongued is a snare of death. [2.5] Your word will not be false or empty, but will be fulfilled in action. [2.6] You will not be covetous, nor greedy, nor a hypocrite, nor spiteful, nor arrogant.[49] You will not plot an evil plan against your neighbor. [2.7] You will not hate any one, but some you will reprove, and for others you will pray, and some you will love more than your soul.
3.7 But be meek,
    since the meek will inherit the earth [Matt 5:5]
[3.8] become long-suffering, and merciful, and harmless, and gentle, and good, and one who trembles always at the words that you have heard.[50] [3.9] You will not exalt yourself, and you will not

---

compare the reconstruction in Huub van de Sandt and David Flusser, *The Didache: Its Jewish Sources and Its Place in Early Judaism and Christianity*, CRINT 3.5 (Assen: Van Gorcum; Minneapolis: Fortress, 2002), 120–30, which differs at several points. For Did. 6.2–3, see their separate essay at 238–70.

49. Compare Exod 20:13–17 (Varner, *Way of the Didache*).
50. Compare Isa 66:2 (Varner, *Way of the Didache*).

	give boldness to your soul. Your soul will not be joined with the haughty, but with just and lowly people you will dwell.[51]
3.10	You will accept the experiences that happen to you as good things,[52] knowing that apart from God, nothing happens.[53]
4.1	My child, the one speaking to you the word of God you will remember night and day,[54] and you will honor him as the Lord. [4.2] And you will seek every day the presence of the saints in order that you may find support in their words. [4.3] You will not cause division, and you will reconcile those who quarrel; you will judge justly, you will not show favoritism when you reprove others for their failings.[55]
4.4	You will not become double-minded, whether it will be or not.[56]
4.5	Do not become one who, on the one hand, stretches out your hands to receive, or on the other hand, draws them back from giving. [4.6] If you should have something through the work of your hands, you will give it as a ransom for your sins.[57] [4.7] You will not hesitate to give, nor will you grumble when you give, for

---

51. Compare Jas 2:1, "My brothers, show no partiality as you hold the faith in our Lord Jesus Christ, the Lord of glory." The egalitarianism of James is one of its salient traits. Economic egalitarianism in the early churches is depicted, in an obviously legendary way, by Luke in Acts 4:32–35. We here see the Didache reflecting a similar situation: it is the "justness" of the community that enables it to be viable, although "lowly."

52. Compare Jas 1:2, "Count it all joy, my brothers, when you meet trials of various kinds."

53. Compare Jas 1:13, "Let no one say when he is tempted, 'I am being tempted by God,' for God cannot be tempted with evil, and he himself tempts no one."

54. Varner (*Way of the Didache*) notes the similarity to Heb 13:7.

55. In the primitive Christian community, each member is in principle liable to judge others. The function of judge has not yet been assigned to a permanent leader.

56. Compare Mark 11:23, "and does not doubt in his heart, but believes that what he says will come to pass, it will be done for him." Sincerity of belief is the requirement for any result of prayer. So also Jas 1:6–7, "But let him ask in faith, with no doubting…. For that person must not suppose that he will receive anything from the Lord."

57. This is the only appearance of "ransom" in the text. Notice that it is not Jesus who ransoms sinners by his death, but the individual who ransoms himself from his sins by doing good deeds. See Jas 5:19–20 ("My brothers, if anyone among you wanders from the truth and someone brings him back, let him know that whoever brings back a sinner from his wandering will save his soul from death and will cover a multitude of sins"), the final passage in that text.

you know who will be the good paymaster of your reward. [4.8] You will not turn away the one in need, but you will share together all things with your brother, and you will not say that such things are your own, for if you are partners in what is immortal, how much more in mortal things?

4.9 You will not take away your hand from your son or from your daughter, but from youth you will teach them the fear of God.[58] [4.10] You will not command your male or female slave, who are hoping in the same God, in your bitterness, lest they should never fear the God who is over you both; for He does not come to call [to salvation] according to social status, but those whom the Spirit has prepared. [4.11] And you, slaves, will be subject to your masters as to the image of God in shame and fear.[59]

4.12 You will hate all hypocrisy, and everything that is not pleasing to the Lord. [4.13] Never forsake the commandments of the Lord, but you will guard the things that you have received, neither adding nor subtracting anything.[60]

4.14 In church, you will confess your wrongdoings, and you will not go to your place of prayer with an evil conscience. This is the way of life!

5.1 The Way of Death, on the other hand, is this.
First of all, it is evil and full of accursedness:[61]

1. murders,	5.2	B1. persecutors of the good,[62]
2. adulteries,		B2. hating truth,
3. lusts,		B3. loving a lie,
4. fornications,		B4. not knowing the wages of righteousness,

---

58. This clause corresponds to Barn. 19.5d; it may have inspired "lack of the fear of God" at Barn. 20.1d (#17 on that list).

59. Didache 4.10–11 are somewhat reminiscent of Col 3:22–4:1 (and its later duplicate, Eph 6:5–9). Those who have felt that the Didache is a second-century text naturally conclude that Didache is the borrower, but it may also be that the widely circulated Didache influenced those who composed some of the deuteroPauline material. I tentatively retain Did. 4.10f–11 as original.

60. Varner (*Way of the Didache*) cites Deut 4:2 or 12:32.

61. This is the original atonement prayer list, repeated from the above discussion.

62. I follow Varner in arranging Did. 5.2 as a B list, parallel to that of 5.1. In the pre-Didache evolution of the Two Ways, it is the final rewrite of the original twenty-two item list. It repeats material from previous passages, and even repeats itself.

5. thefts,	B5. not cleaving to the good,
6. idolatries,	B6. nor to just judgement,
7. feats of magic,	B7. those who are alert not for good but for evil,
8. sorceries,	B8. far from being gentle and patient,
9. robberies,	B9. loving empty things,
10. perjuries,	B10. pursuing retribution,
11. hypocrisies,	B11. not showing mercy to the poor,[63]
12. double-heartedness,	B12. not working for the oppressed,
13. fraud,	B13. not knowing the One who made them,[64]
14. arrogance,	B14. murderers of children,
15. malice,	B15. destroyers of what God has formed,
16. willfulness,	B16. turning away from one in need,
17. covetousness,	B17. oppressing the afflicted,
18. foul speech,	B18. advocates of the rich,
19. jealousy,	B19. unjust judges of the poor,
20. audacity,	B20. totally sinful
21. pride,	
22. boastfulness.	

6.1 *See to it that no one leads you astray from this way of teaching, since he is teaching you apart from God.*

6.2 *For, on the one hand, if you are able to bear the whole yoke of the Lord, you will be perfect, but if, on the other hand, you are not able, that which you are able, do this.*[65]

These transitional passages of Did. 6.1–2 are not original to the Two Ways. They serve as a transition to the following section of the Didache ("Teaching"). They were written at the time when the Two Ways was added and

---

63. The enmity of rich and poor is a major theme in James.

64. This echoes Did. 1.2a and incidentally confirms that passage as integral in the original Didache.

65. The "what you are able" motif is like that of the first passage in the Didache proper (Did. 6.3), and at the time of its interpolation, Did. 6.2 may have imitated that passage.

are not part of the Matthean interpolation layer, which on other evidence comes later.

The Two Ways are in effect a Way of Death warning, elaborated in several ways but remaining essentially a list of things not to do (the prescriptions of the Way of Life is also largely negative). The added Matthean layer provided more positive maxims, for the Didache as a whole and also for the Two Ways as its first section. This positive tone was one of the great merits of Matthew as an authority text.

2.2. The Original Church Order Document: Did. 6.3–12.1

2.2.1. Form

Within the middle part of the Didache, 6.3–12.1 is distinguished by the use of the itemization idiom περὶ δέ ("as for; now concerning").[66] The first such passage, the single verse 6.3, deals with questions of permissible food. It makes an abrupt beginning for the text, if this was indeed the oldest section of the Didache, but it is reasonable to assume that, as with the sections so marked in 1 Corinthians, the ruling dealt with a question concerning which uncertainty already existed in the Didache churches. The context is thus supplied by the concern.[67] The last περὶ δέ passage begins at Did. 11.3 ("Now concerning apostles and prophets"), but where does it end? I suggest that the key discontinuity is the forbidding of long-term resi-

---

66. Περὶ δέ is used as an organizing principle also in 1 Cor 7:1 (introducing the topic of marriage), 7:25 (the unmarried), 8:1 (food offered to idols), 12:1 (spiritual gifts), 16:1 (the collection for Jerusalem), and 16:12 (the visit of Apollos). Some have thought that, as is the case here (1 Cor 7:1, "Now concerning the matters about which you wrote"), περὶ δέ occurs *only* in response to questions raised in a previous letter. Margaret Mitchell ("Concerning PERI DE in 1 Corinthians," *NovT* 3 [1989]: 229–56) has shown that instead, περὶ δέ in Greek generally is "simply a topic marker, a shorthand way of introducing the next subject of discussion" (234). It is not limited to a subject previously mentioned; rather, it introduces "a new topic, the only requirement of which is that it is readily known to both writer and reader" (236). Mitchell mentions the Didache at 251 n. 98, but without discussion. The general usage she describes will serve for περὶ δέ in the Didache, but without excluding the possibility, indeed, the likelihood, that authoritative guidance on these subjects, the "difficult cases" under law or custom, was much desired by the leaders of the various early Alpha churches.

67. Note that one of the περὶ δέ sections in 1 Corinthians also deals with food offered to idols. For considerations of date, see section 3 below.

dence in Did. 11.5 ("But if ever he should remain three [days], he is a false prophet"), but allowed in Did. 12.3 ("If, on the other hand, he wishes to settle down among you"), which in turn is linked by idiom to 12.2 ("If, on the one hand"), which repeats the substance of 11.5 as a preface to discussing the exception. The original "apostles" guideline then seems to end at 12.1, which has a summative function ("and everyone coming in the name of the Lord").[68]

There are several points at which Matthean parallels occur. Most of them can be excised without damage to local continuity. These are italicized and indented on the right. A few (discussed in the notes) are more difficult. Some are indeed difficult, and it is not supposed that the last word has here been said on any of them.

2.2.2. Translation

The format of the preceding section is also followed here. The sections beginning with the structural marked περὶ δέ are printed in *italics*.

Food
6.3   *Concerning food*, bear that which you are able, but from the food sacrificed to idols, especially keep away, for it is the worship of dead gods.

Baptism
7.1   *Concerning baptism*,[69] baptize this way. After you have said all these things beforehand, immerse in the name of the Father, and

---

68. See Clayton N. Jefford and Stephen J. Patterson ("A Note on *Didache* 12.2a [Coptic]," *SecCent* 7 [1989–1990]: 65–75) for an argument, based on the Coptic text, that the Didache ended at 12.2a, and compare F. Stanley Jones and Paul A. Mirecki, "Considerations on the Coptic Papyrus of the Didache," in *The* Didache *in Context: Essays on Its Text, History and Transmission*, ed. Clayton N. Jefford, NovTSup 77 (Leiden: Brill, 1995), 47–87.

69. As in 1 Peter, which with Francis Wright Beare (*The First Epistle of Peter*, 3rd ed. [Oxford: Basil Blackwell, 1970]) and others I regard as in origin a baptismal homily, the Christian life begins with baptism, considered not only as a symbolic purification (the tradition of John the Baptist) but also as a rite of Christian entry. It is thus entirely appropriate as the first part of this section of the Didache, which gives instruction to local church leaders.

of the Son, and of the Holy Spirit[70] in flowing water. [7.2] But if you[71] do not have flowing water, immerse in another water, and if you are not able to do so in cold, in warm; [7.3] and if you should have neither, pour out water on the head three times in the name of the Father, and of the Son, and of the Holy Spirit.

[Fasts][72]

7.4 And prior to the baptism, let the one baptizing fast, also the one being baptized, and if any others are able to do so;[73] and order the one being baptized to fast one or two [days] before.

8.1. *Rules on fasting* [cf. Matt 6:16][74]

[Prayer]

8.2–3. *Rules on Prayer* [Matt 6:9–13][75]

---

70. This formula, which also appears at Matt 28:19, need not imply a Trinitarian theology in the later sense. Its origin even in Matthew has been much discussed and remains unsolved. It is not firmly situated in Matthew, and I here take it as an early formula used by the Didache writer, and also, separately and later, by Matthew. Father, Son, and Spirit all play a role in the Didache scheme of things, as a reading of the whole text will reveal, and the formula is thus not locally anomalous.

71. The "you" in Did. 7.1 is singular; in 7.2–4 it is plural. This has been thought to imply a complex history of the Didache baptismal advice (see Alan J. P. Garrow, *The Gospel of Matthew's Dependence on the* Didache, JSNTSup 254 [London: T&T Clark, 2004], 94–95, with reconstruction). It is possible that the difference can be otherwise accounted for, but the matter cannot be pursued in the space here available.

72. There was no original Didache topic for fasts, as is indicated by the brackets around this heading. The rule on fasting before baptism was simply part of the instructions for baptism; it was thus included under the baptism topic.

73. Note the recurrent motif of permissible relaxation of a known ideal procedure, which pervades this part of the text.

74. When the Matthean material was added, this was the obvious place to include a note on fixed fast days (envisioned, but as an institution of the later church, in Mark 2:18–21. The Didache inhabits the situation predicted by that passage). At that point in the history of the text, there was created an implicit "fasts" topic, though without the περὶ δέ marker. The disuse of that marker perhaps suggests that the person in charge of the Didache at the end was not the same as the one who had been in charge at the beginning. Apart from its use of Matthew rather than Luke (in all probability the later version), the Did. 8.3 prescription of thrice daily prayer seems also late; for a comparison with the Jewish Eighteen Benedictions, see Gordon J. Bahr, "The Use of the Lord's Prayer in the Primitive Church," *JBL* 84 (1965): 153–59.

75. Fasting suggests prayer, and an implicit section on prayer was created at the

The Eucharist

9.1 *Now concerning* the thanksgiving meal, give thanks this way. [9.2] First, concerning the cup: "We give you thanks, our Father, for the holy vine of your servant David, which you revealed to us through your servant Jesus.[76] To you is the glory forever." [9.3] And concerning the broken bread: "We give you thanks, our Father, for the life and knowledge which you revealed to us through your servant Jesus. To you is the glory forever." [9.4] "Just as this broken bread was scattered over the mountains, and was gathered together and became one,[77] in this way may your church be gathered together from the ends of the earth into your kingdom. Because yours is the glory and the power, through Jesus Christ forever."

9.5 And let no one eat or drink from your thanksgiving meal except those baptized in the name of the Lord.

For also the Lord has said concerning this:
"Do not give what is holy to the dogs" [Matt 7:6][78]

10.1 And after being filled, give thanks in this way: [10.2] "We give you thanks, holy Father, for your holy name, which you have caused to dwell in our hearts, and for the knowledge and faith and immortality which you revealed to us through your servant Jesus. To you is the glory forever." [10.3] "You, almighty Master, created all things for the sake of your name, both food and drink you have given to people for enjoyment, in order that they might give thanks. But to us you have graciously bestowed spiritual food and drink and eternal life through your servant." [10.4] "Before all things, we give you thanks because you are powerful; to you is the glory forever."

10.5 "Remember, Lord, your church, to save her from every evil, and to perfect her in your love, and to gather her together from the four

---

same time the preceding note was added (the prayer in question is the Lord's Prayer in its Matthean version), thus creating the two bracketed topics shown above. For another argument concerning the interruptive nature of Did. 8, see Jonathan A. Draper, "Christian Self-Definition against the 'Hypocrites' in Didache 8," in Draper, *The* Didache *in Modern Research*, 223–43.

76. This passage, with its omission of the blood of Jesus, is crucial for the present argument; see nn. 6 and 7 above.

77. The comparison is enigmatic, but the ingathering of the saved at the last day is present already in Mark 13:27.

78. A not wholly appropriate later insertion of a striking Matthean phrase.

	winds,[79] the sanctified into your kingdom which you prepared for her; Because yours is the power and the glory forever."
10.6	"May grace come, and may this world pass away! Hosanna to the God of David!"[80] "If anyone is holy, let him come! If anyone is not, let him repent! Come, Lord! Amen!"[81]
10.7	But allow the prophets to give thanks as much as they wish.[82]
11.1	Therefore, whoever teaches you all these things said previously, receive him. [11.2] If, on the other hand, the one teaching, if he has been turned, and should teach another doctrine for the destroying [of these things], do not listen to him. But if it is for the bringing of righteousness and knowledge of the Lord, receive him as the Lord!

Visiting Apostles

11.3	*Now concerning* the apostles and prophets in accord with the decree of the gospel,[83] act thus:
11.4	Every apostle coming to you, let him be received as the Lord, [11.5] but he will not remain except for one day, and if there is need, also another, but if ever he should remain three, he is a false prophet. [11.6] And when he departs, let the apostle take nothing except bread [that he needs] until he is [next] lodged. If, however, he asks for money, he is a false prophet.[84]

---

79. This is usually referred to Matt 24:31, but the "four winds" of Mark 13:27 will suffice.

80. The unmistakable Davidic strand in Mark's account of Jesus (e.g., Mark 2:25; 10:47–48; 11:10; 12:35–37) is troubling for later exegesis. It is the more remarkable (and perhaps a sign of early date) to find it preserved intact, here and at Did. 9.2.

81. "Come, Lord" translates the Aramaic ejaculation prayer "Maranatha." Paul in 1 Cor 16:22 has just cursed (anathema) Alphas of Corinth, who do not in his specific sense "love the Lord." Paul's sense of "Maranatha" (16:23) is, "Let the Lord indeed come, and judge all, and condemn you for your errors." The prayer appears in Greek translated form in Rev 22:20.

82. The new fixed forms prescribed by the Didache are not meant to inhibit the older way, which presumably featured prayer or prophecy by inspired individuals, as we know was the practice also in the churches of Paul.

83. Not here a written text, but the teaching as apostolically preached. So also in Mark 1:14–15; 10:29; 13:10; 14:9.

84. That apostles are not to carry money, but to rely exclusively on local hospitality, is laid down in Mark 6:8.

11.7 And every prophet speaking in the Spirit you should not test or judge, for every sin will be forgiven, but this sin will not be forgiven.[85] [11.8] But not everyone speaking in the Spirit is a prophet, but only if he has the behavior of the Lord. Therefore, from their behavior will be known the false prophet and the prophet.

11.9 And every prophet ordering a table in the Spirit, will not eat from it; but if he does, he is a false prophet. [11.10] And every prophet teaching the truth, if he does not do what he preaches, he is a false prophet. [11.11] And every prophet who has been put to the test and is genuine, and who acts for the earthly mystery of the church, but not teaching to do what he himself does, he shall not be judged by you, for he has his judgement from God, for so the ancient prophets also acted.

11.12 But whoever should say in the Spirit, "Give me silver" or any other thing, you will not listen to him. But if he should say to give to others in need, let no one judge him.

12.1 And everyone coming in the name of the Lord, let him be received, and then, having put him to the test, you will know, for you will have understanding of right and left.

2.3. The Extension: Did. 12.2–15.4

As above mentioned, we here enter an area that is not formally organized in περὶ δέ sections and that substantively goes beyond the original apostolic visit guidelines to include options not previously discussed. What is happening here historically? The system of itinerant teachers undoubtedly obtained from the beginning, whereas we first hear of the resident apostle variant in the mid 50s. Paul in 1 Cor 9:3–15 makes much of his supporting himself while at Corinth for an extended period, though claiming a right

---

85. The unforgivable nature of the sin of denying the presence of the Spirit is established in Mark 3:29. The wording of Matthew is closer to that of the Didache, which may mark this as after all an interpolation. It also might indicate Matthew's knowledge of the Didache. If two texts, A and B, are literarily related, and A is a growth text whose timespan includes the date of B, then we have a situation where A is both earlier and later than B. Seeming borrowings in both directions then become possible, and the present argument is not entirely incompatible with that of Garrow (*Gospel of Matthew's Dependence*), who sees a uniform Didache > Matthew directionality.

to support if he had asked for it (see also 1 Cor 12:28–31). The Didache text is thus moving into new territory: territory partly witnessed by Paul.

2.3.1. Translation

The format of the preceding section is retained.

[The Resident Apostle][86]

12.2 If, on the one hand, the one coming is passing through, help him as much as you are able. He will not remain, however, among you except for two or three days, if there should be a need. [12.3] If, on the other hand, he wishes to settle down among you, and if he is a craftsman, let him work and let him eat.[87] [12.4] If, on the other hand, he does not have a craft, according to your own understanding, plan beforehand how he will live among you as a Christian, without being idle. [12.5] If, on the other hand, he does not wish to behave in this way, he is a Christ-peddler. Beware of such ones!

13.1 And every genuine prophet wishing to settle down among you is worthy of his food.

Likewise, a genuine teacher is worthy, just as the laborer, of his food [Matt 10:10][88]

---

86. I do not see this as a section subsequent to the previous instructions for apostles and thus dealing with another topic such as ordinary Christian travelers (note the reference to "every genuine prophet," seeming to pick up the ending of the previous section, and the general conformity to the apostolic instructions in Mark). Given further the witness of Paul, noted below, I feel that this material was added precisely to deal with the new situation of prophets taking root in the communities they visited. I do not assume that there were at any one time only twelve apostles, and regard this as a formalism, though it probably has a real history behind it (see E. Bruce Brooks, "The Secret History of the Twelve" [paper presented at the annual meeting of the Society of Biblical Literature, Atlanta, GA, 21 November 2010]).

87. One senses here the barely self-sufficient community, which must be continually watchful of its collective resources. Compare Paul in 1 Cor 9:4–14 (mid 50s), who ends by claiming the apostles' right to "get their living by the gospel." If the chronology here suggested is correct, Did. 12.2 is more or less contemporary with 1 Cor 9:4–14, that is, in the mid 50s. As other statements in this part of the Didache show, and as Paul implies, these questions of support were delicate.

88. The intruded Matthean quote merely echoes the previous line, which probably uses a common saying. The interpolator here seems to be trying to give his production a gloss of support from the widely known and respected Matthew.

[13.3] So you shall take every first fruits of the produce from the wine vat and threshing floor, of both cattle and sheep, and you will give the first fruits to the prophets, for they themselves are your high priests. [13.4] But if you do not have a prophet, give it to the poor. [13.5] But if you should make bread, take the first fruits, and give according to the commandment. [13.6] Similarly, when you open a jar of wine or oil, take the first fruits, and give it to the prophets. [13.7] And of silver and of clothing and of every possession, take the first fruits, as it seems good to you, and give according to the commandment.

[A Ceremony of Reconciliation]

14.1 And on the Lord's Day of the Lord,[89] when you are gathered together, break bread and give thanks, having before confessed your failings, so that your sacrifice may be pure. [14.2] However, let no one having a conflict with his comrade come together with you, until they have been reconciled,

in order that your sacrifice may not be defiled [Matt 5:23-24][90]

[14.3] For this [sacrifice] is that which was spoken by the Lord: "In every place and time, offer to me a pure sacrifice, because I am a great king," says the Lord, "and my name will be wondrous among the gentiles" [Mal 1:11, 14][91]

[Appointed Local Authorities][92]

15.1 Appoint then, for yourselves, overseers and deacons worthy of the Lord:[93] gentle men, and not money lovers, and truthful and

---

89. This curious locution is convincingly explained by Neville L. A. Tidwell, "Didache 14:1 (KATA KYPIAKKHN ΔE KYPIOY) Revisited," *VC* 53 (1999): 197-207, who relates it to Hebrew superlatives on the order of "Sabbath of Sabbaths," and to a Christian version of the annual Yom Kippur observance, which emphasized reconciliation with others, as does Did. 14.2.

90. The Matthean quote in 14.2b merely underlines what was already complete in 14.1.

91. Notice the recurring echoes of Malachi in the Didache, and recall the frequent echoes of Malachi in Mark.

92. That this topic exists at all is a sign that we (and whoever was in charge of putting together the Didache and keeping it current) have now left the apostolic period and entered the age of independent local churches.

93. Compare Phil 1:1 for the existence of these functionaries and 1 Tim 3:2-10 for

tested, for they likewise conduct among you the ministry of the prophets and teachers. [15.2] Do not then look down upon them, for they themselves are your honored ones, along with the prophets and teachers.

[Internal Discipline]

15.3   And correct one another, not in anger but in peace.
As you have it in the Gospel [Matt 18:15–18][94]
And to everyone wronging another, let no one speak to him, nor let anyone hear from you about him, until he repents.

15.4   And *do your prayers and alms and all your actions as you have it from the gospel of our Lord* [Matt 6:1–4, 5–15][95]

Didache 15 ends with a clear reference to the Gospel of Matthew (for "your prayers and alms and all your actions"), these being specified in Matt 6:5–13 (prayers) and 6:2–4 (alms). Since this has no relation to the immediately preceding text and is probably meant as a concluding command, it should be regarded as another Matthean addition to the text. Its summary directions, referring to Matthew for specifics, probably at one point marked the end of the Didache. Then not even Did. 15 can be said to be a composition of the time of Matthew. It is a pre-Matthean composition to which a concluding Matthean touch was later added. I may add that it is noteworthy that some of the small interpolations proposed above begin with a subordinating introductory word: "for, likewise, however." This is a not unreasonable way of appending a comment to a previously existing statement.

---

most of the qualifications here listed. Didache 15.1 is perhaps less likely to be quoting the deutero-Pauline texts than relying on qualifications generally accepted at the time. It is wrong to imagine that the producers of early Christian texts knew nothing more about Christianity than they, or we, can read in other early Christian texts.

94. Another merely decorative quote from Matthew. The wording in 2 Tim 2:25 is actually closer.

95. This Matthean ending, however, was constitutive: it apparently intended to invoke the authority of Matthew generally or to proclaim the consistency of the Didache with Matthew for all the preceding instructions.

2.4. The Concluding Apocalypse: Did. 16.1–11

This final chapter departs from the rest of the text in prescribing neither ceremonial behavior (6.3–12.1), nor institutional structures (12.1–15.4), nor yet rules of personal conduct (the Two Ways, now 1.1–6.2), but in spelling out in detail a cardinal point of belief: the expectation of the last days.

Joseph Verheyden, rightly in my opinion, has argued for the Matthean character of this final chapter.[96] In Did. 16, as is not the case with the preceding material, the Matthean matter cannot be excised as interpolations, leaving a coherent text behind.

2.4.1. Translation

Since the Matthean passages are integral in this final apocalypse, they will here be identified but not separated from the rest of the text.

16.1 Be watchful over your life, do not let your lamps be quenched, and do not let your waists be ungirded [Matt 25:8?], but be prepared, for you do not know the hour in which our Lord is coming [Matt 24:42].

16.2 And frequently be gathered together, seeking what is appropriate for your souls, for the whole time of your faith will not benefit you unless you are perfected in the End Time. [16.3] For, in the last days, the false prophets and corrupters will be multiplied, and the sheep will be turned into wolves, and the love will be turned into hatred. [Matt 24:10]. [16.4]. For, when lawlessness increases, they will hate each other and they will persecute and they will betray each other [Matt 24:12]. And then will appear the world-deceiver as a son of God, and he will do signs and wonders [Matt 24:24], and the earth will be delivered into his hands, and he will do unlawful things that never have happened from eternity.

---

96. See Joseph Verheyden, "Eschatology in the Didache and the Gospel of Matthew," in *Matthew and the Didache: Two Documents from the Same Jewish-Christian Milieu?* ed. Huub van de Sandt (Assen: Van Gorcum; Minneapolis: Fortress, 2005), 214–15.

16.5 Then the human creation will come into the fiery test, and many will be led into sin and will perish, but the ones remaining firm in their faith will be saved [Matt 24:10, 13] by the curse itself.[97]

16.6 And then the signs of the truth will appear [cf. Matt 24:30]: first, a sign of an opening in heaven, then a sign of a trumpet sound [Matt 24:30; 1 Thess 4:16], and the third, a resurrection of the dead, [16.7] but not all, but as it was said, "The Lord will come and all the holy ones with him" [Zech 14:5; 1 Thess 3:13].

16.8 Then the world will see the Lord coming atop the clouds of heaven [Matt 24:30; 26:64; Dan 7:13],[98] with the angels of his power, in the throne of his kingdom, [16.9] to condemn the devil, the deceiver of the world, and to render to every one according to his deeds. [16.10] Then shall the wicked go away into everlasting punishment, but the righteous shall enter eternal life, [16.11] to inherit those things which eye hath not seen, nor ear heard, nor have entered into the heart of man, such things as God has prepared for them that love him.[99]

2.4.2. The Completion Date of the Didache

Unlike other parts of the text in which Matthean touches are merely supplemental and can be construed as latter decorative additions, Did. 16

---

97. "By the curse itself," in that temptation is the opportunity to demonstrate steadfastness. See again Jas 1:2–4, "Count it all joy, my brethren, when ye fall into manifold temptations. Knowing that the proving of your faith worketh patience. And let patience have its perfect work, that ye may be perfect and entire, lacking in nothing." It may have been in part on some such reasoning that the Christians of the late first century and afterward came to seek martyrdom, not to avoid it.

98. From this point on, the defective end of the Bryennios manuscript is supplied, following Aldridge ("Lost Ending of the *Didache*"), from Apostolic Constitutions and Canons and Boniface. See n. 33 above.

99. It may now be possible to reconsider the decision reached in n. 33 about the possibility of indebtedness of this passage to 1 Cor 2:9. Whatever Paul's source may have been, the possible awareness of 1 Thessalonians in Did. 16.7 strengthens the case for 1 Corinthians as a source in this part of the Didache. A text that knows Matthew is chronologically well situated to know the genuine Pauline Epistles as well. For the deutero-Paulines, see further below. Directionality problems that are difficult in the absence of relative dates may become clarified as information about relative dates accumulates. It is also important to remember that not all of the Didache has the same date of composition.

would appear to have been composed with full knowledge of Matthew. To the time of its composition, we may also reasonably assign the Matthean additions to the earlier material: self-interpolations designed to give the entire text something of the authority of Matthew.[100] The apocalypse itself represents a new venture: it adds a doctrinal section to the Didache, giving it representation in all the categories of teaching that Matthew itself provides, though of course in different proportions. It lets the Didache function like something of a gospel on its own, a complete guide to Christian behavior, administration, and hopes. This would be not unlike the Epistle of Barnabas, which though it assumes the form of an epistle, openly claims to provide everything "bearing on salvation" (17.1). These similarities, these novel intentions of completeness, in a context in which Matthew had begun to assume the preeminent place in Christian thinking that the work of Édouard Massaux has shown it to have occupied, would seem to suggest, for this final formative impulse of the Didache group, a date somewhere between 1 Peter (of which it is aware) and 1 Clement (ca. 96).

3. The Beginning Date of the Didache

The preceding argument has arrived at the following stages in the evolution of the text:

- The original liturgical handbook, Did. 6.3–12.1, circularized to the Alpha churches at large.
- The addition of an ethical or Two Ways section, Did. 1.1–6.1, with a new transition at 6.1–2
- The original handbook was kept current with postapostolic times by adding 12.2–15.3

---

100. For self-interpolation in the earlier parts of a growth text, to keep it compatible with material added later, see E. Bruce Brooks and A. Taeko Brooks, *The Original Analects: Sayings of Confucius and His Successors* (New York: Columbia University Press, 1998) for the Analects of Confucius, and Brooks and Brooks, "The Nature and Historical Context of the Mencius," in *Mencius*, ed. Alan K. L. Chan (Honolulu: University of Hawaii Press, 2002), 242–81, for the Mencius. For the interpretation of Did. 16 and the interpolated Two Ways passage Did. 1.3b–2.1 (the so-called *Sectio Evangelica*) as belonging to the same textual layer, see Clayton N. Jefford, *The Sayings of Jesus in the Teaching of the Twelve Apostles*, VCSup 11 (Leiden: Brill, 1989), 113–14.

- It made itself into a more complete guide to Christian life and expectation by adding an apocalypse, Did. 16, derived from Matthew. At the same time, Matthean passages were added to the earlier parts of the text to enhance its authority in a period when Matthew was rapidly gaining acceptance as *the* authority.

If the end of this process was reached somewhere around the year 90, where did it begin? Our best guess will come from analysis of its formation process, in which the liturgical section 6.3–12.1 turns out to be the earliest.

It was above suggested that Did. 6.2 ("if you are able to bear the whole yoke") had in view the whole of the ethical injunctions in the preceding Two Ways (not the whole of the Jewish Torah),[101] but that it also imitated the adjacent and original passage 6.3 ("bear that which you are able"). We may now notice this sense of permissible retreat from a perhaps unattainable ideal runs through the following sections as well:

- Baptism: "but if you do not have flowing water" (Did. 7.2)
- Fasting before baptism: "and if any others are able to do so" (Did. 7.4)
- Praise after Eucharist: "but allow the prophets to give thanks as much as they want" (Did. 10.7)
- Acceptance of apostles: "but if, on the other hand, the one teaching, if he has been turned" (Did. 11.2)
- Duration of apostolic visit: "But if ever he should remain three [days]" (Did. 11.5)

That is, every major area for which the earliest Didache prescribes has its qualifications, its accounting for exceptions, and its tolerance of special situations. The impression one gets is that the first recipients of this document (which was presumably recirculated in revised versions, over time) knew early versions of these things: Johannine running-water baptism, a

---

101. The few and elemental commandments of Jesus, as Jas 2:10 points out, must all be kept ("For whoever keeps the whole law but fails in one point has become guilty of all"). His examples are adultery and murder. But the much longer Two Ways list contains some lesser offenses, such as arrogance (5.1, #14) and boastfulness (#22), which might be considered tolerable in an otherwise perfect person. It is in this context that the extenuations of Did. 6.2–3 seem to make maximum sense.

simple Eucharist, the routine with itinerant apostles that is symbolized in Mark. But they needed guidance for the exceptional and the unexpected cases, and it seems to be just this sort of guidance that the first form of the Didache was designed to provide.

Which of these areas first experienced growth beyond what might have been primitive practice in the early Jesus movement? On present knowledge, it is difficult to say. But we seem to be informed from two sources (the angry Paul in Galatians, and with equal caution, the revisionist Luke in Acts) that the issue of acceptable food came up for central decision somewhere around the year 44 and that it was decided in somewhat the way that Did. 6.3 says. That part of the Didache might then have been functional, as conveying a new ruling to all the Alpha churches in circa 45. The first extensions of apostolic privilege, however, are not reflected until the letters of Paul, specifically until circa 55, about a decade later. The evolution toward increasing local control, which is seemingly the burden of what I have called the Didache extension, seems to have continued in ways that are also attested in the post-Pauline Pastorals, which must be dated somewhat later than Paul's death in circa 60[102] and perhaps also later than the death of Peter, the last of the major apostles, circa 64.

The final increment of the Didache, as was argued above, was from later in the century, perhaps somewhat before the year 90. If so, then the entire growth process of the Didache, from inception to completion as a complete guide to Christian belief and practice, may have comprised about forty-five years, from circa 45 to circa 90, or from a time roughly contemporary with the completion of Mark to the period of the wide acceptance of Matthew.

Forty-five years is as long a span as one can reasonably attribute to a single person in charge of a text. It is perhaps more likely that the continuity of the Didache was not personal but institutional: that it is the prod-

---

102. Or 62. Another tradition is that Paul perished with Peter in the first year of the Neronian persecution (both 1 Clem. 5 and Eusebius, *Hist. eccl.* 3.1, list Paul after Peter as martyred at Rome under Nero). The present argument is not affected by these alternatives. What might be called the major apostolic period ended ca. 64. It cannot be said that there is a consensus about the date of the Pastorals. I regard the evidence of Gnosticism as indecisive (that tendency can probably be attested earlier than the end of the first century, when a more organized Gnosticism existed). Burton Scott Easton (*The Pastoral Epistles* [New York: Scribner's Sons, 1947], 91–92) suggests a date shortly after the death of Paul.

uct of some sort of central authority whose business it was to coordinate apostolic activity and to give approved and standard advice to the local churches founded and at intervals refreshed by apostolic travels. If so, the addition of the Did. 16 apocalypse may well have been the work of a second text proprietor, in succession to the first.[103]

The first location of such an authority will probably have been in Galilee, where Mark shows the Jesus movement as centered.[104] At least some major figures and functions seem to have moved to Jerusalem early in the movement's history.[105] Both Galilee and Jerusalem, though in different ways, were sacred to Jesus history, and from either, the Didache would have been well positioned to have a widespread influence. Egypt and Syria have been proposed for its place of composition, but the Didache was probably not written for one church, but in principle for all churches. Given its continued prominence as the ancestor of more than one later church order document, it must from the beginning have carried considerable authority. As between Capernaum and Jerusalem, the Alpha character of Didache theology suggests the former (Jerusalem, as the *site* of Jesus's death, is more likely to have accepted the Beta soteriology *based* on Jesus's death). The Galilee alternative may also better account for the continuation of the Didache, and thus of whatever agency produced it, after the year 70.[106]

4. Final Considerations

The original Didache was a liturgical reference, meant for the guidance of those in charge of textually fixed observances. In what might have been a second phase, it was extended by adding personal guidance material (the Two Ways) and guidance for new developments: salaried teachers and elected leaders (the extension), the latter reflecting the waning of itinerant or apostolic authority and the beginning of local authority. A similar tran-

---

103. Compare n. 74 above.

104. The shift to Jerusalem is increasingly emphasized in the later Gospels (Brooks, "Gospel Trajectories," 172), which only underlines the importance of the earliest testimony, which is that of Mark among the Gospels.

105. See Brooks, "Secret History of the Twelve."

106. The prominence of Sepphoris in Galilee, the former capital of Herod Antipas, as a center of later Jewish learning may also be relevant. Sepphoris had remained pro-Roman during the First Jewish War.

sition occurs between the Paul of the genuine Epistles and the churches of the post-Pauline Pastoral Epistles. In what might have been a third phase, the text was further supplemented by interpolated material from Matthew, which our text calls "the gospel," and a Matthean-based apocalypse was added at the end, perhaps to let the Didache function as something like a complete gospel, in competition with the other authority texts of the time.

Interest naturally attaches to the earliest form of any growth text, but I wish to conclude by urging that *all* of a growth text is interesting. The whole extent of the text directly shows the passage of time and reflects events occurring during that period of time. It is an invaluable witness to the happening of history. In the case of the Didache, I believe we see a text with its roots firmly in the soil of Alpha Christianity during the age of the itinerant apostle, slowly expanding to annex the function of moral instruction (the Two Ways), then gradually accommodating changes that occurred within the apostolic period, as well as those that immediately followed it, and finally accepting the prominence of Matthew and of the second-tier Gospels generally, and attempting to remain valid in an age when those Gospels had transformed the context and practice of Christian edification.

The heritage of the Didache was not lost. Though it did not develop further, it did bequeath something of its substance to later church order texts.[107] In that final process the Didache itself was transformed, both doctrinally and liturgically, according to the needs and tendencies of those later ages.

---

107. For an overview, see Niederwimmer, *Didache*, 13–18.

The Sectio Evangelica (Didache 1.3b–2.1) and Performance*

Perttu Nikander

The relationship between the Didache and the synoptic tradition has been a subject of a long-lasting scholarly discussion. The question is still open, as implied by the recent interest in the subject. One of the most pertinent problems in this discussion is related to the relationship of the passage usually referred as the Sectio Evangelica (Did. 1.3b–2.1) and its synoptic parallels, Matt 5:44–47 and Luke 6:27–33. The Sectio Evangelica is generally regarded as a later interpolation in the Didache, because it is lacking from other early witnesses of the Two Ways teaching such as the Epistle of Barnabas and the Latin Doctrina apostolorum.

In this essay I will study the Sectio Evangelica within the framework of oral performance. I will first critique the idea of its literary dependence on other written sources, especially Matthew and Luke. Instead, it will be argued that the Sectio Evangelica owes its origin to oral performances of the Two Ways tradition and the constant interplay of oral and written modes of communication. As a heuristic model, I will refer to the elements of Greek prose composition, such as period and colon, and apply these insights to the study of the Sectio Evangelica. Finally, I will present a sound map of this tradition that supports the idea of the oral provenance of this passage.

---

*This article is based on a paper read in the Didache in Context session at the SBL 2011 Annual Meeting. I want to thank my respondent Jonathan Schwiebert for his constructive criticism. I am also indebted to Jonathan Draper, who read the first drafts of my paper and offered his valuable criticism.

288 THE DIDACHE: A MISSING PIECE OF THE PUZZLE

1. The Sectio Evangelica and the Question of Literary Dependence

The previous discussion on the question regarding the dependence of the Didache on the Synoptics can be roughly plotted on a continuum between two poles. While some scholars argue that the Sectio Evangelica is dependent on the written Gospels of Matthew and Luke,[1] other scholars reject this and suggest alternative options such as dependence on the Q source[2] or some other tradition, either written or oral,[3] and even the priority of the Didache over the Synoptic Gospels.[4] Such widely divergent positions in scholarship indicate that the discussion on the relationship between the Sectio Evangelica and the synoptic tradition is still wholly open.

The discussion of the relationship between the Sectio Evangelica and the synoptic tradition usually follows the methodological principle formu-

---

1. Édouard Massaux, *The Influence of the Gospel of Saint Matthew on the Christian Literature before Saint Irenaeus* (Macon, GA: Mercer University Press, 1993); Bentley Layton, "The Sources, Date, and Transmission of *Didache* 1.3b–2.1," *HTR* 61 (1968): 343–83; Christopher M. Tuckett, "Synoptic Tradition in the Didache," in *The Didache in Modern Research*, ed. Jonathan A. Draper (Leiden: Brill, 1996), 92–128; John S. Kloppenborg, "The Use of the Synoptics or Q in *Did*.1:3b–2:1," in *Matthew and Didache*, ed. Huub van de Sandt (Assen: Van Gorcum; Minneapolis: Fortress, 2005), 105–29. Also, the proponents of the so-called "fiction hypothesis" have posited this view; see J. Armitage Robinson, *Barnabas, Hermas and the Didache* (London: SPCK), 1920; R. H. Connolly, "The Didache in Relation to the Epistle of Barnabas," *JTS* 33 (1932): 237–53.

2. Roger Glover, "The Didache's Quotations and the Synoptic Gospels," *NTS* 5 (1958): 12–29; Clayton N. Jefford, *The Sayings of Jesus in the Teaching of the Twelve Apostles*, VCSup 11 (Leiden: Brill, 1989).

3. Helmut Köster, *Synoptische Überlieferung bei den apostolischen Vätern*, TUGAL 65/5.10 (Berlin: Akademie, 1957); Jean-Paul Audet, *La Didachè: Instructions des Apôtres*, Ebib (Paris: Gabalda, 1958); Willy Rordorf, "Does the Didache Contain Jesus Tradition Independently of the Synoptic Gospels?" in *Jesus and the Oral Synoptic Tradition*, ed. Henry Wansbrough (Sheffield: Sheffield Academic, 1991), 394–423; Jonathan A. Draper, "The Jesus Tradition in the Didache," in Draper, *Didache in Modern*, 72–91; Kurt Niederwimmer, *The Didache: A Commentary*, trans. Linda M. Maloney, Hermeneia (Minneapolis: Fortress, 1998); Huub van de Sandt and David Flusser, *The Didache: Its Jewish Sources and Its Place in Early Judaism and Christianity*, CRINT 3.5 (Assen: Van Gorcum; Minneapolis: Fortress, 2002).

4. Alan J. P. Garrow, *The Gospel of Matthew's Dependence on the Didache*, JSNTSup 254 (London: T&T Clark, 2004).

lated by Helmut Koester in 1957.[5] He argued that, if material that is redactional in some text appears in another text, then the former text precedes the latter text. It must be noted that the Sectio Evangelica shows no traces of Markan material and contains only parallels to the double tradition of Matthew and Luke. Most scholars who have dealt with this problem advocate the Two Document hypothesis. Thus the nucleus of the problem lies in the reconstruction of Q and respectively in the redactional activity of Matthew and Luke.[6] The Q text of the synoptic parallels of the Sectio Evangelica (Matt 5:44–47; Luke 6:27–33) is notoriously difficult to reconstruct, and, although the International Q Project took the task in the 1980s and 1990s, the work that finally resulted as the Critical Edition of Q in 2000 has not really advanced the discussion.[7] At this point, there is no agreement regarding the original text of Q or the extent of the redaction on the part of Matthew and Luke. In fact, the exact reconstruction of Q may be itself an anachronistic task that stems from the influence of the modern print culture, assuming that there must have been a fixed text form of Q. Even if Q existed as a written document, it is possible that there were various versions of this document. It is thus possible (or even likely) that Matthew and Luke may not necessarily have used similar versions of Q.[8] If one gives up on the reconstruction of the original wording of Q, the principle posited by Koester is not apt anymore, since the redaction by either Matthew or Luke is no longer detectable. On the other hand, the lack of certainty over the reconstruction of Q naturally weakens the possibilities for any further discussion on the literary dependence of the Didache on Q.

---

5. A prime example of such methodology is provided by Tuckett, "Synoptic Tradition in the Didache."

6. Garrow is a rare exception, because he omits Q from the discussion and argues that Matthew used Luke.

7. James M. Robinson, Paul Hoffmann, and John S. Kloppenborg, eds., *The Critical Edition of Q: Synopsis including the Gospels of Matthew and Luke, Mark and Thomas with English, German and French Translations of Q and Thomas*, Hermeneia (Minneapolis: Fortress; Leuven: Peeters, 2000).

8. See Draper, "Jesus Tradition in the *Didache*," 75; Rordorf, "Does the Didache Contain Jesus Tradition," 422. See also Richard A. Horsley and Jonathan A. Draper, *Whoever Hears You Hears Me: Prophets, Performance, and Tradition in Q* (Harrisburg, PA: Trinity Press International, 1999). Recently, the plurality of early Christian manuscript traditions has been argued convincingly by David C. Parker, who disputes the conception of "original text form." See Parker, *Living Text of Gospels* (Cambridge: Cambridge University Press, 1997).

The criticism above relates to the problem of the definition of "literary dependence" in the first place. In its strictest form the term refers to a literary operation in which a production of a text is based on direct visual copying of a source document. If it is assumed that the editor of the Sectio Evangelica copied a source visually, we are facing the problem regarding the identification or reconstruction of the source. Moreover, to assume *multiple* written sources behind the Sectio Evangelica is equally problematic.[9] On the basis of what we know about ancient book production, such a hypothesis of multiple sources would be implausible. As it has been noted in many studies, ancient text production differed from that of the modern world. In antiquity the actual conditions set certain limitations on the writing process. For example, in the absence of writing desks, it would have been extremely difficult for an author to switch between different source documents such as Matthew and Luke, not to mention the other parallel documents. An image of an ancient author having multiple source books open on the desk simultaneously does not correspond to historical reality.[10] In addition, the "book" formats were difficult to use, especially in the case of scrolls, and the lack of indexing and the common practice of *scriptio continua* made it equally difficult to make random access to certain passages in a source text.[11] Moreover, for such a short passage as the Sectio Evangelica, it is unlikely that the editor would ever consult multiple written sources, picking one saying from here and another from there.

---

9. In addition to the synoptic parallels, the Sectio Evangelica contains parallels to the Shepherd of Hermas (Herm. Mand. 2.4–6) in Did. 1.5. The following passage (Did. 1.6) is rather enigmatic and has invoked questions because of its quotation formula ἀλλὰ καὶ περὶ τούτου δὲ εἴρηται. The most usual suggestion for the parallel is Sir 12:1. Despite these parallels, it seems unlikely that the editor would have used them as literary sources.

10. See the classic study by Bruce M. Metzger, "When Did Scribes Begin to Use Writing Desks?" in *Historical and Literary Studies, Pagan, Jewish, and Christian* (Leiden: Brill, 1968), 123–37. More recently, the absence of writing desks in Greco-Roman antiquity and its consequences for early Christian text production has been discussed by Pieter J. J. Botha, "'I am writing this with my own hand….': Writing in New Testament Times," *VE* 30 (2009): 115–25 (155). See also Botha, *Orality and Literacy in Early Christianity*, BPC 5 (Eugene, OR: Cascade, 2012), 62–88.

11. The question about the codex and random access is discussed by Margaret Ellen Lee and Bernard Brandon Scott, *Sound Mapping the New Testament* (Salem, OR: Polebridge, 2009), 35. See also Robert A. Derrenbacker, *Ancient Compositional Practices and the Synoptic Problem*, BETL 186 (Leuven: Leuven University Press; Peeters, 2005), 32.

Instead, as some recent studies argue, the ancient authors usually used written sources only one at the time.[12] If the author wanted to add some other material to the text, it must have been recalled from the resources of memory. One could, of course, argue that the editor harmonized multiple sources or used an already harmonized source. This would not solve the original problem, however, because even such a harmonization would not have been merely a literary operation, and the process would have involved oral dynamics.

In recent discussion there has been growing interest to elaborate further the concept of "literary dependence" in the direction of oral transmission of tradition. Christopher Tuckett, one of the proponents of the Didache's literary dependence on the Synoptics, has argued on the basis of Koester's principle that the Didache "presupposes" the written texts of Matthew and Luke.[13] This argument was originally rather enigmatic in terms of media culture, and fortunately he has recently cleared up his position by arguing that, while the Didache presupposes these documents, the author did not necessarily use them directly by copying or having them "set out before him or her on a table."[14] In somewhat similar manner, John Kloppenborg has argued that the compiler of the Sectio Evangelica knew

---

12. C. B. R. Pelling, "Plutarch's Method of Work in the Roman Lives," *JHS* 99 (1979): 74–96 (esp. 92). According to Pelling, the ancient authors usually gathered and read their source material before starting the actual writing process. We can easily imagine that the editor of the Sectio Evangelica could have been familiar with the parallel texts (the Synoptic Gospels, Shepherd of Hermas) in one way or another. The writing process, however, did not require visual contact with the text that was being copied. As István Czachesz has recently noted, both the production and the use of text were seldom "solitary activities." See István Czachesz, "Rewriting and Textual Fluidity in Antiquity: Exploring the Socio-Cultural and Psychological Context of Earliest Christian Literacy," in *Myths, Martyrs, and Modernity: Studies in the History of Religions in Honour of Jan N. Bremmer*, ed. by J. H. F. Dijkstra, J. E. A. Kroesen, and Y. B. Kuiper (Leiden: Brill, 2010), 425–41 (esp. 430). This, of course, presupposes that the early Christian authors followed the same conventions of text production as other contemporary Greco-Roman authors. Unfortunately, we know very little about the actual working habits of early Christian authors.

13. Tuckett, "Synoptic Tradition in the Didache," 128. Tuckett presents initial possibilities that the author of the Didache had access to the texts of both gospels or a single harmonized text. On this basis, it would be easy to conclude that Tuckett is presupposing traditional views of literary dependence for both options.

14. Christopher M. Tuckett, "The Didache and the Synoptics Once More: A Response to Aaron Milavec," *JECS* 13 (2005): 509–18.

the text of Luke and either Q or Matthew. He also distances himself from the convictions of the previous study by suggesting the possibility that "the harmonization of Luke with Q (or with Matthew) was not a literary operation." Rather, he sees it possible that it "occurred in oral performance."[15] Finally, Dale Allison, while arguing for Matthean influence on the Sectio Evangelica, suggests that this section "incorporates an oral composition" that is influenced by Matthew while not being fully dependent on it.[16] Unfortunately, despite this fresh perspective on the issue, these scholars stop their analyses at the point where the most interesting questions invoked by their studies begin to emerge. Once strict literary dependence as a result of (at least) exclusive literary activities is rejected, the natural step would be to explore the question of how oral communication influenced the compositional process of the Sectio Evangelica.

2. Orality and Performance

As argued above, instead of a source critical investigation, one should try to find other ways to define the history and the origin of the Sectio Evangelica. While it is likely that it is a later interpolation in the Didache, it is not necessarily a literary creation that combines material from multiple written sources. Rather, I would argue that it was shaped (most likely) through multiple oral performances of this tradition. In the following discussion, I will present some ideas regarding orality and performance that are relevant to the current problem.

As it has been argued on many occasions, orality and writing were constantly intertwined in the ancient world.[17] The production and use of texts were influenced by oral aspects. Technically speaking, the composition of texts was hardly ever a silent and solitary practice. An oral aspect was present, for example, through the usual custom of dictation. Traditions were seldom drawn directly from the source books. Instead, the background of tradition usually lay in the oral register, from which they

---

15. Kloppenborg, "Use of the Synoptics or Q," 129.

16. Dale C. Allison, *Constructing Jesus: Memory, Imagination, and History* (London: SPCK, 2010), 333.

17. See, e.g., Ruth Finnegan, *Literacy and Orality: Studies in the Technology of Communication* (Oxford: Blackwell), 1988; Risto Uro, "Thomas and Oral Gospel Tradition," in *Thomas at the Crossroads: Essays on the Gospel of Thomas* (Edinburgh: T&T Clark, 1998), 8–32 (esp. 15–19).

were transformed into the written register with help of memory. This was not, however, merely transcribing or "recording" the tradition but rather a progressive process that included multiple rewritings of the text that were done on the basis of multiple oral performances to the "test audience."

It is commonly accepted that texts were mostly written to be read aloud in antiquity.[18] While this is true, it is also partly a limiting definition. More than just reading aloud, the use of the texts could be better termed as performing.[19] In fact, "reading aloud" may evoke modern associations regarding reading, as if the content of the text is just being transformed into orality in the reading process. Rather, in antiquity the performer would not read directly from the paper at the event of the performance. This is due to the book formats themselves, such as scrolls and their layout, which required performers to familiarize themselves with the texts in advance. Further, performing may have included some paralinguistic features such as pauses, mimics, and gestures that had to be practiced before the event of performance. Thus, it is evident that performing involved the use of memory.

The role of memory has been discussed in the studies of early Christianity on many occasions. In recent discussion, the classic views of Fredric Bartlett have been reaffirmed.[20] It appears that memory is not just a storage of "frozen" traditions but rather a matter of constantly self-interpreting and constructive processes. In addition to individual memory control and interpretation, traditions can be interpreted socially or even culturally.[21] Thus, for example, a community can exercise control over certain traditions through feedback in performances. The concept of constructive memory supports the idea of the relativity of the "original form" or "origi-

---

18. See the often-referred article by Paul J. Achtemeier, "*Omne verbum sonat*: The New Testament and the Oral Environment of the Late Western Antiquity," *JBL* 109 (1990): 3–27. For more references, see William Johnson, "Toward a Sociology of Reading in Classical Antiquity," *AJP* 121 (2000): 593–627.

19. For example, see Whitney Shiner, *Proclaiming the Gospel: First-Century Performance of Mark* (Harrisburg, PA: Trinity Press International, 2003), esp. 1–35.

20. E.g., John Dominic Crossan, *The Birth of Christianity: Discovering What Happened in the Years Immediately after the Execution of Jesus* (San Francisco: HarperSanFrancisco, 1998); John S. Kloppenborg, "Memory, Performance, and the Sayings of Jesus" (paper presented at the Helsinki Seminar on Memory, Helsinki, Finland, 11 May 2011), esp. 2–3.

21. See the summarizing article on memory by Dennis C. Duling, "Memory, Collective Memory, Orality and the Gospels," *HTS* 67 (2011): 1–11.

nal wording" of a tradition. As argued in many studies on orality, each performance is an original by itself.[22] Thus, if we discuss the performance of the Sectio Evangelica or the Two Ways, there is no reason to suppose that each performance would always contain exactly same wording as previous or subsequent performances.

John Miles Foley has coined the term "word-power" to characterize performance of oral-derived texts.[23] Foley's approach is heavily influenced by the receptionist theories of the literary critic Wolfgang Iser.[24] While Iser studied literary texts, however, Foley applies these insights to performances of oral-derived texts.[25] The starting point in this approach is to underline the importance of the participation of the recipient in the communication event instead of merely concentrating on the speaker and the message. Performance of oral-derived texts implies that an audience performs certain interpretative tasks, especially filling in the "gaps of indeterminacy" in performance. These gaps are active and important meanings that lie outside the received version or text, and the task for the audience is to use its prior knowledge (tradition) to bridge the gaps. Tradition is thus an *enabling referent* in the performance of oral-derived texts, whereas the performance itself is an *enabling event*. Foley's word-power is divided into three aspects: performance arena, register, and communicative economy.

The performance arena is "the locus in which some specialized form of communication is uniquely licensed to take place."[26] In order to achieve a successful oral performance, both the performer and the audience must enter the same performance arena, because each arena is loaded with its own ways of speaking and ways of meaning. Those who are outside a certain performance arena are unable to decode the meanings that are

---

22. Albert B. Lord, *The Singer of Tales*, HSCL 24 (Cambridge: Harvard University Press, 1960), 101; Werner H. Kelber, *The Oral and Written Gospel: The Hermeneutics of Speaking and Writing in the Synoptic Tradition, Mark, Paul and Q* (Philadelphia: Fortress, 1983), 30. The written text was not a matter of frozen tradition in the preprint cultures either. It was only the invention of the printing press that generally allowed the production of multiple identical copies.

23. John Miles Foley, *Singer of Tales in Performance* (Bloomington: Indiana University Press, 1995), xiv.

24. Wolfgang Iser, *The Act of Reading* (Baltimore: The Johns Hopkins University Press, 1978).

25. John Miles Foley, *Immanent Art: From Structure to Meaning in Traditional Epic* (Bloomington: Indiana University Press, 1991), 6–8.

26. Foley, *Singer of Tales in Performance*, 47.

encoded and implied in the oral performance. Thus one will be unable to fill in the gaps of indeterminacy.

The language that is used in certain performance arenas can be termed as registers.[27] In his model, Foley applies Michael Halliday's sociolinguistic theory of *discourse register*, which consists of three factors: *field*, *tenor*, and *mode*.[28] In the study of early Christian performances, Jonathan Draper has recently applied Halliday's theory in the context of the Two Ways and the sermon of the Gospel of Luke.[29] First, *field* defines the area of operation of the language activity, in other words, what discourse is taking place and where.[30] The fields of the Sectio Evangelica and the Two Ways fall within the context of baptismal catechesis. Secondly, *tenor* covers the relationships between those who take part in the discourse. According to Draper, in the context of the Didache the tenor is the "quasi-parental relationship of the teacher to the prospective new members."[31] In addition, *tenor* could also cover a metonymic link to the teachings of Jesus, especially in the case of the Sectio Evangelica. The teacher would thus speak with the authority of the Lord Jesus. The wider context of the Two Ways has a clear metonymic reference to the Decalogue, the nucleus of the Israelite traditions. Thirdly, *mode* covers the method of communication. In oral mode this could contain techniques that are used to help communication, especially memorizing and reception of tradition. This will be covered in more detail below.

An important part of the performance of oral-derived texts is communicative economy, especially in the form of traditional referentiality. According to Foley, traditional referentiality entails the invoking of a context with wider meanings than the text itself invokes. Thus, traditional

---

27. Ibid., 50.

28. Michael Alexander Kirkwood Halliday, *Language as Social Semiotic* (Baltimore: University Park Press, 1978), 33.

29. Jonathan A. Draper, "Jesus' 'Covenantal Discourse' on the Plain (Luke 6:12–7:17) as Oral Performance: Pointers to 'Q' as Multiple Oral Performance," in *Oral Performance, Popular Tradition, and Hidden Transcript in Q*, ed. Richard A. Horsley, SemeiaSt 60 (Atlanta: Society of Biblical Literature, 2006), 71–98; "Vice Catalogues as Oral-Mnemonic Cues: A Comparative Study of the Two-Ways Tradition in the Didache and Parallels from the Perspective of Oral Tradition," in *Jesus, the Voice, and the Text: Beyond the Oral and the Written Gospel*, ed. Tom Thatcher (Waco, TX: Baylor University Press, 2008), 111–13.

30. See Foley, *Singer of Tales in Performance*, 50.

31. Draper, "Vice Catalogues as Oral-Mnemonic Cues," 116.

referentiality is a sort of *pars pro toto*, "a mode of signification wherein the part stands for the whole." Tradition is an enabling referent that allows the audience to understand the performance in a way that the performer intended it to be understood. This can be also applied in the context of the Didache and especially the Two Ways. Whatever the original text of the Two Ways may have been, it seems plausible that both the content and the form of this teaching opened (through its performance and reception) wider meanings than just the teaching of a community. For example, the prohibitions in the way of life undoubtedly invoke the Decalogue and its significance for the Jewish people, in fact, the whole spectrum of Israelite traditions that are preserved in the collective memory of the community.

The inclusion of the Sectio Evangelica in the Two Ways could have been due to traditional referentiality. In a literary critical investigation, the Sectio Evangelica seems a rather awkward passage because it seems to interrupt the flow between Did. 1.3a and 2.2. As it has been argued in previous studies, the editor's attempt to "hide" the interpolation by adding Did. 2.1 is not particularly skillful, at least in the eyes of a modern scholar.[32] Nevertheless, it is safe to assert that the editor knew what he or she was doing when adding the Sectio Evangelica into the Two Ways teaching. These materials did not end up in the Didache by accident. It is certain that the editor knew that most of these traditions were already attributed to Jesus, although there is no sign of reference to him on the textual level of the Didache.[33] Regarding its placement, the Sectio Evangelica would fit better topically in the context of the *anawim* sayings in Did. 3.8–10 and the rules for life and society in Did. 4 and not before the first vice list in Did. 2. I would suggest, however, that its current location could be explained by the occurrence of the negative form of the golden rule in Did. 1.2b, which perhaps worked as a metonymic marker that invoked the Jesus tradition found also in Matthew and Luke. It is possible that the editor knew that these traditions were circulated together elsewhere as well, as in the Gospel of Luke or perhaps even in the Q sermon.[34] The Lukan parallels occur in Luke 6:27–30 and 32, which sandwiches the positive form of the golden rule in Luke 6:31. It must be noted, however, that metonymic

---

32. Niederwimmer, *Didache*, 86–87.

33. See the Didache's references to the Gospel in Did. 8.2, 11.3, and 15.3–4, or the words of Lord in 9.5 and 14.3. The other quotation formulas are found in 1.6 and 16.7.

34. In Matthew, the golden rule works as a conclusion for the Sermon on the Mount in Matt 7:12.

referentiality is not a matter of literary dependence. Thus, if we argue that the golden rule invoked the other Jesus tradition, it does not mean that the Sectio Evangelica would betray literary dependence on the Gospel of Luke.

Whereas the Sectio Evangelica can be regarded literary critically as an interpolation, it also has a connection to the multiple performances of the Two Ways tradition. Following Chris Keith's recent theory on the Pericopae Adultarae in the Gospel of John (7:53–8:11),[35] I would argue that the interpolation of the Sectio Evangelica betrays two levels of performances of tradition. First, the editor most probably belonged to the Didache community and was thus a part of the audience during performances of the Two Ways tradition that lacked the Sectio Evangelica. As I argued above, the Sectio Evangelica became part of this tradition through traditional referentiality, and, further, the interpolation could be characterized as an *interpretation* of the existing Two Ways tradition. Similarly in the case of the Pericopae Adultarae, Keith notes the similar dynamics of oral performance that contain interaction between the audience and the performer. The interpolation is thus the audience's response to the original tradition.[36] In the context of the Didache, the editor practiced creative control over the tradition by adding the interpolation and continued performing the version of the Two Ways that now contained the Sectio Evangelica. As a performer, however, the editor had to take the audience into account, because it was not practical to include material with which the audience would have been unfamiliar. Thus the traditional referents in the interpolated material are important, and most probably have invoked familiar ideas among the audience just as the original content of the Two Ways teaching did.

Since it is likely that few people in the Didache community had access to the actual written text of the Two Ways while the rest had to rely solely on oral performance and aural reception, the interpolation must be studied in this light as well. As seen above, the concept of original wording was a relative matter in oral performance. Actually, even the search for the original wording in the manuscript tradition may be a fantasy of a print

---

35. See Chris Keith, "A Performance of the Text: The Adulteress's Entrance into John's Gospel," in *The Fourth Gospel in First-Century Media Culture*, ed. Anthony Le Donne and Tom Thatcher, LNTS 426 (London: T&T Clark International, 2011), 49–69.

36. Ibid., 62.

culture in itself.[37] Since each and every performance was an original production in its own right, it is safe to assume that the people in the Didache community did not regard the Sectio Evangelica as a later gloss of obscure origin but rather a part of "living tradition" in the community.

3. Tracking the Oral Mode of the Sectio Evangelica

3.1. Sound Mapping

Besides these theoretical approaches to the current problem, I wish to study the oral mode of the Sectio Evangelica, which will make use of more concrete analyses of the text. As we saw in Foley's theory, the oral mode covers the methods that facilitate oral performance. While the Didache exists only in a written register, the oral mode of an oral-derived text such as the Sectio Evangelica can be studied with an analysis that pays attention to the performative features in the text. As it has been noted above, composition and performance were closely tied together in antiquity, and texts were usually composed in order to be performed and to be heard. Performing did not mean merely reading the text aloud, but rather, in many cases, texts worked as aids for memory, thus giving guidelines for creativity on the part of the performer. Even in some cases, texts were composed *in* performance.[38]

In their pioneering work *Sound Mapping the New Testament*, Margaret Ellen Lee and Bernard Brandon Scott study the aural quality of early Christian texts by using a method that they call "sound mapping." This method is based on the sound analysis of a text, the mapping out of certain phonemes and syllables, vowels and consonants in the text. With this approach, as Lee and Scott argue, one is able pay attention to the "sound" of early Christian performances. Since oral performance is a highly situational and time bound event, it requires different type of dynamics than modern silent reading. In oral mode, the special repetition of certain sounds are of great importance, because they help a person to memorize

---

37. This multiformity may be seen even in the sparse manuscript tradition on the Didache. P.Oxy 1782 is a fragment that contains Did. 1.3c, 1.4a, and 2.7b. Interestingly, this fragment contains a slightly longer reading for the Sectio Evangelica in comparison to the Jerusalem manuscript.

38. For example, see the recent study by Antoinette Clark Wire, *The Case for Mark Composed in Performance*, BPC 3 (Eugene, OR: Cascade, 2011).

traditions and create a structure that can be more easily understood by members of the audience, who do not necessarily have a visual contact with the text and are not able to scan it thoroughly, unlike modern readers.[39] It must be noted, however, that sound mapping covers only one dimension of oral mode. Obviously there are limits in this approach, because oral registers can never be captured totally in a graphic chart. Charts do not take into account paralinguistic features of a performance, such as volume level, pitch and tone of voice, mimics, and other gestures. While sound mapping does not cover the whole performance event, it may nevertheless take us *closer* in our understanding to early Christian performances.

3.2. Oral Units within the Composition

Lee and Scott approach texts from within the framework of Greco-Roman prose composition, introducing ideas from classical authors and literary critics. For their analyses, the most crucial ideas are the concepts of the period and colon that they apply to the gospel texts. Here we may briefly refer to classical definitions of period and colon and to their relationship to the different types of prose composition.

In Greek prose composition, the period is the largest unit of expression within a composition. While classical authors offer varying definitions for it, they all share the common idea that a period is a sentence that conveys a complete thought (e.g., Aristotle, *Rhet.* 3.9.5; Demetrius, *Eloc.* 10–11; Dionysius of Halicarnassus, *Comp.* 2; Quintilian, *Inst.* 9.4.125; *Rhet. Her.* 4.27). The name περίοδος carries with it a meaning of a circular path, which reflects its inner logic: the ideas that are presented in the beginning are completed at the end, either by syntactical or grammatical suspension or rhetorical figures such as antithesis.[40] A classic analogy for the period is provided by Demetrius, who compares a speaker (*sic*) to runners in a stadium: after running around the circle, runners arrive at the same position that they started from (*Eloc.* 11). The main component of a period is the colon (κῶλον), which is prose's equivalent to the measure

---

39. Lee and Scott, *Sound Mapping the New Testament,* 135, 141–57.
40. R. Dean Anderson Jr., *Glossary of Greek Rhetorical Terms Connected to Methods of Argumentation, Figures and Tropes from Anaximenes to Quintilian,* CBET 24 (Leuven: Peeters, 2001), 94; Galen O. Rowe, "Style," in *Handbook of Classical Rhetoric in the Hellenistic Period: 330 BC–AD 400,* ed. Stanley E. Porter (Leiden: Brill, 1997), 121–57 (esp. 152).

in poetry. Demetrius discusses the relationship between the period and colon by using the analogy of a hand: the period is a hand, while the colon is a finger (*Eloc.* 2). Thus the latter is subordinated to the former. Classical authors disagree regarding the maximum number of cola in a period. While Aristotle speaks of a maximum of two cola (*Rhet.* 3.9), Demetrius doubles it to up to four (*Eloc.* 16). He argues that anything beyond four cola would destroy the symmetry of the period. Although Cicero uses the Latin term *membrum* in reference to the colon, he states that the period may consists of up to four hexameters (*De or.* 3.181).[41] As Galen Rowe has noted, however, these limits seem to have been sometimes exceeded.[42] For example, Quintilian argues that "the average number [of cola] would appear to be four, but it *often contains even more*" (*Inst.* 9.4.125). The periods were used in a certain type of compositional style that is called by different names by classical authors. For example, for Aristotle there are two types of styles: εἰρομένη λέξις ("strung on") and κατεστραμμένη λέξις ("turned down") (*Rhet.* 3.9). The former style is continuous and uses parataxis with little subordination. According to Aristotle, the continuous style, or running style, can go on until everything has been said on the topic. He finds this type of style unpleasant because of its endlessness. The periodic style again contains periods that make it much easier to follow, because each period should convey a complete thought. Hence the periodic style has a beginning and end, whereas in the running style the end was not in sight. Other classical authors have basically adopted Aristotle's distinction between these two styles, although some have modified his theories to some degree (e.g., Demetrius, *Eloc.* 12; Quintilian, *Inst.* 9.4.19–22).

Because of the plurality of different definitions of a period in antiquity, modern scholars have summarized the period in rather general terms as well. For example, we can cite George Kennedy, who states that a period "refers usually to a complex sentence in which grammatical completion is postponed to the end or almost to the end."[43] According to him, periods are rare in early Christian prose such as the canonical Gospels. Given

---

41. Quintilian (*Inst.* 9.4.125) argues that Cicero limits the length of the period to "four iambic trimeters, or the space between the times of taking breath."

42. Rowe, "Style," 152. Rowe posits two examples, the opening statement of Cicero's *For Archias* and Demosthenes's *On the Crown*.

43. George Kennedy, *New Testament Interpretation through Rhetorical Criticism* (Chapel Hill: University of North Carolina Press, 1983), 30.

this definition, it could be asked whether one can find real periods from the gospel tradition as Lee and Scott do, because instead of containing complex sentences and subordinated clauses, they consist of paratactic cola, structures of grammatical parallelism. On the other hand, Lee and Scott offer a broader definition for periods. According to them, periods can consist of several cola combined *either* paratactically *or* by means of grammatical subordination.[44] Their broad definition of period and especially its application in their method, however, do not match with the classical (although varying) ideas of period. Further, it could be debated whether an early Christian author such as the editor of the Sectio Evangelica would have been familiar with the periodic style, since it is found mostly in sophisticated texts by classical Greco-Roman authors. The problem is related to larger questions about the educational level of the early Christian authors in general. Nevertheless, it is hardly likely that one could have achieved full Greek literacy without any connection to the common educational processes that included certain exercises and compositional training that provided familiarity with the periodic style.[45] In this sense we should not be surprised to find echoes of these elements in early Christian texts. Against this background, it seems that a number of the examples in the study by Lee and Scott are not technically periods but should be termed in some other way.[46] The periodic structure (a sign of an elegant style) could be regarded as some type of ideal topos for early Christian writers who themselves applied more basic approaches in their composition processes. In order to avoid further confusion, it may be better to refer to these "periods," as presented by Lee and Scott, by the alternative designation "units."

Despite some problems with their theory, Lee and Scott have demonstrated that the idea of the periodic structure serves the study of the early Christian texts. The central idea of the periodic structure in this discussion lies in its relation to the performance event: oral delivery and aural

---

44. Lee and Scott, *Sound Mapping the New Testament*, 171.

45. See F. Gerald Downing, "Compositional Conventions and the Synoptic Problem," *JBL* 107 (1988): 69–85 (71).

46. For example, see Matt 6:9–10, 6:11–13, and 6:14–15. See Lee and Scott, *Sound Mapping the New Testament*, 181–82. The category of period was not entirely clear in antiquity either. Interestingly, Augustine regards *Ep.* 5.5 as a period, although it is not really one. I owe this reference to R. Dean Anderson Jr., *Ancient Rhetorical Theory and Paul*, CBET 18 (Leuven: Peeters, 1996), 18 n. 1.

reception. For example, Cicero states that "a speech which is easy for lungs is also pleasant to listen to" (*De or.* 3.181).[47] According to him, the periodic structure (*clausula*) also makes the reception easier for the listener. Hence, in classical definitions the length of the period was connected to breathing. For example, Aristotle famously states that the period is "easy to repeat in a breath." (*Rhet.* 3.9.5).[48] As it was referred above, however, the length of the periods (as well as cola) could vary quite remarkably from very short ones to very complex ones. As a result, the matter of whether the period was always uttered in a single breath remains uncertain. For Lee and Scott, it is the colon, instead of the period, that constitutes a breath unit within performance. As a result, they have presented colometric divisions of the cola in their example texts.

3.3. Oral Units in the Sectio Evangelica

Whereas the materials in the Sectio Evangelica do not fit in the category of the classically defined periods, the section still consists of similar structures to many examples provided by Lee and Scott in their study. Its structure contains units that betray features such as rounding and suspension and resolution of thought that are usually linked with the periods. They lack grammatical suspension and contain paratactic clause structures, however. This excludes the possibility for labeling them as periods in the classical sense. The remarkable feature of these units, though, is the fact that each of them appears to be topically as well as aurally structured. The boundaries of the units are relatively easily defined in terms of their content and aurality, as the material contains an abundance of repetitions of certain sounds and patterns. These are clearly structured into separate units of few cola.

While the performative features of the Matthean and Lukan versions of the Q sermon have been covered in previous studies,[49] it is fascinating to

---

47. See also Quintilian, *Inst.* 9.4.125. The breathing obviously depends on the length of the cola and period.

48. The connection between periodic structured and breathing is discussed also by other classical authors. Demetrius (*Eloc.* 1) argues that the cola give rest for the speaker, because otherwise the speaker would run out of breath. Dionysius of Halicarnassus again uses breath as a meter for the period in his analysis of Thucydides's *History of the Peloponnesian War* (*Comp.* 22).

49. For Matthew, see Bernard Brandon Scott and Margaret E. Dean, "A Sound

notice similar types of features in the Sectio Evangelica as well. If we take a closer look at the Sectio Evangelica, we can find five units that are linked with one another by similar topics, catchwords, and common aural features. In the following, each of these units will be presented with the parallels in the Gospels of Matthew and Luke. First, let us investigate the first unit found in Did. 1.3b–d, as well as its Matthean parallel (5:44b–48). For the sake of convenience, the text will be presented with colometric divisions.[50]

Did. 1.3b–d
εὐλογεῖτε τοὺς καταρωμένους ὑμῖν
καὶ προσεύχεσθε ὑπὲρ τῶν ἐχθρῶν ὑμῶν
νηστεύετε δὲ ὑπὲρ τῶν διωκόντων ὑμᾶς
ποία γὰρ χάρις, ἐὰν φιλῆτε τοὺς φιλοῦντας ὑμᾶς
    οὐχὶ καὶ τὰ ἔθνη τοῦτο ποιοῦσιν
ὑμεῖς δὲ φιλεῖτε τοὺς μισοῦντας ὑμᾶς
καὶ οὐχ ἕξετε ἐχθρόν

Matt 5:44b–48
ἀγαπᾶτε τοὺς ἐχθροὺς ὑμῶν
καὶ προσεύχεσθε ὑπὲρ τῶν διωκόντων ὑμᾶς
ὅπως γένησθε υἱοὶ τοῦ πατρὸς ὑμῶν τοῦ ἐν οὐρανοῖς
    ὅτι τὸν ἥλιον αὐτοῦ ἀνατέλλει ἐπὶ πονηροὺς καὶ ἀγαθοὺς
    καὶ βρέχει ἐπὶ δικαίους καὶ ἀδίκους
ἐὰν γὰρ ἀγαπήσητε τοὺς ἀγαπῶντας ὑμᾶς
τίνα μισθὸν ἔχετε
οὐχὶ καὶ οἱ τελῶναι τὸ αὐτὸ ποιοῦσιν
καὶ ἐὰν ἀσπάσησθε τοὺς ἀδελφοὺς ὑμῶν μόνον
τί περισσὸν ποιεῖτε
οὐχὶ καὶ οἱ ἐθνικοὶ τὸ αὐτὸ ποιοῦσιν
ἔσεσθε οὖν ὑμεῖς τέλειοι
ὡς ὁ πατὴρ ὑμῶν ὁ οὐράνιος τέλειός ἐστιν

There is clear correspondence between the Didache's and Matthew's versions. Both begin with a set of exhortations to love your enemies, and after

---

Map of the Sermon on the Mount," in *SBL Seminar Papers 1993*, ed. Eugene H. Lovering, SBLSP 32 (Atlanta: Scholars Press, 1993), 672–725. For Luke, see Draper, "Jesus' 'Covenantal Discourse' on the Plain," 80–86. For the Q sermon, see Horsley and Draper, *Whoever Hears You Hears Me*, 212–17.

50. The colometric division for Matthew follows the one posited by Scott and Dean, "Sound Map of the Sermon on the Mount," 690–91.

that they move on to rhetorical questions. Overall, the Matthean rhetoric differs from that of the Didache in that, whereas Matthew underlines the importance of becoming sons of the heavenly Father, the Didache contains more practical rhetoric about everyday life. After the three exhortations that employ the rhetorical figure of *auxesis*,[51] the Didache introduces rhetorical questions that give further motivation for the preceding exhortations.[52] Finally, the Didache's unit is resolved with a general exhortation to love your enemies, the activity that will eventually lead to the situation in which one has no enemies at all.[53] The rounding of the unit in the Didache is not totally perfect, but it can be detected, for example, in the occurrence of "enemy" as a catchword in the second and final cola.

As for the Lukan parallel (6:27–28), it is close to the Didache in its choice of vocabulary. There are instances of verbatim agreement, and they both contain four cola of exhortations. The Lukan passage has a straightforward quadripartite structure, however, that lacks (in my opinion) the Didache's or Matthew's rhetorical genius.[54] On the other hand, the Lukan quatrain contains other signs of elegant style, such as total avoidance of hiatus and *homoeoteleuton* with occurrence of the personal pronoun ὑμεῖς:

ἀγαπᾶτε τοὺς ἐχθροὺς ὑμῶν
καλῶς ποιεῖτε τοῖς μισοῦσιν ὑμᾶς
εὐλογεῖτε τοὺς καταρωμένους ὑμᾶς
προσεύχεσθε περὶ τῶν ἐπηρεαζόντων ὑμᾶς

Although the Didache shares elements with both Matthew and Luke, I consider it unlikely that the Didache's unit presented above is a conflation of these two texts. While it is definitely related to the traditions preserved

---

51. Layton ("Sources, Date and Transmission," 353) mistakenly regards it as a *climax* and as a "deliberate 'improvement' of the Lukan text … which has no climactic ordering." For *climax*, see Quintilian, *Inst*. 9.3.54; *Rhet. Her*. 4.34. For an example of Christian text employing *climax*, see Rom 5:3–4.

52. Matthean and Lukan parallels for these rhetorical questions occur in slightly different contexts in Matt 5:46–47 and Luke 6:32.

53. A similar idea is found in P.Oxy 1224, Didascalia apostolorum (Syriac and Latin), Justin Martyr (*Apol*. 1.14.3), and the *Stromata* of Clement of Alexandria (2.19.102.4).

54. A similar quatrain is found in Justin, *Apol*. 1.15.9. Allison (*Constructing Jesus*, 340) regards it as a harmony of Matthew and Luke.

in Matthew and Luke, its structure strongly points towards oral development of similar tradition, any literary operations notwithstanding.

The next unit in the Sectio Evangelica consists of Did. 1.4, excluding the commandment to abstain from bodily passions, which may be a post-Didachist insertion and belongs most likely to the later textual history of the Didache.[55] This unit deals with the theme of nonretaliation and contains parallels in Matt 5:39b–42 and Luke 6:29–30. Both Matthean and Lukan quatrains contain parallelism between the first and the third cola, as well as the second and fourth cola. This structure can be termed as ABAB:[56]

Matt 5:39b–42
ἀλλ' ὅστις σε ῥαπίζει εἰς τὴν δεξιὰν σιαγόνα σου
στρέψον αὐτῷ καὶ τὴν ἄλλην
    καὶ τῷ θέλοντί σοι κριθῆναι καὶ τὸν χιτῶνά σου λαβεῖν ἄφες αὐτῷ
    καὶ τὸ ἱμάτιον
καὶ ὅστις σε ἀγγαρεύσει μίλιον ἕν
ὕπαγε μετ' αὐτοῦ δύο
    τῷ αἰτοῦντί σε δός
    καὶ τὸν θέλοντα ἀπὸ σοῦ δανίσασθαι μὴ ἀποστραφῇς

Luke 6:29–30
τῷ τύπτοντί σε ἐπὶ τὴν σιαγόνα πάρεχε καὶ τὴν ἄλλην
    καὶ ἀπὸ τοῦ αἴροντός σου τὸ ἱμάτιον
    καὶ τὸν χιτῶνα μὴ κωλύσῃς
παντὶ αἰτοῦντί σε δίδου
    καὶ ἀπὸ τοῦ αἴροντος τὰ σὰ μὴ ἀπαίτει

Didache 1.4 again employs a different structure from Matthew and Luke. Here we find a quadripartite of conditional clauses that are balanced with the main clause:

ἐάν τις σοι δῷ ῥάπισμα εἰς τὴν δεξιὰν σιαγόνα
στρέψον αὐτῷ καὶ τὴν ἄλλην καὶ ἔσῃ τέλειος
ἐὰν ἀγγαρεύσῃ σέ τις μίλιον ἕν
ὕπαγε μετ' αὐτοῦ δύο
ἐὰν ἄρῃ τις τὸ ἱμάτιόν σου
δὸς αὐτῷ καὶ τὸν χιτῶνα

---

55. Thus also Niederwimmer, *Didache*, 20; Layton, "Sources, Date and Transmission," 375–76.
56. For Allison's analysis of the ABAB structure, see *Constructing Jesus*, 335–37.

ἐὰν λάβῃ τις ἀπὸ σοῦ τὸ σόν
μὴ ἀπαίτει·οὐδὲ γὰρ δύνασαι

The use of conditional clauses may echo the rhetorical question in Did. 1.3, which also contains ἐάν + subjunctive. It must be noted that all three versions, despite their different structures and wordings, have interesting features: after specific examples of nonretaliation, the last colon universalizes the case with a general admonition not to ask or require anything back.

Interestingly, Did. 1.5a begins with the material παντὶ τῷ αἰτοῦντί σε δίδου καὶ μὴ ἀπαίτει, which parallels closely Luke 6:30b. These sayings have different functions in their respective contexts, however: whereas the Lukan saying works as a conclusion to the unit dealing with nonretaliation (Luke 6:29–30), the Didache's rhetoric employs it in the context of almsgiving that is the topic of the next unit:

παντὶ τῷ αἰτοῦντί σε δίδου καὶ μὴ ἀπαίτει
πᾶσι γὰρ θέλει δίδοσθαι ὁ πατὴρ ἐκ τῶν ἰδίων χαρισμάτων
μακάριος ὁ διδοὺς κατὰ τὴν ἐντολήν·ἀθῷος γάρ ἐστιν

The inner logic of the unit is rather simple. The unit starts with an exhortation of unconditional almsgiving, which is followed by a motivation (*imitatio dei*). The unit is concluded with a maxim that is related to the beatitudes of the Q sermon.

The following unit turns the focus on the receiver, who should not receive any alms in vain:

οὐαὶ τῷ λαμβάνοντι
εἰ μὲν γὰρ χρείαν ἔχων λαμβάνει τις, ἀθῷος ἔσται
ὁ δὲ μὴ χρείαν ἔχων δώσει δίκην, ἵνα τί ἔλαβε καὶ εἰς τί
ἐν συνοχῇ δὲ γενόμενος ἐξετασθήσεται περὶ ὧν ἔπραξε
καὶ οὐκ ἐξελεύσεται ἐκεῖθεν, μέχρις οὗ ἀποδῷ τὸν ἔσχατον κοδράντην

The material of the unit consists of 1.5b. It starts with a woe that is addressed to the unjustifiable receiver, which builds a contrast with the previous unit. One could argue that the woe belongs together with the previous maxim. As we can see below, however, the sound analysis suggests that they belong to different units. The following two cola are structured with the particles μέν and δέ, which underline the opposite cases of receiving. The consequences of unjustifiable receiving are spelled out in the fourth and fifth cola, which again have Matthean and Lukan parallels but occur in totally different contexts (see Matt 5:25–26; Luke 12:58–59). Again, we cannot presume a literary dependence on the Synoptics, but rather a creative performing of the tradition.

The quotation in Did. 1.6 is difficult to interpret, and it seems that it would fall out of the structure of the Sectio Evangelica. Although Did. 1.6 continues the theme of giving, it stands in tension with the earlier commandments that promote giving without any conditions (Did. 1.5a) and underlines the responsibility of the one who receives (Did. 1.5b). The exhortation to consider to whom to give may reflect a different socioeconomic situation in the Didache communities. Changed circumstances may have forced the members of the communities to reconsider the ideal of unconditional almsgiving. One could see also link with Did. 11.5–6 and 12.1–5, which warns the community of false teachers who seek only economical profit.

3.4. The Sound Map of the Sectio Evangelica

After defining the units within the Sectio Evangelica, we may move on to perform a sound analysis of these units based on the pioneering work of Lee and Scott. In the following analysis special attention is given to the repetition of certain sounds (syllables and phonemes) throughout the cola. As has been noted, repetition helps both performing and reception of oral-derived tradition.

As for the Sectio Evangelica, one can clearly see how the tradition is structured throughout by the sound. In the following sound maps I have marked the recurring "sounds" with **bold** letters:

1	εὐλογεῖτε		τοὺς καταρωμένους	ὑμῖν
2	καὶ προσεύχεσθε	ὑπὲρ τῶν	ἐχθρῶν	ὑμῶν
3	νηστεύετε δὲ	ὑπὲρ τῶν	διωκόντων	ὑμᾶς
4	ποία γὰρ χάρις, ἐὰν	φιλῆτε	τοὺς φιλοῦντας	ὑμᾶς
	οὐχὶ καὶ τὰ ἔθνη		τοῦτο ποιοῦσιν	
5	ὑμεῖς δὲ	φιλεῖτε	τοὺς μισοῦντας	ὑμᾶς
	καὶ οὐχ ἕξετε		ἐχθρόν	

In this unit one immediately notes the repetition of second person plural personal pronouns at the end of the cola. In fact, the second person plural dominates the whole unit with the occurrence of similar endings of the finite verb forms. Of course, it can be debated whether these endings should be taken as intentionally structured sounds. It may be that they stem only from syntactic requirements of the sentence. In any case, here we may find an instance of repetition that helps to create a structure in the performance.

Another notable feature is the repetition of common sounds in the fourth and the fifth cola, although τοὺς φιλοῦντας/τοὺς μισοῦντας and τοῦτο ποιοῦσιν represent totally different grammatical forms and thus have different syntactical functions. The correspondence between οὐχὶ καὶ and καὶ οὐχ is also interesting, because they are aurally similar but syntactically different.

1	**ἐάν**	τις	σοι δῷ ῥάπισμα εἰς τὴν δεξιὰν σιαγόνα
	στρέψον	αὐτῷ καὶ τὴν ἄλλην καὶ ἔσῃ τέλειος	
2	**ἐὰν** ἀγγαρεύσῃ σέ τις μίλιον ἕν		
	ὕπαγε μετ'	αὐτοῦ δύο	
3	**ἐὰν** ἄρῃ	τις τὸ ἱμάτιόν	σου
	δὸς	αὐτῷ καὶ τὸν χιτῶνα	
4	**ἐὰν λάβῃ**	τις ἀπὸ	σοῦ τὸ σόν
		μὴ ἀπαίτει· οὐδὲ γὰρ δύνασαι	

This unit is a heavily patterned passage that is built on balanced cola. The repetition of certain sounds is evident: ἐάν, τις, αὐτοῦ /αὐτῷ, σου / σοι / σε. This sound pattern is a prime example of how the repetition has helped performing as well as reception of the tradition.

1	παντὶ τῷ αἰτοῦντί σε	**δίδου** καὶ	**μὴ ἀπαίτει**
2	πᾶσι γὰρ θέλει	**δίδοσθαι** ὁ πατὴρ ἐκ τῶν ἰδίων χαρισμάτων	
3	μακάριος	ὁ **διδοὺς** κατὰ τὴν ἐντολήν **ἀθῷος** γάρ ἐστιν	

In this unit we find a link to the previous one. The repeated expression μὴ ἀπαίτει builds a link with the preceding occurrence of μὴ ἀπαίτει. In addition, the unit is structured with an occurrence of πα-/-α-sounds in the beginning of each colon. The aural nucleus of this unit is, however, the repetition of διδου-/διδο- in the middle of each colon. Finally, the phrase ἀθῷος γάρ ἐστιν anticipates similar sounds in the following unit:

1	οὐαὶ τῷ		λαμβάνοντι	
2	εἰ μὲν γὰρ	χρείαν ἔχων	λαμβάνει τις	ἀθῷος ἔσται
3	ὁ δὲ μὴ	χρείαν ἔχων δώσει δίκην, ἵνα **τί**		ἔλαβε καὶ εἰς **τί**

4 ἐν συνοχῇ δὲ γενόμενος **ἐξετασθήσεται** περὶ ὧν   **ἔπραξε**
5 καὶ οὐκ **ἐξελεύσεται** ἐκεῖθεν, **μέχρις** οὗ ἀποδῷ τὸν ἔσχατον κοδράντην

This unit contains a repetition of sounds that forms a climatic structure. It appears that each colon is linked with the other by common sets of sounds. Especially the aural links between ἔλαβε/ἔπραξε and ἐξετασθήσεται/ἐξελεύσεται are interesting phenomena.

Finally, the last unit is linked with the previous one with the ending -ηται and the reoccurrence of the catchword μέχρις. The second colon also includes repetition with certain sounds σου, -ας, and γνῷς/δῷς:

1 ἀλλὰ καὶ περὶ τούτου δὲ εἴρη**ται**
2 Ἰδρωσάτω ἡ ἐλεημοσύνη **σου** εἰς **τὰς** χεῖρά**ς σου**, **μέχρις** ἂν γν**ῷς**, τίνι δ**ῷς**

On the basis of this short investigation, it is clear that the Sectio Evangelica is full of aural repetition of certain sounds and links. It would be unnatural to suggest that the Sectio Evangelica is merely due to literary redaction by a later editor. Rather, aurality must have played a certain role in the formation of the Sectio Evangelica. More than being just a written text that imitates "oral style," I would argue that the Sectio Evangelica becomes a text through oral performing. Importantly, the sound map can be detected even in a unit such as Did. 1.5b, which does not have a clearly patterned structure. This increases the likelihood for the formation of tradition through oral performance.

4. Summary

This article started with an argument that the traditional methods for studying the tradition history and source criticism of the Sectio Evangelica in the Didache have led to an impasse for two reasons: first, the uncertainty of the reconstruction of Q and the redaction of the Gospels of Matthew and Luke downplay the possibility of establishing any literary dependence between the Synoptics and the Sectio Evangelica; second, the concept of literary dependence as a matter of visual copying is not supported by what we know about the conventions of ancient text production. Instead, it was argued that the composition and origin of the Sectio Evangelica should be studied in its own right, as an oral-derived text that was formed through multiple performances. As a heuristic model, I referred to the elements of the Greek prose composition, the period and colon. Although the units in the Sectio Evangelica are not totally comparable with the periods in Greek prose, they serve a common purpose, that is, oral performing. Regarding the methodology, I applied sound mapping in order to point out the aural structure of the Sectio Evangelica. The sound map revealed repetition of certain sounds and patterns within the units, which strongly suggests an oral provenance for this passage. Interestingly, these two aspects support each other, since the units were structured topically as well as aurally. These examples may bring us closer to the performances of this tradition and further give us a more realistic view of early Christian transmissions of tradition.

The Didache and Oral Theory[*]

Nancy Pardee

The stimulus for this study was a paper presented by Perttu Nikander in November 2010 for the "Didache in Context" section of the Society of Biblical Literature. Nikander's paper, entitled "Orality and Writing in the Context of the Two Ways Teaching and the *Didache*,"[1] made a first attempt at bridging the gap between the recent emphasis on understanding the Two Ways and the Didache overall as fundamentally oral texts and the traditional view that focuses on the Didache and its components as written communication. When looking in particular at the Two Ways, Nikander, in my opinion correctly, stated, "both media—orality and writing—should be studied at the same time as interacting phenomena." But how does one do this for the Two Ways, for the Didache as a whole, and for early Christian texts in general? What is the balance between the two media? Does the acknowledgment that these texts were created in societies that were still very much oriented toward the oral transmission of tradition[2] make illegitimate any attempt to derive from them information on the historical development of the church via comparative and redactional *textual* stud-

---

[*] This study is a revised form of a paper presented at the annual meeting of the Society of Biblical Literature, San Francisco, 21 November 2011.

1. Perttu Nikander, "Orality and Writing in the Context of the Two Ways Teaching and the *Didache*" (paper presented at the annual meeting of the Society of Biblical Literature, Atlanta, 21 November 2010). I am exceedingly grateful for his willingness to share with me a written copy of his oral presentation.

2. Joanna Dewey, e.g., using the oft-cited terminology of Walter Ong, characterizes the first century as "a manuscript culture with high residual orality"; see Dewey, "Textuality in an Oral Culture: A Survey of the Pauline Traditions," *Semeia* 65 (1994): 37–65 (39), with reference to Walter J. Ong, *Orality and Literacy: The Technologizing of the Word* (York, UK: Methuen, 1982; repr. Oxford: Routledge, 2002). See, e.g., Ong, *Orality and Literacy*, 38, 125.

ies? Nikander suggested both that the Two Ways had been influenced by oral performance prior to its inclusion in the Didache and that the Didache as a whole continued to be "influenced by oral performing, feedback and adaptation of new traditions." At the same time, he theorized that the writing of the Didache showed the expansion of influence and subsequent "decontextualization" of the Two Ways tradition and suggested, based on the work of J. Peter Denny, that the reference in Did. 7.1 to reciting chapters 1–6 in the context of baptism was "an attempt to explain the function of the Two Ways teaching to an audience that did not share the same performance arena with the original community."[3] The questions remained, however, as to the precise purpose of this "decontextualization" and the extent to which oral performance might continue to influence the use of the tradition. In my 2002 dissertation, I had suggested that at its earliest stage the Didache had been created through the "overt Christianization of a TW text ... by the addition of 1.3b–5 (6) as well as chapter 16" and that a second stage of composition saw "its development into a basic outline for a gentile community ... of the two necessary Christian rituals, baptism and eucharist."[4] If this reconstruction be correct, would such rituals continue to be open to the influence of oral performance? Thus my goal in this paper is to pick up where Nikander in his very interesting preliminary study left off, expanding on some of his comments, clarifying and evaluating the ways in which I see oral theory being applied to the Didache, and raising questions regarding its role in understanding the form, contents, and function of the text.

The concept of orality, of the oral transmission and "performance" of texts, and of the ancient Greco-Roman world as a primarily oral culture has been an important avenue of investigation for the texts of the New Testament. How texts were "performed," how they would be perceived by their audiences, and what their function would have been have all been

---

3. Nikander cites as his basis the observation by J. Peter Denny that, "the general cause of decontextualization ... is the growth of human societies beyond a size where all members share a common background of information"; see Denny, "Rational Thought in Oral Culture and Literate Decontextualization" in *Literacy and Orality*, ed. D. R. Olson and N. Torrance (Cambridge: Cambridge University Press, 1991), 72.

4. Nancy D. Pardee, "The Genre of the Didache: A Text-Linguistic Analysis" (Ph.D. diss., The University of Chicago, 2002), 195–96. See now also Pardee, *The Genre and Development of the Didache*, WUNT 2/339 (Tübingen: Mohr Siebeck, 2012), 184–85.

illuminated by the concept of these works as texts that would be spoken and heard rather than simply written and read. Beyond this, however, was the impact such a realization had on the search for "original" sayings of Jesus. The early studies of Milman Parry and then Albert Lord[5] on the way in which epics were transmitted in oral form showed, among other things, that while the inclusion of essential themes and formulae kept the stories recognizable, other variations in the performance of these texts were not only acceptable but expected and considered artistic. As Walter Ong summarized it,

> originality consists not in the introduction of new materials but in fitting the traditional materials effectively into each individual, unique situation and/or audience.... The fixed materials in the bard's memory are a float of themes and formulas out of which all stories are variously built.[6]

In these situations there were no "original" texts but rather a variety of similar, yet different, performances, indeed each performance was unique. If true, however, this created problems for scholars endeavoring to recapture the historical Jesus from data provided by his "original" sayings and for those attempting to reconstruct the early Christian communities through studies of the redaction of "original" texts, since in both cases oral theory threatened the very foundation of their methodology: if there were no "original" traditions, the significance of "variations" was much harder to determine, if not entirely undermined.

Of course the possibility of oral transmission has often been raised with respect to the tradition that the Didache shares with the Synoptic Gospels. Indeed, as Nikander pointed out, this had been the primary focus in the past for orality studies on the Didache. Beyond that, however, such ideas have increasingly been brought to bear on other aspects of the Didache, with studies appearing in essentially two categories: (1) those that see the *overall* oral character of the Didache as helping to provide a way out of the scholarly impasse over the question regarding the presence of redactional layers in the text and (2) those that apply such concepts of orality to *particular* sections of the text. Examples of the first category

---

5. Milman Parry, *L'Epithète traditionelle dans Homère* (Paris: Belles Lettres, 1928); Albert B. Lord, *The Singer of Tales*, HSCL 24 (Cambridge: Harvard University Press, 1960).

6. Ong, *Orality and Literacy*, 59–60.

would be the commentary of Aaron Milavec and the work of Ian Henderson, both of whom maintain the compositional unity of the Didache and see the text's primarily oral character as a way to explain what others have cited as evidence of the use and redaction of sources. Examples of the latter include publications of Jonathan Draper, the commentary by Milavec, and the work on the eucharistic prayers by Jonathan Schwiebert. Nikander criticized briefly and to varying degrees the work of Milavec, Draper, and Henderson, while also acknowledging the usefulness of their approach to the Didache from the perspective of oral performance. I believe, however, that these studies require a more in-depth evaluation if one is to achieve a more precise understanding of the composition and function of the Didache, and it is to such an evaluation that this study will now turn.[7]

Among the basic premises of Milavec's 2003 commentary[8] is that the extant Didache represents the "comprehensive, step-by-step program used for the formation of a gentile converting to Christianity,"[9] that it is a "pastoral manual"[10] created by "senior mentors,"[11] and that it had "circulated on the lips of the members of this community for a good many years before any occasion arose that called for a scribe to prepare a textual version."[12] In Milavec's opinion, when one looks at the text as a step-by-step process of training, one recognizes that it exhibits a unity both "marvelous" and "holistic."[13] Moreover, such unity is even more evident when the Didache is viewed from the perspective of orality:

---

7. For my earlier critique of the work of Milavec, see Pardee, review of *The Didache: Text, Translation, Analysis, and Commentary,*" by Aaron Milavec, *JECS* 13 (2005): 525–27; for my evaluation of Henderson, see Pardee, "Genre of the Didache," 53–58; on both now, see *Genre and Development of the Didache,* 53–62.

8. Aaron Milavec, *The Didache: Faith, Hope, and Life of the Earliest Christian Communities, 50–70 CE* (New York: Newman, 2003). The premises are the same in the epitome version of the larger commentary, *The Didache: Text, Translation, Analysis, and Commentary* (Collegeville, MN.: Liturgical Press, 2003).

9. Milavec, *Didache: Faith, Hope, and Life,* xvii.

10. Ibid., vii.

11. Ibid., xi.

12. Ibid., vii.

13. Ibid., xii.

> When the residual clues of orality are ... noted in the *Didache* ..., it becomes possible to understand that its oral creation and oral recitation marked its internal structure long before it was ever a written text.[14]

Such clues Milavec finds in the many references to "words" and "speaking" within the text,[15] as well as oral patterns, key words, and associations, indeed an "oral logic" that lends itself well to memorization and performance.[16] Resorting to source and redaction criticism to explain the text of the Didache is, in his view, unwarranted.

Milavec's reconciliation of seeming inconsistencies/disruptions in the text by resorting to its oral character, however, is altogether unconvincing. One example, and a crucial one of course, is his explanation for the problematic juncture of the text at Did. 7.1 mentioned by Nikander. Here, with the beginning of the new section "concerning baptism" (περὶ δὲ τοῦ βαπτίσματος), the text not only issues the command to recite everything that has been stated in the text heretofore (ταῦτα πάντα προειπόντες), that is, the material on the Two Ways in the previous six chapters, but unexpectedly moves from the singular form of address found just prior to this point in 6.1–3 (and predominant in the Two Ways overall) to a plural form (βαπτίσατε). Given the independent witnesses to virtually the same Two Ways tradition in the Doctrina Apostolorum, the Epistle of Barnabas, and the Apostolic Church Order, most scholars have viewed Did. 7.1 as a somewhat awkward editorial seam connecting a preexistent Two Ways text, now apparently used by this community as part of the baptismal ritual, with the material that followed. Clearly the change in verbal form signals a change in audience that otherwise goes completely unacknowledged in the text. Milavec, however, denies that the Two Ways existed in written form within the community prior to its inscription as part of the Didache and considers the various textual witnesses to the Two Ways as transcriptions of independent oral productions of the same basic oral text found in Did. 1–5.[17] While agreeing that the change from singular to plural in 7.1 signals a different audience, he simply explains the disruption by saying that the audience all along had been the mentors of the community (not their catechumens) and that the text took this form, because "the trainers

---

14. Ibid., 718.
15. Ibid., 719.
16. Ibid., xxxiii.
17. Ibid., 717–18.

need to hear the specific rules in the form in which they will use them to train their novices."[18] Such a solution is problematic on many counts. First, that the true audience would only become clear so far into the text, whether oral or written, seems highly unlikely, especially if the text as a whole had been honed orally over so many years prior to its transcription. Secondly, Milavec's explanation does not account for the fact that a change from singular to plural is also found in the verbs of Did. 1.3b, a passage closely related to Matt 5:44, 46–47 and Luke 6:27–28, 32–35, where the same verbs occur in the second person plural (εὐλογεῖτε, προσεύχεσθε, ἀγαπᾶτε). Indeed, 1.3b is the beginning of a passage (1.3b–2.1) that presents material shared by both Matthew and Luke, which is absent from all other versions of the Two Ways and which of necessity must be deemed a later addition to the shared, preexisting Two Ways source. Finally, the idea that the text would have to be given in the exact form in which the mentors were to present it to catechumens flies in the face of his suggestion that the catechumens themselves would likely have memorized the Two Ways:[19] why would the form used by all not be rendered in indirect speech?

Indeed the "interpolation" of 1.3b–2.1 is another example of Milavec's attribution of a problematic juncture to the oral character of the Didache. In Did. 2.1, one meets with the announcement, "the second command of the teaching is," a surprising statement in light of the fact that nothing heretofore had been designated as a "first command." Again, the fact that this section is missing from other Two Ways texts has led most scholars to see 2.1 as another, awkward, redactional seam created by an editor to incorporate the new material. Milavec, however, based on his premise that the Two Ways is a training program delivered orally, suggests the following explanation:

> Within the progression of a training program … it would have been natural for the spiritual master to give the "rule" of *Did.* 1.5 first and to discuss it at length without making any reference to there even being a "second rule"—a topic that would be taken up at the next training session.[20]

---

18. Ibid., 245.
19. Ibid., 93, 267.
20. Ibid., 118.

Apart from the fact that no data is offered to support such a hypothesis, there is the more difficult problem of reconciling the idea that such a specific cutoff point would be dictated within an oral text.

From the opposite view, Milavec's belief that the Didache is primarily an oral production is difficult to maintain given the potential for confusion that exists in the text as it stands. One example is found in the Two Ways, again a text that catechumens would, according to Milavec, likely have committed to memory, and thus one would expect to find it extremely simple to understand. Yet instructions regarding the giving of charity are found in two places in the Two Ways: 1.(4)5–6 and 4.5–8.[21] The first passage, part of the "interpolated section," occurs within material parallel to Matt 5:39–42 and Luke 6:27–30. In Did. 1.4, one finds the same stance of nonresistance to the seizure of property and person as in Matthew and Luke:

> If someone gives you a blow on your right cheek, turn to him the other as well and you will be perfect. If someone forces you to go one mile, go with him two miles; if someone takes your cloak, give him your tunic also; if someone takes from you what belongs to you, do not demand it back, for you cannot do so.

Following this in Did. 1.5, there is a sort of summary statement where, as also in the synoptic parallels, what Milavec terms a "milder alternative"[22] is presented:

> Give to everyone who asks you, and do not demand it back, for the Father wants something from his own gifts to be given to everyone.

Here the literal sense is that one should give freely to all without question. In Did. 1.6, however, the text continues:

> But it has also been said concerning this: "Let your gift sweat in your hands until you know to whom to give it."

---

21. Milavec seems to begin the first passage on giving in 1.4 (*Didache: Faith, Hope, and Life*, 99).
22. Ibid., 183.

This of course raises the question as to whether one should give "freely" or not? Many scholars see here a later insertion that retreats from the unfettered charity advised in 1.5. Milavec, however, citing the parallels to Did. 1.6 in Augustine, notes how the early father himself dealt with precisely the same contradiction.

> My brethren, it is both said and read, "To everyone who asks, give," and in another place Scripture says, "Let alms sweat in your hand until you find a righteous person to whom to give [it]." One person begs of you, another you ought to seek out. But do not leave empty the person who begs of you, "To everyone who asks, give," but there is another you ought to seek out: "Let alms sweat in your hand until you find a righteous person to whom to give [it]."[23]

The precise source from which Augustine drew the first tradition is uncertain, given the parallels in Matthew and Luke. The source of the second, cited as Scripture, is today still unsatisfactorily identified but bears a resemblance to Sir 12:1–7.[24] For Milavec, however, the fact that Augustine can, in his opinion, successfully reconcile the two instructions shows that they are also not contradictory in the Didache, but rather, the second supplements the first: "The *Didache* can be understood as saying that giving to those who ask of you (*Did.* 1:5) does not suffice; at times one must let the alms sweat in our hands until one finds someone in need of it."[25] In fact Milavec sees the Didache as even less contradictory in this matter, since it does not make explicit that the recipient must be "righteous," as does the rendition of Augustine. For Milavec, both 1.5 and 1.6 advocate giving to all without discernment.[26]

Yet what is more likely the case is that Augustine is himself trying to make sense of the contradiction posed by these teachings. Indeed, he was not the first to do so. Matthew's own insertion of "lending" into the text in 5:42 may have been to moderate the indiscriminate giving advocated in Q (see Luke 6:30) at a time/place when even the first-century Christians realized this was not practical. Interestingly, none of the other witnesses

---

23. Translation follows Milavec, *Didache: Faith, Hope, and Life*, 186–87.
24. On the identification of this tradition, see Kurt Niederwimmer, *The Didache: A Commentary*, trans. Linda M. Maloney, Hermeneia (Minneapolis: Fortress, 1998), 83–86.
25. Milavec, *Didache: Faith, Hope, and Life*, 187.
26. Ibid., 187–88.

to the Didache include 1.6: P.Oxy. 1782 breaks off before that point; the Georgian translation completely lacks 1.5–6; and the Apostolic Constitutions and Canons essentially lacks 1.5b–2.1, although for 1.5a it has substituted the version found in Matthew along with Matt 5:45 and has drawn in Did. 4.6 adding that fellow Christians take priority (7.2.6–7). Exactly when Did. 1.6 crept into the text is unclear, but that Augustine believed it to be "Scripture" and that he discussed it in the same context that is found in the Didache, namely, in the face of a command to give to all freely, may illustrate the widespread knowledge of this tradition.

But the second passage on charity in the Two Ways makes a consistent interpretation even more difficult. Didache 4.5–8 reads:

> Do not be one who stretches out the hands to receive but withdraws them when it comes to giving. If you earn something by working with your hands, you shall give a ransom for your sins. You shall not hesitate to give, nor shall you grumble when giving, for you will know who is the good paymaster of the reward. You shall not turn away from someone in need, but shall share everything with your brother or sister, and do not claim that anything is your own. For if you are sharers in what is imperishable, how much more so in perishable things.[27]

Here the text advocates giving freely, but only to a Christian "brother or sister." Of course, as with 1.5, both are contradictory to the statement in 1.6.

Milavec reconciles these inconsistencies by contrasting the use of the imperative in 1.4–6 with the presence of the future indicative in 4.5–8: the first, in his view, is what is required of catechumens immediately upon conversion; the latter will be required in the future after baptism and full admission to the community. While stating that the future indicative here "could function as a mild imperative," he believes that "this would leave the awkward situation whereby two diverse rules of giving are provided and no attempt is made to harmonize them."[28] Instead, citing specifically the instruction of Did. 4.3 that calls for reconciling conflict and making just and impartial judgments among community members, he maintains that the context of 4.5–8 is clearly postbaptismal, and thus it would be obvious

---

27. Unless otherwise indicated, the English translations of the Didache are taken from Michael W. Holmes, ed. and trans., *The Apostolic Fathers: Greek Texts and English Translations*, 3rd ed. (Grand Rapids: Baker Academic, 2007).

28. Ibid., 99.

to all that the verbs should be understood as pointing to a future point of time. That this would be easily understood in an oral delivery, however, is dubious. Indeed the same future indicative form is found in Did. 2, 3.9–10, and virtually all of chapter 4. Exactly when does the context change from immediate action to a future time? Is the command to "remember [μνησθήσῃ] night and day the one who preaches God's word to you and honor [τιμήσεις] him as though he were the Lord" (4.1) or to "seek out [ἐκζητήσεις] daily the presence of the saints, so that you may find support in their words" (4.2) to apply only after admission to the community? To interpret 4.3 in a future sense in contradistinction to the surrounding material that would seem to require an immediate application is arbitrary. Moreover, not simply a "mild imperative," the negative οὐ + future imitates the Hebrew לֹא + imperfect which, according to E. Kautzsch, denotes "the strongest expectation of obedience" and is "especially used in enforcing the divine commands," for example in the Decalogue.[29] That this is more likely the result of the juxtaposition of sources/later redaction is supported by the fact that the future tense in 4.5-8 is also attested in the parallels in the Doctrina apostolorum and Barnabas, while the imperative in 1.3b-6 is found in the synoptic parallels of Matthew and Luke.

But even beyond the fact that oral theory does not provide a convincing explanation for these individual difficulties within the text of the Didache is the problem that Milavec's characterization of the text as "oral" is not well defined.[30] While suggesting that the Didache would "have been created as a scribal transcription listening to an oral production being recited by someone who had mastered it"[31] and asserting, as noted above, that it is both "comprehensive" and detailed, he elsewhere describes the Way of Life section as "a bare-bones training outline"[32] and suggests, based on the work of Parry and Lord, that, "it could be supposed that the same

---

29. E. Kautzsch, *Gesenius' Hebrew Grammar*, trans. A. E. Cowley, 2nd ed. (Oxford: Clarendon, 1983), 107*o*. Odd is Milavec's statement that the "simple future ... functions as a mild imperative and imitates the language of the Decalogue found in the Septuagint" (*Didache: Faith, Hope, and Life*, 102).

30. Here Nikander also sensed a lack of clarity, briefly stating, "When Milavec argues that the Way of Life was recited from memory, he clearly presupposes that the process of memorizing does not involve a use of any text, but stems rather from oral tradition. In this light, the relationship between the written text and oral performances seems unclear."

31. Milavec, *Didache: Faith, Hope, and Life*, 718.

32. Ibid., 92.

teacher/mentor introduced small variations and pastoral expansions every time he/she recited the Way of Life."[33] But if what one has in the Didache is a transcription of one of these oral productions, it is no longer the "barebones" outline that Milavec envisions. The same contradiction can be seen in his view of the prayers found in Did. 8–10 where, again, seemingly opposed to the idea that the written text is a transcription of an oral production, Milavec states: "none of the prayers given in the *Didache* was ever read or recited word for word from memory. Prayer leaders were expected to be entirely familiar with the prayer synopsis that guided the opening phrases, the thematic flow, and the concluding refrain(s)."[34] Is what we have in the text a "synopsis" or a transcription of an oral performance of the text? Part of the problem is the failure on the part of Milavec to make a distinction between narrative traditions, such as those studied by Parry and Lord, and a "manual," like the Didache: would the variations found in oral storytelling in the ancient world apply to a text providing ritual instruction as does a significant portion of the Didache (1–10)?

Another study that sought to maintain the compositional unity of the Didache by pointing to its oral characteristics was published in 1992 by Henderson, with a later article appearing in 1995.[35] Henderson maintained "that the symbolic, formulaic, and argumentative unity of the Didache can fruitfully be reconciled with its evident episodic and stylistic disunity if we recognize and understand the deliberate, oral quality of the text."[36] In the Didache, "the frequency of speech words (λέγω, λαλέω, διδάσκω, κελεύω, ἐλέγχω, εὐχαριστέω, etc.) and their even distribution contrast vividly with the complete absence of specifically literate symbols."[37] Moreover, Henderson states that, "The *Didache* argues for the complementarity of diverse authorities by receiving them conversationally and pragmatically rather than ideologically, as διδαχή/ἐντολή/δόγμα."[38] In his view the unexpected repetitions and contradictions of the Didache and the seeming disruption

---

33. Ibid., 718.
34. Ibid., xiv.
35. Ian Henderson, "*Didache* and Orality in Synoptic Comparison," *JBL* 111 (1992): 283–306; "Style-Switching in the *Didache*: Fingerprint or Argument?" in *The Didache in Context: Essays on Its Text, History and Transmission*, ed. Clayton N. Jefford, NovTSup 77 (Leiden: Brill, 1995), 177–209.
36. Henderson, "Style-Switching in the *Didache*," 177.
37. Henderson, "*Didache* and Orality in Synoptic Comparison," 295.
38. Ibid., 304.

of the text at various junctures are not due to one or more subsequent redactions but are characteristics of its "oral sensitivity." Recurring symbols of "verbal, spoken authority," in his opinion, provide an overall structure to the text and communicate the intentions of the author to "provide an interpretative framework within which to harmonize conflicting norms"[39] and to "frustrate any interrogation about its specific tradition-historical loyalties and connections."[40] Considering again Did. 7.1, Henderson cites as recurring and thus structurally enhancing features the περὶ δέ of 7.1 that recurs in 6.3, and 9.1, 3 and, in his first study, the "λέγω-citation formula" also found in 1.6, 11.1, 14.3, and 16.7.[41] In his view, ταῦτα πάντα in 7.1 denotes more than chapters 1–6 but is

> understood nonsequentially to imply also ταῦτα πάντα of 11.1, the ἐντολὰς κυρίου of 4.13, 14 and the πάσας τὰς πράξεις ... ὡς ἔχετε ἐν τῷ εὐαγγελίῳ τοῦ κυρίου ἡμῶν of 15.4: *Didache* understands even its own textuality not only as the sequence of monologue and reading but above all as the presence and flexibility of conversation (cf. 4.1).[42]

Indeed, ταῦτα πάντα is

> protreptic not just for baptism but for an indefinitely extended chain of expectations, partly met within the text itself, partly overflowing into the situation of the readership.... ταῦτα πάντα become explicit and actual only in the whole imagined conversation in which tradition, text, and readership all have decisive voices (4.1–2; 6.1–7.1; 11.1–3; 14.1–16.2).[43]

In my opinion, Henderson's attempt to rescue the unity of the Didache is also unconvincing. First of all, the oral terminology found in the text is not part of a "normative hermeneutical strategy"[44] but rather the natural

---

39. Ibid., 302.
40. Henderson, "Style-Switching in the *Didache*," 178.
41. In his later publication, Henderson included Did. 9.5 among examples of this formula, but redefined 7.1 and 11.1 as "marked self-allusions" ("Style-Switching in the *Didache*," 206–7).
42. Henderson, "*Didache* and Orality in Synoptic Comparison," 303. Noted also in Pardee, "Genre of the Didache," 56; *Genre and Development of the Didache*, 61. Nikander also criticized Henderson on this point, noting that "Henderson's 'oral-poetic reading' interprets the text in a way that the plot of the text itself does not endorse."
43. Henderson, "*Didache* and Orality in Synoptic Comparison," 299.
44. Ibid., 305.

result of providing instruction for the recitation of prayers and ritual texts, of quoting sayings of Jesus, and of the use of other ancient literary conventions including περὶ δέ + genitive as a section heading[45] and the λέγω-citation formula to cite the Hebrew Scriptures.[46] Secondly, neither the juxtaposition of conflicting norms nor the citing of a variety of authorities alleviates the tension in the Didache, especially in light of the fact that the text itself warns against deviation from the teaching presented (4.13; 6.1; 11.1). Finally, the detailed nature of the text speaks against viewing it as the representation of a conversation where "there is nothing ... that the reader does not already know."[47]

From examining the studies of Milavec and Henderson, it seems clear that the attribution to the Didache of an originally oral character, even if it is only "oral sensitivity," does not account for the state of the text as we have it. Clearly the lens of orality is more usefully applied to the portions of the Didache designated by the text itself as oral communication, that is, the Two Ways text (1–6 as indicated by 7.1), the Lord's prayer (8.2–3), and the prayers for the eucharistic meal (9–10). These are all subtexts on a level of communication deeper than that of the surface level and have clearly been recorded for the use of the receiving audience. Recognizing anew their oral nature, scholars have been better able to appreciate the flow of these texts as performances, to speculate on how they would have been received and understood, and to understand how and where they fit into the picture in the development of worship, ritual, and liturgy in early Christianity. I completely acknowledge the usefulness of such a perspective to illuminate those areas. The focus of the remainder of this paper, however, will not be on the meaning and function of these subtexts individually but rather on the reason for their inclusion in the Didache and their intended use within the community.

In a 2008 study of the vice lists of the Two Ways text, Draper respectfully challenged the attempt by Huub van de Sandt and David Flusser to reconstruct the Greek Two Ways text lying behind the Didache, Doctrina apostolorum, and Barnabas, a text that they saw as also related to even

---

45. On this see Margaret Mitchell, "Concerning PERI DE in 1 Corinthians," *NovT* 3(1989): 229–56.

46. See "εἶπον," BDAG 1e. Examples of a parallel phenomenon outside of Jewish and Christian texts, including in the work of Epictetus, can be found in "λέγω," BDAG 1bη.

47. Henderson, "*Didache* and Orality in Synoptic Comparison," 292.

earlier traditions used in 1QS and seen also in the *Derek Eretz* materials.[48] On the model of oral performance, Draper suggested instead that the Two Ways, despite its written forms, was primarily an oral tradition and continued to exist in oral forms alongside these written versions. The fact of the matter, according to Draper, was that as an oral tradition the Two Ways likely had no original form from which the others descended. Moreover, he maintains that, because the genre of the Two Ways tradition is that of catechesis, it

> would have been delivered orally by a teacher over a lengthy period, during which the teaching would have been committed to memory. The text would never have been read in a silent or even in a public recital in the form that is found either in the Jerusalem Manuscript of the *Didache* (H54) or in the reconstruction of the Two Ways provided by van de Sandt and Flusser. The text is simply a skeleton, an aide de mémoire for the oral instructor.[49]

In support of this stance, Draper cites studies by Jan Vansina on narratives and Ruth Finnegan on oral poetry and also brings in the interesting example of the lukasa memory board of the Luba people, a mnemonic device used for initiation rites. Attached to the lukasa boards are a number of pegs and shells, each representing some piece of information both in and of itself and in its relationship to the other pegs/shells. Some of the pegs/shells are movable while others are more static and serve as anchors for the rite overall. The information connected with these pegs/shells serves "to recall particular aspects of the history of the Luba, its kings, and its sacred significance."[50] A performance of the initiation always contained approximately the same information, roughly in the same order, but allowed for a good deal of flexibility as well, within the limits set by the anchors. Draper finds here an analogy to the vice lists of the Two Ways, where certain patterns/combinations almost always occur together and where specific vices

---

48. See Huub van de Sandt and David Flusser, *The Didache: Its Jewish Sources and Its Place in Early Judaism and Christianity*, CRINT 3.5 (Assen: Van Gorcum; Minneapolis: Fortress, 2002), 180–82.

49. Jonathan A. Draper, "Vice Catalogues as Oral-Mnemonic Cues: A Comparative Study of the Two-Ways Tradition in the Didache and Parallels from the Perspective of Oral Tradition," in *Jesus, the Voice, and the Text: Beyond the Oral and the Written Gospel*, ed. Tom Thatcher (Waco, TX: Baylor University Press, 2008), 112; see also 115.

50. Ibid., 118.

or combinations anchor the tradition, but where there can also be significant variation in larger sequences, as is seen across the independent Two Ways texts. Although he sees this within the Didache itself between chapters 2, 3, and 5, the similarities in the text here seem to me not to show the patterning necessary to signal a set, albeit still variable, tradition in the background. Better examples, in my opinion, are his comparisons of the lists of the Didache, the Doctrina apostolorum, and Barnabas where a variation of smaller patterns can be more clearly seen, especially between Barnabas and the other two texts. Such is the case in the Way of Life in Did. 2, Doctr. 2, and Barn. 19.4–7. Although Draper concedes here that the Didache and the Doctrina apostolorum are in fact quite close in order, he still does not exclude the possibility that even the slight differences are due to oral rather than written transmission.[51] Similar variations are found also in the way of death in Did. 5, Doctr. 5, and Barn. 20, though again the Didache and the Doctrina apostolorum are much closer to each other, while Barnabas, oddly, differs significantly from the others in the first half (20.1) but is virtually identical to them in the second (20.2). This latter instance, however, especially throws into question, in my opinion, the analogy with the lukasa. Assuming that the lukasa pegs represent content and not actual verbatim texts, it is hard, in my opinion, to reconcile the verbally identical character of large portions of the Two Ways witnesses with the idea that they represent different performances of the same oral tradition or different aide mémoires. Moreover, I keep coming back to the fact that the text itself guards its content in 4.13, warning the audience to neither add nor take away from the Lord's commandments. Draper maintains that this warning "does not necessarily protect the text when the oral tradition changes." He compares it to Matt 5:18 ("not one jot not tittle shall pass away from the Law") and sees it as much weaker (though in line with the similar saying in Rev 22:18–19, which also, in his opinion, attests the "pliable world of oral tradition").[52] Though Nikander agreed with Draper on this point, the question must be raised as to whether one can legitimately compare Matt 5:18 with Did. 4.13, given the different contexts of the two statements. While the Christian Jewish author of Matthew is addressing other Christian Jews regarding the law of Moses, that is, an outside text held by both parties as sacred, the Didache, I would maintain,

---

51. Ibid., 127.
52. Ibid., 114.

presents a Christian Jewish author addressing gentile Christians about the text at hand. Matthew 5:13 was prefixed to the material that follows not as a warning, but as a claim that the teaching of Jesus was not contrary to the law of Moses. The warning of Did. 4.13, however, follows the Way of Life in order to authorize it and to safeguard its contents, in my opinion, because the Way of Life is the law of Moses for gentiles.

Thus, while Draper may indeed be correct in seeing oral influence on the variations of the Two Ways tradition, in my opinion one cannot draw from this the conclusion that the text of the Two Ways in the Didache serves only as an aide mémoire and not as a text to be performed verbatim at an initiation ceremony such as baptism. The comparison with oral renditions of artistic works (songs, poems, narratives, etc.; note that even the initiation represented by the lukasa conveys information of an historical nature) is questionable, since these differ in genre and thus in function from that of a ritual text, and one cannot necessarily transfer the means of transmission for the one category to that of the other. Indeed, when one looks at the Two Ways of the Didache, one finds much more than pegs on which to hang other catechetical material. The text is very explicit and detailed. Surely Draper is correct when he states that the actual catechetical training would have been more extensive, but this does not preclude that the Two Ways as we have it was the text used for the baptismal rite. Moreover, it seems clear that the Two Ways of the Didache existed in written form *before* the addition of chapters 7–10, since the beginning of the text lacks any indication that it will be used for the subsequent baptism ritual. Indeed, I would maintain that it is on the authority of the Two Ways that the chapters on baptism and Eucharist are intended to piggy back.

Similar claims, however, regarding the nature of the eucharistic prayers of Did. 9–10, that is, that they are only models from which the prayer leader would have formulated their own version, have been made by Draper and Milavec, as well as Schwiebert.[53] Clearly these prayers are Jewish in character, and in particular Did. 10.1–5 has often been seen as a Christian version of the Jewish after-meal prayer, the Birkat Hamazon, as reconstructed by Louis Finkelstein.[54] Scholars of Jewish prayer and liturgy,

---

53. Jonathan A. Draper, "Ritual Process and Ritual Symbol in Didache 7–10," *VC* 54 (2000): 121–58 (139); Milavec, *Didache: Faith, Hope, and Life*, 416-21; Jonathan Schwiebert, *Knowledge and the Coming Kingdom: The Didache's Meal Ritual and Its Place in Early Christianity*, LNTS 373 (London: T&T Clark, 2008), 88.

54. Louis Finkelstein, "The Birkat Ha-Mazon," *JQR* NS 19 (1928–1929): 211–62.

such as Joseph Heinemann, however, have contended that the prayers of this period did not yet have a fixed form and that the evidence suggests that there existed simultaneously a number of versions of specific prayers in different communities. While earlier scholars, such as Louis Ginzberg, had drawn from the fact that specific prayers were referred to in the talmudic-midrashic material in an abbreviated, fragmentary fashion the conclusion that readers would have known the full text in a "more or less fixed character,"[55] Heinemann inferred from this data and from the existence of variant versions of the prayers in later witnesses that the texts of the prayers were not yet standardized and only gradually became so, taking on last of all a fixed wording. The entire process, in his opinion, did not end until the Geonic period (600–1100 CE).[56] In this light Draper and others have contended that the prayers of the Didache also were not intended for verbatim recitation but rather provided only a basic model to follow. Draper writes: "The eucharistic prayers of the *Didache* are not literary compositions but oral tradition, which has been reduced to text.... The written text would provide the template for oral performance in the *Didache* as also in the Rabbinic instructions."[57]

But is this conclusion warranted? Even if, as Heinemann contends, the traditional Jewish prayers of this time were not yet fixed, is this evidence applicable to the Didache? As noted above, references to specific prayers in the Jewish literature are *abbreviated,* not written out in full. An example can be found in the instruction for the Eighteen Benedictions in m. Roš Haš. 4:5:

> The order of the *Blessings*: one recites the *Patriarchs*, the *Powers*, the *Holiness of God's Name*, and includes with them *Sovereignty*, but one does not sound, the *Holiness of the Day* and one does sound, the *Remembrances* and one does sound, the *Shofaroth* and one does sound, and he recites the *Temple Service*, and the *Thanksgiving*, and the *Priestly Blessing*; this is the view of R. Jochanan ben Nuri.[58]

---

55. Joseph Heinemann, *Prayer in the Talmud: Forms and Patterns*, SJ 9 (Berlin: de Gruyter, 1977), 45 n. 17, quoting Louis Ginzberg, "Saadia's Siddur," *JQR* NS 33 (1943): 315–63 (315).

56. Heinemann, *Prayer in the Talmud*, 29.

57. Draper, "Ritual Process and Ritual Symbol," 139.

58. Translation from Philip Blackman, ed., *Order Moed*, vol. 2 of *Mishnayoth* (New York: Judaica, 1963), 401.

Indeed, further on in the quotation cited by Heinemann, Ginzberg remarked that

> in the entire talmudic-midrashic literature … one does not find a single principal prayer in full.… [The prayers] are cited only by initial words or have at most a sentence quoted from them.[59]

Heinemann himself goes on to say that

> it is precisely the later prayers (from the Amoraic period onwards) which were instituted with a more or less fixed wording. This would account for the fact that it is the less important prayers which are recorded in their entirety in the two Talmuds, and not the major statutory prayers.… There would be no need to do so since every Jew knew a[t] least some formulation of these prayers. This would not be the case, however, with those prayers which were instituted at a later date and which had not yet become widespread among the people; or with the prayers for special occasions which were not recited daily and hence would not be familiar to the average man.… We cannot necessarily conclude that the version which appears in the sources is the only one that ever existed.… But certainly with respect to these special prayers there never existed the same kind of possibility for a wide range of formulations as was the case with the daily statutory prayers.[60]

In this light, the fact that the prayers of the Didache are given in a full form seems to indicate that they were intended to be recited as written. Support for this view can also be found in the Dead Sea Scrolls. Stefan Reif, remarking on the oral character of Jewish prayer in the early rabbinic period as compared with that of the Dead Sea Scrolls, notes that

> this is not to say that there was no structure to Jewish prayer as far as the talmudic rabbis were concerned and that expression was totally free. The sources indicate at least a basic, and even hardy framework, and differences of opinion about precisely how to complete the picture. Those who argued for a fixed format attempted to lay down the details; those who preferred spontaneity argued the need for the constant introduction of novel elements. But, given the efficiency of the oral transmission

---

59. Heinemann, *Prayer in the Talmud*, 45 n. 17, citing Ginzburg, "Saadia's Siddur," 315.

60. Heinemann, *Prayer in the Talmud*, 65–66.

of the time, such a framework by no means required to be committed to writing to ensure its adoption and survival. The sect from the Dead Sea thought differently and preserved written versions of their prayers.[61]

Moreover, given that the prayers of the Didache occur within a ritual context, it is noteworthy when James Davila, for example, writes that the "liturgical works from the Qumran library … constitute our earliest examples of fixed Jewish liturgical texts."[62] Indeed, it is widely accepted that such liturgical pieces were written in the form in which they were intended to be used. One example, the prayers of 4QDibHam (Words of the Luminaries), of which at least two copies were recovered from among the Dead Sea Scrolls,[63] was to be recited by the community on specific days, seemingly for each day of the week. One section reads:

> Hymns for the Sabbath Day
> Give thanks.… [Bless] His holy Name unceasingly … all the angels of the holy firmament … above] the heavens, the earth and all its deep places, the great [Abyss] and Abaddon and the waters and all that is [in them.] [Let all His creatures [bless Him] unceasingly for everlasting [ages. Amen! Amen!].[64]

Indeed, unlike the majority of the prayers of the Mishnah/Talmud, the prayers in the Qumran texts are not simply fragments, but are prayers in their entirety. One example is that of another liturgical text, 1Q34 [bis]:

> I. Thou wilt cause the wicked to be our ransom and the unfaithful to be our redemption. [Thou wilt] blot out all our oppressors and we shall praise Thy Name for ever [and ever]. For this has Thou created us and [to say to Thee] this: Blessed art Thou.…
> II. the Great Light (of heaven) for the [day]time, [and the Little Light (of heaven) for the night] … without transgressing their laws … and their dominion is over all the world. But the seed of man did not understand all that Thou caused them to inherit; they did not discern Thee in all

---

61. Stefan Reif, *Judaism and Hebrew Prayer: New Perspectives on Jewish Liturgical History* (Cambridge, UK: Cambridge University Press, 1993), 77.
62. James R. Davila, "Liturgical Works from Qumran," *EDEJ* 890.
63. The fragments universally accepted are 4Q504 and 4Q506; the assignment of 4Q505 to this text is disputed.
64. Translation of the Dead Sea Scrolls are taken from Geza Vermes, *The Dead Sea Scrolls in English*, 2nd ed. (New York: Penguin, 1975).

Thy words and wickedly turned aside from every one. They heeded not Thy great power and therefore Thou didst reject them. For wickedness pleases Thee not, and the ungodly shall not be established before Thee. But in the time of Thy goodwill Thou didst choose for Thyself a people. Thou didst remember Thy Covenant and [granted] that they should be set apart for Thyself from among all the peoples as a holy thing. And Thou didst renew for them Thy Covenant (founded) on a glorious vision and the words of Thy Holy [Spirit], on the works of Thy hands and the writing of Thy Right Hand, that they might know the foundations of glory and the steps towards eternity.... [Thou didst raise up] for them a faithful shepherd.

Finally, 4QBerakot is described by Davila as "a liturgy for the sectarian covenant renewal ceremony that is summarized in the *Community Rule* (1QS 1–2)."[65] A portion of this text, 4Q286–287, reads:

council of the Community shall all say together, Amen, amen. Afterwards [they] shall damn Satan and all his guilty lot. They will answer and say, Cursed be [S]atan in his hostile design, and damned in his guilty dominion. Cursed be all the spirits of his [lo]t in their wicked design, and damned in their thoughts of unclean impurity. For they are the lot of darkness and their visitation is for eternal destruction.

That one should conclude that these prayers and other liturgical texts were intended merely as frameworks based on the practice in the Mishnah/Talmud seems unwarranted here as it does also in the Didache. Like the sectarian texts of the Dead Sea Scrolls, the community that generated the Didache felt the necessity to establish correct forms of their prayers and ritual texts, perhaps especially for gentile converts unfamiliar with Jewish practice.

The expectation that the recipients of the Didache will recite the given prayers verbatim is also in line with the comment in 10.7, where it appears that the prophets are the only ones with the authority to pray in any other way. Although Schwiebert argues here for the interpretation that the prophets are being allowed to pray "as long as they wish" in accord with the basic translation of ὅσα as referring to "extent not manner,"[66] τοῖς δὲ

---

65. Davila, "Liturgical Works from Qumran," 890; see also John J. Collins, "Dead Sea Scrolls," *ABD* 2:94.
66. Schwiebert, *Knowledge and the Coming Kingdom*, 92.

προφήταις ἐπιτρέπετε εὐχαριστεῖν ὅσα θέλουσιν, in my opinion, must be translated in accord with the other occurrences of this relative pronoun in Did. 1.2 and 11.11.

1.2 πάντα δὲ ὅσα ἐὰν θελήσῃς μὴ γίνεσθαί σοι καὶ σὺ ἄλλῳ μὴ ποίει

11.11 πᾶς δὲ προφήτης ... μὴ διδάσκων ... ποιεῖν ὅσα αὐτὸς ποιεῖ οὐ κριθήσεται ἐφ' ὑμῶν

Examples of such a translation for ὅσα are also seen in Mark 9:13 and Phil 4:8:

Mark 9:13 ἀλλὰ λέγω ὑμῖν ὅτι καὶ Ἠλίας ἐλήλυθεν καὶ ἐποίησαν αὐτῷ ὅσα ἤθελον καθὼς γέγραπται ἐπ' αὐτόν.

Phil 4:8 Τὸ λοιπόν ἀδελφοί ὅσα ἐστὶν ἀληθῆ ὅσα σεμνά ὅσα δίκαια ὅσα ἁγνά ὅσα προσφιλῆ ὅσα εὔφημα εἴ τις ἀρετὴ καὶ εἴ τις ἔπαινος ταῦτα λογίζεσθε

The meaning in these contexts, according to BDAG, is really "everything that, whatever" and even A. T. Robertson, citing Ludwig Rademacher (who cites Conybeare!), states that in Philo ὅσοι often is simply equivalent to οἵ.[67] Thus prophets who come into the community must be given the freedom to pray in whatever way they want. This freedom is not passed on, however, to community members at large, as indeed this *exception* for prophets indicates. Note that until the mention of prophets in 10.7, no other office of church leadership has been named.[68]

One last clue that supports seeing the prayers of the Didache as intended to be recited verbatim is the comparison of the version of the Lord's Prayer in the Didache with that of Matthew, a community many believe to be closely related to that of the Didache. Aside from the clos-

---

67. A. T. Robertson, *A Grammar of the Greek New Testament in the Light of Historical Research*, 2nd ed. (New York: Hodder & Stoughton; George H. Doran, 1915), 732, citing Ludwig Radermacher, *Neutestamentlich Grammatik: Das Griechisch des Neuen Testaments im Zusammenhang mit der Volkssprache*, HNT 1.1 (Tübingen: Mohr Siebeck, 1911), 63.

68. It is perhaps the case that the prophets in this context perform the same duty as that of the prayer leader within the community of the Jewish synagogue. On this, see Heinemann, *Prayer in the Talmud,* 16 passim.

ing doxology in the Didache, the two versions are extremely close, a sign that the community is concerned with the wording of this prayer (note that this prayer is to be recited by community members three times a day) and that they likely are equally concerned with the wording of the ones that follow.

Such rigid instructions from the creators of the Didache surely give us insight into the function of the text (at least at this stage in its development) as well as into the relationship between the community of origin and the community of reception. From the perspective of the originators at least, the two communities are not equal in status, nor are they identical in culture and background, and for those reasons the recipients cannot be relied upon to perform the central rituals of baptism, prayer, and Eucharist correctly. Indeed, in my opinion, the reason for the inscribing of the Two Ways and the various prayers is reflected in the very title of the Didache in 1.1: Διδαχὴ κυρίου διὰ τῶν δώδεκα ἀποστόλων τοῖς ἔθνεσιν. The text was created for use in gentile congregations where, from the point of view of the Jewish originators of the text, steps must be taken to ensure that these new converts are performing the necessary rituals correctly.[69] To the original "teaching," Did. 1.1–6.2 and 16, a later editor added (possibly 6.3 and) 7.1–11.2 and repurposed the text into a manual on how to conduct the two most important community rituals, baptism and Eucharist. In this sense, rather than "de-" and "recontextualization," it may be better to see the sources incorporated into the Didache as "transcontextualization," that is, the transmission of a text from one community to another for use in identical situations.

In conclusion, one must of course acknowledge the fact that the Didache was a text created in a culture still very much oriented toward oral communication and consequently that the characteristics of oral performance must be taken into consideration in any study of its composition and function. Nonetheless, one must also carefully distinguish between texts of different genres/functions. The preliminary comparison offered here between the traditions of the Didache and the prayer and ritual materials from the Dead Sea Scrolls and Mishnah surely demonstrates the need for a deeper investigation of the transmission of ritual materials within

---

69. For arguments supporting the theory that the second, longer title of the Didache was original to the text, see Pardee, *Genre and Development of the Didache*, 101–25.

Second Temple and rabbinic Judaism, nascent Christianity, and the wider Greco-Roman world.[70]

---

70. A brief look into the Greek magical papyri, e.g., shows that οὕτως can be used to introduce incantations; see PGM IV.937, 977, 2572 (cf. Did. 7.1; 8.2; 9.1; 10.1). The question of indicators of verbatim recitation would be a necessary avenue of investigation.

From the Sermon on the Mount to the Didache

John W. Welch

In spite of numerous meticulous studies over the past century and a half, many issues concerning the Didache's origins still remain puzzling and unsettled.[1] If the wide array of approaches and conclusions found recently in several superb publications is any indication, no clear consensus is close at hand about the nature and setting of this very significant but generally overlooked early Christian text. Reflecting on these vigorous debates, I hope to contribute to the wider discussion of the character of the Didache by looking anew at its relationship to the Sermon on the Mount in Matt 5–7. In the end I am inclined to see the Didache as consciously drawing on, carefully selecting from, and purposefully transforming many elements from the Sermon on the Mount (= SM). If this observation has merit, these transmutations reveal much about the main trajectories of the Didache not only by helping readers to focus on what is said and done in that text, but perhaps even more importantly by drawing attention to what it omits from the SM.

The following analysis proceeds in several steps. First, it is beyond dispute that the SM and the Didache have many words and phrases in common, indeed so many that it would not appear that these texts were independent compositions coming from a common oral or shared communal source. Indeed, according to Seidel's law,[2] eleven inverted word

---

1. See, for example, Huub van de Sandt and Jürgen K. Zangenberg, eds., *Matthew, James, and Didache: Three Related Documents in Their Jewish and Christian Settings*, SBLSymS 45 (Atlanta: Society of Biblical Literature, 2008); Kurt Niederwimmer, *The Didache: A Commentary*, trans. Linda M. Maloney, Hermeneia (Minneapolis: Fortress, 1998).

2. Moshe Seidel, "Parallels between Isaiah and Psalms," in *Hiqrei Miqra* (Jerusalem: Rav Kook Institute, 1978), 1–97 (Hebrew), discussed further below.

orders substantiate a direct relationship between these two texts, and thus it follows either that the SM has drawn upon the Didache or that the Didache has drawn upon the SM. Primarily on thematic grounds, I next argue that it is more likely that the Didache has made use of the SM rather than vice versa, inasmuch as the SM makes heavy use of the Psalms and other temple-related material, whereas the Didache does not, as it moves in other directions. Looking at such subjects as law, ethics, ritual, temple, and eschatology, it then appears that the Didache has reworked the SM for use by "templeless" Christians in general and among gentile Christians in particular. Finally, all this aligns with the idea that some version of the SM existed prior to its use in the Gospel of Matthew, a point that also is consistent with the use of material from the SM throughout the New Testament in ways that are similar to uses of the SM in the Didache.

1. Similarities between the SM and the Didache

In making a comprehensive comparison of these two texts, it is helpful to begin with a careful listing of the main points at which they coincide. Appendix 1 lists in a straightforward manner words, phrases, and distinctive concepts or elements common to both of these texts.[3] The overlaps are remarkable in several ways.

First, the number of congruencies is high, perhaps higher than even most serious readers might have surmised. Appendix 1 is over one hundred entry lines long, an extraordinarily high number of intertextual connections gauged by any standard of comparison between two relatively short texts. Moreover, there does not appear to be any other text that compares with the SM more extensively than does the Didache, and no known text compares with the Didache more frequently than does the SM.

Second, the points of intersection shown on appendix 1 are found consistently throughout most sections of the SM, running sometimes nearly verse by verse. Conversely, although not quite to the same degree of uniformity, words and phrases in the SM can also be found throughout the Didache from beginning to end and in almost every chapter. Appendix 1 associates twenty-one SM elements with words in Did. 1 alone. With the exception of chapters 7 and 13, SM elements can be linked to all other

---

3. Working with the text in Aaron Milavec, *The Didache: Text, Translation, Analysis, and Commentary* (Collegeville, MN: Liturgical Press, 2003).

chapters in the Didache: chapter 2 (three times), chapter 3 (ten times), chapter 4 (eight times), chapter 5 (seven times), chapter 6 (two times), chapter 8 (twelve times), chapter 9 (two times), chapter 10 (three times), chapter 11 (nine times), chapter 12 (three times), chapter 14 (three times), chapter 15 (two times), and chapter 16 (fourteen times). This degree of mutual overlap points to a full-ranging familiarity between these two texts.

While these linkages are not all equally indicative, many are quite strong. On twenty-nine occasions, marked by equal signs on appendix 1, the Greek is identical. On many other occasions the Greek is nearly the same. In six instances, for example, the congruence is quite distinctive and precise: Matt 5:26/Did. 1.5 (about not coming out of prison until you have paid the last κοδράντην); 5:39–42/1.4 (about not returning evil with evil); 5:44/1.3 (blessing and praying for those who oppose you); 6:9–13/8.2 (the Lord's Prayer); 7:6/9.5 (not giving the holy to the dogs); and 7:12/1.2 (positive and negative versions of the golden rule). Interestingly, these passages appear in the SM in chapters 5, 6, and 7. Except for the Lord's Prayer (which stands roughly at the centers of both the SM and the Didache) and the saying of the Lord about not giving "the holy thing to the dogs" (both of which are attributed to the Lord explicitly in Did. 8.2 and 9.5, respectively), the other four of these main passages appear in the opposite order in these two texts: The elements in Matt 5:27, 5:39–42, 5:44, and 7:12 appear in Did. 1.5, 1.4, 1.3, and 1.2, respectively. While much more has been said and remains yet to be said about the intriguing and compelling similarities between these two texts, it is the overall density and structural arrangement of these textual intersections that have not been previously detected or discussed, this last point about reversed ordering in particular.

2. Inverted Quotations

In addition to arguments made by others to support the dependence of the Didache on the SM, I draw attention to eleven instances of inversions that occur when texts in the SM and the Didache are verbally related to each other. Beyond the sequence mentioned above, these eleven other reversals are evident, as indicated in appendix 1 by the term "inverting."

	Sermon on the Mount		Didache
5:15	men do not light/lamp	16.1	lamps/not quenched
5:21–22	murder/anger	3.2	anger/murder
5:40	tunic/cloak	1.4C	cloak/tunic

5:41	someone/you/compels	1.4B	compels/you/someone
5:43	love all/hate enemy	2.7	not hate anyone/love all
5:45	father/on all	1.5	on all/father
5:47	if you love only/what special	1.3C	what favor/if you love only
6:3	left not know what/right gives	12.1	give with understanding right/left
7:11	give/ask	1.5	ask/give
7:12	do/to them	1.2	to others/do not do
7:13–14	way of destruction/life	1.1	way of life/death

Initially, Moshe Seidel located 110 examples of inverted quotations between the book of Isaiah and the Psalms, with additional instances involving inverted parallels between Isaiah and Proverbs, and Micah and the Pentateuch.[4] According to Seidel's law, as it has come to be known, when Hebraic texts draw on earlier texts, they tend to invert the order of the terms found in the earlier text.[5] While this principle does not operate as an iron law and must be controlled sufficiently,[6] with adequate controls one can reach meaningful conclusions. As Shemaryahu Talmon has wisely stressed in analyzing a number of such examples within biblical and rabbinic literature, the process of identifying these reversals is primarily descriptive in nature, one without inherent prescriptive force, and therefore the appraisal of these remote parallels will "depend to some extent on the sensibility of the individual scholar, and of his readers, to such literary intricacies."[7] Proceeding cautiously, Talmon went on to conclude that the employment of this stylistic and structural tool "underlines the deep-seated effect this technique had on biblical literature in the 'creative' and the 'recension-

---

4. As tallied by Isaac Kalimi, *The Reshaping of Ancient Israelite History in Chronicles* (Winona Lake, IN: Eisenbrauns, 2005), 233, n. 8.

5. Seidel, "Parallels between Isaiah and Psalms." For numerous additional examples of Seidel's law, see Kalimi, *Reshaping of Ancient Israelite History*, 232–74; Pancratius C. Beentjes, "Inverted Quotations in the Bible: A Neglected Stylistic Matter," *Bib* 63 (1982): 506–23; Shemaryahu Talmon, "The Textual Study of the Bible: A New Outlook," in *Qumran and the History of the Biblical Text*, ed. Frank M. Cross and Shemaryahu Talmon (Cambridge, MA: Harvard University Press, 1975), 358–80; Bernard M. Levinson, *Deuteronomy and the Hermeneutics of Legal Innovation* (New York: Oxford University Press, 1997), 18–20, 35; Karl William Weyde, *Prophecy and Teaching* (Berlin: de Gruyter, 2000), 121–22; Marc Z. Brettler, "Jud 1,1–2,10: From Appendix to Prologue," *ZAW* 101 (1989): 433.

6. Levinson, *Deuteronomy and the Hermeneutics of Legal Innovation*, 18 n. 51.

7. Talmon, "Textual Study of the Bible," 362–63.

ist' stages" and beyond.[8] In his 1982 article, Pancratius Beentjes in turn identified inverted quotations occurring over a range of interrelated texts, indicating that this practice was widespread and commonly recognized. He analyzed eleven cases of texts within the Hebrew Bible being inversely quoted in other passages within the Hebrew Bible (instances come from Genesis, Leviticus, Numbers, Deuteronomy, Psalms, Isaiah, Micah, Ezekiel, Haggai, Zechariah, and Jonah), seven cases of Sirach quoting from Exodus, 1 Samuel, Job, Proverbs, or Malachi, and five instances of New Testament texts in Romans, 1 Corinthians, and Mark inverting word orders in Isaiah, Hosea, or 1 Kings.[9] From this, he concludes, "It is hard to avoid the impression that [ancient authors created these inversions] *on purpose*," thereby drawing "a moment of extra attention in the listener (or reader), because the latter hears something else than the traditional words."[10] Most recently, Isaac Kalami has discussed 106 instances of chiasmus between parallel texts quoted in Chronicles from the books of Samuel and Kings, from which he deduced that these word orders had been reversed so as "to stress a word, name, or phrase that appeared in the earlier text or to render it more prominent."[11]

In the case of judging the relationship between the SM and the Didache, the frequency, concentration, location, and verbal similarities of their eleven inverted quotations objectively strengthen the hypothesis that either the Didache is consciously quoting or drawing upon the SM or the SM is quoting or drawing upon the Didache. Comparing these examples with those detected by Seidel, Talmon, Beentjes, and Kalami, these inverted quotations are amply numerous, are verbally precise, are drawn only between these two texts and not from widely scattered sources, and are for the more part tightly clustered within the first segment of the Didache. While it is true that the large majority of the linkages or allusions between the SM and the Didache do not involve inverted quotations

---

8. Ibid., 368. On its ongoing "impact," see 371 and 381. The writers at Qumran also considered inversion "a legitimate quotation technique," 378.

9. Beentjes, "Inverted Quotations in the Bible," 506–23.

10. Pancratius C. Beentjes, "Discovering a New Path of Intertextuality: Inverted Quotations and Their Dynamics," in *Literary Structure and Rhetorical Strategy in the Hebrew Bible*, ed. Lénart de Regt, J. de Waard, and Jan P. Fokkelman (Assen: Van Gorcum, 1996), 49 (emphasis original).

11. Kalami, *Reshaping of Ancient Israelite History*, 232.

or allusions, having eleven such reversals is more than insignificant[12] and points to a case of intertextuality that is more than accidental.

Although the question remains open to further debate, it seems more likely for several reasons (structural, sequential, logical, linguistic, dependent, and thematic) that the Didache is quoting the SM rather than vice versa. Structurally, the tight order of borrowing in Did. 1.5, 1.4, 1.3, and 1.2 would seem more likely to be a conscious inversion of passages scattered from Matt 5:27–7:12 than for the SM to have taken this series and diffused it throughout the SM. Sequentially, Did. 16.1 presumes that people have already lit their lamps, as commanded in Matt 5:16. Logically, the assertion that anger leads to murder in Did. 3.2, while natural enough, is used to explain or motivate the command "do not become angry" (μὴ γίνου ὀργίλος). But, because not all anger leads to homicide, this passage would rationally seem to be a truncation of the more clearly motivated statement in Matt 5:22 that anyone who becomes angry (ὀργιζόμενος) with a brother is already in danger of judgment. Linguistically, the word order in Matt 5:41 is a more natural word order than that in Did. 1.4B. Dependently, when Did. 2.7 (which seems tacked onto the rule "do not plan evil against your neighbor") begins with the blanket injunction "do not hate any man" (οὐ μισήσεις πάντα ἄνθρωπον), along with the eventuality that "concerning others you will pray," all this seems to depend on and to take for granted the teachings about loving and praying for one's neighbor in Matt 5:43–44. As will be developed next below, this is also thematic.

3. Differences between the SM and the Didache

Assuming *arguendo* that the Didache is drawing upon and modifying the SM, it proves productive to notice what themes the Didache has omitted or transmuted from the SM and then to ask why those changes or deletions may have been made. Many elements in the SM have not been retained in the Didache, and these seem to come from a single domain. Easily recognizable words and phrases on such a missing-pieces list include: receiving mercy (ἐλεηθήσονται); sons of God (υἱοὶ θεοῦ); rejoicing (χαίρετε)

---

12. Kalami (*Reshaping of Ancient Israelite History*, 232) finds significance even though the number of inverted quotations in Chronicles "is small" compared with "the total number of texts copied [by Chronicles] in the order in which they appear in the books of Samuel–Kings."

and shouting hallelujah (ἀγαλλιᾶσθε; Pss 5:11; 32:11); salt (ἅλας); being a light to the world to bring glory to God (δοξάσωσιν τὸν πατέρα); the lampstand (ἐπὶ τὴν λυχνίαν; the word for the menorah in Exod 25); the altar (θυσιαστήριον, the term commonly used for the altar of the temple); swearing oaths (Ps 50:5, 14; Num 30); God's throne (Ps 11:4); the city of the great king (Ps 48:2); white hair (τρίχα λευκήν; Lev 13:2–10); sun and rain bestowed by God on the earth (Pss 84:11; 147:8); giving in the secret place (ἐν τῷ κρυπτῷ); sounding of trumpets at the time of prayer (Pss 81:3; 105:3); praying where God sees and hears (1 Kgs 8:33); there obtaining forgiveness (1 Kgs 8:34); anointing, washing, treasuring up treasures (θησαυρίζετε ... θησαυροὺς); being pure (ἁπλοῦς) and full of light (Ps 139:12); serving (δουλεύειν) and cleaving unto (ἀνθέξεται) the Lord alone; trusting the Lord to give necessities (Ps 23:1); spinning (νήθουσιν; used ten times in Exod 26–39); glorious garments (ἐνδύματα; Pss 93:1; 104:1); entering a sacred gate (πύλης; Pss 24:4–7; 118:19–20); an archetypal tree of life and goodness (Ps 1:1–3); the wise man (φρόνιμος; Ps 94:8); and being founded upon the rock (ἐπὶ τὴν πέτραν; Judg 13:19; Ps 27:5); as well as the mention of symbolic actions portraying punishments or the ridding of impurities, facing judgment of the συνέδριον, casting away an offending right hand, being trampled underfoot, or being torn in pieces.

Significantly, the list of SM features absent from the Didache is rich in elements that reflect temple themes,[13] as is particularly apparent when these words and practices are characteristically found in the Psalms and other texts that are at home in the temple or tabernacle. Indeed, of the 383 words in the total vocabulary of the SM, one-third of them cast a long temple shadow.[14]

Thus it may be argued that the Didache has systematically eliminated these temple elements altogether or has reduced them to ordinary community rules or daily ethical teachings. This fact about the rhetorical register of the SM leads to many interesting implications, but for present purposes it is to be noted that most of the words in the SM that are most

---

13. On temple themes, see Margaret Barker, *Temple Theology* (London: SPCK, 2004); *Temple Themes in Christian Worship* (London: T&T Clark, 2007); John W. Welch, *The Sermon on the Mount in the Light of the Temple* (London: Ashgate, 2009), 42–45.

14. Each of these elements in the SM and the points discussed below are analyzed and documented from a temple perspective in Welch, *Sermon on the Mount*, 41–182, with the word list regarding the temple register of the SM charted on pages 184–87.

obviously connected with the temple are absent from the Didache or have been resituated for use in what appears to be a community that is without the temple or has distanced itself from the temple.

From the outset, gone from the Didache is any mention of going up into the mountain or any sacred space, the mountain being a thinly veiled allusion to Moses going up into Mount Sinai (Exod 19:3, 20; 24:9) and also to the righteous ascending into the temple, the mountain of the Lord, in Jerusalem (Ps 24:3).

The Didache never promises (at least not in so many words) that the righteous will inherit any heavenly or divine reward. Missing are the exalted blessings of the macarisms, which twice (functioning as an *inclusio*) promise to the righteous the kingdom of the heavens. The future and celestially oriented beatitudes of the SM are replaced with two simple remnants: "be meek, for the meek will inherit the earth" (Did. 3.7), promising a terrestrial reward, and the rule to "be/become merciful" (Did. 3.8), which carries no promise at all, whether present or eschatological. Absent are the blessings of receiving mercy (readily understood as the particular blessing of the mercy-seat), seeing God (a privilege usually reserved for those who enter the holy of holies; Pss 17:5; 63:2), and becoming sons of God (as kings are called who have been anointed in the temple; Ps 2:7; Deut 14:1). The cursing, persecution, and slander by other Jews or enemies, which only makes the followers of Jesus more like the holy prophets of former times, is reduced in the Didache to hatred, persecution, and betrayals by or among the false prophets in the last times (Did. 16.4).

Gone in the Didache is the shouting of hallelujah (so characteristic of cultic joy) and so is any reference to being the salt for the earth (or, as Mark 9:49 understood, the salt of the covenant), along with the drastic consequences of the defilement of failed discipleship, namely being cast out, banned, trodden under foot, in danger of God's judgment and hell fire, or torn in pieces. Lacking is the strong theme of the light of God and of the temple (much is said about light in the SM, but nothing in the Didache). The light on the mountain that, like the light of the Lord, cannot be hid in the SM becomes in the Didache a flicker of a personal lamp, as in the parable of the ten virgins, that one must take care to keep lit (16.1). When the SM talks about putting one's lamp on a candlestick, the word used there is λυχνία, the word that the Septuagint uses for the menorah, concentrated nine times inside of only six verses in the instructions in Exod 25 about building the tabernacle and its utensils and implements. This idea is absent from the Didache.

The Decalogue (which was read twice a day in the temple and is quoted three times in the SM with an overt reference to its ancient origins) is never invoked as such in the Didache, which begins its list of twenty-three vices with prohibitions against murder and adultery. In the Didache, however, these prohibitions are stated, in connection with preparing a candidate for baptism, in a future tense (you *will* not murder; you *will* not be double-tongued) rather than as imperatives.

The centrally important altar of the temple is still mentioned in the SM, but it is not remembered in the Didache, in which the offering had become an immaterial sacrifice through the Eucharist, which retains some temple terminology but is placed in a setting removed from its native rock. The requirement in Matt 5:24 of private reconciliation prior to sacrifice at the altar takes on the additional requirement of prior confession before the congregation (προσεξομολογησάμενοι) in Did. 14.1.

The concern in the Didache is only with false oaths, not with oaths that invoke improperly the holy name of God, his heavenly throne, or his holy city. The Didache's concern with fasting, which appears in the cultic instructions of Matt 6:16–18, is only worried about the days on which one should fast (Did. 6.16), and its only functional application has been moved into the section on praying for one's enemies and fasting for one's persecutors (Did. 1.3).

The goodness of God and the temple, which blesses the entire world with sun, rain, and good gifts to those who ask in the SM is reduced in the Didache to an injunction for fathers to support their children (Did. 4.9). Being perfect (τέλειος) no longer relates to being like God (or completely initiated into the holy mystery), but simply bearing the whole yoke of God's burden, or at least carrying as much as one can bear (Did. 6.2).

Absent are many creation elements that can be found throughout the SM, such as letting there be light, marriage, and divorce (what God put together in Eden); trees distinguished by their fruits (with the tree of life symbolized in the temple); or the thorns and thistles (an allusion in the SM to the thorns and thistles that resulted from the fall of Adam and Eve). The act of creation that is important for the Didache (in Did. 1.2) is God's creation (or re-creation) of the individual convert, not the creation of heaven and earth.

Gone is any instruction about giving in secret, praying in secret, or fasting in secret, or to God seeing in secret and rewarding when all things shall be revealed. Obtaining forgiveness, another crucial temple theme that was of the essence in the atonement sacrifices of the temple, is minimized. Lacking also are continued washing and anointing of ritual significance, as well as consecrating treasures to a heavenly treasury (the temple being an earthly repository of the divine storehouse).

Loving God (Did. 1.2) is given prominence at the outset of the Didache, but the reference to serving (δουλεύειν) the Lord alone as a servant, slave, or temple servant has been dropped. In Did. 9.2 and 10.3, Jesus is presented as a son or boy (παῖς) of God, not as a servant.

In Did. 10.3 the righteous are promised food and drink, but only in a eucharistic context, while the SM in Matt 6:25–34 promises that true disciples will be given care and sustenance beyond food and drink, including garments more glorious than Solomon's. In the Didache there is no promise of clothing of any kind, let alone royal or priestly vestments better than Solomon's.

False prophets in the Didache are not known by their fruits (their results) as in Matt 7:16 (καρπῶν), but by their habits (τρόπων; 11.8), such as whether they stay in the community longer than two or three days. The former requirement of giving of the typical first fruits to the temple has now become the giving of first fruits of bread, wine, oil, silver, or cloth to the prophets in the community (Did. 13.5–7), who are even identified in a nontemple setting as high priests (Did. 13.3).

The climactic objective of the SM is to allow the disciple to find the narrow gate and enter (εἰσελεύσεται) into the heavenly kingdom, qualified to be admitted by the Lord into the holy presence on that final day. The objective of the Didache is quite different, to allow the faithful to withstand the burnings as they watch from the world below as the Lord comes atop the clouds of heaven (Did. 16.8).

In the process of removing or recasting the temple elements in the SM, it is also interesting to note that the Didache appears to have consistently left out almost all of the words or phrases that appear to have been drawn in the SM from the Psalms, which were the hymns of the temple in Jerusalem. The strong presence of psalmodic phraseology in the SM is significant, because the temple is the dominant factor in the Psalms. As people ascended to the temple, they sang the Psalms: psalms of joy, penitence, prayer, and praise. The Psalms were chanted in the temple by Levitical cantors, were repeated by dispersed Jews yearning for the temple, and were sung by families giving thanks for the blessings of God and of his temple. In the ears of Jewish listeners, several words from the Psalms would have accented the SM's temple register.

For example, the word μακάριοι ("blessed") in the SM is also the first word in Ps 1:1, and it goes on to appear twenty-five more times in the Psalms, but only once in the Didache and on that occasion in a rather mundane setting and without any mention of a heavenly reward. The words "filled" and "righteousness" stand together in Ps 17:15 as they do in Matt 5:6, and the words "pure in heart" in "blessed are the pure in heart" clearly come from Ps 24, which has been thought of as a statement of worthiness to enter the temple. But neither of these are included in the Didache. In Ps 32:11 is found a double call: "Be glad in the Lord, and rejoice [ἀγαλλιᾶσθε]!" A double call ("rejoice and be exceeding glad") is also in Matt 5:12, using the same word that is used so often in the Psalms (ἀγαλλιᾶσθε; "hallelujah"). The warning in Matt 7:6 ("lest they trample [your pearls] under their feet, and turn again and rend you") echoes Ps 50:22 ("lest I rend and there be none to deliver"). The distinctive phrase "depart you workers of ἀνομίαν" in Matt 7:23 comes straight from Ps 6:8 ("Depart from me all ye workers of iniquity [ἀνομίαν]"). Psalm 94:8 contrasts the wise man and the foolish man using the same root words (φρονίμῳ and μωρῷ) found in Matt 7:24–26.

Yet none of these psalmic elements are found in the Didache. Only two direct links to the Psalms are arguably reflected in the Didache: the clearest is the promise that the "meek shall inherit the earth," found both in Matt 5:5 and Did. 3.7, which comes from Ps 37:11; and the other is the reference to the two ways in Did. 1.1, which seems to come from Ps 1:1, although less directly so than does the double reference to the two divergent ways in Matt 7:13–14. In the SM, the "way" is mentioned twice: the wide way (ὁδός) that leads to destruction (εἰς τὴν ἀπώλειαν) and the narrow way (ὁδός) that leads to life (εἰς τὴν ζωήν). Likewise, a double occurrence of "way" is found in Ps 1:6, which reads: "the Lord knows the way [ὁδός] of righteousness, but the way [ὁδός] of the wicked will perish." While Did. 1.1, like the book of Psalms, commences with the idea of the Two Ways, the Didache simply takes it as an already understood and formulaically conceptualized axiom that "there are two ways [ὁδοί δύο εἰσί]: one of life [ζωῆς] and one of death [θανάτου]," not repeating the previously double-mentioned word ὁδός.

4. Considerations with Chronological Implications

Might then these fundamental differences between the SM and the Didache help in analyzing when the Didache may have been written? Whereas the

SM makes clear sense in a Jewish context that still accepts the importance of temple imagery, phraseology, and themes, the Didache has removed or repurposed those elements to apply in another context. This development can be seen and substantiated by considering what the Didache says and does not say about the law, ethics, ritual, and eschatology.

Regarding the use of the law, the SM has not separated itself from the law of Moses. Just as the Ten Commandments and the Covenant Code function in Exod 19–24 as the stipulations comprising the substance of the treaty-covenant between Yahweh and the house of Israel, so the legal contents of the SM define the elements of the restored covenant renewed on this occasion between God and the followers of Jesus. Hence, this section in the SM has rightly been compared by Roland Deines "to the preamble of a new treaty that relates what will be in force from now on but based on an existing foundation. No hints in the text indicate that this verse needs to be understood as a demand for a special Law-observant piety."[15] Law in the SM is based on the Decalogue, which was read twice a day "in the Temple, together with the *Shemaʿ* prayer, close to the time of the offering of the Daily Offering,"[16] and the Decalogue may also be seen as a list of negative confessions required for admission into the temple.[17] The Didache, however, has gone over to the more characteristic Hellenistic practice of listing long strings of virtues and vices,[18] a practice that is more at home in Greek ethical discourse and rhetorical polemic than in a temple context where commandments revealing the will of God are of the essence.

Regarding ethics, the sources of ethical authority that stand at the foundation of the temple include divine lawgiving, charisma, covenantal cohesion, group identity, individual commitment, honor and shame, and threats of adverse consequences and exclusion for those who fail to live up to their obligations. All of these are strongly present in the SM with Jesus

---

15. Roland Deines, "Not the Law but the Messiah: Law and Righteousness in the Gospel of Matthew—An Ongoing Debate," in *Built upon the Rock: Studies in the Gospel of Matthew*, ed. Daniel M. Gurtner and John Nolland (Grand Rapids: Eerdmans, 2007), 75.

16. Moshe Weinfeld, "The Decalogue: Its Significance, Uniqueness, and Place in Israel's Tradition," in *Religion and Law: Biblical Judaic and Islamic Perspectives*, ed. Edwin R. Firmage, Bernard G. Weiss, and John W. Welch (Winona Lake, IN: Eisenbrauns, 1990), 3–47 (34).

17. Moshe Weinfeld, "Instructions for Temple Visitors in the Bible and in Ancient Egypt," *ScrHier* 28 (1982): 224–50.

18. See John T. Fitzgerald, "Virtue/Vice Lists," *ABD* 6:857–59.

standing as a new Moses,[19] with charismatic delivery (Matt 7:29), commissioning, group loyalty (no anger with a brother), commitment (seek you first the kingdom of God), honor and shame (shall be the least in the kingdom of heaven), and threats of expulsion, casting out, cutting off, and being trampled underfoot. While some of these elements are preserved in the rabbinical *giyyur* ritual for the admission of proselytes (e.g., b. Yebam. 47a–b),[20] they are largely absent even from the prebaptismal ritual instructions of the Didache. The ethical core of the Didache is to be found in one's conformance with a way of daily life dominated by negative injunctions regarding things to be avoided.

Ritual also has been modified from the SM to the Didache, although perhaps less so than law and ethics. Indeed, there is reason to believe that the most likely ritual use of the SM would have been connected with its role as an "early Christian catechetical instruction to new converts."[21] Hans Dieter Betz and others have marshaled considerable evidence that the SM is precisely the kind of document that would have been used as a cultic text or to instruct or remind baptismal candidates of required rules of Christian conduct.[22] In much the same vein, the Didache explicitly requires that candidates for baptism must be given the training in Did. 1–6 before they can be immersed "in the name of the Father, and of the Son, and of the Holy Ghost, in living [or flowing; ζῶντι] water" (Did. 7.1). But the Didache goes on in a different vein to give handbook-like instructions regarding further rituals, such as fasting, praying, the Eucharist, teaching, presiding, and making first-fruit offerings that go organizationally well beyond these communitarian requirements set forth in the SM.

---

19. Dale C. Allison Jr., *The New Moses: A Matthean Typology* (Minneapolis: Fortress, 1993); John D. Lierman, *The New Testament Moses: Christian Perceptions of Moses and Israel in the Setting of the Jewish* Religion, WUNT 2/173 (Tübingen: Mohr Siebeck, 2004).

20. See Avi Sagi and Zvi Zohar, "The Halakhic Ritual of Giyyur and Its Symbolic Meaning," *JRitSt* 9 (1995): 1–13; see also David Daube, "A Baptismal Catechism," in *The New Testament and Rabbinic Judaism* (London: University of London, 1956), 106–40.

21. Andrej Kodjak, *A Structural Analysis of the Sermon on the Mount* (Berlin: de Gruyter, 1986), 16.

22. Hans D. Betz, *Essays on the Sermon on the Mount*, trans. Lawrence L. Welborn (Philadelphia: Fortress, 1985), 55–70; W. D. Davies, *The Sermon on the Mount* (Cambridge: Cambridge University Press, 1966), 105–6; Joachim Jeremias, *Sermon on the Mount*, trans. Norman Perrin (Philadelphia: Fortress, 1963), 22–23.

Likewise, the eschatology of the SM deals almost entirely with one's personal preparation to face the final judgment, to be forgiven by God as one has forgiven, to be condemned in that day as one has condemned others, and to receive a willing reception by the Lord on the condition that one has done the will of the Father and has personally built upon the rock by hearing and doing the teachings of righteousness that lead to the narrow gate. Judging (κρίνω) is a common theme of the temple, particularly divine judgment. God's judgment is found in several places in the SM, and one encounters this theme often in the Old Testament as well, most elaborately in the Psalms, where God is affirmed as the sole rightful judge of the world: "The Lord judges the peoples; judge me, O Lord, according to my righteousness" (Pss 7:8; 35:24). In God's appearance, he "has made himself known, he has executed judgment" (Ps 9:16; see also Pss 9:8, 19; 10:5; 50:4, 6; 58:1, 11; 72:1–2; 82:8; 96:13; 98:9; 103:6), which brings joy to his people and the whole earth (Pss 67:4; 96:12–13). In a temple-centered worldview, God is solely the rightful and righteous judge of all mankind. Any other forms of judgment are likely flawed and presumptuous, and thus one should take care not to be judgmental. Moreover, it was thoroughly understood in Second Temple Judaism that the temple was the premier place where God's righteous judgment was found. There God dispensed judgment, seated on his throne or mercy seat: "Thou hast sat on the throne giving righteous judgment" (Ps 9:4); "righteousness and justice are the foundation of thy throne" (Pss 89:14; 97:2). These judgments of the temple are both personal (Ps 7:8) and cosmic.[23] In the Didache, however, the eschatological concerns have shifted away from the operation of case-by-case judgment and more toward the cataclysm of universal fire and destruction that will occur when the world-deceiver will come as if he were a son of God, after which the Lord will come with his holy ones and the world will see him coming (16.1–8). The worldview of the SM, according to which the temple rock (the Shetiyyah stone) that held at bay the destructive waters from the deep below and the torrents of rain from above (see Ps 93:1–5), had already yielded in the Didache to an apocalyptic view of the destruction of the wicked world by fire. If by the time of the Didache the temple was distant or perhaps even gone, another model

---

23. The little apocalypse in Isa 24–27 presents a revelation of the mystery of judgment: it portended the collapse of the world, the removal of the veil of mortality, the revelation of the glory of God, the restoration of the earth, its renewal and recreation. Margaret Barker, "Isaiah," *ECB* 516–17.

of the end times was needed to take its place, ensuring the complete parting of the ways between temple Judaism and Christianity in terms of law, ethics, and eschatology.

Thus, while several things carry over from the SM into the Didache (most noticeably being merciful, avoiding anger and lust, turning the other cheek, loving one's enemies, praying the Lord's Prayer, guarding holy things, following the way of life, and being wary of false prophets), those elements are retained in the Didache as social and local congregational concerns. What then can explain the elimination or transmutation of the many elements that were no longer seen as useful by the Didachist? The loss of or removal from the temple would seem to be the obvious answer. The Didache is an effort to construct a "templeless" Christianity. Sooner or later Christianity came to redefine itself after its loss of the temple, as even more so did Judaism.

This view would thus see the SM as stemming from a time when Jesus or his followers were still hoping for a cleansing, restoration, reformation, and rejuvenation of the temple, not its destruction or obsolescence.[24] In looking for the temple to be a house of prayer, Jesus affirmed the "legitimacy of its function" and desired "to see that function restored,"[25] but this view problematized "the parting of the ways" between Jews and Christians, making it a longer and more complicated process than one might otherwise have expected.[26] As Huub van de Sandt has rightly summarized, it was "a gradual process of dissimilarity and definition,"[27] and

---

24. As argued and explored in Welch, *Sermon on the Mount*, 210–19. On the prominent role played by the temple in the Gospel of Matthew, see David M. Gurtner, "Matthew's Theology of the Temple and the 'Parting of the Ways,'" in *Built upon the Rock: Studies in the Gospel of Matthew*, ed. Daniel M. Gurtner and John Nolland (Grand Rapids: Eerdmans, 2007), 128–53. On Jesus's attitudes toward the temple in their cultural, cultic, and noneschatological contexts, see Bruce Chilton, *The Temple of Jesus: His Sacrificial Program within a Cultural History of Sacrifice* (University Park: Pennsylvania State University Press, 1992), 137–54; Jostein Ådna, *Jesu Stellung zum Tempel: Die Tempelaktion und das Tempelwort als Ausdruck seiner messianischen Sendung*, WUNT 2/119 (Tübingen: Mohr Siebeck, 2000).

25. Gurtner, "Matthew's Theology of the Temple," 138.

26. Showing that the separation of Christianity from Judaism was a slow and complex process with the temple being the key issue that distinguished the various Jewish sects and movements, see Richard J. Bauckham, "The Parting of the Ways: What Happened and Why," *ST* 47 (1993): 135–51.

27. Huub van de Sandt, "Introduction," in *Matthew and the Didache*, ed. Huub van de Sandt (Assen: Van Gorcum; Minneapolis: Fortress, 2005), 1–9 (3).

as Richard Bauckham has seminally stated, that parting required Christians to redefine "the covenant people so as to include Gentiles," to recast the law so that gentile converts "were not obligated to keep the whole law," and to reshape "monotheism to include Christology." But perhaps most difficult of all, Christians had to transfigure the temple, which "was the greatest, the most meaningful boundary-marker between Jew and Gentile."[28] This is the transformation one can see occurring in the shift from the SM to the Didache. As Bauckham explains, Christians, who saw their community as the eschatological temple, could either choose to maintain close ties to the temple while it stood or see that temple as no longer relevant.[29] In my view, the SM comes from those of the former persuasion regarding close temple ties, while the Didache stems from the latter view of temple irrelevancy. Thus, although we differ in other respects, I see Bas ter Haar Romeny correct in observing that the SM and the Didache have arisen out of "diametrically opposed circumstances."[30] In the words of Joseph Verheyden, by the time of the Didache "there was no need any more for the Didache to ponder about the destruction of the Temple,"[31] or, I would add, any inclination to perpetuate any of the temple's now unavailable functions.

5. Concluding Observations

While the foregoing points suggest that the Didache has drawn upon the SM, this need not mean that the Didache must be dated after the destruction of the temple in 70 CE, for even if the Gospel of Matthew was composed after the destruction of the temple, it is possible that the SM predates the final composition of the Gospel of Matthew. If it is true, as Betz has argued, that the SM draws heavily on a pre-Matthean text, then the Didache may have done likewise. Although this point remains highly debatable, Betz and others have pointed out that the SM is in some

---

28. Bauckham, "Parting of the Ways," 142–43.
29. Ibid., 144.
30. Bas ter Haar Romeny, "Hypotheses on the Development of Judaism and Christianity in Syria in the Period after 70 CE," in van de Sandt, *Matthew and the Didache*, 41.
31. Joseph Verheyden, "Eschatology in the Didache and the Gospel of Matthew," in van de Sandt, *Matthew and the Didache*, 212.

ways quite un-Matthean and in most ways pre-Matthean.[32] Speaking of the puzzling passage about not giving the holy thing to the dogs, Betz sees this mysterious mandate as "part of the pre-Matthean SM."[33] While the version of the SM finally found in the Gospel of Matthew may have been redacted and emended by Matthew, seeing the SM as beginning as a pre-Matthean text, perhaps earlier than the 40s as Betz ventures, chronologically increases the likelihood that the SM (especially in its pre-Matthean form) influenced the Didache and not vice versa.

Parenthetically, additional support for Betz's thesis can be found in the vocabulary of the SM. As one compares the Greek words in the SM with those used in the rest of the Gospel of Matthew, some sharp contrasts emerge. By my count, of the 383 basic vocabulary words in the SM, 73 words (or 19 percent of the total) appear (sometimes more than once, but counting them only once) never again elsewhere in Matthew. In fact, several are never used again in the entire New Testament. In some cases words used in the SM, such as δόμα (gift, Matt 7:11; see also Eph 4:8 quoting Ps 68:18), appear un-Matthean, for on the two occasions outside the SM when the Gospel of Matthew speaks of gifts, where the context is similar to that of Matt 7:11 (see 2:11; 15:5), it prefers to use the word δῶρόν (gift). Only two words in the SM, γέεννα (hell) and γραμματεῖς (scribes), are used in Matthew in greater preponderance than elsewhere in the New Testament, and in only one case, ῥαπίζει (smite; Matt 5:39; 26:67), is Matthew the sole New Testament book to use a SM vocabulary word outside the sermon. Although these verbal arguments are not conclusive of authorship, especially since the text sample involved is statistically small, the results seem to be indicative. If the hand that composed the Gospel of Matthew played a significant role in drafting, selecting, or reworking the contents of the SM, it seems odd that nearly every fifth vocabulary word

---

32. Betz, *Essays on the Sermon on the Mount*, 1–15, 55–76; and Hans Dieter Betz, *Sermon on the Mount: A Commentary on the Sermon on the Mount, including the Sermon on the Plain (Matthew 5:3–7:27 and Luke 6:20–49)*, Hermeneia (Minneapolis: Fortress, 1995), 70–80. Alfred M. Perry ("The Framework of the Sermon on the Mount," *JBL* 54 [1935]: 103–15) similarly finds evidence that Matthew worked from a written source that he regarded "so highly that he used it for the foundation of his longer Sermon, even in preference to the Q discourse" (115). On the conjectured existence of other pre-Matthean sources, see Georg Strecker, *The Sermon on the Mount: An Exegetical Commentary*, trans. O. C. Dean Jr. (Nashville: Abingdon, 1988), 55–56, 63, 67–68, 72.

33. Betz, *Sermon on the Mount*, 494.

is one that never is used again in that gospel. Nevertheless, the issue is not cut-and-dried.

Pre-Matthean elements in the SM that are developed subsequently in the Gospel of Matthew are seen to include the following: the initial idea of being "the least [ἐλάχιστος] in the kingdom of heaven" (Matt 5:19) is transmuted in Matt 11:11 into the affirmation that even the lesser (μικρότερος) in the kingdom of heaven is greater than John the Baptist and then moralized in Matt 18:4 in its affirmation that the greatest in the kingdom of heaven is one who "humbles himself as this little child." Settling quickly with a brother in private (Matt 5:23–25) is amplified in Matt 18:15–19 in an ecclesiastical instruction about resolving a case of a brother's transgression, first in private and then before witnesses, and then through appropriate church councils, hoping for conciliation. The simple admonition in Matt 5:28 against committing adultery in one's heart is expanded seven times over in Matt 15:18–19: "for out of the heart proceed evil thoughts, murders, adulteries, fornications, thefts, false witness, blasphemies." The two sayings in Matt 5:29–30 about cutting off a hand (or foot) and casting it away and plucking out an eye and casting it away are invoked (significantly, in the reverse order) in Matt 18:8–10, where this extreme measure is connected with injunctions not to offend (σκανδαλίζει) or to despise (καταφρονήσητε) even the smallest child.[34] Matthew 19:3–9 expands widely on the topic of divorce, which had been merely introduced in Matt 5:31–32.[35] Elaborating on Matt 6:14–15, Matt 18 answers the question about how often to "forgive" (ἀφήσω, 18:21) by telling the story of the unforgiving servant. Matthew 19:21 redirects Matt 6:20, about laying up "treasures in heaven" (θησαυροὺς ἐν οὐρανῷ), when the rich young ruler is told to sell all and give to the poor in order to have "treasure in heaven" (θησαυρὸν ἐν οὐρανοῖς) and become perfect (τέλειος), echoing "perfect" (τέλειοι) in 5:48.[36] Matthew 7:7 ("Ask [αἰτεῖτε], and it shall be given you") is clarified in Matt 21:22: "All things, whatever ye shall ask [αἰτήσητε] in prayer, believing, you shall receive" (21:22). Sometimes the wording of the SM is simply invoked authoritatively in Matthew's narrative: The essence

---

34. Betz (*Sermon on the Mount*, 236–39) questions what the right eye and the right hand have to do with adultery, but he agrees that "the connection was made prior to Matthew. That tradition appears to be more specifically the SM itself and not Q."

35. Betz (*Sermon on the Mount*, 258) discusses the relation between Matt 19:3–12, Mark 10:2–12, and the earlier Matt 5:31–32.

36. Welch, *Sermon on the Mount*, 116–20.

of doing "the will of my Father which is in heaven" (ὁ ποιῶν/ὅστις γὰρ ἂν ποιήσῃ τὸ θέλημα τοῦ πατρός μου τοῦ ἐν τοῖς οὐρανοῖς) appears virtually identically in 7:21 and 12:50, along with the proviso that otherwise one cannot "enter into the kingdom of heaven" (7:21; 18:3). The summation "for this is the law and the prophets" (7:12; see also 5:17) marks not only the culmination of the SM, but also the final instruction given in Matt 17–22 and ends with the same "on these two commandments hang all the law and the prophets" (22:40). And in Matt 25, the five foolish bridesmaids come late, saying, "Lord, Lord [κύριε, κύριε], open to us," but are told, "I know [οἶδα] you not" (25:11–12), reiterating the warning of Matt 7:21. Those who have not multiplied their talents (25:13–15) are told: "Depart from me [πορεύεσθε ἀπ᾽ ἐμοῦ], ye cursed" (25:41), carrying the same condemnation that concludes the SM: "Depart from me [ἀποχωρεῖτε ἀπ᾽ ἐμοῦ], ye workers of iniquity" (7:23). The fact that Matt 24–25 concludes by reiterating these final words of the SM is structurally significant. As in the Didache, Matthew's narrative draws on about fourteen elements from the beginning, middle, and ending of the SM. One inverts the key quoted terms and of these about half appear in the Didache, which is at a rate and in transmuted ways that are generally consistent with the Didache's use of elements from the SM.

Interestingly, this same manner of drawing from, even quoting from, the SM also appears in other books of the New Testament. If one may assume that the SM was widely used during the earliest decades of Christianity to instruct baptismal candidates or to teach and complete (and perfect) baptized members, that would lead one to expect that it would have been frequently quoted and that it would have been very influential throughout the first Christian century. Being valued as coin of the sacred realm among early Christians would explain why it would have been used heavily in the Didache. It would also account for the strong influence of pre-Matthean SM materials on the Gospels of Mark and Luke, as well as on the vocabulary of 1 Peter, and the teachings in Romans, as shown further in the following paragraphs.

In 1 Peter, for example, inverting blessed/righteousness in Matt 5:10 (μακάριοι … ἕνεκεν δικαιοσύνης) is 1 Pet 3:14 (διὰ δικαιοσύνην μακάριοι); inverting blessed/cursed in Matt 5:11 (μακάριοι … ὀνειδίσωσιν) is 1 Pet 4:14 (ὀνειδίζεσθε … μακάριοι); and reversing see/good works in Matt 5:16 (ἴδωσιν ὑμῶν τὰ καλὰ ἔργα) is 1 Pet 2:12 (ἐκ τῶν καλῶν ἔργων ἐποπτεύοντες), both of which conclude with thereby glorifying God in the SM (δοξάσωσιν τὸν πατέρα ὑμῶν τὸν ἐν τοῖς οὐρανοῖς) and in 1 Peter (δοξάσωσι τὸν θεὸν ἐν ἡμέρᾳ ἐπισκοπῆς). Hypocrites (Matt 6:2, 5, 16; 7:5) are generalized as hypocrisies in 1 Pet 2:1; anxiety (μεριμνᾶτε) in Matt 6:25-31 is echoed in 1 Pet 5:7, exhorting believers to cast all anxiety (μέριμναν) on the Lord who cares, and both the SM and 1 Peter end with the same metaphor of building or being built (θεμελιόω in Matt 7:25; 1 Pet 5:10) on a solid foundation.

James uses a dozen phrases that also range from the beginning to the end of the SM and several times in inverted order. James 1:12 employs the beatitude formula (μακάριος ... ὅτι). James 2:13 turns Matt 5:7 into a negative in the reverse order, no mercy will be given to the unmerciful. James 1:19-20 (telling brothers to be slow to anger, ὀργὴ) tracks Matt 5:22 (warning brothers against being angry, ὀργιζόμενος). James 1:14-15 (on lust, ἐπιθυμία, leading to sin and death) epitomizes Matt 5:28. James 5:12 and Matt 5:33-37 both speak of not swearing oaths by heaven or earth but only by yes or no, each using ὀμνύω, οὐρανός, γῆ, ναί ναί, and οὒ οὔ. James 1:4 and Matt 5:48 both use the adjective τέλειος. James 1:13 interacts with Matt 6:13 on temptation (πειρασμόν). James 4:11 and Matt 7:1-2 (on not speaking ill or judging a brother), each uses κρίνω. James 1:5-6 and Matt 7:7 (on asking of God) each use αἰτέω in the imperative followed by the future passive form of δίδωμι. James 1:17 and Matt 7:11 deal with good and perfect gifts coming from heaven (πᾶσα δόσις ἀγαθὴ/ δόματα ἀγαθὰ). Inverting grapes (σταφυλάς) and figs (σῦκα) in Matt 7:16 is Jas 3:12, figs (σῦκα) and vine (ἄμπελος). Finally, reversing hear/words/ do (ἀκούει/λόγους/ποιεῖ) from the end of the SM in Matt 7:24 is the opening injunction in Jas 1:22 to be doers of the word and not hearers only (ποιηταὶ/λόγου/ἀκροαταὶ).

Paul also was aware of verbiage from the beginning to the ending of the SM, as reflected in Romans.[37] Whether Paul's rhetoric in general reflects written or oral channels of transmission is debatable,[38] but several parallels can be noted. Romans 4:7 quotes Ps 32:1-2, blessing those who have averted iniquity. These catchwords (μακάριοι and ἀνομία) are used at

---

37. See Helmut Koester, *Ancient Christian Gospels: Their History and Development* (London: SCM; Philadelphia: Trinity, 1990), 52-55, 64-66, 71-75. Regarding these allusions to sayings of Jesus in Rom 12-14, 1 Peter, and James, Koester opines, when such "pieces of tradition are quoted or used in early Christian authors ... it may not even be necessary to refer to them as traditions." Koester, "Written Gospels or Oral Tradition?" *JBL* 113 (1994): 293-97 (297).

38. Betz, *Sermon on the Mount*, 6 n. 12.

the beginning and ending of the SM. Fulfilling the righteousness of the law (τοῦ νόμου πληρωθῇ) in Rom 8:4 compares with the fulfillment of the law (τὸν νόμον ... πληρῶσαι) in Matt 5:17. Being sons of God (υἱοὶ θεοῦ) and children who inherit from God (Rom 8:14, 17) recalls being called sons of God (υἱοὶ θεοῦ) and inheriting the earth (Matt 5:5, 9). Crying unto God as Father (Rom 8:15) aligns with Matt 6:9. The exhortation to bless those who persecute (εὐλογεῖτε τοὺς διώκοντας) and not to curse them (καταρᾶσθε) in Rom 12:14 and its textual variants uses the same words that populate the textual variants of Matt 5:44. Not only is this exhortation followed by the directive not to render evil for evil, to feed the enemy, and conquer evil in the good (Rom 12:17, 20, 24), which precedes the rule of loving one's enemies in Matt 5:39, but also Rom 12:17 reverses the order of evil/render (κακὸν/ἀποδιδόντες) from that of Matthew (ἀντιστῆναι/πονηροί). Two final rhetorical questions about judging a brother (Rom 14:10; Matt 7:2–4) and about disparaging a brother (Rom 14:10; Matt 5:22) strongly imply that Paul's audience in Rome already knew the obligation to "judge not" and not to call a brother a fool.

In sum, even without a fully developed analysis, which would exceed the principal focus of this paper, it is evident that several important early Christian writings draw from all portions of the SM, most of these invert certain quoted material, and as a group they manifest the same wide range of adoptions and types of adaptations of SM words and phrases that are also found in the Didache, as well in the mandates of the Shepherd of Hermas.[39] All of this can most readily be explained by seeing the Didache, along with these other texts, as drawing on the SM and not vice versa. Otherwise, it is clearly not the case that these other New Testament have drawn on the Didache, for only the SM contains the full set the elements that reappear multiple times in these early Christian writings.

Appendix 1

	Matthew			Didache
5:3	Blessed (μακάριοι)		1.5	Blessed (μακάριος) is the giver
5:3	The poor (πτωχοί)		5.2	The poor (πτωχόν)

---

39. For example, Shephard of Hermas, Mand. 2 (give gifts to all as God gives to all), Mand. 4 (prohibiting remarriage after divorce), Mand. 5 (no anger), Mand. 6 (walk the straight path), and Mand. 11 (distinguishing true prophets from false).

5:4	Comfort (παρακληθήσονται)	5.2	Those who are advocates (παράκλητοι) of the rich (B18)
5:5	Blessed are the meek (πραεῖς), inherit the earth (κληρονομήσουσιν τὴν γῆν)	3.7	Be meek (πραΰς), the meek (πραεῖς) will inherit the earth (= κληρονομήσουσι τὴν γῆν)
5:7	Merciful (ἐλεήμονες)	3.8	Be merciful (ἐλεήμων)
		5.2	Showing mercy (ἐλεοῦντες) [in B11]
5:8	Pure in heart (καθαροὶ)	14.1	Confession makes a sacrifice pure (καθαρὰ)
5:8	See (ὄψονται) God	16.8	The world will see (ὄψεται) the Lord coming
5:9	Peacemakers (εἰρηνοποιοί)	4.3	Make peace (εἰρηνεύσεις) to those quarreling
5:11	Persecuted (διώξωσιν)	5.2	Persecutors (διῶκται) [in B1]
		16.4	Persecution by or among the false prophets
5:11	All evil (πᾶν πονηρὸν) spoken	5.1	The first of all evils (πάντων πονηρά)
5:11	Falsely [in some manuscripts]	5.1	False witnessing (ψευδομαρτυρίαι)
5:12	God will reward well (μισθὸς πολὺς)	4.7	God will reward well (ὁ τοῦ μισθοῦ καλὸς)
5:13	Casting out (βληθὲν ἔξω)	15.3	Do not speak to those who misbehave until they repent
5:14	As upon a mountain (ἐπάνω ὄρους)	9.4	As bread scattered on the mountains (ἐπάνω τῶν ὀρέων)
5:15	Light a lamp (καίουσιν λύχνον)	16.1	Lamps not quenched (λύχνοι ὑμῶν μὴ σβεσθήτωσαν) [inverting]
5:16	Your light (φῶς ὑμῶν)	16.1	Your lamps (λύχνοι ὑμῶν)
5:17	Jesus not come to destroy (καταλῦσαι)	11.2	If a teacher destroys (= καταλῦσαι), do not listen
5:19	Don't ignore any commands (ἐντολῶν)	4.13	Don't ignore any commandments (ἐντολὰς)
5:19	Don't teach (διδάξῃ) otherwise	6.1	Beware teachers who teach (διδάσκει) without God
5:21–37	Parts of the Decalogue	2.1–7	List of twenty-three vices
5:21	No murder (οὐ φονεύσεις)	2.2	No murder (= οὐ φονεύσεις)
5:22	No anger (ὀργιζόμενος)	3.2	No anger (μὴ γίνου ὀργίλος)

			Anger leads to murder [inverting murder-anger]
5:22	No anger to your brother (ἀδελφῷ)	15.3	Do not reprove each other in anger (ἀλλήλους μὴ ἐν ὀργῇ)
5:22	Danger of hell fire (πυρός)	16.5	Many led away and burned (πύρωσιν)
5:23	Gift (δῶρόν) proper at the altar	14.1	Your sacrifice (θυσία) may be pure at Eucharist
5:24	If you remember, go settle	4.14	Do not go to your prayers with a bad conscience
5:24	Reconcile (διαλλαγηθι)	14.1–2	Confess and reconcile (διαλλαγῶσιν)
5:25	Judge, prison (εἰς φυλακὴν)	1.5	Trial, prison (ἐν συνοχῇ)
5:26	Not come out (ἐξέλθῃς ἐκεῖθεν)	1.5	Not come out of there (ἐξελεύσεται ἐκεῖθεν)
5:26	Until you pay the last kodrantes (ἕως ἂν ἀποδῷς τὸν ἔσχατον κοδράντην)	1.5	Until he pays the last kodrantes (μέχρις οὗ ἀποδῷ τὸν ἔσχατον κοδράντην)
5:27	No adultery (οὐ μοιχεύσεις)	2.2	No adultery (= οὐ μοιχεύσεις)
5:28	Looking (βλέπων) upon a woman	3.3	No high-minding eye (ὑψηλόφθαλμος)
5:28	Lust (πρὸς τὸ ἐπιθυμῆσαι)	3.3	Lust (ἐπιθυμίᾳ)
5:28	Adultery (ἐμοίχευσεν) in the heart	3.3	The path to adulteries (ὁδηγεῖ … μοιχεῖαι)
5:33	No false oaths (οὐκ ἐπιορκήσεις)	2.3	No false oaths (= οὐκ ἐπιορκήσεις)
5:39	Slap on the right cheek (=)	1.4	Slap on the right cheek (= ῥαπίζει εἰς τὴν δεξιὰν σιαγόνα)
5:39	Turn to him the other also (=)	1.4A	Turn to him the other also (= στρέψον αὐτῷ καὶ τὴν ἄλλην)
5:40	Tunic (χιτῶνά), cloak (ἱμάτιον)	1.4C	Cloak (ἱμάτιον), tunic (χιτῶνά) [inverting]
5:41	If someone compels you one mile (ὅστις σε ἀγγαρεύσει μίλιον ἕν)	1.4B	Compels you someone [to go] one mile (ἀγγαρεύσῃ σέ τις μίλιον ἕν) [inverting someone-compels]
5:41	Go with him two (=)	1.4B	Go with him two (= ὕπαγε μετ' αὐτοῦ δύο)
5:42	Give to those who ask (αἰτοῦντί)	1.4D	Don't ask for it back (μὴ ἀπαίτει)

5:43	Love neighbor (ἀγαπήσεις τὸν πλησίον)	1.2	Love neighbor (= ἀγαπήσεις ... πλησίον)
5:43	Love your enemies (ἐχθροὺς)	1.3D	Love those who hate you, have no enemy (ἐχθρῶν)
		2.7	Hate none, pray for them, love them [inverting love-hate]
5:44	[[Bless those who curse you]] (=)	1.3A	Bless those who curse you (= εὐλογεῖτε τοὺς καταρωμένους)
5:44	Pray for those who persecute you (=)	1.3B	Pray (= προσεύχεσθε) for your enemies
5:45	The Father's sun and rain falls on all	1.5	Upon all wishes to give the Father [inverting Father-all]
5:47	If you love those who love you, what remarkable (περισσὸν) do you do?	1.3C	What favor (χάρις) do you do, if you love those who love you? [inverting if-what]
5:47	Gentiles (ἐθνικοὶ) also do this (=)	1.3C	Gentiles (ἔθνη) also do this (= αὐτὸ ποιοῦσιν)
5:48	Be perfect (ἔσεσθε οὖν ὑμεῖς τέλειοι)	1.4	You will be perfect (ἔσῃ τέλειος)
5:48	As Father is perfect (τέλειός ἐστιν)	6.2	Will be perfect (τέλειος ἔσῃ) by bearing the whole yoke
6:3	Give alms (ποιοῦντος ἐλεημοσύνην)	1.6	Give alms (ἐλεημοσύνη ... δῷς)
6:3	Left hand, what right hand does	12.1	Understanding of right and left hand [inverting δεξιὰν, ἀριστερὰν]
6:3	Hands not know (γνώτω)	1.6	Sweat in hands until you know (γνῷς) to whom to give it
6:5	When you pray (ὅταν προσεύχησθε) not as the hypocrites (ὡς οἱ ὑποκριταί)	8.2	Do not pray (μηδὲ προσεύχεσθε) as the hypocrites (ὡς οἱ ὑποκριταί)
6:9	Pray thus (οὕτως προσεύχεσθε)	8.2	Pray thus (= οὕτως προσεύχεσθε)
6:9	God as Father (= Πάτερ ἡμῶν ὁ ἐν τοῖς οὐρανοῖς)	8.2	God as Father (= πάτερ ἡμῶν ὁ ἐν τῷ οὐρανῷ)
6:9	Hallowed be your name (=)	8.2	Hallowed be your name (= ἁγιασθήτω τὸ ὄνομά σου)

6:10	Kingdom come (=)	8.2	Kingdom come (= ἐλθέτω ἡ βασιλεία σου)
6:10	Let your will be born (=)	8.2	Let your will be born (= γενηθήτω τὸ θέλημά σου)
	on earth as in heaven (=)		on earth as in heaven (= ὡς ἐν οὐρανῷ καὶ ἐπὶ γῆς)
6:11	Our daily bread give us today (=)	8.2	Our daily bread give us today (= τὸν ἄρτον ἡμῶν τὸν ἐπιούσιον δὸς ἡμῖν σήμερον)
6:12	Forgive us our debts (ὀφειλήματα)	8.2	Forgive us our debt (ὀφειλὴν)
	as we forgive (ἀφήκαμεν) our debtors		as we forgive (ἀφίεμεν) our debtors
6:13	Do not lead us into trial (πειρασμόν)	8.2	Do not lead us into trial (= πειρασμόν)
6:13	Deliver us from the evil (πονηροῦ)	8.2	Deliver us from the evil (= πονηροῦ)
		3.1	Flee from all evil (= πονηροῦ)
		10.5	Deliver the church from all evil (= πονηροῦ)
6:13	Kingdom, power, glory, forever	8.2	Power, glory, forever; also 10.5 (= δύναμις, δόξα, αἰῶνας)
6:16	When you fast (νηστεύητε), not as the hypocrites (ὑποκριταὶ)	8.1	Let your fasts (νηστεῖαι), not at the same time with the hypocrites (ὑποκριτῶν)
6:19	No treasuring treasures on earth	3.5	No love of glory
6:19	Thieves steal (κλέπται ... κλέπτουσιν)	3.5	Leads to theft and thefts (κλοπήν, κλοπαὶ)
6:19	Treasures in heaven do not rust	4.8	If you have in common immortal things, then share more easily things that perish
6:24	Do not love or serve Mammon	3.5	No love of money (μηδὲ φιλάργυρος)
6:24	Love the Master (ἀγαπήσει)	1.2	Love (ἀγαπήσεις) the God who made you
6:25	Food (τροφῆς) [and drink (πίητε)]	10.3	Food and drink (τροφήν καὶ ποτὸν)

6:31, 33	food and drink, shall be given		you have given to people for enjoyment
6:33	Seek (ζητεῖτε) God's righteousness	16.2	Seek (ζητοῦντες) the needs of your souls
6:33	Then all things will be added to you	16.2	Faith will not be useful to you in the end time
			if you have not first been perfected
7:1	Judge not (μὴ κρίνετε)	11.7	A true prophet you shall not judge (οὐδὲ διακρινεῖτε)
		11.11	You shall not judge (οὐ κριθήσεται)
7:2	Will be judged [by God] (κριθήσεσθε)	11.11	With God will be their judgment (κρίσιν)
7:3	Speck (καρφός) in own eye	4.3	Fairness in reproving others for their failings
7:6	Give not the holy to the dogs (μὴ δῶτε τὸ ἅγιον τοῖς κυσίν)	9.5	Give not the Eucharist to the unbaptized, quoting the Lord: "give not the holy to the dogs" (= μὴ δῶτε τὸ ἅγιον τοῖς κυσί)
7:7	Seek (ζητεῖτε)	16.2	Seek (ζητοῦντες) things pertaining to your souls
7:9	Give his son bread (ἄρτον)	11.6	Let an apostle accept bread (= ἄρτον) when he leaves
7:11	Give to son (υἱός) and children	4.9	Take not your hand from your son (υἱοῦ) and daughter
7:10–11	Gifts (δόματα)	1.5	Gifts (χαρισμάτων)
7:11	If you give to those who ask (αἰτοῦσιν)	1.5	Give to everyone who asks (αἰτοῦντί)
	much more will the Father give (δώσει)		for [thus] the Father wishes to give (δίδοσθαι) [inverting give-ask]
7:12	All you wish men to do to you,	1.2	All you wish won't happen to you
	and so you do to them (ποιεῖτε αὐτοῖς)		and you to another don't do (ἄλλῳ μὴ ποίει) [inverting do-to]
7:13–14	Way, way (ὁδός, ὁδός)	1.1	Two ways (ὁδοί δύο)
7:13	To destruction (εἰς τὴν ἀπώλειαν)	1.1	Of life, of death (ὁδοὶ ... τῆς ζωῆς, θανάτου) [inverting death-life]

7:14	To life (ὁδὸς ... εἰς τὴν ζωήν)	1.1; 4.14	Way of life (ὁδὸς τῆς ζωῆς)
7:15	Beware (προσέχετε)	6.1	Watch out (ὅρα) for those who lead you astray
	false prophets (ἀπὸ ψευδοπροφητῶν)	16.3	False prophets (ψευδοπροφῆται) [also 11.5]
7:15	Sheepskin, wolves (προβάτων, λύκοι)	16.3	Turn sheep into wolves (πρόβατα εἰς λύκους)
7:16	Known by fruits (ἀπὸ τῶν καρπῶν)	11.8	Known by their behavior (ἀπὸ τῶν τρόπων)
7:19	Cast into the fire (πῦρ)	16.5	Many led away and burned (πύρωσιν)
7:21	Lord, Lord (κύριε, κύριε)	11.2	Of the Lord ... receive as the Lord (κυρίου ... κύριον)
7:21	Coming (εἰσελεύσεται) by doing the Father's will	12.1	Coming (ἐρχόμενος) in the name of the Lord
7:22	In your name (ὀνόματι)	12.1	Receive one who comes in the name (= ὀνόματι) of the Lord
7:22	We cast out demons (δαιμόνια) and did many wonders (δυνάμεις)	16.4	World-deceiver will do signs (σημεῖα) and wonders (τέρατα)
7:23	Being not received (ἀποχωρεῖτε)	10.6	If anyone is not holy, let them repent (μετανοείτω)
		11.2	Do not listen to those who teach another teaching
7:23	Being known (ἔγνων)	12.1	Being known (γνώσεσθε)
		11.2	Receive one who builds knowledge (γνῶσιν) of the Lord
7:23	Workers of iniquity (ἀνομία)	16.4	Iniquity (= ἀνομία) will increase
		5.2	Lawless (ἄνομοι) judges of the poor (πενήτων) (B2)
7:24	Hearing and doing (ποιεῖ)	11.10	The teacher who does not teach what he does (= ποιεῖ)
7:27	Floods, winds, fall (πτῶσις)	16.5	Burning, destruction (ἀπολοῦνται)
7:28	His teaching (διδαχὴ αὐτοῦ)	1.0	The apostles' teaching (διδαχὴ τῶν δώδεκα ἀποστόλων)

The Lord Jesus and His Coming in the Didache

Murray J. Smith

1. Introduction

The eschatological vision of the Didache centers on the "coming of the Lord" (Did. 16.1, 7–8; cf. 10.6). But which "Lord" does the Didache expect to come? In his 2003 commentary, Aaron Milavec argues that the Didache does not employ the title κύριος ("Lord") for Jesus. On this reading, the "coming of the Lord" envisaged in Did. 16.1–8 is not the "second coming" of Christian expectation, but the great and final coming of God expected in the Hebrew Scriptures. "All of the instances of 'Lord' in the *Didache*," Milavec argues, "ought to be understood as referring to the Lord God."[1] "It is quite clear," he concludes, "that it is the Lord God who is awaited."[2] Milavec goes on to suggest that "further study is necessary in order to situate the *Didache* in the spectrum of Christologies that developed during the first two centuries."[3] His own suspicion, following the earlier work of T. F. Glasson and John A. T. Robinson, is that such study will reveal in the Didache "the most primitive Christology of all."[4] The Christology of the Didache, he suspects, is relatively "low": Jesus appears primarily as "servant" rather than as "Lord"; eschatological expectation remains firmly fixed on God the Father.[5]

---

1. Aaron Milavec, *The Didache: Faith, Hope, and Life of the Earliest Christian Communities, 50–70 CE* (New York: Newman Press, 2003), 665.
2. Ibid., 665.
3. Ibid., 663.
4. Ibid., 663 citing T. F. Glasson, *The Second Advent: The Origin of the New Testament Doctrine*, 3rd rev. ed. (London: Epworth, 1963), 162–79; John A. T. Robinson, *Jesus and His Coming*, 2nd ed. (London: SCM, 1979), 56, 140.
5. Milavec, *Didache: Faith, Hope, and Life*, 665: in the Christology of the

This paper makes a modest contribution to the christological question identified by Milavec. The task—perhaps surprisingly one not yet attempted—is to systematically examine the identity of the "Lord" in the Didache, with special reference to the eschatological "coming of the Lord" in Did. 16.1, 7–8 (see also 10.6). The argument proceeds in two stages. First, an examination of the twenty-one occurrences of κύριος in the Didache outside Did. 16 reveals that in the vast majority of cases the term at least includes reference to the Lord Jesus. Second, an analysis of Did. 10.6, 16.1, 7–8 demonstrates that the Didache does not merely repeat the eschatological vision of the biblical theophany tradition, but develops it christologically to present the final "coming of the Lord" as the "coming" of the Lord Jesus.

Thus, like a range of other early Christian texts, the Didache includes Jesus within the identity of the one true God of Israel and so reworks the Jewish "coming of God" tradition around him. It is concluded, therefore, that even if the Christology of the Didache is "primitive," it is, nevertheless, remarkably "high." Like the earliest Christian texts collected in the New Testament, the Didache reserves a central role in the eschatological drama for Jesus.

2. The Identity of the "Lord" in the Didache outside Chapter 16

2.1. Κύριος in the Didache in the Context of the Early Jewish and Christian Literature

The Greek text of the Didache preserved in Codex Hierosolymitanus, the only extant Greek manuscript, employs the crucial term κύριος a total of twenty-four times (Did. 1.0; 4.1 (x 2), 11, 12, 13; 6.2; 8.2; 9.5 (x 2); 10.5; 11.2 (x 2), 4, 8; 12.1; 14.1, 3 (x 2); 15.1, 4; 16.1, 7, 8).[6] The ancient Greek versions of the Hebrew Scriptures habitually employ κύριος to translate the divine name (יהוה). For this reason, Milavec's case that κύριος consistently means "God" deserves serious consideration. Nevertheless, the very earliest Christian texts, namely the Pauline Epistles, routinely

---

Didache "attachment ... to Jesus" does not disrupt "the eschatological roles assigned to the Father."

6. For the text and associated traditions, see esp. Kurt Niederwimmer, *The Didache: A Commentary*, trans. Linda M. Maloney, Hermeneia (Minneapolis: Fortress, 1998), 4–52.

(if remarkably), apply to Jesus a range of texts from the Scriptures of Israel that originally referred to the Lord God. In this way, they regularly include Jesus within the identity of the one true God of Israel, identifying Jesus as "Lord" (= κύριος).[7] This practice is attested as early as 49–50 CE when Paul and his companions wrote 1 Thessalonians (e.g., 1 Thess 3:13 with Zech 14:5; and 1 Thess 4:16–17 with Exod 19:11–19; Mic 1:3; Isa 64:1–3).[8] Indeed, the presuppositional way in which Paul and his companions speak of Jesus as "the Lord" in this letter and then predicate of him a range of prerogatives that from a biblical perspective belong to "the Lord" God alone renders it likely that this understanding of Jesus as "Lord" goes back further still.[9]

These brief considerations, of course, cannot decide the meaning of κύριος in the Didache. They do, however, reveal the range of interpretive possibilities for the title κύριος in the early Jewish and Christian literature. In particular, since the very earliest extant Christian texts present a very "high" Christology by applying the title κύριος to Jesus, there is no a priori reason to expect a "low" Christology in the Didache, even if it is dated amongst the earliest Christian texts.[10] Indeed, the following analysis demonstrates that the twenty-one references to κύριος outside Did. 16 support the recognition of a "high" Christology in the Didache. These references may be classified as follows: (1) five almost certainly refer to the Lord Jesus (Did. 8.2; 9.5 [x 2]; 14.1; 15.4); (2) eleven most likely refer to the Lord Jesus (Did. title; 4.1 [x 2]; 6.2; 10.5; 11.2 [x 2], 4, 8; 12.1; 15.1);

---

7. Compare: 1 Cor 8:4–6 with Deut 6:4; Rom 10:9–13 with Isa 28:16/Joel 2:32 (LXX Joel 3:5); Phil 2:9–11 with Isa 45:22–23 and 1 Cor 15:25; Rom 8:34; Eph 1:20; Col 3:1 with Ps 110:1. See esp. here: Richard Bauckham, *Jesus and the God of Israel: God Crucified and Other Studies on the New Testament's Christology of Divine Identity* (Grand Rapids: Eerdmans, 2008); see also Larry Hurtado, *Lord Jesus Christ: Devotion to Jesus in Earliest Christianity* (Grand Rapids: Eerdmans, 2003); Gordon D. Fee, *Pauline Christology: Devotion to Jesus in Earliest Christianity* (Peabody, MA: Hendrickson, 2007), 631–38.

8. Fee, *Pauline Christology*, 41–55.

9. See Murray J. Smith, "The Thessalonian Correspondance," in *All Things to All Cultures: Paul among Jews, Greeks and Romans*, ed. Mark Harding and Alanna M. Nobbs (Grand Rapids: Eerdmans, 2013), 269–301.

10. On the date of the Didache and the composite nature of the text, see the survey of opinion in Niederwimmer, *Didache*, 52–53, who dates the final form of the text to ca. 110–20 CE.

(3) four quite possibly refer to the Lord Jesus, but remain indeterminate (Did. 4.12, 13; 14.3 [x 2]); (4) one refers to human masters (Did. 4.11).[11]

2.2. Texts in Which the "Lord" is Almost Certainly the Lord Jesus

At five points in the Didache κύριος almost certainly refers to Jesus.

(1) Didache 8.2 introduces a citation of a Lord's Prayer tradition very similar to Matt 6:9–13 as something "the Lord commanded in his gospel":[12]

μηδὲ προσεύχεσθε ὡς οἱ ὑποκριταί ἀλλ᾽ ὡς ἐκέλευσεν ὁ κύριος ἐν τῷ εὐαγγελίῳ αὐτοῦ οὕτω προσεύχεσθε

The question of the form in which the author of the Didache knew the Jesus tradition has received significant scholarly attention in recent years.[13] In relation to this text (Did. 8.2), it seems most likely that the Didache reflects knowledge of the Gospel of Matthew in its finished form, or at least knowledge of some other written gospel source, though this is much debated.[14] Be that as it may, there is no surviving record of the Lord God of

---

11. For a comparable analysis see Niederwimmer, Didache, 135 n. 5, who considers that κύριος refers to Jesus at: "title (= 1.0), 4.1; 6.2; 8.2; 9.5; 10.5; 11.2; 11.4, 8; 12.1; 14.1; 15.1, 4; 16.1, 7, 8. But not: 4.12, 13; 14.3." Consideration of the three references to the "Lord" in Did. 16 is reserved for part 2 below. Didache 4.11 may be safely excluded from the present discussion.

12. English translations from the Didache, except where noted, are those of Michael W. Holmes, ed. and trans., *The Apostolic Father: Greek Texts and English Translations*, 3rd ed. (Grand Rapids: Baker, 2007).

13. See especially the exchange between Christopher Tuckett and Aaron Milavec: Christopher M. Tuckett, "Synoptic Tradition in the Didache," in *The New Testament in Early Christianity*, ed. Jean-Marie Sevrin, BETL 86 (Leuven: Leuven University Press; Peeters, 1989), 197–230; Aaron Milavec, "Synoptic Tradition in the *Didache* Revisited," *JECS* 11 (2003): 443–80; Christopher M. Tuckett, "The Didache and the Synoptics Once More: A Response to Aaron Milavec," *JECS* 13 (2005): 509–18; Aaron Milavec, "A Rejoinder [to Tuckett]," *JECS* 13 (2005): 519–23. For a review see Murray J. Smith, "The Gospels in Early Christian Literature," in *The Content and Setting of the Gospel Traditions*, ed. Mark Harding and Alanna M. Nobbs (Grand Rapids: Eerdmans, 2010), 181–207. The most recent contribution is that of Stephen E. Young, *Jesus Tradition in the Apostolic Fathers: Their Explicit Appeals to the Words of Jesus in Light of Orality Studies*, WUNT 2/311 (Tübingen: Mohr Siebeck, 2011).

14. For dependence on Matthew or a pre-Matthean written gospel, see Eduard Massaux, *The Influence of the Gospel of Saint Matthew on Christian Literature before Saint Irenaeus*, trans. Norman J. Belval and Suzanne Hecht, 3 vols., NGS 5.2 (Leuven:

Israel commanding a prayer such as this (Did. 8.2). In the sources known to us the only "Lord" who commanded such a prayer is the Lord Jesus. Almost certainly, then, the κύριος here is Jesus of Nazareth.[15]

(2–3) Didache 9.5 contains two references to the "Lord."

Μηδεὶς δὲ φαγέτω μηδὲ πιέτω ἀπὸ τῆς εὐχαριστίας ὑμῶν ἀλλ᾽ οἱ βαπτισθέντες εἰς ὄνομα κυρίου καὶ γὰρ περὶ τούτου εἴρηκεν ὁ κύριος·Μὴ δῶτε τὸ ἅγιον τοῖς κυσί

These two references to the "Lord" come in the context of a eucharistic prayer addressed to God "our Father" and exhibiting a Davidic Christology (Did. 9.2, 3).[16] Nevertheless, the considerations below make it almost

---

Peeters; Macon, GA: Mercer University Press, 1990), 3:145; James A. Kelhoffer, "'How Soon a Book' Revisited: ΕΥΑΓΓΕΛΙΟΝ as a Reference to 'Gospel' Materials in the First Half of the Second Century," *ZNW* 95 (2004): 1–34 (22); Christopher M. Tuckett, "The Didache and the Writings that Later Formed the New Testament," in *The Reception of the New Testament in the Apostolic Fathers*, vol. 1 of *The New Testament and the Apostolic Fathers*, ed. Andrew F. Gregory and Christopher M. Tuckett (Oxford: Oxford University Press, 2005), 104–6. The majority, however, argue for independence from Matthew and/or a written gospel source, seeing a reference here to the oral proclamation of the gospel and/or liturgical tradition. See esp. Kirsopp Lake, "The Didache," in *The New Testament and the Apostolic Fathers* (Oxford: Clarendon, 1905), 28; Rudolf Knopf, *Die Lehre der zwölf Apostel: Die zwei Clemensbriefe*, vol. 1 of *Die apostolischen Väter*, HNT.E (Tübingen: Mohr Siebeck, 1920), 23; Helmut Koester, *Synoptische Überlieferung bei den apostolischen Vätern*, TUGAL 65/5.10 (Berlin: Akademie-Verlag, 1957), 10 (but see also 203 where he concedes that "an interpretation in terms of a written gospel is not entirely impossible"); Jean-Paul Audet, *La Didachè: Instructions des Apôtres*, Ebib (Paris: Gabalda, 1958), 173; Richard Glover, "The Didache's Quotations and the Synoptic Gospels," *NTS* 5 (1958): 12–29 (19); Jonathan A. Draper, "The Jesus Tradition in the *Didache*," in *The Didache in Modern Research*, ed. Jonathan A. Draper, AGJU 37 (Leiden: Brill, 1996), 86; Niederwimmer, *Didache*, 136; Milavec, "Synoptic Tradition in the *Didache* Revisted," 452.

15. Milavec, *Didache: Faith, Hope, and Life*, 664–65 suggests that "when it is remembered that Jesus proclaims the 'good news of God' and that those who hear him, hear the Lord God, then it does not seem strange to attribute to the Lord God a rule of praying." But this must surely be regarded as special pleading. In the context of the early Christian recognition of Jesus as "Lord," the most natural assumption is that the "Lord" here is the one who actually taught the prayer.

16. See Jonathan A. Draper, "Eschatology in the Didache," in *Eschatology of the New Testament and Some Related Documents*, ed. Jan G. van der Watt, WUNT 2/315 (Tübingen: Mohr Siebeck, 2011), 569–70.

certain that the Lord Jesus is, at very least, included in the intended referent of the term "Lord" in both instances.

In the first instance, Did. 9.5a commands "let no one eat or drink of your eucharist except those who have been baptized into the name of the Lord" (ἀλλ' οἱ βαπτισθέντες εἰς ὄνομα κυρίου). This brief expression recalls Did. 7.1, 3, which instructs that baptism be into the singular name (τὸ ὄνομα) of the triune God: "Baptize in the name of the Father and of the Son, and of the Holy Spirit." Moreover, the construction here is identical with that found at Matt 28:19 and similar to that presented by Justin (*Apol.* 1.61.3, 10, 13). For our purposes, it is again not necessary to enter the debate about the relationship between Matthew and the Didache.[17] It is enough to note that in the context of Did. 7.1, 3, and the parallel expressions in Matt 28:19 and in Justin, the "Lord" at Did. 9.5a, into whose "name" baptism is to be made, is most naturally understood as the name of the triune God of Christian confession, inclusive of the Lord Jesus.

The second reference to "the Lord" in Did. 9.5b follows immediately, when the Didache introduces a saying identical to Jesus's statement in Matt 7:6 with the words "for the Lord has also spoken concerning this." As at Did. 8.2, it seems most likely that the Gospel of Matthew stands behind this citation, though this is debated.[18] There are some comparative sayings in the ancient wisdom literature[19] and in Jewish sayings about what is holy to the temple being eaten by dogs.[20] Nevertheless, the verbatim correspondence between this saying and Matt 7:6 and the attribution of

---

17. See note 12 above.

18. For dependence on Matthew, see Donald A. Hagner, *The Use of the Old and New Testaments in Clement of Rome*, NovTSup 34 (Leiden: Brill, 1973), 280; Klaus Wengst, *Didache (Apostellehre), Barnabasbrief, Zweiter Clemensbrief, Schrift an Diognet*, SU 2 (Darmstadt: Wissenschaftliche Buchgessellschaft, 1984), 28; Massaux, *Influence of the Gosepl of Saint Matthew*, 3:156. To the contrary, see esp. Koester, *Synoptische Überlieferung*, 198–200, 240.

19. Hermann von Lips, "Schweine füttert man, Hunde nicht—Ein Versuch, das Rätsel von Matthäus 7:6 zu lösen," *ZNW* 79 (1988): 165–86 (177–78) draws attention to a class of sayings in which inappropriate animal food symbolises inappropriate human behaviour (e.g., "to feed water to a frog"; "a dog does not eat cooking herbs").

20. Huub van de Sandt, "'Do Not Give What Is Holy to the Dogs' (Did 9:5d and Matt 7:6a): The Eucharistic Food of the Didache in Its Jewish Purity Setting," *VC* 56 (2002): 223–46 (230 n. 17 and 234–38); see also Milavec, *Didache: Faith, Hope and Life*, 665.

similar sayings to Jesus in other early Christian texts[21] renders it almost certain that the "Lord" intended here is the Lord Jesus.[22]

(4) Didache 14.1a commands the community, "having been gathered together," to "break bread" and "give thanks" "on the Lord's Day":

κατὰ κυριακὴν δὲ κυρίου συναχθέντες κλάσατε ἄρτον καὶ εὐχαριστήσατε

The κύριος, here again, is almost certainly the Lord Jesus. To begin with, the pleonastic expression κατὰ κυριακὴν δὲ κυρίου uses both the adjective κυριακός and the noun κύριος to refer to a day of the week.[23] This usage is distinctively Christian: in addition to the reference here, the "Lord's Day" is widely attested in the early Christian writings (Rev 1:10; Ign. *Magn.* 9.1; Gos. Pet. 9.35; 13.50; Clement of Alexandria, *Strom.* 7.12; Eusebius, *Hist. eccl.* 4.26.2 [Melito of Sardis]; 4.23.8 [Dionysius of Corinth]; Origen, *Cels.* 8.22) and is closely associated with the celebration of Jesus's resurrection (see esp. Ign. *Magn.* 9.1; cf. Barn. 15.9; Justin, *Apol.* 1.67.3, 7; *Dial.* 24.1; 41.4; 138.1).[24] Thus the "Lord" referred to here is almost certainly the Lord Jesus. Moreover, the Didache here commands that on this "Lord's Day," the community "having been gathered together" (συναχθέντες), should "break

---

21. Similar sayings are attributed to Jesus in other early Christian sources. The first half of the saying appears in the Gospel according to Basilides in Epiphanius, *Pan.* 1.24.5, and a similar logion is found in Gos. Thom. 93.

22. So, correctly, Niederwimmer, *Didache*, 153, contra Milavec, *Didache: Faith, Hope, Life*, 665, whose arguments, however, do not stand up under close scrutiny. He argues: (1) the Didache is "focally centered on the Father's revelation"; but this assumes an answer to the very question under discussion; (2) the introductory formula is paralleled at Did. 14.3, where it introduces the word of the Lord God through Malachi. But since there is no biblical citation here, the parallel is not exact; (3) Matt 7:6, unlike Did. 9.5, contains no "oblique reference to the Eucharist," but this can be easily explained as a different application of the same saying by the two texts.

23. The so-called Georgian version supports the more natural καθ'ἡμέραν δὲ κυρίου conjectured by Audet, *Didachè*, 72–73, 240, 460. The value of this Georgian version is, however, highly questionable (see Niederwimmer, *Didache*, 27), and there is at any rate no reason to question the text of Codex Hierosolymitanus. As Niederwimmer, *Didache*, 195 n. 6 notes, Apos. Con. 7.30.1 interprets the phrase with the extended gloss τὴν ἀναστάσιμον τοῦ κυρίου ἡμέραν τὴν κυριακὴν φαμεν ("the day of the resurrection of the Lord, we say the 'Lord's Day'"), which probably reveals that it had both κυριακὴν and κυρίου in its source (i.e., Did. 14.1).

24. See Richard Bauckham, "The Lord's Day," in *From Sabbath to Lord's Day*, ed. D. A. Carson (Grand Rapids: Zondervan, 1982), 221–50.

bread" and "give thanks." Though not without Jewish antecedents, this is once again distinctively Christian language for the practice of remembering and celebrating the death of Jesus (Luke 24:35; 1 Cor 10:16; Acts 2:42, 46; 20:7, 11; 27:35; Ign. *Eph.* 20.2; see also Pseudo-Clement, *Hom.* 14.1.4). The κύριος on whose day the community gathers is undoubtedly the same κύριος celebrated in the breaking of bread and the giving of thanks. The κύριος here is Jesus.

(5) Didache 15.4 encourages its readers to conduct "prayers" and "acts of charity" "just as you find it in the gospel of our Lord":

τὰς δὲ εὐχὰς ὑμῶν καὶ τὰς ἐλεημοσύνας καὶ πάσας τὰς πράξεις οὕτω ποιήσατε ὡς ἔχετε ἐν τῷ εὐαγγελίῳ τοῦ κυρίου ἡμῶν.

"The gospel of our Lord" here almost certainly means "the gospel of Jesus." Milavec, by contrast, asserts that since Jesus proclaimed the "good news of God," not "'the good news of Jesus' … it must be supposed that this is the 'good news of our Lord God.'"[25] Against this, however, three considerations argue that the "Lord," here again, is the Lord Jesus.

First, the phrase "gospel of our Lord" (εὐαγγελίον τοῦ κυρίου ἡμῶν) is a distinctively Christian construction. On the one hand, the phrase does not appear in the LXX or in the extant Greco-Roman literature of the first century. On the other hand, the phrase "gospel of the/our Lord" does appear elsewhere in the early Christian literature and with explicit reference to Jesus (e.g., 2 Thess 1:8: "the gospel of our Lord Jesus Christ" [τῷ εὐαγγελίῳ τοῦ κυρίου ἡμῶν Ἰησοῦ]).[26] Thus, despite the fact that early Christian "gospel" language had its roots in the Scriptures of Israel (e.g., 1 Kgs 1:42; Jer 20:15; Pss 40:9; 68:11; 96:2; Isa 40:9, 27; 52:7; 61:1) and spoke polemically into the Greco-Roman world, the construction "gospel of our Lord" is distinctively Christian.[27] Second, the statement "as you find it/have it in the gospel" (ὡς ἔχετε ἐν τῷ εὐαγγελίῳ), which is repeated from

---

25. Milavec, *Didache: Faith, Hope, and Life*, 663.

26. The New Testament texts do, of course, also speak of the "gospel of God" (Mark 1:14; Rom 1:1; 15:16; 1 Thess 2:2, 8–9; 1 Pet 4:17), but in early Christian texts it can never simply be assumed that θεός and κύριος are synonymous. As a case in point, Rom 1:1–4 speaks of the "gospel of God," but then applies κύριος specifically to Jesus.

27. For the origins of Christian use of the term εὐαγγελίον and its cognates and the subsequent application of this language to written documents, see Smith, "Gospels in Early Christian Literature," 182–89.

the previous verse (Did. 15.3), seems to suggest a written gospel book.[28] In this connection, it is significant that the contents of this "gospel" indicated at Did. 15.3–4 bear significant resemblance to Jesus's instructions in the Gospel of Matthew (see Matt 5:22; 6:2, 5; 18:15–17).[29] The similarities are not close enough to prove that the Didache knew Matthew, but the reminiscences of Jesus's teaching here are surely significant. Third, more briefly, in the context of Jewish–Gentile polemic evident in the Didache (e.g., 8.1–2), the personal pronoun ἡμῶν ("gospel of *our* Lord") most likely indicates the distinctively Christian "Lord." Taken together, these considerations indicate that the "Lord" associated with the "gospel" at Did. 15.4, as already at Did. 8.2, is none other than the Lord Jesus.

2.3. Texts in Which the "Lord" is Most Likely the Lord Jesus

In eleven other cases, κύριος most likely refers to Jesus.

(1) Didache 1.0 (= Title): The longer of the two titles in Codex Hierosolymitanus most likely refers to the "Lord" Jesus.[30] Since most of the ancient witnesses use the short title (without "Lord"), some have questioned the originality of the long title.[31] It is significant, however, that the long title appears as the introduction to the main text, while the short title

---

28. See esp. Kelhoffer, "How Soon a Book," 24–27. Even by those who deny that εὐαγγελίον at Did. 8.2 and 11.3 refers to a written document recognize that the reference here is to a written gospel. E.g., Koester, *Synoptische Überlieferung*, 10–11; Philipp Vielhauer, *Geschichte der urchristlichen Literatur: Einleitung in das Neue Testament, die Apokryphen und die Apostolischen Väter*, dGL (Berlin: de Gruyter, 1975), 253–54; Willy Rordorf and André Tuilier, *La doctrine des douze Apôtres (Didachè)*, SC 248 bis (Paris: Cerf, 1978), 88, 194 n. 4; Niederwimmer, *Didache*, 204.

29. Kelhoffer, "How Soon a Book," 25 notes that Did. 15.4's reference to ἐλεημοσύνη ("alms/acts of charity") serves to connect the Didache to Matt 6, since the only three occurrences of this term in the Gospel of Matthew appear in Matt 6:2–4, and the term otherwise appears in the New Testament only in Luke-Acts and then in quite different contexts (Luke 11:41; 12:33; Acts 3:2–3, 10; 9:36; 10:2, 4, 31; 24:17). There are also partial parallels to Did. 15.3–4 at 1QS V, 24–25 and 1 Clem. 63.2, but these are not as close as the parallels with Matthew and, at any rate, are not found in books identified by the term "gospel."

30. The long title reads "Teaching of the Lord [κυρίου] through the Twelve Apostles to the Nations." The short title has simply διδαχὴ τῶν δώδεκα ἀποστόλων ("Teaching of the Twelve Apostles").

31. E.g., Niederwimmer, *Didache*, 56 n. 5, citing Eusebius, *Hist. eccl.* 3.25.4; Athanasius, *Ep. fest.* 39.11; Pseudo-Athanasius, *Synopsis scripturae sacrae* 76; Indi-

appears in a separate line above the main text.[32] For this reason, the possibility that the long title is original cannot be ruled out. If so, then the mention of the "twelve apostles" and the evident parallels to Acts 2:42 and Matt 28:19 most likely indicate that the κύριος here is Jesus.

(2–3) Didache 4.1: The two references to the "Lord" at Did. 4.1 most likely also refer to Jesus. The text addresses a student as "my child," and encourages the student to respect his teacher "as the Lord" (ὡς κύριον). The reason given is that "wherever the Lord's nature [ἡ κυριότης] is preached, there the Lord is [ἐκεῖ κύριός ἐστιν]." The use of the same noun κυριότης at Hermas, Sim. 5.6.1, with clear reference to Jesus, together with the parallels between this section and other early Christian texts (Heb 13:7; Matt 18:20 and especially Barn. 19.9–10), suggest that the sayings in Did. 4.1 reflect a distinctively Christian context and thus refer to the distinctively Christian "Lord."[33]

(4) Didache 6.2: The encouragement at Did. 6.2 that "if you are able to bear the whole yoke of the Lord [εἰ μὲν γὰρ δύνασαι βαστάσαι ὅλον τὸν ζυγὸν τοῦ κυρίου], you will be perfect" most likely intends the "yoke of the Lord Jesus." To be sure, Jewish texts employ the image of the "yoke" in various ways.[34] Nevertheless, the Jewish sources nowhere explicitly speak

---

cium scriptorium canonicorum sexagesima; Pseudo-Nicephorus, *Stichometry*; Pseudo-Cyprian, *De aleat.* 4.

32. The originality of the long title was defended by Philip Schaff, *The Oldest Church Manual Called the Teaching of the Twelve Apostle (ΔΙΔΑΧΗ ΤΩΝ ΔΩΔΕΚΑ ΑΠΟΣΤΟΛΩΝ): The Didachè and Kindred Documents* (London: T&T Clark; New York: Funk & Wagnalls, 1885), 14, 162. Adolf von Harnack, *Die Lehre der zwölf Apostel nebst Untersuchungen zur ältesten Geschichte der Kirchenverfassung und des Kirchenrechts* TUGAL 2.1, 2 (Leipzig: Hinrichs, 1884; repr., Berlin: Akademie, 1991), 24–37 similarly considered the longer title original and the shorter title to be an abbreviation of it. For what it is worth, the Georgian text, which is probably a modern translation, preserves the longer title (further expanded), including the reference to the "Lord": "Teaching of the Twelve Apostles, Written in the Year 90 or 100 after the Lord Christ: Teaching of the Lord, Conveyed to Humanity through the Twelve Apostles."

33. See the similar judgment of Niederwimmer, *Didache*, 105.

34. The "yoke" of (1) the Torah or the commandments (Jer 5:5; 2 Bar. 41.3; m. 'Abot 3:5; m. Ber. 2:2; see also Acts 15:10; Gal 5:1); (2) written revelation (Liv. Pro. Dan. 6; 2 En. 48.9); (3) wisdom (Sir 51:26); (4) "heaven" (Sipre Deut. 323); (5) the "kingdom of heaven" (b. Ber. 10b); (6) "the kingdom" (3 En. 35.6). See further: Herman L. Strack and P. Billerbeck, *Kommentar zum Neuen Testament aus Talmud und Midrasch* (Munich: Beck, 1922), 1:608–10; G. Bertram and K. Rengstorf, "ζυγός," *TDNT* 2:898–904.

of "the yoke of the Lord." The closest parallels come in the Psalms of Solomon where "Solomon," addressing God in prayer, says (7.9) "we (shall be) under your yoke for ever" (ἡμεῖς ὑπὸ ζυγόν σου τὸν αἰῶνα) and later speaks of the gentiles coming under the "yoke" of the Messiah (17.30). More significant, then, is Jesus's invitation at Matt 11:29–30: "take my yoke upon you ... for my yoke is easy and my burden is light" (ἄρατε τὸν ζυγόν μου ἐφ᾽ ὑμᾶς ... ὁ γὰρ ζυγός μου χρηστὸς καὶ τὸ φορτίον μου ἐλαφρόν ἐστιν). Other early Christian texts similarly refer to the "yoke" of the Lord Jesus. Justin (*Dial.* 53.1) speaks of the disciples "having borne the yoke of his (= Christ's) word" (τὸν ζυγὸν τοῦ λόγου αὐτοῦ βαστάσαντες). Christians are likewise spoken of as those "who through him have come under the yoke of his (= Jesus') grace" (οἱ ὑπὸ τὸν ζυγὸν τῆς χάριτος αὐτοῦ δι᾽ αὐτοῦ ἐλθόντες) in 1 Clem. 16.17.[35] In the context of these significant Christian parallels, it is most likely that the "Lord" intended at Did. 6.2 is the Lord Jesus.

(5) Didache 10.5: This text is the third and final benediction of the extended prayer of thanksgiving in Did. 10.2–5, and also most likely refers to Jesus as "Lord."[36] The prayer is based on the Jewish Birkat Hamazon.[37] It addresses "you, holy Father" (Did. 10.2) in the first benediction and "you, almighty Master" (Did. 10.3) in the second benediction, before it speaks of "your servant" (Did. 10.3) in clear reference to Jesus.[38] In this context, it might be suggested that the "Lord" addressed in the third benediction at Did. 10.5 is the "holy Father" and "almighty master" of the preceding verses. Four considerations, however, suggest to the contrary that the Lord addressed at Did. 10.5 at least includes reference to the Lord Jesus. First, Did. 10.5 begins a new section in which the Christianization already evident in the first two benedictions is taken further.[39] The close of the second

---

35. See also Barn. 2.6, which gives "yoke" a more negative connotation and speaks of "the new law of our Lord Jesus Christ, which is free from the yoke of compulsion" (ὁ καινὸς νόμος τοῦ κυρίου ἡμῶν Ἰησοῦ Χριστοῦ ἄνευ ζυγοῦ ἀνάγκης ὤν).

36. For analysis of the structure of the prayer, see Niederwimmer, *Didache*, 155.

37. For the Birkat Hamazon, see especially Louis Finkelstein, "The Birkat Ha-Mazon," *JQR* NS 19 (1928–1929): 211–62.

38. See the specification of the "servant" as Jesus at Did. 9.2, 3; 10.2. The Coptic translation and the so-called Georgian version (such as it is) both also specify at Did. 10.3 that the servant is Jesus. For the Coptic, see Carl Schmidt, "Das koptische Didache-Fragment des British Museum," *ZNW* 24 (1925): 81–99 (85, 97).

39. Martin Dibelius, "Die Mahl-Gebete der Didache," in *Zum Urchristentum und zur hellenistischen Religionsgeschichte*, vol. 2 of *Botschaft und Geschichte*, ed. Heinz

benediction is clearly marked at Did. 10.4 by the doxological statement "to you be the glory forever." We therefore cannot assume the same addressee for the third benediction as for the first two. Second, the Didache's evident prototrinitarianism (Did. 7.1, 3) makes it perfectly possible that here, as occasionally elsewhere in the early Christian literature, the renewed prayer in Did. 10.5 might be directed to Jesus as "Lord" (see Acts 7:59; Ign. *Eph.* 20.1).[40] Third, the Didache's prayer is reminiscent of a number of dominical sayings in which Jesus himself is the subject: the request for the Lord to "make it (the church) perfect in your love" is reminiscent of Jesus's prayer that the church will be perfected by his presence among them (John 17:23); the reference to the church as "your church Lord" (κύριε, τῆς ἐκκλησίας σου) resembles Jesus's promise "I will build my church" (Matt 16:18: οἰκοδομήσω μου τὴν ἐκκλησίαν); the request for the Lord to "gather it (the church) from the four winds" (σύναξον αὐτὴν ἀπὸ τῶν τεσσάρων ἀνέμων) parallels Jesus's prophesy that the "son of man" at his "coming" will "gather [his] elect from the four winds" (Mark 13:27: ἐπισυνάξει τοὺς ἐκλεκτοὺς [αὐτοῦ] ἐκ τῶν τεσσάρων ἀνέμων);[41] the prayer for the Lord to gather the church "into your kingdom, which you have prepared for it" (εἰς τὴν σὴν βασιλείαν ἣν ἡτοίμασας αὐτῇ) is reminiscent of the words Jesus gives to "the king" in the parable of the sheep and the goats (Matt 25:34).[42] In each of these cases, Jesus's words about *himself* from the canonical gospels appear as *requests* to the Lord in the Didache.[43] Whatever the literary relationships between these texts, these connections suggest that Jesus is

---

Kraft and Günther. Bornkamm (Tübingen: Mohr Siebeck, 1956), 124–25; Niederwimmer, *Didache*, 155–61.

40. For early Christian prayers directed to Jesus, see Hurtado, *Lord Jesus Christ*, 618.

41. At Mark 13:27 the son of man is the subject of the verb ἐπισυνάξει. At Matt 24:31 the son of man's role in gathering the elect is mediated by the angels (καὶ ἀποστελεῖ τοὺς ἀγγέλους αὐτοῦ ... καὶ ἐπισυνάξουσιν τοὺς ἐκλεκτοὺς αὐτοῦ). The phrase is also reminiscent of Zech 2:10 LXX: διότι ἐκ τῶν τεσσάρων ἀνέμων τοῦ οὐρανοῦ συνάξω ὑμᾶς, λέγει κύριος.

42. Massaux, *Influence of the Gospel of Saint Matthew*, 3:163 regards the phrase ἣν ἡτοίμασας αὐτῇ as evidence of literary dependence on the Gospel of Matthew. Whatever the case, the two texts are clearly related; the Didache here reflects influence from Jesus tradition in some form.

43. Note, however, that the request for the Lord to "deliver it (the church) from evil" (Did. 10.5) does not fit this pattern, for here the prayer of the Didache parallels the Lord's Prayer, which is addressed to the Father (Matt 6:13; cf. Did. 8.2).

the "Lord" intended at Did. 10.5.[44] Finally, in support of this reading, it might be noted that the whole prayer is immediately followed, at Did. 10.6, with the distinctively Christian injunction μαραναθά (cf. 1 Cor 16:22; see further below).

(6–10) Didache 11.2 (x 2), 4, 8; 12.1: These five reference to the "Lord" come at the beginning of a new section on "church order" in the context of instructions about the reception of itinerant teachers and evangelists (11.1). It is, again, most likely that the "Lord" repeatedly spoken of here is Jesus.

To be sure, the first use of κύριος at 11.2, taken on its own, is indeterminate. The Didache speaks of the "righteousness and knowledge of the Lord" in a statement which—by itself—could just as easily refer to the Lord God or the Lord Jesus.

The second reference to κύριος at 11.2, and those that follow at 11.4 and 12.1, however, most likely refer to Jesus. To begin with, the repeated command to "receive" the "teacher" (11.2), "apostle" (11.4), or "all who come in the name of the Lord" (12.1) parallels a number of other early Christian texts in which instruction is given regarding receiving teachers or leaders (Matt 10:40–41; Luke 10:16; John 13:20; 2 John 10; Ign. *Eph.* 6.1; 9.1). Most significant among these are the parallels between the command in 11.2, 4 to receive such people "as the Lord" and other early Christian texts in which the Lord Jesus is understood to be present in his messengers (Matt 10:40–41; John 13:20; Ign. *Eph.* 6.1). The correspondence is particularly striking with Matt 10:40–41, which uses δέχομαι for receiving Jesus's disciples as Jesus himself,[45] and Ign. *Eph.* 6.1, which likewise uses δέχομαι to speak of welcoming the bishop "as the Lord." Given these significant parallels, it is most likely that the "Lord" at Did. 11.2, 4 and 12.1 is Jesus.[46]

---

44. The "gathering" of the people of God is, granted, an important motif in the Scriptures of Israel. It is significant, however, that although some texts envisage the Lord God himself gathering his scattered people (e.g., Ezek 34:13), the Jewish literature more commonly sees the gathering of the elect as a messianic task (e.g., Pss. Sol. 8.28; 11.1–4; 17.21–28; Tg. Isa. 53.8; Tg. Hos. 14.8; Tg. Mic. 5.1–3). This expectation of the Messiah gathering the elect comports well with both the synoptic vision of Jesus gathering the elect as the "son of man" and further supports the possibility that the "Lord" here addressed is the Lord Jesus.

45. Among the canonical gospels, the saying is unique to Matthew. Massaux, *Influence of the Gospel of Saint Matthew*, 3:164 hears an echo of Matt 10:40; see also Kelhoffer, "How Soon a Book," 23–24; Tuckett, "*Didache* and the Writings," 107.

46. So also Niederwimmer, *Didache*, 172, 179. Indeed, the probability that the

In addition, the reference to "the name of the Lord" at Did. 12.1 further strengthens the likelihood that the reference to the "Lord" here at least includes Jesus. Granted, "the name of the Lord" is a common biblical phrase that usually refers to the Lord God and that continues to carry this sense in some of the early Christian texts (Mark 11:9; Matt 21:9; Luke 19:38; Matt 23:39//Luke 13:35; John 12:13). In early Christian usage elsewhere, however, the biblical phrase came to include reference to Jesus. In the Gospel of Matthew, Jesus speaks of his followers being gathered "in my name" (Matt 18:20) and charges his disciples to baptize people "in the name [sing.] of the Father and of the Son and of the Holy Spirit." In the Pauline Epistles, the "name of the Lord" formula is expanded to refer specifically to Jesus in the construction "in the name of the Lord Jesus" (1 Cor 5:4; 2 Thess 3:6; cf. Phil 2:9–10 with Isa 45:22–23). In 1 Clem. 58.1 and 59.2-3 believers are exhorted to "obey," "trust," and "hope" in the "name" in a context that strongly implies that Jesus is understood to embody that name.[47] Most significantly, as we saw in the comments on Did. 9.5 (above), the Didache itself uses the expression "name of the Lord" in a manner that clearly evokes the baptism formula of Did. 7.1, 3 and so includes reference to Jesus, "the Son." The reference to the "name of the Lord" at Did. 12.1, then, most likely includes reference to Jesus as "Lord."[48]

Finally, the reference to the "Lord" at Did. 11.8 is closely related to 11.2, 4, and 12.1 but provides the negative corollary. "Not everyone who speaks in the spirit is a prophet," it affirms, but only the one who "has the Lord's way of life" (ἀλλ᾿ ἐὰν ἔχῃ τοὺς τρόπους κυρίου). It is, again, most likely that the κύριος here is Jesus. To begin with, since the κύριος at Did. 11.2, 4, and 12.1 is most likely Jesus, the same referent is also most likely here. Further, the genitive κυρίου most likely functions as a subjective genitive, relying on the action noun τρόπος (cf. the cognate verb τρέπω) and

---

Didache refers to the Lord Jesus in this section is strengthened by the formal parallelism of Did. 11.3 with the earlier 8.2 (see Niederwimmer, Didache, 174 n. 5). Both texts make reference to "the gospel" (εὐαγγελίον) in the singular. Both texts refer to what the Lord "commanded" (ἐκέλευσεν) or his "decree" (δόγμα) contained in this gospel. And both texts conclude with an exhortation "so pray" (οὕτως προσεύχεσθε) or "so do" (οὕτως ποιήσατε). Given this parallelism, the strong indications, noted above, that the "Lord" at Did. 8.2 is the Lord Jesus, also carry force in this later section.

47. So Hurtado, *Lord Jesus Christ*, 617 n. 164.

48. Niederwimmer, *Didache*, 183 n. 2 plausibly suggests that "*Kyrios* = Jesus. Ἐν ὀνόματι κυρίου = ὡς χριστιανός. Such a one comes and speaks the name of Jesus, i.e., declares that he or she is a Christian."

so intending "the way in which the Lord lived." The phrase thus evokes an actual human life, in this case that of the "Lord" Jesus, against which the lives of would-be prophets might be evaluated.[49] Finally, the identification of the κύριος with Jesus at Did. 11.8 is suggested by the significant parallel with Matt 7:15-21, in which Jesus teaches that false prophets may be identified by their way of life, speaks of himself as "Lord" (Matt 7:21), and then goes on to make adherence to his own teaching the single criterion of faithfulness (Matt 7:24).[50] Thus, κύριος at Did. 11.8, as at 11.2, 4, and 12.1, most likely "means Jesus."[51]

(11) Didache 15.1: The Didache here instructs the local congregation to elect "overseers and deacons" who are "worthy of the Lord" (ἀξίους τοῦ κυρίου). It is possible that the κύριος here simply refers to the Lord God, but a reference to Jesus seems most likely, for three reasons. First, the combination of "overseers and deacons" is well attested in the early Christian literature (Phil 1:1; see also 1 Tim 3:1-10; 1 Clem. 42.4-5); its appearance here renders it likely that the specifically Christian "Lord" Jesus is on view. Second, the phrase "worthy of the Lord" parallels Col 1:10 (see Phil 1:27: "worthy of the gospel of Christ") where the specifically Christian Lord Jesus is on view.[52] Third, the reference in the immediate context (Did. 15.4) to "the gospel of our Lord," which almost certainly refers to Jesus (see above), makes a further reference to the κύριος Jesus here most likely.[53]

---

49. Alternatively, it is possible that κυρίου is a genitive of source, with the sense the "way of life *given by* the Lord," in which case the "Lord" could be God or Jesus. Given, however, that the genitive of source is not common and that there is no compelling reason for taking the genitive in this sense here, the subjective genitive is more likely. See Daniel B. Wallace, *Greek Grammar Beyond the Basics: An Exegetical Syntax of the New Testament* (Grand Rapids: Zondervan, 1996), 109 who states of the genitive of source: "since this usage is not common, it is not advisable to seek it as the most likely one for a particular genitive that may fit under another label. In some ways, the possessive, subjective, and source genitives are similar. In any given instance, if they all make good sense, subjective should be given priority."

50. Massaux, *Influence of the Gospel of Saint Matthew*, 3:165-66, who sees Did. 11.8 as a recollection of Matt 7:15-21.

51. Niederwimmer, *Didache*, 179: "the true prophet is in continuity with the lifestyle and praxis of Jesus—the earthly Jesus."

52. The phrase "worthy of God" also appears in the early Christian literature (1 Thess 2:12; Ign. *Eph.* 2.1; 4.1; Ign. *Rom.* 10.2; see also more broadly Eph 4:1; Ign. *Eph.* 15.1; Ign. *Magn.* 12), but this provides no argument against the reading above which specifically refers to the "Lord."

53. So also Niederwimmer, *Didache*, 201.

2.4. Texts in Which the "Lord" is Quite Possibly the Lord Jesus

The remaining four references to the "Lord" outside Did. 16 are indeterminate, but quite possibly intend Jesus.

(1-2) Didache 4.12-13: The "Lord" twice invoked at Did. 4.12-13 could be either the Lord God of Israel or the Lord Jesus. The injunctions here to "hate all hypocrisy and everything that is not pleasing to the Lord" and to "not forsake the Lord's commandments" find a parallel in Barn. 19.2-3, where the instruction is to "hate everything that is not pleasing to God [τῷ θεῷ]" and to "not forsake the Lord's commandments." The clear reference to "God" at Barn. 19.2 might suggest that the parallel "Lord" of Did. 4.12 should be understood as the Lord God, but this parallel cannot be pressed, since the two passages are set in different contexts.[54] The "Lord's commandments," likewise, could be read either as reference to the commandments of the Lord God or the Lord Jesus. The "commandments" intended are most likely those enumerated in the immediate context,[55] which bear some resemblance to early Christian teaching (cf. Did. 4.8 with Acts 4:32; Did. 4.11 with Eph 6:5; Col 3:22; Titus 2:9). At the same time, the injunction to "guard what you have received, neither adding or subtracting anything" is probably inspired by Deut 4:2, 12:32, and finds parallels in a range of both Jewish and Christian texts (Jer 26:2; 33:2 LXX; Prov 30:5-6 LXX; 1 En. 104.10-13; Let. Aris. 310-311; Josephus, *A.J.* 1.17; *Ag. Ap.* 1.42; Rev 22:18b, 19). It is therefore difficult to determine whether the Lord God of Israel or the Lord Jesus is intended in this instance. Given, however, the likelihood that the Lord twice referred to in the immediately preceding verse is the Lord Jesus (Did. 4.11; see above), it is certainly possible that Jesus is the intended referent here also.

(3-4) Didache 14.3: The two references to the "Lord" here are those most likely, of all of the twenty-four occurrences in the Didache, to intend the Lord God. Even here, however, a reference to the Lord Jesus cannot be ruled out.

This text introduces a conflation of Mal 1:11b, 14b as "the saying/word of the Lord" (ἡ ῥηθεῖσα ὑπὸ κυρίου). The Scripture citation itself includes the phrase "I am a great king, says the Lord" (βασιλεὺς μέγας ἐγώ εἰμί λέγει κύριος). The MT here employs the divine name (יהוה), which is

---

54. See ibid., 112 n. 2.
55. See Knopf, *Lehre der zwölf Apostel*, 19.

translated in the LXX in the customary manner as κύριος. It is therefore most probable that the Didache, in citing Malachi, retains the prophet's reference to the Lord God of Israel.[56]

At the same time, it remains quite possible that the intended referent here at least includes the Lord Jesus.[57] Three considerations are significant:

(a) Early Christian christological exegesis: Early Christian texts regularly exhibit, as noted above, a "Christology of divine identity" in which scriptural texts that in their original contexts speak of the "Lord" God are newly applied to Jesus (e.g., 1 Cor 8:6 with Deut 6:5; Phil 2:10–11 with Isa 45:22; Rev 1:12–16 with Dan 7:9–10). More specifically, a number of early Christian texts predicate preexistence of Jesus (John 1:1–4; Col 1:15–17), or assert that Jesus was present with Israel at the time of the exodus (1 Cor 10:4; Jude 5[58]), or attribute scriptural prophecy to the preincarnate Son/Logos (Justin, *Apol.* 1.36.1).[59] Given this wider usage and the evidence above that the Didache clearly uses κύριος for Jesus at a number of points, the possibility that Did. 14.3 refers to Jesus cannot be ruled out.

---

56. For discussion of the scriptural sources known to the Didache at this point, see Niederwimmer, *Didache*, 198 n. 35, who considers that the Didache has "quoted freely" from the Septuagint.

57. So Franz Xaver Funk, ed. *Patres apostolici*, 3d ed. (Tübingen: Laupp, 1913), 2:33: "Jesu Christo dictum Veteris Testamenti attribuitur"; Wengst, *Didache*, 31; contra Niederwimmer, *Didache*, 198: "Kyrios here probably does not refer to Jesus."

58. At Jude 5, there is significant evidence in the MSS for the reading that identifies the one who saved Israel from Egypt as Ἰησοῦς (A B 33 81 322 323 424c 665 1241 1739 1881 2298 2344 vg cop$^{sa, bo}$ eth Origen Cyril Jerome Bede; ὁ Ἰησοῦς 88 915) or θεὸς Χριστός (Π^{72}). The editors of the NA^{28} have now acknowledged the weight of this evidence by printing Ἰησοῦς in the main text. Cf. Bruce M. Metzger, *A Textual Commentary on the Greek New Testament*, 2nd ed. (London: United Bible Societies, 1994), 657, who, despite favouring the reading κύριος at Jude 5, makes the frank admission that "critical principles seem to require the adoption of Ἰησοῦς, which admittedly is the best attested reading among Greek and versional witnesses."

59. Justin, *Apol.* 1.36.1: "But when you hear the utterances of the prophets spoken as it were personally, you must not suppose that they are spoken by the inspired themselves, but by the Divine Word who moves them. For sometimes He declares things that are to come to pass, in the manner of one who foretells the future; sometimes He speaks as from the person of God the Lord and Father of all; sometimes as from the person of Christ; sometimes as from the person of the people answering the Lord or His Father." See discussion in Bruce Chilton, "Justin and Israelite Prophecy," in *Justin Martyr and his Worlds*, ed. Sara Parvis and Paul Foster (Minneapolis: Fortress, 2007), 81–82.

(b) The immediate context: Didache 14.1, as noted above, speaks of the "Lord" gathering his people together to "break bread" and "give thanks" on the "Lord's own day" (Did. 14.1). Since the κύριος at Did. 14.1 is almost certainly Jesus, it is at least possible that the κύριος at Did. 14.3 is also Jesus. Didache 14.2, indeed, is reminiscent of Jesus's word at Matt 5:23–24 and employs the same verb διαλλάσσομαι, which occurs at only these two points in the whole of the New Testament and Apostolic Fathers. Whether the Didache is here dependent on the Gospel of Matthew or not, this contact with Jesus tradition strengthens the possibility that the Lord referred to at Did. 14.3 is Jesus.[60] Finally, Did. 15.1, which immediately follows, also speaks of the "Lord" in what is most likely a reference to Jesus (see above). Although it is possible that Did. 14.3 uses κύριος in a manner different to its immediate context, the surrounding usage at least strengthens the possibility that Jesus is here again the intended referent.

(c) The saying itself: Didache 14.3 (citing Mal 1:14b) records the Lord's declaration that "my name is marvellous among the nations." In the context of Did. 7.1, 3; 9.5; 12.1, where the "name of the Lord" includes reference to Jesus, it is certainly possible that this text also includes reference to Jesus.[61]

When all is considered, it remains most likely that the "Lord" at Did. 14.3 refers primarily to the Lord God of Israel. Even in this case, however, the inclusion of the Lord Jesus in the divine identity cannot be ruled out.

2.5. Conclusion

In view of all this, Milavec's insistence that "all of the instances of 'Lord' in the Didache ought to be understood as referring to the Lord God"[62] cannot be sustained. In at least five instances, κύριος in the Didache almost certainly refers to Jesus. In eleven other cases, a reference to Jesus is most

---

60. A number of scholars affirm that the Didache here reflects the dominical saying. So Harnack, *Lehre, der zwölf Apostel* 55; Paul Drews, "Apostellehre (Didache)," in *Handbuch zu den neutestamentlichen Apokryphen*, ed. Edgar Hennecke (Tübingen: Mohr Siebexk, 1904), 279. Others argue for direct literary dependence on Matthew: Massaux, *Influence of the Gospel of Saint Matthew*, 3:156–57. This is denied by Koester, *Synoptische Überlieferung*, 214, who argues that the Didache here draws on "the treasure of freely circulating community rules."

61. Note, however, Did. 8.2, 10.2, 3, which refer to the "name" (ὄνομα) of God the Father.

62. Milavec, *Didache: Faith, Hope, and Life*, 665.

likely. In a final four cases, a reference to Jesus is possible, even if the text remains indeterminate. Significantly, the evidence nowhere *requires* that κύριος refers to the Lord God of Israel. It is, therefore, a mistake to overdraw the distinction between the Lord God of Israel and the Lord Jesus in the Didache. In common with other early Christian writings, the Didache includes Jesus within the identity of the one true God of Israel, so that ambiguity in some cases is almost inevitable, and perhaps deliberate. Certainly, on the basis of this analysis there is no a priori reason to rule out the possibility that Jesus is the "Lord" whom the Didache expects to "come" (Did. 10.6; 16.1, 7, 8). On the contrary, there is much to suggest that the Didache, in common with other early Christian texts, looks forward to the "coming of the Lord" Jesus.

3. The "Coming of the Lord" Jesus in Did. 10.6 and 16.1, 7–8

The Didache speaks of the future "coming of the Lord" at four points (Did. 10.6; 16.1, 7, 8). In what follows, it is argued that in each case the Didache expects the "second coming" of the Lord Jesus and interprets this event as the final embodiment of the long prophesied "coming of God."

3.1. The Μαραναθά Invocation of Did. 10.6

The first reference to Jesus's coming as Lord is found in the μαραναθά invocation at Did. 10.6. Amongst the Christian literature of the first two centuries, the μαραναθά prayer appears in this form, as a Greek transliteration of Aramaic, only here and at 1 Cor 16:22. The roots of this "earliest Christian prayer"[63] are found in the theophany tradition of the Hebrew Scriptures (Deut 33:2; Judg 5:4–5; Hab 3:3–6; Mic 1:2–5a; Zech 14:5), perhaps especially in the form preserved in the Aramaic Qumran fragment of 1 En. 1.9 (4QAram).[64] Depending on the segmentation of the Aramaic it could mean "Our Lord has come" (μαραν αθα), "Our Lord is coming/will come" (μαραν αθα, if αθα is understood as a participle), or "Our Lord,

---

63. Archibald Macbride Hunter, *Exploring the New Testament* (Edinburgh: Saint Andrew Press, 1971), 98.

64. Matthew Black, "The Maranatha Invocation and Jude 14, 15 (1 Enoch 1:9)," in *Christ and Spirit in the New Testament: In Honour of Charles Francis Digby Moule*, ed. Barnabas Lindars and Stephen S. Smalley (Cambridge: Cambridge University Press, 1973), 193–95.

come!" (μαρανα θα).⁶⁵ Be that as it may, in an early Christian context, there is no doubt that the "Lord" addressed in the prayer is Jesus. Two considerations are decisive.

First, a number of other early Christian prayers call on the Lord Jesus to come again. Most significant here is the parallel prayer at 1 Cor 16:22—also in transliterated Aramaic—which is clearly directed to the Lord Jesus. To be sure, the first part of 1 Cor 16:22, with its reference to "love for the Lord" (φιλεῖ τὸν κύριον) and to "curse" (ἀνάθεμα), evokes the covenant language of Israel's Scriptures.⁶⁶ For this reason, it might be thought to imply a reference to the Lord God, simplistically understood. It is decisive, however, that earlier in the same letter Paul clearly distinguishes the "Lord" Jesus from "God" the Father, while unambiguously including Jesus within the identity of the one God of the Hebrew Shema (1 Cor 8:6; see also 1:2-3). In this context, it is clear that Paul's μαραναθά invocation is addressed to Jesus as "Lord." By it, the apostle calls on Jesus to come again and so gives voice to his expectation that the final "coming" of the covenant Lord for judgment is to be embodied in the return of Jesus.⁶⁷ Also significant here is the parallel Greek prayer at Rev 22:20, "Come, Lord Jesus" (ἔρχου κύριε Ἰησοῦ), which clearly has Jesus's final advent in view. Further, the prophetic vision of Jude 14 (Ἰδοὺ ἦλθεν κύριος: "Behold, the Lord comes"), which similarly draws on the Jewish vision of the "coming of God" (see 1 En. 1.9; Zech 14:5) to speak of Jesus's "second coming" (see Jude 21),⁶⁸ probably also preserves a form of the μαραναθά prayer.

Second, the immediate context of Did. 10.6 indicates that the prayer is addressed to Jesus. To begin with, the location of the prayer in a kind of

---

65. M. Wilcox, "Maranatha," *ABD* 4:513.

66. Anders Eriksson, *Traditions as Rhetorical Proof: Pauline Argumentation in 1 Corinthians*, ConBNT (Stockholm: Almquist & Wiksell, 1998), 289-93.

67. See especially, C. F. D. Moule, "A Reconsideration of the Context of Maranatha," *NTS* 6 (1959-1960): 307-10; Black, "Maranatha Invocation," 189-96; Eriksson, *Traditions as Rhetorical Proofs*, 289-93; Anthony C. Thiselton, *The First Epistle to the Corinthians: A Commentary on the Greek Text*, NIGTC (Grand Rapids: Eerdmans, 2000), 1347-52; Hurtado, *Lord Jesus Christ*, 617: μαραναθά "is an appeal to the exalted Jesus to come in eschatological power."

68. Glasson, *Second Advent*, 186; Black, "Maranatha Invocation," 194; Richard J. Bauckham, *Jude, 2 Peter*, WBC (Waco, TX: Word, 1983), 96-97; Edward Adams, "The Coming of God Tradition and Its Influence on New Testament Parousia Texts," in *Biblical Traditions in Transmission: Essays in Honour of Michael A. Knibb*, ed. Charlotte Hempel and Judith M.Lieu, JSJSup (Leiden: Brill, 2006), 1.

liturgy for the Lord's Supper (Did. 9.1; 10.7) may indicate that it is to be understood, at least in part, as a call for the "Lord" to be present among his people at the meal (see Matt 18:20).[69] If so, then it can be none other than the Lord Jesus who is invoked. At the same time, it is also clear that the prayer ultimately looks for God's eschatological triumph in the world through the Messiah.[70] Indeed, given that the expectation of Jesus's return was an integral part of the Christian celebratory-remembrance meal from the very beginning (Mark 14:25; Matt 26:29; 1 Cor 11:26), it is no surprise to find it here also. Didache 10.5 already has the final state on view in its prayer for the church to be delivered from evil (see Matt 6:13), made perfect in love (see John 17:23), and gathered from the four winds into God's kingdom (see Zech 2:10 LXX; Mark 13:27; Matt 24:31; 25:34; Did. 9.5). As noted above, the way in which Jesus's words about *himself* appear here as *requests* to the "Lord" clearly indicates that Jesus himself is the one expected. Didache 10.6 then continues this eschatological trajectory and brings it to a climax. Indeed, the μαραναθά petition is the last in a series of four prayers that look for the consummation of God's purposes in the world through the Messiah: "may grace come" (ἐλθέτω χάρις);[71] "may this

---

69. Hans Lietzmann, *Messe und Herrenmahl: Eine Studie zur Geschichte der Liturgie*, AK (Bonn: Marcus & Weber, 1926), 229, argued that the μαραναθά invocation at 1 Cor 16:22 primarily concerns the Lord's presence in the Eucharist. He was followed by many others including Günther Bornkamm, "Das Anathema in der urchristlichen Abendmahlsliturgie," *TLZ* 65 (1950): 227–30; John A. T. Robinson, "Traces of a Liturgical Sequence in 1 Cor. xvi. 20–24," *JTS* 4 (1953): 38–41 (38); K. G. Kuhn, "μαραναθά," *TDNT* 4:470; and Ernst Käsemann, "Sentences of Holy Law in the NT," in *New Testament Questions of Today* (London: SCM, 1969), 66–81 (69–70). This reading probably cannot hold for 1 Cor 16:22 and has been ably refuted by Moule, "Reconsideration of the Context," 307–10; Eriksson, *Traditions a Rhetorical Proofs*, 279–98; see also Thiselton, *First Epistle to the Corinthians*, 1347–52. Nevertheless, in the different context of Did. 10.6, a eucharistic reference may well be included. See Hunter, *Exploring the New Testament*, 98 who suggests a threefold reference to the Lord's presence at Easter ("the Lord has come!"), the Eucharist ("The Lord is come!"), and the parousia ("The Lord will come!"); and Black, "Maranatha Invocation," 192 n. 16, 195–96 who supports Hunter's threefold reference.

70. Contra Kuhn, *TDNT* 4:466–72, who excludes any future reference. For the arguments, see esp. Black, "Maranatha Invocation," 195–96.

71. The Coptic text has ἐλθέτω ὁ κύριος and should perhaps be preferred as the more difficult reading (see Draper, "Eschatology in the *Didache*," 571). If so, this further strengthens the eschatological emphasis of the section and confirms the argument above regarding the μαραναθά invocation.

world pass away" (παρελθέτω ὁ κόσμος οὗτος); "Hosanna to the God of David" (ὡσαννὰ τῷ θεῷ Δαυίδ); "Maranatha!"[72] Finally, in the midst of all this, the invitation to the "holy" to "come" and the call for those who are not to "repent" (μετανοείτω), underlines the urgency of the eschatological situation.

Taking all of this together, the μαραναθά prayer at Did. 10.6 is best understood as an invocation for the Lord Jesus to come in final judgment. The "Lord" (Aramaic מרן) here invoked is the Lord Jesus; the "coming" referred to his is final advent.

3.2. The Coming of the Lord in Did. 16

The remaining three references to the "coming of the Lord" in the Didache occur in its final chapter (Did. 16.1, 7, 8). Most commentators assume without argument that Jesus's "second coming" is here on view.[73] Milavec, however, as noted above, considers it "quite clear ... that ... the Lord God ... is awaited."[74] In what follows, it is demonstrated that each of these texts does indeed refer to Jesus's expected "second coming."

To begin with, it is worth noting that the structure of this final chapter makes it highly likely that the same "Lord" is referred to at Did. 16.1, 7, 8. The three references to the "coming of the Lord" frame the other eschatological material and form an *inclusio* that gives unity to the whole section.[75] Within this frame, the material in Did. 16.1c–8 is structured in two halves: first, "a series of four causal clauses introduced by γάρ" address the "present ethical life ... of the community" under persecution in the light of the coming "last time" (Did. 16.1c–4a); second, a further series of "four future clauses introduced by καὶ τότε or τότε" speak more directly of the final

---

72. See Hurtado, *Lord Jesus Christ*, 617–18.

73. E.g., Wengst, *Didache*, 31 who states simply in relation to Did. 16.7b: "Kyrios (as the context shows) refers to Jesus"; Draper, "Eschatology in the *Didache*," 577, who speaks of the "coming of the Son of Man on the clouds" even though "son of man" language is absent from the Didache.

74. Milavec, *Didache: Faith, Hope, and Life*, 665.

75. This analysis concerns the extant text, since the precise contents of the "lost-ending" of the Didache are unknown. For a reconstruction based on Apos. Con. 7.32, see Robert E. Aldridge, "The Lost Ending of the *Didache*," *VC* 53 (1999): 1–15; see also Alan J. P. Garrow, *The Gospel of Matthew's Dependence on the* Didache, JSNTSup 254 (London: T&T Clark, 2004), 44–64.

eschatological events (Did. 16.4b-8).[76] The effect of this structure is to contrast the present life of the community with the expected eschatological events and thus to emphasize the final eschatological event introduced by the fourth τότε in Did. 16.8, namely, the "coming of the Lord … on the clouds of heaven."[77] It is no surprise, then, that this crucial final event is also introduced at the beginning of the eschatological section (Did. 16.1) to form the *inclusio* just noted. The following analysis demonstrates that the presumption created by this structure is correct: the same "Lord" is expected at Did. 16.1, 7, and 8; in each case the "Lord" expected is none other than the "Lord" Jesus.

3.2.1. The "Coming of the Lord" Jesus in Did. 16.1

Didache 16.1 serves as a brief introduction to the eschatological material of Did. 16.1–8. The text reads as follows:

ᵃΓρηγορεῖτε ὑπὲρ τῆς ζωῆς ὑμῶν ᵇοἱ λύχνοι ὑμῶν μὴ σβεσθήτωσαν καὶ αἱ ὀσφύες ὑμῶν μὴ ἐκλυέσθωσαν ᶜἀλλὰ γίνεσθε ἕτοιμοι·οὐ γὰρ οἴδατε τὴν ὥραν ἐν ᾗ ὁ κύριος ἡμῶν ἔρχεται

This verse contains three significant parallels to the synoptic tradition, each of which refers to Jesus's final advent. The argument here is that whether the Didache is directly dependent on the Synoptic Gospels or not, the presence of parallels to those points of the synoptic tradition that refer to Jesus's "second coming" strongly suggests that Did. 16.1 also expects the coming of none other than Jesus as Lord. This will be clearly seen if we first note the connections with the synoptic tradition and then demonstrate that the parallel synoptic texts refer to Jesus's final advent.[78]

---

76. Draper, "Eschatology in the *Didache*," 577.
77. See Vicky Balabanski, *Eschatology in the Making: Mark, Matthew and the Didache*, SNTSMS 97 (Cambridge: Cambridge University Press, 1997), 208: "Unlike Matthew, the author of Didache 16 does not seem to consider the present as part of the 'last days.'"
78. Milavec, *Didache: Faith, Hope, and Life*, 660–63 omits consideration of Did. 16.1 in his discussion of "whether the Lord God comes or the Lord Jesus returns."

3.2.1.1. The Text and Its Intertexts

(a) The call to watch, and the unexpected coming: The Didache's call to "watch" (Did. 16.1a) and its warning regarding the unknown time of the Lord's coming (Did. 16.1c) are similar to Jesus's words recorded at a number of points in the synoptic tradition.

Mark 13:32, 35: περὶ δὲ τῆς ἡμέρας ἐκείνης ἢ τῆς ὥρας οὐδεὶς οἶδεν, οὐδὲ οἱ ἄγγελοι ἐν οὐρανῷ οὐδὲ ὁ υἱός, εἰ μὴ ὁ πατήρ … γρηγορεῖτε οὖν·οὐκ οἴδατε γὰρ πότε ὁ κύριος τῆς οἰκίας ἔρχεται

Matt 24:36: περὶ δὲ τῆς ἡμέρας ἐκείνης καὶ ὥρας οὐδεὶς οἶδεν οὐδὲ οἱ ἄγγελοι τῶν οὐρανῶν οὐδὲ ὁ υἱός εἰ μὴ ὁ πατὴρ μόνος

Matt 24:42, 44: γρηγορεῖτε οὖν ὅτι οὐκ οἴδατε ποίᾳ ἡμέρᾳ ὁ κύριος ὑμῶν ἔρχεται … διὰ τοῦτο καὶ ὑμεῖς γίνεσθε ἕτοιμοι ὅτι ᾗ οὐ δοκεῖτε ὥρᾳ ὁ υἱὸς τοῦ ἀνθρώπου ἔρχεται

Matt 25:13: γρηγορεῖτε οὖν ὅτι οὐκ οἴδατε τὴν ἡμέραν οὐδὲ τὴν ὥραν

Luke 12:40: καὶ ὑμεῖς γίνεσθε ἕτοιμοι ὅτι ᾗ ὥρᾳ οὐ δοκεῖτε ὁ υἱὸς τοῦ ἀνθρώπου ἔρχεται

Did. 16.1a, c: γρηγορεῖτε ὑπὲρ τῆς ζωῆς ὑμῶν … ἀλλὰ γίνεσθε ἕτοιμοι·οὐ γὰρ οἴδατε τὴν ὥραν ἐν ᾗ ὁ κύριος ἡμῶν ἔρχεται

The numerous points of contact between Did. 16.1 and these synoptic texts include: (1) the call to "watch" (γρηγορεῖτε: Mark 13:35; Matt 24:42; 25:13);[79] (2) the combination of γίνεσθε with ἕτοιμοι ("be prepared": Mark 13:35; Matt 24:44; Luke 12:40); (3) the verb οἴδατε ("you know": Mark 13:35; Matt 24:42; 25:13; see also οἶδεν: Mark 13:32; Matt 24:36); (4) the reference to τὴν ὥραν ("the hour": Mark 13:32; Matt 24:36, 44; 25:13; Luke 12:40); (5) the identity of the coming one as ὁ κύριος ("Lord": Mark

---

79. This call is, to be sure, used in a slightly different sense in the Didache than in the Synoptics: in the former the command is to "watch over your life"; in the latter it relates more directly to the unknown timing of the Lord's coming. This difference must not, however, be overplayed, since after some brief additional material (Did. 16.1b), Did. 16.1c grounds the necessity to "watch" in the unknown timing of the Lord's coming. Balabanski, *Eschatology in the Making*, 198 thus overstates the point when she argues for a significant shift in meaning from the imminent end expectation of the synoptics to the concern for care in daily living in the Didache.

13:35; Matt 24:42); (6) the verb ἔρχεται ("come": Mark 13:35; Matt 24:42, 44; Luke 12:40); (7) the reference to ὁ κύριος ἡμῶν ("our Lord": see Matt 24:42, which has Jesus employ the second-person plural ὁ κύριος ὑμῶν ["your Lord"]).

In all, the closest parallels here are with Matt 24:42, 44, which together contain nearly the whole of Did. 16.1a, c. Common to both texts are: γρηγορεῖτε; γίνεσθε ἕτοιμοι; οἴδατε; τὴν ὥραν; ὁ κύριος ἡμῶν/ὑμῶν; ἔρχεται. On this basis it has often been thought that the Didache here depends on Matt 24.[80] This remains quite likely, but the parallels are not so exact as to require direct literary dependence. In particular, there is nothing in Did. 16.1 that so clearly reflects Matthean redaction of Mark that it could only be derived from Matthew's Gospel.[81] Be that as it may, the numerous points of contact between Did. 16.1a, c and the synoptic materials listed above at very least demonstrate that the Didache's expectation of the "coming of the Lord" is firmly located within the synoptic tradition.

(b) The call be prepared (lamps lit and loins girded): Didache 16.1b further exhorts its readers to "not let your lamps go out, and do not be unprepared." There is a significant parallel here with Luke 12:35.

Luke 12:35: Ἔστωσαν ὑμῶν αἱ ὀσφύες περιεζωσμέναι καὶ οἱ λύχνοι καιόμενοι

Did. 16.1b: οἱ λύχνοι ὑμῶν μὴ σβεσθήτωσαν καὶ αἱ ὀσφύες ὑμῶν μὴ ἐκλυέσθωσαν

Once again, the verbal agreement is not close enough to prove direct literary dependence.[82] It has been suggested that the language is stereotypical (see 1 Pet 1:13; Eph 6:14) and therefore provides no information regarding the relationship between Luke and the Didache.[83] Against this,

---

80. Harnack, *Lehre der zwölf Apostel*, 60; Funk, *Patres apostolici*, 35; J. Armitage Robinson, "The Problem of the Didache," *JTS* 13 (1912): 339–56; F. E. Vokes, *The Riddle of the Didache: Fact or Fiction, Heresy or Catholicism?* (London: SPCK, 1938), 111; Massaux, *Influence of the Gospel of Saint Matthew*, 3:167–73; Hagner, *Use of the Old and New Testaments*, 280.

81. So Tuckett, "Synoptic Tradition in the Didache," 212; Tuckett, "Didache and the Writings," 111.

82. Emphasized by Koester, *Synoptische Überlieferung*, 175–76; Audet, *Didachè*, 181; Niederwimmer, *Didache*, 214.

83. Koester, *Synoptische Überlieferung*, 175–76; Wengst, *Didache*, 99.

however, the co-location of the two images ("lamps" and "loins girded") is sufficiently uncommon to suggest a relationship of some kind.[84] Certainty is impossible, but most likely either the Didache and Luke both knew the saying from a common source (perhaps Q),[85] or the Didache presents a modified rendition of a saying it knew from Luke's Gospel.[86] Either way, it is sufficient for our purposes to notice again that the Didache's expectation of the "coming of the Lord" is firmly located within the synoptic tradition.

Indeed, the reference to "lamps" may well also be connected to Jesus's parable of the ten virgins (see Matt 25:1–13), especially since both the call to watch (Did. 16.1a) and the warning regarding the unknown hour (Did. 16.1c) find a parallel at Matt 25:13. Since Matthew's parable uses λαμπάς rather than λύχνος, direct literary dependence is unlikely. Nevertheless, the strong conceptual links may indicate that both Matthew and the Didache here draw on common dominical tradition or that the Didache presents a somewhat garbled reminiscence of the parable as the Didache knew it in Matthean or proto-Matthean form.

To summarise, Did. 16.1 stands in clear parallel with a number of texts in the synoptic tradition. The call to "watch," the saying about preparedness (using the dual image of lamps lit and loins girded), and the warning regarding the unknown hour of the Lord's coming are all reflected in texts in the Synoptic Gospels, where they appear on the lips of Jesus. While direct literary dependence cannot be demonstrated with certainty, the common vocabulary and multiple points of contact strongly locate the Didache's expectation of the coming Lord within the synoptic tradition.

3.2.1.2. The Identity of the Coming Lord in Did. 16.1

This contact between Did. 16.1 and the synoptic tradition is significant for our purposes because, without exception, the synoptic texts in question

---

84. So Tuckett, "Synoptic Tradition in the Didache," 213; Tuckett, "Didache and the Writings," 112.

85. Burnett H. Streeter, *The Four Gospels: A Study of Origins* (London: Macmillan, 1924), 511; Glover, "Didache's Quotations and the Synoptic Gospels," 21–22; Draper, "Jesus Tradition in the *Didache*," 87; Draper, "Eschatology in the *Didache*," 573–74.

86. B. C. Butler, "The Literary Relations of Didache, ch. XVI," *JTS* 11 (1960): 265–83 (265–68), who argues that the dual parallel of Did. 16.1a, 1b with Luke 12:35, 40 is sufficient evidence for literary dependence; see also cautiously Tuckett, "Synoptic Tradition in the Didache," 213–14; Tuckett, "Didache and the Writings," 112.

concern *Jesus's* final advent. In none of the synoptic texts does Jesus speak of a final theophany in which he is uninvolved; in all of them, he speaks of his own final advent, often in theophanic terms. Given the strong connections between the Didache and the synoptic tradition at this point, the "coming of the Lord" in Did. 16.1 almost certainly also refers to the return of the Lord Jesus. A brief consideration of the texts in question will make the point.

(a) Mark 13:32–37: Jesus's parable of the "man going on a journey" and the associated sayings at Mark 13:32–37 have long been understood as a reference to Jesus's own final advent. More recently, however, a significant stream of modern scholarship has rejected this reading, arguing instead that most, if not all, of Mark 13, including the "coming of the son of man" (Mark 13:26), is concerned with Jesus's heavenly enthronement, manifested on earth in the first-century destruction of Jerusalem.[87] Two considerations, however, argue decisively for the traditional reading.

First, the structure of Mark 13 distinguishes "these things," namely, the imminent destruction of Jerusalem and the period of tribulation of which it is part (Mark 13:3–23, 28–31)[88] from the final climactic "coming of the son of man" (Mark 13:24–27, 32–37).[89] While "all these things" are to (begin to) occur within a generation, the "coming of the son of man"

---

87. See, most recently, N. T. Wright, *Jesus and the Victory of God*, vol. 2 of *Christian Origins and the Question of God* (Minneapolis: Fortress, 1996), 339–66, who argues that the whole of Mark 13 is concerned with the destruction of the Jerusalem temple. In his view the "coming of the son of man" (Mark 13:26) does not refer to Jesus's final coming from heaven to earth in glory but is, rather, apocalyptic code for Jesus's vindication, manifested in his own enthronement in heaven, and in the destruction of the city that opposed him. See similarly T. Manson, "The Son of Man in Daniel, Enoch and the Gospels," *BJRL* 32 (1950), 171–93 (174); T. F. Glasson, "The Son of Man Imagery: Enoch xiv and Daniel vii," *NTS* 23 (1976–1977): 82–90; Robinson, *Jesus and His Coming*, 45; Joachim Jeremias, *The Proclamation of Jesus*, vol. 1 of *New Testament Theology*, trans. John Bowden (New York: Scribner's Sons, 1971), 273–74; R. T. France, *Mark: A Commentary on the Greek Text*, NIGTC (Grand Rapids: Eerdmans, 2002), 502, 534, 612.

88. Note esp. Mark 13:4: ταῦτα … ταῦτα πάντα; 13:23: προείρηκα ὑμῖν πάντα; 13:29: ταῦτα; 13:30: ταῦτα.

89. Helpful analyses of the structure of Mark 13 are offered by William L. Lane, *The Gospel of Mark*, NICNT (Grand Rapids: Eerdmans, 1974), 444–48; see also Arthur L. Moore, *The Parousia in the New Testament*, NovTSup 13 (Leiden: Brill, 1966), 131–36; Adela Yarbro Collins, *Mark: A Commentary*, Hermeneia (Minneapolis: Fortress, 2007), 614–20.

will occur after an indeterminate period of time, and at an unknown day and hour (Mark 13:24-27,[90] 32-37[91]). Given this distinction, there is no reason to doubt that when Mark's Jesus speaks of the unknown day and hour (Mark 13:32) and of the "coming" of the "Lord" (Mark 13:35), he speaks of the day of his own final advent as son of man.

Second, the Danielic image of the "coming son of man" itself indicates that Mark 13:24-27 and 32-37 refer to Jesus's own final theophany-like coming from heaven to earth in glory. To begin with, Dan 7:13-14 already presents the coming of the "one like a son of man" in theophanic terms, as a descent from heaven to earth.[92] This is indicated by: (1) the coming of the "one like a son of man" *on the clouds*, which reflects the way God regularly comes "in," "with," or "on" the clouds when making an appearance on earth to bring salvation and judgment (see Exod 16:10; 19:9; 34:5; Num 11:25; 12:5; 2 Sam 22:12; Isa 19:1; Nah 1:3; Pss 18:10-11; 97:2);[93] (2) the coming of the son of man *to* the Ancient of Days, who has

---

90. A change of topic at Mark 13:24 is indicated by (1) the adversative "but" (ἀλλὰ) and the laboured reference to a new period of time: "in those days after that suffering"; (2) the contrast between the second person plural at Mark 13:14 ("but when you see" = ὅταν δὲ ἴδητε; cf. Mark 13:29) and the third person plural at Mark 13:26 ("and then they will see" = καὶ τότε ὄψονται). The introduction of a substantially new topic at Mark 13:24 is recognised by D. M. Roark, "The Great Eschatological Discourse," *NovT* 7 (1964): 123-27 (127); Lane, *Mark*, 473 n. 87; Joachim Gnilka, *Das Evangelium nach Markus*, 2 vols., EKKNT 2 (Zürich: Benziger, 1978), 2:200; Rudolf Pesch, *Das Markus-Evangelium*, 3rd ed., 2 vols., HTKNT 2 (Freiburg: Herder, 1980), 2:302; Robert H. Gundry, *Mark: A Commentary on His Apology for the Cross* (Grand Rapids: Eerdmans, 1993), 745; Collins, *Mark*, 614.

91. The backward reference from Mark 13:32 to 13:24-27 is marked by (1) the adversative περὶ δὲ at Mark 13:32, which customarily introduces a new topic (see also Mark 12:26); (2) the emphatic reference to "that day" (singular: τῆς ἡμέρας ἐκείνης, which naturally takes the [implied] day of the son of man's coming as its antecedent; and (3) the contrast between the timing of "these things" that will most certainly (at least begin to) occur within a generation (13:30) and of "that day," which will come at a time unknown, even to the son (Mark 13:32: "no one knows"; 13:33: "you do not know"; 13:35: "you do not know").

92. For this view, see esp. Maurice Casey, *Son of Man: The Interpretation and Influence of Daniel 7* (London: SPCK, 1979), 22, 24-29; G. R. Beasley-Murray, "The Interpretation of Daniel 7," *CBQ* 45 (1983): 44-58; J.E. Goldingay, *Daniel*, WBC (Dallas: Word, 1989), 147, 164.

93. J. A. Emerton, "The Origin of the Son of Man Imagery," *JTS* 9 (1958): 225-42 (231-32): "The act of coming with clouds suggests a theophany of Yahweh himself. If Dan. vii. 13 does not refer to a divine being, then it is the only exception out of about

already "come" to execute judgment against the beasts and to establish his throne upon the earth (see Dan 7:9–10, 22);[94] (3) the grant of a kingdom to the "one like a son of man," which reflects the earthly kingdom that earlier belonged to Nebuchadnezzar (Dan 4:34) and which unmistakably evokes both the biblical creation paradigm and the prophetic expectation that the king of Israel would rule over the beastly pagan nations (Pss 2:7–9; 80:13–16; 110:1; 144:3). Decisively, however, Mark 13:24–27 does not merely repeat the Danielic vision, but further extends its theophanic presentation of the "coming of the son of man."[95] The son of man "comes," as God regularly does, "with great power and glory" (see Isa 59:19; 66:18; Hab 3:3). He comes, like God, with an angelic entourage (see Deut 33:2; Zech 14:5). His coming, like that of God, causes cosmic convulsions (see Isa 13:10; 34:4; Ezek 32:7–8; Amos 8:9; Joel 2:10; 3:15–16). And he comes, as God does, to gather the elect (see Deut 30:3–4; Ps 50:3–5; Isa 43:6; 66:18; Jer 32:37; Ezek 34:13; 36:24; Zech 2:6–10; Ps 147:2; Tob 14:7; Pss. Sol. 17.28). In this context, the reference to "that day" at Mark 13:32 is

---

seventy passages in the O.T." The same point was made earlier by André Feuillet, "Le Fils de l'homme de Daniel et la tradition biblique," *RB* 60 (1953), 170–202 and 321–46. See also Leopold Sabourin, "The Biblical Cloud: Terminology and Traditions," *BTB* 4 (1974): 290–311 (295): "No other literature … uses so insistently the metaphor of the cloud to describe theophanies as Israel does"; 304: "coming with the clouds is an exclusively divine attribute."

94. The terrestrial location of the Ancient of Day's throne in Dan 7:9–10 is indicated by (1) the terrestrial location of the scene in Dan 7:2–8 (see also 7:17, 23); (2) the echoes of the creation paradigm in the vision of a "son of man" ruling over the beasts (see André Lacocque, "Allusions to Creation in Daniel 7," in *The Book of Daniel: Composition and Reception*, ed. John Joseph Collins and Peter W. Flint, 2 vols., VTSup 83 [Leiden: Brill, 2001], 1:114–31); (3) the lack of any indication at Dan 7:9 that the scene has changed from earth to heaven (see Goldingay, *Daniel*, 164); (4) the "coming" (see 7:22: אֲתָה) of the Ancient of Days to bring judgment upon the earth-bound beasts (see Beasley-Murray, "Interpretation of Daniel 7," 49); (5) the depiction of the divine judgment throne, which Jewish and Christian texts customarily locate upon the earth (Jer 49:38; Ps 9:7–8, 11; 1 En. 25.3–4; 90.20; T. Abr. [Rec. A] 12.4, 11; cf. Matt 19:28; 25:31; Rev 20:11–12); (6) the "fiery" appearance of the Ancient of Days (see Exod 19:18; 24:17; Deut 4:36; 5:4, 22–26; 33:2) and the angelic retinue attending him (see Deut 33:2; Ps 68:18; Zech 14:5; 1 En. 1.9), which both evoke the "coming of God" tradition of the Hebrew Scriptures.

95. See esp. G. R. Beasley-Murray, *Jesus and the Last Days: The Interpretation of the Olivet Discourse* (Peabody, MA: Hendrickson, 1993), 374–75, 424; see also Edward Adams, "The Coming of the Son of Man in Mark's Gospel," *TynBul* 56 (2005): 39–61 (52–59); Adams, "Coming of God Tradition," 10–11.

highly significant: it evokes the scriptural tradition of the "day" of the Lord (e.g., Amos 8:3, 9, 13; 9:11; Mic 4:6; 5:9; 7:11; Zeph 1:9; 3:11, 16; Obad 8; Joel 3:18; Zech 9:16; 12–14) and so serves to confirm the presentation of the final "coming of the son of man" as the embodiment of the final coming of God himself.

In all of this, Mark 13:32–37 clearly presents Jesus's own final advent in terms of the "coming of God" tradition of Israel's Scriptures. The significant point for our purposes is that Did. 16.1c speaks of the "coming of the Lord" in terms very similar to those used in Mark 13:32–37 to speak of the return of Jesus.[96] In the absence of compelling evidence to the contrary, the assumption should be that the Didache also presents the final coming, not of the Lord God simplistically understood, but of the Lord God embodied in the Lord Jesus.

(b) Matthew 24:36, 42-44: The saying at Matt 24:36 ("But about that day") parallels that at Mark 13:32 and clearly has the same referent, namely, the "coming of the son of man" (Matt 24:27, 30). Indeed, Matt 24 indicates even more explicitly that the "day" referred to here is that of Jesus's final advent. To begin with, while Matt 24 retains the basic structure of Mark 13, the disciples' double question at Matt 24:3 emphasizes the distinction between "these things" that will (at least begin to) occur within a generation (Matt 24:4–28, 32–35), and "that day" of Jesus's "coming," the timing of which is unknown to all but the Father (Matt 24:29–31, 36-51; see also 24:27).[97] In this context, it is clear that the emphatic reference at

---

96. It is also significant here that the key verb at Mark 13:32 and Did. 16.1a, γρηγορέω, regularly appears in the New Testament in contexts focussed on Jesus's return; see Luke 12:37, 39 (some MSS); 1 Thess 5:6; and Rev 3:2-3; 16:15 (see also 1 Cor 16:13).

97. Wright, *Jesus and the Victory of God*, 346 n. 105 believes that Matthew does not "divide his chapter into two halves (vv. 4–35, 36-51) on the basis of this double question, the first dealing with the destruction of Jerusalem and the second with the 'second coming.'" Against this, however, is the clear distinction in the disciples' double question (Matt 24:3), the transitional περὶ δὲ at Matt 24:36, and contrast between Jesus's confident prediction that "all these things" will (at least begin to) occur within a generation, and his profession of ignorance regarding the timing of "that day and hour" (see R. T. France, *The Gospel of Matthew*, NICNT [Grand Rapids: Eerdmans, 2007], 890-94). While it is sometimes suggested that Jesus's ignorance at Matt 24:36 is confined only to the specific day and hour, within a generation, when the temple will fall (e.g., John Nolland, *The Gospel of Matthew*, NIGTC [Grand Rapids: Eerdmans, 2005], 991), this reading fails to account for the clear distinction in the structure of the

Matt 24:36 to "that day and hour" (τῆς ἡμέρας ἐκείνης καὶ ὥρας), looks back to Jesus's brief references to the παρουσία of the "son of man" in Matt 24:27, 30 and thus refers to the "day" of his own final advent. Finally, the term παρουσία itself, which appears in the gospels only here (Matt 24:3, 27, 37, 39), is widely applied to Jesus's final advent in the early Christian literature (1 Cor 15:23; 1 Thess 2:19; 3:13; 4:15; 5:23; 2 Thess 2:1, 8, 9; Jas 5:7-8; 2 Pet 1:16; 3:4, 12; 1 John 2:28) and should probably be regarded as something of a technical term for Jesus's royal "coming" from heaven to earth in glory at the end of the age. Clearly, then, the "day and hour" Jesus refers to at Matt 24:36 is the "day and hour" of his return.

Similarly, the brief parable of the thief in the night, which follows (Matt 24:42-44), is also concerned with Jesus's final advent. To begin with, the image of a thief in the night (ὁ κλέπτης ἔρχεται) is used elsewhere in the early Christian literature as an image of the future coming of Jesus (1 Thess 5:4; 2 Pet 3:10; Rev 3:3; 16:15), but nowhere as an image of the coming of God to Israel.[98] Moreover, in case there was any doubt, the reference to the "coming of the Lord" at Matt 24:42 is explicitly interpreted at Matt 24:44 as the "coming of the son of man" (ὁ υἱὸς τοῦ ἀνθρώπου ἔρχεται). Matthew 24:36, 42, 44, then, also do not refer to the final coming of God to Israel simplistically understood, but to that final coming manifested in the return of the Lord Jesus. In the absence of compelling reasons to the contrary, the presumption must be that the similar language employed at Did. 16.1 also refers to the final coming of the Lord Jesus.

(c) Matthew 25:1-13: Jesus's parable of the ten virgins (Matt 25:1-13) also refers to the return of Jesus at the end of the age.[99] The parable is clearly set in the final phase of the eschatological drama, and, in the light of Matt 9:15, there is no doubt that the bridegroom (νυμφίος) is Jesus.[100]

---

discourse between the destruction of Jerusalem and the period of tribulation of which it is a part and the final coming of the son of man.

98. For the argument that 2 Pet 3:10 refers to the "day" of Jesus's final advent, see my "Jesus as the Logic of his Coming" (Ph.D. diss., Macquarie University, forthcoming).

99. Contra Glasson, *Second Advent*, 89: "The parable of the Ten Virgins probably referred to the situation of Israel when Jesus came.... We think of other sayings in which he complained of unreadiness and the failure of the people to recognise the crisis in their history."

100. The finality of the parable's vision is indicated by: (1) the temporal marker τότε at Matt 25:1 links the parable to the final fate of the wicked servant in the previous verse (Matt 24:51); (2) the stark image of the shut door (Matt 25:10) suggests eschatological finality; (3) the plea of the foolish virgins, addressing the bridegroom

Indeed, the related image of the "wedding feast" (Matt 25:10: γάμος) evokes Matthew's earlier use of the same image in the parable of the king and his son (Matt 22:2, 3, 4, 8, 9, 10: γάμος), but the final decisive coming of the king there is now seen to be embodied in the coming of the bridegroom (= Jesus). The return of the bridegroom, then, is the return of Jesus, somehow embodying the great and final return of the Lord God himself.[101] As such, the parallel to this parable in Did. 16.1 most likely also has the final coming of Jesus on view and not simply a great final theophany.

(d) Luke 12:35–40: Luke 12:35–40 presents two parables of unexpected coming (Luke 12:35–38: master from a wedding feast; Luke 12:39: thief) interpreted as the unexpected "coming of the son of man" (Luke 12:40). It is sometimes denied that these Lukan parables refer to Jesus's final advent.[102] The majority view, however, that these parables refer to Jesus's future return, has much to commend it. The first parable of a returning κύριος (Luke 12:35–38) evokes Luke's larger narrative Christology where Jesus is regularly identified as "the Lord" (see especially Luke 12:41, 42).[103] Moreover, the unexpected "service" (διακονήσει) offered by the master upon his return (Luke 12:37) anticipates Jesus's striking self-designation as the "one who serves" (Luke 22:27: ὁ διακονῶν) so that competent readers of the gospel associate the returning κύριος with Jesus.[104] The second brief parable employs the image of the thief (Luke 12:39), which—as noted—is

---

as "Lord, Lord," and especially the bridegroom's response, "Truly I say to you, I do not know you," evokes Jesus's word of eschatological judgment at Matt 7:23; (4) the final warning, "you do not know the day or the hour' echoes Matt 24:36 and its vision of the final day.

101. Nolland, *Gospel of Matthew*, 1010 suggests that Jesus originally told the parable to speak of the imminent coming of the kingdom of God, rather than his own "return." In the absence of textual evidence this remains speculative.

102. E.g., Wright, *Jesus and the Victory of God*, 640 argues that "the right way to take this whole kaleidoscopic sequence of parables is as further stories about the imminent return of YHWH to Zion, and the awesome consequences which will ensue if Israel is not ready"; David E. Garland, *Luke*, ZECNT (Grand Rapids: Zondervan, 2011), 528 on Luke 12:36–39: "The parable does not require that Jesus be the returning master to make its point, just as the next one, the thief coming in the night (12:39), need not refer to Jesus."

103. C. Kavin Rowe, *Early Narrative Christology: The Lord in the Gospel of Luke* (Grand Rapids: Baker, 2006), 153–54, demonstrates how the reference to the master in the parable as "his Lord" "ties the parable to the larger Lukan story."

104. See Luke Timothy Johnson, *The Gospel of Luke*, SP (Collegeville: Liturgical Press, 1991), 206; Garland, *Luke*, 528.

used elsewhere in the early Christian literature for the future coming of Jesus (Matt 24:44; 1 Thess 5:4; 2 Pet 3:10; Rev 3:3; 16:15), but never for the coming of God. The section concludes with Jesus's injunction to "be ready, for the son of man is coming at an hour you do not expect" (καὶ ὑμεῖς γίνεσθε ἕτοιμοι ὅτι ᾗ ὥρᾳ οὐ δοκεῖτε ὁ υἱὸς τοῦ ἀνθρώπου ἔρχεται), which unambiguously concerns Jesus's own final advent. Once again, when similar language appears in Did. 16.1, the presumption must be that Jesus' final advent is on view there also.

The synoptic texts from the tradition in which Did. 16.1 stands consistently refer to Jesus's final advent in glory (Mark 13:32–37; Matt 24:36; 42–44; 25:1–13; Luke 12:35–40). It is, of course, theoretically possible that the Didache employs the same language and imagery with different import, to speak only of the final coming of God. In the absence of compelling reasons to indicate such divergent usage, however, it seems clear that Did. 16.1 expects Jesus as the coming Lord.

3.2.2. The "Coming of the Lord" Jesus in Did. 16.7–8

The final two references to the coming of the Lord in Did. 16.7–8 are distinct but closely related. The text reads as follows:

⁷ ἀλλ᾽ ὡς ἐρρέθη "Ἥξει ὁ κύριος καὶ πάντες οἱ ἅγιοι μετ᾽ αὐτοῦ ⁸ τότε ὄψεται ὁ κόσμος τὸν κύριον ἐρχόμενον ἐπάνω τῶν νεφελῶν τοῦ οὐρανοῦ

The reference to the "coming of the Lord" here relies on a citation of Zech 14:5 and an allusion to Dan 7:13. In what follows we first note these intertextual connections and then demonstrate that these two texts are consistently combined in the early Christian literature in reference to Jesus's final advent, thus creating the presumption that the combination here also refers to Jesus's final coming as Lord.

3.2.2.1. The Text and Its Intertexts
The first of these two final references to the "coming of the Lord," at Did. 16.7b, takes the form of a citation from Zech 14:5, introduced with the formula ἀλλ᾽ ὡς ἐρρέθη.[105]

---

105. See the use of the aorist passive form of λέγω at Did. 14.3 to introduce the scriptural citation from Mal 1:11, 14.

Zech 14:5b (LXX): καὶ ἥξει κύριος ὁ θεός μου καὶ πάντες οἱ ἅγιοι μετ' αὐτοῦ

Did. 16.7b: ἥξει ὁ κύριος καὶ πάντες οἱ ἅγιοι μετ' αὐτοῦ

Dichache 16.7b here reproduces Zech 14:5 LXX verbatim, except that it omits the phrase ὁ θεός μου and attaches the article to κύριος. Although there are allusions to Zech 14:5 in a number of early Christian texts (1 Thess 3:13; 2 Thess 1:7; Mark 8:38; Matt 16:27; 25:31; Justin, *Apol.* 1.51; *Dial.* 31), the close correspondence between Did. 16.7b and the LXX renders it most likely that the Didache depends directly on the LXX.[106]

The function of this citation, following the third τότε in Did. 16.4b-8, is to explain the immediately preceding affirmation that not all the dead will be raised: the Lord will come with "all his holy ones with him." The "holy ones" are thus the righteous dead; the rest of the dead, presumably, will be left in the grave.[107] The citation from Zech 14:5, then, is not primarily introduced to affirm the coming of the Lord, but to explain that the resurrection will be limited to the righteous. It is a text well chosen, however, since it leads immediately to the fourth τότε and final event in the eschatological sequence, namely, the "coming of the Lord ... upon the clouds of heaven."

The final reference to the "coming of the Lord" in the Didache, then, is also the primary reference in this section (Did. 16.8). It completes the *inclusio* begun at Did. 16.1 and is the climax the Didache's eschatological conclusion. Like the one before it, this final reference to the "coming of the Lord" relies on an allusion to the Scriptures of Israel, this time to Dan 7:13. The situation here is more complex, however, since the text of the Didache reflects not only the Greek translations of Dan 7:13, but also the appropriation of Dan 7:13 in the synoptic tradition. Milavec, for his part, ignores the significance of the Danielic motif and discounts any relationship between the Didache and synoptic tradition at this point, arguing

---

106. Correctly: Koester, *Synoptische Überlieferung*, 187; Niederwimmer, *Didache*, 225. The theory of John S. Kloppenborg, "Didache 16.6–8 and Special Matthean Tradition," *ZNW* 70 (1979): 54–67 (66), that both Matthew and the Didache drew the Zechariah quotation from a common apocalyptic tradition, is unnecessarily complicated.

107. Discussion in Jonathan A. Draper, "Resurrection and Zechariah 14.5 in the Didache Apocalypse," *JECS* 5 (1997): 154–79, who argues that Zech 14:5 was used in early Jewish and Christian exegesis to affirm the assumption of righteous martyrs and their return with the Lord at the end.

instead that Did. 16.7–8 is solely derived from Zech 14:5.[108] The following analysis, however, demonstrates that Did. 16.8 does indeed rely on an allusion to Dan 7:13, while also reflecting the common early Christian application of the Danielic "coming son of man" motif to Jesus.

Dan 7:13 OG: ἐθεώρουν ἐν ὁράματι τῆς νυκτὸς καὶ ἰδοὺ ἐπὶ τῶν νεφελῶν τοῦ οὐρανοῦ ὡς υἱὸς ἀνθρώπου ἤρχετο

Dan 7:13 Θ: ἐθεώρουν ἐν ὁράματι τῆς νυκτὸς καὶ ἰδοὺ μετὰ τῶν νεφελῶν τοῦ οὐρανοῦ ὡς υἱὸς ἀνθρώπου ἐρχόμενος

Justin, Dial. 31.3b–4: ἐθεώρουν ἐν ὁράματι τῆς νυκτός καὶ ἰδοὺ μετὰ τῶν νεφελῶν τοῦ οὐρανοῦ ὡς υἱὸς ἀνθρώπου ἐρχόμενος [109]

Mark 13:26–27: καὶ τότε ὄψονται τὸν υἱὸν τοῦ ἀνθρώπου ἐρχόμενον ἐν νεφέλαις μετὰ δυνάμεως πολλῆς καὶ δόξης καὶ τότε ἀποστελεῖ τοὺς ἀγγέλους καὶ ἐπισυνάξει τοὺς ἐκλεκτοὺς [αὐτοῦ] ἐκ τῶν τεσσάρων ἀνέμων

Matt 24:30–31: καὶ τότε φανήσεται τὸ σημεῖον τοῦ υἱοῦ τοῦ ἀνθρώπου ἐν οὐρανῷ καὶ τότε κόψονται πᾶσαι αἱ φυλαὶ τῆς γῆς καὶ ὄψονται τὸν υἱὸν τοῦ ἀνθρώπου ἐρχόμενον ἐπὶ τῶν νεφελῶν τοῦ οὐρανοῦ μετὰ δυνάμεως καὶ δόξης πολλῆς καὶ ἀποστελεῖ τοὺς ἀγγέλους αὐτοῦ μετὰ σάλπιγγος μεγάλης καὶ ἐπισυνάξουσιν τοὺς ἐκλεκτοὺς αὐτοῦ ἐκ τῶν τεσσάρων ἀνέμων

Did. 16.6, 8: καὶ τότε φανήσεται τὰ σημεῖα τῆς ἀληθείας πρῶτον σημεῖον ἐκπετάσεως ἐν οὐρανῷ εἶτα σημεῖον φωνῆς σάλπιγγος καὶ τὸ τρίτον ἀνάστασις νεκρῶν … τότε ὄψεται ὁ κόσμος τὸν κύριον ἐρχόμενον ἐπάνω τῶν νεφελῶν τοῦ οὐρανοῦ

---

108. Milavec, *The Didache: Faith, Hope, and Life*, 660–61.
109. Justin, *Dial.* 31.2–7 cites Dan 7:9–28 at length. The text Justin cites has readings that agree with both the OG and Θ, while also differing from both in important respects. See Henry B. Swete and H. S. J. Thackeray, *An Introduction to the Old Testament in Greek*, 2nd ed. (Cambridge: Cambridge University Press, 1902), 421–22 for synopsis and comments. It seems most likely that Justin used one of the καίγε group of recensions: see Dominique Barthélemy, "Redécouverte d'un chaînon manquent de l'histoire de la Septante," *RB* 60 (1953): 18–29; Oskar Skarsaune, *The Proof from Prophecy: A Study in Justin Martyr's Proof-text Tradition: Text-type, Provenance Theological Profile*, NovTSup 56 (Leiden: Brill, 1987), 90.

The basic allusion at Did. 16.8 to Dan 7:13 is clear. It is established by: (1) the phrase τῶν νεφελῶν τοῦ οὐρανοῦ, which is unique in the LXX to Dan 7:13; (2) the use of the key verb ἔρχομαι, which appears in one form or another in all the Greek versions of Daniel, as well as in the most important early Christian appropriations of the Danielic motif (Did. 16.8: ἐρχόμενον; see Dan 7:13 OG: ἤρχετο; Dan 7:13 Θ, and Justin, *Dial.* 31.3b–4: ἐρχόμενος; Mark 13:26; Matt 24:30: ἐρχόμενον).

The Danielic motif is here, however, reworked in terms very similar to those adopted in the synoptic tradition. In particular, Did. 16.8 shares the following significant similarities with Mark 13:26–27 and Matt 24:30–31: (1) the sequence of elements (the world will see—Lord—coming—clouds) reflects that of Mark 13:26 and Matt 24:31 (they will see—son of man—coming—clouds) rather than that of Dan 7:13 (clouds—son of man—coming);[110] (2) the future middle indicative form of the verb to see (ὄψεται) parallels Mark 13:26 and Matt 24:30 (both ὄψονται); (3) the sign of the "resurrection of the dead" (Did. 16.6: ἀνάστασις νεκρῶν) may be related to the expectation expressed in the synoptic texts that the son of man's angels will "gather the elect" (Mark 13:27, Matt 24:31).[111]

In addition, Did. 16.6–8 shares significant similarities with the peculiar emphases of Matt 24:30–31: (1) the reference to "signs of the truth" (Did. 16.6: καὶ τότε φανήσεται τὰ σημεῖα τῆς ἀληθείας) is identical to Matt 24:30–31 (καὶ τότε φανήσεται τὸ σημεῖον τοῦ υἱοῦ τοῦ ἀνθρώπου), except the Didache has the plural for Matthew's singular (the connection is strengthened by the fact that both texts make reference to an eschatological "trumpet" [σάλπιγγος] and locate at least the first sign "in heaven" [ἐν οὐρανῷ]); (2) improper preposition ἐπάνω with τῶν νεφελῶν reflects Matt 24:30 (cf. Dan 7:13 OG: ἐπὶ), rather than Mark 13:26 (ἐν νεφέλαις) or Dan 7:13 Θ/Justin (μετὰ τῶν νεφελῶν); (3) the addition of τοῦ οὐρανοῦ after τῶν νεφελῶν is similar to Matt 24:30 (cf. Dan 7:13 OG, Θ, Justin).

Of these parallels, number 1 may perhaps be explained in terms of Matthew and the Didache independently adapting the "signs" of the holy war tradition (Jer 51:27; Isa 11:10–12).[112] Similarly numbers 2 and 3 may

---

110. Niederwimmer, *Didache*, 226; see also Koester, *Synoptische Überlieferung*, 187.

111. The roots of the expectation are perhaps to be found in the combination of Dan 7:13–14 with Dan 12:1–3. The Scriptures of Israel also associate the resurrection of the dead with the coming of God himself (e.g., Isa 26:19, 21).

112. Certainly, the "trumpet" is a standard motif from the theophany tradition

simply reflect the influence of Dan 7:13 in its various forms. Nevertheless, given the other similarities with Matt 24:30–31, it is quite possible that the Didache here reflects knowledge either of the Gospel of Matthew or, at least, of a source common to it and Matthew.

Finally, the Didache contains two unique elements: (1) Did. 16.8 substitutes "the Lord" for the "one like a son of man" found at Dan 7:13, Mark 13:26, and Matt 24:30. The identification of the "son of man" with "the Lord" is, to be sure, also clear in Matt 24:42, 44 (see also Luke 12:36, 40–42, where Lord = son of man = Jesus). Nevertheless, Did. 16.8 takes this one step further by inserting "the Lord" directly into the Danielic motif. Nowhere else amongst the texts of the New Testament and the Apostolic Fathers is the "Lord" said to come, like the Danielic "son of man," "on the clouds of heaven"; (2) Did. 16.8 asserts that "the world will see" (ὄψεται ὁ κόσμος) the Lord coming on the clouds. The Didache's universal vision here completes a trajectory of ever-widening witness to the "coming of the son of man" that runs from Daniel's first hand eyewitness account of the vision (ἐθεώρουν) through Jesus's prophecy in Matthew that "all the tribes of the earth" will see him (πᾶσαι αἱ φυλαὶ τῆς γῆς … ὄψονται). To be sure, such a universal vision is already implied in the universal kingship granted to the "one like a son of man" in Dan 7:14. In Daniel, however, this kingship is only seen by the visionary; in the Didache it is seen by "the world."

This pattern of parallels makes it clear that Did. 16.8: (1) relies on the "coming son of man" motif, which ultimately derives from Dan 7:13; (2) has reworked that motif in terms similar to the synoptic tradition found at Mark 13:26–27 and especially Matt 24:30–31; (3) has further added some developments of its own. The relationship between Did. 16.6–8 and the Synoptic Gospels has, therefore, been much debated. A number of scholars argue that Did. 16.8 is independent of the Synoptic Gospels. Helmut Koester suggested that Did. 16.8 and Matt 24:30 both rely on an earlier version of Mark, which read ἐπὶ τῶν νεφελῶν.[113] The postulation of an early, unknown source is, however, unnecessarily complicated and must

---

stemming from Sinai (Exod 19:19; Isa 27:13; Zech 9:14) and is elsewhere associated with the Jesus's final advent in the early Christian texts (1 Thess 4:16; 1 Cor 15:52). See Jonathan A. Draper, "The Development of 'The Sign of the Son of Man' in the Jesus Tradition," *NTS* 39 (1993): 1–21; see also Draper, "Eschatology in the *Didache*," 579–80.

113. Koester, *Synoptische Überlieferung*, 188.

surely be considered a refuge of last resort.¹¹⁴ Richard Glover suggested that the similarities between Did. 16.8, Mark 13:26, and Matt 24:30 may be explained by "joint borrowing from Dan. vii. 13." The suggestion, however, fails to explain the points at which Mark, Matthew, and the Didache agree against Dan 7:13 (the inverted order of elements, the use of ὄψεται/ ὄψονται).¹¹⁵ John Kloppenborg argued that since Did. 16.8 "agrees with Mt 24.30" only "at those points where Matthew disagrees with Mark," the Didache and Matthew rely on a common apocalyptic source. If the Didache knew Matt 24:30, he reasoned, we would expect it to retain not only elements unique to Matt 24:30 (from the pre-Matthean source), but also some elements common to Matt 24:30 and Mark 13:26.¹¹⁶ In fact, however, Did. 16.8 does contain some elements common to Matt 24:30 and Mark 13:26, namely, the inverted order of the elements and the use of ὄψεται/ὄψονται.¹¹⁷ It is possible, then, that the Didache and Matthew both relied on a common source, but more likely that Did. 16.6-8 reflects knowledge of Matt 24:30-31.¹¹⁸

---

114. See the critiques in Kloppenborg, "Didache 16.6-8," 61; Tuckett, "Synoptic Tradition in the Didache," 204.

115. Glover, "Didache's Quotations and the Sypoptic Gospels," 24.

116. Kloppenborg, "Didache 16.6-8," 63. Kloppenborg also appeals to (1) the lack of reference to the "sign in heaven" of Matt 24:29 (but see Did. 16.6); (2) the lack of reference to the coming in "great power and glory" as at Mark 13:26 and Matt 24:30 (but this argument from silence is particularly weak given the uncertain ending of the Didache in the extant manuscripts). See also Draper, "Eschatology in the *Didache*," 577-79, who follows Kloppenborg in arguing that "since the *Didache* contains only the material found in Matthew that is not in Mark, it is inconceivable that it derives directly from Matthew and far more conceivable that Matthew has utilized a source to modify the framework he has received from Mark."

117. See Tuckett, "Synoptic Tradition in the Didache," 204.

118. For a defense of this view, see Streeter, *Four Gospels*, 510; Burnett H. Streeter, "The Much Belaboured Didache," *JTS* 37 (1936): 369-74 (370); Vokes, *Riddle of the Didache*, 111; Butler, "Literary Relations of the Didache," 265-83; F. F. Bruce, "Eschatology in the Apostolic Fathers," in *The Heritage of the Early Church: Festschrift for G. V. Florovsky*, ed. D. Neiman and G. Schatkin, OrChrAn 195 (Rome: Pontificium Institutum Studiorum Orientalium, 1973), 84; Tuckett, "Synoptic Tradition in the Didache," 205; Tuckett, "Didache and the Writings," 115-16; Tuckett, "Didache and the Synoptics Once More," 509-18. To say that the Didache "reflects knowledge of Matthew" is not, of course, the same as saying that the Didache here "cites" or "quotes" Matthew.

3.2.2.2. The Identity of the Coming Lord in Did. 16.7–8

Didache 16.7–8, then, clearly juxtaposes Zechariah's vision of the "coming of God" to Daniel's vision of the "coming of the son of man," mediated by the synoptic tradition. Milavec, for his part, ignores the allusion to Dan 7:13 and claims that "*Did.*16 presents an early and formative eschatology that is much closer to Zechariah than to the Synoptics."[119] In this way he is able to conclude that Did. 16.7–8 refers to the coming of the Lord God and not to the return of Jesus. In what follows, however, it is demonstrated that the juxtaposition of these two texts is not an unusual innovation of the Didache. The early Christian texts regularly combine Zechariah's vision of the "coming of the Lord God" with Daniel's vision of the "coming son of man" to speak of Jesus final advent in glory at the end.

Four sets of texts are particularly important here. First, as early as Paul's first letter to the Thessalonians (ca. 49–50 CE), both Zech 14:5 and Dan 7:13–14 could be used to speak of Jesus's final advent. On the one hand, 1 Thess 3:13 transforms Zechariah's vision of the "coming of the Lord my God and all the holy ones with him" into a prophecy of the "coming of the Lord *Jesus* with all *his* holy ones" (ἐν τῇ παρουσίᾳ τοῦ κυρίου ἡμῶν Ἰησοῦ μετὰ πάντων τῶν ἁγίων αὐτοῦ).[120] On the other hand, at 1 Thess 4:16–17 Paul and his companions announce, with clear reference to Jesus' return, that the "Lord himself will descend" (καταβήσεται) with the sound of a "trumpet" (σάλπιγξ) to raise the dead so that all of his people may come to him "in clouds" (ἐν νεφέλαις) and "meet" (εἰς ἀπάντησιν) him "in the air" (εἰς ἀέρα). The primary echoes here are of the original theophany at Sinai when the Lord God "descended" (Exod 19:11, 18, 20; 34:5 LXX: καταβαίνω),[121] in "clouds" (Exod 19:9, 16: ἐν στύλῳ νεφέλης) and with the sound of a "trumpet" (Exod 19:16, 19: σάλπιγξ), to "meet" his people (Exod 19:17: εἰς συνάντησιν). There are, however, also echoes of the Dan-

---

119. Milavec, *Didache: Faith, Hope, and Life*, 663.

120. See 2 Thess 1:7, where the author relies on Zech 14:5 to speak of a time "when the Lord Jesus is revealed from heaven with his mighty angels" (ἐν τῇ ἀποκαλύψει τοῦ κυρίου Ἰησοῦ ἀπ᾽ οὐρανοῦ μετ᾽ ἀγγέλων δυνάμεως αὐτοῦ).

121. The verb καταβαίνω became the standard LXX translation of the Hebrew ירד in later allusions to the Sinai theophany (2 Sam 22:10; Ps 18:9; Neh 9:13; Ps 144:5; Mic 1:3). It is significant, therefore, that 1 Thess 4:16 is the only instance in the New Testament where the same verb is applied to the future "coming" of Christ (see John 3:13; 6:38, 41, 42, 50, 52, 58 for Jesus's incarnation). Since the word was not commonly used to speak of Christ's future advent, the choice of it here most likely reflects a deliberate allusion to the "descent" of the Lord at Sinai.

ielic "son of man" coming on the "clouds" to the Ancient of Days. Just as the "son of man," representing the "saints of the Most High' (Dan 7:13–14 with 18, 22, 29) "comes" to the Ancient of Days on the clouds, so here those who belong to Jesus come to the Lord "in clouds."[122] Significantly, it seems quite likely that Paul here relies not only on Dan 7:13, but on the dominical tradition he had received, which already associated the "trumpet" and "angels" with the eschatological gathering of the elect at the final coming of the son of man (Matt 24:30–31; cf. Mark 13:26–27).[123] Thus in what is one of the very earliest extant Christian texts, Paul and his companions employ both Zechariah's vision of the "coming of the Lord" God and Daniel's vision of the "coming son of man" to speak of the return of the Lord Jesus. The combination of these two Scriptures at Did. 16.8 to speak of Jesus's "second coming" is, then, not unique to the Didache.[124]

Second, Mark 8:38 has Jesus himself apply Dan 7:13–14 and Zech 14:5 to his own future "coming" when he says that the "son of man" will "come in the glory of his Father with the holy angels" (ὅταν ἔλθῃ ἐν τῇ δόξῃ τοῦ

---

122. The allusion to Dan 7:13 is recognised by F. F. Bruce, *1 and 2 Thessalonians*, WBC (Grand Rapids: Word, 1982), 102; Charles A. Wanamaker, *The Epistles to the Thessalonians: A Commentary on the Greek Text*, NIGTC (Grand Rapids: Eerdmans, 1990), 175; Gordon D. Fee, *The First and Second Letters to the Thessalonians*, NICNT (Grand Rapids: Eerdmans, 2009), 180.

123. Christopher M. Tuckett, "Synoptic Tradition in 1 Thessalonians?" in *The Thessalonian Correspondence*, ed. Raymond F. Collins, BETL 87 (Leuven: Peeters, 1990), 160–82 (177–80), questions this connection on the basis that Matt 24:30–31 and Mark 13:26–27 do not mention resurrection, which is "the key point of Paul's argument." In response, Seyoon Kim, "The Jesus Tradition in 1 Thess 4.13–5.11," *NTS* 48 (2002): 225–42 (234–35), plausibly suggests that Paul most likely considered the gathering of the elect to presuppose the resurrection of the dead, especially given the prominence of resurrection in the Danielic tradition on which Jesus's saying depends (Dan 12:1–3; see also John 5:27–29, which similarly connects the son of man's "voice" with "resurrection"). See Ben Witherington III, *1 and 2 Thessalonians: A Socio-Rhetorical Commentary* (Grand Rapids: Eerdmans, 2006), 133–37, who suggests that Paul here "combines a saying of Jesus with his own reflections on Dan 7:13–14 and 12:2–3" (135).

124. Alan J. P. Garrow, "The Eschatological Tradition behind 1 Thessalonians: Didache 16," *JSNT* 32 (2009): 191–215, raises the interesting possibility that Did. 16 preserves the "eschatological tradition behind 1 Thessalonians" (211). It is far more likely, however, that the Didache, as an anonymous, composite document, is a later source reflecting similar emphases to 1 Thess 4:16–17 and Matt 24:30–31 than that the Didache is itself the source of Paul's or Matthew's eschatology.

πατρὸς αὐτοῦ μετὰ τῶν ἀγγέλων τῶν ἁγίων). The basic allusion here to the throne-room scene of Dan 7 is secured by the reference to the son of man by the use of ἔρχομαι for his "coming" (Dan 7:13) and by the mention of his δόξα (Dan 7:14 OG). A secondary allusion to Zech 14:5 (cf. Deut 33:2), however, is also secured by the mention of the son of man coming with the "holy angels" (μετὰ τῶν ἀγγέλων τῶν ἁγίων).[125] Mark's Jesus thus speaks of his own future "coming" by weaving together the "coming of the son of man" from Dan 7:13 with the dramatic coming of God depicted in Zech 14:5.[126] Indeed, the combination of Dan 7:13 with Zech 14:5 is also evident in the parallel saying at Matt 16:27.[127] To be sure, in contrast to Mark, Matthew does not use the attributive adjective ἅγιος ("holy") to describe the angels, and this weakens the allusion to some extent. Matthew does, however, more firmly connect the angels to the son of man by calling them "his angels" (μετὰ τῶν ἀγγέλων αὐτοῦ), which strengthens the presentation of the son of man's coming as theophany. Once again, it is clear that in associating Dan 7:13 and Zech 14:5, and in applying both texts to Jesus's final advent, Did. 16.8 follows a well-worn path in early Christian exegesis.

Third, Matt 25:31–32 also combines a primary allusion to Dan 7:13 with a secondary allusion to the theophany of Zech 14:1–21, in which the Lord God comes to gather the nations for judgment.[128] The basic allusion to Dan 7 is secured by the references to the "coming" of the son of man

---

125. Adams, "Coming of the Son of Man in Mark," 51–52.

126. E.g., Adams, "Coming of the Son of Man in Mark," 52, suggests that Mark's Jesus here modifies the original meaning of Daniel's vision: what was a vision of "heavenly enthronement" is transformed into a vision of a divine coming from heaven to earth. It is much more likely, however, that the association of the two texts (Dan 7:13–14 and Zech 14:1–5) was facilitated by their common subject matter. Mark's Jesus combines Dan 7:13–14 with Zech 14:1–5 because he saw in both texts a prophecy of the climactic divine theophany.

127. France, *Gospel of Matthew*, 639, recognises the probable allusion, but fails to see its significance in presenting the son of man's coming as a theophany.

128. France, *Gospel of Matthew*, 960–61, recognizes that Matt 25:31 alludes to Zech 14:5 and suggests that Matt 25:32 alludes to Joel 4:2 (English translation, 3:2). In both cases, however, his "heavenly enthronement" reading of Dan 7:13–14 dominates, so that he fails to recognize the implications of these allusions for the terrestrial location of Matthew's vision. He does not note the probable allusion to Zech 14:2 at Matt 25:32. N. T. Wright, *The New Testament and the People of God* (London: SPCK, 1992), 462 n. 66, explains Matt 25:31 as "a reference to Zech. 14.5 which 'attracts' the idea of the 'coming of the son of man' from Daniel 7, and places it in a different context." He

(ὅταν δὲ ἔλθῃ ὁ υἱὸς τοῦ ἀνθρώπου; cf. Dan 7:13 OG: ὡς υἱὸς ἀνθρώπου ἤρχετο; Θ: ὡς υἱὸς ἀνθρώπου ἐρχόμενος), along with the references to "his glory" (ἐν τῇ δόξῃ αὐτοῦ; cf. Dan 7:14 OG: δόξα), "his glorious throne" (ἐπὶ θρόνου δόξης αὐτοῦ; Dan 7:9: θρόνος), and to the judgment of "all the nations" (πάντα τὰ ἔθνη; Dan 7:14 OG: πάντα τὰ ἔθνη; Θ: πάντες οἱ λαοί, φυλαί, γλῶσσαι). Indeed, Matt 25:31–32 extends the Danielic vision further in the direction of theophany by: (1) affirming that he "comes in *his* glory" (rather than merely receiving glory after his coming as at Dan 7:14); (2) depicting the son of man himself as judge (rather than as the mere beneficiary of judgment as in Daniel); (3) designating the son of man as "king" (in extension of him being granted a "kingdom" in Dan 7:14). These theophanic extensions of the Danielic vision comport well with the secondary allusion to Zech 14. This secondary allusion is secured by: (1) Jesus's announcement that the son of man shall come and "all his angels with him" (Matt 25:31: καὶ πάντες οἱ ἄγγελοι μετ' αὐτοῦ; cf. Zech 14:5: πάντες οἱ ἅγιοι μετ' αὐτοῦ);[129] (2) Jesus's announcement that "all the nations will be gathered before him" (Matt 25:32: συναχθήσονται ἔμπροσθεν αὐτοῦ πάντα τὰ ἔθνη; cf. Zech 14:2: ἐπισυνάξω πάντα τὰ ἔθνη);[130] (3) Jesus's identification of the "son of man" as the "king" (Matt 25:34: ὁ βασιλεὺς; cf. Zech 14:9: καὶ ἔσται κύριος εἰς βασιλέα; 14:17 τῷ

---

thus notes the allusion to Zech 14:5 at Matt 25:31 but, likewise, does not allow this to significantly inform his understanding of the scene.

129. Of course, Dan 7:10 reports that the heavenly beings serve the Ancient of Days. The striking development here, however, as at Matt 16:27, is that the angels form a heavenly retinue for the "son of man" (see Matt 13:41 and 24:31 where the son of man sends the angels out). Matthew's Jesus thus implies that the "coming of the son of man" will embody nothing less than the coming of the Lord God himself.

130. See also Zech 12:3. The judgment of the nations is, to be sure, already implied at Dan 7:14, where the "son of man" is given authority over "all peoples, nations, and languages" (OG: πάντα τὰ ἔθνη τῆς γῆς κατὰ γένη; Θ: πάντες οἱ λαοί φυλαί γλῶσσαι). Daniel's vision however, lacks any reference to the "gathering of the nations." The verbal similarity between Zechariah and Matt 25:32 at this point is striking. The texts employ the near-synonymous verbs ἐπισυνάγω and συνάγω and use the identical phrase πάντα τὰ ἔθνη. Indeed, Matthew's use of the future passive indicative form of συνάγω in place of Zechariah's future active indicative of ἐπισυνάγω may well be intended as a "divine passive" designed to preserve the Lord God's role in gathering the nations. If so, then the difference in verbal form represents a theological unity: Matthew's Jesus, like Zechariah, speaks of the Lord God gathering the nations for judgment.

βασιλεῖ κυρίῳ παντοκράτορι).[131] Matthew's Jesus thus weaves three significant allusions to Zech 14:1–21 into the primary allusion to Dan 7:9–14 and applies both texts to his own future advent. Like Paul and the Gospel of Mark, Matthew's Gospel understands that the coming of the Lord God, prophesied in Zech 14:5, is to find its fulfilment in the coming of the Lord Jesus as the Danielic "son of man." Once again, the Didache is not alone in combining these texts. Since, Paul, Mark, and Matthew all deploy the combination in order to speak of Jesus's final advent, it is most likely that Did. 16.7–8 also refers to the final "coming of the Lord" Jesus.

Fourth and finally, Justin Martyr in similar manner twice combines Dan 7:13 with a reference to the son of man's angelic retinue, which probably relies on Zech 14:5. At *Apol.* 1.51, Justin writes: "Behold, as the son of man he comes in the clouds of heaven, and his angels with him" (υἱὸς ἀνθρώπου ἔρχεται ἐπάνω τῶν νεφελῶν τοῦ οὐρανοῦ καὶ οἱ ἄγγελοι αὐτοῦ σὺν αὐτῷ). Similarly, at *Dial.* 31, Justin writes: "For he shall come on the clouds as the son of man, so Daniel foretold, and his angels shall come with him" (Ὡς υἱὸς γὰρ ἀνθρώπου ἐπάνω νεφελῶν ἐλεύσεται ὡς Δανιὴλ ἐμήνυσεν ἀγγέλων σὺν αὐτῷ ἀφικνουμένων). In both instances, the references to the son of man's angelic retinue cannot be explained on the basis of Dan 7 alone. In that chapter the angelic host serve the Ancient of Days, not the son of man (Dan 7:9–10). It seems most likely, then, that as at Matt 16:27 and 25:31, the reference to "angels" accompanying the coming Lord reflects the "holy ones" of Zech 14:5 (cf. Deut 33:2 LXX).[132] If so, then, we have a fourth example outside Did. 16.7–8 of an early Christian text combining Dan 7:13 and Zech 14:5 to speak of Jesus's final advent.

Clearly, then, the early Christian literature from Paul to Justin regularly combines Daniel's vision of the coming of the son of man with Zechariah's vision of the coming of the Lord God to speak of the future return of the Lord Jesus.[133] In this context, the references to the "coming of the

---

131. This connection is not widely recognized. While the "kingly" role granted the son of man in Dan 7:14 may go some way towards accounting for Matthew's Jesus's presentation here, the linguistic link with Zech 14:9, 17 in the context of other connections to Zech 14 is compelling.

132. Certainly Justin regularly takes texts from the Scriptures of Israel that clearly refer to the Lord God and applies them to the Lord Jesus. This is evident, to take just one example, at *Apol.* 1.51 just prior to the citation of Dan 7:13 + Zech 14:5, where Justin applies Ps 24:7 to Jesus's ascension.

133. Wright, *New Testament and the People of God*, 463 n. 72, suggests that the combination of Dan 7:13 and Zech 14:5 in Did. 16 is best read "like Justin, as the begin-

Lord" in Did. 16.7–8 most naturally refer to the "coming of the Lord" Jesus. Indeed, once the allusion to Dan 7:13 at Did. 16.8 is recognised, it can be no other way. For, while we have ample evidence of both "son of man" language and theophany traditions being applied to Jesus in the early Christian literature, there is not one example of the "coming of the son of man" imagery being applied to the Lord God. If the κύριος of Did. 16.8 is indeed the Lord God, as Milavec insists, then the Didache is highly idiosyncratic at this point. Much more likely, the κύριος at Did. 16.7 and 16.8 is none other than the Lord Jesus.

3.3. Conclusion

At four points the Didache clearly refers to the future return of Jesus. Didache 10.6 deploys the μαραναθά invocation to call on the Lord Jesus to return in judgment. Didache 16.1 speaks of the "coming of the Lord" in terms that parallel Jesus's sayings about his own final advent in the Synoptic Gospels. Didache 16.7–8, in common with a number of other early Christian texts, combines Zech 14:5 and Dan 7:13 (mediated by the synoptic tradition) to present Jesus's final "coming" as the embodiment of the great and final coming of God.

4. Conclusion

The foregoing analysis leads to a twofold conclusion. First, the κύριος repeatedly referred to in the Didache at least includes reference to Jesus. Of the twenty significant occurrences of κύριος outside Did. 16, five almost certainly refer to Jesus, a further eleven most likely refer to Jesus, and the final four quite possibly refer to Jesus. Second, the "coming of the Lord" expected in the Didache is the "second coming" of Jesus. The μαραναθά

---

ning of a rereading of Jewish apocalyptic in an un-Jewish way." Given the parallels between the Didache, Mark, Matthew, and Paul at this point, however, Wright's position requires that all of these major witnesses to early Christian thought were guilty of the same error. Much more likely, Wright's understanding of Dan 7:13 (as "heavenly enthronement" rather than "theophany-like descent") is itself mistaken. The reason these early Christian texts were able to combine Dan 7:13 with Zech 14:5 to speak of Jesus's final descent in glory is that both texts belong together in the theophany tradition of Israel's Scriptures. The reading of Dan 7:13 as a theophany-like descent from heaven to earth is thoroughly "Jewish." The Christian innovation consists not in reading Dan 7:13 as a "descent" from heaven to earth, but in applying this text to Jesus.

invocation at Did. 10.6 and the three references to the "coming of the Lord" in Did. 16 each take the "coming of God" tradition from the Scriptures of Israel and rework it, in terms similar to those found across the early Christian literature, to speak of the final return of the Lord Jesus. The Christology of the Didache, then, is remarkably "high." In common with a range of other early Christian texts, the Didache includes Jesus within the identity of the one true God of Israel and attributes to him the dignity and prerogatives that belong to God alone.

Matthew and the Didache: Some Comments on the Comments

Joseph Verheyden

Matthew and the Didache—I have on purpose inverted the order of the two components as mentioned in the title of this section—is a "classic question" in studies on the Didache. The change of order is symbolic and symptomatic for a particular way of looking at the relationship between these two entities that has received quite some attention in recent years and that is also present in some of the essays to be presented here.

It begins already right with the first one. E. Bruce Brooks's "Before and After Matthew" picks up on his overall thesis about the development of early Christian theology, which gives a significant place to its oldest form dating back to a time when Christianity was not yet "obsessed" by the resurrection and can be characterized as reflecting "a preresurrection form of belief and practice."[1] The thesis he wishes to argue is stated most clearly in the very first clause: "In this paper I will argue that the Didache is a growth text, that it makes contact with Matthew only at the end of its formation period, and that its core is best understood if it is related to the period *before* Matthew and Luke: the time of Mark."[2] The argument is developed in nine sections of very different lengths and character. Brooks begins by explaining and illustrating the concept of "growth text," that is, a text that was composed in stages and over a period of time. The evidence that is cited includes an instance of an ancient legal text and three of the canonical gospels—Mark and Luke (and John, who is mentioned only in passing). The strength and clarity of the argument is marred in part because the author also conflates in this survey his views on the

---

1. See in the present volume Brooks, "Before and After Matthew," above 247.
2. Ibid., 247.

relationship between Luke and Matthew, a critique of the Q hypothesis, and further also debatable evidence from Paul for the existence of this earliest form of Christianity, which he labels "Alpha Christianity." The last element is of some importance for identifying the Didache, but it had better been separated more clearly from the question of the growth text. The argument is further weakened by the observation that a growth text exists in many different forms. Urban von Wahlde's three-stage composition history of John is, of course, very different from the extension of legal texts, as is the case in the Gortyn law code,[3] and very different also from what is supposed to have happened in Mark and in Luke. The evidence in Mark is disappointingly sober and quite diverse. Brooks is not looking for recovering a form of Ur-Mark, as some might have expected, or at least he does not use this kind of vocabulary. Of the many interpolations he reckons with, only a few are mentioned. He mentions Adela Collins's "pre-Markan passion narrative," but adds that this is not what he is looking for or how he sees it: as he sees it, this earlier form is not "pre-Markan" in the strict sense, but "an early state in a continuous process of additions to Mark";[4] but how to distinguish between the two and what is there against calling this "pre-Markan"? Mark 14:28 and 16:7 are cited as instances of "progressive divinization of Jesus," which may well be what they are,[5] but this in turn raises the question whether all such passages dealing with divinization are to be removed as interpolations or only those that are less well integrated in their immediate context. Layering the Markan apocalypse is a tricky business, as the history of research on this chapter has proven. Vincent Taylor's reconstruction is but one among many attempts at making sense of the text in this way, and it was not developed for use "within the Markan formation process," but to identify part of the chapter as that which instigated Mark to compose his apocalyptic discourse as such.[6] The atonement doctrine may be marginally present, difficult to read within the whole of the gospel, and easy to remove—"without detriment" and "with benefit,"[7] but that does not make it a later addition. There is a lot more in Mark that can easily be removed, yet was most probably part of the original.

---

3. Ibid., 247.
4. Ibid., 249 n. 7.
5. Ibid., 248.
6. Ibid., 249.
7. Ibid., 249.

Just as with Mark, it is not a "pre-Lukan" stage Brooks is after when bringing Luke on the table. Proto-Luke is not mentioned (and indeed a horror for the author). The evidence he is dealing with are such texts that "occupy different positions in the narrative from their counterparts in Mark and create inconcinnities in their new positions."[8] The one example that is cited is the Nazareth pericope and the difficulty that Jesus is asked to do the same kind of wonders he had done before in Capernaum at a moment he had not yet been there. The difficulty has of course long been noticed, and many scholars get away with it without having recourse to stratifications or later interpolations in Luke. At most it could indicate that a later redactor has transposed and anticipated a passage from its initially correct place to a wrong one, but that is not so much an instance of "growth" as of transposition. By the way, it is a pity that Brooks cannot cite Q and John Kloppenborg's stratification model for his position, because he does not accept the hypothesis. Finally, this evidence from the Gospels is preliminary at most. It can be used for illustrating the existence of a particular phenomenon. Now it has to be demonstrated that the Didache has gone through a similar kind of process.

The introductory information on the contents and structure of the work is a bit confusing: "three readily distinguishable parts" (1.1–6.2; 6.3–12.1; and 16; with an extra that is preserved in Apostolic Constitutions and Canons) and not a word on 12.2–15.4.[9] Each of the parts, including the fourth one, is then commented upon in the light of the overall hypothesis and in view of reconstructing the composition history of the document. The latter is summarized on pages 282–83 as follows: 6.3–12.1 (a liturgical handbook); 1.1–5.2, with a transition in 6.1–2 added later on (the Two Ways section); 12.2–15.4 (updating the handbook for later times); 16 (completing and transforming the handbook into a guide for Christian life). I must say I had quite some difficulties following the argument.

The partial parallel between the Didache and Barnabas in the list of vices is "evidently" explained in terms of the latter depending on the former. Brooks notes that an orderly list is not usually disordered by a second user,[10] but then proceeds to show that this is exactly what has happened here when Barnabas first scales down the original list in Did. 5.1 from twenty-two to seventeen, combining some of the vices and adding in a few others, which

---

8. Ibid., 250.
9. Ibid., 259–60.
10. Ibid., 264.

Brooks calls tidying up, but then also appears to have destroyed the original intended structure (as described by James Rendel Harris), which is then regarded as a second form of "disordering." So how does that function as proof for a "directionality" of Didache > Barnabas? Brooks then goes on by listing those sections that have no parallel in Barnabas and concludes by translating those sections that he considers to be part of the Two Ways. I do not see the force of the argument, and there is certainly no indication here of why this section would have been the second one in the composition history of the document or of why it came to be added in.

The "comments" on 6.3–12.1, "the original church order document," are perhaps even more disturbing. This section is singled out by repetitive use of περὶ δέ, surely a distinctive marker, but apparently not the only one, for in 7.4 a short section on fasting is delineated (unless this should be seen as originally forming part of the section on baptism, only to be separated from it at a later stage?). The reason to have this section end with 12.1 is the tension Brooks sees between what is said about a longer stay of wandering prophets in 11.5 and in 12.3. For Brooks the tension amounts to outright contradiction, hence proof of a later redaction. If contradictory, one might have expected the later redactor, who was responsible for adding on the section beginning with 12.2 immediately to the end of 6.3–12.1 and that deals with the same topic of receiving prophets, to have harmonized the two passages in some way, preferably by copying out 11.5. But maybe contradiction is too strong a word, for 12.3 can also be read as a specification or further clarification of the rule stated in 11.5. Prophets are not expected to stay on for more than three days. That is the rule in 11.5, and it still is the rule in 12.3; only, now it is further specified that a longer stay is possible if the prophets provide for themselves. But why should this of necessity reflect the interests and concerns of a later generation? The rule stands and is not made more flexible; it has just been refined without undoing its core element.

On to the extension then. This is not structured or composed in the same way as the larger part of the previous section (no περὶ δέ), but it was noted that even there it was not the sole principle. Four items are mentioned. Two of these could (but should not) be linked to a later development (the resident apostle and the installation of local authorities); but there is no reason to think that the two others (which are actually very closely linked: a ritual of reconciliation and the prescript that members should correct one another) point to a later time and can only have come on the table at a later stage. The resident apostle providing for himself, or claiming so and making an issue of this, is documented in the letters of Paul. However, it does not mean it was not an issue already before that time, for which documentation is sparse or just lacking. Moreover, the question does not seem to have bothered any of the evangelists too much and is left unmentioned in the various versions of the mission discourse. The issue of local authorities is likewise documented from Paul's time on, but community leaders there must have been right from the beginning wherever there was a small group gathering in the name of Christ, and the way the issue is formulated in 15.1 allows for a lot of initiative to be left to the local community in this regard ("Appoint then [yourself], for yourselves"). This can hardly be subsumed under the heading "increasing local control."[11] So again, in Paul's time, or earlier, or later....

I am glad to read that Brooks agrees with me on the important issue of the origins of the final chapter. This one is thoroughly shaped by Matthew's version of the apocalyptic discourse, indeed to the extent that such elements that stem from Matthew cannot be excised from the rest: there simply would not be left anything else! It is an important conclusion and a key issue in dating the composition of the Didache, but as for the previous sections, here again I miss an argument why this chapter was added later on. Of course, it must have been composed after Matthew started to be circulating (unless one would turn the order around and make Matthew depend on the Didache, as has also been argued with little or no attention for distinctively Matthean elements that object against such a view). More problematic still is the suggestion—and as a matter of fact, it really is not more than a suggestion—that the same redactor who was responsible for adding on chapter 16 was also responsible for the relatively many Matthean elements that can be found all through the document. These had carefully been sifted out by Brooks in his reconstruction of the earlier sections with no clue for the reader of where these came from. Now they are massively assigned to this one author who wrote up chapter 16. But the whole procedure in handling this "Matthean material" is very different and no explanation is given for this. This is a difficulty also for those arguing for Matthean dependence without giving in to the hypothesis of "the growth text," but it is still more of a difficulty for the latter, because the options are multiplied and the suggestion that this material all comes from the same hand is but one among others. Maybe (some of) these

---

11. Ibid., 284.

earlier sections originated at a much later date than Brooks suggests—after Matthew was around and accessible also already to their authors. Or maybe these Matthean interpolations have to be assigned to a still later redactor who got the taste and inspiration for it when reading a version of the Didache with chapter 16; or maybe it was the other way around and it was these earlier interpolations that inspired the author of chapter 16. This is not just poking around from my side. The point I wish to make is the following: once multiple stages are allowed to pop up in a text, stages that are not convincingly and stringently argued for, everything, or almost everything becomes possible and there is no reason why the composition history was not more complicated still, or more nuanced, than Brooks's model allows it to be. Finally, as to the reason for why these additions were made, Brooks says they were "designed to give the entire text something of the authority of Matthew."[12] It could be a valid reason, but as said, the authority is obtained in a rather loose way and without a clear pattern, which makes one wonder whether and why there was this sudden need to be or become "more Matthean"; and it is certainly one step too far to promote the Didache to "something of a gospel" for a very simple reason: Jesus is missing from the larger part of it!

Perttu Nikander invites the reader to a journey in the land of sound and vision, so it seems, but I am afraid he did not really manage to escape altogether the bookish world that is ours. He studies the so-called Sectio Evangelica at the beginning of the Didache from the perspective of performance theory and in arguing against any form of literary dependence theory. I do not see why the two cannot be somehow connected, and I have not found an argument or indication in the paper that this would be totally impossible. Nikander begins by explaining at some length why theories or hypotheses of literary dependence do not work, not only in this particular case, but also on a more general level. Two objections are raised. First, literary dependence does not work in this instance, and it never does. Q cannot be reconstructed with absolute certainty; so there is no way to find out what may be redaction in Matthew's or Luke's version of a Q passage; hence the "golden rule" of literary dependence theories, which is to look for such elements in the text under scrutiny that can be led back to the author of the supposed source text, cannot be applied or verified. The criticism is formulated here with regard to Did. 1.3b–2.1, but from the way it is

---

12. Ibid., 282.

formulated, I assume the author wishes to extend it to any form of literary dependence (e.g., we do not know for sure which form of Mark that Luke or Matthew have used, hence there is no way of obtaining certainty about what they altered to the source). Second, literary dependence, apparently regardless of how it is defined, was simply not used as a method in antiquity, which was focused much more on orally informed text production. The objections are formulated in this order, though one might think that the inverted order would have been the more logical one: if the method in general was never used, it is futile to discuss particular forms of it. It is an extreme position and, in my opinion, too general a conclusion. There is no room, it would seem, for nuances in defining literary dependence: there is no "weak" form of dependence—the author has read or heard a text, interiorized or memorized (parts of) it, and reproduces this in writing—and certainly no "strong" one—an author works from a text *de visu*. There is no room for nuances in the type of text that is reproduced—whole books or short sections, texts never heard before and such passages that are familiar to the author: it is all the same. All that is left is a world of sound.

Nikander spends the whole second section of his paper (pp. 292–98) devoted to the issue of orality and performance in antiquity; the pages are in a sense well spent, for these are issues that are important, that have perhaps for too long been neglected, and that are still not sufficiently known to some of us. Ancient authors wrote to be heard, and they often "wrote" while hearing the text they were producing, as composing could happen through dictation. This is all true and well. Ancient writing and text producing differed from the way most texts come about today. Yet it must be noted that a significant part of text producing today also takes into account the orality factor, and this not just in writing speeches, or a piece for the theatre, or poetry and lyrics. We still have our daily share of oral-oriented text consumption: one just has to listen to the news report on television. A much more important difference, to me, is how written texts were produced in antiquity using other written texts. There was no way of endlessly "scrolling through scrolls"; writing habits and the book format used just prevented this or made it an incredibly complex process. But again, it all depends on what kind of text one is producing and what kind of sources there are available. Historians doubtlessly did not produce their work (solely) on the basis of hearing tradition. They consulted the works of their predecessors, read sections from them or had them read out, and then proceeded to produce their version of the events they had chosen to deal with. The same procedure may also have been at work in reproducing sections from the gospel accounts (or one of their sources); and here it would have been much easier to work "from the text" as the source was probably even better known than the average historian knew the work of his predecessors on the same topic. So books are in the background and often also "in the picture" as well, in producing other books in antiquity. The source may have been mediated through hearing and performing the text, but it does not of necessity mean the author heard a completely or significantly different text. The difference may have been his decision to "work" with the source text.

In the third and final part, Nikander then proceeds to "tracking the oral mode" of Did. 1.3b–2.1.[13] His comments on sound mapping, phrase units and their role in performing a text, and the division of the material according to "oral units" are interesting and correct, but they are purely descriptive and at no point do they offer an argument, let alone a demonstration, for the conclusion that this section was composed without any consideration for or any link with the written counterpart in the Gospels or their common source. The latter are never in sight, not even merely to compare the various attempts made by other authors to compose such a *Sectio Evangelica* and maybe say something on the quality of each of them. And that is a pity, for on Nikander's own hypothesis, Matthew's and Luke's version (and Q's) of the *Sectio Evangelica* would have come about in very much the same way as that of the Didache. It could be instructive to see who has come up with the "best" result, as this could say something about the qualities of the respective authors. But an even sorrier thing, in my view, is the unidimensional character of Nikander's approach. If redaction and source critics all too often and sadly have ignored the aural factor, Nikander risks obscuring without reason the textual factor. It does not have to be a matter of "either-or" (actually, for Nikander there is no "or" left, as in his opinion literary dependence can no longer claim any place or role in text producing in antiquity). Ancient authors heard texts, which they then turned into other texts. Aurality is an important factor, but the text had not of necessity disappeared altogether. Ancient authors had ways for composing with an eye for the "ear" and for the "eye"—for the fact that their work would most probably be heard rather than read and for the fact that a source text could be heard but not infrequently also be seen

---

13. See in the present volume, Perttu Nikander, "The *Sectio Evangelica* (Didache 1.3b–2.1) and Performance," above 298–309.

and consulted. In this respect it would have been worthwhile to check, in parallel and if only by way of experiment, whether the "sound" of Did. 1.3b–2.1 was perhaps more likely inspired by hearing Luke 6:27–30, 32–36 than Matt 5:39–42, 44–48 or an even a more ancient version. In Nikander's approach, we have no clue of what the Didache has heard, hence no clue what its author has been doing; but apparently we should not care too much about this.

One person at least seems to care. Nancy Pardee's "The Didache and Oral Theory" is an answer to Nikander, not, however, to the essay that is included in this volume, but to a paper he read at the SBL Didache session of 2010 on the Two Ways section. But of course the basic principles that guide Nikander in that paper are present also in the later one, as is clear from a line cited by Pardee on the relation between orality and writing: "both media … should be studied at the same time as interacting phenomena."[14] The point of Pardee's concerns with this way of presenting things and the core issue in her reply can be formulated in her own words as follows: "But how does one do this for the Two Ways, for the Didache as a whole, and for early Christian texts in general?"[15] An easy partial answer would be to say that what applies for the first of the three categories mentioned does not necessarily also go for the other two, but that would probably not really be in the spirit of Nikander's approach, which indeed wants the interplay of the two media to be at work in all sorts of ancient text production.

In the world of o/aurality, as Pardee describes it, there are no "originals" any longer, there are only performances, and each of these is unique.[16] This poses a giant problem, as Pardee notices, to those who would like to recover the original wording of, say, a saying of Jesus. Such a project would become very complicated, "if not entirely undermined."[17] The bulk of Pardee's paper is given to a critical presentation of several authors (and of Nikander's criticism of these same authors) who have given a place to orality in studying the way the Didache came about, be it for explaining parts of the process and the text or, in a more general way, of the whole process as such, at the exclusion of any form of redaction- or source-critical factor.

---

14. See in the present volume, Nancy Pardee, "The Didache and Oral Theory," above 311–33.

15. Ibid., 311.

16. Ibid., 313.

17. Ibid..

I must say I have a lot of sympathy for the criticism and the comments of Pardee. To mention only two of these: Aaron Milavec's interpretation of the change from singular to plural in Did. 7.1 just does not convince; the same is true of Draper's comments on the Two Ways section: variations there certainly are among the various witnesses to the Two Ways tradition, but these cannot be called upon to "demote" (my qualification) the Didache's use of it to that of "an aide mémoire" and not consider it as "a text to be performed verbatim at an initiation ceremony such as baptism."[18] The differences that exist among different texts cannot be used to make any conclusions on the status and purpose of one particular text, especially not if it can be argued (and in my opinion, proven) that the author of the Didache cannot have known any of these other witnesses. In a similar vein, it is tricky to argue for a first-century text on the basis of an interpretation of the status and role of similar texts (in genre, not in wording) that have been collected and preserved in much later and probably quite different sorts of texts.[19] The prayers in the Didache are "fixed," that is, meant to be used in this form and format. The one exception that is mentioned is found in 10.7, and it is meant to remain an exception.[20]

To conclude, picking up on Pardee's final comment about distinguishing "between texts of different genres/functions"[21] and at the same time going beyond her essay, I assume that even in a world of "performance only," this does not also have to mean that all performances are on principle equally valid, should be regarded as such, and cannot be criticized or commented upon by an audience that is acquainted also with other performances of the same text. I also assume it does not have to mean that this description of necessity goes for all texts. There are some texts for which the text—the wording—is crucial and unchangeable. Magical formulas are one such group, liturgical formulas may be another. In these cases, the performance may differ—in the reciting, in the pronunciation, in the chanting perhaps—but the text, the wording, is and stays the same. It remains to be seen to which category the Didache belongs or wished to belong. If the work is to be defined as a handbook for oral use, how would this have to be understood: should the text—the wording—be read exactly as it is found in the Didache; or is the work only a help for reciting

---

18. Ibid., 326.
19. See ibid., 327–30, on the comparison with prayers in rabbinic literature.
20. Ibid., 330.
21. Ibid., 332.

the text and the formulas it contains in performing a ritual without this recitation to be exact; or is this just one way for reciting the necessary formulas that for whatever reason happened to be laid down in writing without any thought of being normative or helpful to others? The fact that a text whose wording is very similar to that of the Didache was taken up, with some comments, in a work such as the Apostolic Constitutions and Canons would indicate that at least the collector/redactor of the latter, if working from "our" Didache, rather considered the first of the three options just mentioned to be the more and perhaps the sole correct one. Of course, maybe that was just this one redactor/collector's position and decision; but after all, it is that of an ancient author.

John Welch addresses the very important issue of the relationship between the Didache and Matthew's Sermon on the Mount (= SM). The author is "inclined to see the Didache as consciously drawing on, carefully selecting from, and purposefully transforming many elements from the Sermon on the Mount."[22] The second and third movement mentioned here also allow for asking what was omitted form the source text and why. Welch first lists and briefly comments on the similarities; he then has a section on "inverted quotations"; this is followed by one on the differences and another section on the "chronological implications"; the evidence is then drawn together for some concluding observations on the relationship between the Didache and SM.[23]

The similarities as listed by Welch are numerous and, in his words, "remarkable."[24] With over one hundred entries, the list in appendix 1 is long indeed and turns the relationship with SM into something unique: no other known text has so many corresponding words and phrases. The overlaps are found almost all through the Didache, chapters 7 and 13 being the sole exceptions. The list is qualified in terms of verbatim and other types of agreement and Welch is not blind to the differences in arrangement and in density of the overlaps that do exist; but these are not considered to be sufficient to give up on the hypothesis of literary dependence. Welch draws attention to the inversions, of which he lists eleven, which is not an extraordinary number for a phenomenon that is well attested also in Hebrew Scripture, though one might rather have preferred to find

---

22. See in the present volume, John W. Welch, "From the Sermon on the Mount to the Didache," 335–61 (335).
23. Ibid., 350–55.
24. Ibid., 336.

here a comparison with other Greek texts (the LXX or maybe also Mark-Matthew/Luke?) to give more force to the argument. Some readers certainly will be surprised to find out that the question of the direction of the dependence (SM > Didache, or perhaps Didache > SM) is mentioned only briefly at the end of the section on inversions (even before the differences have been listed!) and is decided rather quickly and in general terms for the former option ("for several reasons—structural, sequential, logical, linguistic, dependent, and thematic").[25]

The "missing-pieces" list contains a bit of everything, but in particular quite a lot of words that have to do with the temple and temple cult. Not everything in Welch's survey is equally important and in the same way linked to the temple, but overall the list is quite impressive and would seem to allow for the conclusion that the Didache has more or less systematically done away with anything in SM that has a link to the temple.[26] Welch builds on it (in line with Richard Bauckham) to explain the Didache's redaction in terms of transforming (or modifying) old Jewish concerns for the interest of gentile newcomers and to conclude that with the Didache we have shifted from the Jewish ambit of SM into a gentile one,[27] or as he formulates it in, to my taste, somewhat strange wording, "the SM comes from those of the former persuasion regarding close temple ties, while the Didache stems from the latter view of temple irrelevancy."[28]

So it seems we have landed in Matthew's world, for it is with Matthew's version of SM that the Didache is compared and have been given a plausible explanation for the differences between the two. But in the conclusion this then turns out to be an illusion, for Welch's SM is not Matthew's but the highly speculative pre-Matthean variant of it. Welch knows this latter entity "remains highly debatable," but he nevertheless proves to be a loyal follower of Hans Dieter Betz's position on this matter, up to the point of claiming to bring on "additional support" for it.[29] I am afraid the support is not that impressive. The rare, "un-Matthean" words and phrases Welch lists on page 351 had of course also already been noted by Betz himself and made to use for his hypothesis; it is not really much of a help when Welch then ends his paragraph offering support with a mere, "neverthe-

---

25. Ibid., 340.
26. See the comment ibid., 340 and the list on 340–41.
27. Ibid., 349–50.
28. Ibid., 350.
29. Ibid., 351.

less, the issue is not cut-and-dried."[30] Likewise, the list of un-Matthean words in SM that occur elsewhere in Matthew and are thought to have been introduced there from SM (see pages 352–53) is far from supporting the hypothesis; if the presence of the word "the lesser/least" (μικρότερος) in Matt 11:11 were to be derived from ἐλάχιστος in 5:19,[31] how does one account for the fact that Luke uses the very same word in his parallel to 11:11 in 7:28, unless, of course, one reckons with the possibility that Luke too (and many other books of the New Testament!) was influenced by SM and made the same reasoning as Matthew did in "transmuting" ἐλάχιστος into μικρότερος. I would like to see evidence for this. And I would have preferred Welch to offer evidence for the hypothesis that the Didache must depend on pre-Matthean SM and cannot be explained from Matthew's version itself. In its current form, the hypothesis is too easy a prey for the "oralists" in Didache studies (how can we ever be sure of what the Didache really did with SM if we do not have it and cannot reconstruct it with any certainty—see Nikander's comment on working from Q referred to above) and the "textualists" alike (why reconstruct an hypothetical SM if Matthew's SM can explain things in the same way).

Murray Smith, in what is the longest and best documented essay of this section, significantly broadens the perspective and the range of texts that are discussed in relation to or for interpreting the Didache, while largely staying away from the question of whether and how the latter knew Matthew or his tradition. The first half of the essay is given to a survey and detailed discussion of the references to the title "Lord" and how to identify the one addressed in this way. In the second part, Smith offers a lengthy analysis of the motif of the "coming of the Lord Jesus" as it appears in the Didache in comparison to other ancient texts dealing with the same question. All of the instances of "Lord" in the Didache outside chapter 16 can with more or less certainty be said to refer to Jesus. In combination with parallel use in other ancient documents, this observation may prove to offer sufficient ground for the conclusion that the Didache is familiar with the motif of the parousia of the Lord Jesus and his judgemental role that goes with it, and that the work displays a "remarkably 'high'" christology.[32] So far I am with the author. I am less happy with the way he formulates his

---

30. Ibid., 352.
31. Ibid., 351.
32. See in the present volume, Murray J. Smith, "The Lord Jesus and His Coming in the Didache," above 363–407.

position then also as, "the Didache includes Jesus within the identity of the one true God of Israel and attributes to him the dignity and prerogatives that belong to God alone."[33]

Smith's position with regard to the identification of the Lord in the passages reviewed by him is probably correct. The major question one might have is not so much with the contents but with the way he integrates the question of the relationship with Matthew into his analysis and hence whether and how this essay belongs in this section of the volume. If the comments on Did. 8.2, the first passage to be discussed among the instances of "Lord," can be taken as typifying the author's position, not much can be gained here for the question of the relation between the Didache and Matthew; for indeed, after pointing out the two options that are found in the literature—"knowledge of the Gospel of Matthew in its finished form," which seems to be the author's privileged position, or "knowledge of some other written gospel source"—Smith continues with a slightly disappointing, "be that as it may."[34] A similar comment is found at 9.5: "For our purposes, it is again not necessary to enter the debate about the relationship between Matthew and the Didache."[35] Smith may feel this way, and one might well agree with his reading of 9.5a as (somehow) including Jesus, but it is a bit easy and dissatisfying and also methodologically not completely sound if part of the argument for the reading is built on Matt 28:19. What does it mean that the comparable phrase of Did. 7.1, 3 "is identical with that found at Matt 28:19"?[36] It certainly means something different if the Didache is supposed to have drawn on Matthew's final form (probably Smith's own position) or on a phrase that was circulated before Matthew and ended up in his Gospel. So, while being supportive and sympathetic of Smith's analysis, arguments, and conclusions with regard to the identification of the Lord, I fear the argument suffers from this lack of clarity on the relationship with Matthew. It is also a bit disturbing to notice that Smith does not seem to take the trouble to argue why the genitive in the phrase "the gospel of the Lord" (see Did. 15.4) should be a genitive of the subject, not of the object.

---

33. Ibid., 407.
34. Ibid., 366.
35. Ibid., 368.
36. Ibid.

Four out of the twenty-one occurrences of the title "Lord" outside chapter 16 are said to be "indeterminate, but quite possibly" refer to Jesus.[37] The latter of these qualifications has the author's preference and appears in the title of this section. The author of Barn. 19.2–3 interpreted the parallel to Did. 4.12–13 undoubtedly as referring to God. The different context in which the two passages figure may not be sufficient ground to say that this says nothing about Did. 4.12–13.[38] I am afraid Smith is overdoing the argument. Even if there are a couple of cases in the Didache in which the Lord would refer to God, this would not invalidate the identification with Jesus Smith argues for in chapter 16. The parallel use elsewhere in the Didache is an important argument for identifying the use of the title in chapter 16, but it is not an absolute or the only one. The immediate context in which the word appears and the way it is used in parallel passages to this particular one are also important and perhaps even stronger arguments. Now Smith risks becoming liable to the same charge of overgeneralising that can easily be brought against Aaron Milavec, arguing for the opposite position and identifying all such instances of Lord as referring to God, which is certainly an even more impossible position than Smith's.[39]

The same comments and reservations apply to the passages on the coming of the Lord that are dealt with in the second half of the essay. The μαραναθά invocation in Did. 10.6 (in combination with 10.5) has something for it to be understood with reference to the Lord Jesus. Its origins are to be found in Hebrew Scripture and are there obviously applied to God, but the process of transposing the motif to Jesus had already begun and is documented in the earliest Christian tradition—most explicitly in Rev 22:20, rather less clearly in 1 Cor 16:22 and Jude 14. Hence, there remain some doubts about Did. 10.5–6, notwithstanding Smith's enthusiasm for the Lord = Jesus option. The conclusion "almost certainly the Lord Jesus" may be just a little bit too strong in view of the reference to "the God of David," the double doxology (in 10.4 and 5), the double mention of the Lord's "power," and the motif of preparing the kingdom (10.5).[40] Of course, the first of these could be interpreted in a strongly messianic way, as if David was not speaking about the coming of a political and earthly messiah, but of the divine one, the Christ Jesus. But one needs almost a

---

37. Ibid., 378.
38. Against Smith (378).
39. See, ibid., 380 n. 62.
40. Ibid., 383–84.

detour over Mark 12:35–37 to make this work. Likewise, the last of the objections could be rendered futile by arguing that it is a somewhat awkward way to say that the Lord Jesus left to prepare a place in heaven for his disciples, now in line with John 14:2–3, but are all of us prepared to make this detour?

Perhaps a stronger case can be made for the three references to the coming of the Lord in Did. 16.1, 7, 8. In this instance parallels with the Synoptic Gospels abound, but again their force and use for the argument is significantly reduced when reading such phrases as, "it has often been thought that the Didache here [on 16.1a] depends on Matt 24. This remains quite likely, but the parallels are not so exact as to require direct literary dependence.... Be that as it may."[41] But if not "direct literary dependence," what then? Dependence on synoptic tradition? But then at the risk that this tradition interpreted the motif differently from what Smith thinks Matthew makes of it and (still) applied it to God instead of to Christ? It is the same reasoning and the same kind of, in my view, overcautious hesitation that is found in the comments on the lamps and the girded robes in 16.1b. The least that can be said, I would think, is that "the co-location of the two images ... is sufficiently uncommon to suggest a relationship of some kind" between this passage and Luke 12:35.[42] It is all a bit discouraging. "A common source (perhaps 'Q')," or "a modified rendition" of Luke 12:35 are the two options mentioned,[43] and Smith is happy to leave it there, for as far as he is concerned he has made his point: the motif has its place in the synoptic tradition. But again, how sure can we be that the common source used the motif in exactly the same way; what about calling in Q for a verse that is not attested also in Matthew; and why can the common source not also be further evaporated into a form of common tradition? After all, the imagery is not particularly Christian or christological and could also have been in use in the context of Jewish eschatological expectations. I may be driving my scepticism too far, but I do so on purpose, because it should not be forgotten that not all of the parallels Smith cites explicitly identify the coming one with Jesus, contrary to what he seems to suppose when writing, "in all of them, he speaks of his own final advent, often in theophanic [sic] terms."[44] Such an identification can be found in the par-

---

41. Ibid., 387.
42. Ibid., 388.
43. Ibid.
44. Ibid., 389.

able in Matt 24:36, 42–44 and its parallel in Luke 12:35–40 (that is, if the Son of man refers to Jesus, which it most probably does), but not in the quasiparallel in Mark 13:32–37, nor in the parable of the virgins in Matt 25:1–13. Why would this have been different in "the synoptic tradition"? So caution there should be, but maybe for a different reason.

In the last, double-reference to the Lord in 16.7–8, the Didachist seems to go his own way when citing from Zech 14:5 and alluding quite openly to Dan 7:13–14. However much I sympathize with his position, it is slightly ironic to note that this is the only instance in which Smith thinks it "more likely" that the Didache reflects knowledge of Matthew (24:30–31) than turning to the alternative of positing a common source.[45] And it is again a bit disappointing to see that, while the Didachist is now given his freedom to act as a "real" author—that is with the right to write out his mind—Smith does not wish to extend this conclusion to other such instances in the work and accept that elsewhere as well the Didache may have used this freedom to work with and from the Gospels without betraying these, but without slavishly copying any of them. If Matthew is allowed to get in here in this instance, he should be allowed to enter elsewhere as well. And if the Didache is said to have changed here Matthew's (double!) son of man into Lord, he should be given credit for systematically referring to Jesus in a way all through his work. It makes me a bit sad not to read such a conclusion, and it takes away something of the joy I felt in studying an otherwise well-documented essay.

I conclude most briefly. In reading through the five essays that constitute this section one might be recalled of the saying "quot capita, tot sensus" ("as many heads, so many opinions"). In essence, there is nothing wrong with such an observation. Unfortunately, however, it turns out that not all the "sensus" are equally sound and strongly argued. I refrain from commenting on the "capita."

---

45. Ibid., 400.

Part 4
The Didache and Other Early Christian Texts

Without Decree: Pagan Sacrificial Meat and the Early History of the Didache[*]

Matti Myllykoski

The prohibition of pagan sacrificial meat in Did. 6.2–3 is often viewed as evidence for the influence of the Apostolic Decree (Acts 15:20, 29) on early Syrian Jewish Christianity.[1] According to a similarly popular theory, behind Did. 1.1–6.1 lies a Jewish catechism presumably used by Jewish Christians.[2] The prohibition of the consumption of pagan sacrificial meat in Did. 6.2–3 is regarded as an addition, which conveys the basic content of the decree to the gentiles. This article proposes an alternative reconstruction of this history. First, I will ask whether there was a *vorlukanisch* Apostolic Decree at all and, second, I will argue that the teaching of the Two Ways in the Didache was from the outset a Jewish Christian text,

---

[*] This essay was previously published under the title "Ohne Dekret: Das Götzenopferfleisch und die Frühgeschichte der Didache," in *Apostedekret und antikes Vereinwesen: Gemeinschaft und ihre Ordnung*, ed. Markus Öhler, WUNT 280 (Tübingen: Mohr Siebeck 2011), 113–37.

1. So e.g., Jean-Paul Audet, *La Didachè: Instructions des Apôtres*, Ebib (Paris: Gabalda, 1958), 209, 354–57; Marcel Simon, "De l'observance ritual à l'asceticism: Recherches sur le décret Apostolique," *RHR* 193 (1978): 27–104 (89–90); Clayton N. Jefford, *The Sayings of Jesus in the Teaching of the Twelve Apostles*, VCSup 11 (Leiden: Brill, 1989), 96–97; and Huub van de Sandt and David Flusser, *The Didache: Its Jewish Sources and Its Place in Early Judaism and Christianity*, CRINT 3.5 (Assen: Van Gorcum; Minneapolis: Fortress, 2002), 24–243. Otherwise e.g., Kurt Niederwimmer, *Die Didache: A Commentary*, KAV 1 (Göttingen: Vandenhoeck & Ruprecht, 1993), 157 n. 37.

2. Most scholars embrace the theory by Charles Taylor, *The Teaching of the Twelve Apostles, with Illustrations from the Talmud* (Cambridge: Deighton Bell, 1886), and Benjamin B. Warfield, "Text, Sources and Contents of the 'Two Ways' or First Section of the Didache," *BSac* 43 (1886): 81–97; see Audet, *Didachè*, 131–37; Niederwimmer, *Didache*, 67–69; and others.

which in a certain phase of development was supplemented with the prohibition of pagan sacrificial meat.

1. To the Formation of the So-Called Apostolic Decree

Without Acts we would not know the so-called Apostolic Decree. Only Luke reports that the dispute about the circumcision of the gentiles in Antioch was resolved with a formal decree sent from Jerusalem. None other than Luke himself tells us about an epistle that the apostles and elders sent through Paul, Barnabas, Judas, and Silas to the Christians in Antioch, Syria, and Cilicia (Acts 15:22–23). Only Luke tells us that the apostles admonished the gentiles with a written document to stay away from pagan sacrificial meat, blood, strangled animals, and fornication (v. 29).

Luke describes the beginning of the conflict as a serious situation: some (τινες) have caused "no small" conflict by claiming that the gentiles who converted to the faith in Christ without circumcision and obedience to the law cannot be saved. Curiously enough Luke does not say whether these Torah-observant Jews are Christians. Luke's account reveals (v. 5) that he numbers them among the members of the Jerusalem community, although he freely acknowledges that actually these people are no real insiders. At the last visit of Paul to Jerusalem, Luke mentions these believers who are so zealous for the law and counts their number in myriads (Acts 21:20). Luke falters between two tendencies that pull in opposite directions: on the one hand, the zealots of the law must be understood as a serious minority, which is able to cause a serious strife in the community; on the other hand, they must appear as a fringe group that can by no means shake the consensus of the faithful.

Because of the demand of these "some," Paul, Barnabas, "and some others" must travel from Antioch to Jerusalem in order to hold a meeting with the apostles and elders (15:1–2, 5). There is a notable contrast between the serious issue originally at stake and the description of events that follows. Luke tells how Paul and his colleagues who travel towards Jerusalem are welcomed in Phoenicia and Samaria with joy (v. 3). When they arrive in Jerusalem and report about their activities, Luke seems to indicate that all others except "some of the sect of the Pharisees" seem to relate very positively to their news (vv. 4–5; see next v. 12).[3]

---

3. Biblical quotations are from the NRSV; translations of the Didache are my own.

In the assembly, the requirement of those zealots for the law is unanimously denied after a fierce dispute (πολλῆς δὲ ζητήσεως γενομένης, v. 7) with the breathtaking speeches of Peter and James (vv. 7–11, 13–21),[4] both in complete agreement with each other and reading like Pauline statements. Now that God has cleansed the hearts of the gentile Christians and they also have received the Holy Spirit—according to Peter—there is no difference between them and Jews who believe in Christ. The zealots for the law "put God to the test" with their claim. The law is a yoke that even the fathers of the faithful could not bear (see 7:53; 13:38–39), while the salvation of the Jews and gentiles relies merely on faith in Jesus Christ (vv. 7–11). The subsequent testimony of Paul and Barnabas about the wonderful impact of God among the gentiles underscores the futility of the demand of those zealous for the law (v. 12). James continues in perfect agreement with the speech of Peter that God has made himself a people among the gentiles, as the "words of the prophets" prove.[5] Through the restoration of Israel in Jesus Christ and the inclusion of the gentiles in his people, God has fulfilled his promise. In the strict sense, it is Lord's brother James, who, according to Luke, decides the issue (v. 19: ἐγὼ κρίνω).[6]

According to Luke, the specific proposal of James (v. 20) is adopted by the assembly as such (vv. 23–29) and is repeated in the letter (v. 29). The four things from which the gentiles should abstain are named slightly differently in these two versions:

v. 20:[7] τῶν ἀλισγημάτων τῶν εἰδώλων καὶ τῆς πορνείας καὶ τοῦ πνικτοῦ καὶ τοῦ αἵματος

---

4. Peter and Paul silence the whole crowd (vv. 12–13) and, after the speech of James (v. 22), the matter is completely settled.

5. Some scholars assume that it is the historical James who is speaking here; see particularly, Richard J. Bauckham, "James and the Jerusalem Church," in *The Book of Acts in Its Palestinian Setting*, vol .4 of *The Book of Acts in Its First Century Setting*, ed. Richard Bauckham (Grand Rapids: Eerdmans; Carlisle: Paternoster, 1995), 455.

6. Jacob Jervell, *Die Apostelgeschichte*, 17th ed., KEK 3 (Göttingen: Vandenhoeck & Ruprecht, 1998), 389; see also Ernst Haenchen, *Die Apostelgeschichte*, 14th ed., KEK 6 (Göttingen: Vandenhoeck & Ruprecht, 1965), 394 (= κρίνω "I mean"). The course of events indicates that James as the author of the decision also has the last word.

7. Codex D has in the end the so-called golden rule καὶ ὅσα μὴ θέλουσιν ἑαυτοῖς γίνεσθαι ἑτέροις μὴ ποιεῖτε, and the words καὶ τῆς πορνείας are missing in P[45]. Irenaeus already knows the text transmitted by D: *a uanitatibus idolorum et a fornicatione et a sanguine et quaecumque nolunt sibi fieri aliis ne faciant* (Haer. 3.12.14–15).

v. 29:[8] εἰδωλοθύτων καὶ αἵματος καὶ πνικτῶν καὶ πορνείας

The speeches of the two apostles clearly show that Luke relates the decree to cult and not to ethics: the hearts of the gentile Christians are pure (vv. 8–9), but the decree is necessary for their external or ritual purity (v. 28: ἐπάναγκες).[9] The list in verse 29 is directly derived from the essential prohibitions mentioned in Lev 17–18. The taboos concerning pagan sacrificial meat (17:7, idolatry), blood (17:10), what is strangled (17:13, hunting prey for food), and fornication (18:6, sexual contact between blood relatives) stem—even in the right order—from these chapters that should rule the life of the Israelites and the aliens living among them. The real problem in this supposedly traditional list is fornication, which when taken without further explanation, does not refer to ritual practices but to ethical conduct. Therefore it has been assumed that the prohibitions of the decree should be traced back to the interpretation of Lev 17–18 in the Targums.[10] If this is true, it is also possible to understand fornication in a broader sense. In his formulation of verse 20, however, Luke shows that he has a problem with the expression πορνεία: he stresses the ritual character of the decree with the expression "polluted things" (pl. ἀπέχεσθαι τῶν ἀλισγημάτων) and moves πορνεία to the end of the list. Luke clearly recognized the problem, but did not want to change the expression to make it clear that the decree points to the ritual issues related to fornication. This in turn indicates that he considers the specific content of the decree less important than the purpose that the decree has in his salvation-historically motivated narrative.

For Luke, the purpose of the decree is clear: if the converted gentiles follow these rules, they are full members of the people of God, which is

---

Only some modern scholars prefer the Western text. For an interesting argument for the Western text and the origin of the decree in the Noachide prohibitions (Gen 9:4–6; Jub. 7:20, 21a; t. ʿAbod. Zar. 8:4; t. Šabb. 16:17; b. Pesaḥ. 25a), see van de Sandt and Flusser, *Didache*, 245–53.

8. As in v. 22, Codex D also here concludes with the golden rule καὶ ὅσα μὴ θέλετε ἑαυτοῖς γίνεσθαι ἑτέρῳ μὴ ποιεῖν. A few Vulgate manuscripts do not mention the fornication. The earliest witness of the original text is Clement of Alexandria (*Paed.* 2.7.56; *Strom.* 4.15.97).

9. Thus rightly Jervell, *Apostelgeschichte*, 391–92.

10. Jürgen Wehnert, *Reinheit des "christlichen Gottesvolkes" aus Juden und Heiden: Studien zum historischen und theologischen Hintergrund des sogenannten Aposteldekrets*, FRLANT 173 (Göttingen: Vandenhoeck & Ruprecht, 1997), 209–32.

made up of Jews and gentiles according to the will of God. According to Luke, the strict Jewish Christians raise absolutely no objections against the thin ritual content of the decree proposed by James. The reader of Acts must further assume that these zealots stay in the Jerusalem community only to reappear in chapter 21 with their new protests and demands. In Acts 15, Luke wants to point out that with the decree the apostles reached a *reconciliation*. In the report of Paul (Gal 2:1–10), there are traces neither of a decree nor of a reconciliation. According to Paul, the "pillars" in Jerusalem *accepted* his law-free gentile mission, regardless of what they themselves or the zealots for the law thought about it.

It is characteristic of Luke's narration that, in the argument concerning the decree in Acts 15:21, he makes James leave the zealots aside and instead take up the synagogues "everywhere." This reasoning is hard to follow, but in any case it must be assumed that it legitimizes the authority of the decree with the Mosaic law.[11] Luke wants to show how patiently and peacefully the Christian gentile mission approached the synagogues. When Paul and his associates return to Antioch, the content of the apostolic letter makes the local gentile Christians rejoice (vv. 30–31). This joy cannot be understood as anything other than an expression of pious relief: Luke indicates that the prohibitions of the decree are easy to fulfill and that the Antiochene gentile Christians have already naturally followed them. In verse 41, where Luke portrays Paul's journey among the communities in Syria and Cilicia, he keeps quiet about the decree,[12] and after the statement in 16:4 he no longer refers to the statutes of the apostles.

Behind the Lukan narrative only some specific elements can be confidently included in a traditional source: the starting point of the dispute, the meeting of the major participants, and the basic acceptance of the gentile mission. It is very difficult to reconstruct an original letter of the apostles and elders behind the document reported by Luke in verses 23–29. Except for the four items of the decree, everything in this letter is dependent on the Lukan report and that alone. Both the language of the letter and the description of the main actors and their roles correspond to the Lukan presentation in the other chapters. In the light of these observations, it is

---

11. According to Haenchen, *Die Apostelgeschichte*, 396, the presence of the synagogue in all cities indicates that the local gentile Christians knew the four things mentioned in the decree.

12. Codex Bezae and some other manuscripts add the words παραδιδοὺς τὰς ἐντολὰς τῶν πρεσβυτέρων.

reasonable to ask whether it is at all possible to trace a traditional letter or decree from the Lukan text. My conclusion is that Luke knew the four prohibitions as a rule, which some Christians followed and attributed to the authority of the apostles.[13]

A parallel to the decree can be found in Rev 2:14–15. Here the community of Pergamum is blamed for their toleration of the Nicolaitans, who "hold the doctrine of Balaam" by "eating pagan sacrificial meat" and "adultery" (φαγεῖν εἰδωλόθυτα καὶ πορνεῦσαι).[14] Some scholars think that these verses are influenced by the decree,[15] but the polemical connection of eating pagan sacrificial meat and fornication does not necessarily indicate a ritually oriented Apostolic Decree as its background.

Although some scholars assume that the Lukan report about the decree and its sending to Syria and Cilicia is historically reliable,[16] nothing in the Pauline letters indicates that the apostle would have known such a decree. Paul says in Gal 2:6 that the pillars did not impose anything on him (οὐδὲν προσανέθεντο). These words hardly imply an implicit reference to the decree, because in verse 10 Paul pointedly stresses that he and Barnabas should *only* (μόνον) take care of the poor. Many scholars conclude therefore that Paul and his coworkers did not take the decree to Antioch immediately after the meeting. They assume that the decree was sent to the communities in Syria and Cilicia only later, without the knowledge and approval of Paul.[17] This theory presupposes that Luke knew a letter of the apostles in Jerusalem, used it in a stylized form, and simply added a reference to Paul and Barnabas.

That is possible, but there is no plausible way from Gal 2 to the decree: the division of mission in Paul's account in Gal 2:9 does not fit well with

---

13. Haenchen, *Apostelgeschichte*, 417–18; see also John Painter, *Just James: The Brother of Jesus in History and Tradition* (Columbia: University of South Carolina Press, 1997), 52–53.

14. Simon, "Observance ritual à l'ascéticism," 71 interprets this passage similarly.

15. Ibid., 67–75: 73: "que le décret soit sous-jacent aux lettres de l'Apocalypse ne paraît pas ... faire de doute."

16. So for example Simon, "Observance ritual à l'ascéticism," 76–78, who thinks that Paul does not take up the decree, because he did not want to act in obvious contradiction to it.

17. Thus first, Carl von Weizsäcker, *The Apostolic Age of the Christian Church* trans. James Miller, 3rd ed. (London: Williams & Norgate; New York: Putnam's Sons, 1902), 173. Jervell, *Apostelgeschichte*, 406–7, suggests that the decree had been proposed to Paul in the council, but he rejected it.

the decree. If the Jerusalem apostles were responsible only for the mission to the Jews, it would be hard to understand how they could have been able to interfere with the Pauline mission to the gentiles. Furthermore, the conflict at Antioch (Gal 2:11–14) demonstrates that James and his party did not recognize the fellowship between Jewish and gentile Christians at Antioch. Thereby they made themselves outsiders in the eyes of the gentile Christians who could and should not control their lives.

Paul's first letter to the Corinthian community, written five to six years after the meeting in Jerusalem, also speaks against rather than for the originality of the decree. In 1 Cor 5:1–13, Paul treats the case of an incestuous man without any hint or reference to an apostolic condemnation of immorality of this kind. Paul does not categorically prohibit the Corinthians from eating food offered to idols, but defends the conscience of the weak brother against the freedom of the strong who know that eating idol food does not hurt them (8:1–13). In principle, it is possible that Paul knew the decree, but did not care about it or interpreted it quite differently from the apostles in Jerusalem. In both cases, however, the basis of his decision is completely independent of the decree: he advises the Corinthians to leave the incestuous man to Satan, while those who eat sacrificial meat do nothing evil at all. Even the Jewish Christian adversaries of Paul, on whose animosity towards Paul we have ample information in the genuine epistles of the apostle, did not criticize Paul because he neglected a very specific apostolic decision in his gentile communities.

Irenaeus and Clement of Alexandria are the first authors known to us who clearly rely on Luke's decree in Acts 15. It is significant that Irenaeus, like Codex Bezae, quotes the decree in an ethically interpreted version, which includes the golden rule. The ethical version is clearly of later origin, but nevertheless stems already from the first half of the second century. Distancing from a ritual rule becomes visible also in other Christian sources. The later witnesses of the decree cite neither the report of Luke nor a formal apostolic decision, but point instead and independently of each other to particular prohibitions known from the decree without citing the apostolic decision in its entirety.[18]

---

18. Consumption of pagan sacrificial meat is more or less strongly prohibited by some authors in separate references (Justin, *Dial.* 34.8; Aristides, *Apol.* 15.5; Minucius Felix, *Oct.* 38.1; Tertullian, *Apol.* 9.15), and we have some evidence against eating meat of dead animals (Justin, *Dial.* 20.1; Tertullian, *Apol.* 9.13; Origen, *Comm. Matth.* 10) and blood (Minucius Felix, *Oct.* 30.6; Tertullian, *Apol.* 9.13; Eusebius, *Hist. eccl.*

In the Pseudo-Clementine *Homilies* (7.8.1), the components of the decree linked to the eating of meat are mentioned: εἰδωλοθύτων, νεκρῶν, πνικτῶν, θηριαλώτων, αἵματος, and in the narrow context of a list commenting on the meaning of the "table of demons" (cf. 1 Cor 10:22); however, we find here no reference to an apostolic letter or decision.

2. The Prohibition of Pagan Sacrificial Meat in the Didache

The prohibition of eating sacrificial meat in Did. 6 is often seen as a parallel to the decree in Acts 15:20, 29. It is not at all clear in what context the prohibition is incorporated into the text and how it should be interpreted in detail. In the following analysis, I will study the early history of the Didache in order to cast some light on the background of the prohibition. The prohibition of idol food does not belong to the original tract of the Two Ways, but I believe that it can be located in the literary history of the Didache and even dated on the basis of literary analysis. The composition of the Didache demonstrates how the essential teachings of the Christian Jews were received and transmitted in the Syrian region. It can be shown that the explicit prohibition of eating idol food played a relatively limited but nevertheless significant role.

2.1. Development of the Two Ways Tract

Even before the discovery and publication of the Didache by Bryennios,[19] scholars were aware that the Two Ways tract known by Rufinus (*Duae viae vel Iudicium Petri*)[20] had notable similarities with the epistle of Barnabas, the so-called Apostolic Ecclesiastical Canon and the Apostolic Constitutions and Canons.[21] The discovery of the Latin Doctrina apostolorum by

---

5.1.26). Tertullian's references are revealing. He interprets the decree ethically (*Pud.* 12.4; Codex Bezae is close to the text), and when he condemns eating meat offered to idols (*Spect.* 13.4), blood (*Mon.* 5.3), and strangled animals (*Apol.* 9.13), he does not refer to Acts 15 but to quite different passages in the Scriptures (1 Cor 10:21, 28; Gen 9:4; and Lev 17:15 [?] respectively).

19. Philotheos Bryennios, Διδαχὴ τῶν δώδεκα ἀποστόλων … (Constantinople: Voutyra, 1883).

20. Rufinus, *Symb.* 36: *siue pastoris in nouo Stiefel testamento libellus qui dicitur hermae, et qui appellatur duae is via, vel iudicium secundum petrum*.

21. On this subject, see Robert E. Aldridge, "Peter and the 'Two Ways,'" *VC* 53

Otto von Gebhardt (1884) and its publication by Josef Schlecht (1901)[22] has made the comparison between the documents still easier. The so-called Sectio Evangelica in Did. 1.3–2.1 is missing in these and other more distant parallels. Right at the outset it was clear that the treatise behind Did. 1–6 had to stem from much earlier times.

In his lectures of 1885 at the Royal Institute, Charles Taylor demonstrated the thoroughly Jewish character of the Didache with many contemporary and rabbinic parallels.[23] Most of these parallels can be found in chapters 1–5, which in their original form refer neither to Jesus nor include any christological features. The reason for being meek ("because the meek shall inherit the earth," Did. 3.7) seems to be formulated on the basis of Ps 36:11 LXX and has no parallel in Barn.19.4. Correspondingly, the reference to the Lord in Did. 4.1 ("you shall honor him [i.e., the teacher of the word] like the Lord"), together with the rationale ("because wherever the Lordly rule is preached, there is the Lord"), are later christological statements, since the parallel passage of Barn. 19.9 is formulated without reference to Jesus. The saying only tells the hearer of the word to love his teacher as the apple of his eye. Taylor thinks that pseudo-Barnabas has here retained the original form of the saying. Since the whole passage has notable close and "non-Christian" parallels in Barn. 18–20, Taylor and others have concluded that the so-called treatise of the Two Ways was a text that must have originated in non-Christian Jewish circles.[24] In the

---

(1999): 233–64 (233–42). In his own contribution, Aldridge argues for the thesis that the tract of the Two Ways circulated under the name of the apostle Peter.

22. Joseph Schlecht, *Doctrina XII Apostolorum: Die Apostellehre in der Liturgie der katholischen Kirche* (Freiburg im Breisgau: Herder, 1901).

23. Taylor, *Teaching of the Twelve Apostles*, 6–45.

24. Jonathan A. Draper, "A Continuing Enigma: The 'Yoke of the Lord in *Didache* 6:2–3 and Early Jewish-Christian Relations," in *The Image of Judaeo-Christians in Ancient Jewish and Christian Christian Literature*, ed Peter J. Tomson and D. Lambers-Petry, WUNT 158 (Tübingen: Mohr Siebeck, 2003), 111–12, offers a good summary of the theories for the origin of the tract: (1) according to the majority of scholars, the Two Ways treatise is an intra-Jewish or sectarian writing (thus, e. g., Niederwimmer, *Didache*, 35–41); (2) some earlier scholars, such as Adolf Harnack, *Die Apostellehre und die jüdischen Beiden Wege* (Leipzig: Heinrichs, 1886), 14–15, considered the treatise as a Jewish proselyte catechism; (3) Draper himself argues for the view that the treatise was originally a Jewish Christian catechism (this is also the view defended in this article); and, (4) in the 1920s and 1930s, some scholars assumed that the treatise was a later version of the corresponding text in the epistle of Barnabas. This thesis has for a long time been but *neiges d'antan*.

1950s, the discovery of a close parallel in the Rule of the Community of Qumran (1QS III, 13–IV, 26) supported this theory further.[25]

This commonly accepted assumption is not without problems. It is based on a sharp division between the "Jewish" and "Christian" paraenesis in a time in which all "Christian" texts were basically "Jewish."[26] The theory further indicates that the followers of Jesus could not have created such a text with their own resources, but must have adopted it from a group that was not oriented towards Jesus. One could perhaps propose how this might actually have happened. Nevertheless, it is much easier to assume that the Two Ways treatise was produced by the Jewish Christians themselves during a particular phase in their development. Both observations on the composition history of the treatise as well as a comparison with the structure and content of the Matthean Sermon on the Mount indicate that the treatise fits very well in the evolving teaching situations of the Jewish Christian communities. The assumption of the Jewish Christian origin of the treatise implies that the "commandments of the Lord" to which the epilogue of the Two Ways refers should be understood as the commandments of the Lord Jesus Christ already in the context of the original treatise.

For the reconstruction of the original form of the treatise, our sources offer two possible starting points: the text of the epistle of Barnabas on the one hand and the Didache (and the Doctrina apostolorum) on the other. Unlike the Didache, in the introduction of the treatise Barnabas speaks not about the ways of life and death but about those of light and darkness, while the Doctrina apostolorum has both characteristics. The reference to the angels of God and of Satan in Barn. 18.1 resembles the passage about the two angels in the Rule of the Community of Qumran (1QS III, 13–IV, 26). The connection in the tradition between the tropes of two roads and two angels is found also in the description of the Two Ways in the Testament of Asher (T. Ash. 1.8–9; 6.4–5).

A significant group of scholars assumes that the apocalyptic frame (light and darkness) in Barn. 18.1 (with reference to the angels of God and the angels of Satan), 19.1, and Doctr. 1.1 is original.[27] In the light of

---

25. Audet, *Didachè*, 159–61.

26. Following the same logic, a text from Qumran which has a non-Qumranic parallel should automatically be regarded as having non-Qumranic origins.

27. Most recently, John Kloppenborg has argued for this theory in his article, "The Transformation of Moral Exhortation in *Didache* 1–5," in *The* Didache *in Con-*

this assumption, it is problematic that Pseudo-Barnabas emphasizes the eternal reward and eternal punishment in his own version of the treatise (18.2; 19.1b; 20.1). On the other hand, it can be shown that the secondary *teknon* passage in Did. 3.1–6 points to a deepening of the interpretation of the law in the Two Ways tradition (see section 2.2 below). By and large, the Two Ways treatise in Did. 1–6 is by no means noneschatological, since it concerns the ways of life and death.

The arbitrary sequence of sayings in Barn. 19–20 makes it difficult to believe that we should seek the source or prototype of the treatise precisely here.[28] In the Didache (Doctrina apostolorum), however, the parallel material is organized very well, since it is structured according to the commandments of the Decalogue. It is hardly a coincidence that there is a nearly perfect parallelism between the commandments of Did. 2.2–7 and the evil deeds in Did. 5.1. If it is assumed that the author of Barnabas has preserved a common source better, it must also be accepted that an editor has compiled the beautiful Decalogue-oriented structure in chapters 2 and 5 from disparate, apocalyptic sayings. For these reasons, I think that it is likely that the tradition of Barnabas is a secondary, apocalyptically-oriented redaction of an original tradition that was modeled on the pattern of the Decalogue. Pseudo-Barnabas calls his hearers or readers to the right kind of orientation and inner motivation. This internalization, which has led to a reordering of the text, is based on the commandments of the Decalogue.

Because the two titles "way of life" (introduced with the golden rule in Did. 1.2) and "way of death" bind these two pieces together, I think it is correct to assume with Jean-Paul Audet that Did. 1.1–2a, 2.2–7, and 5.1 form the core of the tradition, regardless of the differences in details between the Didache and the Doctrina apostolorum.[29]

---

text: *Essays on Its Text, History and Transmission*, ed. Clayton N. Jefford, NovTSup 77 (Leiden: Brill, 1995), 100–102. A thorough and convincing argument against this thesis is offered by Kari Syreeni, "The Sermon on the Mount and the Two Ways Teaching of the Didache," in *Matthew and the Didache: Two Documents from the Same Jewish-Christian Milieu?* ed. Huub van de Sandt (Assen: Van Gorcum; Minneapolis: Fortress, 2005), 93–97.

28. With Niederwimmer, *Didache*, 61; Syreeni, "Sermon on the Mount and the Two Ways," 92; and others.

29. Audet, *Didachè*, 309–12.

2.2. Two Ways Treatise and the Matthean Sermon on the Mount

Because the way of life in the epistle of Barnabas knows nothing of the *teknon* passage in Did. 3.1–6, it is well-founded to assume that this piece is a later addition to the treatise. It does not stem from the author of the Didache, but from an earlier editor of the treatise.[30] In the Didache, the *teknon* sayings deepen the list of prohibitions of the original short treatise. It is not enough to forbid murder, fornication, idolatry, theft, and blasphemy, but also all emotional impulses and smaller acts that lead to these great sins. With his warm and sympathetic tone, the teacher gives these exhortations and internalizes and psychologizes the statutes of the Torah.[31] In a tradition-historical sense, the *teknon* sayings belong to a middle stage between the Decalogue and the Matthean antitheses: only Matthew goes so far as to identify hate with murder and lust with adultery.[32] The addition of the *teknon* sayings clearly belongs to a pre-Matthean stage of development that has led to a more stringent interpretation of the Decalogue. They are not introduced by the Didachist but belong to the history of the development of the Two Way tract.[33]

The so-called *anawim* sayings in Did. 3.7–10, which because of a striking Qumran parallel are regarded as particularly Jewish and therefore not originally Christian, offer in their original context (i.e., immediately after

---

30. With Niederwimmer, *Didache*, 123–24; Kloppenborg, "Transformation of Moral Exhortation in *Didache* 1–5," 105; Alan J. P. Garrow, *The Gospel of Matthew's Dependence on the Didache*, JSNTSup 254 (London: T&T Clark, 2004), 83–85; and others.

31. Many scholars, like Charles Taylor, *Teaching of the Twelve Apostles*, 23, have referred at this point in the rabbinic idea of a fence around the Torah. Audet, *Didachè*, 301–2, however, correctly argues that the rabbinic practice is far removed from the passage of the Didache, because the latter is designed to protect the specific commandments through detailed legalistic discussion. See also Syreeni, "Sermon on the Mount and the Two Ways," 95.

32. Looking backwards from the Gospel of Matthew it can be said that the *teknon* sayings belong to a process that finally leads to the Matthean interpretation of the Law; thus Kloppenborg, "Transformation of Moral Exhortation in *Didache* 1–5," 109. Syreeni, "Sermon on the Mount and the Two Ways," 96, however, argues that this process cannot be traced back to the history of the Didache, because in Did. 1.3–4 the idea of completeness is proclaimed without antitheses and scriptural references.

33. Niederwimmer, *Didache*, 124, Syreeni, "Sermon on the Mount and the Two Ways," 96, and Jefford, *Sayings in the Teaching of the Twelve Apostles*, 68, think that the *teknon* sayings of the Didachist are inserted.

the list of prohibitions; 2.2–7) a positive model for a believer. He or she should be gentle, patient and merciful, stay humble, and accept all her or his experiences as good. The similarity of this passage with some Matthean beatitudes (Matt 5:5, 7) is striking, while the Q sayings in Luke 6:20–23 are not comparable with the text of the Didache. The particular details of the social relations that the Two Ways treatise suggests is presented in the special tradition of Matthew as the motivation for the eschatological exaltation of its bearers.

Most scholars assume that Matthew has developed the first chapter of the Sermon on the Mount quite independently of the Two Ways treatise.[34] I find it more likely, however, that Matthew or the tradition used by him knew either the Two Ways treatise or a similar teaching and interpreted it as he did with corresponding sayings from Q. If this is correct, the tradition of the early Jewish Christians has been developed here in a threefold sense *ad majorem gloriam* of the Matthean community:

(1) especially in Matt 5:10–12, the first half of the so-called *anawim* proverbs (Did. 3.7–8a) and corresponding Q sayings are developed as a sympathetic representation of the community.[35]
(2) Together with Q sayings (Q 14.34–35; 8.16), the passive teaching of the *anawim* sayings (Did. 3.8b–10) is replaced with an active image of community members as the light and salt of the world (Matt 5:13–16).
(3) The prohibitions based on the Decalogue (Did. 2.2–7) and the *teknon* sayings (3.1–6) are replaced by the rough antitheses (Matt 5:21–48), which also treat the sixth and seventh commandment first.

Here the ethical teaching of Jesus transcends the barriers of the Torah. Only those who fulfil this form of the law completely are perfect.[36]

---

34. Thus e.g., Jefford, *Sayings in the Teaching of the Twelve Apostles*, 67, who sees a connection between the texts in their special interest in the Torah.

35. Christopher M. Tuckett, "Synoptic Tradition in the Didache," in *The* Didache *in Modern Research*, ed. Jonathan A. Draper, AGJU 37 (Leiden: Brill, 1996), 108, sees the origin of Did. 3.7 in Matt 5:5, while Garrow, *Gospel of Matthew's Dependence on the Didache*, 240, derives this saying and the preceding verses from Ps 36. According to Garrow, Matthew drew upon the Didache and not upon the Two Ways treatise.

36. The common features between Did. 3.2–6 and Matt 5:21–48 are described

This theory must remain completely unproven, because a strong parallelism can be shown only between Did. 3.7–8 and Matt 5:5, 7. Other parallels are rather related to the content, theme, and partly to the structure of the texts. The comparison shows, however, that the antitheses in Matt 5 represent a higher level of the traditional material of the Two Way treatise. It is possible that it motivated Matthew to the pointed statements in his own presentation.

Like the Matthean Sermon on the Mount, the Two Ways treatise of the Didache is community-oriented, but the latter reveals no traces of a conflict with other strands of Judaism. In this respect, Did. 3.7–4.10 is a very revealing passage. It is motivated by the exhortation in 2.7: the believer is called to love all people, but some in particular. In Didache 4, numerous features indicate the carefully regulated life of the members of a particular community: the authority of teachers (4.1), the communion of the saints (4.2, 14), the threat of schisms (4.3), the ideal of common property (4.8), and the regulation of the private sphere (4.9–11). All this is followed by a reference to evil people outside the community (5.2). The community portrayed here is neither threatened from outside nor affected by notable internal schisms.

In this context, the idea of common property is striking. It has a parallel both in the early Jesus movement (Acts 2:44–45; 4:32–37) and in Qumran (1QS I, 11–12; V, 2; VI, 2–3, 19–20; VII, 6; cf. Josephus, *B.J.* 2.122; *A.J.* 18.20). Since giving alms indicates private property, Did. 4.8 does not point to common property in a strict sense, but rather to an increased demand for economical equalization. The note, however, is so vague and general that it cannot tell us anything more about the community of the treatise or its social practices. It can be assumed that such a community has drawn a clear line between insiders and outsiders, as well as strived towards economic independence.[37]

To summarize, the original Two Ways tract behind the Didache fits into the picture well when it is compared with the development of the Jewish-Christian paraenesis in Q and Matthew. That there is no sign of conflict with the other forms Judaism indicates that the treatise dates back to a time before the Jewish War.

---

exhaustively by van de Sandt and Flusser, *Didache*, 225–28. They assume (229–30) that the Matthean antitheses and Did. 3.1 6 can be traced back to a common tradition.

37. For the state of research, see Marcello Del Verme, *Didache and Judaism: Jewish Roots of an Ancient Christian-Jewish Work* (London: T&T Clark, 2004), 113–42.

2.3. Didache 6 and Idol Meat

In the Didache, the Two Ways treatise is followed by a piece that culminates in the prohibition of idol meat. Comparison with the Doctrina apostolorum shows that only Did. 6.1, the exact wording of which cannot be reconstructed, belonged to an earlier form of the treatise. A secondary end of the treatise can be found in Doctr. 6.4–5: The reader is encouraged to follow these rules daily, so that he or she remains close to the living God. He or she should keep all of it in the soul and not lose hope. Thus he or she will obtain the athlete's laurel wreath by holy struggles. Ultimately, this pastoral advice means that the believer should live through hard times and remain faithful to the community, especially its teachers.[38] Instead of this ending, there is in Did. 6.2–3 a different secondary conclusion that supplements the ideas of the original treatise with teaching about the Mosaic law.

This passage, which clearly addresses gentile Christians, is motivated by the content of the treatise. But instead of the strong imperative tone of the treatise, the phrasing in 6.2–3 is instead concessive. The editor of the treatise knows that not all listeners can be perfect followers of the teaching: the imperfect should do what they can. This also applies to food. But there is one particularly important prohibition: idol meat shall be avoided, because it is a cult of "dead gods." Only the total meaning of these sayings can illuminate what "perfection" means in this context. The passage does not indicate a particularly strict asceticism, and it is also difficult to see in the addition a reference to the golden rule added in Did. 1.3–6 and to the other *mandata Christi*.[39] We do not know when the Sectio Evangelica was inserted as an explanation to the golden rule after Did. 1.2, but the absence of this piece in most parallels indicates that it is a very late addition.[40] There are further no differences between the sentences of the Sectio

---

38. Van de Sandt and Flusser, *Didache*, 38, note correctly that Doctr. 6.4–5 "just faintly echoes some allusion to the End while the Didache's rendering of the Two Ways' conclusion lacks any eschatological preoccupation."

39. Niederwimmer, *Didache*, 155–56.

40. For various theories about the sources of Sectio Evangelica, see Niederwimmer, *Didache*, 98–100: the dependency (1) of Matt 5:39–46 and Luke 6:27–32 and possibly of Herm. Mand. 2.4–6; (2) of the sayings source Q (Q 6:27–32); (3) of an apocryphal collection of sayings; and (4) of the oral tradition, the age of which is assessed in various ways. John S. Kloppenborg, "The Use of the Synoptics or Q in *Did.* 1:3b–2:1," in van de Sandt, *Matthew and the Didache*, 105–29, pleads with convincing arguments that Did. 1.3b–5 goes back to Luke and either Matthew or Q.

Evangelica and the commandments of the original treatise: both advise the reader to love instead of hate and promote alms-giving (2.7; 4.5–8). In the Sectio Evangelica, it is said that the one who turns the left cheek to an aggressor is perfect.[41] But that is not a programmatic sentence, since it does not indicate different levels of perfection.[42] Perfection means here that in front of an adversary (i.e., an outsider) one can do nothing except quietly endure injustice, but then one will be perfectly just before God.

For these reasons, I find it credible to suggest that the yoke of the Lord in 6.2 is not associated with the Sectio Evangelica,[43] but belongs rather with the commandments of the Lord in 4.13. In the treatise, the commandments of the Lord are portrayed in an overarching sense: nothing necessary (to salvation) is missing here. The sentence added by the first editor of the original Two Ways treatise in 6.2 wants to say something about the *entire* yoke of the Lord. The perfect one is anybody who follows not only the ethical,[44] but also the ritual, commandments of the Lord.[45] Just because this question is related to circumcision and purity and food laws, the editor recommends that gentile readers bear the entire yoke of the Lord: even though the whole law is still in force, the faithful from among the gentiles are exhorted to do what they can. Positively this means that they can (even as nonperfect members of mixed communities) observe such ritual com-

---

41. Niederwimmer, *Didache*, 107, thinks that the words καὶ ἔσῃ τέλειος are added by the Didachist.

42. Willy Rordorf, "Le problème de la transmission textuelle de *Didache* 1,3b–2,1," in *Überlieferungsgeschichtliche Untersuchungen*, ed. Franz Paschke (Berlin: Akademic, 1981), 512. He sees in Did. 1.3 the same logic as in Did. 6.2: the perfect can fulfill the doctrine of 1.3b–5, but less than perfect Christians can obey the prohibitions listed in 2.2.

43. Thus Rordorf, "Problème de la transmission," 511–12; Niederwimmer, *Didache*, 155–56; and others.

44. Willy Rordorf and André Tuilier. *La doctrine des douze Apôtres (Didachè)*, SC 248 bis (Paris: Cerf, 1998), 32–33, see in Did. 6.2 a note on the *Sectio Evangelica* in 1.3–5, while Aaron Milavec, *The Didache: Faith, Hope, and Life of the Earliest Christian Communities, 50–70 CE* (New York: Newman, 2003), 776, suggests that the verse refers to the whole Two Ways tract.

45. Jonathan A. Draper, "Torah and Troublesome Apostles in the Didache Community," *NovT* 33 (1991): 347–72 (367–68), also connects the idea of perfection of the whole law, including the cultic rules. He further suggests (with Alfred Stuiber, "Das ganze Joch des Herrn [Didache 6,2-3]," *StPatr* 4 [1961]: 323–29 [328]) that, according to Did. 6.2, in the course of this process the gentiles have to accept the whole law and thus also become perfect.

mandments, the fulfilment of which is possible for them. Negatively, they may refrain from doing anything that is impossible for them. Unlike the case of the ethical commandments, here it is not necessary to go into details. The gentiles addressed by the editor know very well what is at stake. The perfect ones have a special spiritual dignity and authority, which reinforces the integrity of the mixed communities. The editor of the treatise takes for granted that the readers and listeners naturally recognize this.[46] This also applies to other practical demands, which the Jewish Christians had posed to converted gentiles. In mixed communities in which the decree of Acts 15 was taught, the Jewish Christian teachers had the authority to interpret these prohibitions for gentile Christians.

It is further interesting that in the Doctrina apostolorum any parallel to the exhortation οὐ μὴ ἐγκαταλίπῃς ἐντολὰς κυρίου in Did. 4.13a is missing. According to the parallels in Did. 4.12, Doctr. 4.12, and Barn. 19.2, the believer should do nothing that does not please *God*, while in the Didache it is the *Lord* who should be pleased. One can therefore assume that the original treatise here did not refer to Jesus as the Lord. Already the original treatise, however, spoke of Jesus as the Lord in Did. 4.1 (par. Doctr. 4.1), where the authority of the teacher is founded on the authority of the Lord.[47] This sentence is missing in Barn. 19.9b–10, because the author has moved the reader's attention toward responsibility in the day of the eschatological judgment.

If this interpretation is correct, the question of food in 6.3 must not be viewed as something completely different from the previous contents. Among all cultic rules of the law, only the prohibition of idol food is considered to be absolutely necessary for gentiles. The editor of the Didache does not go as far as those who expressly say that gods are demons. For the editor they are, at least in this context, in the traditional sense "dead gods" (Ps 115:3–8; Isa 44:12–20; Wis 15:17). Eating idol food is obviously a practice that some gentile members of the communities have not given up. The editor of the treatise does not quote the Apostolic Decree. If the decree were known, there was no obligation in the least to point to the authority of the Apostolic decision, although the decree has its background in the prohibitions of the Mosaic law regarding aliens (Lev 17–18). I do not find

---

46. Audet, *Didachè*, 355–56, interprets the consequences of the exhortation quite differently: everyone who follows the entire law can hardly resist the temptation to judge such brothers who enjoy all food.

47. See Niederwimmer, *Didache*, 136.

it likely that the isolated exhortation in Did. 6.3 would have been based on the so-called Apostolic Decree.[48] It is difficult to date the insertion of 6.2–3 and to put it into a social context. In any case, the concessive tone of the addition indicates that the converted gentiles were able to continue living their previous status. But only those "who are able to carry the full yoke of Lord Jesus are 'perfect,'" that is, those who obey not only the moral but also the cultic law. I find it reasonable to conclude that Did. 6.2–3 refers to the yoke of the Lord Jesus and to the perfect practice of the law by strict Jewish Christians, who propagated the fulfilment of the whole law as an expression of their faith in Jesus.

2.4. The Apocalypse in Didache 16 and the Two Way Tract

The apocalypse of the final chapter, however, is something entirely different. It points at a hard tribulation that will take place at the end of time. I think that it is not very easy to imagine this passage as an editorial addition of the Didachist to the foregoing church order. Some scholars have seen in it (correctly, I think) the final chapter of the Two Way treatise.[49] Brevity of the apocalypse and lack of parallels, however, have raised doubt against this theory.[50] Barnabas offers no parallel to the apocalypse in Did. 16, but this does not speak against the original connection between the apocalypse and the Two Ways treatise. Even though pseudo-Barnabas stresses

---

48. For the various theories on the origin and meaning of Did. 6.2–3, see Draper, "Continuing Enigma," 112–14: (1) these verses are part of an original Jewish Two Ways tract that is directed to pagan converts (thesis by Stuiber, "Ganze Joch des Herrn," 323–29, assumed by Klaus Wengst, *Didache (Apostellehre), Barnabasbrief, Zweiter Klemensbrief, Schrift an Diognet*, SU 2 [Darmstadt: Wissenschaftliche Buchgesellschaft, 1984], 94–96); (2) they were an independent Jewish Christian tradition; (3) they come from the Didachist alone (thus especially Rordorf and Tuilier, *Doctrine des douze Apôtres*, 32–34); and (4) they teach abstaining from sex and food. Draper himself is inclined to accept the first theory.

49. See, e.g., Helmut Koester, *Synoptische Überlieferung bei den apostolischen Vätern*, TUGAl 65/5.10 (Berlin: Akademie, 1957), 160; Syreeni, "Sermon on the Mount and the Two Ways," 88 ("possibly … the starting point of the literary evolution"); Del Verme, Didache *and Judaism*, 245; etc. Against this hypothesis, see Rordorf and Tuilier, *Doctrine des douze Apôtres*, 81–83.

50. Niederwimmer, *Didache*, 248, suggests that the Didachist found the apocalypse among his sources as a separate epilogue to the whole and added it for compositional reasons to the end of the entire writing.

that he and the recipients of his writing live at the end of time (Barn. 2.1), the specific features of Did. 16 (the false prophets, which cause the believers to hate and betray each other, as well as the appearance of a seducer of the world) do not fit in his own situation. In spite of this, he does not hesitate to quote Did. 16.2 in Barn. 4.9b.

Shortly after the introduction of his presentation, pseudo-Barnabas mentions "the new law of our Lord Jesus Christ, which is not a forced yoke" with which the offerings are done away. Later, in Barn. 10.10,[51] he ends his long allegorical interpretation of the Mosaic food laws with the following sentence: "Also in terms of the food, you are perfect." With these thoughts he reacts in my opinion against the idea of the Two Ways treatise (Did. 6.2), according to which those are perfect can bear the entire yoke of the Lord. The generalizing sentence in Barn. 10.10 (ἔχετε τελείως καὶ περὶ τῆς βρώσεως) is designed to replace the rule in Did. 6.3 (περὶ δὲ τῆς βρώσεως). Therefore, I think that it is well-founded to assume that pseudo-Barnabas knew the Two Ways tract in an extended form (Did. 1–6, 16).[52]

A literary seam between Did. 5.2 and 6.1 is helpful here. The closing warning about the way of death in Did. 5.2 is in the plural (ῥυσθείητε τέκνα ἀπὸ τούτων ἁπάντων), and it seems clear that it has replaced an original singular formulation (Doctr. 5.2: *abstine te, fili, ab his omnibus*). It is possible that an editor of the treatise wanted to close the list of warnings with the generalizing plural statement. In the light of the address in the singular in 6.1, this is somewhat strange. Therefore, it is possible that the salutation in the plural once had a natural connection to the beginning of the apocalypse. Also, the shortness of the apocalypse is best explained with its original connection to the Two Ways treatise. Both the exemplary life of individual believers and their absolute loyalty to their community form a basis on which the exhortations in Did. 16.1–2 are based.

The comparison of the individual verses of the apocalypse to the synoptic apocalypses shows that the traditions of Did. 16 were alive at the time of the Jewish War. This chapter has its closest parallels with Matthean special material (Matt 24):

---

51. See the reference to the "perfect knowledge" in Barn. 1.5.

52. As for the connection of Did. 5.2 and 16.1, see also Del Verme, *Didache and Judaism*, 244, who rightly emphasizes the moral motivation of the apocalypse.

Did. 16.3   Matt 24:11–12 (cf. 7:15)
Did. 16.4a   Matt 24:10, 12
Did. 16.4b   Matt 24:24 = Mark 13:22
Did. 16.4c1   Matt 24:21 = Mark 13:19
Did. 16.5   Matt 24:10
                    Matt 24:13 = Mark 13:13
Did. 16.6   Matt 24:30a, 31
Did. 16.7   Matt 24:31 (cf. Zech 14:5)
Did. 16.8   Matt 24:30b = Mark 13:26 (cf. Dan 7:13)

These parallels have been explained with two[53] different theories: either the Didache is dependent on Matt 24 and possibly also Mark 13[54] or the parallels between Did. 16 and Matt 24 can be traced back to a common apocalyptic tradition.[55] The former theory presupposes that the editor of Did. 16 posed the Matthean source some specific questions and got the answers from an intensive reading of the text. Further, it must be assumed that this editor has seen himself as a transmitter of an authorized tradition.[56] Thus, according to this theory, Did. 16 is a condensed apocalypse, which has to be seen rather as traditional instruction and exhortation, than a text oriented towards vivid expectation of the end.[57] Here lies also

---

53. Garrow, *Gospel of Matthew's Dependence on the* Didache, 190–215, has proposed a new third theory. He thinks that Matthew is in chapter 24 dependent on Did. 16. According to Garrow, Matthew has combined some elements of Mark 13:1–13 and Did. 16.3–5 in Matt 24:1–12. In Matt 24:30–31, in turn, the author has melted Mark 13:24–27 and Did. 16.6, 8 together. The sources of Matt 25:31 can be found in Mark 8:38 and Did. 16.8.

54. Thus, especially Tuckett, "Synoptic Tradition in the Didache," 197–230; and Joseph Verheyden, "Eschatology in the Didache and the Gospel of Matthew," van de Sandt, *Matthew and the Didache*, 193–215.

55. Thus John S. Kloppenborg, "*Didache* 16:6–8 and Special Matthaean Tradition," *ZNW* 70 (1979): 54–67; Jonathan A. Draper, "The Jesus Tradition in the Didache," in *The Jesus Tradition Outside the Gospels*, vol. 5 of *Gospel Perspectives*, ed. David Wenham (Sheffield: JSOT, 1985), 269–89; Del Verme, Didache and Judaism, 254; and others.

56. Verheyden, "Eschatology in the Didache and the Gospel of Matthew," 201–14.

57. Victoria Balabanski, *Eschatology in the Making: Mark, Matthew and the Didache*, SNTSMS 97 (Cambridge: Cambridge University Press, 1997), 205. Verheyden, "Eschatology in the Didache and the Gospel of Matthew," 212, thinks somewhat

the weakness of this theory, because it is very difficult to see how the apocalypse as a post-Matthean instructively and morally oriented desk work could have been a credible exhortation among those who expected the end to come very soon.

Didache 16 is apocalypse oriented toward paraenesis,[58] which points to a determined scenario of the end of times.[59] The shortness of the text[60] and its urgent message, however, raise the question of its specific purpose.[61] The author of the text lives in a situation in which ignorance of the eschatological hour forces vigorous vigilance (vv. 1–2). It is noteworthy, however, that the sheep turn into wolves and love turns into hate (v. 3), which means nothing else than that the former believers become enemies.[62] This description of the crisis in the community of believers is a common apocalyptical theme, but in my opinion it cannot be explained merely in terms of animal symbolism.[63]

---

differently: "One still needs a good deal of eschatological hope kept alive to make this presentation work."

58. Del Verme, Didache *and Judaism*, 226–30, correctly stresses that the literary genre of the apocalypse can contain different theological elements.

59. Especially the sequence of verbs in the future tense and use of the word τότε create this impression; see also Del Verme, Didache *and Judaism*, 231–32.

60. It is controversial whether the conclusion of Did. 16 could be reconstructed partly on the basis of Apos. Con. 7.32, which includes a short description of the final judgment: the Lord will judge the world seducer (the devil) and all people; the wicked will go to eternal punishment, and the righteous to eternal life. According to Niederwimmer, *Didache*, 269, this text is "a very free rendering of Did 16." Milavec, *Didache: Faith, Hope, and Life*, 833–34, thinks that the final sentences of Apos. Con. 7.32 are not the lost ending of Did. 16, because these sentences are in line with dispensing with Did. 16.5. Unlike Apos. Con. 7.32.1–5, Did. 16 does not say that the Lord repays "each according to his deed." Furthermore, in Did. 16 only the destruction of the world seducer is proclaimed, which does not include the separate punishment of hell for the unjust.

61. Usually the text of Did. 16 is evaluated more on the basis of its form than its content. So, del Verme, *Didache and Judaism*, 236–51, emphasizes its ideological connection to the dualistically colored Enoch traditions and Qumran texts.

62. Koester, *Synoptische Überlieferung*, 179.

63. Thus Del Verme, Didache *and Judaism*, 232, who emphasizes the question of genre. In his summary he describes the purpose of the author as follows: "His aim was to provide a sort of 'synthesis' of specific traditions and doctrines, previously active but which were now being re-interpreted in the light of the new community context of which he is a member" (262).

An alternative interpretation of the apocalypse takes as its starting point the most likely idea that the author addresses believers who know quite well the false prophets, serious divisions in their communities, as well as the growing hostility of the outsiders by their social position and their own lives. In such times, it is necessary for their salvation that they come together often and focus on the essential things in their lives (v. 2). In the final days this is precisely the way to "perfection." In the middle stands the oppressed and persecuted community whose members may betray their own brothers and sisters. The crucial question for the interpretation is whether this situation of persecution and betrayal is a present reality for the first readers of the text. If this is acknowledged, there is no other credible Syro-Palestinian context in which these instructions might be conceivable except the situation of the Jewish War (see Mark 13:12; Matt 24:10, 12). In contrast to the Markan apocalypse, the synagogue and the leading Jews are not stamped as enemies of the community (Mark 13:9; par. Luke 21:12; see also Matt 10:17). Its only enemy is Roman power, the emperor of which is described as the seducer of the world. It is hard to imagine another specific person or merely mythological figure that the author might wish to indicate for his readers. It is meaningful to claim that the Roman emperor believes himself to be the son of God and that he wants to have the world in his power. His signs, wonders, and sacrilegious acts culminate in the destruction of Jerusalem and its temple.[64] Compared to the synoptic apocalypses, it is noteworthy that the eschatological turn following the persecution is not directly related to the destruction of the temple and its consequences (Matt 24:15–20). In spite of this, it is possible that the outrageous evil deeds (ἀθεμίτα) of the world seducer point to the acts of war, which lead to the destruction of the temple.[65]

For these reasons I think it is justified to assume that the apocalypse of the Didache used, independently of Mark and Matthew, the apocalyptic tradition known from the Synoptic Gospels. Further, it can be assumed that Did. 16 was added to the Two Ways treatise in the context of the

---

64. Suetonius, *Vesp.* 5 reports how Emperor Vespasian during his stay in Judea got a very favorable answer to all his plans from Carmelus, an oracle of God.

65. Some scholars see in the evil deeds, which have not happened since eternity (see Dan 12:1), the persecution of Christians; thus Niederwimmer, *Didache*, 262–63; Verheyden, "Eschatology in the Didache and the Gospel of Matthew," 205. This interpretation is based on v. 5 in which the "fire of testing" would point at the situation of the Christians. Verses 4–5, however, are separated from each other with the word τότε.

Jewish War. The *vaticinium ex eventu* covers Did. 16.3–4, while verses 5–6 point toward future events.

2.5. Didache 6 between the Two Ways Treatise and the Apocalypse (Didache 16)

Following the argument presented above, the author of the epistle of Barnabas knew the extended version of the Two Ways treatise (Did. 1–6, 16) and used it as a source. Because of the address in the plural in 5.2 and the thematic transition from the teaching of the Two Ways to the apocalypse, I suppose that Did. 6 was added in two stages to Did. 1–5, 16. First, an editor added 6.1 to make a connection between the treatise and the apocalypse. The words μή τις σε πλανήσῃ stem from the language of the apocalypse (see Matt 24:4), but are introduced following the style of the Two Ways treatise as a general warning: the believers should walk on the way of life and listen to no one who try to teach them "without God," that is, without the law. Therefore, it is easiest to assume that with this expression the editor condemns those who reject the law; it is not hard to imagine that he has in mind those who follow the teachings of Paul (cf. Rom 3:21).

In the Didache (unlike in the Doctrina apostolorum[66]), verses 2–3 follow the first verse. It is wrong to teach without the law, and only such a believer who is completely faithful to the law can be called "perfect" (see 1 Cor 2:6). The yoke of the law and the yoke of the Lord are identical.

If the dating of the apocalypse immediately after the Jewish War is correct, Did. 6 should be seen as a relatively late addition to the treatise. Here there is nothing left of the fervent eschatological expectation of Did. 16. The idea of perfection, which in Did. 16 is related to the close expectation of the end and attachment to the community, is here seen in the context of perfect fulfilment of the law. The lack of anti-Jewish polemics in the Two Ways treatise as well as in the apocalypse indicates that the two pieces were

---

66. The individual eschatology in Doctr. 6.1, 4–5 cannot prove the theory presented here, but it makes the rejection of the apocalypse at least understandable. Verse 1 is formulated in more general terms than its parallel in Did. 6.1, because there have been a lot of teachers who teach *extra disciplinam*. Verses 4–5 emphasize the daily exercise of the way of life as a guarantee for salvation. The struggle of the believer is portrayed as a mental process, and the community dimension of the treatise has been completely set aside. I think it is quite possible that these two verses have replaced the apocalypse; v. 6 is a later addition.

produced among Jewish Christians loyal to the Torah. Didache 6.2-3, in turn, indicates a later situation in which a Jewish Christian teacher draws the attention of believers among the gentiles to the *whole* yoke of the Lord. The concessive tone of these verses indicates that he knows well that it has become very difficult to encourage gentile Christians to perfect obedience to the Mosaic law.

Some scholars have seen an original connection between 6.2-3 and the instruction for baptism in 7.1-4.[67] Both passages are formulated as concessive. Nothing seems to indicate that the executor of the baptism should necessarily be a leader. It is nevertheless important to see that the address in 7.1 is formulated in the plural. Willy Rordorf suggests that the address in 6.3 must have been in the plural, because eating of idol meat in Apos. Con. 7.21 is forbidden in the plural (ἀπὸ δὲ τῶν εἰδωλοθύτων φεύγετε).[68] This assumption is problematic, because the baptismal instruction in Did. 7.2-4 is thoroughly formulated in the singular, which is probably the original formulation. The editor who has inserted the piece on baptism into the extended treatise (Did. 1-6, 16) considered it necessary to formulate the first sentence in the plural, despite the preceding singular address in the treatise. Therefore, I think that it is justified to assume that in the baptismal instruction the community was originally addressed as a collective and the focus on the individual performer of the rite was developed later. Precisely here is the difference between the exhortations in Did. 1-6 and 7.1: in the Two Ways treatise an individual believer is instructed about the way of life, while in 7.1 the discourse is about a collective cultic act. It depends on the community who is allowed to perform baptisms.

Behind Did. 7.1-4, there is an earlier Jewish Christian version of baptismal instruction. Both the reference to the Father, Son, and the Holy Spirit, as well as the plural form of address in 7.1, are secondary. Through the addition of the baptismal instructions, the treatise became a kind of catechism, and the discourse as a whole was on the way to becoming a church order. The apocalypse had already become an integral part of the text before this stage. Later it was considered to reflect an eschatological outlook, details of which no longer corresponded to the social reality of the readers.

---

67. Willy Rordorf, "Le baptême selon la *Didachè*," in *Mélanges liturgiques*, ed. Bernard Botte (Leuven: Abbaye du Mont César, 1972), 500-503; Draper, "Continuing Enigma," 115-17.

68. Rordorf, "Le baptême selon la *Didachè*," 500.

3. Summary

In my presentation I have tried to argue for the following theses and conclusions:

(1) The Apostolic Decree in Acts 15:20, 29 does not go back to a formal decision of an apostolic meeting, but to a tradition known by Luke.
(2) The Two Ways treatise in Did. 1–5 originated in Jewish Christian circles.
(3) The short Jewish Christian apocalypse in Did. 16 is a piece added to the Two Ways treatise immediately after the sentence in the plural in 5.2. It stems from the situation of the Jewish War.
(4) The following addition Did. 6.1 (and Doctr. 6.1) is influenced by the seductive topic of the apocalypse, but its original form in the Didache indicates that it targeted people who taught about faith without the law, that is, to Paulinists.
(5) In the next stage of the literary development of the Didache, the Jewish War already lay in the past and the treatise is more and more extended to gentile Christians. Next, the prohibition of idol meat is added in 6.2–3 after 6.1. The bearing of the whole yoke of the Lord, both the ethical and ritual law, is presented to the gentiles as perfection. But at the same time, these verses are concessive: not all believers can or must be perfect. Only eating idol meat is expressly prohibited.
(6) Bearing the entire yoke of the Lord as a sign of perfection in Did. 6.2 points to those who fulfill not only the Decalogue, but also the ritual law. These people have special dignity in mixed communities. Corresponding to the concessive tone of the prohibition in Did. 6.2 reflects a situation in which the "perfect" Christian teachers have full authority to interpret the prohibition in these communities. The same also applies to the four statutes that Luke lists in Acts 15:29 as the so-called Apostolic Decree.

Another Gospel: Exploring Early Christian Diversity with Paul and the Didache

Taras Khomych

The issue of diversity in early Christianity has recently attracted a lively scholarly interest. In this field of research, the Didache has received relatively limited attention. This essay seeks to contribute to the discussion by juxtaposing the notion of εὐαγγέλιον as found in the Didache to that of the Pauline Epistles. It is generally recognized that the Pauline gospel was focused unambiguously on the Lord Jesus Christ, particularly emphasizing his death and resurrection. As opposed to Paul, the Didache is notably not centered on Christology. This document presents Jesus as God's servant, who revealed the will of the Lord God. Accordingly, the term εὐαγγέλιον, which reappears four times in this short text, can hardly be associated with the death and resurrection of Jesus Christ. As a matter of fact, these topics, which are crucial for Paul, are not even mentioned in the Didache. The notion of εὐαγγέλιον, however, is found there predominantly in the paraenetical context. The evidence of the Didache, remarkably different from that of the Pauline Epistles, which is echoed in the rest of the New Testament, yields invaluable information about the origins of Christianity. This article highlights the importance of the Didache, insisting that its investigation would advance on-going research on the diversity in early Christianity.

1. Research into Primitive Christian Diversity

The research into diversity in early Christianity tends to become an increasingly divided area of investigations today. Whereas Walter Bauer, whose groundbreaking study marked an important leap in the critical reflection on this subject matter,[1] included a broad scope of early Christian literature,[2] most of contemporary scholarship tends to focus instead on a more limited number of sources. As a result, some early Christian documents receive a lot of scholarly attention, while others are often dealt with only occasionally. New Testament theology, for instance, which attracts an impressive scholarly interest nowadays, focuses only on canonical books. In this field of research the question of diversity is related mainly to the differences between, and individuality of, particular New Testament writings.[3] This diversity is then usually interpreted through the prism of an overarching unity of the New Testament.[4] On the other hand, a growing body of studies of early Christian gnostic literature points to a radical diversity of theological viewpoints even within so-called "Gnosticism,"[5] to

---

1. Walter Bauer, *Rechtgläubigkeit und Ketzerei im ältesten Christentum*, 2nd ed., BHT 10 (Tübingen: Mohr Siebeck, 1964). For an overview of early reactions to Bauer's thesis, see the following English version of a supplementary essay to the second German edition of the *Rechtgläubigkeit und Ketzerei*: Georg Strecker, "The Reception of the Book," in *Orthodoxy and Heresy in Earliest Christianity*, ed. Robert A. Kraft and Gerhard Krodel (Philadelphia: Fortress, 1971), 286–316. For evaluations of later discussions, see Daniel J. Harrington, "The Reception of Walter Bauer's Orthodoxy and Heresy in Earliest Christianity during the Last Decade," *HTR* 73 (1980): 289–98; Lewis Ayres, "The Question of Orthodoxy," *JECS* 14 (2006): 395–98. One of the recent discussions of Bauer's thesis can be found in Bart D. Ehrman, *Lost Christianities: The Battles for Scripture and the Faiths We Never Knew* (New York: Oxford University Press, 2003), 172–80.

2. Although in *Rechtgläubigkeit und Ketzerei*, Bauer focuses mostly on the second and the third century evidence, he deals there also with the New Testament sources, albeit to a lesser extent. His engagement with biblical scholarship, however, is well known thanks to his monumental work *Griechisch-Deutsches Wörterbuch zu den Schriften des Neuen Testaments und der übrigen urchristlichen Literatur* (BDAG).

3. For helpful overviews of recent (and not only recent) research on the matter, see Frank Matera, "New Testament Theology: History, Method, and Identity," *CBQ* 67 (2005): 1–21; C. Kavin Rowe, "New Testament Theology: The Revival of a Discipline. A Review of Recent Contributions to the Field," *JBL* 125 (2006): 393–410; Jens Schröter, *Von Jesus zum Neuen Testament: Studien zur urchristlichen Theologiegeschichte und zur Entstehung des neutestamentlichen Kanons*, WUNT 204 (Tübingen: Mohr Siebeck, 2007), 355–77. See also Don A. Carson, "Locating Udo Schnelle's *Theology of the New Testament* in the Contemporary Discussion," *JETS* 53 (2010): 133–41.

4. There is currently no consensus, however, as to what exactly constitutes the unity of New Testament theology.

5. See, e.g., Elaine Pagels, The Gnostic Gospels (New York: Random House, 1979); Karen L. King, *What is Gnosticism?* (Cambridge: Harvard University Press, 2003);

use a conventional, although not unproblematic, umbrella term.[6] In this case, however, scholars deal with documents from the second century on, which have rather limited value for the reconstruction of the first century developments in the Jesus movement.[7] More general historical-theological investigations of Christian origins usually do not follow strictly the *sola scriptura* approach, characteristic for New Testament theology, and yet they tend to pay only scant attention to the extrabiblical sources, especially such as the writings of the apostolic fathers composed in the first and second centuries.[8] Accordingly, the New Testament books (particularly the Pauline Epistles and Acts) serve as the only source for the reconstruction of the most primitive stages of developing Christianity,[9] notwithstanding that many scholars would recognize that reconstruction as rather simplified.[10] In the present article, I would like to address this issue by pointing

---

Christoph Markschies, *Gnosis: An Introduction* (London: T&T Clark, 2003); David Brakke, *The Gnostics: Myth, Ritual, and Diversity in Early Christianity* (Cambridge: Harvard University Press, 2010).

6. On the problems related to the use of the term and the category of "Gnosticism," see Michael A. Williams, *Rethinking "Gnosticism": An Argument for Dismantling a Dubious Category* (Princeton: Princeton University Press, 1996); King, *What is Gnosticism*, 5–19, 218–38.

7. Some scholars tend to interpret the Gospel of Thomas as a first-century document; see e.g. Elaine Pagels, *Beyond Belief: The Secret Gospel of Thomas* (New York: Vintage, 2003. There is, however, no consensus regarding this issue. A number of researchers prefer to date this text to the mid-second century, arguing in particular for its dependence on the Synoptics; so recently Mark Goodacre, *Thomas and the Gospels: The Case for Thomas's Familiarity with the Gospels* (Grand Rapids: Eerdmans, 2012).

8. See, e.g., N. T. Wright, *Christian Origins and the Question of God*, 3 vols. (Minneapolis: Fortress, 1992–2003; James D. G. Dunn, *Christianity in the Making*, 2 vols. (Grand Rapids: Eerdmans, 2003–2008); Ron Cameron and Merrill P. Miller, eds., *Redescribing Christian Origins*, SBLSymS 28 (Atlanta: Society of Biblical Literature, 2004)

9. The value of Pauline evidence for the reconstruction of the theological milieu of first generation Christians has recently been emphasized in Larry H. Hurtado, *Lord Jesus Christ: Devotion to Jesus in Earliest Christianity* (Grand Rapids: Eerdmans, 2003), 79–216, and even more strongly in Jeffrey Peterson, "The Extent of Christian Theological Diversity: Pauline Evidence," *ResQ* 47 (2005): 1–12. While Peterson's insistence on the importance of the *corpus Paulinum* for our understanding of Christian origins should not be undermined, his view that Paul provides reliable evidence for a theological uniformity in the first three decades of the Christian movement needs to be challenged.

10. Burton L. Mack, "On Redescribing Christian Origins," *MTSR* (1996): 247–67.

to a valuable first century piece of evidence, namely the Didache, one of the writings regarded as a part of the *corpus patrum apostolicorum*, which receives very limited attention in the present quest for Christian origins.[11] This contribution seeks to fill in this gap by comparing the message of the Didache with that of the Pauline Epistles. In order to make our investigation more specific we choose the notion of εὐαγγέλιον, which expresses the core of Paul's teaching and is important also in the Didache. Our examination of this term will be accompanied by further observations about and comparison of more general theological message(s) of the two writings.

2. Pauline Epistles and the Didache: Introductory Issues

Before comparing the letters of Paul with the Didache, it is important to establish how these two pieces of literature relate to each other. The question of the possible literary relationship between the Didache and the New Testament in general is highly complex.[12] Whereas early scholarship on the Didache tended to argue for its literary dependence on virtually all the New Testament writings,[13] most contemporary scholars have become

---

11. It is worth noting, however, that the Didache has received increasing attention in the field of liturgical studies; see Paul F. Bradshaw, *Eucharistic Origins* (Oxford: SPCK, 2004); Gerard Rouwhorst, "Didache 9–10: A Litmus Test for the Research on Early Christian Liturgy Eucharist," in *Matthew and the Didache: Two Documents from the Same Jewish Christian Milieu?* ed. Huub van de Sandt (Assen: Van Gorcum; Minneapolis: Fortress, 2005), 143–56; Jonathan Schwiebert, *Knowledge and the Coming Kingdom: The Didache's Meal Ritual and Its Place in Early Christianity*, LNTS 373 (London: T&T Clark, 2008); etc.

12. For a useful survey of research on this question see Kurt Niederwimmer, *The Didache: A Commentary*, trans. Linda M. Maloney, Hermeneia (Minneapolis: Fortress, 1998), 42–52.

13. Thus, J. Armitage Robinson characterized the Didache as a "perverse imitation, almost a parody" of certain New Testament texts ("The Problem of the Didache," *JTS* 13 (1912): 339–56 [347]; *Barnabas, Hermas and the Didache* [London: SPCK, 1920]). This view gained much support from a number of scholars, including R. H. Connolly, "The Use of the Didache in the Didascalia," *JTS* 24 (1923): 147–57; "The Didache in Relation to the Epistle of Barnabas," *JTS* 33 (1932): 237–53; "The Didache and Montanism," *DRev* 55 (1937): 339–47; James Muilenburg, *The Literary Relations of the Epistle of Barnabas and the Teaching of the Twelve Apostles* (Ph.D. Diss., University of Marburg, 1929); F. C. Burkitt, "Barnabas and the Didache," *JTS* 32 (1931): 25–27; and W. Telfer, "The 'Didache' and the Apostolic Synod in Antioch," *JTS* 40 (1939): 133–46, 258–271; "The 'Plot' of the Didache," *JTS* 45 (1944): 141–51.

increasingly skeptical about this issue.[14] With respect to the Pauline Epistles, there is an overwhelming consensus that the Didache and the Pauline writings do not exhibit any literary relationship.[15] To point to further distinctions between the two sources, the Didache and Epistles belong to two different literary genres. The *corpus Paulinum* is an example of epistolary genre, whereas the Didache is usually classified as a church order,[16] although an increasing number of scholars today find this definition misleading[17] and tend to identify the text as a "community rule," analogous

---

14. This difference can clearly be demonstrated by comparing two publications by the same author, F. E. Vokes, on the Didache. In *The Riddle of the Didache: Fact or Fiction, Heresy or Catholicism?* (London: SPCK, 1938), Vokes followed closely the thesis of Armitage Robinson about the Didache's dependence on the letter of Barnabas and on various New Testament writings. Later on, however, he presented this issue in a much more nuanced way; see "Life and Order in an Early Church: The Didache," *ANRW* 2.27.1, 209–33. With respect to the writings of the apostolic fathers more generally, a comparison of the influential reference work of the Oxford Society of Historical Theology, *The New Testament in the Apostolic Fathers* (Oxford: Clarendon, 1905) with the relevant contributions in Andrew F. Gregory and Christopher M. Tuckett, eds., *The New Testament and the Apostolic Fathers: The Reception of the New Testament in the Apostolic Fathers*, 2 vols. (Oxford: Oxford University Press, 2005), published to celebrate the centenary of the earlier volume is illuminating. As a matter of fact, the change of the general approach to this field of study is readily visible from the very titles of these publications, as the preposition "in" of the 1905 publication is substituted by the coordinating conjunction "and" in 2005.

15. Christopher M. Tuckett, "The *Didache* and the Writings that Later Formed the New Testament," in *Reception of the New Testament in the Apostolic Fathers*, vol. 1 in Gregory and Tuckett, *New Testament and the Apostolic Fathers*, 91–93. See also Andreas Lindemann, *Paulus im ältesten Christentum: Das Bild des Apostels und die Rezeption der paulinischen Theologie in der frühchristlichen Literatur bis Marcion*, BHT 58 (Tübingen: Mohr Siebeck, 1979); "Paul in the Writings of the Apostolic Fathers," in *Paul and the Legacies of Paul*, ed. William S. Babcock (Dallas: Southern Methodist University Press, 1990), 25–45.

16. See, e.g., Niederwimmer, *Didache*.

17. So recently, Joseph G. Mueller, "The Ancient Church Order Literature: Genre or Tradition?" *JECS* 15 (2007): 337–80. Mueller argues that the expression "church order literature" is misleading and inappropriate not only for the Didache, but also for all other early Christian documents composed during the period of the first six centuries CE, which are usually called so from the seventeenth century on. The author observes that this expression refers primarily to the collections of laws governing church life that were composed during the period of the Reformation. Despite apparent similarities between the Reformation *Kirchenordnungen* and the ancient Chris-

to that of the Qumran Scrolls.[18] Whatever the correct definition of the literary form of the Didache, the basic difference of genre for these two consists in the fact that the Epistles tend to focus on a particular situation, while the Didache provides more general regulations,[19] unrelated (at least ostensibly) to any specific circumstances. These differences should not prevent us, however, from comparing these writings. One of the most important reasons for such comparisons is the *antiquity* of the documents. The undisputed Pauline Epistles are usually recognized to have been written between 50 and 65 CE. Although there is no consensus regarding the time of the final composition of the Didache,[20] many scholars place it at the end of the first century. Taking into consideration the Didache's explicitly Jewish character and a very primitive form of institutions and ministries reflected in the document,[21] more recent studies tend to favor an even earlier date of its composition.[22] However that may be, most researchers

---

tian texts, the association is rather misleading. The latter should better be understood against the background of ancient Jewish exegetical tradition.

18. Jonathan A. Draper, "The *Didache* in Modern Research: An Overview," in *The Didache in Modern Research*, ed. Jonathan A. Draper, AGJU 37 (Leiden: Brill, 1996), 1–42; Aaron Milavec, *The Didache: Faith, Hope, and Life of the Earliest Christian Communities, 50–70 CE* (New York: Newman, 2003), xvi–xvii.

19. The text of the Didache can roughly be divided into four unequal parts: (1) the Two Ways teaching (chapters 1–6), (2) liturgical instructions (chapters 7–10), (3) regulations concerning community life (chapters 11–15), and (4) eschatological warnings (chapter 16).

20. For the *status quaestionis* on the Didache, see Clayton N. Jefford, *The Sayings of Jesus in the Teaching of the Twelve Apostles*, VCSup 11 (Leiden: Brill, 1989), 1–21; Vokes, "Life and Order in an Early Church," 209–33; Draper, "*Didache* in Modern Research," 1–42. For an annotated bibliography, see Marcello Del Verme, Didache *and Judaism: Jewish Roots of an Ancient Christian-Jewish Work* (London: T&T Clark, 2004).

21. Interestingly, the document refers to the ministry of itinerant apostles, which appear as present-day functionaries visiting the addresses of the Didache (11.3–6). See Jonathan A. Draper, "Apostles, Teachers and Evangelists: Stability and Movement of Functionaries in Matthew, James, and the Didache," in *Matthew, James, and Didache: Three Related Documents in their Jewish and Christian Settings*, ed. Huub van de Sandt and Jürgen K. Zangenberg, SBLSymS 45 (Atlanta: Society of Biblical Literature, 2008), 155–58; Taras Khomych, "Diversity of the Notion of Apostolicity in the Writings of the Apostolic Fathers," in *Heiligkeit und Apostolizität der Kirche*, ed. Theresia Hainthaler, Franz Mali, and Gregor Emmenegger (Innsbruck: Tyrolia, 2010), 44.

22. Milavec argues forcefully for a very early date behind the composition of the Didache as a whole, as the title of his book implies (see n. 18). Draper (ibid.), on the other hand, suggests that an earlier form of this document preceded the Gospel of

are inclined to agree that at least some parts of the Didache, such as the Two Ways section (1–6) and the eucharistic prayers (9–10), could be dated to the mid-first century CE.²³ Since a number of scholars recognize the antiquity of the (parts of the) Didache, it is not unwarranted to compare the Pauline Epistles and the Didache as precious evidence of the earliest developments in the Jesus movement.²⁴ Before examining and comparing the use of the notion of εὐαγγέλιον in both writings, we will address briefly the question of its derivation.

3. Early Christian Use of Εὐαγγέλιον

Origins of Christian usage of the term εὐαγγέλιον remain quite obscure. The available literary evidence permits at best a fragmentary reconstruction of the usage of this word prior to the mid-first century CE. The εὐαγγέλ- words appear in ancient Greek and Hellenistic literature.²⁵ In classical Greek the noun had the meaning of "reward for good news," whereas in Roman times εὐαγγέλιον was used to designate the "good news" itself.²⁶

Matthew. In a similar vein, Alan Garrow argues that Matthew is dependent on various redactional layers of the Didache; see Alan J. P. Garrow, *The Gospel of Matthew's Dependence on the* Didache, JSNTSup 254 (London: T&T Clark, 2004).

23. For an excellent study of the Jewish background of the Didache, see Huub van de Sandt and D. Flusser, *The Didache: Its Jewish Sources and Its Place in Early Judaism and Christianity*, CRINT 3.5 (Assen: Van Gorcum; Minneapolis: Fortress, 2002).

24. So recently, Magnus Zetterholm, "The Didache, Matthew, James, and Paul: Reconstructing Historical Development in Antioch," in van de Sandt and Zangenberg, *Matthew, James, and Didache*, 73–90. See also David Flusser, "Paul's Jewish-Christian Opponents in the *Didache*," Draper, *Didache in Modern Research*, 195–211. The author focuses, however, only on Did. 6.2–3, dealing with the question of perfection. Flusser argues that this passage "reflects the position of the majority in the Mother Church towards the Gentile Christian believers while Paul's attitude was more unusual and therefore revolutionary" (195). Joel Willitts, however, criticizes Flusser's attempt to juxtapose Paul and the Didache, suggesting that Did. 6.2–3 is not in conflict with Pauline perspective ("Paul and Jewish Christians in the Second Century," in *Paul and the Second Century*, ed. Michael F. Bird and Joseph R. Dodson, LNTS 412 (London: T&T Clark, 2011), 152–54.

25. See "εὐαγγέλιον," LSJ 704–5. See also "εὐαγγέλιον," BDAG 402–3; G. Strecker, "εὐαγγέλιον," EDNT 2:70–74; G. Friedrich, "εὐαγγελίζομαι κτλ," TDNT 2:707–37 (here 708–12, 719–23).

26. Helmut Koester, *Ancient Christian Gospels: Their History and Development* (London: SCM; Philadelphia: Trinity, 1990), 1–2.

For our present purpose it is sufficient to mention two features relative to use prior to the emergence of Christianity.

(1) In the Septuagint the verb εὐαγγελίζεσθαι is used in a theological context, referring to the proclamation of the rule of YHWH. In Deutero-Isaiah in particular, εὐαγγελίζεσθαι, a Greek equivalent of the Hebrew root בשר,[27] appears in the sense "to proclaim good news" of the salvation of Israel.[28] This verb relates to the activity of the God of Israel during and after the return of the people from Babylon to Zion in this context. The messenger of the good news (מבשר) proclaims peace, salvation, and the victory of YHWH over the entire world (Isa 52:7). This very proclamation ushers in the new era so that the proclamation itself, expressed through the verb εὐαγγελίζεσθαι, has an effective power. Although it might be tempting to draw parallels with the New Testament use of the same notion, it cannot be proven that the same idea of the good news was widespread in first-century Judaism,[29] and, even if it was, a more problematic question of its impact on the New Testament authors remains.[30] This problem of the relationship between the Old Testament and New Testament use of the notion comes into sharper focus in the light of a philological problem that the singular neuter τὸ εὐαγγέλιον, characteristic of Christian usage, does not appear in the Septuagint. Besides the verb, the LXX employs only the feminine singular noun ἡ εὐαγγελία for "good news" (2 Kgdms 18:20, 22, 25, 27; 4 Kgdms 7:9) and the neuter plural τὰ εὐαγγέλια for "reward for the good news" (2 Kgdms 4:10),[31] both related to victory in the battlefield.

(2) The neuter εὐαγγέλιον, however, appears in nonbiblical literature. Besides the classical Greek usage (see above), it is noteworthy that the noun occurs as an important religious notion in the context of the imperial cult, referring to significant events such as birth and accession to the

---

27. R. Ficker, "*mlk*," *TLOT* 2:669.

28. See *EDNT* 2:69; *TDNT* 2:708–709, 716–17.

29. There is too little evidence for this. Philo and Josephus tend to employ the cognate verb εὐαγγελίζειν in the sense in which it is used in the Roman imperial cult. See *EDNT* 2:69; *TDNT* 2:712–14.

30. Koester, *Ancient Christian Gospels*, 3.

31. So Albert Pietersma and Benjamin G. Wright, eds., *A New English Translation of the Septuagint* (Oxford: Oxford University Press, 2007); T. Muraoka, *A Greek-English Lexicon of the Septuagint* (Leuven: Peeters, 2009), 297. But J. Lust et al., eds., *A Greek-English Lexicon of the Septuagint* (Stuttgart: Deutsche Bibelgesellschaft, 2003), 247, translates the latter instance as "good tidings, good news."

throne of a deity in human form, the emperor.[32] In particular, this term appears in the famous Priene inscription (9 BCE) related to the introduction of the Julian calendar, which came into force in 45 BCE as part of the religious political propaganda of Julius Caesar.[33] The most interesting lines for our purposes read as follows:

ἦρξεν δὲ τῷ κόσμῳ τῶν δι᾽ αὐτὸν εὐαγγελί[ων ἡ γενέθλιον] τοῦ θεοῦ[34]
But the birthday of the god was for the world the beginning of tidings of joy on his account.[35]

Augustus is presented here as savior and god, proclaiming a new rule that ushers in the new age of peace and salvation.[36] In this context the combination of the terms σωτήρ, θεός, and εὐαγγέλιον are particularly reminiscent of Christian use.[37] Would it be surprising if early followers of Jesus,

---

32. Adolf Deismann, *Light from the Ancient East*, trans. Lionel R. M. Strachan (London: Hodder & Stoughton, 1910), 370–72; trans. of *Licht vom Osten: Das Neue Testament und die neuentdeckten Texte der hellenistisch-römischen Welt* (Tübingen: Mohr Siebeck, 1908), 313–14. For more recent surveys of the ancient documentary examples of the εὐαγγελ- words and excellent discussions of them, see G. H. R. Horsley, *New Documents Illustrating Early Christianity* (Syndey: Macquarie University, 1981), 3:10–15; Ceslas Spicq, *Notes de lexicographie néo-testamentaire*, OBO 22.1–3 (Göttingen: Vandenhoeck & Ruprecht, 1982), 3:296–306. See also William Horbury, "'Gospel' in Herodian Judaea," in *The Written Gospel*, ed. Markus Bockmuehl and Donald A. Hagner (Cambridge: Cambridge University Press, 2005), 7–30.

33. It is worth noting, however, that the plural τὰ εὐαγγέλια was used in a similar context of ruler worship even earlier, as it is attested by Hellenistic inscriptions from the fourth century BCE; see Wilhelm Dittenberger, *Orientis Graeci Inscriptiones Selectae* (Leipzig: Hirzel, 1903), 1:4.42 (εὐαγγέλια καὶ σωτήρια ε[θ]υσε); see also 1:6.31–32 (θῦσαι δὲ καὶ [εὐ]αγγέλια τὴν πόλιν).

34. The Greek text is quoted according to Dittenberger, *Orientis Graeci Inscriptiones Selectae*, 2:458.40–42.

35. The English translation is taken from Deismann, *Light from the Ancient East*, 371.

36. A similar use of the term εὐαγγέλιον is also attested in Josephus. In *B.J.* 2.420, it appears in singular but without the article in the sense of "good news" to Florus about the civil strife. In 4.618 and 4.656, it occurs in the plural referring to the elevation of Vespasian as Caesar. See Steve Mason, ed., *Judean War 2*, vol. 1b of *Flavius Josephus: Translation and Commentary*. Leiden: Brill, 2008, 321 n. 2641. In Philo the noun is not attested, see Peder Borgen, Kåre Fuglseth, and Roald Skarsten, *The Philo Index* (Grand Rapids: Eerdmans; Leiden: Brill, 2000).

37. The term σωτήρ appears a few lines above the quoted text; see Dittenberger,

proclaiming the gospel just a few decades later, were influenced to some extent by this Augustan use of the term εὐαγγέλιον?[38]

The two points mentioned above, the meaning of the verb εὐαγγελίζεσθαι in the LXX and use of the noun τὸ εὐαγγέλιον in the Roman imperial cult, yield valuable material illuminating early Christian background to the use of the notion εὐαγγέλιον. Scholars discussing this subject matter tend to emphasize alternately either the scriptural influence[39] or impact of the Greco-Roman ruler-cult[40] on the Christian use of εὐαγγελ- words. Some disputants take a mediating position, suggesting that both factors exercised important influence on primitive Christianity.[41] It must be acknowledged, however, that arguments in the discussion are not conclusive.[42] With the evidence available to date, it is not possible to

---

Orientis Graeci Inscriptiones Selectae, 2:458.36. Note further the plural form of εὐαγγέλιον in the inscription.

38. So Koester, *Ancient Christian Gospels*, 4, mentioning, however, that many scholars are rather hesitant to make this connection. Thus Nigel Turner, for instance, preoccupied with a rather speculative idea of a "sacred Greek" presumably developed in primitive Christianity, confidently states that "the first Christians would not be aware of so definitive a use of the word and would be likely to avoid the association even if they were" (Nigel Turner, *Christian Words* [Edinburgh: Nelson, 1980], 190). Criticising this way of dealing with the evidence, Horsley correctly points out that "Turner's case depends on the transparent fallacy that if only one attestation survives the word was employed only once" (Horsley, *New Documents Illustrating Early Christianity* 5:4).

39. For a useful summary of this position and bibliographical references, see H. Frankemölle, *Evangelium—Begriff und Gattung: Ein Forschungsbericht* (Stuttgart: Katholisches Bibelwerk, 1994), 76–86. The following references can be added now: P. Stuhlmacher, "The Theme: The Gospel and the Gospels" and "The Pauline Gospel," in *The Gospel and the Gospels*, ed. Peter Stuhlmacher (Grand Rapids: Eerdmans, 1991), 1–25 and 149–72; Martin Hengel and A. M. Schwemer, *Paulus Zwischen Damascus und Antiochien: Die unbekannten Jahre des Apostels*, WUNT 108 (Tübingen: Mohr Siebeck, 1998).

40. See again Frankemölle, *Evangelium*, 86–93; and also Koester, *Ancient Christian Gospels*, 3–4; Graham N. Stanton, *Jesus and Gospel* (New York: Cambridge University Press, 2004), 20–35.

41. More recently, Horbury ("Gospel"), offering a helpful fresh overview of the subject matter, argued at first for the convergence of the influences of the Hebrew Scriptures and of the emperor cult in Herodian Judaea (i.e., the Roman province of Judea in the period between 40 BCE till about 100 CE). Eventually, however, he emphasized the importance of the Scripture over against the ruler cult.

42. So Frankemölle, *Evangelium*, 93–96.

clearly demonstrate whether, how, and to what extent the ideas and the vocabulary mentioned above influenced the earliest Christian writings. The question of the origin of early Christian use of the term thus cannot be answered unequivocally. For the particular meaning(s) of εὐαγγέλιον and its cognates, we need to rely on the pertinent Christian texts, although the two points mentioned above should not be neglected either.

4. Gospel of Christ Jesus: Pauline Evidence

Many scholars tend to ascribe the application of the singular noun τὸ εὐαγγέλιον, in the sense of "the salvific good news," to Pauline authorship.[43] While this can be debated, in terms of the use of the notion εὐαγγέλιον Paul certainly holds a place of honor, as most of the New Testament references to this term appear in his epistles. Out of seventy-six occurrences in the entire New Testament, this noun reappears some forty-eight times[44] in the undisputed Pauline Epistles,[45] and this frequent use of the notion testifies to its importance for the apostle.

---

43. So James D. G. Dunn, *The Theology of Paul the Apostle* (Grand Rapids: Eerdmans, 1998), 168. Two points are worth mentioning in this respect. First of all, in almost half of the instances, including the earliest epistles (e.g., 1 Thess 2:4), Paul uses the noun in the absolute, τὸ εὐαγγέλιον, without any further explanation. This suggests that the word already functions as a technical term in the Pauline Epistles, which in turn implies that this notion was introduced *prior* to the appearance of Paul's writings. Secondly, in his early letters Paul refers to the teaching(s) of his opponents with the same term εὐαγγέλιον (Gal 1:6; 2 Cor 11:4). This use of the noun might suggest that εὐαγγέλιον has the technical meaning not only for Paul and his followers, but also for those whose teaching(s) Paul renounces and who could scarcely be suspected of accepting any Pauline innovation. This evidence, however, is not conclusive, since in this case we rely on the words of Paul and do not know whether the opponents themselves used the term. Taking all of this into account, it may be concluded that the noun τὸ εὐαγγέλιον was known within the early Jesus movement *prior* to the appearance of Pauline writings. It is not possible to establish, however, whether this term was introduced by the apostle to the gentiles or not.

44. Out of the forty-eight references, the following ones are absolute: Rom 1:16; 10:16; 11:28; 1 Cor 4:15; 9:14 (twice); 9:18 (twice); 9:23; 2 Cor 8:18; Gal 2:5, 14; Phil 1:5, 7, 12, 16, 27; 2:22; 4:3, 15; 1 Thess 2:4. The other references are with a genitive (of object or subject).

45. Robert Morgenthaler, *Statistik des neutestamentlichen Wortschatzes*, 4th ed. (Zürich: Gotthelf, 1992), 101. For a more detailed overview of the occurrences in Paul,

For Paul the εὐαγγέλιον is a *message*, first and foremost. This message is to be proclaimed (1 Thess 2:9; Gal 2:2), made known (1 Cor 15:1), taught (Gal 1:12), presented for discussion (Gal 2:2), and received (2 Cor 11:4).[46] It is worth noting that Paul does not refer to any written source with the term εὐαγγέλιον. This notion instead stands for the proclaimed[47] message in his epistles.

As for the content, in the Pauline writings the core of the gospel message is encapsulated in passages such as Rom 1:1–4 and 1 Cor 15:1–5. The former passage runs as follows:[48]

> ¹Paul, a slave of Christ Jesus, called [to be] an apostle, set apart for the gospel of God, ²which he promised previously through his prophets in the holy scriptures, ³concerning his Son, who was born a descendant of David according to the flesh, ⁴who was declared Son of God in power according to the Holy Spirit by the resurrection from the dead of Jesus Christ our Lord.
>
> ¹Παῦλος δοῦλος ‹Χριστοῦ Ἰησοῦ› κλητὸς ἀπόστολος ἀφωρισμένος εἰς εὐαγγέλιον θεοῦ ²ὃ προεπηγγείλατο διὰ τῶν προφητῶν αὐτοῦ ἐν γραφαῖς ἁγίαις ³περὶ τοῦ υἱοῦ αὐτοῦ, τοῦ γενομένου ἐκ σπέρματος Δαυὶδ κατὰ σάρκα ⁴τοῦ ὁρισθέντος υἱοῦ θεοῦ ἐν δυνάμει κατὰ πνεῦμα ἁγιωσύνης ἐξ ἀναστάσεως νεκρῶν Ἰησοῦ Χριστοῦ τοῦ κυρίου ἡμῶν

At the beginning of this passage (1:1) the term appears in a genitive construction with a modifying θεοῦ. This phrase can either be an objective or

---

see Peter Stuhlmacher, *Vorgeschichte*, vol. 1 of *Das paulinische Evangelium*, FRLANT 95 (Göttingen: Vandenhoeck & Ruprecht, 1968), 56–60.

46. *TDNT* 2:730.

47. Most scholars tend to use the term "to preach" in this context, emphasizing thus a *verbal* aspect in the process of transmission of the "good news." Paul, however, employs different terms, as mentioned above. In this respect, following more recent research (see especially Dominka A. Kurek-Chomycz, "Performing the Passion, Embodying Proclamation: The Story of Jesus's Passion in the Pauline Letters?" in *Gospel Images of Jesus Christ in Church Tradition and in Biblical Scholarship*, ed. Chrestos Karakolis, Karl-Wilhelm Niebuhr, and S. Rogalsky, WUNT 1/288 (Tübingen: Mohr Siebeck, 2012], 373–402), I prefer the verb "to proclaim," which has a broader spectrum of meanings than "to preach."

48. The letters of Paul are quoted according to the edition of the Michael W. Holmes, *The Greek New Testament: SBL Edition* (Atlanta: SBL Press, 2010); the English translation is that of the LEB, a new translation based on the Holmes, *Greek New Testament* (http://www.lexhamenglishbible.com/).

a subjective genitive. In this case God is probably the source of the gospel, since its content is mentioned further in 1:3 (περὶ αὐτοῦ τοῦ υἱοῦ). The apostle then points out that the εὐαγγέλιον was "promised previously through his [God's] prophets," thus claiming scriptural foundation for the "gospel" (1:2). Having said this, Paul discloses the kernel of his gospel message, focusing on God's Son (1:3). Paul exalts Jesus first as the "seed of David," implying most probably his messianic descent.[49] Because of the power shown in Jesus's resurrection, at the same time he is celebrated as the divinely appointed "Son of God."[50] From then on Paul emphasizes the role of the Son of God, counterbalancing eventually the initial expression the "gospel of God" with the phrase the "gospel of [God's] Son" (τὸν εὐαγγέλιον τοῦ υἱοῦ αὐτοῦ) in Rom 1:9.[51] This focus on Jesus is even more clearly expressed in 1 Cor 15:1–5, which offers one of the most elaborate presentations of the εὐαγγέλιον message. The passage runs as follows:

> [1]Now I make known to you, brothers, the gospel which I proclaimed to you, which you have also received, in which you also stand, [2]by which you are also being saved, if you hold fast to the message I proclaimed to you, unless you believed to no purpose. [3]For I passed on to you as of first importance what I also received, that Christ died for our sins according to the scriptures, [4]and that he was buried, and that he was raised up on the third day according to the scriptures, [5]and that he appeared to Cephas, then to the twelve.
> [1]Γνωρίζω δὲ ὑμῖν ἀδελφοί τὸ εὐαγγέλιον ὃ εὐηγγελισάμην ὑμῖν ὃ καὶ παρελάβετε ἐν ᾧ καὶ ἑστήκατε [2]δι' οὗ καὶ σῴζεσθε τίνι λόγῳ εὐηγγελισάμην ὑμῖν εἰ κατέχετε ἐκτὸς εἰ μὴ εἰκῇ ἐπιστεύσατε [3]Παρέδωκα γὰρ ὑμῖν ἐν πρώτοις ὃ καὶ παρέλαβον ὅτι Χριστὸς ἀπέθανεν ὑπὲρ τῶν ἁμαρτιῶν ἡμῶν κατὰ τὰς γραφάς [4]καὶ ὅτι ἐτάφη καὶ ὅτι ἐγήγερται τῇ ⟨ἡμέρᾳ τῇ τρίτῃ⟩ κατὰ τὰς γραφάς [5]καὶ ὅτι ὤφθη Κηφᾷ εἶτα τοῖς δώδεκα

At first Paul reminds the Corinthians that it was through him (Paul) that they received the εὐαγγέλιον. He then explains that "the good news" is not his own invention. Instead the apostle underscores that he transmits

---

49. Romans Jewett, *Romans: A Commentary*, Hermeneia (Minneapolis, Fortress, 2007), 104.

50. Gordan D. Fee, *Pauline Christology: An Exegetical-Theological Study* (Peabody, MA: Hendrickson, 2007), 243, sees "the climax of the Son of God Christology" in this passage.

51. In Rom 1:1–4, Paul shortly presents these ideas, which he elaborates then in 1:16–8:39; see Jewett, *Romans*, 97.

something he has received himself. Paul proclaims the gospel "that Christ died for our sins." While the previous pericope (Rom 1:1–4) does not mention Jesus's death explicitly, the passage at hand emphasizes the death of Jesus first, as well as its salvific significance (ὑπὲρ τῶν ἁμαρτιῶν ἡμῶν). The other elements of the gospel include the subsequent events of Jesus's story, namely, his burial, resurrection, and appearance to Cephas and the twelve. Overall, the gospel denotes here the most crucial moments in the story of Jesus Christ, especially his death and resurrection, and their saving power.[52] We may observe thus that in Rom 1:1–4 and, even more explicitly in 1 Cor 15:1–5, "the good news" refers primarily to the Christ-event.

It is worth noting that Paul sometimes uses the absolute τὸ εὐαγγέλιον or genitive construction (such as in 2 Cor 11:7; Gal 1:7; etc.), which serve the purpose of abbreviated references to the entire gospel message. In a similar way, he employs the verb εὐαγγελίζεσθαι or even some other verbs expressing an action of proclamation, such as in 1 Cor 11:26. The latter reference is interesting, since in this context Paul introduces his instruction concerning the Lord's Supper with the same formula (ἐγὼ γὰρ παρέλαβον … ὃ καὶ παρέδωκα ὑμῖν ὅτι) as in 1 Cor 15:3, which presents the gospel message. In the passage dealing with the meal (more particularly 1 Cor 11:23–26), Paul emphasizes again the importance of the death of the Lord and its proclamation.

It can be concluded that Paul's gospel is focused unambiguously on Jesus Christ, the Son of God, and to proclaim Christ is equal to proclaiming the gospel. As Joseph Fitzmyer succinctly put it: "'Gospel' is *par excellence* Paul's *personal* way of summing up the significance of the Christ-event, the meaning that the person, life, ministry, passion, death, resurrection, and lordship of Jesus of Nazareth had and still has for human history and existence."[53] This Pauline use of the term evokes the LXX notion of εὐαγγέλιον in as much as both refer to the proclamation of the salvific news of God. Paul, however, emphasizes further the centrality of the Christ-event, especially the birth, death, and resurrection, resembling

---

52. Athony C. Thiselton, *The First Epistle to the Corinthians: A Commentary on the Greek Text*, NIGTC (Grand Rapids: Eerdmans, 2000), 1184–85. See also Joseph A. Fitzmyer, *First Corinthians*, AYBC 32 (New Haven: Yale University Press, 2008), 539–49.

53. Joseph A. Fitzmyer, "The Gospel in the Theology of Paul," *Int* 33 (1979): 339–50 (italics original).

the use of the term in the Roman imperial cult with its focus on the significant events in the life of the emperor.

5. Gospel in the Didache

The evidence of the Didache, however, is remarkably different. As opposed to Paul, the Didache is not centered on Christology. Accordingly, the term εὐαγγέλιον, which reappears four times in this short document, can hardly be associated with the birth, death, and resurrection of Jesus Christ. Instead, it is found predominantly in the paraenetical context. For the first time the Didache refers to the "good news" as follows:[54]

> 8.2 And do not pray as the hypocrites. But as the Lord ordered in his good news. Pray thus:
> μηδὲ προσεύχεσθε ὡς οἱ ὑποκριταί ἀλλ᾽ ὡς ἐκέλευσεν ὁ κύριος ἐν τῷ εὐαγγελίῳ αὐτοῦ, οὕτως προσεύχεσθε [The text of the Lord's Prayer follows.]

It is worth noting that the text of the prayer that follows agrees, although not entirely,[55] with the Matthean version of the Lord's Prayer (Matt 6:9–13) over against that of Luke (11:2–4).[56] Based on the strong verbal correspondence between the two versions of the prayer and some other parallels between Matthew and the Didache, many scholars tend to conclude that in this and all other passages where the term εὐαγγέλιον appears, the Didache refers directly to Matthew. This would imply then that the Didachist, relying on the Gospel of Matthew, shares with or takes over from the latter its message about the significance of the Christ event, which in turn appears to correspond to the Pauline teaching.[57] This way of reason-

---

54. In this article, the text and the English translation of the Didache are quoted according to Milavec, *Didache: Faith, Hope, and Life*, 12–45 with some slight alterations.

55. The differences include (1) ἐν τῷ οὐρανῷ instead of the plural in Matthew; (2) τὴν ὀφειλήν in place of Matthew's τὰ ὀφειλήματα; (3) ἀφίεμεν for ἀφήκαμεν in Matthew, although ἀφίεμεν is also attested in some manuscripts; (4) and the Didache's doxology, which is found in some late and less reliable manuscripts of Matthew. Further on these points, see Niederwimmer, *Didache*, 136.

56. It is also worth noting that when the Didache deviates from Matthew in this passage, it does not follow Luke.

57. An overlap between Pauline and Matthean Christology includes an impor-

ing, however, needs to be questioned by challenging the basic assumption that the Didache presupposes the written Gospel of Matthew. Since the 1950s, an increasing number of scholars have questioned the alleged link between the term εὐαγγέλιον in the Didache and Matthew, or any other gospel book, pointing out that the passage in question is more likely to refer to a *proclaimed* than to a *written* material.[58] It is very unlikely that the author of the Didache needed to copy this short prayer, prescribed as *lex orandi* to be recited three times daily (!), from a written source. Most probably the Didachist quoted it from memory.[59] Accordingly, the variants in the form of the prayer in Matthew and the Didache most likely reflect the difference in liturgical practices behind the two documents.[60] If the Lord's

---

tant affirmation of Jesus as "Christ" and "Lord" (see Joel Willitts, "Paul and Matthew: A Descriptive Approach from a Post-New Perspective Interpretative Framework," in *Paul and the Gospels: Christologies, Conflicts and Convergences*, ed. Michael F. Bird and Joel Willitts, LNTS 411 [London: T&T Clark, 2011], 62–85; Paul Foster, "Paul and Matthew: Two Strands of the Early Jesus Movement with Little Sign of Connection," in Bird and Willits, *Paul and the Gospels*, 86–114). It is worth remembering, however, that whereas Paul associates the good news primarily with Jesus's death and resurrection, Matthew does not use the term εὐαγγέλιον with this meaning, combining it instead with the idea of the kingdom of God. Koester, *Ancient Christian Gospels*, 12. See also M. Eugene Boring, "Gospel, Message," NIDB 2:629–36 (esp. 635–36).

58. So, e.g., Helmut Koester, *Synoptische Überlieferungen bei den Apostolischen Vätern*, TUGAL 65/5. 10 (Berlin: Akademie, 1957), 11; Richard Glover, "The Didache's Quotations and the Synoptic Gospels," *NTS* 5 (1958): 12–29.

59. Contra James A. Kelhoffer, "'How Soon a Book' Revisited: ΕΥΑΓΓΕΛΙΟΝ as a Reference to 'Gospel' Materials in the First Half of the Second Century," *ZNW* 95 (2004): 1–34 n. 58. Objecting to Koester's view that a Christian author would know the Lord's Prayer by heart and would not need to copy it from a written source, Kelhoffer observes that "the instruction of *Did.* 8.2 is given because of the Didachist's view of how the faithful should be—but apparently are not—praying. It is precisely for this reason that the Lord's 'commandment' in 'the Gospel' is cited at length, because the Didachist's audience—*un*like so many Christians today—need this information" (italics original). This observation, however, does not dismiss the view that the Didachist is quoting from memory. It only problematizes the assumption that the Lord's Prayer was part of a local liturgical tradition. However, even if the *audience* of the Didache did not know this prayer, this ignorance cannot be attributed to the person who penned Did. 8.2, including the instruction to repeat the prayer three times a day.

60. On the variants as reflecting different liturgical practices, see already Kirsopp Lake, "Didache," in *The New Testament and the Apostolic Fathers* (Oxford: Clarendon, 1905), 30–31. For a useful recent discussion of the liturgical character of the Lord's Prayer in the Didache, see Stephen E. Young, *Jesus Tradition in the Apostolic Fathers:*

Prayer in the Didache derives from oral/liturgical tradition, then the term εὐαγγέλιον in 8.2 refers to an orally transmitted message and not written material. The rest of the Didache appears to use εὐαγγέλιον in a similar manner. The relevant passages run as follows:

> 11.3 And concerning the apostles and prophets, in accordance with the decree of the good news, act thus
> περὶ δὲ τῶν ἀποστόλων καὶ προφητῶν κατὰ τὸ δόγμα τοῦ εὐαγγελίου οὕτω ποιήσατε

> 15.3 And reprove each other not in anger, but in peace, as you have it in the good news.
> ἐλέγχετε δὲ ἀλλήλους μὴ ἐν ὀργῇ, ἀλλ᾽ ἐν εἰρήνῃ ὡς ἔχετε ἐν τῷ εὐαγγελίῳ

> 15.4 And your prayers and alms and all actions, do thus as you have it in the good news of our Lord.
> τὰς δὲ εὐχὰς ὑμῶν καὶ τὰς ἐλεημοσύνας καὶ πάσας τὰς πράξεις οὕτω ποιήσατε ὡς ἔχετε ἐν τῷ εὐαγγελίῳ τοῦ κυρίου ἡμῶν

It is worth noting that although the quotations above employ εὐαγγέλιον in different ways, none of the passages makes it clear whether the "gospel" is written or not. In this respect, the use of the term in early Christian literature may prove illuminating. In the sense of a written book, the word εὐαγγέλιον is securely attested only in Justin Martyr's works, composed in the middle of the second century CE (*Apol.* 1.66.3).[61] The same term in the Didache, which is usually dated to the turn of the first century at the latest, should not be interpreted in light of the latter work. Instead, it is better understood against the backdrop of the first century writings, using

---

Their Explicit Appeals to the Words of Jesus in Light of Orality Studies, WUNT 2/311 (Tübingen: Mohr Siebeck, 2011), 201–25.

On the whole, the question of the Didache's relationship to the Synoptic Gospels has not yet been settled. See a recent exchange in the *Journal of Early Christian Studies*: Christopher M. Tuckett, "The Didache and the Synoptics Once More: A Response to Aaron Milavec," *JECS* 13 (2005): 509–18. This was intended as a response to the following article: Aaron Milavec, "Synoptic Tradition in the *Didache* Revisited," *JECS* 11 (2003): 443–80. Tuckett's contribution was immediately followed by Milavec's reply: Aaron Milavec, "A Rejoinder [to Tuckett]," *JECS* 13 (2005): 519–23.

61. "Apostles' memoirs, which are called gospels [ἀπομνημονεύματα τῶν ἀποστόλων ἅ καλεῖται εὐαγγέλια]" (ca. 155). See also *Dial.* 10.2; 100.1 (ca. 160).

εὐαγγέλιον as a reference to the "good news" proclaimed by the Jesus movement.[62] In comparison to Justin Martyr's writings, there is indeed no clear indication of "writtenness" of εὐαγγέλιον in the Didache.[63] We can observe instead a correspondence with the Pauline Epistles: the Didache appears to use the term "gospel" in a similar manner as Paul does, namely, as a reference to a *proclaimed* message.

Interestingly enough, εὐαγγέλιον is used to support several exhortations in the Didache. Thus, besides the dominical instructions concerning the daily prayer (8.2), the reference to the εὐαγγέλιον appears to reinforce regulations about treatment of itinerant functionaries (11.3), relationships between the community members (15.3), as well as prayer, almsgiving, and the way of life more in general (15.4) in the Didache. In these passages overall, the term εὐαγγέλιον is related to different regulations.

Although focused on praxis, the εὐαγγέλιον of the Didache is not devoid of theological elements. In the discussion of the content of this term scholars usually pay surprisingly little attention to the content of the Lord's Prayer, which is presented as a part of the "good news." It is important to note that this prayer is directed to God the Father, exhibiting in this way the *theo*-logical component of the εὐαγγέλιον. It is equally worth observing that at no point in the Didache does εὐαγγέλιον refer to the incarnation, death, and resurrection of Jesus as opposed to the Pauline usage of the term. The Didache gospel is not about the death and resurrection of Jesus. Instead, it is a message about God the Father and God's instructions to the faithful.[64] This focus on God in the Didache is

---

62. Helmut Koester, "From the Kerygma-Gospel to Written Gospels," *NTS* 35 (1989): 361–81; *Ancient Christian Gospels*, 1–43; R. H. Gundry, "ΕΥΑΓΓΕΛΙΟΝ: How Soon a Book?" *JBL* 115 (1996): 321–25; Milavec, *Didache: Faith, Hope, and Life*, 701–2.

63. Gundry, "ΕΥΑΓΓΕΛΙΟΝ," 323. Contra James A. Kelhoffer, "How Soon a Book"; "'Gospel' as a Literary Title in Early Christianity and the Question of What Is (and Is Not) a 'Gospel' in Canons of Scholarly Literature," in *Jesus in apokryphen Evangelienüberlieferungen*, ed. Jörg Frey and Jens Schröter, WUNT 254 (Tübingen: Mohr Siebeck, 2010), 399–422. Kelhoffer aptly problematizes the scholarly view that Marcion of Sinope was the first to use the term "gospel" as a designation for a written book/material. His suggestion that the Didache provides the earliest surviving evidence of such a use of the term εὐαγγέλιον is attractive but not entirely convincing. It is not possible to enter into discussion with Kelhoffer's thesis here, but see my critique of one of his points in n. 59 above.

64. It needs to be recognized that besides clear references to God (θεός and πάτερ) on the one hand and to Jesus (Ἰησοῦς) on the other, the Didache uses a more

closer to the LXX use of the notion than is that of Paul. This particular use of the word in itself does not obviously imply that the christological kerygma is absent in the Didache. If we turn to the rest of the document, however, we encounter the same lack of elaborate Christology.

5.1. Eucharist in the Didache

One of the most important theological expressions in the Didache occurs in the body of the eucharistic prayers (Did. 9–10). Kurt Niederwimmer expresses a majority opinion when he states that "this material is without peer in the early Christian literature," as it represents "the oldest formula for Christian Eucharistic liturgy"[65] dating most probably to the mid-first century.[66] In this case we have a piece of evidence roughly contemporary with Paul's missionary activities. This text, however, provoked passionate scholarly debates about the nature of the celebration to which it refers. The problem consists first of all in the fact that Did. 9–10 provides us only with the text of prayers mixed with some instructions on how to conduct the celebration. There is no explanation of the ritual provided. We can hardly expect, however, to find such an explanation in this early Christian document. Secondly, and more importantly, although the text of the prayers contains very transparent references to the Eucharist—using in particular the noun εὐχαριστία (9.1, 5) and the verb εὐχαριστέω (9.1, 2, 3; 10.1, 2, 3, 4, 7), mentioning cup (9.2) and bread (9.3, 4), and even interpreting the eucharistic food and drink as τὸ ἅγιον to be consumed only by those who have been baptized (9.5)—it does not conform to a "normative" pattern of

---

ambiguous term, κύριος (lord). Some scholars suggest that the meaning of κύριος fluctuates in this document, referring sometimes to the "Lord-God" and sometimes—to the "Lord-Jesus"; so, e.g., J. A. Draper, "The Didache," in *The Apostolic Fathers*, ed. Wilhelm Pratscher (Waco, TX: University of Baylor Press, 2010), 7–26. It is worth mentioning, however, that while the Didache employs πάτερ and κύριος interchangeably (e.g., in chapter 10), it never does the same with the terms κύριος and Ἰησοῦς. In view of this and some other features of this document, such as the absence of an elaborate Christology, Milavec's suggestion that the Didache consistently uses κύριος in the sense of the "Lord-God" appears particularly convincing (see his contribution in this volume).

65. Niederwimmer, *Didache*, 139.
66. So Schwiebert, *Knowledge and the Coming Kingdom*, 110, 121; compare Enrico Mazza, *The Origins of the Eucharistic Prayer*, trans. Ronald E. Lane (Collegeville, MN: Liturgical Press, 1995), 40–41.

the sacramental Eucharist, which would include the words of institution or at least a reference to Christ's death and resurrection.[67] In this respect its overall theological message is remarkably different from that of Paul and the Pauline Lord's Supper with its focus on Jesus's death in particular (1 Cor 11:23-26).[68] For the purposes of our research, suffice it to quote here only the beginning of the eucharistic prayers of the Didache, 9.1-2:

> 9.1 (And) concerning the Eucharist, eucharistize thus:
> Περὶ δὲ τῆς εὐχαριστίας οὕτως εὐχαριστήσατε
>
> 9.2 First, concerning cup: We give you thanks, our Father, for the holy vine of *your servant David* which you revealed to us through *your servant Jesus*. To you [is] the glory forever. (emphasis added)
> πρῶτον περὶ τοῦ ποτηρίου Εὐχαριστοῦμέν σοι πάτερ ἡμῶν ὑπὲρ τῆς ἁγίας ἀμπέλου Δαυεὶδ τοῦ παιδός σου ἧς ἐγνώρισας ἡμῖν διὰ Ἰησοῦ τοῦ παιδός σου σοὶ ἡ δόξα εἰς τοὺς αἰῶνας

This passage and the rest of the prayers are directed to God (our Father: πάτερ ἡμῶν). Jesus, on the other hand, is presented here as God's "servant" (παῖς),[69] who "revealed/made known" (ἐγνώρισας) the work of the Lord God.[70] It is worth noting that the prayers designate Jesus as the "servant" only after they have referred to King David with exactly the same title first. In this context the link between David and Jesus as servant implies comparison between their missions, as Aaron Milavec amply notes in his commentary:

> David was the servant sent to rescue powerfully and to protect "the holy vine" Israel in the name of the Father. Jesus, on the other hand, is not named as succeeding David but rather *as revealing* the election and care

---

67. For succinct summaries of research on Did. 9-10, see Niederwimmer, *Didache*, 141-43; Bradshaw, *Eucharistic Origins*, 26-35; Gunnar Garleff, *Urchristliche Identität in Matthäusevangelium, Didache und Jakobusbrief*, BVB 9 (Münster: LIT, 2004), 150-62.

68. See a detailed comparison of the two (Pauline and Didache) meal traditions in Schwiebert, *Knowledge and the Coming Kingdom*, 98-110.

69. The term παῖς may be translated both as "servant" and "child." The latter meaning, however, is also expressed by the Greek word τέκνον, which appears in Did. 3. Given the presence of τέκνον in the text, it seems more probable that in the eucharistic prayers the notion παῖς is used with the meaning of "servant."

70. Milavec, *Didache: Faith, Hope, and Life*, 365-71.

of Israel established through the agency of David. According to Did. 9:2, therefore, Jesus ... is the "servant" who revealed to us how God once established his kingdom on earth and how, in the future, God will do so again.[71]

This celebration, in contrast to the Pauline Lord's Supper, shows no reference to Jesus's death and resurrection. Instead, the Didache Eucharist emerges essentially as a thanksgiving to the Lord God for the election of the shoot of David,[72] which God made known through Jesus. This message is consistent with the content of εὐαγγέλιον as reflected in 8.2, focusing on God the Father. The eucharistic prayers (Did. 9–10), which express most sharply the Didache's teaching about God and Jesus, present the παῖς-Christology, very distinct from that found in the Pauline Epistles.

6. Concluding Remarks

The comparison of the notion εὐαγγέλιον in the *corpus Paulinum* and in the Didache offers striking results. As far as the meaning of the term is concerned, both writings similarly use εὐαγγέλιον in the sense of a proclaimed message. The content of the good news, however, is remarkably different in these two cases. Whereas in the Pauline Epistles εὐαγγέλιον refers primarily to the death and resurrection of Jesus, the Didache is notably silent about these events, focusing instead on the Lord God and mentioning Jesus as God's servant. In other words, Paul's gospel features above all a message of salvation in/through Christ, a christologically centered soteriology. In comparison to Paul, the message of the Didache is more theocentric and focused on ethics. These differences between the Pauline Epistles and the Didache should be interpreted in the light of the respective views on Jesus and his mission in these writings. In his epistles,

---

71. Ibid., 368. Compare Jens Schröter, *Das Abendmahl: Frühchristliche Deutungen und Impulse für die Gegenwart*, SBS 210 (Stuttgart: Katholisches Bibelwerk, 2006), 69; Schwiebert, *Knowledge and the Coming Kingdom*, 83–88.

72. The expression "the holy vine of David" is notably imprecise. It might refer to the grape vine, taking into account that this phrase forms part of the blessing over the cup (of wine). The presence of the adjective "holy" and the reference to David, however, indicate that this expression has a wider field of significance. It appears to refer to Israel as the kingdom of David, drawing on a rich symbolic traditions of ancient Judaism; see Jonathan A. Draper, "Ritual Process and Ritual Symbol in Didache 7–10," *VC* 54 (2000): 148–51.

Paul elaborates an exalted Christology, presenting Jesus as God's Christ, Savior, and Lord. This perspective is evidently missing in the Didache, which envisages Jesus as God's παῖς who revealed the will of the Lord God. The two types of teachings probably coexisted in the same period, although obviously in different communities/milieus. The evidence of the Didache, remarkably different from that of the Pauline Epistles, yields invaluable information about the origins of Christianity. Further investigation of this document remains a critical scholarly desideratum for ongoing research on diversity in the early Jesus movement.

The First Century Two Ways Catechesis and Hebrews 6:1–6

Matthew Larsen and Michael Svigel

1. Introduction

Three ambiguities within Heb 6:4–6 have led many interpreters astray. First, the text seems to describe actual members of the Christian community, not pretenders (6:4–5). Second, it seems to speak of a true falling away (6:6). And third, it warns of the real impossibility of repentance after the apostasy (6:4, 6). These three obstacles have proved nettlesome for interpreters throughout the reception history of this text. Perhaps as early as the Shepherd of Hermas (Mand. 4.3.1–7), the belief that Christians could not repent of certain sins—based partly on Heb 6:4–6—has vexed many readers.[1]

What does all this have to do with the Didache? In this chapter, we ask what happens when we read Heb 6:1–6 in conjunction with the Didache. While arguing for an analogical, not genealogical, relationship between the Didache and Hebrews, we will place the Didache alongside Hebrews in order to offer a new reading that we believe will lead to a better interpretation of Hebrews. We will suggest that the first-century Two Ways catechetical pattern presents an intriguing historical context for Heb 6:1–6, demonstrated through compelling conceptual parallels between the Didache and Heb 6:1–2. Consequently, in our reading, παραπίπτω in Heb 6:6 does not refer to irreversible apostasy, but to a failure to advance on the way of life from the level of catechumen to teacher (5:12–14).

---

1. See Carolyn Osiek, *The Shepherd of Hermas: A Commentary*, Hermeneia (Philadelphia: Fortress, 1999), 29, 114–15.

Likewise, the impossibility of renewal to repentance does not refer to an inability to return to the faith, but to the impossibility of repeating the initiatory baptism of repentance associated with preliminary catechesis.

2. Preliminary Comments

Understandably, modern scholarship has attempted to steer a course around the difficulties of Heb 6:1–6 by illuminating the path with a variety of suggested historical backgrounds, none of which has achieved anything like a consensus.[2] For example, some have suggested that the author refers to only apparent converts in 6:4–5, not to authentic Christians who would have borne the true fruit of salvation (6:9).[3] Others consider the "falling away" to refer not to actual cases of apostasy among the readers, but to the hypothetical possibility of such apostasy from which there would have been no recovery. The text then serves as a warning against the readers' dullness and lack of spiritual progress (5:11–14), which, if left unchecked, would have plunged them into an irreversible condition.[4] Finally, the third obstacle can be dodged if the impossibility of repentance is limited to human effort, the author leaving room for God's gracious work that could

---

2. Numerous examples could be listed. Brent Nongbri, for instance, provides a Second Temple apocalyptic background ("A Touch of Condemnation in a Word of Exhortation: Apocalyptic Language and Graeco-Roman Rhetoric in Hebrews 6:4–12," *NovT* 45 [2003]: 265–79). Martin Emmrich suggests a Second Temple pneumatological reading ("Heb 6:4–6—Again! [A Pneumatological Inquiry]," *WTJ* 65 [2003]: 83–85). For an Old Testament background, i.e., Kadesh-Barnea, see Dave Mathewson, "Reading Heb 6:4–6 in Light of the Old Testament," *WTJ* 61 (1999): 209–25. David deSilva reads the text in light of a social and Mediterranean cultural (patron/client) milieu ("Exchanging Favor for Wrath: Apostasy in Hebrews and Patron-Client Relationships," *JBL* 115 [1996]: 91–116). For an oral critical reading, see Casey W. Davis, "Hebrews 6:4–6 from an Oral Critical Perspective," *JETS* 51 (2008): 753–67. Andreas H. Snyman argues from a discourse perspective ("Hebrews 6:4–6: From a Semiotic Discourse Perspective," in *Discourse Analysis and the New Testament*, ed. Stanley E. Porter and Jeffrey T. Reed, JSNTSup 170 [Sheffield: Sheffield Academic, 1999], 354–68). See also Scot McKnight, "The Warning Passages of Hebrews: A Formal Analysis and Theological Conclusions," *TJ* n.s. 13 (1992): 21–59.

3. This is often the interpretation of confessional readings that cite passages such as 1 John 2:19. This view has too many adherents to name.

4. Luke Timothy Johnson, *Hebrews: A Commentary*, NTL (Louisville: Westminster John Knox, 2006), 160–64; Alan C. Mitchell, *Hebrews*, SP 13 (Collegeville, MN: Liturgical Press, 2007), 123–30.

transcend human impossibility.⁵ Many commentators, however, taking the language at its apparent face value, have simply affirmed that the author of Hebrews taught that, through intentional apostasy or neglected faith, members of the Christian community could fall away from salvation, resulting in a condition in which restoration to repentance was simply impossible.⁶

Acknowledging the complexity of the interpretive questions, this article presents a fresh examination of Heb 6:1–6 in light of a neglected and heretofore underutilized historical context: the first century Two Ways catechesis. Though some have drawn on the Two Ways didactic pattern of early Jewish and Jewish-Christian communities to shed light on certain elements of Heb 6:1–6,⁷ we submit that the entire passage can be explained in light of this context. When interpreted in the context of a community that has been initiated into the Christian faith through a Two Ways catechesis, Heb 6:1–6 takes on a different meaning that coheres well with the rest of the document. We will argue that the author of Hebrews shows an awareness of a common early Christian Two Ways catechesis and initiation in Heb 6:1–6, the cognizance of which would have been shared by the original readers of Hebrews who had experienced the catechism and initiation. The Hebrews version of the Two Ways catechesis and its initiatory rites were similar to that pattern preserved for us in the Didache.⁸ Contextually, this Two Ways background synchronizes with the theme of pilgrimage suggested by several scholars as a major motif in Hebrews.⁹

---

5. F. F. Bruce, *The Epistle to the Hebrews*, NICNT (Grand Rapids: Eerdmans, 1990), 144; Thomas G. Long, *Hebrews*, IBC (Louisville: Westminster John Knox, 1997), 72–74; Brooke Westcott writes, "There may be, through the gift of GOD, a corresponding change, a regaining of the lost view with the consequent restoration of the fullness of life, but this is different from the freshness of the vision through which the life is first realised" (Brooke F. Westcott, *The Epistle to the Hebrews: The Greek Text with Notes and Essays*, 3rd ed. [London: Macmillan, 1914], 152).

6. Harold W. Attridge, *The Epistle to the Hebrews: A Commentary on the Epistle to the Hebrews*, Hermeneia (Philadelphia: Fortress, 1989), 166–77; Craig R. Koester, *Hebrews*, AB 36 (New York: Doubleday, 2001), 311–23; James Moffatt, *A Critical and Exegetical Commentary on the Epistle to the Hebrews*, ICC (New York: Scribner's Sons, 1924), 77–80.

7. See, e.g. Bruce, *Epistle to the Hebrews*, 140.

8. For a discussion of the origin, development, and date of the final form of the Didache in current scholarship, see below.

9. Most recently, Johnson, *Hebrews*, 7–9, 161. Johnson connects παραπεσόντας in

It is important to clarify that we are not arguing that the author of Hebrews knew the Didache itself or vice versa. There need be no literary dependence here. Rather, we hope to demonstrate compelling lexical and conceptual parallels between the two documents, reaffirming the common view that at least an oral Two Ways didactic pattern similar to that found in the Didache existed when the writer of Hebrews addressed his readers. To use the language of Jonathan Z. Smith, we present these two texts not as genealogically but as analogically related, making no claims about the genetic relationship between the Didache and Hebrews.[10] The author of Hebrews could have reasonably assumed the original readers to be aware of such a pattern. Thus, an understanding of the catechetical experience of many early Christian communities provides an intriguing historical context within which Heb 6:1–6 may be read.[11]

3. The Two Ways Didactic Pattern in the First Century

The "Two Ways" refers to a didactic pattern that compares the way of life (or sometimes "light" or "truth") and the way of death (or sometimes "darkness" or "error"). The way of life section explains the virtuous lifestyle expected of an initiated member of the community. In stark contrast, the way of death illustrates the sinful and destructive lifestyle of an outsider (see, e.g., Did. 1.1, 5.1–2). While the early church used the Two Ways didactic pattern, most scholars agree that it came into existence before

---

Heb 6:6 with the pilgrimage motif. See also Ernst Käsemann, *The Wandering People of God: An Investigaton of the Letter to the Hebrews*, trans. Roy A. Harrisville and Irving L. Sandberg (Minneapolis: Augsburg, 1984); William G. Johnsson, "The Pilgrimage Motif in the Book of Hebrews," *JBL* 97 (1978): 239–51; Raymond Brown, "Pilgrimage in Faith: The Christian Life in Hebrews," *SwJT* 28 (1985): 28–35; D. W. Perkins, "A Call to Pilgrimage: The Challenge of Hebrews," *TTE* 32 (1985): 69–78.

10. Jonathan Z. Smith, *Drudgery Divine: On the Comparison of Early Christianities and the Religions of Late Antiquity* (Chicago: University of Chicago Press, 1990), 46–50.

11. A helpful analog to our approach may be found in Alan J. P. Garrow, "The Eschatological Tradition behind 1 Thessalonians: *Didache* 16," *JSNT* 32 (2009): 191–215. Garrow suggests the tradition preserved in Did. 16 as the foundational eschatological teaching behind 1 Thess 4:15–17 (pp. 210–11), though he leaves open the question of whether Paul knew the Didache or its sources (210 n. 27). We approach the texts of Hebrews and the Didache in a comparable manner.

the birth of Christianity.[12] The Two Ways finds echoes in early Hellenistic literature (see, e.g., Xenophon, *Mem.* 2.1.21–34; Hesiod, *Op.* 287–292), but the early Christian form appears to have taken its cues from Jewish religious themes. The Two Ways pattern can be seen in the Hebrew Scriptures (see, e.g., Deut 30:15; Pss 1:6; 139:24; Prov 2:8–22; and Jer 21:8), at Qumran (see esp. 1QS III, 13–IV, 26),[13] in the Pseudepigrapha (see, e.g., 1 En. 91–107; 2 En. 30.14–15; 2 Esd 7.3–8; T. Ash. 1.3–6.5),[14] the Mishnah (see, e.g., m. 'Abot 2:9), and the Babylonian Talmud (see, e.g., b. Ber. 28b). It is also discerned in similar form in the early Jesus movement (see, e.g., Matt 7:13–14; Luke 13:24; Acts 2:28; 18:25),[15] the Apostolic Fathers (see Did. 1.2–6.2; Barn. 18–20; Herm. Mand. 6.2), later church writings (see Aristides, *Apol.* 15; Apos. Con. 7.1–19, and *Vita Shenudi*), and in texts often labeled by scholars as apocryphal New Testament texts.[16]

---

12. M. Jack Suggs, "The Christian Two Ways Tradition: Its Antiquity, Form and Function," in *Studies in New Testament and Early Christian Literature: Essays in Honor of Allen P. Wikgren*, NovTSup 33 (Leiden: Brill, 1972), 60–74. For a scholarly reconstruction of the Two Ways, see Huub van de Sandt and David Flusser, *The Didache: Its Jewish Sources and Its Place in Early Judaism and Christianity*, CRINT 3.5 (Minneapolis: Fortress, 2002), 112–31.

13. This is a particularly interesting usage, because it models the Two Ways didactic pattern found in the Didache: it begins with the Two Spirits/Ways [dogmatic section], followed by a catalog of virtues and vices [ethical section], and ends with an eschatological tone. Suggs notes that 1QS III, 13–IV, 26 is irrefutable evidence of the Two Ways Jewish tradition with an introduction dealing with the Two Spirits and their role in human life, a double catalog of vices and virtues, an eschatologically colored threat-promise conclusion (Suggs, "Christian Two Ways Tradition," 64–65). 1QS V, 13 states that participation in pure food should follow water purification (see Did. 9.5). For a discussion of the Two Ways in the Essene and pre-Essene form and the two spirits, see van de Sandt and Flusser, *Didache*, 147–55. Interestingly, 1QS VII, 23–24 and VIII, 21–23 also speak of the impossibility of an apostate re-entering the covenant community.

14. T. Ash. 5.2–3, like 1QS III, 13–IV, 26, also ends the section with eschatological judgment, which indicates that the early Jewish Two Ways didactic pattern seemed to have a tendency to climax with an eschatological warning, as does the Didache in chapter 16.

15. See Hans Dieter Betz, *The Sermon of the Mount: A Commentary on the Sermon on the Mount, including the Sermon on the Plain (Matthew 5:3–7:27 and Luke 6:20–49)*, Hermeneia (Minneapolis: Fortress, 1995), 522–23. Betz sees a Two Ways pattern in the Sermon on the Mount, and one that is congruous with Did. 1.2; 5.1–2. Additionally, according to Acts the Jesus movement was often referred to as "the Way" (Acts 9:2; 19:9, 23; 22:4; 24:14, 22). See also van de Sandt and Flusser, *Didache*, 81–111.

16. On the *Vita Shenudi*, see Ludwig Emil Iselin and Andreas Heusler, *Eine bisher*

The Two Ways was an early, widespread, and enduring didactic pattern in the Jewish and early Christian religious traditions. Therefore, the possibility that this pattern may have occupied a place in the cultural world of Heb 6:1–6 should not be surprising. Yet this raises several questions. How formal were the expressions of this didactic pattern at the time Hebrews was written? Was the pattern stable enough that the letter's readers would have been familiar with a specific catechetical form? That is, since there was a general Two Ways catechetical pattern common by the latter half of the first century, may the specific form of this catechesis expressed in the Didache provide insight into understanding catechetical language and imagery in Heb 6:1–6?

This essay does not provide a full exploration of such questions, yet we will highlight some issues. While some scholars date the Didache to the early second century and regard it as a composite work that brings together various early texts and traditions developed over the course of several decades,[17] other scholars date it from 50 to 70 CE,[18] and a growing consensus of scholars holds that the Didache (as we have it in Codex Hierosolymitanus) reached its final redacted form by the turn of the first century CE with traditions reaching back well into the first century CE.[19] Furthermore, scholars recognize that the Two Ways didactic pattern possessed a common form that began in pre-Christian Judaism and was adopted in its various forms in earliest Christianity: (1) a dogmatic section, (2) fol-

---

unbekannte Version des ersten Teiles der "Apostellehre," TUGAL 13.1b (Leipzig: Hinrichs, 1895), 1–30. For an apocryphal New Testament text, see reference to Peter's Two Ways catechism in the *Preaching of Peter* of Pseudo-Clement, Hom. 7.

17. Leslie W. Barnard, *Studies in the Apostolic Fathers and Their Background* (New York: Schocken Books, 1966), 99; Bart D. Ehrman, *The Apostolic Fathers*, 2 vols., LCL 24 (Cambridge: Harvard University Press, 2003), 411; Claudio Moreschini and Enrico Norelli, *Early Christian Greek and Latin Literature: A Literary History*, trans. Matthew J. O'Connell, 2 vols. (Peabody, MA: Hendrickson, 2005), 1:128. See scholarly views of the date and provenance of the Didache in Clayton N. Jefford, *The Sayings of Jesus in the Teaching of the Twelve Apostles*, VCSup 111 (Leiden: Brill, 1989), 3–17.

18. See Jean-Paul Audet, *La Didachè: Instructions des Apôtres*, Ebib (Paris: Gabalda, 1958), 187–210; John A. T. Robinson, *Redating the New Testament* (Philadelphia: Westminster, 1976), 96–100, 322–27; Aaron Milavec, *The Didache: Faith, Hope, and Life of the Earliest Christian Communities, 50–70 CE* (New York: Newman, 2003).

19. For a list of such scholars, see van de Sandt and Flusser, *Didache*, 48–49, esp. n. 128; Kurt Niederwimmer, *The Didache: A Commentary*, trans. Linda M. Maloney, Hermeneia (Minneapolis: Fortress, 1998), 52–53; Willy Rordorf and André Tuilier, *La doctrine des douze apôtres (Didachè)*, SC 248 bis (Paris: Cerf, 1998), 96–97.

lowed by an ethical section, (3) associated with initiatory activity, and (4) concluding with an eschatological conclusion.[20] The Didache also exhibits this same pattern with a dogmatic section in 1.1–2.1, an ethical section in 2.2–5.2, initiatory rites in 7.1–10.7, and an eschatological conclusion in 16.1–8. Thus we reasonably may accept the likelihood of a stable Christian Two Ways didactic pattern in the second half of the first century CE.

Because our thesis does not allege direct literary dependence of Hebrews on the Didache itself, the questions of unity and development are of no immediate importance. Our suggestion here is that they inhabit some of the same intellectual space. The Didache reflects a specific form of a more general pattern of catechesis in the last half of the first century CE. It is sufficient to place these texts (and traditions or both) broadly in the latter half of the first century.

4. Similarities between the Two Ways Catechesis in Heb 6.1–6 and the Didache

The Didache Two Ways catechesis includes distinctively Christian logia (Did. 1.1–6.3), followed by a liturgical section (7.1–10.7), which addresses the proper parameters for baptism (7), prayer and fasting (8), and the Eucharist (9–10). A section follows on apparently primitive and transitional church leadership and order (11.1–15.4), concluding rather abruptly with a brief but dense eschatological summary (16.1–8).[21] The

---

20. Suggs, "Christian Two Ways Tradition," 63–74. See also Willy Rordorf, "An Aspect of the Judeo-Christian Ethic: The Two Ways," in *The Didache in Modern Research*, ed. Jonathan A. Draper, AGJU 37 (Leiden: Brill, 1996), 148–64 (153).

21. The Didache lends itself to a successive temporal reading, as evidenced by the presence of an antecedent temporal participle of προλέγω (the aorist προειπόντες in 7.1; the perfect προειρημένα in 11.1) that links the Two Ways in 1–6 temporally to the liturgical section of baptism, fasting and prayer, and Eucharist in 7–10, and 7–10 to the church order section in 11–15. As such, it is structured more for use as something like a didactic catechetical manual than a reference manual for church order or discipline. See Niederwimmer, *Didache*, 1; Rordorf and Tuilier, *Doctrine des douze Apôtres*, 22–83. Even if the catechetical section is limited to Did. 1–6, however, the entire book could have been used for the instruction of initiates toward maturity, a trajectory clearly emphasized in Hebrews (5:12). In this light, our thesis may actually be strengthened if the Didache served a dual purpose as a catechesis for initiates as well as a manual for developing leaders. The latter is merely the intended trajectory of the former.

Didache presents this outline as the basic catechetical method for new converts moving from the initial act of repentance (μετανοέω) and baptism (βάπτισμα)[22] to maturity (τέλειος).[23]

The basic idea of progressing from repentance to maturity is found in Heb 5–6, forming the broader context of Heb 6:1–6.[24] The point of Heb 5 and 6 was to contrast between immature novices and mature teachers, that is, those who lack discernment and those who are trained and experienced. The writer's purpose was to encourage spiritual infants (νήπιος; 5:13) to grow toward spiritual maturity (τέλειος; 5:14). David DeSilva writes, "The author here uses another expression that will reinforce the overarching agenda he has been proposing for the addressees from the beginning, namely, pressing ever forward toward the end of the journey begun at their conversion, baptism, and early catechesis in the Christian worldview."[25] In the final analysis, the idea of new converts and mature teachers is found in both Heb 5–6 and the Didache. But this is not the only parallel between these two passages. Hebrews 6:1–2 reads:

Διὸ ἀφέντες τὸν τῆς ἀρχῆς τοῦ Χριστοῦ λόγον ἐπὶ τὴν τελειότητα φερώμεθα μὴ πάλιν θεμέλιον καταβαλλόμενοι μετανοίας ἀπὸ νεκρῶν

---

22. The Didachist seems to use repentance (μετανοείτω) to refer to the act of baptism. Didache 9.5 links taking the Eucharist with holiness and explicitly forbids the unbaptized from participating (see 1QS V, 13). Then in Did. 10.6 we read, Εἴ τις ἅγιός ἐστιν, ἐρχέσθω εἴ τις οὐκ ἐστί μετανοείτω, which can then be paraphrased as follows: "If anyone is baptized, let that person come. If anyone is unbaptized, let that person enter into catechesis (1.1–6.3) culminating in baptism." The ideas of repentance and baptism are also closely linked in the New Testament at Matt 3:11; Mark 1:4; Luke 3:3; Acts 2:38; 13:24; and 19:4. They are also connected in Herm. Mand. 4.3.1 and in Gos. Eb. 1 and Acts Pil. 18.2.

23. See Did. 1.4; 6.2; 10.5; and 16.2. At the culmination of the Two Ways initiatory catechesis, Did. 6.2 indicates that the purpose of the catechesis is movement towards maturity (τέλειος). Thus, the goal of the Two Ways catechesis was for one to arrive at τέλειος, i.e., maturity and wholeness (G. Delling, "τέλος, τελέω, κτλ," *TDNT* 8:49–87, especially 73–78; BDAG 996. Such a notion can also be confirmed by considering the usage of τελε* in Did. 1.4, 10.5, and 16.2.

24. Repentance (μετάνοια) is found in Heb 6:1, 6. Maturity (τέλειος) is found in Heb 5:9, 14, and 6:1. As will be shown later, we believe the way the author of Hebrews used both μετάνοια and τέλειος in a way parallel to the Didachist is due to their dependence upon a shared Two Ways didactic pattern.

25. David A. deSilva, *Perseverance in Gratitude: A Socio-Rhetorical Commentary on the Epistle "to the Hebrews"* (Grand Rapids: Eerdmans, 2000), 215.

ἔργων καὶ πίστεως ἐπὶ θεόν βαπτισμῶν διδαχῆς ἐπιθέσεώς τε χειρῶν
ἀναστάσεώς τε νεκρῶν καὶ κρίματος αἰωνίου

We can identify several notable parallels between what the author of Hebrews considers to be the elementary teachings and the didactic pattern seen in the Didache.[26] Both can be divided into four parts. The possible didactic parallels between Heb 6:1c–2 and the Didache can be seen in the following chart:

Heb 6:1c: Initial Repentance and Faith	Did. 1–6: Initiatory Catechism
Heb 6:2a: Teaching on Baptisms	Did. 7–10: Teaching on Christian Liturgy
Heb 6:2b: Teaching on Church Leadership	Did. 11–15: Teaching on Church Leadership
Heb 6:2c: Teaching on Eschatology	Did. 16: Eschatological Conclusion

Let us examine these parallels in greater depth. First, the author of Hebrews regards μετανοίας ἀπὸ νεκρῶν ἔργων καὶ πίστεως ἐπὶ θεόν as a foundational theme among the Christian community. Similarly, the heart of the Didache is the Two Ways catechesis. Didache 1.1–6.3 contains instruction about the ὁδοὶ δύο (two paths): the path of life (1.2–4.14) and the path of death (5.1–2). Once a person has chosen the path of life, the journey begins by the initiation of water baptism. The path of life is the proper response of repentance from the path of death (= "dead works"?) and faith toward God. Further, the verb μετανοέω is used in Did. 10.6b as a call to baptism, which would be preceded by catechesis in the Two Ways.[27] Thus,

---

26. The phrase τὰ στοιχεῖα τῆς ἀρχῆς τῶν λογίων τοῦ θεοῦ in Heb 5:12 is conceptually equivalent to the τὸν τῆς ἀρχῆς τοῦ Χριστοῦ λόγον in 6:1. These therefore refer to elementary, foundational Christian teachings, i.e., catechesis. Cf. Moffatt, *Critical and Exegetical Commentary on the Epistle*, 70, 74; Westcott, *Epistle to the Hebrews*, 142; Otto Michel, *Der Brief an die Hebräer*, 8th ed., KEK 14 (Göttingen: Vandenhoeck & Ruprecht, 1984), 238.

27. When read in conjunction with Did. 9.5 (μηδεὶς δὲ φαγέτω μηδὲ πιέτω ἀπὸ τῆς εὐχαριστίας ὑμῶν ἀλλ᾽ οἱ βαπτισθέντες εἰς ὄνομα κυρίου καὶ γὰρ περὶ τούτου εἴρηκεν ὁ κύριος·μὴ δῶτε τὸ ἅγιον τοῖς κυσί), it would seem that the phrase Εἴ τις ἅγιός ἐστιν ἐρχέσθω in Did. 10.6 would refer to those who have gone through catechesis and been baptized, while μετανοείτω would be a call to enter into the way of life through catechesis and baptism. All of this is predicated on the understanding that

μετανοίας ἀπὸ νεκρῶν ἔργων καὶ πίστεως ἐπὶ θεόν in Heb 6:1 and Did. 1–6 exhibits strong conceptual links: God had laid out a path of life and people are to respond appropriately by repenting of their dead works (the path of death) and acting faithfully towards God (the path of life).[28]

Second, the author of Hebrews mentions βαπτισμῶν διδαχῆς as another foundational understanding within the Christian community. This section displays conceptual and lexical similarities to the Didache. Hebrews 6:2 refers to a singular foundational teaching (διδαχῆς) concerning multiple washings (βαπτισμῶν). Interestingly, Did. 7.1–3 reads:

> Περὶ δὲ τοῦ βαπτίσματος οὕτω βαπτίσατε·ταῦτα πάντα προειπόντες βαπτίσατε εἰς τὸ ὄνομα τοῦ πατρὸς καὶ τοῦ υἱοῦ καὶ τοῦ ἁγίου πνεύματος ἐν ὕδατι ζῶντι ἐὰν δὲ μὴ ἔχῃς ὕδωρ ζῶν εἰς ἄλλο ὕδωρ βάπτισον εἰ δ' οὐ δύνασαι ἐν ψυχρῷ ἐν θερμῷ ἐὰν δὲ ἀμφότερα μὴ ἔχῃς ἔκχεον εἰς τὴν κεφαλὴν τρὶς ὕδωρ εἰς ὄνομα πατρὸς καὶ υἱοῦ καὶ ἁγίου πνεύματος

Here we see intriguing similarities between Heb 6:2 and Did. 7.1–3. The passage in the Didache contains instructions concerning baptism that would apply generally to changing contexts and conditions, implying the intention for geographical distribution of the document. Didache 7.1–3 creates provision for a variety of geographical contexts that would have access to running water, cold water, warm water, or only enough water to pour over a person's head. Hence, the Didachist made provisional instruction for all four scenarios, including distinct modes of baptism, that is, a variety of "baptisms." Put more straightforwardly, the Didache contains one teaching for multiple modes of baptism (see βαπτισμῶν διδαχῆς in Heb 6:2a). It is not difficult to see a conceptual parallel with Hebrews' reference to βαπτισμόι.[29] Moreover, Otto Michel notes several interpretations

---

the Didache lends itself to being read and used in a temporally successive manner. See n. 21 above.

28. Michel (*Brief an die Hebräer*, 239) also suggests an allusion between "dead works" and "the way of death" in Did. 5.1, mentioning a possible Semitism in the Greek syntax of νεκρῶν ἔργων.

29. Heb 6:2 uses βαπτισμός, a common term for Jewish ritual washings (see Mark 7:4), as it is later used in Hebrews itself (9:10). The more frequent word for Christian baptism is, of course, βάπτισμα. Both terms can be used to refer to the rite of initiation, as shown by Col 2:12, clearly a reference to baptism. Though the external textual evidence appears evenly split between βάπτισμα and βαπτισμός in Col 2:12, the *lectio difficilior* would be the dative singular of βαπτισμός. In any case, even if Jewish ritual

of the plural "baptisms" in Heb 6:2: Jewish Christian washings and oblations; a distinction between Jewish proselyte baptism, John's baptism, and Jesus's baptism; or even a reference to a threefold immersion.[30] This latter possibility is important, considering that Did. 7.3 mentions pouring three times on the head, which practice might be generally referred to as Christian βάπτισμα, but could more particularly be described with the plural βαπτισμοί because of the multiple "washings" involved. While the exact lexical and conceptual parallels are found only with 7.1–3, it is clear that all of Did. 7–10 belongs to a single unit held together by many linguistic features. The περὶ δέ refrain found in 7.1 and 9.1, 3 creates a lexically unified progression of thought. Also, similar doxological refrains can be found in 8.2, 9.2, 3, 4, 10.2, 4, and 5. Fasting (νηστεία/νηστεύω) links chapters 7 and 8. Further, similar liturgical words are used throughout: κελεύω in 7.4 and 8.2; ἁγιάζω in 8.2 and 10.5; and ῥύομαι in 8.2 and 10.5. Lastly, the construction οὕτως followed by a second person present imperatival command appears in 7.1, 8.1, 2, 3, 9.1, 4, and 10.1. Thus, Did. 7–10 represents one whole unit concerning Christian rites, with different modes of baptisms heading the section.

Third, the author of Hebrews refers to ἐπιθέσεώς τε χειρῶν as another foundational theme within the Christian community. The practice of laying on hands was an ancient sign of ordination to church leadership (Acts 6:6; 13:3; and 1 Tim 5:22). Church leadership is also the dominant topic throughout Did. 11–15. Didache 11.3 reads, "Now concerning the apostles and prophets, deal with them as follows in accordance with the rule of the gospel." It then describes how one can distinguish a true from a false prophet, gives instructions for dealing with leadership, and tells how to discern good and bad leaders (11.4–13.7). In light of an early Christian pastoral admonition not to neglect the gift given by the laying on of hands of the elders in 1 Tim 4:14 (μὴ ἀμέλει τοῦ ἐν σοὶ χαρίσματος ὃ ἐδόθη σοι διὰ προφητείας μετὰ ἐπιθέσεως τῶν χειρῶν τοῦ πρεσβυτερίου),[31] ἐπιθέσεώς

---

washings were at least partly in view in Heb 6:2, this would not rule out the possibility that instruction regarding these diverse ritual washings was, at least in the first century, an important aspect of catechism in preparation for the distinctive Christian rite.

30. Michel, *Brief an die Hebräer*, 239.

31. Commenting on 1 Tim 4:14, David Daube concludes: "Surely, as *semikhath zeqenim* denotes not the ordination of specified individuals, not the appointment of certain men as elders, but the rite of ordination in general" (*The New Testament and Rabbinic Judaism* [New York: Arno, 1973], 245).

τε χειρῶν ("laying on of hands") in Heb 6:1 may refer to instructions concerning legitimate leadership in the church and legitimate church order.[32]

Fourth, the author of Hebrews refers to ἀναστάσεώς τε νεκρῶν καὶ κρίματος αἰωνίου as the final facet of the elementary understanding of the Christian community. Again, clear lexical and conceptual parallels can be seen between Hebrews and the Didache. Lexically, Did. 16.6 also uses the words ἀνάστασις νεκρῶν. Conceptually, Did. 16 moves the reader toward the κύριος as coming judge. Both documents clearly posit an eschatological climax to their foundational catechesis.

Given the demonstrable widespread use of the Two Ways didactic pattern by the time of the first century CE,[33] as well as the particular expression of this pattern in the Didache, these apparent similarities should not be ignored as a potential background to Heb 6:1-2. As such, this same catechetical pattern would also constitute the historical background of the warning passage in 6:4-6, serving as an important aid for interpreting its most difficult features.

5. Marks of the Two Ways Catechesis in Heb 6:4-6

As we have shown in the introduction of this study, the rather harsh assertion of Heb 6:4, 6 (ἀδύνατον ... πάλιν ἀνακαινίζειν εἰς μετάνοιαν) has vexed many throughout the history of its interpretation. In our reading however, we submit that if a Two Ways catechetical context similar to that of the Didache stands behind Heb 6:1-6, the concept of irreversible apostasy will be seen in a different light. When the author of Hebrews wrote the warning in 6:1-6, he was not primarily addressing soteriological questions—especially those asked in post-Reformation contexts. Rather, the author primarily faced the overarching problem of a spiritual "failure to thrive" (Heb 5:12-14), arguing within the context of a first century Two Ways catechesis designed to move new converts from initiation toward

---

32. It is also possible that Heb 6:2 refers to the impartation of the Holy Spirit associated with baptism (Acts 8:17-18; 9:6; see Bruce, *Epistle to the Hebrews*, 142). The latter interpretation would then be parallel with being made "partakers of the Holy Spirit" in 6:4. This construal would be less likely, however, if a catechetical background similar to that of the Didache can be argued for Heb 6.

33. See section 3 above.

maturity. The same danger that is made explicit in Heb 10:26–27 and 12:16–17 is implicit in the warning in 6:1–6.³⁴

The author uses four descriptors to speak of members of the covenant community. The first is ἅπαξ φωτισθέντας. The author of Hebrews uses the verb φωτίζω in 10:32 to refer not to a state of spiritual enlightenment, but rather with reference to a concrete point of initiation into the faith: "But remember the former days in which after you were enlightened [φωτισθέντες] you endured a great conflict of suffering."³⁵ The concept of light was embedded in the pre-Christian Two Ways didactic pattern (Prov 4:18; 6:23; 13:9; 1QS III, 13; T. Ash. 5.2-3). And already in the Two Ways section of Barnabas, the author replaces "way of life" and "way of death" with the way "of light" (φῶς) and way "of darkness" (Barn. 18.1).³⁶ It should therefore not be surprising that φωτίζω, along with its synonyms, rather quickly became a widely used figure for a person's conversion through baptism.³⁷ For example, around 155 CE Justin Martyr wrote:

> And this washing [baptism] is called illumination [φωτισμός], as those who learn these things are illuminated [φωτιζομένων] in the mind. And he who is illuminated [ὁ φωτιζόμενος] is washed in the name of Jesus Christ, who was crucified under Pontius Pilate, and in the name of the Holy Spirit, who through the prophets foretold all the things about Jesus. (*Apol.* 1.61)³⁸

Though we must caution against anachronism, the widespread image of baptism as φωτισμός/φωτίζω in the early church must have had a prior history. It may very well be that the Two Ways catechesis behind

---

34. The important question of the relationship between Heb 6:1–6 and other warning passages in Hebrews will also be addressed further below.

35. See Attridge, who notes the Syriac translation, *qabeltun ma'muditha*, "receive baptism" (*Epistle to the Hebrews*, 298).

36. For a New Testament connection between baptism and new life, see, e.g., Col 2:12–13 and Rom 6:4. This imagery of new life or "regeneration" could very well have been derived from baptism as the point of one's conversion from the way of death to the way of life. Similarly, those communities like that of Barnabas that referred to the way of light and way of darkness could have quickly begun referring to baptism as "illumination" or "enlightenment."

37. PGL 1508–9.

38. Leslie W. Barnard, ed., *St. Justin Martyr: The First and Second Apologies*, ACW 56 (New York: Paulist, 1997), 67; Miroslav Marcovich, ed., *Iustini Martyris Apologiae pro Christianis*, PTS 38 (Berlin: de Gruyter, 1994).

Heb 6:1–6 was a possible source of initially equating baptism and illumination.[39] Indeed, in Did. 7.1 and 9.5, the act of baptism marked the beginning of the new convert's spiritual journey on the way of life— their transfer from the kingdom of darkness into the kingdom of light (see Acts 26:18; Rom 13:12; Eph 5:8; Col 1:13; 1 Pet 2:9). Therefore, the author of Hebrews refers to the one-time (ἅπαξ) experience of illumination (φωτίζω). In our reading, this refers to the converts' once-for-all initiation of baptism that followed the Two Ways catechetical instruction. Though illumination in general may be used in reference to a repeatable experience for believers (Eph 1:18), the illumination mentioned in Heb 6:4 refers to a once-for-all event (ἅπαξ), like baptism itself (Eph 4:5), or as Ernst Käsemann put it, "this enlightenment is related to a concrete action that can only be baptism."[40]

The second descriptor of members of the Christian community in Hebrews is γευσαμένους τε τῆς δωρεᾶς τῆς ἐπουρανίου. Some scholars take this metaphorically to mean a cognitive spiritual experience.[41] In our reading, however, the author of Hebrews referred to partaking in the eucharistic meal that followed baptism.[42] Joachim Jeremias holds that Heb 6:1–6, especially γεύεσθαι in Heb 6:4, refers to the Eucharist in an intentionally veiled manner so as not to profane the eucharistic words, which were meant only for the τέλειοι.[43] It is notable that not only is γεύομαι used to refer to physical tasting or partaking in New Testament literature (Matt 27:34; Luke 14:24; John 2:9; Acts 10:10; 23:14; Col 2:21), but it is also used more particularly in connection with Christians breaking bread together and sharing a meal on the first day of the week in Acts 20:11. Further, there seems to be a strong conceptual link between "tasted the

---

39. Hans Conzelmann suggests that water baptism is already in view in Heb 6:4 ("φῶς, φωτίζω, κτλ," *TDNT* 9:355).

40. See Käsemann, *Wandering People of God*, 187.

41. See, e.g., deSilva, *Perseverance in Gratitude*, 223–24; Attridge, *Epistle to the Hebrews*, 170.

42. This reading is also argued in Johannes Betz, *Die Realpräsenz des Leibes und Blutes Jesu im Abendmahl nach dem Neuen Testament*, vol. 2.1 of *Die Eucharistie in der Zeit der griechischen Väter* (Freiburg im Breisgau: Herder, 1961), 157. See also Paul Andriessen, "L'Eucharistie dans l'Épître aux Hébreux," *NRTh* 3 (1972): 269–77 (272); Bruce, *Epistle to the Hebrews*, 146; Geoffrey Wainwright, *Eucharist and Eschatology* (New York: Oxford University Press, 1981), 151–52.

43. Joachim Jeremias, *Die Abendmahlsworte Jesu* (Göttingen: Vandenhoeck & Ruprecht, 1967), 127, esp. n. 3.

heavenly gift" in Heb 6:4 and "you have graciously given to us spiritual food and drink" in Did. 10.3, along with the general tenor of the eucharistic prayers in Did. 9–10.[44]

The concept of eating and drinking the bread and wine of the Eucharist as partaking of a "gift" can be found in other early Christian writings. In *Smyrn.* 7.1, Ignatius of Antioch writes: "They [the docetists] abstain from eucharist and prayer, on account of not confessing the eucharist to be the flesh of our savior Jesus Christ, which suffered for our sins, which by goodness the Father raised up. Therefore, those speaking against the gift [δωρεά] of God, disputing, die." "False teachers" were failing to confess that the Eucharist was the flesh of the Savior and in their contentiousness they were "confessing against" the "gift of God," that is, against the Eucharist.[45] In this light, the eucharistic interpretation of the "heavenly gift" (δωρεά) of Heb 6:4 occurs among what can be regarded as a eucharistic expression.

Furthermore, if "illumination" in Heb 6:4 refers to the one-time initiation of baptism, then participation in the Eucharist would have been the natural experience of catechumens following that rite of initiation, since the Eucharist would have followed baptism in many situations.[46] In light of these considerations, we find it reasonable to understand γευσαμένους τε τῆς δωρεᾶς τῆς ἐπουρανίου in Heb 6:4 as a reference to partaking of the Eucharist as a part of postconversion Christian experience.

---

44. Johannes P. Louw and Eugene A. Nida list both δωρεά and χαρίζομαι under semantic domain 57: "possess, transfer, exchange" (*Introduction and Domains*, vol. 1 of *Greek-English Lexicon of the New Testament Based on Semantic Domains* [New York: United Bible Societies, 1988], 558–85). And ἐπουράνιος with πνευματικός may be considered semantically related under domain group 12: "supernatural beings and supernatural powers" (136–49).

45. See William R. Schoedel, *Ignatius of Antioch: A Commentary on the Letters of Ignatius of Antioch*, Hermeneia (Philadelphia: Fortress, 1985), 241.

46. The antecedent temporal participle in Did. 7.1 (προειπόντες) links the Two Ways tractate (1.1–6.3) in immediate temporal succession with the liturgical section (7–10). Furthermore, the form of doxology in 8.2 is also found in Did. 9.2, 3, 4 and 10.2, 4, 5 (ἁγιάζω and ῥύομαι are also found in both 8.2 and 10.5), binding these liturgical sections together conceptually. Thus, the Didache itself seems to indicate that the catechumen was instructed in the Two Ways tractate, followed by baptism and then Eucharist. See also n. 21 above.

Finally, many scholars understand παραπεσόντας as referring explicitly to apostasy.[47] Παραπίπτω, however, is a New Testament *hapax legomenon*, is not the normal word for apostasy, which more commonly would be ἀφίστημι.[48] It is used in this sense even by the author of Hebrews (3:12). The most literal understanding of παραπίπτω is not to apostatize from the faith, but "to fall beside."[49] Its use in this sense can be illustrated by Polybius, *Hist.* 3.54.5: "For the path down was narrow and precipitous, and the snow made it impossible for the men to see where they were treading, while to step aside from the path [παραπεσόν τῆς ὁδοῦ], or to stumble, meant being hurled down the precipices."[50]

The image here is that of a person wandering off a path, thus "falling aside." It does not suggest "falling away" from the faith per se but falling beside "a way" or path. Here we suggest that the Two Ways background of Heb 6:1–6 comes into play. Because the author and original readers of Hebrews already had a Two Ways catechetical background as part of their foundational Christian experience, the use of the verb παραπίπτω refers to a falling aside from the way of life or light toward maturity, not apostatizing from the faith *per se*. Though absolute apostasy similar to the conditions described in Heb 10:26–27 and 12:15–17 may remain implied, it is not the main thrust of παραπίπτω in Heb 6:6, which is that only those who resume their journey on the way of life will arrive at their destination. Implied is that those who do not resume their journey face death, as only Two Ways exist. This point, though implicit in 6:4–6, is explicit in

---

47. Attridge, *Epistle to the Hebrews*, 171. See also McKnight, "Warning Passages of Hebrews," 21–59.

48. See Luke 8:13; 13:27 (though in the sense of Jesus actively moving someone away from him); Acts 15:38 (Mark forsaking Paul); 1 Tim 4:1; Heb 3:12; Herm. Sim. 8.8.2; Irenaeus, *Haer.* 1.13.7. See also its usage in the LXX: Num 31:16; Deut 13:11; 32:15; Josh 22:19, 23; 1 Sam 28:15; 3 Kgdms 18:22; Jdt 13:14; 1 Macc 11:43; Odes Sol. 2:15; Isa 59:13; Jer 3:14; 17:5, 13; and Bar 3:8. See also LSJ 291.

49. BDAG 770. See Wis 6:9, where παραπίπτω refers to turning aside or going astray from wisdom, and Esth 6:10, which refers to "falling to the side" from a promise.

50. English translation from Evelyn S. Schuckburgh, trans., *The Histories of Polybius*, vol. 1 (London: Macmillan, 1889), 214. While this usage was clearly literal, Polybius also meant παραπίπτω in a metaphorical manner to refer to falling along the path of truth (see *Hist.* 12.12.2). This is actually quite similar to the sense we believe the author of Hebrews used παραπίπτω in 6:6. Even when used metaphorically, the image of falling beside a path or way is retained.

10:26–27 and especially in 12:15–17. Nonetheless, 12:15 and 6:9 show that the author remains hopeful about his immediate audience.

Read in this way, the referent of ἀδύνατον γὰρ ... πάλιν ἀνακαινίζειν εἰς μετάνοιαν in Heb 6 was not a person who lost their salvation and was therefore unable to regain it. Rather, in light of the Two Ways reading of Heb 6:4–6, the author of Hebrews was referring to the inability of baptized members of the community to return to their catechetical state and repeat their rite of initiation into the community.[51] The phrase πάλιν ἀνακαινίζειν εἰς μετάνοιαν thus refers not to repentance from an apostatized state to a state of grace, but to repeated baptism, πάλιν in 6:6 intentionally contrasted with ἅπαξ of 6:4. Just as repentance is associated with conversion and baptism in other early Christian literature,[52] repentance was associated with baptism in the Two Ways didactic pattern (Did. 9.5 and 10.6). Further, in Barn. 6.11, ἀνακαινίζω is used to refer to being made "new" through the forgiveness of sins in baptism, and Herm. Mand. 4.3.1 refers to the descent into the water and remission of sins as "repentance" (μετάνοια).

At this point, the final piece of the puzzle finds its place. Trying to return to the waters of baptismal initiation would have been tantamount to ἀνασταυροῦντας ἑαυτοῖς τὸν υἱὸν τοῦ θεοῦ καὶ παραδειγματίζοντας ("crucifying again the son of God and disgracing him publicly"). Baptism, of course, was connected to the death and the resurrection of Christ in the writings of Paul and in 1 Peter.[53] Paul's rhetorical question, "Or do you not know" (ἢ ἀγνοεῖτε), in Rom 6:3 implies that the interpretation of baptism as participation in the crucifixion of Christ was a Pauline innovation.[54] While Hebrews is neither Pauline nor Petrine, it does share a

---

51. "Patristic authors frequently took the pericope in this sense, as a rejection of the position of Cyprian, the Donatists, and the Meletians that heretics and apostates should be rebaptized" (Attridge, *Epistle to the Hebrews*, 167 n. 17). See also Epiphanius, *Pan.* 2.59. The recourse of those who had fallen away from the way of life was not to repeat their rite of initiation, but to resume their journey down the way of life. Implicitly, those who remain "lazy" (νωθροὶ; Heb 6:12) and refuse to resume their journey will find their end to be destruction and rejection (see Heb 10:26–27; 12:16–17).

52. See BDAG s.v. 2, esp. Acts 2:38; 13:24; *PGL* 856.

53. See Rom 6:1–11, where Christian baptism was linked with being united with Christ's death. See also Gal 2:20, where Paul declares that he had been "crucified with Christ." See 1 Pet 3:21, where the salvific benefits of baptism are wrought through the resurrection (δι' ἀναστάσεως) of Jesus Christ.

54. See Rudolf Bultmann, *Theology of the New Testament*, trans. K. Grobel, 2 vols. (Waco, TX: Baylor University Press, 2007), 1:141.

certain amount of common Christian tradition with Paul[55] and 1 Peter.[56] Moreover, Hebrews connects baptism with application of the sacrifice of Christ.[57] Thus it is not difficult to imagine how for the audience of Hebrews rebaptism could be spoken of metonymically as a recrucifixion of the Son of God. In the mind of the author of Hebrews, it seems this act would expose him to open shame.

The author of Hebrews was stating that it was impossible for the stagnant, dull, immature Christian (5:12–14) who had fallen to the side of the way of life to undergo catechesis and baptism a second time. That is, it was foolish for such a person to remain in a state no better than unbaptized catechumens, as if they could return to the waters of illumination and begin their walk on the way of life all over again. The only good option available to such a person was to get back on the path and resume a walk toward maturity, reversing the deviation from the way of life. Those who have strayed from the way of life will find themselves on the way of death, resulting in destruction. Although the author does not specifically describe the ultimate effect of falling aside from the way of life, the readers would likely have understood that a prolonged divergence from this path would result in severe consequences, described more fully and explicitly in major warning passages such as Heb 10:26–31 and 12:12–17.[58]

---

55. See C. P. Anderson, "Hebrews among the letters of Paul," *SR* 5 (1975–1976): 258–66; Johnson, *Hebrews*, 30. E.g., Johnson notes both Paul and Hebrews speak of Christ giving access to God (Heb 4:16; 10:19–22; Rom 5:1), both understand Jesus's faith as obedience (Heb 5:1–10; Rom 5:12–21), both ascribe an important position to Abraham (Heb 6:13–18; Gal 3:16–18), and his response of faith (Heb 11:8–12; Rom 4:1–25). See also Attridge, *Epistle to the Hebrews*, 6, 30.

56. See Ceslas Spicq, *L'Epître aux Hébreux*, 2 vols. (Paris: Gabalda, 1952-1953), 1:139–44. Johnson, *Hebrews*, 30; Attridge, *Epistle to the Hebrews*, 30–31. Attridge elucidates several points of parallel tradition.

57. Attridge, *Epistle to the Hebrews*, 30 n. 238.

58. The exhortation in Heb 6:1–6 takes a more positive form by encouraging advancement on the way of life without explicitly describing the consequences of straying from that path and returning to the way of death (see Heb 6:9–12), as the author does in Heb 10:26–27 and 12:16–17. In Heb 6, however, the author likely relies on the readers' implicit awareness of the consequences of returning to the way of death, much like those described in Did. 5.1–2 and Barn. 20.1–2. Barnabas especially spells out certain doom for the one who, "having knowledge of the way of righteousness, departs to the way of darkness" (Barn. 5.4). Barnabas specifically describes the way of darkness as "the way of eternal death with punishment, in which are things that destroy the soul" (Barn. 20.1; see also 21.1). For the original readers of Hebrews, an

6. Conclusion

We have argued in this essay that the author of Hebrews appears to be drawing on a Two Ways didactic pattern similar to that exampled in the Didache. This thesis dovetails nicely with the use of the Old Testament wilderness journey narrative in Heb 3:1–4:11, the warnings therein, and with Käsemann's understanding of journey as a primary motif in Hebrews.[59] We have argued that the author of Hebrews assumed knowledge of the Two Ways catechetical pattern. He assumed that they would readily remember their instruction in the way of life/light/truth and their subsequent baptism and participation in the Christian rites. Believing that some of his audience were failing to progress and develop as Christians, he reminds them that rebaptism, preceded by recatechesis, is not a viable option. Though his stance is more hopeful in this text (Heb 6:9), darker insinuations concerning failure are still to come in Heb 10:26–27 and 12:16–17. At bottom, when read in light of the Two Ways didactic pattern, the purpose of the author of Hebrews in Heb 6:1–6 is to warn the stagnant Christians of the impossibility of a second baptism, implicitly urging them to return to the Christian way of life.[60]

---

acute warning stood behind the exhortation of Heb 6, not unlike the harsher warnings throughout the book of Hebrews. See also 1QS IV, 14. Additionally, we must keep in mind that the exhortation to advance along the way of life in Heb 6 is part of a digression from the author's teaching concerning Melchizedek, set aside in Heb 5:10 and picked up again in Heb 7:1. The main purpose of this digression was to encourage the readers to wake from their dullness, reverse their failure to thrive, and press on toward maturity (5:11–14). One should therefore expect that such a digression from the main argument would contribute to the overall argument of Hebrews only in an indirect manner.

59. Käsemann, *Wandering People of God*. More recently, see Johnson, *Hebrews*, 7–9. If true, it could perhaps even be argued that the Two Ways catechesis provided one of the conceptual backdrops for the whole of Hebrews, energizing the journey/pilgrimage motif. Our conclusion also coincides nicely with the conclusion of Emmrich—perseverance and obedience is *sine qua non* in the Christian pilgrimage ("Heb 6:4–6—Again!" 94).

60. It is interesting to compare our conclusion with that of the fourth-century comments on Heb 6:4–6 of Ephrem the Syrian. In light of a Two Ways catechetical background to Heb 6:1–6, Ephrem's interpretation coheres well with our reading of Heb 6:4–6, albeit in a different ecclesiastical context, of course: "'It is impossible to restore again to repentance' through a second baptism 'those who have once been baptized, who have tasted the heavenly gift' through the medicine which they received

… but now 'have fallen away' again. Those who propose two baptisms ask for the crucifixion again of the Son of God and for his dishonor. But crucifixion was performed once and will not be performed once more, and baptism was conceded as an 'absolve' and is not conceded a second time to the sinner" (M. Conti, trans., *Hebrews*, ACCS 10 [Downers Grove, Ill.: InterVarsity Press, 2005], 84–85).

The Didache and Revelation

Alan J. P. Garrow

Is the Didache a matriarch, a great-niece, or a forgotten half-sister in relation to the New Testament? Elements of family resemblance suggest some form of relationship, but greater precision remains elusive. Most previous attempts to address this type of question have focussed understandably on the Didache's numerous and well known points in common with Matthew's Gospel. Despite the discussion of every possible interpretation of the evidence, however, opinion remains divided as to whether the Didache is a source for Matthew, dependent upon Matthew, or dependent on sources independently shared with Matthew.[1] One way to refresh the discussion is to approach it from an entirely different angle. This essay, accordingly, seeks to locate the Didache in terms of its relationship to Revelation, a text with affinities to the Didache in its ethics, eucharistic references, and eschatology.[2]

---

1. Christopher M. Tuckett, "Synoptic Tradition in the Didache," in *The Didache in Modern Research*, ed. Jonathan Draper, AGJU 37 (Leiden: Brill, 1996) is among those who see the Didache as dependent on Matthew. Clayton N. Jefford, *The Sayings of Jesus in the Teaching of the Twelve Apostles*, VCSup 11 (Leiden: Brill, 1989), esp. 91, 160–61, and Jonathan A. Draper, "The Jesus Tradition in the *Didache*," in Draper, *The Didache in Modern Research*, esp. 83, represent the majority view that both texts depend on a common source or sources. Alan J. P. Garrow, *The Gospel of Matthew's Dependence on the* Didache, JSNTSup 254 (London: T&T Clark, 2004) explores the possibility of Matthew's direct dependence on more ancient sections of the Didache (see also Jonathan A. Draper, "The *Didache*," in *The Writings of the Apostolic Fathers: An Introduction*, ed. Paul Foster (London: SPCK, 2007), 13–20.

2. Because of the composite nature of the Didache, the current study is strictly speaking concerned only with Revelation's relationship with specific ethical, eucharistic, and eschatological material in the Didache. Garrow (*Gospel of Matthew's Dependence*, 13–156) offers detailed consideration of compositional issues.

1. Ethics

That the Didache and Revelation share similar ethics is not especially surprising given that broadly speaking a common ethical base underlies most early Christian literature. They are distinctly similar, however, in their attitudes to eating food sacrificed to idols and the practice of sorcery.

In both the Didache and Revelation, eating food sacrificed to idols receives specific and pointed attention as an activity to be avoided at all costs. In Did. 6.2–3, this is articulated as the only requirement of the law where no compromise is permitted. In the messages to Pergamum and in particular Thyatira, eating food sacrificed to idols is held up as an ultimate betrayal (2:14, 20). All the churches are uniquely warned against this activity (2:23), while those who have resisted this temptation have no other burden laid on them (2:24).

The Didache and Revelation are also unusual in early Christian literature in their strong and explicit condemnation of sorcery and magic (Did. 2.2; 3.4; and Rev 9:21; 18:23; 21:8; 22:15).[3] In Rev 9:21, sorcery is condemned alongside murder, fornication and theft, a combination similar to that of murder, adultery, child abuse, fornication, theft, magic and sorcery in Did. 2.2. This is not to suggest that the lists of proscribed actions in Revelation and the Didache are necessarily directly related. It is to note, however, that their ethical attitudes are more closely related to one another than to any other early Christian text. In terms of illuminating the relationship between the Didache and Revelation this observation serves to indicate the likely presence of a relationship of some kind.

2. Eucharist

A striking set of parallels is noted by David Barr:

> Nearly every aspect of [Did. 9 and 10] is paralleled in the Apocalypse, but the concentration of elements in the closing scene is remarkable. There are no less than seven specific points of correlation with the final scene in the Apocalypse: (a) both mention David; (b) both say only some are worthy to participate; (c) both compare outsiders to "dogs"; (d) both

---

3. The only other mention of sorcery in the New Testament is in the vice list of Gal 5:20.

promise a drink of life; (e) both invite some to come; (f) both invite the Lord to come; (g) both close with Amen.[4]

Barr also identifies other connections between Revelation and the Didache's Eucharist:

> Numerous other correlations can be made with other parts of the Apocalypse as well: "We give you thanks" (*Did.* 9:1; Rev 11:17); "to you be glory unto the ages" (*Did.* 9:2; Rev 7:12, etc.); Jesus as the agent of revelation (*Did.* 9:3; Rev 1:1); plea for gathering of the church (*Did.* 9:4; Rev 7:1–10; 21:9–10); God said to "tabernacle" with humanity (*Did.* 10:3; Rev 21:3; 13:6); God addressed as "Almighty" (παντοκράτωρ: *Did.* 10:3; Rev 1:8; [4:8; 11:17; 15:3; 16:7,14; 19:6,15] 21:22; etc.); God said to "create all things" (*Did.* 10:3; Rev 4:11); the call to repentance (*Did.* 10:6; Rev 2–3). The Eucharistic service in the *Didache* also includes two themes that pervade the Apocalypse: the plea to deliver the church from all evil and perfect it in love (*Did.* 10:5), and the prayer "May grace come and may this world pass away" (*Did.* 10:6). This association of the Eucharist with the passing away of this world and the gathering of the church into the Kingdom is to be stressed.[5]

By highlighting these correlations while also drawing attention to the curious instruction at Did. 10.7 "but permit the prophets to give thanks [εὐχαριστεῖν] however they wish,"[6] Barr hints at the possibility that Revelation is an example of a prophet exercising such freedom to create an extended eucharistic prayer.

Barr's intimation is suggestive. Some form of link between Revelation and the Didache Eucharist[7] does seem likely. Meaningful precision about the nature of that relationship, however, requires believable

---

4. David L. Barr, "The Apocalypse of John as Oral Enactment," *Int* 40 (1986): 243–56 (254).

5. Ibid., 254–55.

6. Ibid., 254.

7. My own view, expressed in Garrow, *Gospel of Matthew's Dependence*, 13–28, is that Did 9–10 are two parallel and originally separate eucharistic prayers. See also Paul F. Bradshaw, *Reconstructing Early Christian Worship* (London: SPCK, 2009), 41–42. An important feature of this view relevant to the current discussion is that the reception of bread and wine is perceived as taking place after Did. 10.6. For a contrary view, see Dietrich-Alex Koch, "Die Eucharistischen Gebete von Didache 9 und 10 und das Rätsel von Didache 10:6," in *Jesus, Paul, and Early Christianity: Studies in Honour*

answers to two practical questions. First, how much of Revelation was performed on any given liturgical occasion? As Barr himself notes, "the length of the Apocalypse makes it unlikely that it was actually and repeatedly read aloud as part of a service. It would seem to take up the whole service."[8] This is not to say that it is impossible that the whole text was performed on each occasion, but it is to say that such an arrangement seems ungainly and, to that extent, implausible. Second, what was the relationship between hearing Revelation and physically receiving bread and wine? This question is generated by the observation that Revelation does not include any acts of thanksgiving over food or drink and so to this extent is unlikely to represent an equivalent act to that described in the Didache's eucharistic chapters.

The problem of the length of reading at each service may be solved by observing that Revelation's narrative regularly sets up conditions suitable for the creation of cliff-hanging installment breaks. For example, in Rev 5–7 the scroll of "what must soon take place," which only the Lamb may open, is sealed shut with seven seals. As each seal is broken the hearers (see 1:3) are brought closer and closer to accessing the scroll's contents directly.[9] A high point of suspense is generated, therefore, just before the final seal is broken: as the hearers stand on the brink of being able to "see" the contents of the scroll. These conditions are ideal for a cliff-hanging installment break, whereupon the audience must return to a future gathering to find out what happens next.

A similar pattern occurs as the narrative continues. Now that the seven seals are broken, the audience might reasonably expect at their next meeting to learn the contents of the Lamb's scroll. Instead, however, they are treated to a further series of announcements, this time in the form of trumpet blasts and woes (Rev 8–9). Eventually an angel declares (10:6, 7): "There will be no more delay, but in the days when the seventh angel is to blow his trumpet, the mystery of God will be fulfilled, as he announced to his servants the prophets." Up until now there has been a delay. When the seventh trumpet blows, however, the delay will be over. The seventh trumpet is blown at Rev 11:15. Surely now the contents of the scroll will be

---

of Henk Jan de Jonge, ed. Rieuwerd Buitenwerf, Harm W. Hollander, and Johannes Tromp (Leiden: Brill, 2008): 195–210.

8. Barr, "Apocalypse of John as Oral Enactment," 253.

9. Translations of the Didache are my own. Translations of Revelation are from the NRSV.

revealed to the expectant congregation? This point of heightened suspense is once again ideally suited for the insertion of a cliff-hanging installment break. The audience must return on a further occasion to hear how the story unfolds.

A further installment break between Rev 15:1–4 and 15:5–7 would explain a well-known curiosity in the flow of Revelation's narrative. Revelation 15:1 describes angels carrying the seven last plagues with which the wrath of God is ended. Just four verses *later*, these same angels emerge from the temple as if being introduced for the first time. They also receive the bowls that only moments previously they had already been described as holding. An installment break between these two appearances after 15:4 would explain this surprising arrangement. In this case, the installment would also end on a high point of suspense just as the final bowls of judgment are about to be poured out. The next installment would then open where the previous one had left off, with a description of the angels emerging from the temple and receiving the bowls of ultimate wrath.

In all, it is possible to identify a pattern of features that signal installment breaks after 3:22, 7:1, 11:18, 15:4, and 19:10, thus creating a text designed to be read in six separate installments (see appendix 1 at the end of this essay).[10] If Revelation was designed to be read in installments, then this removes the need to make the implausible suggestion that the whole text was read prior to a single Eucharist.

The second puzzle generated by Barr's proposal is not, however, immediately resolved by the installment theory. The question here is the functional relationship between the reading of Revelation and the receiving of bread and wine. Barr notes that "Nearly every aspect of [Did. 9–10] is paralleled in the Apocalypse."[11] Crucially, however, the one aspect that is notable by its absence is any kind of thanksgiving over the food or drink. This means that it is not possible simply to characterize the installments of Revelation as complete eucharistic prayers. At the same time, however, the parallels between the two texts do suggest that Revelation's installments relate in some way to Didache-style Eucharist. So far as the particular nature of that relationship is concerned, the following paragraphs seek to illustrate how each installment could serve as a "prophetic preface" to a conventional prayer of thanksgiving, such as those described in Did.

---

10. Alan J. P. Garrow, *Revelation*, NTR (London: Routledge, 1997), 14–53, offers a detailed presentation of this hypothesis.

11. Barr, "Apocalypse of John as Oral Enactment," 254.

9–10. In each case, the preface has the effect of charging the subsequent eating and drinking with a particular set of significances. Each preface also links into a following thanksgiving over bread and wine by picking up the language of the conventional prayer and/or by issuing an explicit invitation to the eschatological meal that follows.

2.1. Installment One: Rev 1:1–3:22

Links to the Didache Eucharist include the following: the description of God as Father (Rev 2:27; Did. 9.2, 10.2); God described as παντοκράτωρ (Rev 1:8; Did. 10.3); reference to the power and glory of God (Rev 1:6; Did. 9.2, 3, 4; 10.2, 4, 5); references to the kingdom and authority over the nations (Rev 1:6; 2:26, 27; 3:21; Did. 9.4; 10.5); the Lord's coming (Rev 1:4, 7, 8; Did. 10.6); reference to David (Rev 3:7; Did. 9.2; 10.6); calls to holiness (Rev 3:4, 7, 18; Did. 10.6); and repeated calls to repentance (Rev 2:5, 16, 21, 22; 3:3, 19; Did. 10.6). Most significantly, the installment concludes with an invitation to eat with Christ: "Listen, I am standing at the door, knocking. If you hear my voice and open the door, I will come in to you and eat with you and you with me" (Rev 3:20). This statement marks a moment of decision, an opportunity to choose between two groups identified in the preceding seven messages. On the one hand, there are those who follow Jezebel and Balaam whose infidelity, likened to fornication, is demonstrated by the eating of food sacrificed to idols (Rev 2:14, 20). On the other, there are those who endure faithfully and who will be rewarded, for example, with food from the tree of life (Rev 2:7) and the hidden manna (Rev 2:17).

2.2. Installment Two: Rev 4:1–8:1

This installment has a particularly large number of parallels to the Didache's eucharistic prayers. These include the following: numerous references to God's holiness (Rev 4:8; Did. 10.2); God described as παντοκράτωρ (Rev 4:8; Did. 10.3) and creator of everything (Rev 4:7–8, 11; Did. 10.3); repeated liturgical refrains giving power and glory to God (Rev 4:11; 5:12, 13; 7:12; Did. 9.2, 3, 4; 10.2, 4, 5); ingathering from every tribe, people, and nation to reign on earth (Rev 5:9; 7:9; 5:10; Did. 9.4; 10.5); and the requirement of holiness/the wearing of white robes for those who enter God's presence (Rev 7:9, 13, 14; Did. 10.6). Heard in a liturgical setting, the conclusion of this installment offers two opportunities to cement identification between the earthly hearers and their faithful heavenly counterparts. First, a closing hymn with which a congregation might also participate begins to break down the boundary between the world of the hearer and the world of the text. Second, the forthcoming reception of bread and wine will enable hearers to begin to participate in the feast enjoyed by those who, having been through the great tribulation, have access to the water of life and neither hunger nor thirst (Rev 7:16, 17).

2.3. Installment Three: Rev 8:1–11:18

Unlike the preceding installment, which focuses on the fate of those who make the right choices in terms of exclusive allegiance to Christ, this installment majors on the fate of those who make the opposite decision. As the installment comes to a close, the message is reinforced once again: God will ultimately be victorious and will reward those allied to him and punish those allied to other gods (Rev 11:15–18). The concluding hymn includes the promise of a coming kingdom (Rev 11:15; Did. 9.4; 10.5) and links to the following Eucharist with the phrase εὐχαριστοῦμέν σοι κύριε ὁ παντοκράτωρ (Rev 11:17; Did. 9.2, 3; 10.2, 3).

2.4. Installment Four: Rev 11:19–15:4

In this installment, the hearers are offered a clear choice between fidelity and infidelity to God. The consequences of infidelity are played out in the description of the blasphemous beast and those induced to worship him (Rev 13:3–8, 11–16; 14:7, 8, 10, 11). In counterpoint, there are two calls to fidelity (Rev 13:7; 14:12) matched with the benefits of such a decision (Rev 14:1–5, 13, 16). This contrast is also expressed in the harvest of grapes for the wine press of God's wrath (Rev 14:17–20) and the ingathering of his good grain (Rev 14:14–16; see Did. 9.4; 10.5). These two harvests provide the raw materials for the forthcoming eucharistic eating at which point the hearers have a further opportunity to confirm their allegiance to Christ. The concluding hymn leads into this participation by inviting the hearers to identify in song and in eating with those who have conquered the beast and his image (Rev 15:2). This song links to the Didache Eucharist by praising God as holy (Rev 15:4; Did. 10.2) and as παντοκράτωρ (Rev 15:3; Did. 10.3). At the close of the installment, as the hearers stand on the brink of the impending final judgments (Rev 15:1), they are reminded that the time to confirm their allegiance to Christ is now.

2.5. Installment Five: Rev 15:5–19:10

This installment is dominated by the perils of false allegiance. Those who fornicate with Babylon the whore will find themselves caught up in her destruction. A vehicle of such allegiance, also characterized as fornication, is the sharing of a common cup (Rev 17:2, 4; 18:3; see also 18:9). There is, however, an alternative to such fornication. The installment links to the following Eucharist by praising God as παντοκράτωρ (Rev 19:6; Did. 10.3) and with the invitation, "Blessed are those who are invited to the marriage supper of the Lamb" (Rev 19:9, see also 19:7). As in Did. 10.6, those who wish to participate in this imminent marriage supper must be "holy" or, in the language of Revelation, "clothed with fine linen, bright and pure" (Rev 19:8).

2.6. Installment Six: Rev 19:11–22:21

As noted at the start of this section, Barr recognizes a large number of parallels between the Didache Eucharist and the concluding chapters of Revelation. Reception of the bread and wine provides a final opportunity to receive the gift of the water of life and to demonstrate a readiness to receive the Lord at his imminent coming.

As noted above, there are two obvious objections to the idea that Revelation is in some sense an example of a prophet exercising the freedom offered by Did. 10.7: it is too long for practical use in a worship setting and does not contain thanksgivings over food and drink. These objections do not apply, however, if Revelation was read in installments that linked into thanksgivings over food and drink. It remains feasible, therefore, that the numerous connections between Did. 9–10 and Revelation are due after all to John's exercising of the privilege afforded to prophets by Did. 10.7.

3. Eschatology

A third set of connections between the Didache and Revelation occurs in their narration of the events of the end of time. Before attempting to consider these similarities, however, it is necessary to deal with an important preliminary issue: the lost ending of the Didache.

There is good reason to suppose that the manuscript of Bryennios (= the Jerusalem MS), which contains the only surviving direct record of the

Didache, is incomplete. This raises the question of the likely original form of the Didache's concluding apocalypse.[12] Clues as to the content of the missing lines may be found in Apos. Con. 7 and in the *Renunciation* of Boniface, which independently support a continuation of the narrative into a scene of final judgment and reward. This continuation in turn highlights the secondary nature of Did. 16.7.[13] After removing Did. 16.7, an analysis of the witness of Apos. Con. 7 and the *Renunciation* of Boniface establishes an initial case for the reconstruction of Did. 16.8b–9.[14]

> 16.3 For in the last days false prophets and corruption will be multiplied and sheep will turn into wolves and love will turn into hate.
> 16.4a For with the increase of lawlessness they will hate, persecute and betray one another.
> 16.4b And then will appear the world-deceiver as a son of God and he will do signs and wonders and the earth will be betrayed into his hands

---

12. Garrow, *Gospel of Matthew's Dependence*, 38–43, observes that the case for seeing the Didache as originally extending beyond 16.8a is supported by the need for a resolution of the conflict between the Lord and the world-deceiver, comparison with New Testament eschatological storylines, evidence from the punctuation and layout of the Jerusalem MS, and by comparison of the Jerusalem MS with the versions of Did. 16 preserved in the Apostolic Constitutions and Canons, the reported (and now lost) Georgian version of the Didache, and the eighth-century *Renunciation* of Boniface.

13. Kurt Niederwimmer, *The Didache: A Commentary*, trans. Linda M. Maloney, Hermeneia, (Minneapolis: Fortress, 1998), 46, 225 n. 27, and Garrow, *Gospel of Matthew's Dependence*, 38–44. If, as Robert E. Aldridge ("The Lost Ending of the *Didache*," VC 53 [1999]: 5–13), and Garrow (*Gospel of Matthew's Dependence*, 38–43) propose, the original text of Did. 16 continued into a description of a general judgment, then the secondary nature of Did. 16.7 becomes particularly apparent. In the face of a general judgment, the selective resurrection of the dead portrayed in Did. 16.7 generates a narrative anomaly. This aberration from the narrative flow of Did. 16 in combination with Did. 16.7's deviation from the style and structure of the surrounding text, all point towards its status as a later insertion. Possible motivations for this insertion are offered in Garrow, *Gospel of Matthew's Dependence*, 44, and Alan J. P. Garrow, "The Eschatological Tradition behind 1 Thessalonians: *Didache* 16," *JSNT* 32 (2009): 191–215 (202).

14. This reconstruction is taken from Garrow, *Gospel of Matthew's Dependence*, 44–64. It shares numerous features with that of Aldridge, "Lost Ending of the *Didache*," 1–15. Taking into account the necessarily speculative character of any reconstruction, one point may be affirmed with some confidence: the original form of the narrative is highly likely to have continued into a scene of judgment and reward.

and he will do godless things that have not been done since the beginning of the age.

16.5 Then human creation will pass into the fire of testing and many will fall away and perish but those who persevere in their faith will be saved by the curse itself.

16.6 And then shall appear the signs of truth first the sign of stretching out in heaven next the sign of the trumpet call and third the resurrection of the dead.

16.7 *not of all the dead, but, as it says, "the Lord shall come, and all the holy ones with him"*

16.8 Then the world will see the Lord coming upon the clouds of heaven … [and all the holy ones with him, on his royal throne, to judge the world-deceiver and to reward each according to his deeds.

16.9 Then the evil will go away to eternal punishment but the righteous will enter into life eternal inheriting those things which eye has not seen and ear has not heard and which has not arisen in the heart of man. Those things which God has prepared for those who love him.]

Having addressed the preliminary issue of the lost ending, it is possible to consider the correlations between this narrative and the story of "what must soon take place" as told by Revelation.[15]

3.1. Signs Preceding the Arrival of the World-Deceiver (Did. 16.3, 4a)

For in the last days false prophets and corruption will be multiplied and sheep will turn into wolves and love will turn into hate. For with the increase of lawlessness they will hate, persecute and betray one another.

The Didache expresses the conviction that one of the signs of the end will be an increase in false prophecy. The context indicates that these are people who arise from inside, rather than outside, the fold of Jesus's followers. They are sheep who turn into wolves.

This kind of character is also described in Revelation. In the messages to Pergamum and Thyatira, two church insiders acquire names designed to reveal their identity as false prophets: Balaam, "who put a stumbling block before the people of Israel" (Rev 2:14), and Jezebel, "who calls herself

---

15. Garrow's *Revelation* offers a detailed analysis of the story told by Revelation. According to John Sweet's review (*JTS* 49 [1998]: 940–41), reading Revelation in installments solves the disputed question of where the contents of the Lamb's scroll, the story of "what must soon take place," are located within the overall narrative.

a prophetess" (Rev 2:20). "The false prophet" is a name also attributed to the second beast (Rev 13:11–17) when it reappears in Rev 19:20. This beast is described as having two horns "like a lamb," even while it speaks like a dragon (Rev 13:11), a description that might also be taken as suggesting that, while the beast has the appearance of innocently belonging to the Lamb, it is in reality a traitor to that cause.[16]

3.2. The Appearance of the World-Deceiver (Did. 16.4b)

> And then shall appear the world-deceiver as a son of God and he will do signs and wonders and the earth will be betrayed into his hands and he will do godless things that have not been done since the beginning of the age.

The antichrist, as witnessed for example in 2 Thess 2:3–12 and 1 John 2:18, is a central figure in the mainstream Christian apocalyptic tradition from the earliest period. In their descriptions of this character, the Didache and Revelation share a number of distinctive features: his influence is global (Rev 13:3, 7, 8; see also 13:12, 14); he has divine pretensions (Rev 13:1, 5, 6, 8); and he performs deceptive miracles (Rev 13:3; see also 13:13, 14). Further, as the narrative progresses, he engenders persecution (see below).

3.3. The Test Engendered by the World-Deceiver (Did. 16.5)

> Then human creation will pass into the fire of testing and many will be caused to stumble and lost but those who persevere in their faith will be saved by the curse itself [σωθήσονται ὑπ' αὐτοῦ τοῦ καταθέματος].

At this point it is necessary to consider the meaning of the obscure phrase σωθήσονται ὑπ' αὐτοῦ τοῦ καταθέματος. The great majority of scholars favor "saved by the accursed one himself," as in "saved by Christ himself."[17] If correct, this interpretation represents a significant disjunction between

---

16. Garrow (*Revelation*, 88–91) presents a case for seeing the second beast/false prophet as a pseudo-Christian rather than pagan figure.

17. For discussions of the mainstream position see, for example, Niederwimmer, *Didache*, 221–22; Aaron Milavec, "The Saving Efficacy of the Burning Process in *Didache* 16.5" in *The* Didache *in Context: Essays on Its Text, History and Transmission*, ed. Clayton N. Jefford, NovTSup 77 (Leiden: Brill, 1995), 139–142; Nancy Pardee, "The Curse that Saves (*Didache* 16.5)," in Jefford, *The* Didache *in Context*, 157;

the Didache and Revelation. In Revelation the highly unusual word κατάθεμα is used to assure hearers that in the New Jerusalem there will no longer be any curse (22:3). On this occasion, therefore, it is impossible that κατάθεμα could be a reference to "Christ."

While the traditional interpretation of the Didache's καταθέματος counts against a link with Revelation, the association between "curse" and Christ has an extremely fragile basis. First, there is no evidence to suggest that "the curse" was ever or could ever have been a reverent title for Christ. More particularly, even if in some very remarkable circumstance Jesus was known by this name, it is unclear why "Lord" would not have been preferable in Did. 16.5. "Those who persevere in their faith shall be saved by the Lord himself" more than adequately expresses the meaning favored by those who see "the curse" as a reference to Jesus.

The popularity of the view that καταθέματος refers to Christ, despite the awkwardness of this interpretation, may be attributed to the lack of credible alternative. Aaron Milavec,[18] however, observes that the burning process (Did. 16.5a) has the power both to save and to destroy, much as a furnace reveals the pure metal from amidst the dross.[19] The fact that the burning process immediately follows the arrival of the world-deceiver suggests the possibility that τὸ κατάθεμα refers not to Christ, but to the persecution engendered by the world-deceiver. During this persecution some fall away and are lost, but others by their perseverance prove their faith true and thereby are saved.[20]

This reading, rather than creating a disjunction with Revelation, creates three points of connection between the two texts. First, the association between faithful endurance and consequent salvation coheres with Revelation's repeated affirmation of the same correlation (Rev 2:10; 3:9–10; 6:9–10; 7:14–17; 12:11; 20:4; 21:7).[21] Second, Revelation and the Didache both closely associate the coming persecution with the advent of the beast/

---

and Hans Reinhard Seeliger, "Considerations on the Background and Purpose of the Apocalyptic Conclusion of the Didache," in Draper, Didache *in Modern Research*, 379.

18. Aaron Milavec, "Saving Efficacy of the Burning Process," 131–55.

19. This interpretation was first proposed in the unpublished doctoral dissertation of Jonathan Draper and is discussed further by him in "Resurrection and Zechariah 14.5 in the Didache Apocalypse," *JECS* 5 (1997): 154–79 (155–56).

20. Garrow, *Gospel of Matthew's Dependence*, 29–38 provides a fuller account of this exegetical debate.

21. This logic is also expressed by Mark 13:9–13; Luke 21:19; Matt 10:22; 24:13; 2 Thess 1:4–6; 1 Pet 4:12–13.

world-deceiver (Rev 13:7; see also 13:10). Third, as already noted, they both share the very rare term κατάθεμα. Revelation 22:3 otherwise appears to allude to Zech 14:11 (LXX), where the more common term ἀνάθεμα is used. This raises the question of Revelation's motive for replacing ἀνάθεμα with κατάθεμα. Given that Did. 16.5 is the only other recorded use of the term in the relevant literature,[22] it is credible that Did. 16.5 provided the motivation for this change. If the Didache's καταθέματος was understood as referring to the ultimate persecution, then there is every reason for Revelation to assure its readers that in the New Jerusalem there will no longer be any κατάθεμα.

3.4. Signs Announcing the Coming of the Lord (Did. 16.6)

> And then shall appear the signs of truth first the sign of spreading out in heaven next the sign of the trumpet call and third the resurrection of the dead.

The meaning of ἐκπετάσεως ἐν οὐρανῷ is very obscure. Read literally, the sign is of a "spreading out" in heaven, but scholars are divided as to how this might be rendered as a visible sign. Kurt Niederwimmer discusses three alternatives:[23] (1) An opening in the heavens as a precondition for the following descent of the Lord and his holy ones. A difficulty with this proposal is that, if this were the intention, it is not clear why ἐκπετάσεως τοῦ οὐρανοῦ was not preferred. (2) A cross in the heavens, as witnessed, for example, in Apoc. Pet. 1 (Ethiopic): "so shall I come on the clouds of heaven with a great host in my glory; with my cross going before my face will I come in my glory." This option has the advantage of examples in the later tradition. If this were the intention, however, it is unclear why such an obscure description of the cross was used. (3) The standard of the Son of Man in the form of banners spread out in the heavens. This suggestion more readily reflects the sense of "spreading out" than the preceding options, but is more difficult to detect in the tradition.[24]

---

22. κατάθεμα occurs only in Revelation and Didache in first century Christian literature. Niederwimmer, *Didache*, 221–22 lists seven later occurrences. See also Pardee, "Curse that Saves," 158.

23. Niederwimmer, *Didache*, 223–24.

24. A reference to the Lord stretching out his hand, as in Isa 11:1, is a further possibility; see Garrow, "Eschatological Tradition," 208.

When it comes to considering how this sign might have been represented by Revelation, there are two possibilities. First, the concept of an enlarging opening in heaven may be reflected in John's reference to an "open door in heaven" in Rev 4:1, which develops through the sequence of installment "openings" until John sees οὐρανὸν ἠνεῳγμένον in Rev 19:11. The second possibility is that the action of "stretching out" refers not to banners, but to a scroll being opened and stretched out in the heavens. The "spreading out" of the Lamb's scroll is, of course, an important element in Revelation's narrative. Further, it is immediately followed by an equivalent to the Didache's second sign, the trumpet call, in Revelation's sequence of seven trumpets (Rev 8:6, 8, 10, 12; 9:1, 13; 11:15). The Didache's third sign, the resurrection of the dead, has a more complex relationship with Revelation's narrative. Revelation does include a description of the resurrection of the dead (Rev 21:13–14), but this description is placed alongside the account of the general judgment (Rev 20:12; see also Did. 16.8b).[25]

3.5. The Arrival of the Lord (Did. 16.8a)

> Then the world shall see the Lord coming upon the clouds of heaven and all his holy ones with him, on his royal throne.

Revelation 1:7 demonstrates an awareness of the expectation that the Lord will come "on the clouds." In Rev 19:11 he is described as riding on a white horse. Both texts agree, if the independently reconstructed ending of the Didache is correct, that the Lord is accompanied by faithful followers. Revelation's equivalent to the Didache's "holy ones" is the accompanying army of riders who wear fine linen white and clean (Rev 19:14). A parallel to the Didache's "royal throne" may be present in Revelation's thrones of reign and judgment (Rev 20:4, 11).

---

25. Revelation refers to more than one resurrection and then not altogether straightforwardly. On the one hand, the martyrs are apparently caught up at a relatively early stage to join the heavenly army on Mount Zion (14:1–5; see also 11:12). At the same time, however, this group appears to enjoy a form of resurrection after the Messiah's return (20:4–5). So far as the general resurrection is concerned, the sequence is also curiously presented. When the throne is set up in Rev 20:11, the dead might be taken as already resurrected (20:12). The description of general resurrection is delayed, however, until the two verses that follow (20:13–14).

3.6. The Consequences of the Lord's Arrival (Did. 16.8b–9)

> to judge the world-deceiver and to reward each according to his deeds. Then the evil will go to eternal punishment but the righteous will enter into life eternal inheriting those things which eye has not seen and ear has not heard and which has not arisen in the heart of man. Those things which God has prepared for those who love him.

In both the Didache and Revelation, the Lord returns for judgment. Both texts specifically mention the judgment of the world-deceiver/beast (Rev 19:20–21; Did. 16.8b), and both texts also specify that each will be rewarded according to their actions/deeds (Rev 20:12, 13; Did. 16.9). The Didache is succinct in its description of the rewards and punishments in prospect. It describes them as "eternal" in both cases and elaborates with regard to the inheritance prepared for the righteous to the extent that they are beyond anything previously experienced or imagined. Revelation also uses the image of God preparing an inheritance for the righteous in its more extensive description of their eternal destiny (Did. 16.8b–9; Rev 21:1–22:5, esp. 21:2, 7).

What is striking about this set of comparisons is that Revelation echoes every major element of the Didache's presentation and does so in a greatly elaborated form. This suggests not only that Did. 16.3–6, 8–9 and Revelation belong to a common stream of eschatological tradition, but also that Revelation falls later in that stream than does the Didache.

4. The Didache's Relationship to Revelation

The preceding observations about the similarities between the Didache and Revelation indicate the likelihood of some form of relationship between the two texts. Further, Revelation's much more elaborate forms suggest that it falls later in the stream of developing tradition than does the Didache. A credible assessment of the more precise relationship between the two texts must explain, however, not only their similarities but also their marked differences. Critical to such an explanation is Did. 10.7: "allow the prophets to give thanks as much as they wish." It is this advice that explains how it is possible that the Didache's simple instructions regarding the Eucharist could be combined with its very brief eschatological narrative to create the extraordinary book of Revelation.[26] On this basis, I conclude not merely that the Didache predates Revelation, but that the Didache's eucharistic and eschatological patterns provided the creative fountainhead out of which Revelation was born.[27]

5. The Didache's Relationship to the New Testament

As well as having implications for the study of Revelation, the above conclusion has implications for the Didache's placement in relation to the wider New Testament. The Didache shares points of connection with almost every strand of New Testament tradition. In addition to the well-known connections with Matthew's Gospel and those with Revelation outlined above, such links include Mark 13:26–27 and Did. 16.8;[28] Luke 6:27–36 and Did. 1.2–5;[29] John's Gospel and Did. 9–10;[30] Acts 15:23–29 and Did. 6.1–3;[31] Rom 12:14, 16, 20, 13:9, 10 and Did. 1.2–4; 1 Cor 2:9 and Did. 16.9;[32] 1 Thess 4:15–17 and Did. 16.3–6, 8–9;[33] James and the Didache;[34] and 1 Pet 2:11, 3:9, 4:12 and Did. 1.4, 1.3, 16.5. This very broad pattern of association suggests either that the Didache was written at a relatively late date in the light of several other texts or that it was written so early as to belong to the shared heritage of several divergent traditions.

---

26. Barr ("Apocalypse of John as Oral Enactment," 253–54) notes the close relationship between apocalypse and Eucharist: "The Eucharist—like the Apocalypse itself—looks back to the death of Jesus and forward to the messianic banquet in the Kingdom of God. An apocalypse is a dramatic portrayal of the coming of the Kingdom of God; Eucharist is an active celebration of the coming of that Kingdom. What the Apocalypse does in word, the Eucharist does in deed; it is the myth that corresponds to the ritual."

27. Revelation is commonly dated to either ca. 95 CE or 68–69 CE. Garrow (*Revelation*, 66–79) discusses the weaknesses of both options, while also making a positive case for 80–81 CE.

28. Garrow, *Gospel of Matthew's Dependence*, 191–96.

29. Ibid., 224–27.

30. Johannes Betz, "The Eucharist in the *Didache*," in Didache *in Modern Research*, 249, 255–56.

31. Clayton N. Jefford, "Tradition and Witness in Antioch: Acts 15 and Didache 6," in *Perspectives on Contemporary New Testament Questions: Essays in Honor of T.C. Smith*, ed. Edgar V. McKnight (Lewiston: Mellen, 1992), 86–88.

32. Garrow, *Gospel of Matthew's Dependence*, 196.

33. Garrow, "Eschatological Tradition."

34. See the papers collected in Huub van de Sandt and Jürgen K. Zangenberg, eds. *Matthew, James, and Didache: Three Related Documents in Their Jewish and Christian Settings*, SBLSymS 45 (Atlanta: Society of Biblical Literature, 2008).

If, as this paper concludes, the Didache's eucharistic and eschatological traditions were the fountainhead from which Revelation was born, then this has the corollary effect of increasing the likelihood that the Didache deserves to be regarded, not as a granddaughter or half-sister in relation to the New Testament, but as its matriarch.

APPENDIX 1: CRITERIA FOR REVELATION'S INSTALLMENT BREAKS (see Garrow, *Revelation*, 50–51)

Break after:	3:22	8:1 (reopening 8.1)	11:18	15:4	19:10
Suspense at end of installment	Must wait for description of "what must soon take place"	Must wait for scroll's contents (now unsealed)	Must wait for scroll's contents (no more announcements)	Must wait for final bowls to be emptied	Must wait for Armageddon and messianic supper
Use of ἀνοίγω	4:1 After this I looked and there in heaven a door stood open	8:1 When the Lamb opened the seventh seal	11:19 Then God's temple in heaven was opened	15:5 After this … the temple of the tent of witness in heaven was opened	19:11 Then I saw heaven opened
Action derived from heaven	4:1	8:1	11:19	15:5	19:11
Signs of the coming of God (see Exod 19)	4:5 Lightning, rumblings, thunder	8:5 Thunder, rumblings, lightning, earthquake	11:19 Lightning, rumblings, thunder, earthquake, heavy hail	15:8 Smoke fills the temple	19:11 The messianic rider arrives
Closing hymn	2:7, 11, 17, 29; 3:6, 13, 22	7:15–17	11:17–18	15:3–4	19:6–8
Final outcome picture	2:7, 10, 17, 26–28; 3:5, 12, 21	7:9–17	11:15–18	15:2–4	19:6–9
Length: ((1:1–3:22) 1,811 words	(4:1–8:1) 1,620 words	(8:1–11:18) 1,728 words	(11:19–15:4) 1,729 words	(15:5–19:10) 2,055 words	(19:11–22:21) 1,928 words

The Didache as a Source for the Reconstruction of Early Christianity: A Response

D. Jeffrey Bingham

Allow me to begin this response with a brief review of the theses of the foregoing papers. First, we review the work of Matti Myllykoski. His primary concern is the early history of the Didache's development and the changing ethnic and ethical identity of its community, which he analyzes in terms of the Two Ways treatise, the apocalypse of Did. 16, the prohibition to eat meat offered to idols, and the question of perfection within the developing community. He sets forth that:

> In my presentation I have tried to argue for the following theses and conclusions:
> (1) The Apostolic Decree in Acts 15:20, 29 does not go back to a formal decision of an apostolic meeting, but to a tradition known by Luke.
> (2) The Two Ways treatise in Did. 1–5 originated in Jewish Christian circles.
> (3) The short Jewish Christian apocalypse in Did. 16 is a piece added to the Two Ways treatise immediately after the sentence in the plural in 5.2. It stems from the situation of the Jewish War.
> (4) The following addition Did. 6.1 (and Doctr. 6.1) is influenced by the seductive topic of the apocalypse, but its original form in the Didache indicates that it targeted people who taught about faith without the Law, that is, to Paulinists.
> (5) In the next stage of the literary development of the Didache, the Jewish War already lay in the past and the treatise is more and more extended to gentile Christians. Next, the prohibition of idol meat is added in 6.2–3 after 6.1. The bearing of the whole yoke of the Lord, both the ethical and ritual Law, is presented to the gentiles as perfection. But at the same time, these verses are concessive: not all believers can or must be perfect. Only eating idol meat is expressly prohibited.

(6) Bearing the entire yoke of the Lord as a sign of perfection in Did. 6.2 points to those who fulfill not only the Decalogue, but also the ritual law. These people have special dignity in mixed communities. Corresponding to the concessive tone of the prohibition in Did. 6.2 reflects a situation in which the "perfect" Christian teachers have full authority to interpret the prohibition in these communities. The same also applies to the four statutes that Luke lists in Acts 15:29 as the so-called Apostolic Decree.[1]

Taras Khomych's interest is a contrast between Paul and the Didache on the subject of εὐαγγέλιον. He seeks thereby to demonstrate an aspect of diversity within early Christianity. He argues that:

Whereas in the Pauline epistles εὐαγγέλιον refers primarily to the death and resurrection of Jesus, the Didache is notably silent about these events, focusing instead on the Lord God and mentioning Jesus as God's servant. In other words, Paul's gospel features above all a message of salvation in/through Christ, a christologically-centered soteriology. In comparison to Paul, the message of the Didache is more theocentric and focused on ethics. These differences between the Pauline letter and the Didache should be interpreted in the light of the respective views on Jesus and his mission in both writings. In his epistles, Paul elaborates an exalted Christology, presenting Jesus as God's Christ, Savior, and the Lord. This perspective is evidently missing in the Didache, which envisages Jesus as God's παῖς, who revealed the will of the Lord God. The two types of teachings probably co-existed in the same period, although obviously in different communities/milieus. The evidence of the Didache, remarkably different from that of the Pauline Epistles, yields invaluable information about the origins of Christianity.[2]

The claim of Matthew Larsen and Michael Svigel relates to a didactic pattern common in the first century. They argue that:

The first-century Two Ways catechetical pattern forms the background of Heb 6:1-6, demonstrated through compelling conceptual parallels between the Didache and Heb 6:1-2. Consequently, in our reading,

---

1. See in the present volume, Matti Myllykoski, "Without Decree: Pagan Sacrificial Meat and the Early History of the Didache," 453.

2. See in the present volume, Taras Khomych, "Another Gospel: Exploring Early Christian Diversity with Paul and the Didache," 476.

παραπίπτω in Heb 6:6 does not refer to irreversible apostasy, but to a failure to advance on the way of life from the level of catechumen to teacher (5:12–14).... Believing that some of his audience were failing to progress and develop as Christians, he reminds them that rebaptism, preceded by recatechesis, was not a viable option.... At bottom, when read in light of the Two Ways didactic pattern [which the author assumes his audience received in catechesis], the purpose of the author of Hebrews in Heb 6:1–6 is to warn the stagnant Christians of the impossibility of a second baptism, implicitly urging them to return to the Christian way of life.[3]

Finally, we revisit the essay by Alan Garrow that treats the relationship of the book of Revelation and the Didache to a developing early Christian tradition. His thesis is as follows:

Revelation's much more elaborate forms suggest that it falls later in the stream of developing tradition than does the Didache. A credible assessment of the more precise relationship between the two texts must explain, however, not only their similarities but also their marked differences. Critical to such an explanation is Did. 10.7: "allow the prophets to give thanks as much as they wish." It is this advice that explains how it is possible that the Didache's simple instructions regarding the Eucharist could be combined with its very brief eschatological narrative to create the extraordinary book of Revelation. On this basis, I conclude not merely that the Didache predates Revelation, but that the Didache's eucharistic and eschatological patterns provided the creative fountainhead out of which Revelation was born.[4]

My response to these essays is ultimately aimed at focusing our attention on issues important to the reconstruction of early Christianity. Allowing these chapters to inform us as to their interests, we will then move to examining how their theses open up larger themes within the superstructure of ancient Christianity. I will concentrate upon four issues raised by these papers that are central to the task of reconstructing elements of that superstructure. After summarizing the four basic claims of our authors, we will give our attention to the problem of unity and diversity, the relationship of early Christianity to its Jewish heritage, the fundamental role

---

3. See in the present volume, Matthew Larsen and Michael Svigel, "The First Century Two Ways Catechesis and Hebrews 6:1–6," 495.
4. See in the present volume, Alan J. P. Garrow, "The Didache and Revelation," 513.

of liturgy within its development, and finally the manner in which it read texts, its hermeneutics.

Four broad arguments emerge from these papers: (1) the diverse ways in which the same evolving Christian community embraced the same received tradition in different phases of its ethnic and social makeup (Myllykoski); (2) the existence of simultaneous (Paul's and the one evidenced in the Didache), but conceptually different versions of the gospel, one focused on Jesus's death and resurrection, the other upon Jesus as the servant who reveals the Lord God (Khomych); (3) the presence of a first-century Two Ways catechetical pattern influencing both the Didache and Hebrews (Larsen and Svigel); and (4) the early development of a Christian tradition evident in the Didache's earlier eucharistic and eschatological patterns and Revelation's later, dependent, more elaborate teachings (Garrow).

1. Unity and Diversity

Both Myllykoski and Khomych develop within their papers the theme of diversity within Christian antiquity. For Myllykoski, the developing community about which he informs us displays and is permitted different concepts of perfection, different senses of obligation to the Mosaic law, different interpretations of the yoke of the Lord Jesus.[5] In Khomych's mind, "the evidence of the Didache, remarkably *different* from that of the Pauline epistles, yields invaluable information about the origins of Christianity" (emphasis added).[6] However, this collection of papers also indicates significant unity in late first-century Christianity, at least in those communities represented by the texts under consideration. Even though each stage of the changing ethnic structure of Myllykoski's mixed community embraces certain teachings differently (and it may have been read differently), still, for each stage the yoke of the Lord Jesus, the Mosaic law, and the apocalyptic language of the apocalypse are the subjects at issue and all have application to various constituencies within the community.[7] Along the same lines, although different aspects of the acts and character of Jesus may be emphasized in Khomych's portrayal of Paul and the Didache's gospel proclamation and although he sees a christological-theological contrast, the gospel, in the material of both, concerns Jesus. And,

---

5. Myllykoski, "Without Decree," 446.
6. Khomych, "Another Gospel," 476.
7. Myllykoski, "Without Decree," 446.

of course, Larsen and Svigel demonstrate a common Two Ways tradition passed on through catechesis, while Garrow suggests a link between the worship and future expectation of the Didache community and that of Revelation. Pointing out such commonality, no matter how small, in the contemporary scholarly atmosphere, is not done without inviting controversy. It seems that since Walter Bauer published his paradigm-shaping book, *Orthodoxy and Heresy in Earliest Christianity*,[8] and the studies of those who have followed his thesis, the prejudice has been for recognizing diversity. Although I could duplicate more recent sentiments, it seems, without end, I note here only Rudolph Bultmann's words as an early, but poignant example of the bias:

> Hellenistic Christianity is no unitary phenomenon, but, taken by and large, a remarkable product of syncretism. It is full of tendencies and contradictions, some of which were to be condemned later on by orthodox Christianity as heretical. Hence also the struggles between the various tendencies, of which the Pauline Epistles give such vivid impression.[9]

The history of the study of development and diversity within early Christianity is not free from metaphysical conceptions, and Bauer and Bultmann were similarly imprisoned. No one merely goes wherever the data leads. One's metaphysic helps to lead the data. Some have been upfront about their metaphysical bias, others less so. Two contrasting examples come to mind. Each states clearly their metaphysical orientation, a step lacking in many such studies, which attempt to keep alive a myth of complete detachment and objectivity. On the one hand, I mention the work of James Robinson and Helmut Koester, *Trajectories through Early Christianity*. For them, the problem with New Testament scholarship is its metaphysics and the integration of its metaphysics into its historiography. They believe that a shift from "essentialist" to "historic" metaphysics is required.[10] In this vein they wrote:

---

8. Walter Bauer, *Orthodoxy and Heresy in Earliest Christianity*, trans. Robert A. Kraft and Gerhard Krodel (Philadelphia: Fortress, 1971); trans. of *Rechtgläubigkeit und Ketzerei im ältesten Christentum*, 2nd ed., BHT 10 (Tübingen: Mohr Siebeck, 1964).

9. Rudolf Bultmann, *Primitive Christianity in Its Contemporary Setting*, trans. R. H. Fuller (London: Thames & Hudson, 1956), 177; trans. of *Das Urchristentum im Rahmen der antiken Religionen* (Zürich: Artemis, 1949).

10. James M. Robinson and Helmut Koester, *Trajectories through Early Christianity* (Philadelphia: Fortress, 1971). Four of the essays were published previously (1964–

> The traditional static, substantial, essence/accidence-oriented metaphysics which gave our inherited categories their most basic form [needs to be replaced] with a dynamic, historic, existence/process-oriented new metaphysics, in terms of which a whole table of restructured categories may be envisaged.[11]

Robinson and Koester acknowledge the benefits of "modern historicism," but they are unhappy with the manner in which it is being practiced; they wish to drive it toward a dynamic metaphysics.[12]

On the other hand is Andreas Kostenberger and Michael Kruger's, *The Heresy of Orthodoxy*. They argue, layer by layer, for the failure of the Bauer thesis and its contemporary resurgence. For them, it fails to account reliably for the history of communities, texts, and ideas that flourished in the era of early Christianity. But, more than that, they set forth a self-conscious, distinctive historiography. Kostenberger and Kruger contend for an "anti-supernatural bias in Bauer's historical method."[13] In turn, they state that such a prejudice "underscores the importance of using the proper philosophical grid in the study of Christian origins. In the end, arriving at the truth of the matter is not just a matter of sifting through data, but of making sense of the data in light of one's worldview."[14] They conclude, then, "that the Bauer-Ehrman thesis is wrong not just because these scholars' *interpretation of the data* is wrong, but because their interpretation proceeds *on the basis of a flawed interpretive paradigm*."[15]

Here, I wish to draw our attention quickly to their third chapter. I found the argument of this chapter on the New Testament especially helpful, because it presented a claim concerning early Christian doctrine that I believe we can also make for the years immediately following the apostolic

---

1971) to their appearance in the book, while the introduction is an enlarged version of an earlier publication. Only the final three chapters/essays are original to the volume. See also Helmut Koester, "The Theological Aspects of Primitive Christian Heresy," in *The Future of Our Religious Past: Essays in Honour of Rudolph Bultmann*, ed. James M. Robinson, trans. C. E. Cariston and R. P. Scharlemann (New York: Harper & Row, 1971), 65–83.

11. Robinson and Koester, *Trajectories the Early Christianity*, 9.

12. Ibid., 2, 5, 9.

13. Andreas Kostenberger and Michael Kruger, *The Heresy of Orthodoxy* (Wheaton, IL: Crossway, 2010), 101.

14. Ibid., 101.

15. Ibid., 101, emphasis original.

ones. Our authors note that "Bauer surprisingly neglected the New Testament data itself" as he investigated the question of the diversity of early Christianity and whether orthodoxy preceded heresy.[16]

Chapter three argues that the New Testament itself "bears credible and early witness to the unified doctrinal core, in particular with regard to christology, centered on Jesus and his apostles, a core that is, in turn, grounded in Old Testament messianic prophecy."[17] This christological core is manifested in the apostolic and early Christian preaching, early Christian liturgical material, and early theological language all of which centers around the death, burial, and resurrection of Jesus in concurrence with Old Testament expectation. Together these witnesses testify to an early, doctrinally unified New Testament Christianity that not only finds common voice in Jesus and his apostles, but which is also in harmony with the Hebrew Scriptures.[18] This chapter also provides a discussion that recognizes and defines a "legitimate diversity" in the New Testament, a diversity that does not compromise a unified doctrinal core in the collection of different documents, but that recognizes the different, but reconcilable language and perspectives of different human authors.[19]

The reconstruction of early Christianity definitely involves investigation of aspects of continuity and diversity as well as the analysis of concepts like heresy and orthodoxy. But this analysis is complicated (or simplified) by the scholar's presuppositions concerning metaphysics and historiography. It is not a simple issue, and I fear that some theses have, at times, been accepted less than critically. These chapters we are discussing help us appreciate the complexity that faces us.

---

16. Ibid., 17.
17. Ibid., 81.
18. Ibid., 81.
19. Ibid., 81–101. See, for another, earlier treatment of both unity and diversity in the New Testament, James D. G. Dunn, *Unity and Diversity in the New Testament: An Inquiry into the Character of Earliest Christianity* (Philadelphia: Westminster, 1977). Dunn argues that the unity concerns the affirmation that the man Jesus is the risen Lord while the diversity concerns the differences between Jewish, Hellenistic, apocalyptic, and Catholic Christianity.

2. Jewish Heritage

Two of the essays under review also help us appreciate the way certain Jewish material underwent development in early Christianity. On the one hand, the heritage and traditions of Israel, particularly in regard to the Torah, the Mosaic law, are shown by Myllykoski to develop within the same socially evolving community; Larsen and Svigel demonstrate the influence of a Two Ways tradition received from earlier "Jewish religious themes."[20]

Contrary to the theses that Marcion will eventually propagate in Rome and the attitude that we occasionally witness in some early *Adversus Judaeos* literature, we see here an enduring respect for Christianity's Jewish heritage through several stages of communal development and catechesis. This is not unlike the more developed understanding of Christianity's relationship to Israel's law that we will witness in Irenaeus. In him we find the law praised and esteemed throughout history, although certain of its external forms end or are augmented. The "natural precepts" are common to both the church and Jews. The Jews had them in "their commencement and origin," while in the church "they received augmentation and amplification" (*Haer.* 4.13.4 [SC 100.2:534,79–82]). This development is neither as the Marcionites would contend, "a contradiction nor an abolition" of the Jew's precepts, "but their fulfillment and amplification" (4.13.1 [SC 100.2:524,12–526,16]). There is in Irenaeus no "abandonment of the law," no devaluation of the Jews as less moral or with a different recompense than the church.[21] He doesn't seek to legitimize Christianity's relationship with God "apart from Torah," but to explain the transeconomical essence of Torah.[22] The Jew and the Christian are equally of the same humankind, but they are humans within two different economies. Thus, Hans Conzelmann is correct when he writes that for Irenaeus "salvation history is not

---

20. Myllykoski, "Without Decree," *passim*; Larsen and Svigel, "First Century Two Ways Catechesis," 481.

21. See the summary in Miriam Taylor, *Anti-Judaism and Early Christian Identity: A Critique of the Scholarly Consensus*, StPB 46 (Leiden: Brill, 1995), 132–34, on other studies concerning the Jews in early Christian writings.

22. See Lloyd Gaston, "Retrospect," in *Separation and Polemic*, vol. 2 of *Anti-Judaism in Early Christianity*, ed. S. G. Wilson, 2 vols., SCJ 2 (Waterloo: Wilfrid Laurier University, 1986), 163–74 (167).

of a national character, but a universal one."²³ For Irenaeus the tension between any supposed redemptive-historical bias for or against certain peoples relaxes within his view of the economies. As he concludes at the end of book 5: "there is one human-kind" (5.36.3 [SC 153:464,66]).

3. LITURGY

But this rich collection of essays does not merely indicate the positive role of Jewish material in the development of some early Christian texts and communities. Garrow shows how the distinctive liturgy and meal of the Christians, the Eucharist, stood behind the composition and liturgical use of texts (by all means, the Eucharist may be related to Jewish meal practices, but this is not Garrow's point). Early Christianity developed out of its Jewish roots, without doubt, but it also developed out of its own liturgical identity.

This last dynamic is crucial to our understanding the development of the texts and practice of early Christians. The liturgical character of Revelation has not been overlooked by scholarship, but the relationship between liturgy and the composition of early Christian texts goes far beyond the Apocalypse.[24] As Roch Kereszty argues:

> A critical reading of the New Testament shows that a widespread Eucharistic practice has preceded the composition of even the earliest extant documents. The succinct narrative on the Lord's Supper that Paul handed on to the Corinthians in 50/51, expresses a tradition he himself had received from the liturgical practice of the Church (1 Corinthians 11:23–26).... [Denis] Farkasfalvy made a strong case for the Eucharistic provenance of the New Testament in general and of the four Gospels in particular. It is in the Eucharistic liturgy that the accounts of what Jesus did and said in his earthly life were formulated and fixed into oral patterns.... The liturgy of the word, then, is not a separate form of worship but intrinsically linked to the liturgy of the Eucharist where it unfolds its power. In other words, the various texts read at the eucharistic service expresses the various aspects of what the Lord does in and through the

---

23. Hans Conzelmann, *Gentiles, Jews, Christians: Polemics and Apologetics in the Greco-Roman Era*, trans. M. Eugene Boring (Minneapolis: Fortress, 1992), 319.

24. See Pierre Prigent, *Apocalypse et Liturgie* (Neuchatel: Delachaux & Niestle, 1964); André Feuillet, *The Apocalypse* (New York: Alba, 1965), 85; Ugo Vanni, "Liturgical Dialogue as a Literary Form in the Book of Revelation," *NTS* 37 (1991): 348–72.

Eucharist. If the Eucharist was the defining *sitz im leben* for the Gospel traditions we may expect that it will obtain a central place within the structure of the Gospels themselves.[25]

Farkasfalvy, in his helpful essay "The Eucharistic Provenance of New Testament Texts," argues, "all New Testament Scripture has a Eucharistic provenance" and that those texts "arose with an eye on the Eucharistic assembly and that assembly was the locus and framework for their ecclesial and sacramental exegesis."[26] The essay treats the apostolic letters, the gospel narratives, and the book of Revelation. Within John's Apocalypse, he sees the eucharistic framework unfolding in this way: (1) Jesus's coming and appearance on Sunday, the Lord's Day (1:7–14); (2) the letters given to the churches (2:1–3:22); (3) the heavenly liturgy of praise with the prophet John as witness and participant (4:1–5:14); and (4) the opening of the seven seals with their apocalyptic signs followed by the eucharistic blessing in 19:9: "Write happy are those invited to the wedding banquet of the Lamb."[27]

For Farkasfalvy, Rev 19:11–22:8 serves as parentheses, while John's vision continues with Rev 22:10–21.[28] In quick succession, then, the Apocalypse moves the congregation from the command not to seal the book and the repeated christological title, "Alpha and Omega," to the three concluding eucharistic references: (1) the tree of life; (2) the exclusion of the wicked from communion; and then, (3) finally, what is in Farkasfalvy's framework the pronouncement of "the concluding Eucharistic exclamation," μαραναθά. This final exclamation in Aramaic, preserved in both 1 Corinthians and the Didache, forms an *inclusio* with the beginning of John's Apocalypse, where we read in 1:7 of Jesus who comes (ἔρχεται), and demonstrates the expectation upon the gentile churches to be faithful to the earliest tradition. In conclusion he writes:

> While the apostolic letters were intended to be presented to the communities assembled in liturgical worship, the book of Revelation was patterned according to an outline of the Sunday assembly as it was

---

25. Denis Farkasfalvy, *Wedding Feast of the Lamb: Eucharistic Theology from A Biblical, Historical, and Systematic Perspective* (Chicago: Hillenbrand, 2004), 15–16.

26. Denis Farkasfalvy, *Inspiration and Interpretation* (Washington, DC: Catholic University of America, 2010), 63–87.

27. Ibid., 85.

28. Ibid., 85–86.

customarily celebrated in the late first century in Asia Minor. But even more important, I intended to show that the way our canonical Gospels were composed presupposes the spread of the Jesus tradition to communities gathered in cultic assemblies to witness, experience, and respond to the coming of the Lord.[29]

4. Hermeneutics

Also, we should note a feature of early Christian hermeneutics highlighted by Myllykoski's essay. He shows us that the members of the various stages of the community that reflected on the issue of perfection, the law of Moses, and apocalyptic language demonstrate a common identity as followers of the Lord Jesus, Moses, and the inherited apocalyptic tradition of early Christianity.[30] Each stage, then, is faithful to these traditions. But, his essay demonstrates that each stage engages in its own reading strategy of the material and that the community's leaders apply it in different ways. Each stage's reading shows both continuity and discontinuity with the hermeneutical approach of the other two stages. What is clear is that, for each of them, the interpretations of Jesus cannot be done away with. They cannot be ignored or rejected. Somehow, they must be managed hermeneutically.

We see this challenge displayed and answered in a very important way in the polemics of Tertullian against Marcion, as he reads John's Apocalypse. His methodology in *Adversus Marcionem* will help us appreciate more fully another facet of the structure of early Christianity raised by our essays on the Didache.

Adversus Marcionem, of course, is Tertullian's answer to what Eric Osborne has called the "foremost threat to emerging Christian theology:" the dualism that overwhelmingly bothered Marcion.[31] To him, apparent contradictions, shadows, changes, and dialectic were unacceptable.[32] The solution, in Marcion's mind, was the separation of deities and scriptures in very systematic detail. In light of this strategy, the catholic responses to Marcion needed to be systematic as well. Therefore, Tertullian's argument

---

29. Ibid., 86.
30. Myllykoski, "Without Decree," *passim*.
31. Eric Osborne, *Tertullian: First Theologian of the West* (Cambridge: Cambridge University Press, 1997), 88.
32. Ibid., 88–89.

in *Adversus Marcionem* is quite intricate.[33] He shows that apparent antitheses exist within God and within the world, apparent antitheses that appear to be opposites but that are manifested in "perfect proportion."[34] For example, Christ is indeed, for him, the jealous God (*Marc.* 2.29.4).

Books 1 and 2 confront and deny the notion that there can exist two gods and argue that there can exist only one unique supreme being. The world is a harmony of apparent opposites. God both creates and redeems; God is both eternal and rational, both good and just, both the God of the Old Testament and the New Testament.[35] Book 3 treats prophecy and its fulfillment and the deity and unity of Jesus Christ. The messianic promises of the Old Testament, Tertullian argues, are in concord with the Christ of the Gospels.[36] For Tertullian, Christ the redeemer is a necessary corollary to the one God creator.[37] His fourth book uses Marcion's own text against him: Marcion's version of Luke reflects the catholic teaching. The mutilated edition of Luke still presents Christ who is in continuity with the Old Testament's prophecies and expectations. The final book is the African father's reply to Marcion's account of Paul. Tertullian argues that Paul does not preach the destruction of Judaism or a separation between creator, flesh, punishment, cross, and God of grace.[38]

It is in proving the thesis of book 3 that Tertullian employs John's Apocalypse in a manner that allows us a glimpse of his hermeneutical approach. Tertullian, as it is well recognized, sometimes to the point of frustration, it seems, has a variety of interpretive methods.[39] Each method is used within a particular context to accomplish a certain task and argue a particular point. Thus he would embrace allegorical, typological, spiritual, or figurative interpretations as well as interpretations that were literal and strict. Tertullian's exegesis was deeply polemical in its principle, as it was overwhelmingly focused upon winning the argument at hand within the parameters established by the rule of faith.

---

33. Ibid., 90.
34. Ibid., 90–91.
35. Ibid., 91–104.
36. Ernest Evans, ed. and trans., *Tertullian Adversus Marcionem, Books 1–3* (Oxford: Clarendon, 1972), xvii.
37. Osborne, *Tertullian*, 104–5.
38. Ibid., 113–15.
39. See Geoffrey D. Dunn, *Tertullian* (London: Routledge, 2004), 22–23.

We observe his sympathies toward a more figurative approach in his attempt to develop and explain a catholic Christology that pleads a unity between Old Testament and New Testament. At one point (*Marc.* 3.12–14), he is concerned with presenting the continuity between Isaiah's vision of the messianic child and peacemaker, who is Emmanuel, from Isa 7:14 and 8:4 and certain New Testament language of christological description, such as Rev 1:16. This apocalyptic text presents a problem: it seems to portray Christ as a warrior, for it "describes a sharp two-edged sword as proceeding from the mouth of God," or in the words of the text, "one like a son of man" (*Marc.* 3.14.3). The apparent contradiction is solved hermeneutically: "this has to be understood as the divine word, doubly sharp in the two testaments of the Law and the Gospel, sharp with wisdom, directed against the devil, arming us against the spiritual hosts of wickedness and evil concupiscence, and cutting us off even from our dearest for the sake of the name of God."[40] A similar use of the language, Tertullian insists, can be found in the Pauline discussion of the armor of spiritual warfare in Eph 6, where he specifically identifies the "sword of the Spirit" as "the Word of God." Thus, the sword of Revelation is an "allegorical sword," allowing for harmony between prophet and apostle. In Tertullian's own words, "And so the Christ who has come will be Isaiah's Christ, for the very reason that he was not a warrior, because he is not by Isaiah described as such (*Marc.* 3.14.7)."[41]

Here, then, the Apocalypse presents itself as a problem to be solved. In polemics, canonical material can pose a challenge to be overcome. Tertullian, unlike Marcion, will not depart from the catholic rule in order to have another definition of what must be read, of what constitutes scripture. His tradition, his rule of faith, his community has received the Apocalypse. He must face up to its language. Marcion chose and selected his language based upon his own rule of faith. Not so Tertullian. However, although he cannot select his scripture, he can select his hermeneutic. And here he selects an allegorical one. Apparently, such a metaphorical or allegorical reading of the Apocalypse by Tertullian is not strange. Elsewhere, in 3.13, he speaks of the metaphorical approach he selected one in which John uses Babylon to refer to "the Roman city."

---

40. Evans, *Tertullian Adversus Marcionem*, 213.
41. Ibid., 215.

Apocalyptic, to the catholic polemicist, frequently presents more conundrum than contribution to the argument. This is the first time in the second and early third century that we have seen this dynamic this forcefully. The church, against the formidable antithesis of Marcion, finds itself in polemical response, hindered and challenged by its own scripture. Apocalyptic, by virtue of its language, can be an irritating element in the attempt to provide a simplistic, naïve argument in accordance with a rule of faith. Since the catholic polemicist cannot solve an apparent dilemma canonically, the only recourse is hermeneutical. In early Christianity, it was not simply the Old Testament that had to be integrated into the faith of the church through various hermeneutical approaches. The Apocalypse, perhaps because of aspects of its language, which echo so clearly difficult portions of the law, also forced the church to embrace variant hermeneutical visions. And really, here is perhaps one of the most important contributions Tertullian makes within the confines of his reply to Marcion. Catholicity would stand or fall, in struggle upon struggle, upon its hermeneutical skill as it attempted to demonstrate concord between variant portions of its scripture. Departures from orthodoxy would bask in the ease of compartmentalization, antitheses, and segregation.

5. Conclusion

In conclusion, I wish to express my gratitude for these four papers and the way in which they have informed my thinking. The task of reconstructing early Christianity is an arduous, but fruitful enterprise. I have attempted to orient our discussion of that enterprise to ancient issues, often travelling away from the Didache into the later second and even third centuries, and to contemporary issues, as we examined pertinent, but diverse metaphysics and historiographies. I hope that future work on the reconstruction of Christianity in antiquity will note aspects of its unity along with its diversity, as well as aspects of its faithfulness to its Jewish heritage along with those cases where it was disparaged. I hope, too, that that work, as it follows the ways of redaction criticism, will renew its appreciation for the liturgical provenance of early Christian texts and the enduring manner in which accepted texts were respected by means of hermeneutics.

Conclusion: Missing Pieces in the Puzzle or Wild Goose Chase? A Retrospect and Prospect

Jonathan A. Draper

1. Why the Riddle?

In his groundbreaking commentary written soon after its first publication by Bishop Bryennios in 1883, Adolf von Harnack[1] highlighted its significance:

> The more one immerses oneself in the context of the *Didache*, the more clearly one sees that its author has exhausted, to his mind, everything which belonged in a short evangelical-apostolic manual for the Christian life of the individual (in everyday dealings and in the community). One could not deny that the evidence provided by this writing is quite first rate.

So impressed was Harnack with its evidence, that it formed the key to his picture of the evolution of the early church from the writings of the New Testament to the emerging institution of "early Catholicism" in his massive two volume work, *Das Mission und Ausbreitung des Christentums in den ersten drei Jahrhunderten* (1902).[2] After one hundred and thirty years,

---

1. Adolf von Harnack, *Die Lehre der zwölf Apostel nebst Untersuchuingen zur ältesten Geschichte der Kirchenverfassung und des Kirchenrechts*, TUGAL 2.1, 2 (Leipzig: Hinrichs, 1884), 36–37 (my translation). Harnack's contention concerning the comprehensiveness of the instructions has been specifically questioned by Georg Schöllgen, "Die Didache als Kirchenordnung: Zur Frage des Abfassungszweckes und sinen Konsequenzen für die Interpretation," *JAC* 29 (1986): 5–26. Schöllgen argues that the Didache simply presents an ad hoc collection of burning issues of the day and what is absent from the text is irrelevant for its interpretation.

2. Translated into English as Adolf von Harnack, *The Mission and Expansion of*

such confidence has proved to be short-lived. Almost every aspect of the evidence has been contested, almost to the point where scholars ceased to use its evidence at all for the reconstruction of early Christianity.

Although there is still no consensus on the exact date, the range of possible dates suggested does seem to have narrowed significantly among modern scholars, with few arguing for a date later than the beginning of the second century CE, with others arguing for a much earlier date from the mid- to late-first century.[3] Yet if this is indeed a genuine document of the first or even early second century CE, it is hard to see how pessimism with regard to its use in the reconstruction of the emergence of early Christianity can be justified, given that it contains practical rules for community rituals and common life as practiced at such an early time, evidence which is not really available elsewhere except incidentally from odd clues here and there in writings with other purposes. On the other hand, it is not surprising that the document is contested and has been from the outset, because it touches in a fundamental way on deep-rooted historical constructions of the early church that relate to legitimations and vested interests of particular denominations and their ecclesiologies. It presents a challenge to any theory of a straightforward evolution from origins to the institutional church of later times, representing a subjugated voice of an alternative strand of the Christian tradition which fell silent. Consequently, any theory of origins that ignores this inconvenient and

---

Christianity in the First Three Centuries (London: Williams & Norgate; New York: Putnam, 1908), esp. 319–68.

3. Most recently Aaron Milavec, *The Didache: Faith, Hope, and Life of the Earliest Christian Communities, 50–70 CE* (New York: Newman, 2003), has made a claim that the work represents an oral catechesis dating from 50–70 CE. He is followed in this by Thomas O'Loughlin, *The Didache: A Window on the Earliest Christians* (Grand Rapids: Baker; London: SPCK, 2010), 26, although he leaves open the question of the final version of the text within the broad range of the first century CE: "In all probability a version of the *Didache* was being committed to memory by groups of followers of Jesus by the middle of the first century—and what we have reflects a very early stage in that text's life and influence." Proponents of a later date at around 110–20 CE include, hesitantly, Kurt Niederwimmer, *The Didache: A Commentary*, Hermeneia (Minneapolis: Fortress, 1998), 53; Huub van de Sandt and David Flusser, *The Didache: Its Jewish Sources and Its Place in Early Judaism and Christianity*, CRINT 3.5 (Assen: Van Gorcum; Minneapolis: Fortress, 2002), 45, "turn of the first century"; and Clayton N. Jefford, "Didache," *EDB*, 345a–46a, who allows 70–150 CE as the furthest extremes but prefers the early second century.

enigmatic voice that was lost in the march of time is left with a missing piece or pieces of the puzzle—rather like infuriating puzzle pieces of the plain sky that just will not fit in at the end of the puzzle or, worse still, that fell off the table and got lost.

Whatever date is advocated for its final redaction, there is broad agreement that it contains early source material, whether originating in oral form or already in written form, so that its final date does not determine its value entirely. For instance, historians of the Eucharist mostly see very early material here, older than the Didache itself, deriving from Jewish prototypes.[4] However, an alternative origin in the Hellenistic symposium is proposed by Matthias Klinghardt,[5] although while one should allow for the influence of Hellenism on first century Judaism on a wide front as argued by Martin Hengel's epic work,[6] this should also not be allowed to suggest the complete eclipse of culture-specific elements of Jewish society.[7] Almost all scholars since Jean-Paul Audet's comparison of the Two Ways in the Didache and the Manual of Discipline (1QS III,

---

4. So Enrico Mazza, *The Origins of the Eucharistic Prayer*, trans. Ronald E. Lane (Collegeville, MN: Liturgical Press, 1995), places it at the center of his reconstruction of origins, while Jonathan Schwiebert, *Knowledge and the Coming Kingdom: The Didache's Meal Ritual and Its Place in Early Christianity*, LNTS 373; (London: T&T Clark, 2008), traces it to the early originating moment of an alternative tradition of the Christian Eucharist to that represented by the words of institution. Gerard Rouwhorst, "Didache 9-10: A Litmus Test for the Research on Early Christian Liturgy Eucharist," in *Matthew and the Didache: Two Documents from the Same Jewish Christian Milieu?* ed. Huub van de Sandt (Assen: Van Gorcum; Minneapolis: Fortress, 2005), 143–56, takes a middle line arguing that early meal thanksgiving prayers like those presented by the Didache may have existed alongside the Eucharist offered using the words of institution at a yearly "Quartodeciman Passover with an etiological function which gradually replaced the communal meal prayers."

5. Matthias Klinghardt, *Gemeinschaftsmahl und Mahlgemeinschaft: Soziologie und Liturgie frühchristlicher Mahlfeiern*, TANZ 13 (Tübingen: Francke, 1996). He is followed by Dennis E. Smith, *From Symposium to Eucharist: The Banquet in the Early Christian World* (Minneapolis: Fortress, 2002), and Hal Taussig, *In the Beginning was the Meal* (Minneapolis: Fortress, 2009).

6. Martin Hengel, *Judaism and Hellenism: Studies in their Encounter in Palestine during the Early Hellenistic Period*, 2 vols. (London: SCM, 1974).

7. The experience of the modern form of imperial domination on a far more widespread scale than was possible in the ancient world shows that subjugated cultures are certainly influenced, even changed in important respects, by the imperial culture, but are not obliterated, reemerging after the collapse of imperial control even after hundreds of years.

13–IV, 26) agree that the material is older than the Didache and represents an originally independent and widespread early Jewish and Christian text or trope.[8] The theory of a late literary fiction does not seem tenable any more, since at every turn new textual discoveries tend to support the authenticity of the kind of world described in the Didache. The many echoes it finds in multiple early Christian texts evidenced in this volume indicate that it stands in a continuing and evolving tradition. In any case, even if it were to represent a fictional and imagined ideal community, it could only be constructed on the possibilities offered by real historical experience in its day. Even dreams and visions are rooted in a particular cultural and social reality.

2. The Didache and Jewish Christianity

One significant development in recent study of the Didache is the result of a greater awareness of the broad span and diversity of first century Jewish/Israelite culture, which tends to confirm that this text originates in a Jewish Christian context. There was no overarching monolithic Jewish/Israelite religious expression in the first two centuries CE but rather a contested public space. Rabbinic Judaism represents only one strand in an evolving tradition battling for hegemony after the collapse of the Judean temple state. The Didache represents another such strand of Judaism, basing its claims on the acceptance of Jesus as the descendent of David and the Messiah who would return as the Son of Man on the clouds. Its rituals and Christology diverge significantly from other types of Christianity known through Pauline Christianity, which became dominant in the West and erased earlier memories, but it can now be seen to be close to patterns found in other Jewish and Jewish Christian groups—in particular Matthew and James and Revelation. The correlation of the Didache with these texts and other known Jewish Christian writings, such as the Pseudo-Clementine texts and the Odes of Solomon, might provide a focal point for the reconstruction of early Jewish Christianity.[9] A particular point of

---

8. Jean-Paul Audet, "Affinités Littéraires et Doctrinales du 'Manuel de Discipline,'" *RB* 59 (1952): 219–38.

9. In his response to papers in the SBL seminar of 2007 in Washington, Marcus Bockmuehl argued that the traces of Jewish Christianity found in the Didache might reflect a much later romanticization of Judaism for which a gentile community is nostalgic. However, this does not match the very early textual traces of the Didache nor

interest is the way in which such a Jewish Christian community orientated itself to a mission to the gentiles while seeking to remain Torah observant (6.2–3). Such a stance is well-known from Matt 5, but here it is fleshed out by the instructions provided for community life. In the Didache there is a major focus on purity and holiness: from a *koinonia* of property in chapter 4,[10] to the right kind of water to remove impurity and effect such a holy community in chapter 7, to an insistence on the exclusion of those not washed in this way from the pure meal of the community, since they are as unclean as dogs (9.5).[11] This insistence on purity is repeated in the instructions after the meal (10.6) and in the instructions on the Lord's Day (14). Such an obsession with purity goes with a concern about boundaries in the construction of a new community facing a pressing external threat[12] and matches the similar concern in other Jewish groups in the first and

---

the way in which the arguments and practice of the Didache follows the inner logic discernible in early Jewish sources. See especially the work of Huub van de Sandt, "Didache 3:1–6:1: A Transformation of an Existing Jewish Hortatory Pattern," *JSJ* 23 (1992), 21–24; "Was the Didache Community a Group within Judaism? An Assessment on the Basis of its Eucharistic Prayers," in *A Holy People: Jewish and Christian Perspectives on Religious Communal Identity*, ed. Marcel J. H. M. Poorthuis and Joshua Schwartz, JCP 12 (Leiden: Brill, 2006), 85–107; van de Sandt and Flusser, *Didache*; and Peter J. Tomson, "The Halakhic Evidence of *Didache* 8 and Matthew 6 and the *Didache* Community's Relation to Judaism," in van de Sandt, *Matthew and the Didache*, 131–41; "Transformations of Post-70 Judaism: Scholarly Reconstructions and Their Implications for our Perception of Matthew, Didache, and James," in *Matthew, James and Didache: Three Related Documents in Their Jewish and Christian Settings*, ed. Huub van de Sandt and and Jürgen K. Zangenberg, SBLSymS 45 (Atlanta: Society of Biblical Literature, 2008), together with his paper ("The Lord's Prayer [Didache 8] at the Faultline of Judaism and Christianity") in this volume; Jonathan A. Draper, "The Holy Vine of David Made Known to the Gentiles through God's Servant Jesus: 'Christian Judaism' in the *Didache*," in *Jewish Christianity Reconsidered: Rethinking Ancient Groups and Texts*, ed. Matt Jackson-McCabe (Minneapolis: Fortress, 2007), 257–83; and "Pure Sacrifice in Didache 14 as Jewish Christian Exegesis," *Neot* 42 (2008): 223–52.

10. See too my paper ("Children and Slaves in the Community of the Didache and the Two Ways Tradition") in this volume.

11. Note the paper of Huub van de Sandt ("Baptism and Holiness: Two Requirements Authorizing Participation in the Didache's Eucharist") in this volume.

12. According to the widely accepted anthropological model of Mary Douglas developed in *Purity and Danger: An Analysis of the Concepts of Pollution and Taboo* (London: Routledge, 1966), and *Natural Symbols: Explorations in Cosmology*, 2nd ed. (New York: Pantheon, 1982).

second century CE, such as the *haburoth* of the Pharisees and the *yahad* of the community of the Dead Sea Scrolls.

3. The Relationship of the Didache and Matthew

The links with Matthew's Gospel are very close and demand attention at every turn. The traditional argument has been about whether the Didache is dependent on Matthew, whether they are both dependent on a prior source such as is traditionally designated "Q,"[13] or whether Matthew is dependent on the Didache, as some recent scholars have argued.[14] A number of scholars, including myself, have argued for a more complex relationship between Matthew and the Didache as an "evolved text," namely, a text which has had a long history of redaction as the community rule of a living and developing community, so that the earliest layers of the text may be among Matthew's sources, while the latest layers of the text may reflect a knowledge of Matthew.[15] Such an approach allows for the continuing influence of orality and performance on the production and transmission of texts over time.

A resurgence of interest in oral tradition has also raised the possibility that what are taken as literary sources in most of the scholarly literature may in fact be reflections of a common oral tradition used by both texts. This is a particularly forceful argument if the Didache contains catechetical material which was designed to be memorized by catechumens under the guidance of an elder or teacher.[16] However, oral tradition cannot, in my

---

13. As argued by Helmut Koester, *Synoptische Überlieferung bei den apostolischen Vätern*, TUGAL 65/5.10 (Berlin: Akademie, 1957), 159–241. Heavy counter arguments are offered by Christopher M. Tuckett, "The *Didache* and the Writings that later formed the New Testament," in *The Reception of the New Testament in the Apostolic Fathers*, vol. 1 of *The New Testament and the Apostolic Fathers*, ed. Andrew F. Gregory and Christopher M. Tuckett (Oxford: Oxford University Press, 2005), 83–127.

14. See Alan J. P. Garrow, *The Gospel of Matthew's Dependence on the Didache*, JSNTSup 254 (London: T&T Clark, 2004).

15. The concept was developed by Robert Kraft, *Barnabas and the Didache*, AF 3 (New York: Nelson, 1965), 1–3; also by Stanislav Giet, *L'énigme de la Didachè* (PFLUS 149; Paris: Ophrys, 1970). Giet was published posthumously, but the manuscript is dated 1967.

16. See Jonathan A. Draper, "Vice Catalogues as Oral-Mnemonic Cues: A Comparative Study of the Two Ways Tradition in the Didache and Parallels from the Perspective of Oral Tradition," in *Jesus, the Voice, and the Text: Beyond the Oral and the*

opinion, replace studies of literary composition, because the first century Mediterranean world was not a context of primary orality. Text and oral tradition were in a continuing and dialectic relationship, which continued to affect even the manuscript traditions of any writing.[17] The question has far reaching consequences for the dating of the Didache, of course, but the question does not seem likely to be easily settled, as the diverse papers and positions reflected in this volume testify.

A more constructive way forward may be to explore the relationship between the praxis of the Didache and the clues in Matthew, asking different questions to chart the dimensions of a Jewish-Christian community life. In other words, could one read them together in the act of historical reconstruction, while leaving open the question of the direction of influence? Such an approach certainly produced dividends in the two Tilburg conferences hosted by Huub van de Sandt in 2003 and 2007, which resulted in a rich and helpful discourse. The very intensity of the debate indicates the importance of the relationship. The continuing disagreements do not indicate a scholarly crisis but a creative vortex of research. Clearly the evidence is inconclusive and its interpretation depends on prior understandings of the researcher concerning the evolution of the earliest Christian communities. Perhaps instead of trying to determine the direction of their literary composition, future research should read the evidence of Matthew and the Didache (and possibly the epistle of James) together as data for the reconstruction of the praxis and beliefs of a particular community or set of communities that stand in the same early Christian trajectory. The Tilburg Conferences of 2003 and 2007 mentioned above have already opened up this possibility.

Although the disagreements remained wide and are reflected again in the current volume of papers from a decade of meetings by the SBL seminar so that one could not really speak of an emerging consensus, the range of issues has narrowed somewhat. Matthew and the Didache, whatever

---

Written Gospel, ed. Tom Thatcher (Waco, TX: Baylor University Press, 2008), 111–36. See also the papers of Nancy Pardee ("The Didache and Oral Theory") and Perttu Nikander ("The *Sectio Evangelica* [Didache 1.3b–2.1] and Performance") in this volume. Note, however, the cautions expressed by John S. Kloppenborg, "Memory, Performance, and the Sayings of Jesus" (paper presented at the Hensinki Seminar on Memory, Helsinki, Finland, 11 May 2011).

17. See the seminal work of David C. Parker, *The Living Text of the Gospels* (Cambridge: Cambridge University Press, 1997).

the direction of supposed dependence, are both now usually regarded as Jewish-Christian/Christian-Jewish texts. Secondly, if the Didache reached its final form by the end of the first and beginning of the second centuries CE, this puts it roughly in the same time zone as the composition of Matthew advocated by most Matthean scholars (give or take a decade or two). Given the difference in genre between the Didache and Matthew then, the question of literary dependence may be a red herring that has prevented scholars from moving on to delineate the nature of the community(ies) which used both texts simultaneously and found no contradiction in doing so.

4. The Didache, the Book of Revelation, and the Johannine Tradition

The relationship between the Didache and Revelation has received little attention except from Alan Garrow,[18] but seems to call for further analysis—again taking into account their difference in genre. The Didache has prophets who "do a cosmic mystery of the ekklesia" within strictly prescribed rules; Revelation offers just such a "cosmic mystery of the ekklesia." No one has imagined the Didache to be a text of early Jewish Christian mysticism, and yet it not only allows but privileges (10.7) and regulates such a practice (13.7–12) in its community rule. Besides this, there are clear traces of the Two Ways trope in Revelation and a similar strict insistence of the avoidance of εἰδωλόθυτον. Relating two such enigmatic texts as the Didache and Revelation may present a daunting task, but may be a productive exercise. Given a date for the Didache between the end of the first and beginning of the second century CE in the new emerging consensus, it is no longer appropriate to describe it as a Montanist document. Was there, however, a continuing early Christian mystical practice based on the work of "prophets" speaking in the spirit (evidenced not only in the Didache but also in Matthew; e.g., the false prophets of 7:15–23 and the true ones implied in 10:41)? Could this prophetic tradition have issued in Montanism not as an innovation, but as a practice the emerging orthodox church sought to suppress? Its links with other works in the Johannine tra-

---

18. So van de Sandt, *Matthew and the Didache*; Huub van de Sandt and Jürgen K. Zangenberg, eds., *Matthew, James and Didache*; Gunnar Garleff, *Urchristliche Identität in Matthäusevangelium, Didache und Jakobusbrief*, BVB 9 (Münster: LIT, 2004); and Alan Garrow ("The Didache and Revelation") in this volume.

dition, such as John's Gospel, 1 John, 2 John, and 3 John, have hardly been explored except by Johannes Betz's brief study of the Eucharist.[19]

5. The Didache in Jewish and Christian Mysticism

Despite the extensive instructions on Christian prophets and prophecy in Did. 10.7, 11.7–12, 13, and 15.1–2, there has been relatively little interest shown in this material on the part of Didache scholars or in the burgeoning study of Jewish and Christian mysticism emerging from a new understanding of apocalyptic as different from (though sometimes overlapping with) eschatology which arose from the work of Alan F. Segal,[20] Christopher Rowland,[21] John J. Collins,[22] Peter Schäfer,[23] and many others. It has been the focus of a long running section of the SBL's "Early Jewish and Christian Mysticism." The nature and evolution of this widespread influence and practice of mystical ascent continues to be debated, but its existence as an influence in Judaism can no longer be doubted in the light of recent studies of mysticism in the Dead Sea Scrolls[24] and Philo of Alexandria.[25] So it is surprising that none of the participants in the SBL seminar series on the Didache took up this quest with respect to the text.

---

19. Johannes Betz, "The Eucharist in the *Didache*," in *The* Didache *in Modern Research*, ed. Jonathan A. Draper, AGJU 37 (Leiden: Brill, 1996), 244–75. Like the Didache, John's Gospel lacks the words of institution, utilizes the trope of the vine in the context of the meal, and applies the vine to Jesus. It is still an open question whether there are any connections between John and the Didache beyond the eucharistic parallels (e.g., could John's failure to describe Jesus's baptism by the Baptist reflect a rejection of Christian baptism as one of "repentance for the forgiveness of sins" which is absent also in the Didache?).

20. Alan F. Segal, *Two Powers in Heaven: Early Rabbinic Reports about Christianity and Gnosticism*, SJLA 25 (Leiden: Brill, 1977).

21. Christopher Rowland, *The Open Heaven: A Study of Apocalyptic in Judaism and Early Christianity* (London: SPCK, 1982).

22. John J. Collins, *The Apocalyptic Imagination: An Introduction to Jewish Apocalyptic Literature* (New York: Crossroad, 1984).

23. Peter Schäfer, *The Hidden and Manifest God* (Albany, NY: State University of New York Press, 1992).

24. See most recently the excellent study of Samuel I. Thomas, *The "Mysteries" of Qumran: Mystery, Secrecy, and Esotericism in the Dead Sea Scrolls*, SBJLEJL 25 (Atlanta: Society of Biblical Literature, 2009).

25. See, e.g., Baudouin Decharneux, *L'Ange, le devin et le prophète: Chemins de la*

The Didache provides instructions to regulate *how* things are to be done and what is to be forbidden. The rules on Christian prophecy that it provides are often seen as merely demonstrating the decline of Christian prophecy and the beginning of its demise, yet they encourage it and value it positively as the spirit speaking through the prophet, so that to silence the voice would be blasphemy. Moreover, prophets are allowed to speak "as they will" at the Christian Eucharist (10.7). Indeed, true and tested prophets speak "cosmic mysteries of the ekklesia" (11.11), the kind of language for the mystical ascent to view the risen Christ enthroned in heaven in a number of New Testament texts, according to Rowland and Christopher Morray-Jones.[26] Prophets, and to a lesser extent teachers, are the only resident leaders in the Didache community who are entitled to material support (13), and their work is so highly rated that they are to receive the same honor as the bishops and deacons—who are in danger of being overshadowed by the prophets (15.1–2). It is time that this aspect of research into early Christian mysticism was taken up in the light of recent studies of mysticism. An earlier generation of British scholars, led by R. H. Connolly[27] and F. E. Vokes,[28] regarded the Didache as a Montanist work because of its teaching on prophecy and prophets, but this assumes that Montanists were the originators of Christian mysticism and prophecy rather than direct descendants of earliest Christianity. Harnack, with his usual acumen, remarked rather off-handedly:

> Down to the close of the second century the prophets retained their position in the church; but the Montanist movement brought early Christian prophecy at once to a head and to an end. Sporadic traces of it are still to be found in later years, but such prophets no longer possessed any significance for the church; in fact, they were quite summarily condemned

---

parole dans l'oeuvre de Philon d'Alexandrie dit "Le Juif," SPL 2 (Bruxelles: Editions de l'Université de Bruxelles, 1994).

26. Christopher C. Rowland and Christopher Morray-Jones, *The Mystery of God: Early Jewish Mysticism and the New Testament*, CRINT 12 (Leiden: Brill, 2009). They see 2 Cor 12:2–4, Colossians, Ephesians, Hebrews, and perhaps 1 John as reflecting such a Christian mysticism.

27. R. H. Connolly, "The Didache and Montanism," *DRev* 55 (1937): 339–47.

28. F. E. Vokes, *The Riddle of the Didache: Fact or Fiction, Heresy or Catholicism?* (London: SPCK, 1938).

by the clergy as false prophets. Like the apostles, the prophets occupied a delicate and risky position. It was easy for them to degenerate.[29]

Sadly, the possibilities of this observation for further research into the Didache have not yet been taken up, particularly in the light of its clear and enduring influence in North Africa and Ethiopia, to which Montanists from Asia Minor fled for refuge.[30]

6. The Didache and Paul

Since the early enthusiasm after its publication in 1883 to find traces of the Didache in every text of the New Testament and early Christianity or vice versa, there has been little research exploring points of contact or opposition relating the letters of Paul to the Didache. A notable exception was the work of Alfred Seeberg, who sought in many volumes to find in the Didache an early Christian catechesis lying behind all the early Christian writings and particularly Paul.[31] In his recent doctoral thesis, *Paul's Witness to Formative Early Christian Instruction*, Benjamin A. Edsall[32] reexamines Seeberg's thesis again in the context of Paul's practice

---

29. Harnack, *Mission and Expansion of Christianity*, 352–53.

30. Besides the manuscript evidence of the Coptic translation and Oxyrhyncus Papyrus 1782, there is the *Vita Shenudi*, the Ecclesiastical Canons, the *Fides Nicanae*, and the presence of large sections of the Didache in the Ethiopic version of the Ethiopian Church Order from the pre-Arabic period, including the whole section on apostles and prophets with chapters 11–13 excerpted. See the new text and translation of Allesandro Bausi, "La Nuova version etiopica della Traditio apostolica: Edizione e traduzione preliminare," in *Christianity in Egypt: Literary Production and Intellectual Trends: Studies in Honor of Tito Orlandi*, ed. Paola Buzi and Alberto Camplani, SEAug 125 (Rome: Institutum Patristicum Augustinianum, 2011), 19–69. The Ethiopian church was evangelized by priests from Asia Minor. This newly discovered text of the Ethiopic version of the Didache lends support to Jean-Paul Audet's contention (*La Didachè: Instructions des Apôtres*, Ebib [Paris: Gabalda, 1958], 35–45) that the Ethiopic version is an important and early (fourth century CE) witness.

31. Alfred Seeberg, *Der Katechismus der Urchristenheit* (Leipzig: Deichert, 1903); *Die beiden Wege und das Apostoldreket* (Leipzig: Deichert, 1906); and *Die Didache des Judentums und der Urchristenheit* (Leipzig: Deichert, 1908). See also Gunther Klein, *Der älteste christliche Katechismus und die jüdische Propaganda-Literatur* (Berlin: Georg Reimer, 1909), who provides a commentary on the text of the Didache from this perspective.

32. Benjamin Edsall, "'As I Said to You Before': Paul's Witness to Formative Early

of Christian initiation. It seems that the time is right for a reexamination of the questions raised by suggestive parallels and oppositions between Paul and the Didache, without necessarily invoking the kind of grand scheme suggested by Seeberg.[33] To what extent does the Didache stand together with Matthew and the epistle of James as evidence of reaction to or as a counter community(ies) to Paul's mission? If the Didache presents ancient catechesis for Christian initiation of gentiles, especially the earlier Two Ways tradition that was incorporated into it,[34] to what extent might such a pattern of catechesis have been known to and perhaps even utilized by Paul? Might the Christian community in which Paul himself was catechized have used such an (oral perhaps) Two Ways pattern which he modified in his own practice, as argued over-elaborately by Seeberg a century ago?

7. The Didache and Early Christian Initiation

This raises a question as to whether the Didache as a whole represents the earliest manual providing rules to initiate new members and regulate their life in an early Christian community.[35] It cannot, of course, be fitted into some supposed genre of the "church order," which did not exist until much later, but it does stand at the beginning of an emerging and multifarious tradition taking up a prior (oral or written) Two Ways teaching and being taken up in its turn into other later such manuals (e.g., the Didascalia, the Apostolic Constitutions and Canons, and the Testamentum Domini). At the heart of it seems to be the practice of Christian initiation for new members who are depicted as gentiles in the "longer title" of the work. The

---

Christian Instruction" (Ph.D. diss., Oxford University, 2013); see also his "*Kerygma, Catechesis and Other Things We Used to Find: Twentieth-Century Research on Early Christian Teaching Since Alfred Seeberg (1903),*" *CurBS* 10 (2012):410–41.

33. See the paper of Taras Khomych ("Another Gospel: Exploring Early Christian Diversity with Paul and the Didache") in this volume; also Jonathan A. Draper, "The Two Ways and Eschatological Hope: A Contested Terrain in Galatians 5 and The Didache," *Neot* 45 (2011): 221–51; and "Paul's Epistle to the Romans and the Catechesis of Gentiles in the *Didache*," *Reflecting on Romans: Essays in Honour of Andrie du Toit's 80th Birthday*, ed. G. J. Steyn, BTS (Leuven: Peeters, forthcoming).

34. This would be especially likely if van de Sandt and Flusser (*Didache*) are right that the Two Ways in the Didache is evidence of a pre-existing Jewish Greek Two Ways.

35. As was claimed by Aaron Milavec, *Didache: Hope, Faith, and Life*.

community into which they are initiated appears to be either a Jewish-Christian/Christian-Jewish community or to stand in the tradition of such a community. Further research into Christian initiation and identity formation in the Didache and a comparison with other such early documents would seem to be called for, moving beyond older debates.[36]

While liturgists have long valued the Didache in their reconstructions of the earliest form(s) of the Eucharist, as we have seen, particularly because of its divergence from the accounts of the Last Supper in the Synoptics and Paul and because of the absence of the words of institution, they have tended to use chapters 9–10 in isolation from the ritual praxis of the whole text. Likewise, the instructions on baptism have been isolated from a consideration of its place in the rest of the Didache. Can the Didache be analyzed as a coherent manual of an early Christian community's life and praxis at a particular moment in its development, whatever the origin of the tradition in prior sources which may have been used in the process? The purpose of the collecting and codifying of the tradition would have been to stabilize and regulate the new community. What appears important and appropriate to modern scholars seeking to define the form of the Didache as a "church order" does not mean that it would have appeared that way to a first century Jewish-Christian/Christian-Jewish community. The material in the Didache cannot be simply dismissed as the result of an ad hoc and therefore random evolution simply because it does not meet our expectations.

---

36. Social Identity Theory seems to offer a promising way forward. This theory was developed by Henri Tajfel and John Turner: see "An Integrative Theory of Intergroup Conflict," in *The Social Psychology of Intergroup Relations*, ed. William G. Austin and Stephen Worchel (Monterey, CA: Brooks/Cole, 1979), 33–48; Henri Tajfel et al., "Social Categorization and Intergroup Behaviour," *EuroJSP* 1 (1971): 149–77. A useful overview of the theory is provided by Stephen Reicher, Russell Spears, and S. Alexander Haslam, "The Social Identity Approach in Social Psychology," *Sage Identities Handbook*, ed. Margaret S. Wetherell and Chandra T. Mohanty (London: Sage, 2010). Social Identity Theory provides a particularly interesting perspective from which to view a text oriented towards initiation into a "sectarian" community. Garleff (*Urchristliche Identität*) took up this challenge, seeking to use the theory dynamically to determine the direction of the trajectory of the tradition from Matthew to the Didache to James. See also Stephen Finlan's paper ("Identity in the Didache Community") in this volume and Jonathan A. Draper, "Mission, Ethics and Identity in the Didache," in *Sensitivity towards Outsiders*, ed. Jacobus Kok et al., WUNT 2 (Tübingen: Mohr Siebeck, 2014), 470–89.

8. Conclusion

Despite a hundred and thirty years of research into the Didache and a renewed flurry of research on this text in the last three decades, it remains a challenge to any reconstruction of early Christianity that cannot be ignored. The later the text is dated, the more puzzling its data. Where does one place a late community that still speaks of visiting apostles, prophets, and teachers and values speaking in the spirit and mystical revelation; a community that practices community of goods; a community that seems to regard circumcision and Torah as "perfection" without requiring it; a community whose baptism does not mention repentance for the forgiveness of sins and focuses on the ritual quality of the water; a community whose Eucharist makes no mention of the words of institution, the body and blood of Christ, the new covenant; a community that believes in the imminent return of the Lord with the holy ones and a resurrection of the righteous only? The later the text is dated, the more its data presents a problem to reconstructions of Christian origins: those scholars who date the text late end up consigning it to some forgotten rural backwater, a fiction or a romantic reconstruction based on nostalgia for a bygone era—without explaining how in that case it came to have such a widespread influence. Or the earlier the text is dated, the more plausible its data but the more challenging its picture of the early church and its relation to Pauline Christianity. Yet it makes the continuance of the traditions of Jewish Christianity (such as the Pseudo-Clementine writings) into the second and third centuries, and perhaps even beyond, more understandable. Perhaps it exercised an influence in the emergence of the twin streams of Montanism and Donatism, which contributed to its marginalization and final disappearance in the West, but with continuing influence in North Africa and Ethiopia as well as in Syrian Christianity and Edessa. It speaks with a "subjugated voice" from the earliest period of the emergence of Christianity, an alternative trajectory that was not in the end triumphant, but that has left traces in or together with a body of Jewish Christian or Christian Jewish texts that the emergent orthodox Church sought to co-opt (as in the Apostolic Constitutions and Canons) or suppress. The contours of this alternative trajectory are important for our understanding of the canonical texts but also in its own right as a different understanding of and response to the life and teaching of Jesus. It is certainly not a wild goose chase in an age where the rigid orthodoxies of Western Christianity are being questioned by Christians seeking alternative expressions of their faith![37] If we "understand all this," perhaps we might affirm the Jesus saying in Matt 13:52 that, "Every scribe who has been trained for the kingdom of heaven is like the master of a household who brings out of his treasure what is new and what is old."

---

37. These orthodoxies rightly have their place in the canons of Christian tradition, but they are rooted contextually in historical debates that no longer necessarily match the debates facing Christians today. Understandings and practices of ancient Christian texts such as the Didache, which was also regarded as orthodox and useful for catechesis although its authorship was disputed (e.g., by Eusebius, *Hist. eccl.* 3.25), may provide helpful material for reflection.

Bibliography

Achtemeier, Paul J. "Omne verbum sonat: The New Testament and the Oral Environment of Late Western Antiquity." *JBL* 109 (1990): 3–27.

Adams, Edward. "The Coming of God Tradition and Its Influence on New Testament Parousia Texts." Pages 1–19 in *Biblical Traditions in Transmission: Essays in Honour of Michael A. Knibb*. Edited by Charlotte Hempel and Judith M.Lieu. JSJSup. Leiden: Brill, 2006.

———. "The Coming of the Son of Man in Mark's Gospel." *TynBul* 56 (2005): 39–61.

Ådna, Jostein. *Jesu Stellung zum Tempel: Die Tempelaktion und das Tempelwort als Ausdruck seiner messianischen Sendung*. WUNT 2/119. Tübingen: Mohr Siebeck, 2000.

Aldridge, Robert E. "The Lost Ending of the *Didache*." *VC* 53 (1999): 1–15.

———. "Peter and the 'Two Ways.'" *VC* 53 (1999): 233–64.

Allison, Dale C. *Constructing Jesus: Memory, Imagination, and History*. London: SPCK, 2010.

———. *The New Moses: A Matthean Typology*. Minneapolis: Fortress, 1993.

Alon, Gedalyahu. "The Bounds of the Laws of Levitical Cleanness." Pages 190–234 in *Jews, Judaism and the Classical World: Studies in Jewish History in the Times of the Second Temple and Talmud*. Translated by I. Abrahams. Jerusalem: Magnes, 1977.

———. *The Jews in Their Land in the Talmudic Age*. Jerusalem: Magnes, 1980–1984.

Amélineau, Émile. *Monuments pour servir à l'histoire de l'Égypte chrétienne aux IVe, Ve, VIe, et VII siècles*. Vol. 4 of *Mémoires publiés par les membres de la Mission archéologique française au Caire, 1885–1886*. Paris: Leroux, 1888.

Anderson, C. P. "Hebrews among the Letters of Paul." *SR* 5 (1975–1976): 258–66.

Anderson, R. Dean, Jr. *Ancient Rhetorical Theory and Paul*. CBET 18. Leuven: Peeters, 1996.

———. *Glossary of Greek Rhetorical Terms Connected to Methods of Argumentation, Figures and Tropes from Anaximenes to Quintilian.* CBET 24. Leuven: Peeters, 2001.

Andriessen, Paul. "L'Eucharistie dans l'Épître aux Hébreux." *NRTh* 3 (1972): 269–77.

Arnold, Russell C. D. *The Social Role of Liturgy in the Religion of the Qumran Community.* STDJ 60. Leiden: Brill, 2006.

Attridge, Harold W. *The Epistle to the Hebrews: A Commentary on the Epistle to the Hebrews.* Hermeneia. Philadelphia: Fortress, 1989.

Audet, Jean-Paul. *La Didachè: Instructions des Apôtres.* Ebib. Paris: Gabalda, 1958.

———. "Literary and Doctrinal Affinities of the 'Manual of Discipline.'" Pages 129–47 in *The* Didache *in Modern Research.* Edited by Jonathan A. Draper. Leiden: Brill, 1996. Translation of "Affinités Littéraires et Doctrinales du 'Manuel de Discipline.'" *RB* 59 (1952): 219–38.

Austin, J. L. *How to Do Things with Words.* Oxford: Clarendon, 1962.

Avemarie, Friedrich. "'Tohorat ha-Rabbim' and 'Mashqeh ha-Rabbim': Jacob Licht Reconsidered." Pages 215–29 in *Legal Texts and Legal Issues: Proceedings of the Second Meeting of the International Organization for Qumran Studies, Cambridge 1995.* Edited by M. Bernstein, Florentino García Martínez, and J. Kampen. STDJ 23. Leiden: Brill, 1997.

Ayres, Lewis. "The Question of Orthodoxy." *JECS* 14 (2006): 395–98.

Bahr, Gordon J. "The Use of the Lord's Prayer in the Primitive Church." *JBL* 84 (1965): 153–59.

Baker, Coleman A. "Social Identity Theory and Biblical Interpretation." *BTB* 42 (2012): 129–38.

Balabanski, Vicky. *Eschatology in the Making: Mark, Matthew and the Didache.* SNTSMS 97. Cambridge: Cambridge University Press, 1997.

Balz, Hortz, and Gerhard Schneider. *Exegetical Dictionary of the New Testament.* ET. Grand Rapids: Eerdmans, 1990–1993.

Barker, Margaret. *Temple Themes in Christian Worship.* London: T&T Clark, 2007.

———. *Temple Theology: An Introduction.* London: SPCK, 2004.

Barnard, Leslie W. "The Epistle of Barnabas and the Tannaitic Catechism." *AThR* 41 (1959): 177–90.

———, ed. *St. Justin Martyr: The First and Second Apologies.* ACW 56. New York: Paulist, 1997.

———. *Studies in the Apostolic Fathers and Their Background*. New York: Schocken Books, 1966.
Barr, David L. "The Apocalypse of John as Oral Enactment." *Int* 40 (1986): 243–56.
Barr, James. "Abbā Isn't 'Daddy.'" *JTS* 39 (1988): 28–47.
Bar-Tal, Daniel. "Group Beliefs as an Expression of Social Identity." Pages 93–113 in *Social Identity: International Perspectives*. Edited by Stephen Worchel, J. Francisco Morales, Darío Páez, and Jean-Claude Deschamps. London: Sage, 1998.
Barthélemy, Dominique. "Redécouverte d'un chaînon manquent de l'histoire de la Septante." *RB* 60 (1953): 18–29.
Bauckham, Richard J. "James and the Jerusalem Church." Pages 415–80 in *The Book of Acts in Its Palestinian Setting*. Vol. 4 of *The Book of Acts in Its First Century Setting*. Edited by Richard Bauckham. Grand Rapids: Eerdmans; Carlisle: Paternoster, 1995.
———. *Jesus and the God of Israel: God Crucified and Other Studies on the New Testament's Christology of Divine Identity*. Grand Rapids: Eerdmans, 2008.
———. *Jude, 2 Peter*. WBC. Waco, TX: Word, 1983.
———. "The Lord's Day." Pages 221–50 in *From Sabbath to Lord's Day*. Edited by D. A. Carson. Grand Rapids: Zondervan, 1982.
———. "The Parting of the Ways: What Happened and Why." *ST* 47 (1993): 135–51.
Bauer, Walter. *Orthodoxy and Heresy in Earliest Christianity*. Translated by Robert A. Kraft and Gerhard Krodel. Philadelphia: Fortress, 1971. Translation of *Rechtgläubigkeit und Ketzerei im ältesten Christentum*. 2nd ed. BHT 10. Tübingen: Mohr Siebeck, 1964.
Bauer, Walter. F. W. Danker, W. F. Arndt, and F. W. Gingrich, eds. *Greek-English Lexicon of the New Testament and Other Early Christian Literature*. 3rd ed. Chicago, 1999.
Bausi, Allesandro. "La Nuova version etiopica della Traditio apostolica: Edizione e traduzione preliminare." Pages 19–69 in *Christianity in Egypt: Literary Production and Intellectual Trends: Studies in Honor of Tito Orlandi*. Edited by Paola Buzi and Alberto Camplani. SEAug 125. Rome: Institutum Patristicum Augustinianum, 2011.
Beall, Todd S. *Josephus' Description of the Essenes Illustrated by the Dead Sea Scrolls*. Cambridge: Cambridge University Press, 1988.
Beare, Francis Wright. *The First Epistle of Peter*. 3rd ed. Oxford: Blackwell, 1970.

Beasley-Murray, G. R. "The Interpretation of Daniel 7." *CBQ* 45 (1983): 44–58.

———. *Jesus and the Last Days: The Interpretation of the Olivet Discourse*. Peabody, MA: Hendrickson, 1993.

Beentjes, Pancratius C. "Discovering a New Path of Intertextuality: Inverted Quotations and Their Dynamics." Pages 31–49 in *Literary Structure and Rhetorical Strategy in the Hebrew Bible*. Edited by Lénart de Regt, J. de Waard, and Jan P. Fokkelman. Assen: Van Gorcum, 1996.

———. "Inverted Quotations in the Bible: A Neglected Stylistic Matter." *Bib* 63 (1982): 506–23.

Benoit, André. *Le baptême chrétien au second siècle: La théologie des Pères*. EHPR 43. Paris: Presses Universitaires de France, 1953.

Betz, Hans Dieter. *Essays on the Sermon on the Mount*. Translated by Lawrence L. Wellborn. Philadelphia: Fortress, 1985.

———. *The Sermon of the Mount: A Commentary on the Sermon on the Mount, including the Sermon on the Plain (Matthew 5:3–7:27 and Luke 6:20–49)*. Hermeneia. Minneapolis: Fortress, 1995.

Betz, Johannes. "The Eucharist in the *Didache*." Pages 244–75 in *The Didache in Modern Research*. Edited by Jonathan A. Draper. AGJU 37. Leiden: Brill, 1996.

———. *Die Realpräsenz des Leibes und Blutes Jesu im Abendmahl nach dem Neuen Testament*. Vol. 2.1 of *Die Eucharistie in der Zeit der griechischen Väter*. Freiburg im Breisgau: Herder, 1961.

Black, Matthew. "The Maranatha Invocation and Jude 14, 15 (1 Enoch 1:9)." Pages 189–96 in *Christ and Spirit in the New Testament: In Honour of Charles Francis Digby Moule*. Edited by Barnabas Lindars and Stephen S. Smalley. Cambridge: Cambridge University Press, 1973.

Blackman, Philip. *Mishnayoth*. 7 vols. New York: Judaica, 1963.

Bloch, Maurice. "Symbols, Songs, Dance and Feature of Articulation: Is Religion an Extreme Form of Traditional Authority?" *EuroJS* 5 (1974): 55–81.

Borgen, Peder, Kåre Fuglseth, and Roald Skarsten. *The Philo Index*. Grand Rapids: Eerdmans; Leiden: Brill, 2000.

Bornkamm, Günther. "Das Anathema in der urchristlichen Abendmahlsliturgie." *TLZ* 65 (1950): 227–30.

Botha, Pieter J. J. "'I am writing this with my own hand….': Writing in New Testament Times." *VE* 30 (2009): 115–25.

———. *Orality and Literacy in Early Christianity*. BPC 5. Eugene, OR: Cascade, 2012.

Bradshaw, Paul F. *Eucharistic Origins*. Oxford: SPCK, 2004.
——. *Reconstructing Early Christian Worship*. London: SPCK, 2009.
——. *The Search for the Origins of Christian Worship*. New York: Oxford University Press, 1992.
Bradshaw, Paul F., Maxwell E. Johnson, and L. Edward Phillips. *The Apostolic Tradition: A Commentary*. Hermeneia. Minneapolis: Fortress, 2002.
Brakke, David. *The Gnostics: Myth, Ritual, and Diversity in Early Christianity*. Cambridge: Harvard University Press, 2010.
Braumann, Georg. "Zum Traditionsgeschichtlichen Problem der Seligpreisungen MT V 3–12." *NovT* 4 (1960): 253–60.
Bredin, Mark. Review of *Faith, Hope, and Life of the Earliest Christian Communities, 50–70 CE*, by Aaron Milavec. *RBL* 6 (2005). Online: http://www.bookreviews.org/pdf/4439_4472.pdf.
Brettler, Marc Z. "Jud 1,1–2,10: From Appendix to Prologue." *ZAW* 101 (1989): 433–35.
Broadhead, Edwin. *Jewish Ways of Following Jesus*. WUNT 1/266. Tübingen: Mohr Siebeck, 2010.
Brooks, E. Bruce. "Acts-Luke." *WSP* 2 (forthcoming).
——. "The Epistle of James." *WSP* 2 (forthcoming).
——. "Gospel Trajectories." *WSP* 1 (2010): 171–72.
——. "Mark's Apocalyptic Discourse." *WSP* 3 (forthcoming).
——. "Prolegomena to Proto-Luke." Paper presented at the annual meeting of the Society of Biblical Literature. San Diego, CA, November 17, 2007.
——. "The Resurrection of Jesus in Mark." *WSP* 3 (forthcoming).
——. "The Secret History of the Twelve." Paper presented at the annual meeting of the Society of Biblical Literature. Atlanta, Ga., November 21, 2010.
——. "Structured Evolution in Mark." Paper presented at the New England regional meeting of the Society of Biblical Literature. Cambridge, MA, April 21, 2006.
Brooks, E. Bruce, and A. Taeko Brooks. "The Nature and Historical Context of Mencius." Pages 242–81 in *Mencius: Contexts and Interpretations*. Edited by Alan K. L. Chan. Honolulu: University of *Hawaii* Press, 2002.
Brooks, E. Bruce, and A. Taeko Brooks. *The Original Analects: Sayings of Confucius and His Successors*. New York: Columbia University Press, 1998.

Brown, Raymond E. *An Introduction to the New Testament*. ABRL. New York: Doubleday, 1997.

———. "Pilgrimage in Faith: The Christian Life in Hebrews." *SwJT* 28 (1985): 28–35.

Bruce, F. F. *1 and 2 Thessalonians*. WBC. Grand Rapids: Word, 1982.

———. *The Epistle to the Hebrews*. NICNT. Grand Rapids: Eerdmans, 1990.

———. "Eschatology in the Apostolic Fathers." Pages 77–89 in *The Heritage of the Early Church: Festschrift for G. V. Florovsky*. Edited by D. Neiman and G. Schatkin. OrChrAn 195. Rome: Pontificium Institutum Studiorum Orientalium, 1973.

Bryennios, Philotheos. Διδαχὴ τῶν δώδεκα ἀποστόλων ἐκ τοῦ ἱεροσολυμιτικοῦ χειρογράφου νῦν πρῶτον ἐκδιδομένη μετὰ προλεγομένων καὶ σημειώσεων ἐν οἷς καὶ τῆς Συνόψεως τῆς ΙΙ. Δ., τῆς ὑπὸ Ἰωάνν. τοῦ Χρυσοστόμου, σύγκρισις καὶ μέρος ἀνέκδοτον ἀπὸ τοῦ αὐτοῦ χειρογράφου. Constantinople: Voutyra, 1883.

Bultmann, Rudolf. *Primitive Christianity in Its Contemporary Setting*. Translated by R. H. Fuller. London: Thames & Hudson, 1956. Translation of *Das Urchristentum im Rahmen der antiken Religionen*. Zürich: Artemis, 1949.

———. *Theology of the New Testament*. Translated by K. Grobel. 2 vols. Waco, TX: Baylor University Press, 2007.

Burkitt, F. C. "Barnabas and the Didache." *JTS* 32 (1931): 25–27.

Butler, B. C. "The Literary Relations of Didache, ch. XVI." *JTS* 11 (1960): 265–83.

Cameron, Ron, and Merrill P. Miller, eds. *Redescribing Christian Origins*. SBLSymS 28. Atlanta: Society of Biblical Literature, 2004.

Carleton-Paget, James. "Jewish-Christianity." Pages 731–75 in *The Early Roman Period*. Vol. 3 of *The Cambridge History of Judaism*. Edited by William Horbury, W. D. Davies, and John Sturdy. Cambridge: Cambridge University Press 1999.

Carson, Don A. "Locating Udo Schnelle's *Theology of the New Testament* in the Contemporary Discussion." *JETS* 53 (2010): 133–41.

Casey, Maurice. *Son of Man: The Interpretation and Influence of Daniel 7*. London: SPCK, 1979.

Chilton, Bruce. "Justin and Israelite Prophecy." Pages 77–87 in *Justin Martyr and His Worlds*. Edited by Sara Parvis and Paul Foster. Minneapolis: Fortress, 2007.

———. *The Temple of Jesus: His Sacrificial Program within a Cultural History of Sacrifice*. University Park: Pennsylvania State University, 1992.

Clabeaux, John. "Purity Regulations in the Didache." Paper presented at the annual meeting of the Society of Biblical Literature. Washington, DC, November 19, 2006.

Cohen, Naomi. "Ma hideish Shmuel Hakatan ba-virkat ha-minim?" *Sinai* 94 (1984–1985): 57–70.

———. "The Nature of Shim'on Hapekuli's Act." *Tarbiz* 52 (1982–1983): 547–55. (Hebrew)

Cohen, Shaye J. D. "The Significance of Yavneh: Pharisees, Rabbis, and the End of Jewish Sectarianism." Pages 44–70 in *The Significance of Yavneh and Other Essays in Jewish Hellenism.* TSAJ 136. Tübingen: Mohr Siebeck, 2010.

———. "The Temple and the Synagogue." Pages 298–325 in *The Early Roman Period.* Vol. 3 of *Cambridge History of Judaism.* Edited by William Horbury, W. D. Davies, and John Sturdy. Cambridge: Cambridge University Press, 1999.

———. "Were Pharisees and Rabbis the Leaders of Communal Prayer and Torah Study in Antiquity? The Evidence of the New Testament, Josephus, and the Early Church Fathers." Pages 266–81 in *The Significance of Yavneh and Other Essays in Jewish Hellenism.* TSAJ 136. Tübingen: Mohr Siebeck, 2010.

Collins, Adela Yarbro. *Mark: A Commentary.* Hermeneia. Minneapolis: Fortress, 2007.

Collins, John J. *The Apocalyptic Imagination: An Introduction to Jewish Apocalyptic Literature.* New York: Crossroad, 1984.

Collins, John J., and Daniel C. Harlow. *Eerdmans Dictionary of Early Judaism.* Grand Rapids: Eerdmans, 2010.

Connolly, R. H. "The Didache and Montanism." *DRev* 55 (1937): 339–47.

———. "The Didache in Relation to the Epistle of Barnabas." *JTS* 33 (1932): 237–53.

———. "The Use of the Didache in the Didascalia." *JTS* 24 (1923): 147–57.

Conti, M., trans. *Hebrews.* ACCS 10. Downers Grove, IL: InterVarsity Press, 2005.

Conzelmann, Hans. *Gentiles, Jews, Christians: Polemics and Apologetics in the Greco-Roman Era.* Translated by M. Eugene Boring. Minneapolis: Fortress, 1992.

Crossan, John Dominic. *The Birth of Christianity: Discovering What Happened in the Years Immediately after the Execution of Jesus.* San Francisco: HarperSanFrancisco, 1998.

Crossley, James G. *The Date of Mark's Gospel: Insight from the Law in Earliest Christianity*. LNTS 266. London: T&T Clark, 2004.
Crouch, James E. *The Origin and Intention of the Colossian Haustafel*. FRLANT 109. Göttingen: Vandenhoeck & Ruprecht, 1972.
Czachesz, István. "Rewriting and Textual Fluidity in Antiquity: Exploring the Socio-Cultural and Psychological Context of Earliest Christian Literacy." Pages 425–41 in *Myths, Martyrs, and Modernity: Studies in the History of Religions in Honour of Jan N. Bremmer*. NBS 127. Edited by J. H. F. Dijkstra, J. E. A. Kroesen, and Y. B. Kuiper. Leiden: Brill, 2010.
Daly, Robert J. *Christian Sacrifice: The Judaeo-Christian Background before Origen*. CUASCA 18. Washington, DC: Catholic University of America Press, 1978.
———. Review of *The Didache: Faith, Hope, and Life of the Earliest Christian Communities, 50–70 CE*, by Aaron Milavex. *Catholic Books Review* (2004). Online: http://catholicbooksreview.org/2004/milavec.htm.
Danielou, Jean. *The Theology of Jewish Christianity*. Translated and edited by John A. Baker. Chicago: Henry Regnery, 1964.
Daube, David. *The New Testament and Rabbinic Judaism*. London: University of London, Athlone, 1956. Repr., New York: Arno, 1973.
Davies, W. D. *The Sermon on the Mount*. Cambridge: Cambridge University Press, 1966.
Davies, W. D., and Dale C. Allison. *A Critical and Exegetical Commentary on the Gospel according to Saint Matthew*. 3 vols. ICC. Edinburgh: T&T Clark, 1988–1997.
Davila, James R. "Liturgical Works from Qumran." *EDEJ* 890–92.
Davis, Casey W. "Hebrews 6:4–6 from an Oral Critical Perspective." *JETS* 51 (2008): 753–67.
Decharneux, Baudouin. *L'Ange, le devin et le prophete: Chemins de la parole dans l'oeuvre de Philon d'Alexcandrie dit "Le Juif."* SPL 2. Brussels: Editions de l'Université de Bruxelles, 1994.
Deines, Roland. *Jüdische Steingefässe und pharisäische Frömmigkeit: Ein archäologisch-historischer Beitrag zum Verständnis von Joh 2,6 und der jüdischen Reinheitshalacha zur Zeit Jesu*. WUNT 2/52. Tübingen: Mohr Siebeck, 1993.
———. "Not the Law but the Messiah: Law and Righteousness in the Gospel of Matthew—An Ongoing Debate." Pages 53–84 in *Built upon the Rock: Studies in the Gospel of Matthew*. Edited by Daniel M. Gurtner and John Nolland. Grand Rapids: Eerdmans, 2007.

Deismann, Adolf. *Light from the Ancient East: The New Testament Illustrated by Recently Discovered Texts of the Graeco-Roman World*. Translated by Lionel R. M. Strachan. London: Hodder & Stoughton, 1910. Translation of *Licht vom Osten: Das Neue Testament und die neuentdeckten Texte der hellenistisch-römischen Welt*. Tübingen: Mohr Siebeck, 1908.

Del Verme, Marcello. *Didache and Judaism: Jewish Roots of an Ancient Christian-Jewish Work*. London: T&T Clark, 2004.

Denny, J. Peter. "Rational Thought in Oral Culture and Literate Decontextualization." Pages 66–89 in *Literacy and Orality*. Edited by D. R. Olson and N. Torrance. Cambridge: Cambridge University Press, 1991.

Derrenbacker, Robert A. *Ancient Compositional Practices and the Synoptic Problem*. BETL 186. Leuven: Leuven University Press; Peeters, 2005.

deSilva, David. "Exchanging Favor for Wrath: Apostasy in Hebrews and Patron-Client Relationships." *JBL* 115 (1996): 91–116.

———. *Perseverance in Gratitude: A Socio-Rhetorical Commentary on the Epistle "to the Hebrews."* Grand Rapids: Eerdmans, 2000.

Deutsch, Celia. *Hidden Wisdom and the Easy Yoke: Wisdom, Torah and Discipleship in Matthew 11.25–30*. JSNTSup 18. Sheffield: JSOT Press, 1987.

Dewey, Joanna. "Textuality in an Oral Culture: A Survey of the Pauline Traditions." *Semeia* 65 (1994): 37–65.

Dibelius, Martin. *James: A Commentary on the Epistle of James*. Revised by H. Greeven. Translated by M. A. Williams. Hermeneia. Philadelphia: Fortress, 1976.

———. "Die Mahl-Gebete der Didache." Pages 117–27 in *Zum Urchristentum und zur hellenistischen Religionsgeschichte*. Vol. 2 of *Botschaft und Geschichte*. Edited by Heinz Kraft and Günther Bornkamm. Tübingen: Mohr Siebeck, 1956.

Dittenberger, Wilhelm. *Orientis Graeci Inscriptiones Selectae*. Leipzig. Hirzel, 1903–1905.

Donfried, Karl Paul. *Paul, Thessalonica, and Early Christianity*. London: T&T Clark, 2002.

Douglas, Mary. *Natural Symbols: Explorations in Cosmology*. 2nd ed. New York: Pantheon, 1982.

———. *Purity and Danger: An Analysis of the Concepts of Pollution and Taboo*. London: Routledge, 1966.

Downing, F. Gerald. "Compositional Conventions and the Synoptic Problem." *JBL* 107 (1988): 69–85.

Draper, Jonathan A. "Apostles, Teachers and Evangelists: Stability and Movement of Functionaries in Matthew, James, and the Didache." Pages 139–76 in *Matthew, James and Didache: Three Related Documents in their Jewish and Christian Settings*. Edited by Huub van de Sandt and Jürgen K. Zangenberg. SBLSymS 45. Atlanta: Society of Biblical Literature, 2008.

———. "Barnabas and the Riddle of the Didache Revisited." *JSNT* 58 (1995): 89–113.

———. "Christian Self-Definition against the 'Hypocrites' in *Didache* 8." Pages 223–43 in *The* Didache *in Modern Research*. Edited by Jonathan A. Draper. AGJU 37. Leiden: Brill, 1996.

———. "A Commentary on the Didache in the Light of the Dead Sea Scrolls and Related Documents." Ph.D. diss., Cambridge University, 1983.

———. "A Continuing Enigma: The 'Yoke of the Lord' in *Didache* 6.2-3 and Early Jewish-Christian Relations." Pages 106–23 in *The Image of Judaeo-Christians in Ancient Jewish and Christian Literature*. Edited by Peter J. Tomson and D. Lambers-Petry. WUNT 158. Tübingen: Mohr Siebeck, 2003.

———. "The Development of 'The Sign of the Son of Man' in the Jesus Tradition." *NTS* 39 (1993): 1–21.

———. "The Didache." Pages 13–20 in *The Apostolic Fathers: An Introduction*. Edited by Wilhelm Pratscher. Waco, TX: University of Baylor Press, 2010.

———. "The *Didache*." Pages 13–20 in *The Writings of the Apostolic Fathers*. Edited by Paul Foster. London: SPCK, 2007.

———. "The *Didache* in Modern Research: An Overview." Pages 1–42 in *The* Didache *in Modern Research*. Edited by Jonathan A. Draper. AGJU 37. Leiden: Brill, 1996.

———. "Do the Didache and Matthew Reflect an 'Irrevocable Parting of the Ways' with Judaism?" Pages 217–41 in *Matthew and the Didache: Two Documents from the Same Jewish-Christian Milieu?* Edited by Huub van de Sandt. Assen: Van Gorcum; Minneapolis: Fortress, 2005.

———. "Eschatology in the *Didache*." Pages 567–82 in *Eschatology of the New Testament and Some Related Documents*. Edited by Jan G. van der Watt. WUNT 2/315. Tübingen: Mohr Siebeck, 2011.

———. "First-fruits and the Support of Prophets, Teachers, and the Poor in *Didache* 13 in Relation to New Testament Parallels." Pages 223–43 in *Trajectories through the New Testament and the Apostolic Fathers*. Vol. 2 of *The New Testament and the Apostolic Fathers*. Edited by Andrew

F. Gregory and Christopher M. Tuckett. Oxford: Oxford University Press, 2005.

———. "The Holy Vine of David Made Known to the Gentiles through God's Servant Jesus: 'Christian Judaism' in the *Didache*." Pages 257–83 in *Jewish Christianity Reconsidered: Rethinking Ancient Groups and Texts*. Edited by Matt Jackson-McCabe. Minneapolis: Fortress, 2007.

———. "Jesus' 'Covenantal Discourse' on the Plain (Luke 6:12–7:17) as Oral Performance: Pointers to 'Q' as Multiple Oral Performance." Pages 71–98 in *Oral Performance, Popular Tradition, and Hidden Transcript in Q*. Edited by Richard A. Horsley. SemeiaSt 60. Atlanta: Society of Biblical Literature, 2006.

———. "The Jesus Tradition in the *Didache*." Pages 269–89 in *The Jesus Tradition Outside the Gospels*. Vol. 5 of *Gospel Perspectives*. Edited by David Wenham. Sheffield: JSOT, 1985. Repr. pages 72–91 in *The* Didache *in Modern Research*. Edited by Jonathan A. Draper. AGJU 37. Leiden: Brill, 1996.

———. "Mission, Ethics and Identity in the Didache." In *Sensitivity towards Outsiders: Exploring the Dynamic Relationship between Mission and Ethos in the New Testament and Early Christianity*. Edited by Jacobus Kok, Tobias Nicklas, Dieter T. Roth, and Christine Hays. WUNT 2/364. Tübingen: Mohr Siebeck, forthcoming.

———. "The Moral Economy of the *Didache*." *HTS.TS* 67 (2011). Art. no. 907. DOI:10.4102/hts.v67il.907.

———. "Paul's Epistle to the Romans and the Catechesis of Gentiles in the *Didache*." *Reflecting on Romans: Essays in Honour of Andrie du Toit's 80th Birthday*. Edited by G. J. Steyn. BTS. Leuven: Peeters, forthcoming.

———. "Pure Sacrifice in Didache 14 as Jewish Christian Exegesis." *Neot* 42 (2008): 223–52.

———. "Resurrection and Zechariah 14.5 in the Didache Apocalypse." *JECS* 5 (1997): 154–79.

———. Review of Aaron Milavec, *The Didache: Faith, Hope, and Life of the Earliest Christian Communities, 50–70 C.E.*, *Neot* 39 (2005): 203–7.

———. "Ritual Process and Ritual Symbol in Didache 7–10." *VC* 54 (2000): 121–58.

———. "Torah and Troublesome Apostles in the Didache Community." *NovT* 33 (1991): 347–72.

———. "The Two Ways and Eschatological Hope: A Contested Terrain in Galatians 5 and the *Didache*." *Neot* 45 (2011): 221–51.

———. "Vice Catalogues as Oral-Mnemonic Cues: A Comparative Study of the Two Ways Tradition in the Didache and Parallels from the Perspective of Oral Tradition." Pages 111–35 in *Jesus, the Voice, and the Text: Beyond the Oral and the Written Gospel*. Edited by Tom Thatcher. Waco, TX: Baylor University Press, 2008.

Drews, Paul. "Apostellehre (Didache)." Pages 256–83 in *Handbuch zu den neutestamentlichen Apokryphen*. Edited by Edgar Hennecke. Tübingen: Mohr Siebeck, 1904.

Duling, Dennis C. "Memory, Collective Memory, Orality and the Gospels." *HTS* 67 (2011): 1–11.

Dunn, Geoffrey D. *Tertullian*. London: Routledge, 2004.

Dunn, James D. G. *Christianity in the Making*. 2 vols. Grand Rapids: Eerdmans, 2003–2008.

———. *The Epistles to Colossians and to Philemon*. NIGTC. Grand Rapids: Eerdmans, 1996.

———. *The Partings of the Ways between Christianity and Judaism and Their Significance for the Character of Christianity*. London: SCM; Philadelphia: Trinity, 1991.

———. *The Theology of Paul the Apostle*. Grand Rapids: Eerdmans, 1998.

———. *Unity and Diversity in the New Testament: An Inquiry into the Character of Earliest Christianity*. Philadelphia: Westminster, 1977.

Dunn, James D. G., and John W. Rogerson, eds. *Eerdmans Commentary on the Bible*. Grand Rapids: Eerdmans, 2003.

Easton, Burton Scott. *The Pastoral Epistles*. New York: Scribner's Sons, 1947.

Edsall, Benjamin. "'As I Said to You Before': Paul's Witness to Formative Early Christian Instruction." Ph.D. diss., Oxford University, 2013.

———. "*Kerygma*, Catechesis and Other Things We Used to Find: Twentieth-Century Research on Early Christian Teaching Since Alfred Seeberg (1903)." *CurBS* 10 (2012): 410–41.

Edwards, James R. "Markan Sandwiches." Pages 192–215 in *The Composition of Mark's Gospel: Selected Studies from Novum Testamentum*. Edited by David E. Orton. BRBS 3. Leiden: Brill, 1999.

Ehrman, Bart D. *The Apostolic Fathers*. 2 vols. LCL. Cambridge: Harvard University Press, 2003.

———. *Lost Christianities: The Battles for Scripture and the Faiths We Never Knew*. New York: Oxford University Press, 2003.

Elbogen, Ismar. *Der jüdische Gottesdienst in seiner geschichtlichen Entwicklung*. Hildesheim: Olms, 1913. Repr, 1962.

Emerton, J. A. "The Origin of the Son of Man Imagery." *JTS* 9 (1958): 225–42.
Emmrich, Martin. "Heb 6.4–6—Again! (A Pneumatological Inquiry)." *WTJ* 65 (2003): 83–95.
Epstein, Jacob Nachum, and Ezra Zion Melamed, eds. *Mekhilta d'Rabbi Šimon b. Jochai*. Jerusalem: Mekize Nirdamim, 1955.
Eriksson, Anders. *Traditions as Rhetorical Proof: Pauline Argumentation in 1 Corinthians*. ConBNT. Stockholm: Almquist & Wiksell, 1998.
Evans, Ernest, ed. and trans. *Tertullian Adversus Marcionem, Books 1–3*. Oxford: Clarendon, 1972.
Farkasfalvy, Denis. "The Eucharistic Provenance of New Testament Texts." Pages 63–87 in *Inspiration and Interpretation*. Washington, DC: Catholic University of America Press, 2010.
———. *Wedding Feast of the Lamb: Eucharistic Theology from A Biblical, Historical, and Systematic Perspective*. Chicago: Hillenbrand, 2004.
Fee, Gordon D. *The First and Second Letters to the Thessalonians*. NICNT. Grand Rapids: Eerdmans, 2009.
———. *Pauline Christology: An Exegetical-Theological Study*. Peabody, MA: Hendrickson, 2007.
Ferguson, Everett. *Baptism in the Early Church: History, Theology, and Liturgy in the First Five Centuries*. Grand Rapids: Eerdmans, 2009.
Feuillet, André. *The Apocalypse*. New York: Alba, 1965.
———. "Le Fils de l'homme de Daniel et la tradition biblique." *RB* 60 (1953): 170–202, 321–46.
Fine, Steven. *This Holy Place: On the Sanctity of the Synagogue during the Greco-Roman Period*. CJA 11. Notre Dame: University of Notre Dame Press, 1997.
Finkelstein, Louis. "The Birkat Ha-Mazon." *JQR* NS 19 (1928–1929): 211–62.
Finnegan, Ruth. *Literacy and Orality: Studies in the Technology of Communication*. Oxford: Blackwell, 1988.
Fitzmyer, Joseph A. "The Ascension of Christ in Pentecost." Pages 265–94 in *To Advance the Gospel: New Testament Studies*. 2nd ed. Grand Rapids: Eerdmans, 1998.
———. *First Corinthians*. AYBC 32. New Haven: Yale University Press, 2008.
———. *The Gospel according to Luke*. AB 28–28A. Garden City, NY: Doubleday, 1981–1985.
———. "The Gospel in the Theology of Paul." *Int* 33 (1979): 339–50.

Fleischer, Ezra. "On the Beginnings of Obligatory Jewish Prayer." Pages 3–47 in *Statutory Jewish Prayers: Their Emergence and Development* [Hebrew]. Vol. 1. Edited by Shulamit Elizur and Tova Beeri. Jerusalem: Magnes, 1989. Repr., 2012.

Flusser, David. "Paul's Jewish-Christian Opponents in the *Didache*." Pages 195–211 in *The* Didache *in Modern Research*. Edited by Jonathan A. Draper. AGJU 37. Leiden: Brill, 1996.

Foley, John Miles. *Immanent Art: From Structure to Meaning in Traditional Epic*. Bloomington: Indiana University Press, 1991.

———. *Singer of Tales in Performance*. Bloomington: Indiana University Press, 1995.

Foster, Paul. "Paul and Matthew: Two Strands of the Early Jesus Movement with Little Sign of Connection." Pages 86–114 in *Paul and the Gospels: Christologies, Conflicts and Convergences*. Edited by Michael F. Bird and Joel Willitts. LNTS 411. London: T&T Clark, 2011.

France, R. T. *The Gospel of Matthew*. NICNT. Grand Rapids: Eerdmans, 2007.

———. *Mark: A Commentary on the Greek Text*. NIGTC. Grand Rapids: Eerdmans, 2002.

Frankemölle, Hubert. *Evangelium—Begriff und Gattung: Ein Forschungsbericht*. Stuttgart: Katholisches Bibelwerk, 1994.

Freedman, David N., ed. *Anchor Bible Dictionary*. 6 vols. New York: Yale University Press, 1992.

———, ed. *Eerdmans Dictionary of the Bible*. Grand Rapids: Eerdmans, 2000.

Friedmann, M., ed. *Seder Eliahu Rabba* and *Eliahu Zuta* and *Nispachim le-Seder Eliahu Zuta*. Vienna: 1904. Repr., Jerusalem: Wahrmann, 1969.

Fuchs, M. Z. "Teshuvot li-shenei mehapkhanim." *Sinai* 114 (1994–1995): 162–70.

Funk, Franz Xaver, ed. *Patres apostolici*. 3rd ed. Tübingen: Laupp, 1913.

Furstenberg, Yair. "Defilement Penetrating the Body: A New Understanding of Contamination in Mark 7.15." *NTS* 54 (2008): 176–200.

Garland, David E. *Luke*. ZECNT. Grand Rapids: Zondervan, 2011.

Garleff, Gunnar. *Urchristliche Identität in Matthäusevangelium, Didache und Jakobusbrief*. BVB 9. Münster: LIT, 2004.

Garrow, Alan J. P. "The Eschatological Tradition behind 1 Thessalonians: Didache 16." *JSNT* 32 (2009): 191–215.

———. *The Gospel of Matthew's Dependence on the* Didache. JSNTSup 254. London: T&T Clark, 2004.

———. *Revelation*. NTR. London: Routledge, 1997.
Gaston, Lloyd. "Retrospect." Pages 163–74 in *Separation and Polemic*. Vol. 2 of *Anti-Judaism in Early Christianity*. Edited by S. G. Wilson. 2 vols. SCJ 2. Waterloo: Wilfrid Laurier University, 1986.
Giet, Stanislas. *L'énigme de la Didachè*. PFLUS 149. Paris: Ophrys, 1970.
Ginzburg, Louis. "Saadia's Siddur." *JQR* NS 33 (1942): 315–63.
Glasson, T. F. *The Second Advent: The Origin of the New Testament Doctrine*. 3rd rev. ed. London: Epworth, 1963.
———. "The Son of Man Imagery: Enoch xiv and Daniel vii." *NTS* 23 (1976–1977): 82–90.
Glover, Richard. "The Didache's Quotations and the Synoptic Gospels." *NTS* 5 (1958): 12–29.
Gnilka, Joachim. *Das Evangelium nach Markus*. 2 vols. EKKNT 2. Zürich: Benziger, 1978.
Goguel, Maurice. *L'Eucharistie: Des origins à Justin Martyr*. Paris: Fischbacher, 1910.
Goldberg, Abr. "The Tosefta: Companion to the Mishna." Pages 283–98 in *Oral Tora, Halakha, Mishna, Tosefta, Talmud, External Tractates*. Vol. 1 of *The Literature of the Sages*. Edited by Shmuel Safrai. CRINT 2.3a. Assen: Van Gorcum; Philadelphia: Fortress, 1987.
Goldberg, Arnold. "Service of the Heart: Liturgical Aspects of Synagogue Worship." Pages 195–211 in *Standing before God: Studies on Prayer in Scriptures and in Tradition*. Edited by A. Finkel and L. Frizzell. New York: Ktav, 1981.
Goldingay, John E. *Daniel*. WBC. Dallas: Word, 1989.
Goodacre, Mark. *Thomas and the Gospels: The Case for Thomas's Familiarity with the Gospels*. Grand Rapids: Eerdmans, 2012.
Goodspeed, Edgar J. "The *Didache*, Barnabas and the Doctrina." *AThR* 27 (1945): 228–47.
Gordon, Robert P. "Targumic Parallels to Acts XIII 18 and Didache XIV 3." *NovT* 16 (1974): 285–89.
Goulder, Michael. *Luke: A New Paradigm*. 2 vols. JSNTSup 10. Sheffield: JSOT, 1989.
Grant, Frederick C. "The Gospel According to St. Mark." *IB* 7:627–917.
Gregory, Andrew F., and Christopher M. Tuckett, eds. *The New Testament and the Apostolic Fathers: The Reception of the New Testament in the Apostolic Fathers*. 2 vols. Oxford: Oxford University Press, 2005.
Gundry, Robert H. "ΕΥΑΓΓΕΛΙΟΝ: How Soon a Book?" *JBL* 115 (1996): 321–25.

———. *Mark: A Commentary on His Apology for the Cross.* Grand Rapids: Eerdmans, 1993.

Gurtner, Daniel M. "Matthew's Theology of the Temple and the 'Parting of the Ways.'" Pages 108–53 in *Built upon the Rock: Studies in the Gospel of Matthew.* Edited by Daniel M. Gurtner and John Nolland. Grand Rapids: Eerdmans, 2007.

Haar Romeny, Bas ter. "Hypotheses on the Development of Judaism and Christianity in Syria in the Period after 70 CE." Pages 13–33 in *Matthew and the Didache: Two Documents from the Same Jewish-Christian Milieu?* Edited by Huub van de Sandt. Assen: Van Gorcum; Minneapolis: Fortress, 2005.

Haenchen, Ernst. *Die Apostelgeschichte.* 14th ed. KEK 6. Göttingen: Vandenhoeck & Ruprecht, 1965.

Hagner, Donald A. *The Use of the Old and New Testaments in Clement of Rome.* NovTSup 34. Leiden: Brill, 1973.

Hakola, Raimo. "Social Identities and Group Phenomena in Second Temple Judaism." Pages 259–76 in *Explaining Christian Origins and Early Judaism: Contributions from Cognitive and Social Science.* Edited by Petri Luomanen, Ilkka Pyysiäinen, and Risto Uro. Leiden: Brill, 2007.

Hall, Stuart G. Review of *The Didache: Text, Translation, Analysis, and Commentary*, by Aaron Milavec. *JTS* 55 (2004): 704–6.

Halliday, Michael Alexander Kirkwood. *Language as Social Semiotic: The Social Interpretation of Language and Meaning.* Baltimore: University Park Press, 1978.

Harnack, Adolf von. *Die Apostellehre und die jüdischen Beiden Wege.* Leipzig: Heinrichs, 1886.

———. *Die Lehre der zwölf Apostel nebst Untersuchungenzuraltesten Geschichte der Kirchenverfassung und des Kirchenrechts.* TUGAL 2.1, 2. Leipzig: Hinrichs, 1884. Repr., Berlin: Akademie, 1991.

———. *The Mission and Expansion of Christianity in the First Three Centuries.* London: Williams & Norgate; New York: Putnam, 1908.

Harrington, Daniel J. "Pseudo-Philo." Pages 297–377 in volume 2 of *The Old Testament Pseudepigrapha.* Edited by James H. Charlesworth. New York: Doubleday, 1985.

———. "The Reception of Walter Bauer's Orthodoxy and Heresy in Earliest Christianity during the Last Decade." *HTR* 73 (1980): 289–98.

Harrington, Daniel J., and Jacques Cazeaux, eds. *Pseudo-Philon: Les antiquités bibliques.* 2 vols. SC 229. Paris: Cerf, 1976.

Harrington, Hannah K. "Did the Pharisees Eat Ordinary Food in a State of Ritual Purity?" *JSJ* 26 (1995): 42–54.

———. *The Purity Texts*. CQS 5. London: T&T Clark, 2004.

Harris, J. Rendel. *The Teaching of the Apostles*. London: C. J. Clay; Baltimore: Johns Hopkins University Press, 1887.

Heinemann, Joseph. *Prayer in the Talmud: Forms and Patterns*. SJ 9. Berlin: de Gruyter, 1977.

Henderson, Ian H. "*Didache* and Orality in Synoptic Comparison." *JBL* 111 (1992): 283–306.

———. "Style-Switching in the *Didache*: Fingerprint or Argument?" Pages 177–209 in *The Didache in Context: Essays on Its Text, History and Transmission*. Edited by Clayton N. Jefford. NovTSup 77. Leiden: Brill, 1995.

Hengel, Martin. *Judaism and Hellenism: Studies in their Encounter in Palestine during the Early Hellenistic Period*. 2 vols. London: SCM, 1974.

Hengel, Martin, and A. M. Schwemer. *Paulus Zwischen Damascus und Antiochien: Die unbekannten Jahre des Apostels*. WUNT 108. Tübingen: Mohr Siebeck, 1998.

Himmelfarb, Martha. *A Kingdom of Priests: Ancestry and Merit in Ancient Judaism*. JCC. Philadelphia: University of Pennsylvania Press, 2006.

Hogg, Michael A., and Craig McGarty. "Self-categorization and Social Identity." Pages 10–47 in *Social Identity Theory: Constructive and Critical Advances*. Edited by Dominic Abrams and Michael A. Hogg. New York: Springer, 1990.

Holmes, Michael W., ed. and trans. *The Apostolic Fathers: Greek Texts and English Translations*. 3rd ed. Grand Rapids: Baker, 2007.

———, ed. *The Greek New Testament: SBL Edition*. Atlanta: SBL Press, 2010.

Holtzmann, Heinrich J. *Die Synoptiker*. HKNT 1/1. Tübingen: Mohr Siebeck, 1901.

Horbury, William. "The Benediction of the *Minim* and Early Jewish-Christian Controversy." Pages 67–110 in *Jews and Christians in Contact and Controversy*. Edinburgh: T&T Clark, 1998.

———. "'Gospel' in Herodian Judaea." Pages 7–30 in *The Written Gospel*. Edited by Markus Bockmuehl and Donald A. Hagner. Cambridge: Cambridge University Press, 2005.

Horovitz, Haym S., ed. *Siphre d'be Rab I: Siphre ad Numeros adjecto Siphre zutta*. CT 3/3.1. Leipzig: 1917. Corr. repr., Jerusalem: Wahrmann, 1966.

Horovitz, H. S., and I. A. Rabin, eds. *Mechilta d'Rabbi Ismael.* Jerusalem: Wahrmann, 1930. Repr., 1970.

Horsley, G. H. R. *New Documents Illustrating Early Christianity.* Sydney: Macquarie University, 1981.

Horsley, Richard A., and Jonathan A. Draper. *Whoever Hears You Hears Me: Prophets, Performance, and Tradition in Q.* Harrisburg, PA: Trinity Press International, 1999.

Horst, Pieter W. van der. "The Birkat Ha-minim in Recent Research." Pages 113–24 in *Hellenism, Judaism, Christianity: Essays on Their Interaction.* Leuven: Peeters, 1998.

Hunter, Archibald Macbride. *Exploring the New Testament.* Edinburgh: Saint Andrew Press, 1971.

———. *Paul and His Predecessors.* 2nd ed. London: SCM, 1961.

Hurtado, Larry H. *Lord Jesus Christ: Devotion to Jesus in Earliest Christianity.* Grand Rapids: Eerdmans, 2003.

Iselin, Ludwig Emil, and Andreas Heusler. *Eine bisher unbekannte Version des ersten Teiles der "Apostellehre."* TUGAL 13.1b. Leipzig: Hinrichs, 1895.

Iser, Wolfgang. *The Act of Reading: A Theory of Aesthetic Response.* Baltimore: Johns Hopkins University Press, 1978.

Jackson-McCabe, Matt, ed. *Jewish Christianity Reconsidered: Rethinking Ancient Groups and Texts.* Minneapolis: Fortress, 2007.

Jaubert, Annie. *La date de la Cène: Calendrier biblique et liturgie chrétienne.* Paris: Gabalda, 1957.

Jefford, Clayton N. *The Apostolic Fathers: An Essential Guide.* Nashville: Abingdon, 2005.

———. "Conflict at Antioch: Ignatius and the *Didache* at Odds." *StPatr* 36 (2001): 262–69.

———. "Didache." *EDB*: 345a–46a.

———. "The Milieu of Matthew, the Didache, and Ignatius of Antioch: Agreements and Differences." Pages 35–47 in *Matthew and the Didache: Two Documents from the Same Jewish-Christian Milieu?* Edited by Huub van de Sandt. Minneapolis: Fortress, 2005.

———. *Reading the Apostolic Fathers: An Introduction.* Grand Rapids: Baker, 2012.

———. Review of *The Didache: Faith, Hope, and Life of the Earliest Christian Communities, 50–70 CE,* by Aaron Milavec. *CBQ* 66 (2004): 662–64.

———. *The Sayings of Jesus in the Teaching of the Twelve Apostles.* VCSup 11. Leiden: Brill, 1989.

———. "Social Locators as a Bridge between the *Didache* and Matthew." Pages 245–64 in *Trajectories through the New Testament and the Apostolic Fathers*. Vol. 2 in *The New Testament and the Apostolic Fathers*. Edited by Andrew F. Gregory and Christopher M. Tuckett. Oxford: Oxford University Press, 2005.

———. *Teaching of the Twelve Apostles: Didache*. Santa Rosa, CA: Polebridge, 2013.

———. "Tradition and Witness in Antioch: Acts 15 and Didache 6." Pages 75–89 in *Perspectives on Contemporary New Testament Questions: Essays in Honor of T.C. Smith*. Edited by Edgar V. McKnight. Lewiston: Mellen, 1992.

———. "'The Wisdom of Sirach and the Glue of the Matthew-*Didache* Tradition.' In *Intertextuality in the Second Century*. Edited by D. Jeffrey Bingham and Clayton N. Jefford. BAC. Leiden: Brill, forthcoming.

Jefford, Clayton N., with Kenneth J. Harder and Louis D. Amezaga Jr. *Reading the Apostolic Fathers: An Introduction*. Peabody, MA: Hendrickson, 1996. Repr., Grand Rapids: Baker, 2012.

Jefford, Clayton N., and Stephen J. Patterson. "A Note on *Didache* 12.2a (Coptic)." *SecCent* 7 (1989–1990): 65–75.

Jenni, E., with assistance from C. Westermann. *Theological Lexicon of the Old Testament*. Translated by M. E. Biddle. 3 vols. Peabody, MA: Hendrickson, 1997.

Jeremias, Joachim. *Die Abendmahlsworte Jesu*. Göttingen: Vandenhoeck & Ruprecht, 1967.

———. *Sermon on the Mount*. Translated by Norman Perrin. Philadelphia: Fortress, 1963.

———. *Die Verkündigung Jesu*. Vol. 1 of *Neutestamentliche Theologie*. Gütersloh: Gütersloher Verlagshaus, 1973. Repr. as *The Proclamation of Jesus*. Vol. 1 of *New Testament Theology*. Translated by John Bowden. New York: Scribner's Sons, 1971.

Jervell, Jacob. *Die Apostelgeschichte*. 17th ed. KEK 3. Göttingen: Vandenhoeck & Ruprecht, 1998.

Jewett, Robert. *Romans: A Commentary*. Hermeneia. Minneapolis, Fortress, 2007.

Johnson, Luke Timothy. *Hebrews: A Commentary*. NTL. Louisville: Westminster John Knox, 2006.

———. *The Gospel of Luke*. SP. Collegeville: Liturgical Press, 1991.

Johnson, William. "Toward a Sociology of Reading in Classical Antiquity." *AJP* 4 (2000): 593–627.

Johnsson, William G. "The Pilgrimage Motif in the Book of Hebrews." *JBL* 97 (1978): 239–51.

Jones, F. Stanley, and Paul A. Mirecki. "Considerations on the Coptic Papyrus of the Didache." Pages 47–87 in *The Didache in Context: Essays on Its Text, History and Transmission*. Edited by Clayton N. Jefford. NovTSup 77. Leiden: Brill, 1995.

Käsemann, Ernst. "Sentences of Holy Law in the NT." Pages 66–81 in *New Testament Questions of Today*. London: SCM, 1969.

———. *The Wandering People of God: An Investigation of the Letter to the Hebrews*. Translated by Roy A. Harrisville and Irving L. Sandberg. Minneapolis: Augsburg, 1984.

Kalimi, Isaac. *The Reshaping of Ancient Israelite History in Chronicles*. Winona Lake, IN: Eisenbrauns, 2005.

Kautzsch, E. *Gesenius' Hebrew Grammar*. Translated by A. E. Cowley. 2nd ed. Oxford: Clarendon, 1983.

Kazen, Thomas. *Jesus and Purity Halakhah: Was Jesus Indifferent to Impurity?* ConBNT 38. Winona Lake, IN: Eisenbrauns, 2010.

Keith, Chris. "A Performance of the Text: The Adulteress's Entrance into John's Gospel." Pages 49–69 in *The Fourth Gospel in First-Century Media Culture*. Edited by Anthony Le Donne and Tom Thatcher. LNTS 426. London: T&T Clark International, 2011.

Kelber, Werner H. *The Oral and Written Gospel: The Hermeneutics of Speaking and Writing in the Synoptic Tradition, Mark, Paul and Q*. Philadelphia: Fortress, 1983. Repr., Bloomington, IN: Indiana University Press, 1997.

———. "The Oral-Scribal-Memorial Acts of Communication in Early Christianity." Pages 235–62 in *Jesus, the Voice, and the Text: Beyond the Oral and the Written Gospel*. Edited by Tom Thatcher. Waco, TX: Baylor University Press, 2008.

Kelhoffer, James A. "'Gospel' as a Literary Title in Early Christianity and the Question of What Is (and Is Not) a 'Gospel' in Canons of Scholarly Literature." Pages 399–422 in *Jesus in apokryphen Evangelienüberlieferungen*. Edited by Jörg Frey and Jens Schröter, with Jakob Späth. WUNT 254. Tübingen: Mohr Siebeck, 2010.

———. "'How Soon a Book' Revisited: ΕΥΑΓΓΕΛΙΟΝ as a Reference to 'Gospel' Materials in the First Half of the Second Century." *ZNW* 95 (2004): 1–34.

Kennedy, George. *New Testament Interpretation through Rhetorical Criticism*. Chapel Hill: University of North Carolina Press, 1983.

Khomych, Taras. "Diversity of the Notion of Apostolicity in the Writings of the Apostolic Fathers." Pages 37–55 in *Heiligkeit und Apostolizität der Kirche*. Edited by Theresia Hainthaler, Franz Mali, and Gregor Emmenegger. Innsbruck: Tyrolia, 2010.

Kilmartin, Edward J. "Sacrificium Laudis: Content and Function of Early Eucharistic Prayers." *TS* 35 (1974): 268–87.

Kim, Seyoon. "The Jesus Tradition in 1 Thess 4.13–5.11." *NTS* 48 (2002): 225–42.

Kimelman, Reuven. "Birkat Ha-minim and the Lack of Evidence for an Anti-Christian Prayer in Late Antiquity." Pages 226–44 in *Aspects of Judaism in the Graeco-Roman World*. Vol. 2 of *Jewish and Christian Self-Definition*. Edited by E. P. Sanders. London: SCM, 1981.

———. "Rabbinic Prayer in Late Antiquity." Pages 573–611 in *The Late Roman-Rabbinic Period*. Vol. 4 of *The Cambridge History of Judaism*. Edited by Steven Katz. Cambridge: Cambridge University Press, 2006.

King, Karen L. *What is Gnosticism?* Cambridge: Harvard University Press, 2003.

Kirby, Peter. "The Case against the Empty Tomb." *JHC* 9 (2002): 175–202.

Kirk, Alan. "Manuscript Tradition as a *Tertium Quid*: Orality and Memory in Scribal Practices." Pages 215–34 in *Jesus, the Voice, and the Text: Beyond the Oral and the Written Gospel*. Edited by Tom Thatcher. Waco, TX: Baylor University Press, 2008.

———. "Memory, Scribal Media and the Synoptic Problem." Pages 459–66 in *New Studies in the Synoptic Problem*. Edited by Paul Foster, Andrew Gregory, John Kloppenborg, and Joseph Verheyden. BETL 239. Leuven: Peeters, 2011.

Kittel, G., and G. Friedrich, ed. *Theological Dictionary of the New Testament*. Translated by G. W. Bromiley. 10 vols. Grand Rapids: Eerdmans, 1964–1976.

Klauser, Theodor. "Taufet in Lebendigem Wasser! Zum religions- und kulturgeschichtlichen Verständnis von Didache 7,1–3." Pages 177–83 in *Gesammelte Arbeiten zur Liturgiegeschichte, Kirchengeschichte und Christlichen Archäologie*. Edited by Ernst Dassmann. JAC.E 3. Münster: Aschendorff, 1974.

Klawans, Jonathan. *Impurity and Sin in Ancient Judaism*. Oxford: Oxford University Press, 2000.

———. "The Impurity of Immorality in Ancient Judaism." *JJS* 48 (1997): 1–16.

———. "Pure Violence: Sacrifice and Defilement in Ancient Israel." *HTR* 94 (2001): 135–57.

———. *Purity, Sacrifice, and the Temple: Symbolism and Supersessionism in the Study of Ancient Judaism*. Oxford: Oxford University Press, 2006.

Klein, Gunther. *Der älteste christliche Katechismus und die jüdische Propaganda-Literatur*. Berlin: Georg Reimer, 1909.

Kleist, James A. *The Didache; the Epistle of Barnabas; the Epistles and the Martyrdom of St. Polycarp; the Fragments of Papias; the Epistle to Diognetus*. ACW 6. Westminster, MD: Newman, 1948.

Klinghardt, Matthias. *Gemeinschaftsmahl und Mahlgemeinschaft: Soziologie und Liturgie frühchristlicher Mahlfeiern*. TANZ 13. Tübingen: Francke, 1996.

Kloppenborg, John S. "*Didache* 1.1–6.1, James, Matthew, and the Torah." Pages 193–221 in *Trajectories through the New Testament and the Apostolic Fathers*. Vol. 2 in *The New Testament and the Apostolic Fathers*. Edited by Andrew F. Gregory and Christopher M. Tuckett. Oxford: Oxford University Press, 2005.

———. "*Didache* 16 6–8 and Special Matthaean Tradition." *ZNW* 70 (1979): 54–67.

———. "Memory, Performance, and the Sayings of Jesus." Paper presented at the Helsinki Seminar on Memory, Helsinki, Finland, May 11, 2011.

———. "The Transformation of Moral Exhortation in *Didache* 1–5." Pages 88–109 in *The Didache in Context: Essays on Its Text, History and Transmission*. Edited by Clayton N. Jefford. NovTSup 77. Leiden: Brill, 1995.

———. "The Use of the Synoptics or Q in *Did*. 1:3b–2:1." Pages 105–29 in *Matthew and the Didache: Two Documents from the Same Jewish-Christian Milieu?* Edited by Huub van de Sandt. Assen: Van Gorcum; Minneapolis: Fortress, 2005.

Knopf, Rudolf. *Die Lehre der zwölf Apostel: Die zwei Clemensbriefe*. Vol. 1 of *Die apostolischen Väter*. HNT.E. Tübingen: Mohr Siebeck, 1920.

Koch, Dietrich-Alex. "Die Eucharistischen Gebete von Didache 9 und 10 und das Rätsel von Didache 10:6." Pages 195–210 in *Jesus, Paul, and Early Christianity: Studies in Honour of Henk Jan de Jonge*. Edited by Rieuwerd Buitenwerf, Harm W. Hollander, and Johannes Tromp. Leiden: Brill, 2008.

Kodjak, Andrej. *A Structural Analysis of the Sermon on the Mount*. Berlin: de Gruyter, 1986.

Koester, Craig R. *Hebrews*. AB 36. New York: Doubleday, 2001.

Koester, Helmut. *Ancient Christian Gospels: Their History and Development*. London: SCM; Philadelphia: Trinity, 1990.

———. "From the Kerygma-Gospel to Written Gospels." *NTS* 35 (1989): 361–81.

———. *Synoptische Überlieferung bei den apostolischen Vätern*. TUGAL 65/5.10. Berlin: Akademie, 1957.

———. "The Theological Aspects of Primitive Christian Heresy." Pages 65–83 in *The Future of Our Religious Past: Essays in Honour of Rudolph Bultmann*. Edited by James M. Robinson. Translated by C. E. Cariston and R. P. Scharlemann. New York: Harper & Row, 1971.

———. "Written Gospels or Oral Tradition?" *JBL* 113 (1994): 293–97.

Köhler, Wolf-Dietrich. *Die Rezeption des Matthäusevangeliums in der Zeit vor Irenaeus*. WUNT 2/24. Tübingen: Mohr Siebeck, 1985.

Kollmann, Bernd. *Ursprung und Gestalten der frühchristlichen Mahlfeier*. GTA 43. Göttingen: Vandenhoeck & Ruprecht, 1990.

Kostenberger, Andreas, and Michael Kruger. *The Heresy of Orthodoxy*. Wheaton, IL: Crossway, 2010.

Kraft, Robert A. *Barnabas and the Didache*. AF 3. Toronto: Nelson, 1965.

Kuhn, Thomas S. *The Structure of Scientific Revolutions*. Chicago: University Press, 1962.

Kurek-Chomycz, Dominika A. "Performing the Passion, Embodying Proclamation: The Story of Jesus's Passion in the Pauline Letters?" Pages 373–402 in *Gospel Images of Jesus Christ in Church Tradition and in Biblical Scholarship*. Edited by Chrestos Karakolis, Karl-Wilhelm Niebuhr, and S. Rogalsky. WUNT 1/288. Tübingen: Mohr Siebeck, 2012.

Kutscher, Edward Yechezkel. *Words and Their History*. Jerusalem: Kiryath Sepher, 1974. (Hebrew).

Lachs, Samuel Tobias. *A Rabbinic Commentary on the New Testament: The Gospels of Matthew, Mark, and Luke*. Hoboken, NJ: Ktav, 1987.

Lacocque, André. "Allusions to Creation in Daniel 7." Pages 114–31 in *The Book of Daniel: Composition and Reception*. Edited by John Joseph Collins and Peter W. Flint. 2 vols. VTSup 83. Leiden: Brill, 2001.

Ladd, George Eldon. "The Eschatology of the Didache." Ph.D. diss., Harvard University, 1949.

Lagarde, P. A. de. *Constitutiones apostolorum*. London: Williams & Norgate; Leipzig: Teubner, 1862.

Lake, Kirsopp, trans. *The Apostolic Fathers*. 2 vols. LCL. Cambridge: Harvard University Press, 1912.

———. "The Didache." Pages 24–36 in *The New Testament and the Apostolic Fathers*. Oxford: Clarendon, 1905.

Lane, William L. *The Gospel of Mark*. NICNT. Grand Rapids: Eerdmans, 1974.

Langer, R. "Revisiting Early Rabbinic Liturgy: The Recent Contributions of Ezra Fleischer." *Prooftexts* 19 (1999): 179–94.

LaPorte, Jean. *Eucharistia in Philo*. New York: Mellen, 1983.

Lawrence, Jonathan D. *Washing in Water: Trajectories of Ritual Bathing in the Hebrew Bible and Second Temple Literature*. SBLAB 23. Atlanta: Society of Biblical Literature, 2006.

Layton, Bentley. "The Sources, Date and Transmission of *Didache* 1.3b–2.1." *HTR* 61 (1968): 343–83.

Lee, Margaret Ellen, and Bernard Brandon Scott. *Sound Mapping the New Testament*. Salem, OR: Polebridge, 2009.

Lerner, Myron B. "The External Tractates." Pages 367–404 in *The Literature of the Sages*. Edited by Shmuel Safrai. CRINT 2.3. Assen: Van Gorcum; Philadelphia: Fortress, 1987.

Levinson, Bernard M. *Deuteronomy and the Hermeneutics of Legal Innovation*. New York: Oxford University Press, 1997.

Licht, Jacob. *The Rule Scroll: A Scroll from the Wilderness of Judaea: 1QS-1QSa-1QSb*. Jerusalem: Bialik Institute, 1965. (Hebrew).

Liddell, H. G., R. Scott, and H. S. Jones. *A Greek-English Lexicon*. 9th ed. with revised supplement. Oxford: Oxford University Press, 1996.

Lierman, John D. *The New Testament Moses: Christian Perceptions of Moses and Israel in the Setting of the Jewish Religion*. WUNT 2/173. Tübingen: Mohr Siebeck, 2004.

Lietzmann, Hans. *Messe und Herrenmahl: Eine Studie zur Geschichte der Liturgie*. AK. Bonn: Marcus & Weber, 1926.

Lightfoot, Joseph B. *The Apostolic Fathers: Revised Texts with Short Introductions and English Translations*. Edited by J. R. Harmer. London: MacMillan, 1912.

Lindemann, Andreas. "Paul in the Writings of the Apostolic Fathers." Pages 25–45 in *Paul and the Legacies of Paul*. Edited by William S. Babcock. Dallas: Southern Methodist University Press, 1990.

———. *Paulus im ältesten Christentum: Das Bild des Apostels und die Rezeption der paulinischen Theologie in der frühchristlichen Literatur bis Marcion*. BHT 58. Tübingen: Mohr Siebeck, 1979.

Lips, Hermann von. "Schweine füttert man, Hunde nicht—Ein Versuch, das Rätsel von Matthäus 7:6 zu lösen." *ZNW* 79 (1988): 165–86.

Liubinskas, Susann. "Identification by Spirit Alone: Community-Identity Construction in Galatians 3:19–4:7." *AJ* 67 (2012): 27–55.

Lockett, Darian R. "Structure or Communicative Strategy? The 'Two Ways' Motif in James' Theological Instruction." *Neot* 42 (2008): 269–87.

Lohmeyer, Ernst. *Das Evangelium des Markus*. KEK 1.2. Göttingen: Vandenhoeck & Ruprecht, 1937.

Long, Thomas G. *Hebrews*. IBC. Louisville: Westminster John Knox, 1997.

Lord, Albert B. *The Singer of Tales*. HSCL 24. Cambridge: Harvard University Press, 1960.

Louw, Johannes P., and Eugene A. Nida. *Introduction and Domains*. Vol. 1 of *Greek-English Lexicon of the New Testament Based on Semantic Domains*. New York: United Bible Societies, 1988.

Lust, J., Erik Eynikel, K. Hauspie, and G. Chamberlain, eds. *A Greek-English Lexicon of the Septuagint*. Stuttgart: Deutsche Bibelgesellschaft, 2003.

Luz, Ulrich. *Das Evangelium nach Matthäus*. 5th ed. Vol. 1. EKKNT 1. Zürich: Benzinger; Neukirchen: Neukirchener, 2002.

MacDonald, Margaret Y. "Beyond Identification of the Topos of Household Management: Reading the Household Codes in Light of Recent Methodologies and Theoretical Perspectives in the Study of the New Testament." *NTS* 57 (2011): 65–90.

Mack, Burton L. "On Redescribing Christian Origins." *MTSR* (1996): 247–67.

Macpherson, John. "Was There a Second Imprisonment of Paul in Rome?" *AJT* 4 (1900): 23–48.

Magness, Jodi. *The Archaeology of Qumran and the Dead Sea Scrolls*. SDSSRL. Grand Rapids: Eerdmans, 2002.

Manson, T. W. "The Son of Man in Daniel, Enoch and the Gospels." *BJRL* 32 (1950): 171–93.

Manson, William. *The Gospel of Luke*. MNTC. London: Hodder & Stoughton, 1930.

Marcovich, Miroslav, ed. *Iustini Martyris Apologiae pro Christianis*. PTS 38. Berlin: de Gruyter, 1994.

Markschies, Christoph. *Gnosis: An Introduction*. London: T&T Clark, 2003.

Mason, Steve. "Chief Priests, Sadducees, Pharisees and Sanhedrin in Acts." Pages 115–77 in *The Book of Acts in its Palestinian Setting*. Vol. 4 of *The Book of Acts in Its First Century Setting*. Edited by Richard Bauckham. Grand Rapids: Eerdmans; Carlisle: Paternoster, 1995.

———, ed. *Judean War 2*. Vol. 1b of *Flavius Josephus: Translation and Commentary*. Leiden: Brill, 2008.
Massaux, Edouard. *The Influence of the Gospel of Saint Matthew on the Christian Literature before Saint Irenaeus*. Translated by Norman J. Belval and Suzanne Hecht. 3 vols. NGS 5.2. Leuven: Peeters, 1990; Macon, GA: Mercer University Press; repr., 1993.
Matera, Frank. "New Testament Theology: History, Method, and Identity." *CBQ* 67 (2005): 1–21.
Mathewson, Dave. "Reading Heb 6:4–6 in Light of the Old Testament." *WTJ* 61 (1999): 209–65.
Mazza, Enrico. "Elements of a Eucharistic Interpretation." Pages 276–99 in *The* Didache *in Modern Research*. Edited by Jonathan A. Draper. AGJU 37. Leiden: Brill, 1996.
———. *The Origins of the Eucharistic Prayer*. Translated by Ronald E. Lane. Collegeville, MN: Liturgical Press, 1995.
McKenzie, John L. "The Social Character of Inspiration." *CBQ* 24 (1962): 115–25.
McKnight, Scot. "The Warning Passages of Hebrews: A Formal Analysis and Theological Conclusions." *TJ* NS 13 (1992): 21–59.
Mees, Michael. "Die Bedeutung der Sentenzen und ihrer auxesis für den Formung der Jesusworte nach Didache 1,3b–2,1." *VetChr* 8 (1971): 55–76.
Metzger, Bruce M. *A Textual Commentary on the Greek New Testament*. 2nd ed. London: United Bible Societies, 1994.
———. "When Did Scribes Begin to Use Writing Desks?" Pages 123–37 in *Historical and Literary Studies, Pagan, Jewish, and Christian*. Leiden: Brill, 1968.
Michel, Otto. *Der Brief an die Hebräer*. 8th ed. KEK 14. Göttingen: Vandenhoeck & Ruprecht, 1984.
———. "κύνω, κυνάριον." *TDNT* 3:1101–4.
Milavec, Aaron. *The Didache: Faith, Hope, and Life of the Earliest Christian Communities, 50–70 CE*. New York: Newman, 2003.
———. *The Didache: Text, Translation, Analysis, and Commentary*. Collegeville, MN: Liturgical Press, 2003.
———. "The *Didache*: A Window on Gentile Christianity before the Written Gospels." *The Fourth R* 18 (2005): 7–11, 15–16
———. "A Rejoinder [to Tuckett]." *JECS* 13 (2005): 519–23.
———. "The Saving Efficacy of the Burning Process in *Didache* 16.5." Pages 131–55 in *The* Didache *in Context: Essays on Its Text, History*

and Transmission. Edited by Clayton N. Jefford. NovTSup 77. Leiden: Brill, 1995.

———. "Synoptic Tradition in the *Didache* Revisited." *JECS* 11 (2003): 443–80.

———. "When, Why, and for Whom Was the *Didache* Created? Insights into the Social and Historical Setting of the *Didache* Communities." Pages 63–84 in *Matthew and the Didache: Two Documents from the Same Jewish-Christian Milieu?* Edited by Huub van de Sandt. Assen: Van Gorcum; Minneapolis: Fortress, 2005.

Milgrom, Jacob. "The Dynamics of Purity in the Priestly System." Pages 29–32 in *Purity and Holiness: The Heritage of Leviticus*. Edited by Marcel J. H. M. Poorthuis and Joshua Schwartz. JCP 2. Leiden: Brill, 2000.

———. *Leviticus 1–16: A New Translation with Introduction and Commentary*. AB 3. New York: Doubleday, 1991.

Mitchell, Alan C. *Hebrews*. SP 13. Collegeville, MN: Liturgical Press, 2007.

Mitchell, Margaret. "Concerning PERI DE in 1 Corinthians." *NovT* 3 (1989): 229–56.

Mitchell, Nathan. "Baptism in the *Didache*." Pages 226–55 in *The Didache in Context: Essays on Its Text, History and Transmission*. Edited by Clayton N. Jefford. NovTSup 77. Leiden: Brill, 1995.

Moffatt, James. *A Critical and Exegetical Commentary on the Epistle to the Hebrews*. ICC. New York: Scribner's Sons, 1924.

Moll, Helmut. *Die Lehre von der Eucharistie als Opfer: Eine dogmengeschichtliche Untersuchung vom Neuen Testament bis Irenäus von Lyon*. Theophaneia 26. Köln: Hanstein, 1975.

Moore, Arthur L. *The Parousia in the New Testament*. NovTSup 13. Leiden: Brill, 1966.

Moore, George Foot. *Judaism in the First Centuries of the Christian Era*. 3 vols. Cambridge: Harvard University Press, 1927–1930.

Moreschini, Claudio, and Enrico Norelli. *Early Christian Greek and Latin Literature: A Literary History*. Translated by Matthew J. O'Connell. 2 vols. Peabody, MA: Hendrickson, 2005.

Morgenthaler, Robert. *Statistik des neutestamentlichen Wortschatzes*. 4th ed. Zürich: Gotthelf, 1992.

Moule, C. F. D. "A Reconsideration of the Context of *Maranatha*." *NTS* 6 (1959–1960): 307–10.

Moxnes, Halvor. *The Economy of the Kingdom: Social Conflict and Economic Relations in Luke's Gospel*. Philadelphia: Fortress, 1988.

Mueller, Joseph G. "The Ancient Church Order Literature: Genre or Tradition?" *JECS* 15 (2007): 337–80.

———. Review of *The Didache: Faith, Hope, and Life of the Earliest Christian Communities, 50–70 CE* and *The Didache: Text, Translation, Analysis, and Commentary*, by Aaron Milavec. *TS* 66 (2005): 890–91.

Muilenburg, James. "The Literary Relations of the Epistle of Barnabas and the Teaching of the Twelve Apostles." Ph.D. Diss., University of Marburg, 1929.

Muraoka, T. *A Greek-English Lexicon of the Septuagint*. Leuven: Peeters, 2009.

Myllykoski, Matti. "Ohne Dekret: Das Götzenopferfleisch und die Frühgeschichte der Didache." Pages 113–37 in *Aposteldekret und antikes Vereinwesen: Gemeinschaft und ihre Ordnung*. Edited by Markus Öhler. WUNT 280. Tübingen: Mohr Siebeck 2011.

Neusner, Jacob. *The Idea of Purity in Ancient Judaism: The Haskell Lectures 1972–1973*. SJLA. Leiden: Brill, 1973.

———. *The Incarnation of God: The Character of Divinity in Formative Judaism*. Philadelphia: Fortress, 1988.

———. *A Life of Rabban Yohanan ben Zakkai c. 1–80 CE*. StPB 6. Leiden: Brill, 1962.

Neusner, Jacob, and Richard S. Sarason, trans. *The Tosefta: Translated from the Hebrew, with a New Introduction*. Peabody, MA: Hendrickson, 2002.

Niederwimmer, Kurt. *The Didache: A Commentary*. Translated by Linda M. Maloney. Hermeneia. Minneapolis: Fortress, 1998. Translation of *Die Didache*. KAV 1. Göttingen: Vandenhoeck & Ruprecht, 1993.

———. "Der Didachist und seine Quellen." Pages 15–36 in *The* Didache *in Context: Essays on Its Text, History and Transmission*. Edited by Clayton N. Jefford. NovTSup 77. Leiden: Brill, 1995.

Nikander, Perttu. "Orality and Writing in the Context of the Two Ways Teaching and the Didache." Paper presented at the annual meeting of the Society of Biblical Literature. Atlanta, November 21, 2010.

Noam, Vered. *Megillat Ta'anit: Versions, Interpretation, History*. Jerusalem: Yad Ben-Zvi, 2003. (Hebrew).

Nolland, John. *The Gospel of Matthew*. NIGTC. Grand Rapids: Eerdmans, 2005.

Nongbri, Brent. "A Touch of Condemnation in a Word of Exhortation: Apocalyptic Language and Graeco-Roman Rhetoric in Hebrews 6:4–12." *NovT* 45 (2003): 265–79.

O'Loughlin, Thomas. *The Didache: A Window on the Earliest Christians.* Grand Rapids: Baker; London: SPCK, 2010.

———. "Reactions to the *Didache* in Early Twentieth-Century Britain: A Dispute over the Relationship of History and Doctrine?" Pages 177–94 in *Religion, Identity and Conflict in Britain: From the Restoration to the Twentieth Century: Festschrift for Prof. Keith Robbins.* Edited by Stewart J. Brown, Frances Knight, and John Morgan-Guy. Farnham, Surrey, UK: Ashgate, 2013.

O'Neill, John Cochrane. *The Recovery of Paul's Letter to the Galatians.* London: SPCK, 1972.

Ong, Walter J. *Orality and Literacy: The Technologizing of the Word.* York, UK: Methuen, 1982. Repr., Oxford: Routledge, 2002.

———. *The Presence of the Word: Some Prolegomena for Cultural and Religious History.* Minneapolis: University of Minnesota Press, 1967.

Osborne, Eric. *Tertullian: First Theologian of the West.* Cambridge: Cambridge University Press, 1997.

Osiek, Carolyn. *The Shepherd of Hermas: A Commentary.* Hermeneia. Philadelphia: Fortress, 1999.

Osiek, Carolyn, and Margaret Y. MacDonald, with Janet H. Tulloch. *A Woman's Place: House Churches in Earliest Christianity.* Minneapolis: Fortress, 2006.

Oxford Society of Historical Theology. *The New Testament in the Apostolic Fathers.* Oxford: Clarendon, 1905.

Pagels, Elaine. *Beyond Belief: The Secret Gospel of Thomas.* New York: Vintage, 2003.

———. *The Gnostic Gospels.* New York: Random House, 1979.

Painter, John. *Just James: The Brother of Jesus in History and Tradition.* Columbia: University of South Carolina Press, 1997.

Pardee, Nancy. "The Curse that Saves (*Didache* 16.5)." Pages 156–76 in *The* Didache *in Context: Essays on Its Text, History and Transmission.* Edited by Clayton N. Jefford. NovTSup 77. Leiden: Brill, 1995.

———. *The Genre and Development of the Didache.* WUNT 2/339. Tübingen: Mohr Siebeck, 2012.

———. "The Genre of the Didache: A Text-Linguistic Analysis." Ph.D. diss., The University of Chicago, 2002.

———. Review of *The Didache: Text, Translation, Analysis, and Commentary,* by Aaron Milavec. *JECS* 13 (2005): 525–27.

Parker, David C. *The Living Text of the Gospels.* Cambridge: Cambridge University Press, 1997.

Parry, Milman. *L'epithète traditionelle dans Homère.* Paris: Société Editrice Les Belles Letters, 1928.

Pelling, C. B. R. "Plutarch's Method of Work in the Roman Lives." *JHS* 99 (1979): 74–96.

Perkins, D. W. "A Call to Pilgrimage: The Challenge of Hebrews." *TTE* 32 (1985): 69–78.

Perry, Alfred M. "The Framework of the Sermon on the Mount." *JBL* 54 (1935): 103–15.

Pesch, Rudolf. *Das Markus-Evangelium.* 3rd ed. 2 vols. HTKNT 2. Freiburg: Herder, 1980.

Peterson, Jeffrey. "The Extent of Christian Theological Diversity: Pauline Evidence." *ResQ* 47 (2005): 1–12.

Philonenko, Marc. *Joseph et Aséneth: Introduction, texte critique, traduction et notes.* Leiden: Brill, 1968.

Pietersma, Albert, and Benjamin G. Wright, eds. *A New English Translation of the Septuagint.* Oxford: Oxford University Press, 2007.

Poirier, John C. "Purity beyond the Temple in the Second Temple Era." *JBL* 122 (2003): 247–65.

Polanyi, Michael. *Tacit Dimension.* Garden City, NY: Doubleday, 1966.

Popkes, Wiard. *Adressaten, Situation und Form des Jakobusbriefes.* SBS 125–126. Stuttgart: Katholisches Bibelwerk, 1986.

———. "Die Gerechtigkeitstradition im Matthäus-Evangelium." *ZNW* 80 (1989): 1–23.

Prigent, Pierre. *Apocalypse et Liturgie.* Neuchatel: Delachaux & Niestle, 1964.

———. *Les testimonia dans le christianiasme primitif: L'épître de Barnabé I–XVI.* Paris: Gabalda, 1961.

Prigent, Pierre, and Robert A. Kraft. *Epître de Barnabé.* SC 172. Paris: Cerf, 1971.

Pritz, Ray A. *Nazarene Jewish Christianity Jewish Christianity: From the End of the New Testament Period until Its Disappearance in the Fourth Century.* StPB 37. Leiden: Brill; Jerusalem: Magnes, 1988.

Radermacher, Ludwig. *Neutestamentlich Grammatik: Das Griechisch des Neuen Testaments im Zusammenhang mit der Volkssprache.* HNT 1.1. Tübingen: Mohr Siebeck, 1911.

Regev, Eyal. "Moral Impurity and the Temple in Early Christianity in Light of Ancient Greek Practice and Qumranic Ideology." *HTR* 97 (2004): 383–411.

———. "Non-Priestly Purity and Its Religious Aspects According to Historical Sources and Archaeological Findings." Pages 223–44 in *Purity and Holiness: The Heritage of Leviticus*. Edited by Marcel J. H. M. Poorthuis and Joshua Schwartz. JCP 2. Leiden: Brill, 2000.

———. "Pure Individualism: The Idea of Non-priestly Purity in Ancient Judaism." *JSJ* 31 (2000): 176–202.

Reicher, Stephen, Russell Spears, and S. Alexander Haslam. "The Social Identity Approach in Social Psychology." *Sage Identities Handbook*. Edited by Margaret S. Wetherell and Chandra T. Mohanty. London: Sage, 2010.

Reif, Stefan C. "The Development of Ancient Jewish Prayer." *Tarbiz* 60 (1990–1991): 677–81. (Hebrew).

———. *Judaism and Hebrew Prayer: New Perspectives on Jewish Liturgical History*. Cambridge: Cambridge University Press, 1995.

Repschinski, Boris. "Purity in Matthew, James and the Didache." Pages 370–95 in *Matthew, James and Didache: Three Related Documents in their Jewish and Christian Settings*. Edited by Huub van de Sandt and Jürgen K. Zangenberg. SBLSymS 45. Atlanta: Society of Biblical Literature, 2008.

Ridderbos, Herman N. "The Earliest Confession of the Atonement in Paul." Pages 76–89 in *Reconciliation and Hope: New Testament Essays on Atonement and Eschatology Presented to L. L. Morris on his 60th Birthday*. Edited by Robert L. Banks. Carlisle: Paternoster, 1974.

Roark, D. M. "The Great Eschatological Discourse." *NovT* 7 (1964): 123–27.

Robertson, A. T. *A Grammar of the Greek New Testament in the Light of Historical Research*. 2nd ed. New York: Hodder & Stoughton; George H. Doran, 1919.

Robinson, J. Armitage. *Barnabas, Hermas and the Didache*. London: SPCK, 1920.

———. "The Problem of the Didache." *JTS* 13 (1912): 339–56.

Robinson, James, and Helmut Koester. *Trajectories through Early Christianity*. Philadelphia: Fortress, 1971.

Robinson, James M., Paul Hoffmann, and John S. Kloppenborg, eds. *The Critical Edition of Q: Synopsis including the Gospels of Matthew and Luke, Mark and Thomas with English, German and French Translations of Q and Thomas*. Hermeneia. Minneapolis: Fortress; Leuven: Peeters, 2000.

Robinson, John A. T. *Jesus and His Coming.* 2nd ed. London: SCM; Philadelphia: Westminster, 1979.

———. *Redating the New Testament.* Philadelphia: Westminster, 1976.

———. "Traces of a Liturgical Sequence in 1 Cor. xvi. 20–24." *JTS* 4 (1953): 38–41.

Rordorf, Willy. "An Aspect of the Judeo-Christian Ethic: The Two Ways." Pages 148–64 in *The Didache in Modern Research.* Edited by Jonathan A. Draper. AGJU 37. Leiden: Brill, 1996.

———. "Le baptême selon la *Didachè*." Pages 499–509 in *Mélanges liturgiques.* Edited by Bernard Botte. Leuven: Abbaye du Mont César, 1972.

———. "Does the Didache Contain Jesus Tradition Independently of the Synoptic Gospels?" Pages 394–423 in *Jesus and the Oral Synoptic Tradition.* Edited by Henry Wansbrough. Sheffield: Sheffield Academic Press, 1991.

———. "Le problème de la transmission textuelle de *Didache* 1,3b–2,1." Pages 499–513 in *Überlieferungsgeschichtliche Untersuchungen.* Edited by Franz Paschke. TUGAL 125. Berlin: Akademic, 1981.

———. *Der Sonntag: Geschichte des Ruhe- und Gottesdiensttages im ältesten Christentum.* ATANT 43. Zürich: Zwingli-Verlag, 1962.

Rordorf, Willy, and André Tuilier. *La doctrine des douze Apôtres (Didachè).* SC 248 bis. Paris: Cerf, 1998.

Rouwhorst, Gerard. "Didache 9–10: A Litmus Test for the Research on Early Christian Liturgy Eucharist." Pages 143–56 in *Matthew and the Didache: Two Documents from the Same Jewish Christian Milieu?* Edited by Huub van de Sandt. Assen: Van Gorcum; Minneapolis: Fortress, 2005.

Rowe, C. Kavin. *Early Narrative Christology: The Lord in the Gospel of Luke.* Grand Rapids: Baker, 2006.

———. "New Testament Theology: The Revival of a Discipline. A Review of Recent Contributions to the Field." *JBL* 125 (2006): 393–410.

Rowe, Galen O. "Style." Pages 121–57 in *Handbook of Classical Rhetoric in the Hellenistic Period: 330 BC–AD 400.* Edited by Stanley E. Porter. Leiden: Brill, 1997.

Rowland, Christopher C. *The Open Heaven: A Study of Apocalyptic in Judaism and Early Christianity.* London: SPCK, 1982.

Rowland, Christopher C., and Christopher Morray-Jones. *The Mystery of God: Early Jewish Mysticism and the New Testament.* CRINT 12. Leiden: Brill, 2009.

Sabourin, Leopold. "The Biblical Cloud: Terminology and Traditions." *BTB* 4 (1974): 290–311.
Safrai, Shmuel. "Bikkureihem shel hakhamei Yavne be-Roma." Pages 365–81 in *In Times of Temple and Mishnah*. Edited by Shmuel Safrai. Jerusalem: Magnes, 1996.
———. "Gathering in the Synagogues on Festivals, Sabbaths and Weekdays." *BARIS* 499 (1989): 7–15.
———. "Hasidim we-Anshei Maase." *Zion* 50 (1984–1985): 133–54.
———. "Jesus and the Hasidic Movement." Pages 413–36 in *The Jews in the Hellenistic-Roman World: Studies in Memory of Menahem Stern*. Edited by Isaiah M. Gafni, A'haron Oppenheimer, and Daniel R. Schwartz. Jerusalem: The Zalman Shazar Center for Jewish History; The Historical Society of Israel, 1996.
———. "Jesus and the Hasidim." *JP* 42–44 (1994): 3–22.
———. "Religion in Everyday Life." Pages 793–833 in *The Jewish People in the First Century: Historical Geography, Political History, Social, Cultural and Religious Life and Institutions*. Vol. 2. Edited by Shmuel Safrai and Menahem Stern. CRINT 1.2. Assen:Van Gorcum, 1976.
———. "Teaching of Pietists in Mishnaic Literature." *JJS* 16 (1965): 15–33.
———. "Yeshu veha-tenua he-hasidit." Pages 413–36 in *The Jews in the Hellenistic-Roman World: Studies in Memory of Menahem Stern*. Edited by Isaiah M. Gafni, A'haron Oppenheimer, and Daniel R. Schwartz. Jerusalem: The Zalman Shazar Center for Jewish History; The Historical Society of Israel, 1996.
Safrai, Shmuel, and Zeev Safrai. *Mishnat Eretz Israel: Tractate Brachot*. Jerusalem: Liphshitz, 2010.
Sagi, Avi, and Zvi Zohar. "The Halakhic Ritual of Giyyur and Its Symbolic Meaning." *JRitSt* 9 (1995): 1–13.
Sakenfeld, K. D, ed. *The New Interpreter's Dictionary of the Bible*. Nashville: Abingdon, 2009.
Sanders, James A. *Torah and Canon*. Philadelphia: Fortress, 1972.
Sandt, Huub van de. "Didache 3:1–6:1: A Transformation of an Existing Jewish Hortatory Pattern." *JSJ* 23 (1992): 21–41.
———. "The Didache Redefining Its Jewish Identity in View of Gentiles Joining the Community." Pages 247–65 in *Empsychoi Logoi: Religious Innovations in Antiquity*. Edited by Alberdina Houtman, Albert de Jong, and Magda Misset-van de Weg. AJEC 73. Leiden: Brill, 2008.

———. "'Do Not Give What Is Holy to the Dogs' (Did 9:5d and Matt 7:6a): The Eucharistic Food of the Didache in Its Jewish Purity Setting." *VC* 56 (2002): 223–46.

———. "The Gathering of the Church in the Kingdom: The Self-Understanding of the *Didache* Community in the Eucharistic Prayers." Pages 69–88 in *SBL Seminar Papers 2003*. SBLSP 42. Atlanta: Society of Biblical Literature, 2003.

———. "Introduction." Pages 1–9 in *Matthew and the Didache: Two Documents from the Same Jewish-Christian Milieu?* Edited by Huub van de Sandt. Assen: Van Gorcum; Minneapolis: Fortress, 2005.

———. "James 4,1–4 in the Light of the Jewish Two Ways Tradition 3,1–6." *Bib* 88 (2007): 38–63.

———. "Law and Ethics in Matthew's Antitheses and James's Letter: A Reorientation of Halakah in Line with the Jewish Two Ways 3:1–6." Pages 315–38 in *Matthew, James and Didache: Three Related Documents in their Jewish and Christian Settings*. Edited by Huub van de Sandt and Jürgen K. Zangenberg. SBLSymS 45. Atlanta: Society of Biblical Literature, 2008.

———, ed. *Matthew and the Didache: Two Documents from the Same Jewish-Christian Milieu?* Assen: Van Gorcum; Minneapolis: Fortress, 2005.

———. "Two Windows on a Developing Jewish-Christian Reproof Practice: Matt 18:15–17 and *Did*. 15:3." Pages 173–92 in *Matthew and the Didache: Two Documents from the Same Jewish-Christian Milieu?* Edited by Huub van de Sandt. Assen: Van Gorcum; Minneapolis: Fortress, 2005.

———. "Was the Didache Community a Group within Judaism? An Assessment on the Basis of its Eucharistic Prayers." Pages 85–107 in *A Holy People: Jewish and Christian Perspectives on Religious Communal Identity*. Edited by Marcel J. H. M. Poorthuis and Joshua Schwartz. JCP 12. Leiden: Brill, 2006.

———. "Why Does the Didache Conceive of the Eucharist as a Holy Meal?" *VC* 65 (2011): 1–20.

Sandt, Huub van de, and David Flusser. *The Didache: Its Jewish Sources and Its Place in Early Judaism and Christianity*. CRINT 3.5. Assen: Van Gorcum; Minneapolis: Fortress, 2002.

Sandt, Huub van de, and Jürgen K. Zangenberg, eds. *Matthew, James and Didache: Three Related Documents in Their Jewish and Christian Settings*. SBLSymS 45. Atlanta: Society of Biblical Literature, 2008.

Saulnier, Stéphane. *Calendrical Variations in Second Temple Judaism: New Perspectives on the "Date of the Last Supper" Debate*. JSJSup 159. Leiden: Brill, 2012.

Schäfer, Peter. *Der Bar Kochba-Aufstand: Studien zum zweiten jüdischen Krieg gegen Rom*. Tübingen: Mohr Siebeck, 1981.

———. *The Hidden and Manifest God: Some Major Themes in Early Jewish Mysticism*. Albany, NY: State University of New York Press, 1992.

———. "Die sogenannte Synode von Jabne; Zur Trennung von Juden und Christen im ersten/zweiten Jh. n. Chr." *Judaica* 31 (1975): 54–64, 116–24.

Schaff, Philip. *The Oldest Church Manual Called the Teaching of the Twelve Apostles (ΔΙΔΑΧΗ ΤΩΝ ΔΩΔΕΚΑ ΑΠΟΣΤΟΛΩΝ): The Didachè and Kindred Documents*. London: T&T Clark; New York: Funk & Wagnalls, 1885.

Schiffman, Lawrence H. *The Eschatological Community of the Dead Sea Scrolls: A Study of the Rule of the Congregation*. SBLMS 38. Atlanta: Scholars Press, 1989.

———. *Reclaiming the Dead Sea Scrolls*. Philadelphia: Jewish Publication Society of America, 1994.

———. *Sectarian Law in the Dead Sea Scrolls: Courts, Testimony and the Penal Code*. Chico, CA: Scholars Press, 1983.

Schlecht, Joseph. *Doctrina XII Apostolorum: Die Apostellehre in der Liturgie der katholischen Kirche*. Freiburg im Breisgau: Herder, 1901.

Schmidt, Carl. "Das koptische Didache-Fragment des British Museum." *ZNW* 24 (1925): 81–99.

Schnackenburg, Rudolf. *The Gospel According to St. John*. 3 vols. London: Burns & Oates, 1968.

Schnelle, Udo. *The History and Theology of the New Testament Writings*. Translated by M. Eugene Boring. Minneapolis: Fortress, 1998.

Schoedel, William R. *Ignatius of Antioch: A Commentary on the Letters of Ignatius of Antioch*. Hermeneia. Philadelphia: Fortress, 1985.

Schöllgen, Georg. "The Didache as a Church Order: An Examination of the Purpose for the Composition of the Didache and Its Consequences for Its Interpretation." Pages 43–71 in *The Didache in Modern Research*. Edited by Jonathan A. Draper. AGJU 37. Leiden: Brill, 1996. Translation of "Die Didache als Kirchenordnung: Zur Frage des Abfassungszweckes und sinen Konsequenzen für die Interpretation." *JAC* 29 (1986): 5–26.

Schöllgen, Georg, and Wilhelm Geerlings, eds. *Didache: Zwölf-Apostle-Lehre; Traditio Apostolica: Apostolische Überlieferung.* FC 1. Freiburg im Breisgau: Herder, 1991.

Schremer, Adiel. *Brothers Estranged: Heresy, Christianity, and Jewish Identity in Late Antiquity.* Oxford: Oxford University Press, 2010.

Schröter, Jens. *Das Abendmahl: Frühchristliche Deutungen und Impulse für die Gegenwart.* SBS 210. Stuttgart: Katholisches Bibelwerk, 2006.

———. *Von Jesus zum Neuen Testament: Studien zur urchristlichen Theologiegeschichte und zur Entstehung des neutestamentlichen Kanons.* WUNT 204. Tübingen: Mohr Siebeck, 2007.

Schuckburgh, Evelyn S., trans. *The Histories of Polybius.* London: Macmillan, 1889.

Schürer, Emil. *The History of the Jewish People in the Age of Jesus Christ (175 BC–AD 135).* Edited by Geza Vermes, Emil Schürer, and Fergus Millar. 4 vols. Edinburgh: T&T Clark, 1973–1987.

Schüssler Fiorenza, Elisabeth. *In Memory of Her: A Feminist Theological Reconstruction of Christian Origins.* London: SCM; New York: Crossroads, 1983.

Schwartz, Joshua, and Peter J. Tomson. "When Rabbi Eliezer was Arrested for Heresy." *JSIJ* 10 (2012): 1–37. Online: http://www.biu.ac.il/JS/JSIJ/10-2012/SchwartzandTomson.pdf.

Schwartz, Seth. *Imperialism and Jewish Society, 200 BCE to 640 CE.* Princeton: Princeton University Press, 2001.

Schwiebert, Jonathan. *Knowledge and the Coming Kingdom: The Didache's Meal Ritual and Its Place in Early Christianity.* LNTS 373. London: T&T Clark, 2008.

Scott, Bernard Brandon, and Margaret E. Dean. "A Sound Map of the Sermon on the Mount." Pages 672–725 in *SBL Seminar Papers 1993.* Edited by Eugene H. Lovering. SBLSP 32. Atlanta: Scholars Press, 1993.

Scott, James C. *Domination and the Arts of Resistance: Hidden Transcripts.* New Haven: Yale University Press, 1990.

Seeberg, Alfred. *Die beiden Wege und das Aposteldekre.* Leipzig: Deichert, 1906.

———. *Die Didache des Judentums und der Urchristenheit.* Leipzig: Deichert, 1908.

———. *Der Katechismus der Urchristenheit.* Leipzig: Deichert, 1903.

Seeliger, Hans Reinhard. "Considerations on the Background and Purpose of the Apocalyptic Final Chapter of the *Didache*." Pages 373–82 in *The*

Didache *in Modern Research*. Edited by Jonathan A. Draper. Leiden: Brill, 1996.

Segal, Alan F. *Two Powers in Heaven: Early Rabbinic Reports about Christianity and Gnosticism*. SJLA 25. Leiden: Brill, 1977.

Seidel, Moshe. "Parallels between Isaiah and Psalms." Pages 1–97 in *Hiqrei Miqra*. Jerusalem: Rav Kook Institute, 1978. (Hebrew).

Shiner, Whitney. *Proclaiming the Gospel: First-Century Performance of Mark*. Harrisburg, PA: Trinity Press International, 2003.

Shukster, Martin B., and Peter Richardson. "Temple and Bet Ha-midrash in the Epistle of Barnabas." Pages 17–31 in *Separation and Polemic*. Vol. 2 of *Anti-Judaism in Early Christianity*. Edited by Stephen G. Wilson. SCJ 2. Waterloo, ON: Wilfrid Laurier University Press, 1986.

Simon, Marcel. "De l'observance ritual à l'asceticism: Recherches sur le décret Apostolique." *RHR* 193 (1978): 27–104.

Simoons, Frederick J. *Eat Not This Flesh: Food Avoidances from Prehistory to the Present*. Madison, WI: University of Wisconsin Press, 1994.

Skarsaune, Oskar. *The Proof from Prophecy: A Study in Justin Martyr's Proof-Text Tradition: Text-Type, Provenance Theological Profile*. NovTSup 56. Leiden: Brill, 1987.

Skarsaune, Oskar, and Reidar Hvalvik, eds. *Jewish Believers in Jesus: The Early Centuries*. Peabody, MA: Hendrickson, 2007.

Skehan, Patrick W. "*Didache* 1,6 and Sirach 12,1." *Bib* 44 (1963): 533–36.

Smith, Dennis E. *From Symposium to Eucharist: The Banquet in the Early Christian World*. Minneapolis: Fortress, 2002.

Smith, Jonathan Z. *Drudgery Divine: On the Comparison of Early Christianities and the Religions of Late Antiquity*. Chicago: University of Chicago Press, 1990.

Smith, Murray J. "The Gospels in Early Christian Literature." Pages 181–207 in *The Content and Setting of the Gospel Traditions*. Edited by Mark Harding and Alanna M. Nobbs. Grand Rapids: Eerdmans, 2010.

———. "Jesus as the Logic of his Coming." Ph.D. diss., Macquarie University, forthcoming.

———. "The Thessalonian Correspondance." In *All Things to All Cultures: Paul among Jews, Greeks and Romans*. Edited by Mark Harding and Alanna M. Nobbs. Grand Rapids: Eerdmans, forthcoming.

Snyman, Andreas H. "Hebrews 6:4–6: From a Semiotic Discourse Perspective." Pages 354–68 in *Discourse Analysis and the New Testament*. Edited by Stanley E. Porter and Jeffrey T. Reed. JSNTSup 170. Sheffield: Sheffield Academic Press, 1999.

The Soncino Classics Collection: The Soncino Talmud, the Soncino Midrash Rabbah, the Soncino Zohar, the Bible, in Hebrew and English. Judaic Classics Library. New York: Davka. Electronic text.

Spicq, Ceslas. *L'Epître aux Hébreux*. 2 vols. Paris: Gabalda, 1952–1953.

———. *Notes de lexicographie néo-testamentaire*. 3 vols. OBO 22.1–3. Göttingen: Vandenhoeck & Ruprecht, 1982.

Stanton, Graham N. *Jesus and Gospel*. New York: Cambridge University Press, 2004.

Stemberger, G. *Einleitung in Talmud und Midrasch*. 8th ed. Munich: Beck, 1992.

———. "Die sogenannte 'Synode von Jabne' und das frühe Christentum." *Kairos* 19 (1977): 14–21.

Stevenson, Kenneth W. *The Lord's Prayer: A Text in Tradition*. London: SCM, 2004.

Stewart, Alistair C. "Didache 14: Eucharistic?" *QL* 93 (2012): 3–16.

Stewart-Sykes, Alistair. *The Apostolic Church Order: The Greek Text with Introduction, Translation and Annotation*. ECS 10. Strathfield, AU: St. Paul's, 2006.

———. "Ἀποκύησις λόγῳ ἀληθείας: Paraenesis and Baptism in Matthew, James, and the Didache." Pages 341–59 in *Matthew, James and Didache: Three Related Documents in their Jewish and Christian Settings*. Edited by Huub van de Sandt and Jürgen K. Zangenberg. SBLSymS 45. Atlanta: Society of Biblical Literature, 2008.

Strack, Herman L. *Introduction to the Talmud and Midrash*. New York: Atheneum, 1931.

Strack, Herman L., and Paul Billerbeck. *Kommentar zum Neuen Testament aus Talmud und Midrasch*. Munich: Beck, 1922–1974.

Strecker, Georg. "The Reception of the Book." Pages 286–316 in *Orthodoxy and Heresy in Earliest Christianity*. Edited by Robert A. Kraft and Gerhard Krodel. Philadelphia: Fortress, 1971.

———. *The Sermon on the Mount: An Exegetical Commentary*. Translated by O. C. Dean Jr. Nashville: Abingdon, 1988.

Streeter, Burnett H. *The Four Gospels: A Study of Origins*. London: Macmillan, 1924.

———. "The Much Belaboured Didache." *JTS* 37 (1936): 369–74.

Stuhlmacher, Peter. "The Pauline Gospel." Pages 149–72 in *The Gospel and the Gospels*. Edited by Peter Stuhlmacher. Grand Rapids: Eerdmans, 1991.

———. "The Theme: The Gospel and the Gospels." Pages 1–25 in *The Gospel and the Gospels*. Edited by Peter Stuhlmacher. Grand Rapids: Eerdmans, 1991.

———. *Vorgeschichte*. Vol. 1 of *Das paulinische Evangelium*. FRLANT 95. Göttingen: Vandenhoeck & Ruprecht, 1968.

Stuiber, Alfred. "Das ganze Joch des Herrn (Didache 6,2–3)." *StPatr* 4 (1961): 323–29.

Suggs, M. Jack. "The Christian Two Ways Tradition: Its Antiquity, Form and Function." Pages 60–74 in *Studies in New Testament and Early Christian Literature: Essays in Honor of Allen P. Wikgren*. NovTSup 33. Leiden: Brill, 1972.

Sweet, John. Review of Alan J. P. Garrow's *Revelation*. *JTS* 49 (1998): 940–41.

Swete, Henry B., and H. S. J. Thackeray. *An Introduction to the Old Testament in Greek*. 2nd ed. Cambridge: Cambridge University Press, 1902.

Syreeni, Kari. "The Sermon on the Mount and the Two Ways Teaching of the Didache." Pages 87–103 in *Matthew and the Didache: Two Documents from the Same Jewish-Christian Milieu?* Edited by Huub van de Sandt. Assen: Van Gorcum; Minneapolis: Fortress, 2005.

Tajfel, Henri, Claude Flament, M. Billig, and R. F. Bundy. "Social Categorization and Intergroup Behaviour." *EuroJSP* 1 (1971): 149–77.

Tajfel, Henri, and John C. Turner. "An Integrative Theory of Intergroup Conflict." Pages 33–48 in *The Social Psychology of Intergroup Relations*. Edited by William G. Austin and Stephen Worchel. Monterey, CA: Brooks/Cole, 1979.

Talmon, Shemaryahu. "The Textual Study of the Bible: A New Outlook," Pages 358–80 in *Qumran and the History of the Biblical Text*. Edited by Frank M. Cross and Shemaryahu Talmon. Cambridge: Harvard University Press, 1975.

Taussig, Hal. *In the Beginning Was the Meal*. Minneapolis: Fortress, 2009.

Taylor, Charles. *The Teaching of the Twelve Apostles, with Illustrations from the Talmud*. Cambridge: Deighton Bell, 1886.

Taylor, Miriam. *Anti-Judaism and Early Christian Identity: A Critique of the Scholarly Consensus*. StPB 46. Leiden: Brill, 1995.

Taylor, Vincent. *The Gospel According to St. Mark*. London: Macmillan, 1959.

Telfer, W. "The 'Didache' and the Apostolic Synod in Antioch." *JTS* 40 (1939): 133–46, 258–271.

———. "The 'Plot' of the Didache." *JTS* 45 (1944): 141–45.

Thiselton, Anthony C. *The First Epistle to the Corinthians: A Commentary on the Greek Text*. NIGTC. Grand Rapids: Eerdmans, 2000.

Thomas, Samuel I. *The "Mysteries" of Qumran: Mystery, Secrecy, and Esotericism in the Dead Sea Scrolls*. SBLEJL 25. Atlanta: Society of Biblical Literature, 2009.

Tidwell, Neville L. A. "Didache 14:1 (ΚΑΤΑ ΚΥΡΙΑΚΚΗΝ ΔΕ ΚΥΡΙΟΥ) Revisited." *VC* 53 (1999): 197–207.

Tomson, Peter J. "The Didache, Matthew, and Barnabas as Sources for Jewish and Christian History." Pages 348–82 in *Jews and Christians in the First and Second Centuries: How to Write Their History*. Edited by Peter J. Tomson and Joshua Schwartz. CRINT 13. Leiden: Brill, 2014.

———. "Gamaliel's Counsel and the Apologetic Strategy of Luke-Acts." Pages 585–604 in *The Unity of Luke-Acts*. Edited by Joseph Verheyden. BETL 142. Leuven: Leuven University Press; Peeters, 1999.

———. "The Halakhic Evidence of *Didache* 8 and Matthew 6 and the *Didache* Community's Relationship to Judaism." Pages 131–41 in *Matthew and the Didache: Two Documents from the Same Jewish-Christian Milieu?* Edited by Huub van de Sandt. Assen: Van Gorcum; Minneapolis: Fortress, 2005.

———. *"If This Be from Heaven": Jesus and the New Testament Authors in Their Relationship to Judaism*. Translated by Janet Dyk. BS 76. Sheffield: Sheffield Academic Press, 2001.

———. "Das Matthäusevangelium im Wandel der Horizonte: Vom 'Hause Israels' (10,6) zu 'allen Völkern' (28,19)." Pages 313–33 in *Judaistik und neutestamentliche Wissenschaft: Feschrift*. Edited by Lutz Doering, Hans-Günther Waubke, and Florian Wilk. FRLANT 226. Göttingen: Vandenhoeck & Ruprecht, 2008.

———. "Transformations in Post-70 Judaism: Scholarly Reconstructions and Their Implications for Our Perception of Matthew, Didache, and James." Pages 91–121 in *Matthew, James and Didache: Three Related Documents in Their Jewish and Christian Settings*. Edited by Huub van de Sandt and Jürgen K. Zangenberg. SBLSymS 45. Atlanta: Society of Biblical Literature, 2008.

———. "The Wars against Rome, the Rise of Rabbinic Judaism and of Apostolic Gentile Christianity, and the Judaeo-Christians: Elements for a Synthesis." Pages 1–31 in *The Image of the Judaeo-Christians in Early Jewish and Christian Christian Literature*. Edited by by Peter J. Tomson and Doris Lambers-Petry. WUNT 158. Tübingen: Mohr Siebeck, 2003.

Tönges, Elke. *Unser Vater im Himmel: Die Bezeichnung Gottes als Vater in der tannaitischen Literatur.* BWANT 8/7. Stuttgart: Kohlhammer, 2003.

Tuckett, Christopher M. "The Didache and the Synoptics Once More: A Response to Aaron Milavec." *JECS* 13 (2005): 509–18.

———. "The *Didache* and the Writings that Later Formed the New Testament." Pages 83–127 in *The Reception of the New Testament in the Apostolic Fathers.* Vol. 1 of *The New Testament and the Apostolic Fathers.* Edited by Andrew F. Gregory and Christopher M. Tuckett. Oxford: Oxford University Press, 2005.

———. "Synoptic Tradition in 1 Thessalonians?" Pages 160–82 in *The Thessalonian Correspondence.* Edited by Raymond F. Collins. BETL 87. Leuven: Peeters, 1990.

———. Synoptic Tradition in the Didache." Pages 197–230 in *The New Testament in Early Christianity.* Edited by Jean-Marie Sevrin. BETL 86. Leuven: Leuven University Press; Peeters, 1989. Repr. pages 92–128 in *The* Didache *in Modern Research.* Edited by Jonathan A. Draper. AGJU 37. Leiden: Brill, 1996.

Turner, Nigel. *Christian Words.* Edinburgh: Nelson, 1980.

Uro, Risto. "Thomas and Oral Gospel Tradition." Pages 8–32 in *Thomas at the Crossroads: Essays on the Gospel of Thomas.* Edinburgh: T&T Clark, 1998.

VanderKam, James C. *Calendars in the Dead Sea Scrolls: Measuring Time.* London: Routledge, 1998.

Vanni, Ugo. "Liturgical Dialogue as a Literary Form in the Book of Revelation." *NTS* 37 (1991): 348–72.

Varner, William. "The Didache 'Apocalypse' and Matthew 24." *BSac* 165 (2008): 309–22.

———. "The Didache's Use of the Old and New Testaments." *MSJ* 16 (2005): 127–51.

———. *The Way of the Didache: The First Christian Handbook.* Lanham, MD: University Press of America, 2007.

Verheyden, Joseph. "Eschatology in the Didache and the Gospel of Matthew." Pages 193–215 in *Matthew and the Didache: Two Documents from the Same Jewish-Christian Milieu?* Edited by Huub van de Sandt. Assen: Van Gorcum; Minneapolis: Fortress, 2005.

Vermes, Geza. *The Dead Sea Scrolls in English.* 2nd ed. New York: Penguin, 1975.

Vielhauer, Philipp. *Geschichte der urchristlichen Literatur: Einleitung in das Neue Testament, die Apokryphen und die Apostolischen Väter.* dGL. Berlin: de Gruyter, 1975.

Vokes, F. E. "Life and Order in an Early Church: The Didache." *ANRW* 2.27.1: 209–33.

———. *The Riddle of the Didache: Fact or Fiction, Heresy or Catholicism?* London: SPCK, 1938.

Vööbus, Arthur. *Liturgical Traditions in the Didache.* Stockholm: ETSE, 1968.

———. "Regarding the Background of the Liturgical Traditions in the Didache." *VC* 23 (1969): 81–87.

Wainwright, Geoffrey. *Eucharist and Eschatology.* New York: Oxford University Press, 1981.

Walker, Joan Hazelden. "A Pre-Marcan Dating for the Didache: Further Thoughts of a Liturgist." *StudBib* 3 (1978): 405–8.

Walker, William O., Jr. *Interpolations in the Pauline Letters.* London: Sheffield, 2001.

Wallace, Daniel B. *Greek Grammar Beyond the Basics: An Exegetical Syntax of the New Testament.* Grand Rapids: Zondervan, 1996.

Wanamaker, Charles A. *The Epistles to the Thessalonians: A Commentary on the Greek Text.* NIGTC. Grand Rapids: Eerdmans, 1990.

Warfield, Benjamin B. "Text, Sources and Contents of the 'Two Ways' or First Section of the Didache." *BSac* 43 (1886): 81–97.

Wehnert, Jürgen. *Reinheit des "christlichen Gottesvolkes" aus Juden und Heiden: Studien zum historischen und theologischen Hintergrund des sogenannten Aposteldekrets.* FRLANT 173. Göttingen: Vandenhoeck & Ruprecht, 1997.

Weidemann, Hans-Ulrich."Taufe und Taufeucharistie: Die postbaptismale Mahlgemeinschaft in Quellen des 2. und 3. Jahrhunderts." Pages 1483–530 in *Ablution, Initiation, and Baptism: Late Antiquity, Early Judaism, and Early Christianity.* Edited by David Hellholm, TorVegge, Øyvind Norderval, and Christer Hellholm.Vol. 2. BZNW 176. Berlin: de Gruyter, 2011.

Weinfeld, Moshe. "The Decalogue: Its Significance, Uniqueness, and Place in Israel's Tradition." Pages 3–47 in *Religion and Law: Biblical Judaic and Islamic Perspectives.* Edited by Edwin R. Firmage, Bernard G. Weiss, and John W. Welch. Winona Lake, IN: Eisenbrauns, 1990.

———. "Instructions for Temple Visitors in the Bible and in Ancient Egypt." *ScrHier* 28 (1982): 224–50.

Weizsäcker, Carl von. *The Apostolic Age of the Christian Church*. Translated by James Miller. 3rd ed. London: Williams & Norgate; New York: Putnam's Sons, 1902.

Welch, John W. "Law, Ethics, Ritual, and Eschatology from the Sermon on the Mount to the Post-Temple Didache." Paper presented at the annual meeting of the Society of Biblical Literature. Boston, November 25, 2008.

———. *The Sermon on the Mount in the Light of the Temple*. London: Ashgate, 2009.

Wengst, Klaus. *Didache (Apostellehre), Barnabasbrief, Zweiter Klemensbrief, Schrift an Diognet*. SU 2. Darmstadt: Wissenschaftliche Buchgesellschaft, 1984.

Werrett, Ian C. *Ritual Purity and the Dead Sea Scrolls*. STDJ 72. Leiden: Brill, 2007.

Westcott, Brooke Foss. *The Epistle to the Hebrews: The Greek Text with Notes and Essays*. 3rd ed. London: Macmillan, 1914.

Weyde, Karl William. *Prophecy and Teaching*. Berlin: de Gruyter, 2000.

Willetts, Ronald F. *The Law Code of Gortyn*. KSup 1. Berlin: de Gruyter, 1967.

Williams, Michael A. *Rethinking "Gnosticism": An Argument for Dismantling a Dubious Category*. Princeton: Princeton University Press, 1996.

Willitts, Joel. "Paul and Jewish Christians in the Second Century." Pages 140–68 in *Paul in the Second Century*. Edited by Michael F. Bird and Joseph R. Dodson. LNTS 412. London: T&T Clark, 2011.

———. "Paul and Matthew: A Descriptive Approach from a Post-New Perspective Interpretative Framework." Pages 62–85 in *Paul and the Gospels: Christologies, Conflicts and Convergences*. Edited by Michael F. Bird and Joel Willitts. LNTS 411. London: T&T Clark, 2011.

Wire, Antoinette Clark. *The Case for Mark Composed in Performance*. BPC 3. Eugene, OR: Cascade, 2011.

Witherington, Ben, III. *1 and 2 Thessalonians: A Socio-Rhetorical Commentary*. Grand Rapids: Eerdmans, 2006.

Wohlenberg, Gustav. *Die Lehre der zwölf Apostel in ihrem Verhältnis zum neutestamentlichen Schrifttum: Eine Untersuchung*. Erlangen: Deichert, 1888.

Wright, Brian J. "Greek Syntax as a Criterion of Authenticity: A New Discussion and Proposal." *CBQ* 74 (2012): 84–100.

Wright, N. T. *Christian Origins and the Question of God*. 3 vols. Minneapolis: Fortress, 1992–2003.

———. *The New Testament and the People of God*. London: SPCK, 1992.
Young, Stephen E. *Jesus Tradition in the Apostolic Fathers: Their Explicit Appeals to the Words of Jesus in Light of Orality Studies*. WUNT 2/311. Tübingen: Mohr Siebeck, 2011.
Zangenberg, Jürgen K. "Reconstructing the Social and Religious Milieu of the Didache: Observations and Possible Results." Pages 43–69 in *Matthew, James, and Didache: Three Related Documents in Their Jewish and Christian Settings*. Edited by Huub van de Sandt and Jürgen K. Zangenberg. SBLSymS 45. Atlanta: Society of Biblical Literature, 2008.
Zetterholm, Magnus. "The Didache, Matthew, James, and Paul: Reconstructing Historical Development in Antioch." Pages 73–90 in *Matthew, James, and Didache: Three Related Documents in Their Jewish and Christian Settings*. Edited by Huub van de Sandt and Jürgen K. Zangenberg. SBLSymS 45. Atlanta: Society of Biblical Literature, 2008.
———. *The Formation of Christianity in Antioch: A Social-Scientific Approach to the Separation of Judaism and Christianity*. London: Routledge, 2003.

Contributors

D. Jeffrey Bingham is Associate Dean of Biblical and Theological Studies and Professor of Theology at Wheaton College (Illinois). He has authored *Irenaeus's Use of Matthew's Gospel in Adversus haereses* (Brill), published many articles and essays on second-century studies and patristic biblical interpretation, edited the *Routledge Companion to Early Christian Thought*, and serves as the general editor for the Bible in Ancient Christianity monograph series (Brill).

E. Bruce Brooks (PhD, University of Washington) is Research Professor in the Warring States Project at the University of Massachusetts at Amherst. He has written on text and corpus formation in classical Chinese (*The Original Analects*, Columbia University Press) and Biblical Greek ("The Reader in the Text" and "Gospel Trajectories," *Warring States Papers*) and has presented more than a dozen papers at national and regional meetings of the Society of Biblical Literature.

John J. Clabeaux is Professor of Sacred Scripture at Pope St. John XXIII Seminary in Weston, Massachusetts. His research has been focused on the second century CE since the 1990s, publishing "Eucharist Prayers from Didache 9 and 10" (trans. and intro.), in *Prayer from Alexander to Constantine* (Routledge), and "Abraham in Marcion's Gospel and Epistles: Marcion and the Jews," in *When Judaism and Christianity Began* (Brill).

Jonathan A. Draper is Senior Professor in New Testament and Fellow of the University of KwaZulu-Natal, Pietermaritzburg Campus, South Africa. He has published widely on the Didache, including as editor, translator, and contributor to *The Didache in Modern Research* (Brill). He co-authored with Richard A. Horsley *Whoever Hears You Hears Me: Prophets, Performance and Tradition in Q* (Trinity Press International) and edited, among other volumes, *Orality, Literacy, and Colonialism in Southern Africa* and

Orality, Literacy, and Colonialism in Antiquity (both Society of Biblical Literature).

Stephen Finlan is seeking ordination in the United Church of Christ. He has taught at Fordham University, Drew University, and the University of Durham. He has written *Problems with Atonement* (Liturgical Press), *The Apostle Paul and the Pauline Tradition* (Liturgical Press), and *The Family Metapor in Jesus' Teaching* and *Bullying in the Churches* (both Wipf & Stock).

Alan Garrow is a Visiting Scholar at the Sheffield Interdisciplinary Institute for Biblical Studies at the University of Sheffield. Related publications include *Revelation* (Routledge) and *The Gospel of Matthew's Dependence on the* Didache (T&T Clark International).

Andrew Gregory is Chaplain and Fellow of University College, Oxford. He is currently preparing an edition of the Gospel according to the Hebrews and the Gospel of the Nazoraeans. His other publications include *The Reception of Luke and Acts in the Period before Irenaeus* (Mohr Siebeck) and, as co-editor and contributor, *The Oxford Handbook of Early Christian Apocrypha* (Oxford University Press), *New Studies in the Synoptic Problem* (Peeters), *The Reception of the New Testament in the Apostolic Fathers* (Oxford University Press) and *Trajectories through the New Testament and the Apostolic Fathers* (Oxford University Press).

Clayton N. Jefford is Professor of Scripture at Saint Meinrad Seminary and School of Theology in St. Meinrad, Indiana. He has published widely in the apostolic fathers and related literature, including more recently *The Epistle To Diognetus (With The Fragment Of Quadratus)* (Oxford University Press) and *Didache: The Teaching Of The Twelve Apostles* (Polebridge).

Taras Khomych is Lecturer in Patrology at the Ukrainian Catholic University (Lviv, Ukraine) and a free research assistant at the Faculty of Theology and Religious Studies at the Katholieke Universiteit Leuven (Belgium). His publications include numerous articles in international journals and collected volumes. He is also co-editor of *The Image of the Perfect Christian in Patristic Thought* (Studia Patristica 51).

Matthew D. Larsen is a doctoral student at Yale University. He has published on the Didache and is currently working on writing practices and modes of authorship in the ancient world.

Aaron Milavec, Professor Emeritus, served as a seminary and university professor for twenty-five years. From 2007 to 2014 he pioneered and administered Catherine of Siena Virtual College. During 2003–2005 he chaired a new program unit of the Society of Biblical Literature, "The Didache in Context." His thousand-page commentary, *The Didache: Faith, Hope, and Life of the Earliest Christian Communities, 50–70 C.E.*, received a 2004 Catholic Press Club award recognizing the best books in theology. He is currently completing his final study, *Didache Research at the Crossroads*, a volume in the series, Studia Traditionis Theologiae, at Nottingham University (Brepols).

Joseph G. Mueller, S.J., has taught theology at Marquette University in Milwaukee, Wisconsin, since 1999. He has published *L'Ancien Testament dans l'ecclésiologie des Pères: Une lecture des* Constitutions apostoliques (Brepols) and "The Ancient Church Order Literature: Genre or Tradition?" *Journal of Early Christian Studies*.

Matti Myllykoski is a Doctor of Theology of the University of Helsinki and lecturer in New Testament at the Faculty of Theology. He also serves as chief information specialist at Helsinki University Library. His published dissertation was on the last days and resurrection of Jesus, *Die letzten Tage Jesu* (Suomalainen Tiedeakatemia). He is the author of a number of papers on early Christianity.

Perttu Nikander (MTh) is a doctoral student in the University of Helsinki, Finland. He is working on a dissertation on the Didache and early Christian literary culture.

Nancy Pardee is the administrator for the Center for Jewish Studies at the University of Chicago and also teaches biblical studies as an adjunct in the Chicago area. She served on the steering committee for the SBL "Didache in Context" section (2003–2011) and is currently a member of the steering committee for the SBL International Meeting "Apostolic Fathers and Related Early Christian Literature" section and the section leader of the "Early Christianity/Patristics" unit of the Midwest Region of the Society of Biblical Literature (2006–present). A revised and expanded version of her dissertation, *The Genre and Development of the Didache: A Text-Linguistic Analysis* was published in 2012 by Mohr Siebeck.

Jonathan Schwiebert is Associate Professor of Religious Studies at Lenoir-Rhyne University, a Lutheran college in Hickory, North Carolina. He is the author of *Knowledge and the Coming Kingdom: The Didache's Meal Ritual and Its Place in Early Christianity* (T&T Clark), and is an active participant in the Society of Biblical Literature's "Ritual in the Biblical World" section, which he currently co-chairs.

Murray Smith is Lecturer in Biblical Studies (Greek and New Testament) at Christ College, Sydney, Australia. His forthcoming Macquarie University doctoral dissertation concerns "Jesus and the Logic of His Coming" in the Synoptic Gospels. His publications include chapters on the canonical gospels and their reception in the second century in *The Content and Setting of the Gospel Tradition* (Eerdmans) and chapters on Pauline scholarship and the Thessalonian correspondence in *All Things to All Cultures: Paul among Jews, Greeks and Romans* (Eerdmans).

Michael J. Svigel is Department Chair and Associate Professor of Theological Studies at Dallas Theological Seminary, in Dallas, Texas, where he teaches graduate and doctoral courses in historical theology and patristics. His studies in historical and patristic themes have appeared in *Studia Patristica, Trinity Journal*, and *Bibliotheca Sacra*.

Peter J. Tomson retired as Dean and Professor of New Testament, Jewish Studies, and Patristics at the Faculty for Protestant Theology in Brussels and is currently Guest Professor at the Catholic University of Leuven. He is Joint General Editor of Compendia Rerum Iudaicarum ad Novum Testamentum, along with Joshua Schwartz of Bar-Ilan University.

Huub van de Sandt is retired Associate Professor in New Testament Studies at the Tilburg School of Humanities. He published several books, including (with the late David Flusser) *The Didache: Its Jewish Sources and Its Place in Early Judaism and Christianity* (Van Gorcum/Fortress).

Joseph Verheyden (STD 1987) studied Theology, Religious Studies, Philosophy, and Oriental Studies at the University of Leuven and is currently Professor of New Testament Studies at the same institution. Recent publications include *Studies in the Gospel of John and Its Christology* (co-editor; Peeters) and *The Elijah-Elisha Narrative in the Composition of Luke* (co-editor; Bloomsbury).

John W. Welch is the Robert K. Thomas Professor of Law at Brigham Young University in Provo, Utah, where he focuses on biblical studies. Among his publications are *The Sermon on the Mount in the Light of the Temple* (Ashgate); *Chiasmus in Antiquity* (Gerstenberg), and "Miracles, Maleficium, and Maiestas in the Trial of Jesus," in *Jesus and Archaeology* (Eerdmans).

Index of Primary Texts

Hebrew Bible/Old Testament

Genesis
2:8	78
9:4	436
9:4–6	432

Exodus
16:10	390
19–24	346
19:3	342
19:9	390, 401
19:11	401
19:11–19	365
19:16	64, 401
19:17	401
19:18	391, 401
19:19	399, 401
19:20	342, 401
20:1–17	255
20:12	117, 118
20:13–15	52
20:13–17	51, 52, 267
20:16	52
20:17	52
21:17	52
24:9	342
24:17	391
25	341, 342
26–39	341
29:33	143
34:5	390, 401

Leviticus
2:3	143
11:24–28	143
12:1–8	143
13–14	143
13:2–10	341
14:5	149
14:50	149
14:52	149
15:1–32	143
15:13	53
15:31	150
17–18	432, 445
17:7	432
17:10	432
17:13	432
17:15	436
18:6	432
18:24–30	153
19:15	52
19:17–18	95
19:17–28	52
19:18	51, 52
19:26	52
19:31	52, 153
20:1–3	153
21:17–23	144
22:6	143
22:7	143
22:10	143, 148
22:10–16	143

Numbers
11:25	390
12:5	390
13:23	27
15:20–21	54

Numbers (cont.)		1 Samuel	
18:8–19	143	28:15	492
19:11–19	143		
19:17	149	2 Samuel	
19:20	149	22:10	401
30	341	22:12	390
31:16	492		
35:33–34	153	2 Kingdoms	
		4:10	462
Deuteronomy		18:20	462
1:16–17	52	18:22	462
1:17	116	18:25	462
4:2	39, 53, 269, 378	18:27	462
4:7–21	255		
4:36	391	1 Kings	
5:4	391	1:42	370
5:17–19	52	8:33	341
5:17–21	51, 52	8:34	341
5:20	52		
5:21	52	3 Kingdoms	
5:22–26	391	18:22	492
6:4	365		
6:5	51, 52, 379	4 Kingdoms	
12:15	76	7:9	462
12:32	39, 269, 378		
13:1	53	Ezra	
13:11	492	2:63	143
14:1	342	9:4	64
15:7–8	52		
18:10	52	Nehemiah	
18:10–11	52	1:9	53
30:3–4	391	7:65	143
30:15	51, 52, 481	9:13	401
32:15	492		
33:2	381, 391, 403, 405	Esther	
		6:10	492
Joshusa			
22:19	492	Job	
22:23	492	33:14	51, 52
Judges		Psalms	
5:4–5	381	1:1	345
11:30–31	147	1:1–3	341
13:19	341	1:6	345, 481
		2:7	342

INDEX OF PRIMARY TEXTS

2:7–9	391	80:8–12	27
5:11	341	80:13–16	391
6:8	345	80:15	27
7:8	348	81:3	341
9:4	348	82:8	348
9:7–8	391	84:11	341
9:8	348	89:14	348
9:11	391	93:1	341
9:16	348	93:1–5	348
9:19	348	94:8	341, 345
10:5	348	96:2	370
11:4	341	96:12–13	348
17:5	342	96:13	348
17:15	345	97:2	348, 390
18:9	401	98:9	348
18:10–11	390	103:6	348
23:1	341	104:1	341
24	345	105:3	341
24:3	342	110:1	365, 391
24:4–7	341	115:3–8	445
24:7	405	117:26	54
27:5	341	118:19–20	341
32:1–2	354	139:12	341
32:11	341, 345	139:24	481
35:24	348	144:3	391
36:11	52, 437	144:5	401
37:11	345	147:2	391
40:9	370	147:8	341
48:2	341		
50:3–5	391	Proverbs	
50:4	348	2:5	29
50:5	341	2:8–22	481
50:6	348	4:18	489
50:14	341	6:23	489
50:22	345	12:28	51, 52
55:18	173	13:9	489
58:1	348	15:27	116, 118
58:11	348	16:6	116, 118
63:2	342	19:17	52, 116, 118
67:4	348	19:18	117, 118
68:11	370	21:6	52
68:18	351, 391	21:13	117, 118
72:1–2	348	24:26	99
79:9	192	30:5–6	378
79:15	192	30:6	39, 53, 117

Isaiah		21:8	51, 52, 481
5	229	23:8	27
7:14	527	26:2	378
8:4	527	31:8–12	27
11:1	509	32:37	391
11:1–12	194	33:2 LXX	378
11:9	29	49:38	391
11:10–12	398	51:27	398
11:12	27		
13:10	391	Lamentations	
19:1	390	3:28	94
24–27	348		
25:8	78	Ezekiel	
26:19	398	15:1–5	27
26:21	398	32:7–8	391
27:13	27, 399	34:13	375, 391
28:16	365	36:24	391
34:4	391		
40:9	370	Daniel	
40:27	370	4:34	391
43:6	27, 391	6:11	144, 173
44:12–20	445	7	403
45:22	379	7:2–8	391
45:22–23	365, 376	7:7–8	263
49:22	27	7:9	391, 404
52:7	370, 462	7:9–10	379, 391, 405
58:7	117, 118	7:9–14	405
59:2–4	260	7:9–28	397
59:13	492	7:10	404
59:19	391	7:13	54, 281, 395, 396, 397, 398, 399, 400, 401, 402, 403, 404, 405, 406, 448
61:1	370		
64:1–3	365		
64:4	261	7:13–14	390, 398, 401, 402, 425
66:2	52, 64, 267	7:14	399, 403, 404
66:18	391	7:17	391
66:20	27	7:18	402
		7:22	391, 402
Jeremiah		7:23	391
2:21	27, 192	7:29	402
3:14	492	11:31	250
5:5	372	12:1	450
9:24	29	12:1–3	398, 402
17:5	492	12:2–3	402
17:13	492		
20:15	370		

INDEX OF PRIMARY TEXTS

Hosea
  4:1   29
  10:1   27

Joel
  2:2   54
  2:10   391
  2:32   365
  3:2   403
  3:15–16   391
  3:18   392

Amos
  8:3   392
  8:9   391, 392
  8:13   392
  9:11   392

Obadiah
  8   392

Micah
  1:2–5   381
  1:3   365, 401
  4:6   392
  5:9   392
  7:11   392

Nahum
  1:3   390

Habakkuk
  2:14   29
  3:3   391
  3:3–6   381
  3:16   64

Zephaniah
  1:9   392
  3:11   392
  3:16   392

Zechariah
  2:6–10   391
  2:10   53, 374, 383
  2:11   31
  5:3   52
  7:10   52
  8:17   52
  9:12–14   392
  9:14   399
  9:16   392
  10:10   27
  12:3   404
  13:8–9   54
  14:1–5   403
  14:1–21   403, 405
  14:2   403, 404
  14:5   44, 45, 50, 54, 281, 365, 381, 382, 391, 395, 396, 397, 401, 402, 403, 404, 405, 406, 425, 448
  14:9   72, 404, 405
  14:11   509
  14:17   404, 405

Malachi
  1:6–10   43
  1:11   28, 42, 43, 48, 54, 57, 75, 77, 278, 378, 395
  1:14   28, 42, 43, 48, 54, 57, 278, 378, 380, 395
  3:5   255
  3:16   94

Deuterocanonical Books

Tobit
  4:8–10   52
  4:15   51, 52
  14:7   391

Judith
  13:14   492

Wisdom of Solomon
  1:11   52
  1:14   53
  6:9   492
  15:17   445

Sirach	
2:4	52
4:5	52
4:9	52
4:30	53
4:31	52
5:14	52
6:1	52
6:28	52
6:34–36	52
7:29–31	52, 54
7:30	52
12:1	46, 290
12:1–7	318
15:17	51, 52
18:1	53
28:13	52
51:26	372
51:26–27	52, 53

Baruch	
3:8	492
1 Macc 11:43	492
2 Esd 7.3–8	481
2 Esd 12:31–36	80
3 Macc 2:9	53

Pseudepigrapha

2 Baruch	
41.3	372

1 Enoch	
1.9	381, 382, 391
25.3–4	391
90.20	391
91–107	481
104.10–13	378

2 Enoch	
30.14–15	481
48.9	372

3 Enoch	
35.6	372

4 Ezra	
5:23	192

Joseph and Aseneth	
10.14	147

Jubilees	
6	241
6:23–28	241
6:23–38	172
7:20	432
7:21	432
50:13	241

Liber antiquitatum biblicarum	
39.11	147

Letter of Aristeas	
310–311	378

Lives of the Prophets Daniel	
6	372

Odes Solomon	
2:15	492

Psalms of Solomon	
7.9	373
8.28	375
11.1–4	375
17.21–28	375
17.28	391
17.30	373

Dead Sea Scrolls

1Q34	329

1QM, War Scroll	
II, 5–6	148

1QS, Community Rule	
I, 11–12	442
III, 4–5	155
III, 4–6	159

III, 6–9	154	ANCIENT JEWISH WRITERS	
III, 13	489		
III, 13–IV, 26	438, 481, 531	Josephus, *Against Apion*	
V	145	1.42	378
V, 2	442		
V, 13	161, 481	Josephus, *Antiquitates judaicae*	
V, 13–14	155, 160	1.17	378
V, 13–15	159	18.20	442
V, 24–25	371		
VI, 2–3, 19–20	442	Josephus, *Bellum judaicum*	
VI, 13–23	160	2.129	145
VI, 16–17	160	2.122	442
VI, 24–25	160	2.420	463
VI, 25	161	4.618	463
VII, 2–3	160	4.656	463
VII, 6	442		
VII, 15–17	160	Josephus, *Life*	
VII, 16	161	428–429	180
VII, 19	161		
VII, 23–24	481	Philo, *De specialibus legibus*	
VIII, 16–17	160	2.175	202
VIII, 21–23	481		
VIII, 22–24	160	NEW TESTAMENT	
4Q286–287	330	Matthew	
		2:11	351
4Q514		3:6	150
1 I	145	3:11	484
		4:31	116
4QDibHam	329	5	17, 51, 533
		5–7	173, 335
4QMMT		5:3	355
58–62	147	5:4	356
		5:5	52, 267, 345, 355, 356, 441, 442
11QT[a]		5:6	345
XLIX, 20–21	145	5:7	354, 356, 441, 442
		5:8	356
CD, Cairo Genizah copy of the Damascus Document		5:9	355, 356
		5:10	353
VI, 11–16	148	5:10–12	441
XI, 16–21	148	5:11	353, 356
		5:12	345, 356
		5:13	326, 356
		5:13–16	441
		5:14	356

Matthew (cont.)
5:15	337, 356
5:16	340, 353, 356
5:17	353, 355, 356
5:17–20	48
5:18	325
5:19	352, 356, 421
5:21	356
5:21–22	337
5:21–37	52, 356
5:21–48	441
5:22	340, 354, 355, 356, 357, 371
5:23	357
5:23–24	48, 54, 278, 380
5:23–25	352
5:23–26	222
5:24	343, 357
5:25	357
5:25–26	307
5:26	220, 337, 357
5:27	337, 357
5:27–7:12	340
5:28	352, 354, 357
5:29–30	352
5:31–32	352
5:33	52, 220, 357
5:33–37	354
5:39	17, 220, 351, 357
5:39–42	305, 317, 337, 417
5:39–46	443
5:40	259, 337, 357
5:41	220, 259, 338, 340, 357
5:42	37, 318, 357
5:43	338, 358
5:43–44	340
5:44	17, 316, 337, 355, 358
5:44–47	287, 289
5:44–48	303, 417
5:45	319, 338, 358
5:46–47	304, 316
5:47	174, 338, 358
5:48	17, 220, 352, 354, 358
6	234, 241, 371
6:1–4	258, 279
6:1–18	54, 167, 173, 174, 220
6:2	47, 49, 354, 371
6:2–4	279, 371
6:3	338, 358
6:5	47, 49, 53, 170, 354, 358, 371
6:5–13	279
6:5–15	258, 279
6:6	181
6:7	47, 174
6:7–8	173
6:7–15	173, 174
6:9	24, 53, 355, 358
6:9–10	301
6:9–13	19, 39, 53, 73, 273, 337, 366, 469
6:10	359
6:11	359
6:11–13	301
6:12	359
6:12–15	170
6:13	53, 354, 359, 374, 383
6:14–15	173, 222, 301, 352
6:16	47, 49, 53, 273, 354, 359
6:16–18	343
6:19	359
6:20	352
6:24	359
6:25	359
6:25–31	354
6:25–34	178, 344
6:31	360
6:33	360
7:1	360
7:1–2	354
7:1–5	41
7:2	360
7:2–4	355
7:3	360
7:5	354
7:6	41, 47, 53, 75, 144, 274, 337, 345, 360, 368, 369
7:7	352, 354, 360
7:9	360
7:10–11	360
7:11	338, 351, 354, 360
7:12	51, 52, 296, 337, 338, 353, 360

Reference	Pages	Reference	Pages
7:13	360	16:27	51, 54, 396, 403, 404, 405
7:13–14	51, 52, 338, 345, 360, 481	16:27–28	78
7:13–27	222	17–22	353
7:14	361	17:4	174
7:15	54, 361, 448	18	352
7:15–21	377	18:3	353
7:15–23	49, 54, 536	18:4	352
7:16	344, 354, 361	18:8–10	352
7:19	361	18:15	54
7:21	353, 361, 377	18:15–17	52, 371
7:22	361	18:15–18	279
7:23	345, 353, 361, 394	18:15–19	352
7:24	354, 361, 377	18:15–35	222
7:24–26	345	18:17	174
7:25	354	18:20	52, 94, 372, 376, 383
7:27	361	18:21	352
7:28	361	19:3–9	352
7:29	347	19:3–12	352
9:15	393	19:18	51, 52, 220
10:10	49, 54, 277	19:21	352
10:17	450	19:28	391
10:22	54, 508	20:10–12	54
10:23	78	21:9	54, 376
10:40	52, 72, 375	21:13	176
10:40–41	375	21:15	54, 79
10:41	536	21:22	352
11:11	352, 421	22:1–14	253
11:25	169	22:2	394
11:28–29	52	22:3	394
11:29–30	53, 373	22:4	394
12:31	49, 54	22:8	394
12:50	353	22:9	394
13:3–24	56	22:10	394
13:37–43	56	22:14	262
13:41	404	22:37	52
13:52	230, 543	22:38–39	51
14:23	171	22:39	52
15:1–20	145	22:40	353
15:3–6	178	23	173
15:4	52	23:2	252
15:5	351	23:7–10	174
15:18–19	352	23:13	173
15:19	53	23:15	173
15:26–27	76	23:23	173
16:18	374	23:25	173

Matthew (cont.)
23:27	173
23:29	173
23:39	376
24	49, 67, 220, 392, 424, 447, 448
24–25	353
24:1–12	448
24:3	392, 393
24:4	451
24:4–28	392
24:4–35	392
24:10	50, 54, 280, 281, 448, 450
24:11–12	50, 448
24:12	50, 280, 448, 450
24:13	54, 281, 448, 508
24:15	250, 251
24:15–20	450
24:21	448
24:24	54, 280, 448
24:27	392, 393
24:29	400
24:29–31	392
24:30	50, 54, 281, 392, 393, 398, 399, 400, 448
24:30–31	50, 54, 397, 398, 399, 400, 402, 425, 448
24:31	53, 220, 275, 374, 383, 398, 404, 448
24:32–35	392
24:36	386, 392, 393, 394, 395, 425
24:36–51	392
24:37	393
24:39	393
24:42	50, 54, 280, 386, 387, 393, 399
24:42–44	392, 393, 395, 425
24:44	54, 386, 387, 393, 395, 399
24:50	50
24:51	393
25	353
25:1	393
25:1–13	388, 393, 395, 425
25:8	280
25:10	393, 394
25:11–12	353
25:13	50, 54, 386, 388
25:13–15	353
25:14–30	253
25:31	44, 50, 54, 391, 396, 403, 404, 405, 448
25:31–32	403, 404
25:31–46	78
25:32	403, 404
25:34	374, 383, 404
25:41	353
25:46	51
26:25	174
26:29	383
26:31	262
26:39	169
26:42	169
26:49	174
26:64	54, 78, 281
26:67	351
27:34	490
28:19	47, 53, 75, 219, 273, 368, 372, 422

Mark
1:4	70, 484
1:5	150
1:14	370
1:14–15	275
1:35	171
2:18–21	273
2:25	275
3:29	276
3:30	49
5:22–24	249
5:34	249
5:35–43	249
6:8	275
6:46	171
7:1–23	145
7:4	486
7:6	173
7:9–13	178
7:26–27	76
8:38	396, 448
9:5	174
9:13	331

9:30–32	249	13:32–37	389, 390, 392, 395, 425
9:33	249	13:33	54, 390
9:49	342	13:35	54, 386, 387, 390
10:2–12	352	13:37	54
10:19	52, 254, 255, 265	14:9	275
10:29	275	14:24	249
10:39	250	14:25	383
10:45	249	14:28	248, 410
10:47–48	275	14:36	169
10:51	174	14:45	174
11:9	376	15:38	249
11:10	275	16:7	248, 410
11:17	176		
11:21	174	Luke	
11:22–24	181	1:17	53
11:23	268	1:33	28
11:25	169, 170, 173, 175, 183, 240	1:49	53
12:14	266	3:1–2	253
12:26	390	3:3	484
12:30	52	4:16–30	251
12:31	52	5:5	174
12:35–37	275, 424	5:16	171
13	220, 389, 392, 448	6:12	171, 179
13:1–13	448	6:20–23	441
13:3–23	389	6:27–28	304, 316
13:4	389	6:27–30	296, 317, 417
13:9	450	6:27–32	443
13:9–13	508	6:27–33	287, 289
13:10	275	6:27–36	512
13:12	450	6:29	220
13:13	54, 448	6:29–30	305, 306
13:14	250, 251, 390	6:30	37, 259, 306, 318
13:19	448	6:31	52, 296
13:22	54, 448	6:32	296, 304
13:23	389	6:32–35	316
13:24	390	6:32–36	417
13:24–27	389, 390, 391, 448	6:42	173
13:26	54, 389, 390, 398, 399, 400, 448	7:28	421
		8:13	492
13:26–27	397, 398, 399, 402, 512	8:24	174
13:27	274, 275, 374, 383, 398	9:12	171
13:28–31	389	9:28	171
13:29	389, 390	9:33	174
13:30	389, 390	9:48	72
13:32	386, 390, 391, 392	9:49	174

Luke (cont.)		24:35	370
10:7	49, 54		
10:16	375	John	
10:21	169	1:1–4	379
10:27	52	1:38	174
11:1–5	167	1:49	174
11:2	53	2:9	490
11:2–4	39, 53, 73, 469	3:2	174
11:38	145	3:13	401
11:41	371	3:26	174
12:1–5	178, 240	4:31	174
12:33	371	5:27–29	402
12:35	54, 387, 388, 424	6	212
12:35–37	50	6:25	174
12:35–38	394	6:38	401
12:35–40	394, 395, 425	6:41	401
12:36	399	6:42	401
12:36–39	394	6:50	401
12:37	392, 394	6:52	401
12:39	392, 394	6:58	401
12:40	54, 386, 387, 388, 394	7:23	178
12:40–42	399	7:53–8:11	297
12:41	394	9:2	174
12:42	394	9:22	185
12:46	50	11:8	174
12:56	173	11:41	169
12:58–59	307	12:13	376
13:15	173	12:42	185
13:24	481	13:20	375
13:27	492	14:2–3	424
13:35	376	15:1–11	221, 228
14:16–24	253	15:4–5	228
14:24	490	15:6	228
17:13	174	16:2	185
18:1	181	17:1	169
18:20	52	17:6–8	228
19:8	255	17:11	46, 53, 216, 228
19:11–27	253	17:12	228
19:38	376	17:23	46, 53, 374, 383
21:12	450	20:16	174
21:19	508		
21:20	250, 252	Acts	
21:22–32	178	1:11	78
21:27	54	2:28	481
22:27	394	2:38	74, 484, 493

2:42	370, 372	15:28	432
2:44	176	15:29	46, 53, 429, 430, 431, 432, 436, 453, 515, 516
2:44–45	46, 52, 442		
2:46	370	15:30–31	433
3:1	176	15:38	492
3:2–3	371	15:41	433
3:10	371	16:4	433
4:32	46, 52, 378	16:13	150
4:32–35	268	17:18	255
4:32–37	442	18:25	481
6:6	487	19:4	484
7:53	431	19:5	74
7:59	374	19:9	481
8:16	74	19:23	481
8:17–18	488	20:7	370
8:36	150	20:11	370, 490
9:2	481	20:35	46, 52
9:6	488	21	433
9:36	371	21:20	430
10:2	371	21:28	251
10:4	371	22:4	481
10:10	490	23:6	256
10:31	371	23:14	490
10:48	74	24:5	80
13:3	487	24:14	481
13:24	484, 493	24:17	371
13:38–39	431	24:21	256
15	12, 433, 435, 436, 445	24:22	481
15:1–2	430	26:18	490
15:3	430	27:35	370
15:4–5	430	28:30–31	252
15:5	430		
15:7	431	Romans	
15:7–11	431	1:1	70, 370, 466
15:8–9	432	1:1–4	370, 466, 467, 468
15:10	372	1:2	254, 467
15:12	430, 431	1:3	28, 467
15:12–13	431	1:16	465
15:13–21	431	1:16–8:39	467
15:19	431	1:18–2:29	260
15:20	429, 431, 432, 436, 453, 515	1:19–2:29	260
15:21	433	2:23	264
15:22	431, 432	3:20–24	251
15:22–23	430	3:21	451
15:23–29	431, 433, 512	3:24–25	21

Romans (cont.)		3:13	46, 54
4:1–3	251	4:15	465
4:1–25	494	5–6	91
4:7	354	5:1–13	435
4:15	264	5:4	376
5:1	494	5:5	46
5:3–4	304	5:11	46, 54
5:8–11	29	6:8	255
5:12–21	494	7:1	271
5:14	264	7:23	21
6:1–11	493	7:25	271
6:3	493	8:1	271
6:4	489	8:1–13	435
6:5	29	8:4–6	365
8:4	355	8:6	74, 379, 382
8:14	355	9:3–15	276
8:15	355	9:4–14	277
8:16	169	9:13–14	46, 49, 54
8:17	355	9:14	465
8:34	365	9:18	465
10:9–13	365	9:23	465
10:16	465	10:2	203
11:28	465	10:4	379
12	225	10:16	370
12:13	46, 54	10:17	229
12:14	355, 512	10:21	436
12:16	512	10:22	436
12:17	355	10:25–29	19
12:20	355, 512	10:28	436
12:24	355	11	212
13:9	512	11:5	253
13:10	512	11:23–26	468, 474, 523
13:12	490	11:26	383, 468
14:5–6	133	12:1	271
14:10	355	12:11	254
15:6	74	12:28–31	277
15:16	370	15:1	466
15:27	134	15:1–5	466, 467, 468
		15:3	468
1 Corinthians		15:5	255
1:2–3	382	15:14	254, 255
1:7–8	78	15:23	393
1:13	74	15:25	365
2:6	451	15:28	72
2:9	51, 261, 281, 512	15:52	46, 54, 399

16:1	271	5:14		46, 52
16:12	271	5:20		498
16:13	392	6:16		28
16:22	46, 54, 221, 275, 375, 381, 382, 423				
		Ephesians			
16:23	275	1:3		74
		1:17		74
2 Corinthians		1:18		490
1:3	74	1:20		365
2:7	70	4:1		377
5:16	254	4:5		490
6:16	28	4:8		351
8:8–15	134	5:8		490
8:18	465	6		527
9:6–15	134	6:5		102, 378
11:4	465, 466	6:5–8		46, 53
11:7	468	6:5–9		269
11:31	74	6:7		117, 118
12:2–5	254	6:9		46, 53
		6:14		387
Galatians		Philippians			
1:6	465	1:1		278, 377
1:7	468	1:5		465
1:12	466	1:7		465
1:13–14	254	1:12		465
1:14	254	1:16		465
2:1–10	433	1:27		377, 465
2:2	466	2		11, 257
2:5	465	2:9–10		376
2:6	434	2:9–11		365
2:9	434	2:10–11		379
2:10	434	2:14		46, 52
2:11–14	435	2:22		465
2:14	465	3:2		76
2:20	493	3:6		254
3:7	31	4:3		465
3:16–18	494	4:8		331
3:19	264	4:15		465
3:27	74			
4:5	31	Colossians			
4:6	169	1:3		74
4:10	133	1:10		377
4:21–31	56	1:13		490
5:1	372	1:15–17		379
5:13–6:10	260			

Reference	Pages
Colossians (cont.)	
2:12	486
2:12–13	489
2:21	490
3:1	365
3:22	378
3:22–23	102
3:22–25	46, 53
3:22–4:1	269
4:1	46, 53
1 Thessalonians	
2:2	70, 370
2:4	465
2:8–9	370
2:9	70, 466
2:12	377
2:19	393
3:13	44, 46, 50, 54, 281, 365, 393, 396, 401
4	80
4:15	393
4:15–17	480, 512
4:16	46, 54, 281, 399
4:16–17	78, 365, 401, 402
5:4	393, 395
5:6	392
5:22	52
5:23	393
2 Thessalonians	
1:4–6	508
1:7	396, 401
1:8	370
2:1	393
2:3–12	507
2:8	393
2:8–9	50
2:9	393
3:6	376
3:7–12	46, 54
3:10	46
1 Timothy	
2:14	264
3:1–10	377
3:2–10	278
4:1	492
4:14	487
5:18	46, 49, 54
5:22	487
2 Timothy	
2:8	254
2:25	279
4:6–18	252
Titus	
2:9	378
Hebrews	
3:1–4:11	495
3:12	492
4:16	494
5	484
5:1–10	494
5:9	484
5:10	495
5:11–14	478, 495
5:12	483, 485
5:12–14	477, 488, 494, 517
5:13	484
5:14	484
6	484, 495
6:1	484, 485, 486, 488
6:1–2	477, 484, 488, 516
6:1–6	12, 477, 478, 479, 480, 482, 484, 488, 489, 490, 494, 495, 516, 517
6:2	485, 486, 487, 488
6:4	477, 488, 490, 491, 493
6:4–5	477, 478
6:4–6	477, 488, 492, 493, 495
6:6	477, 484, 488, 492
6:9	478, 493, 495
6:9–12	494
6:12	493
6:13–18	494
7:1	495
9:10	486

9:15	264	4:12	46, 53
10:19–22	494		
10:26–27	489, 492, 493, 494, 495	2 John	
10:26–31	494	7	46, 54
10:32	489	10	46, 54, 375
11:8–12	494		
12:12–17	494	1 Peter	
12:15	493	1:3	74
12:15–17	492, 493	1:7	46
12:16–17	489, 493, 494, 495	1:13	387
13:7	52, 268, 372	1:17	54
		2:1	354
James		2:9	28, 31, 490
1:2	268	2:11	46, 512
1:2–4	281	2:12	353
1:4	354	3:9	512
1:5–6	354	3:14	353
1:6–7	268	3:21	493
1:12	354	4:12	512
1:13	268, 354	4:12–13	508
1:14–15	354	4:14	353
1:17	354	4:17	70, 370
1:19–20	354	5:7	354
1:22	354	5:10	354
2:1	268		
2:8	46, 52	2 Peter	
2:10	283	1:16	393
2:13	354	2:22	76
2:20	251	3:4	393
2:21–24	251	3:10	393, 395
3:12	354	3:12	393
4:11	354		
5:4	255	Jude	
5:7–8	393	5	379
5:12	354	14	382, 423
5:16	46, 53	21	382
5:19–20	268	22–23	52
5:20	266		
		Revelation	
1 John		1:1	499
1:9	46, 53	1:1–3:22	502, 514
2:18	46, 54, 507	1:3	500
2:22	46, 54	1:4	502
2:28	393	1:6	502
4:3	46, 54	1:7	78, 502, 510, 524

Revelation (cont.)

Reference	Pages
1:7–14	524
1:8	499, 502
1:10	369
1:12–16	379
1:16	527
2–3	499
2:1–3:22	524
2:5	502
2:7	502, 514
2:10	508, 514
2:11	514
2:14	498, 502, 506
2:14–15	434
2:16	502
2:17	502, 514
2:20	498, 502, 507
2:21	502
2:22	502
2:23	498
2:24	498
2:26	502
2:26–28	514
2:27	502
2:29	514
3:2–3	392
3:3	393, 395, 502
3:4	502
3:5	514
3:6	514
3:7	502
3:9–10	508
3:12	514
3:13	514
3:18	502
3:19	502
3:20	502
3:21	502, 514
3:22	501, 514
4:1	510, 514
4:1–5:14	524
4:1–8:1	502, 514
4:5	514
4:7–8	502
4:8	499, 502
4:11	46, 53, 499, 502
5–7	500
5:5	28
5:9	78, 502
5:10	502
5:12	78, 502
5:13	502
6:9–10	508
7:1	501
7:1–10	499
7:9	502
7:9–17	514
7:12	499, 502
7:13	502
7:14	502
7:14–17	508
7:15–17	514
7:16	503
7:17	503
8–9	500
8:1	514
8:1–11:18	503, 514
8:5	514
8:6	510
8:8	510
8:10	510
8:12	510
9:1	510
9:13	510
9:21	498
10:6	500
10:7	500
11:12	510
11:15	500, 503, 510
11:15–18	503, 514
11:17	499, 503
11:17–18	514
11:18	501, 514
11:19	514
11:19–15:4	503, 514
12:11	508
13:1	507
13:3	507
13:3–8	503
13:5	507

13:6	499, 507	19:10	501, 514
13:7	503, 507, 509	19:11	510, 514
13:8	507	19:11–22:8	524
13:10	509	19:11–22:21	504, 514
13:11	507	19:14	510
13:11–16	503	19:15	499
13:11–17	507	19:20	507
13:12	507	19:20–21	511
13:13	507	20:4	508, 510
13:14	507	20:4–5	510
14:1–5	503, 510	20:11	510
14:7	503	20:11–12	391
14:8	503	20:12	510, 511
14:10	503	20:13	511
14:11	503	20:13–14	510
14:12	503	21:1–22:5	511
14:13	503	21:2	511
14:14–16	503	21:3	499
14:16	503	21:3–5	78
14:17–20	503	21:7	508, 511
15:1	501, 503	21:8	498
15:1–4	501	21:9–10	499
15:2	503	21:13–14	510
15:2–4	514	21:22	499
15:3	499, 503	21:23–25	79
15:3–4	514	22:3	508, 509
15:4	501, 503, 514	22:10–21	524
15:5	514	22:15	498
15:5–7	501	22:17–20	221
15:5–19:10	504, 514	22:18	378
15:8	514	22:18–19	103, 325
16:7	499	22:19	378
16:14	499	22:20	275, 382, 423
16:15	392, 393, 395		
17:2	504	RABBINIC WORKS	
17:4	504		
18:3	504	b. Bekorot	
18:9	504	15a	76, 147
18:23	498		
19:6	499, 504	b. Berakot	
19:6–8	514	10b	372
19:6–9	514	22a	64
19:7	504	27b–28a	182
19:8	504	28b	182, 481
19:9	504, 524	29b	178, 184

b. Baba Meṣiʻa		3:3	94
59b	183	4:12	72
b. Ḥagigah		m. Berakot	
4a	99	2:2	372
		4	241
b. Megillah		4:1	173
17b	182, 184	4:1–4	181, 240, 241
		4:3	73, 177
b. Pesaḥim		4:4	177
25a	432	5:1	170
29a	76		
		m. ʻEduyyot	
b. Sanhedrin		7:7	179
98a	80		
		m. Megillah	
b. Šebuʻot		1:3	172
11b	147	3:6	24, 172
		4:1	24, 172
b. Šebiʻit			
11b	76	m. Miqwaʼot	
		1:1–4	239
b. Taʻanit		1:1–8	149, 238, 239
12a	24	1:3	239
		1:4	239
b. Temurah		1:5	239
17a	147	1:5–6	239
31a	147	1:7–8	239
33a–b	147		
17a	76	m. Nedarim	
30b	76	9:1	178
b. Yebamot		m. Peʼah	
47a–b	347	3:8	99
Exodus Rabbah		m. Roš Haššanah	
21:4	99	4.5	327
Kallah Rabbah		m. Taʻanit	
52b	72	1:6	172
		2:2	73
m. ʼAbot		2:9	172
1:1	266	3:1	172
2:9	481	3:8	169
3:5	372	4:2	24

INDEX OF PRIMARY TEXTS

m. Temurah
6:5   26, 76, 146, 147

Numbers Rabbah
11:8   99

Pirqe Rabbi Eliezer
29   26

Sipre Deuteronomy
323   372

Sipre Numbers
108   31
118   146

Targum Hosea
14.8   375

Targum Isaiah
53.8   375

Targum Micah
5.1–3   375

t. 'Abodah Zarah
8:4   432

t. Berakot
3:1–3   173
3:5   179
3:7   178
3:12   177
4:4   178

t. Ḥullin
2:19–24   185

t. Pe'ah
1:13   99

t. Roš Haššanah
2:17   177

t. Šabbat
15:16   178
16:17   432

t. Temurah
4:11   147

Testament of Abraham
12.4   391
12.11   391

Testament of Asher
1.3–6.5   481
1.8–9   438
5.2–3   481, 489
6.4–5   438

y. Berakot
4:3, 8a   184

y. Ma'aśer Šeni
2:5, 53c   147

EARLY CHRISTIAN WRITINGS

Acts of Pilate
18.2   484

Apostolic Constitutions and Canons
7   260, 505
7.1–19   481
7.2.6–7   319
7.9–17   115
7.21   452
7.25.4   216
7.25–26   225, 230
7.25.5–7   41
7.26.5   79
7.30.1   369
7.30.2   130
7.32   384
7.32.1–5   449
7.32.5   260
7.32.4   45

Apostolic Tradition		18–29	87
21	162	18.1	111, 259, 262, 438, 489
25	162	18.2	439
26	162	19–20	439
28–37	162	19.1	438, 439
		19.2	263, 266, 378, 445
Athanasius, *Epistulae festales*		19.2–3	378, 423
39.11	371	19.4–7	325
		19.4–12	112
Augustine, *Epistula*		19.5	269
5.5	301	19.6–7	121
		19.9	437
Barnabas		19.9–10	372, 445
1–17	120	20	325
1.5	447	20.1	269, 325, 439, 494
1.8	112	20.1–2	494
2	262	20.2	325
2.1	447	21.1	494
2.6	373	21.1–9	266
3	262		
3.6	112	1 Clement	
4	262	5	284
4.4	263	16.17	373
4.6	112	42.4–5	377
4.9	111, 112, 447	58.1	376
4.14	262	59.2–3	376
5–8	262	63.2	371
5.4	494		
5.12	262	Clement of Alexandria, *Paedagogus*	
6.11	493	2.7.56	432
9	262		
10	262	Clement of Alexandria, *Stromata*	
10.10	447	2.19.102.4	304
11–12	263	4.15.97	432
13	263	7.6.31.7–8	224
14	263	7.12	369
15	263		
15.9	369	Didache	
16	263	1	17, 336
16.4	263	1–4	93, 151
16.4–5	263	1–5	315, 437, 451, 453, 515
17	111, 262, 263	1–6	18, 86, 142, 151, 153, 156, 162, 312, 322, 323, 347, 439, 447, 451, 452, 460, 461, 483, 485, 486
17.1	120, 282		
17.2	111, 260		
18–20	120, 151, 260, 263, 437, 481	1–7	155

INDEX OF PRIMARY TEXTS

1–10	139, 212, 227	2.2–7	439, 441
1.0	361, 364, 366, 371	2.2–3.6	33
1.1	33, 51, 52, 267, 338, 345, 360, 361, 480	2.2–3.8	51
		2.2–5.2	483
1.1–2	439	2.3	52, 56, 63, 112, 267, 357
1.1–2.1	483	2.4	52, 113, 267
1.1–5.2	411	2.5	63, 267
1.1–6.1	282, 429	2.6	22, 267
1.1–6.2	259, 261, 280, 332, 411	2.6–7	95
1.1–6.3	483, 484, 485, 491	2.7	22, 31, 52, 112, 267, 338, 340, 358, 442, 444
1.2	33, 46, 51, 52, 56, 64, 119, 267, 270, 296, 331, 337, 338, 340, 343, 344, 358, 359, 360, 439, 443, 481	3	337
		3.1	52, 359
		3.1–6	34, 110, 266, 439, 440, 441
1.2–4	512	3.2	22, 337, 340, 356
1.2–4.14	485	3.2–3	100
1.2–5	512	3.2–6	52, 441
1.2–6.2	481	3.3	357
1.2b–6	266	3.4	52, 498
1.3	46, 63, 296, 303, 306, 316, 337, 338, 340, 343, 358, 444, 512	3.5	113, 359
		3.6	46, 52
1.3–4	17, 440	3.7	28, 52, 56, 112, 267, 342, 345, 356, 437
1.3–5	444		
1.3–6	103, 443	3.7–8	441, 442
1.3b–5	65, 312, 443, 444	3.7–10	440
1.3b–6	320	3.7–4.10	442
1.3b–2.1	35, 38, 46, 52, 282, 287, 316, 414, 416, 417, 437	3.8	22, 31, 52, 62, 63, 112, 267, 342, 356
1.4	46, 220, 259, 305, 317, 337, 338, 340, 357, 358, 484, 512	3.8–10	296, 441
		3.9	113, 267
1.4–6	319	3.9–10	320
1.5	22, 37, 38, 42, 46, 77, 91, 96, 104, 105, 118, 220, 259, 290, 306, 307, 309, 316, 317, 318, 337, 338, 340, 355, 357, 358, 360	3.10	52, 113, 268
		4	91, 112, 296, 320, 337, 533
		4.1	34, 52, 62, 71, 92, 95, 103, 107, 108, 113, 268, 320, 322, 364, 365, 366, 372, 437, 442, 445
1.5–6	317, 319	4.1–2	322
1.5b–2.1	319	4.1–8	105
1.6	46, 62, 290, 296, 307, 312, 317, 318, 319, 322, 358	4.2	52, 92, 95, 103, 107, 108, 113, 268, 320, 442
2	296, 320, 325, 337, 357	4.3	52, 80, 92, 95, 103, 104, 107, 109, 112, 114, 268, 319, 320, 356, 360, 442
2.1	38, 267, 296, 316		
2.1–7	356		
2.2	22, 52, 112, 267, 296, 356, 357, 498	4.4	92, 95, 104, 107, 112, 268
2.2–4	220	4.5	52, 92, 104, 107, 109, 113, 268

Didache (cont.)
- 4.5–8 317, 319, 320, 444
- 4.6 21, 52, 92, 96, 104, 105, 107, 109, 113, 266, 268
- 4.7 52, 92, 95, 96, 104, 105, 107, 109, 113, 268, 356
- 4.8 46, 52, 63, 93, 96, 104, 105, 107, 109, 113, 269, 359, 378, 442
- 4.9 93, 104, 108, 112, 269, 343, 360
- 4.9–10 110
- 4.9–11 34, 85, 133, 442
- 4.10 22, 46, 53, 93, 101, 104, 113, 269
- 4.10–11 269
- 4.11 46, 53, 93, 101, 104, 113, 233, 269, 364, 366, 378
- 4.12 93, 102, 104, 108, 113, 269, 364, 366, 378, 445
- 4.12–13 378, 423
- 4.13 18, 24, 38, 39, 53, 56, 80, 93, 104, 108, 109, 113, 269, 322, 323, 325, 326, 356, 364, 366, 444, 445
- 4.14 31, 46, 53, 63, 93, 104, 108, 109, 114, 269, 322, 357, 361, 442
- 5 151, 325, 337
- 5–7 145
- 5.1 33, 53, 95, 263, 269, 283, 356, 411, 439, 486
- 5.1–2 480, 481, 485, 494
- 5.2 269, 355, 356, 361, 442, 447, 451, 453, 515
- 6 337, 436, 451
- 6.1 30, 53, 80, 151, 242, 259, 270, 323, 356, 361, 443, 447, 451, 453, 515
- 6.1–2 266, 270, 282, 411
- 6.1–3 512
- 6.1–7.1 322
- 6.2 18, 19, 31, 53, 259, 270, 283, 343, 358, 364, 365, 366, 372, 373, 444, 447, 453, 484, 516
- 6.2–3 19, 115, 151, 283, 429, 443, 446, 451, 452, 453, 498, 515, 533
- 6.3 20, 21, 25, 46, 53, 237, 266, 270, 271, 272, 283, 284, 322, 332, 445, 446, 447, 452
- 6.3–12.1 260, 271, 280, 282, 283, 411, 412
- 6.16 343
- 7 139, 141, 142, 143, 149, 151, 153, 155, 156, 161, 163, 212, 238, 239, 240, 336, 337, 419, 483, 533
- 7–8 214
- 7–10 212, 214, 215, 218, 231, 326, 460, 483, 485, 487, 491
- 7.1 25, 31, 34, 47, 53, 63, 70, 74, 75, 105, 151, 172, 219, 220, 237, 238, 272, 273, 312, 315, 322, 323, 333, 347, 368, 374, 376, 380, 418, 422, 452, 483, 487, 490
- 7.1–2 219
- 7.1–3 142, 143, 149, 150, 162, 201, 239, 486, 487
- 7.1–4 98, 452
- 7.1–10.7 483
- 7.1–11.2 332
- 7.2 150, 219, 220, 237, 273, 283
- 7.2–3 21
- 7.2–4 273, 452
- 7.3 25, 31, 34, 47, 53, 74, 75, 237, 273, 368, 374, 376, 380, 422, 487
- 7.4 24, 172, 237, 273, 283, 412, 487
- 7.4–8.1 201
- 8 49, 139, 172, 174, 212, 215, 216, 217, 218, 220, 234, 241, 274, 337, 483
- 8–10 40, 43, 214, 215, 321
- 8.1 24, 53, 133, 172, 240, 241, 273, 359, 487
- 8.1–2 167, 371
- 8.2 19, 24, 28, 34, 39, 40, 47, 53, 66, 70, 72, 73, 213, 214, 258, 296, 333, 337, 358, 359, 364, 365, 366, 367, 368, 371, 374, 376, 380, 422, 469, 470, 471, 472, 475, 487, 491
- 8.2–3 31, 241, 273, 323
- 8.3 72, 273, 487
- 9 191, 192, 211, 214, 215, 216, 217, 232, 337, 498
- 9–10 7, 40, 139, 158, 162, 190, 199, 209, 211, 212, 213, 214, 217, 219,

INDEX OF PRIMARY TEXTS

224, 225, 226, 227, 228, 229, 231, 232, 233, 234, 235, 236, 323, 326, 461, 473, 474, 475, 483, 491, 499, 501, 502, 504, 512
9.1   25, 148, 172, 201, 221, 235, 274, 322, 333, 383, 473, 487, 499
9.1–2   474
9.1–3   157
9.2   27, 29, 40, 141, 189, 191, 213, 214, 229, 266, 274, 275, 344, 367, 373, 473, 475, 487, 491, 499, 502, 503
9.2–3   27, 74
9.3   29, 31, 40, 70, 78, 189, 213, 214, 217, 266, 274, 322, 367, 373, 473, 487, 491, 499, 502, 503
9.3–4   25, 141, 157
9.4   27, 28, 29, 31, 40, 53, 77, 79, 190, 213, 214, 220, 223, 259, 274, 356, 473, 487, 491, 499, 502, 503
9.5   26, 34, 40, 42, 47, 53, 62, 70, 74, 75, 76, 140, 141, 142, 143, 144, 146, 147, 148, 156, 157, 159, 162, 163, 201, 203, 219, 228, 235, 236, 238, 240, 274, 296, 322, 337, 360, 364, 365, 366, 367, 368, 369, 380, 383, 422, 473, 481, 484, 485, 490, 493, 533
10   191, 211, 214, 215, 216, 217, 223, 224, 232, 337, 498
10.1   25, 142, 201, 211, 235, 236, 237, 274, 333, 473, 487
10.1–4   157
10.1–5   237, 326
10.1–11.2   54
10.2   23, 28, 29, 31, 40, 46, 53, 70, 77, 189, 213, 214, 220, 228, 266, 274, 373, 380, 473, 487, 491, 502, 503
10.2–3   74
10.2–5   140, 142, 373
10.3   25, 29, 43, 46, 53, 76, 77, 78, 214, 217, 236, 274, 344, 359, 373, 380, 473, 491, 499, 502, 503, 504
10.3–4   191
10.3–5   31
10.4   40, 131, 213, 274, 374, 423, 473, 487, 491, 502
10.5   27, 28, 31, 40, 46, 53, 78, 79, 190, 213, 214, 220, 274, 359, 364, 365, 366, 373, 374, 375, 383, 423, 484, 487, 491, 499, 502, 503
10.5–6   423
10.6   46, 54, 78, 79, 140, 142, 156, 157, 159, 163, 211, 214, 221, 226, 227, 236, 237, 238, 239, 255, 275, 361, 363, 364, 375, 381, 382, 383, 384, 406, 407, 423, 484, 485, 493, 499, 502, 504, 533
10.7   80, 203, 235, 275, 283, 330, 331, 383, 418, 473, 499, 504, 511, 517, 536, 537, 538
11   95, 101, 337
11–12   95
11–13   139, 539
11–15   139, 163, 460, 483, 485, 487
11.1   63, 275, 322, 323, 375, 483
11.1–2   48, 80
11.1–3   322
11.1–13.4   80
11.1–15.4   483
11.2   30, 46, 54, 71, 242, 275, 283, 356, 361, 364, 365, 366, 375, 376, 377
11.3   40, 66, 70, 271, 275, 296, 371, 376, 471, 472, 487
11.4   71, 275, 364, 365, 366, 375, 376, 377
11.4–13.7   487
11.5   272, 275, 283, 412
11.5–6   307
11.6   275, 360
11.7   49, 54, 276, 360
11.7–12   201, 203, 537
11.8   49, 54, 276, 344, 361, 364, 365, 366, 375, 376, 377
11.9   276
11.10   242, 276, 361
11.11   31, 276, 331, 360, 538
11.12   276
11.13   537

Didache (cont.)
- 12   337
- 12.1   46, 54, 56, 70, 71, 272, 276, 338, 358, 361, 364, 365, 366, 375, 376, 377, 380, 412
- 12.1–5   307
- 12.1–15.4   280
- 12.2   272, 277, 412
- 12.2–15.3   282
- 12.2–15.4   276, 411
- 12.3   80, 272, 277, 412
- 12.4   21, 46, 54, 80, 277
- 12.4–5   131
- 12.5   80, 277
- 13   95, 145, 336, 419, 538
- 13.1   46, 49, 54
- 13.2   49
- 13.3   54, 278, 344
- 13.4   278
- 13.5   38, 39, 278
- 13.6   278
- 13.7   38, 39, 278
- 13.7–12   536
- 14   95, 142, 156, 157, 162, 163, 203, 209, 232, 337, 533
- 14–15   139
- 14.1   24, 48, 158, 233, 237, 278, 343, 356, 357, 364, 365, 366, 369, 380
- 14.1–2   21
- 14.1–3   77, 159, 238, 239
- 14.1–16.2   322
- 14.2   28, 48, 54, 158, 237, 278, 380
- 14.2–3   76, 157
- 14.3   31, 42, 48, 54, 57, 62, 75, 130, 158, 278, 296, 322, 364, 366, 369, 378, 379, 380, 395
- 14.5   54
- 15   92, 95, 279, 337
- 15.1   279, 364, 365, 366, 377, 380, 413
- 15.1–2   158, 537, 538
- 15.2   279
- 15.3   40, 46, 54, 63, 66, 70, 95, 142, 158, 159, 163, 279, 356, 357, 371, 471, 472
- 15.3–4   296, 371
- 15.4   40, 54, 67, 70, 80, 258, 279, 322, 364, 365, 366, 370, 371, 377, 422, 471, 472
- 16   49, 67, 220, 260, 280, 281, 282, 283, 285, 312, 332, 337, 365, 407, 411, 413, 414, 423, 446, 447, 448, 449, 450, 451, 452, 453, 460, 480, 485, 488, 515
- 16.1   48, 50, 54, 280, 337, 340, 342, 356, 363, 364, 366, 381, 384, 385, 386, 387, 388, 389, 392, 394, 395, 396, 406, 424
- 16.1–2   80, 447, 449
- 16.1–8   34, 348, 363, 384, 385, 483
- 16.1–11   280
- 16.2   20, 30, 280, 360, 447, 450, 484
- 16.2–3   30
- 16.2–5   242
- 16.3   28, 50, 54, 280, 361, 448, 449, 505, 506
- 16.3–4   80, 451
- 16.3–5   448
- 16.3–6   511, 512
- 16.3–8   79
- 16.4   22, 28, 30, 46, 50, 54, 280, 342, 356, 361, 448, 505, 506, 507
- 16.4–5   50, 450
- 16.4–8   385, 396
- 16.5   28, 46, 50, 54, 281, 357, 361, 448, 450, 506, 507, 508, 509, 512
- 16.5–6   451
- 16.6   46, 50, 54, 281, 397, 400, 448, 488, 506, 509
- 16.6–8   50, 399
- 16.6–11   261
- 16.7   44, 46, 50, 54, 62, 281, 296, 322, 364, 366, 381, 384, 385, 396, 406, 424, 448, 505, 506
- 16.7–8   79, 130, 363, 364, 395, 397, 401, 405, 406, 425
- 16.8   28, 50, 51, 54, 281, 344, 356, 364, 366, 381, 384, 385, 396, 397, 398, 399, 400, 402, 403, 406, 424, 448, 505, 506, 510, 511, 512
- 16.8–9   505, 511, 512

INDEX OF PRIMARY TEXTS

16.8–11	261	6.1	375
16.9	281, 506, 511, 512	9.1	375
16.10	281	15.1	377
16.11	261, 281	20.1	374
16.12	261	20.2	370

Doctrina apostolorum 151

1.1	438
2	325
4	114
4.1	445
4.12	445
5	325
5.2	447
6.1	451, 453, 515
6.2–3	103
6.4–5	443, 451
6.6	451

Epiphanius, *Panarion*

1.16	172
2.59	493
1.24.5	369

Eusebius, *Historia ecclesiastica*

3.1	284
3.25	543
3.25.4	371
4.23.8	369
4.26.2	369
5.1.26	435

Gospel of the Ebionites

1	484

Gospel of Peter

9.35	369
13.50	369

Gospel of Thomas

93	369

Ignatius, *To the Ephesians*

2.1	377
4.1	377

Ignatius, *To the Magnesians*

9.1	233, 369
12	377

Ignatius, *To the Romans*

10.2	377

Ignatius, *To the Smyrnaeans*

7.1	491

Irenaeus, *Adversus haereses*

1.13.7	492
3.12.14–15	431
4.13.1	522
4.13.4	522
5.36.3	523

Justin, *Apologia*

1.14.3	304
1.15.9	304
1.36.1	379
1.51	396, 405
1.61	489
1.61.3	368
1.61.10	368
1.61.13	368
1.66.3	471
1.67	233
1.67.3	369
1.67.7	369

Justin, *Dialogus cum Tryphone*

20.1	435
24.1	369
31	396, 405
31.2–7	397
31.3b–4	397, 398
34.8	435
41	233

Justin, Dialogus cum Tryphone (cont.)	
41.4	369
53.1	373
138.1	369
Origen, Commentarium in evangelium Matthaei	
10	435
Origen, Contra Celsum	
8.22	369
Origen, De oratione	
2.4–5	179
18	170
31	170
Pseudo-Athanasius, De virginitate	
13	223
14	224
Pseudo-Athanasius, Synopsis scripturae sacrae	
76	371
Pseudo-Clement, Homilies	
1.22	26
7.8.1	436
8.22	26
14.1.4	370
Pseudo-Clement, Recognitions	
1.19	26
1.22	26
Pseudo-Cyprian, De aleatoribus	
4	372
Shepherd of Hermas, Mandates	
2	355
2.4–6	290, 443
4	355
4.3.1	484, 493
4.3.1–7	477
5	355
6	355
6.2	481
11	355
Shepherd of Hermas, Similitudes	
8.8.2	492
Syntagma doctrinae	
4.1–2	110
4.2	120
Tertullian, Adversus Marcionem	
2.29.4	526
3.12–14	527
3.14.3	527
3.14.7	527
Tertullian, Apology	
9.13	435, 436
9.15	435
Tertullian, De jejunio adversus psychicos	
16	24
Tertullian, De monogamia	
5.3	436
Tertullian, De pudicitia	
12.4	436
Tertullian, De spectaculis	
13.4	436
Valentinian Expositions	
XI 44, 1–37	224
XI 43, 20–38	224
Vita Shenudi	481

Greco-Roman Literature

Aristides, Apology	
15	481
15.5	435

INDEX OF PRIMARY TEXTS

Aristotle, *Rhetorica*
3.9   300
3.9.5   299, 302

Cicero, *De oratore*
3.181   300, 302

Dionysius of Halicarnassus, *De compositione verborum*
2   299
22   302

Demetrius, *De elocutione*
1   302
2   300
10–11   299
11   299
12   300
16   300

Hesiod, *Opera et dies*
287–292   481

Minucius Felix, *Octavius*
30.6   435
38.1   435

Polybius, *General History*
3.54.5   492
12.12.2   492

Pseudo-Nicephorus, *Stichometry*   372

Quintilian, *Institutio oratoria*
9.3.54   304
9.4.19–22   300
9.4.125   299, 300, 302

Quintilian, *Rhetorica ad Herennium*
4.27   299
4.34   304

Rufinus, *Commentarius in symbolum apostolorum*
36   436

Suetonius, *Vespasianus*
5   450

Xenophon, *Memorabilia*
2.1.21–34   481

Index of Modern Authors

Achtemeier, Paul J. 62, 293
Adams, Edward 382, 391, 403
Adna, Jostien 349
Aldridge, Robert E. 35–36, 51, 261, 281, 384, 436–37, 505,
Allison, Dale C. 252, 292, 304–5, 347, 545
Alon, Gedalyahu 145, 175, 179–80, 184
Amélineau, Émile 108
Amezaga, Louis D. Jr. 563
Anderson, Charles P. 494
Anderson, R. Dean, Jr. 299, 301, 494
Andriessen, Paul 490
Arnold, Russell C. D. 161
Attridge, Harold W. 479, 489–90, 492–94
Audet, Jean-Paul 2, 34, 38, 51, 61, 65, 68, 90, 159, 166, 288, 367, 369, 387, 413, 422–24, 429, 482, 531–32, 539
Austin, John Langshaw 200
Avemarie, Friedrich 161
Ayres, Lewis 456
Bahr, Gordon J. 273
Baker, Coleman A. 18
Baker, John A. 257
Balabanski, Vicky 49, 385–86, 448
Barker, Margaret 341, 348
Barnard, Leslie W. 88, 482, 489
Barr, David L. 12, 498–501, 504, 512
Barr, James 169
Bar-Tal, Daniel 23
Barthélemy, Dominique 397
Bauckham, Richard J. 171, 349–50, 365, 369, 382, 420, 431
Bauer, Walter 4, 255, 455–56, 519–21

Bausi, Allesandro 539
Beall, Todd S. 145
Beare, Francis Wright 272
Beasley-Murray, George R. 390–91
Beentjes, Pancratius C. 338–39
Beeri, Tova 176
Benoit, André 151
Betz, Hans Dieter 217, 347, 350–52, 354, 420, 481
Betz, Johannes 228–29, 490, 512, 537
Billerbeck, Paul 170–71, 372
Billig, Michael 583
Bingham, D. Jeffrey 13
Black, Matthew 381–83
Blackman, Philip 327
Bloch, Maurice 10, 196–202, 204–5, 231–32, 234–35
Bockmuehl, Markus 463, 532
Borgen, Peder 463
Bornkamm, Günther 383
Botha, Pieter J. J. 290
Bradshaw, Paul F. 72, 162, 209, 458, 474, 499
Brakke, David 456
Braumann, Georg 155
Bredin, Mark 125
Brettler, Marc Z 338
Broadhead, Edwin 1249
Brooks, A. Taeko 282
Brooks, E. Bruce 11, 247–51, 253, 277, 282, 285, 409–14, 541
Brown, Raymond E. 185, 479
Bruce, F. F 400, 402, 479, 488, 490
Bryennios, Philotheos 7, 258–60, 262, 281, 436, 504, 529

Bultmann, Rudolf 256, 493, 519
Bundy, Robert F. 541, 583
Burkitt, F. C. 458
Butler, B. C. 388, 400
Cameron, Ron 457
Carleton-Paget, James 124
Carson, Don A. 456
Casey, Maurice 390
Cazeaux, Jacques 147
Chilton, Bruce 349, 379
Clabeaux, John 10–11, 154, 231, 237, 241–43
Cohen, Naomi 177, 184
Cohen, Shaye J. D. 144, 180, 185
Collins, Adela Yarbro 249, 389–90, 410
Collins, John J. 330, 537
Connolly, R. H. 288, 458, 538
Conti, M. 495
Conzelmann, Hans 148, 490, 522–23
Crossan, John Dominic 69–70, 81, 293
Crossley, James G. 250
Crouch, James E. 88
Czachesz, István 291
Daly, Robert J. 82–83, 125, 158
Danielou, Jean 257
Daube, David 347, 487
Davies, William David 252, 347
Davila, James R. 329–30
Davis, Casey W. 478
Dean, Margaret E. 302–3
Decharneux, Baudouin 537
Deines, Roland 146, 346
Deismann, Adolf 463
Denny, J. Peter 312
Derrenbacker, Robert A. 290
deSilva, David 478, 484, 490
Deutsch, Celia 94
Dewey, Joanna 311
Dibelius, Martin 88, 110, 192, 373
Dittenberger, Wilhelm 463
Donfried, Karl Paul 256
Douglas, Mary 533
Downing, F. Gerald 301
Draper, Jonathan A. 1, 5, 7–10, 13, 17–20, 22, 24–27, 29–30, 35, 39–40, 43, 47, 60, 64–65, 72, 75–76, 85–87, 90–91, 95, 111, 123–27, 130–31, 133–35, 139, 148, 154, 157–58, 162, 165, 194, 209–10, 212, 214–15, 218, 228, 233, 237, 258, 263, 274, 287–289, 295, 303, 314, 323–27, 367, 383–85, 388, 396, 399–400, 418, 437, 444, 430, 448, 452, 460–61, 473, 475, 483, 497, 508–9, 533, 534, 537, 540–41
Drews, Paul 380
Duling, Dennis C. 293
Dunn, Geoffrey D. 526
Dunn, James D. G. 63, 74, 86, 457, 465, 521
Easton, Burton Scott 284
Edsall, Benjamin 87, 539
Edwards, James R. 249
Ehrman, Bart D. 456, 482, 520
Elbogen, Ismar 175–76, 184–85
Elizur, Shulamit 176
Emerton, John A. 390
Emmrich, Martin 478, 495
Epstein, Jacob Nachum 178
Eriksson, Anders 382–83
Evans, Ernest 526–27
Farkasfalvy, Denis 523–24
Fee, Gordon D. 365, 402, 467
Ferguson, Everett 149–50
Feuillet, André 390, 523
Fine, Steven 144
Finkelstein, Louis 326, 373
Finnegan, Ruth 292, 324
Fitzmyer, Joseph A 166, 168–69, 257, 261, 468
Flament, Claude 541, 583
Fleischer, Ezra 176, 181
Flusser, David 6, 18, 23, 25, 27, 55, 65, 87, 89–90, 98, 150–53, 166, 202, 220, 267, 288, 323–24, 429, 432, 442, 443, 461, 481–82, 530, 533, 540, 558
Foley, John Miles 294–95, 298
Foster, Paul 379, 470, 497
France, Richard T. 151, 389, 392, 403
Frankemölle, Hubert 464
Friedmann, Me'ir 169

INDEX OF MODERN AUTHORS

Friedrich, Gerhard 461
Fuchs, M. Z. 176
Fuglseth, Kåre 463
Funk, Franz Xaver 379, 387
Furstenberg, Yair 161
Garland, David E. 394
Garleff, Gunnar 474, 536, 541
Garrow, Alan J. P. 5, 7, 12–13, 33, 36, 51, 57, 191, 220, 222, 273, 276, 288–89, 384, 402, 440–41, 461, 480, 497, 499, 501, 505–9, 512, 514, 517–19, 523, 534, 536
Gaston, Lloyd 522
Geerlings, Wilhelm 163
Giet, Stanislas 1, 37, 61, 159, 534
Ginzburg, Louis 328
Glasson, T. Francis 79, 363, 382, 389, 393
Glover, Richard 35, 288, 367, 388, 400, 470
Gnilka, Joachim 390
Goguel, Maurice 191
Goldberg, Abraham 178, 180
Goldberg, Arnold 144
Goldingay, John E 390–91
Goodacre, Mark 259, 457
Goodspeed, Edgar J. 65
Gordon, Robert P. 43
Goulder, Michael 253
Grant, Frederick C. 248
Gregory, Andrew F. 6–7, 9, 34, 123, 367, 459, 534,
Gundry, Robert H. 390, 472
Gurtner, Daniel M. 349, 552
Haar Romeny, Bas ter 350, 560
Haenchen, Ernst 415, 417–18
Hagner, Donald A. 368, 387, 463
Hakola, Raimo 18, 23
Hall, Stuart G. 125
Halliday, Michael 295
Harder, Kenneth J. 313
Harnack, Adolf von 2, 34, 59, 64, 81, 191, 372, 380, 387, 437, 529, 538–39, 560
Harrington, Daniel J. 147, 456, 560–61

Harrington, Hannah K. 146, 160–61
Harris, J. Rendel 2, 258, 265, 412
Haslam, S. Alexander 541
Hauspie, Katrin 569
Heinemann, Joseph 175, 327–28, 331
Henderson, Ian H. 37, 314, 321–23
Hengel, Martin 464, 531
Heusler, Andreas 481
Himmelfarb, Martha 144 146
Hoffmann, Paul 289
Hogg, Michael A. 26
Holmes, Michael W. 319, 366, 466
Holtzmann, Heinrich J. 248
Horbury, William 180, 185, 463–64
Horovitz, Haym S. 146, 178
Horsley, G. H. R. 463–64
Horsley, Richard A. 289, 295, 303
Horst, Pieter W. van der 184
Hunter, Archibald Macbride 257, 381, 383
Hurtado, Larry H. 365, 374, 376, 382, 384, 457
Hvalvik, Reidar 581
Iselin, Ludwig Emil 481
Iser, Wolfgang 294
Jackson-McCabe, Matt 124
Jaubert, Annie 172
Jefford, Clayton N. 2, 5, 7, 22, 47, 61, 67, 125, 128–29, 135, 139, 272, 282, 288, 429, 439, 440–41, 460, 482, 497, 512, 530
Jeremias, Joachim 169, 347, 389, 490
Jewett, Robert 467
Johnson, Luke Timothy 394, 478–79, 494–95
Johnson, Maxwell E. 162–63
Johnson, William 293
Johnsson, William G. 480
Jones, F. Stanley 272
Kalimi, Isaac 338
Käsemann, Ernst 383, 480, 490, 495
Kautzsch, E. 320
Kazen, Thomas 146
Keith, Chris 297
Kelber, Werner H. 63, 68, 136, 294

Kelhoffer, James A. 367, 371, 375, 470, 472
Kennedy, George 300
Khomych, Taras 12, 72–73, 460, 516, 518, 540
Kilmartin, Edward J. 76
Kim, Seyoon 402
Kimelman, Reuven 176, 184, 214
King, Karen L. 456–57
Kirby, Peter 249
Kirk, Alan 136
Kittel, Gerhard 565
Klauser, Theodor 149
Klawans, Jonathan 144, 150, 153–55, 210
Klein, Gunther 87, 539
Kleist, James A. 260
Klinghardt, Matthias 157, 531
Kloppenborg, John S. 7, 35, 38, 49, 65, 69, 288–89, 291–93, 396, 400, 411, 438, 440, 443, 448, 535
Knopf, Rudolf 367, 378
Koch, Dietrich-Alex 499
Kodjak, Andrej 347
Koester, Craig R. 479
Koester, Helmut 33, 40, 44, 69–70, 210, 219–20, 222, 289, 291, 354, 367–68, 371, 380, 387, 396, 398–399, 446, 449, 461–62, 464, 470, 472, 519–20, 534
Köhler, Wolf-Dietrich 258
Kollmann, Bernd 140
Kostenberger, Andreas 520
Kraft, Heinz 553
Kraft, Robert A. 35, 88, 110, 123, 148, 192, 258, 262, 266, 373, 456, 519, 534
Kruger, Michael 520
Kuhn, K. G. 383
Kuhn, Thomas S. 81
Kurek-Chomycz, Dominika A. 466
Kutscher, Edward Yechezkel 169
Lachs, Samuel Tobias 178
Lagarde, P. A. de 115
Lacocque, André 391, 567
Ladd, George Eldon 49
Lake, Kirsopp 28, 146, 262, 338, 346, 367, 470

Lampe, Geoffrey W. H. 78, 337, 342, 356, 568
Lane, William L. 389–90
Langer, Ruth 176
Langer, Jean 202
Lawrence, Jonathan D. 145–46
Layton, Bentley 35, 288, 304–5
Lee, Margaret Ellen 11, 290, 298–99, 301–2, 307
Lerner, Myron B. 152
Levinson, Bernard M. 338
Licht, Jacob 161
Liddell, H. G. 568
Lierman, John D. 347
Lietzmann, Hans 383
Lightfoot, Joseph B. 263
Lindemann, Andreas 459
Lips, Hermann von 368
Liubinskas, Susann 19
Lockett, Darian R. 156
Lohmeyer, Ernst 248, 257
Long, Thomas G. 479
Lord, Albert B. 313
Louw, Johannes P. 491
Lust, Johan 462
Luz, Ulrich 166, 168–71, 173–74, 176
MacDonald, Margaret Y. 86, 100
Mack, Burton L. 457
Macpherson, John 252
Magness, Jodi 161
Manson, Thomas Walter 389, 463
Manson, William 253
Marcovich, Miroslav 489
Markschies, Christoph 457
Mason, Steve 171, 463
Massaux, Edouard 39, 44, 257–58, 282, 288, 366, 368, 374–75, 377, 380, 387
Matera, Frank 456
Mathewson, Dave 478
Mazza, Enrico 76, 140, 473, 531
McGarty, Craig 26
McKenzie, John L. 63
McKnight, Scot 478, 492
Mees, Michael 35
Melamed, Ezra Zion 178

INDEX OF MODERN AUTHORS 629

Metzger, Bruce M. 290, 379
Michel, Otto 76, 485–487
Milavec, Aaron 5, 7, 9, 17–18, 22, 29–30, 35, 38, 44–45, 49, 64–66, 73, 76, 79, 82–83, 87, 89, 91, 98, 125–31, 135–36, 141, 162, 193–94, 291, 314–21, 323, 326, 336, 363–64, 366–70, 380, 384–85, 396–97, 401, 406, 418, 423, 444, 449, 460, 469, 471–74, 482, 507–8, 530, 540
Milgrom, Jacob 145
Miller, Merrill P. 457
Mirecki, Paul A. 272
Mitchell, Alan C. 478
Mitchell, Margaret 271, 323
Mitchell, Nathan 151
Moffatt, James 261, 479, 485
Moll, Helmut 158
Moore, Arthur L. 389
Moore, George Foot 31
Moreschini, Claudio 482
Morgenthaler, Robert 465
Morray-Jones, Christopher 538
Moule, Charles F. D. 381–83
Moxnes, Halvor 9, 85–86
Mueller, Joseph G. 10, 59, 125, 459, 572
Muilenburg, James 458
Muraoka, Takamitsu 462
Myllykoski, Matti 12, 515–16, 518, 522, 525
Neusner, Jacob 68, 78, 99, 155, 160, 179
Nida, Eugene A. 491
Niederwimmer, Kurt 2–3, 33–34, 37, 44–45, 60–61, 65, 71–72, 75, 79, 81, 97, 101, 126, 130–31, 135, 139, 157, 159, 166, 190, 192–94, 209, 214, 219, 221, 259, 286, 288, 296, 305, 318, 335, 364–67, 369, 371, 377, 379, 387, 396, 398, 429, 437, 439–40, 443–46, 449–50, 458–59, 469, 473–74, 482–83, 505, 507, 509, 530
Nikander, Perttu 11, 64, 136, 287, 311–15, 320, 322, 325, 414–17, 421, 535
Noam, Vered 183
Nolland, John 346, 349, 392, 394, 552

Nongbri, Brent 478
Norelli, Enrico 482
O'Loughlin, Thomas 6, 64, 88, 91, 530
O'Neill, John Cochrane 260
Ong, Walter J. 62, 311, 313
Osborne, Eric 525–26
Osiek, Carolyn 86, 100, 477
Pagels, Elaine 456–57
Painter, John 434
Pardee, Nancy 5, 8, 11, 125–26, 136, 311–12, 314, 322, 332, 417–18, 507, 509, 535,
Parker, David C. 89, 134, 289, 535
Parry, Milman 313, 320–21
Patterson, Stephen J. 272
Pelling, C. B. R. 291
Perkins, David W. 480
Perry, Alfred M. 351
Pesch, Rudolf 390
Peterson, Jeffrey 457
Philonenko, Marc 147
Pietersma, Albert 462
Poirier, John C. 145–46
Polanyi, Michael 81
Popkes, Wiard 156
Prigent, Pierre 88, 110, 523
Pritz, Ray A. 257
Rabin, I. A. 178
Radermacher, Ludwig 331
Regev, Eyal 145–46, 155
Reicher, Stephen 541
Reif, Stefan C. 176, 328–29
Repschinski, Boris 157
Richardson, Peter 88
Ridderbos, Herman N. 256
Roark, Dallas M. 390
Robertson, A. T. 331
Robinson, J. Armitage 288, 387, 458–59
Robinson, James M. 289, 519–20
Robinson, John A. T. 79, 363, 383, 389, 482
Rordorf, Willy 2, 34, 37, 61, 65–66, 90, 103, 139, 151, 157, 159, 162, 165, 191, 194, 288–89, 371, 444, 446, 452, 482–83

Rouwhorst, Gerard 458, 531
Rowe, C. Kavin 394, 456
Rowe, Galen O 299–300
Rowland, Christopher C 537–38
Sabourin, Leopold 391
Safrai, Shmuel 143, 152, 169, 177–78, 180
Safrai, Zeev 177
Sagi, Avi 347
Sanders, James A. 36, 57
Sandt, Huub van de 5–6, 10, 17–18, 21–25, 27, 31, 34–35, 41, 47, 49, 55, 65, 67, 87, 89–90, 95, 98, 139, 144, 147–48, 150–53, 155, 157, 159, 165–66, 179, 202, 219, 231, 233, 236–40, 266, 280, 288, 323–24, 335, 349–50, 368, 413, 415, 422, 425, 427, 432, 458, 460–61, 481–82, 512, 530–33, 535–36, 540, 554, 560, 562, 566, 571, 575–76, 578–79, 582–86, 588
Sarason, Richard S. 99
Saulnier, Stéphane 172
Schäfer, Peter 179, 184, 537
Schaff, Philip 2, 34, 372
Schiffman, Lawrence H. 145, 155, 161
Schlecht, Joseph 437
Schmidt, Carl 373
Schnackenburg, Rudolf 229
Schnelle, Udo 39, 456
Schoedel, William R. 491
Schöllgen, Georg 60–61, 64, 123, 158, 163, 529
Schremer, Adiel 185
Schröter, Jens 456, 472, 475
Schuckburgh, Evelyn S. 492
Schürer, Emil 143
Schüssler Fiorenza, Elisabeth 85–86
Schwartz, Joshua 174, 185
Schwartz, Seth 179
Schwemer, Anna Maria 464
Schwiebert, Jonathan 7, 10–11, 157, 189–91, 209–14, 216–27, 230–38, 240–43, 287, 314, 326, 330, 458, 473–75, 531
Scott, Bernard Brandon 11, 290, 298–99, 301–3, 307

Scott, James C. 9, 85, 89, 91, 581
Seeberg, Alfred 87, 539–40
Seeliger, Hans Reinhard 508
Segal, Alan F. 537
Seidel, Moshe 11, 335, 338–39
Shiner, Whitney 293
Shukster, Martin B. 88
Simon, Marcel 429, 434
Simoons, Frederick J. 76
Skarsaune, Oskar 124, 397
Skarsten, Roald 463
Skehan, Patrick W. 46
Smith, Dennis E. 531
Smith, Jonathan Z. 480
Smith, Murray J. 11, 363, 365–66, 370, 421–25
Snyman, Andreas H. 478
Spears, Russell 541
Spicq, Ceslas 463, 494
Stanton, Graham N. 464
Stemberger, Günter 180, 184
Stevenson, Kenneth W. 170
Stewart, Alistair C. 64, 158
Stewart-Sykes, Alistair 107, 155
Strack, Herman L. 98, 170–71, 372
Strecker, Georg 351, 456, 461
Streeter, Burnett H. 388, 400
Stuhlmacher, Peter 464, 466
Stuiber, Alfred 444, 446
Suggs, M. Jack 481, 483
Sweet, John 506
Swete, Henry B. 397
Syreeni, Kari 34, 439, 440, 446
Tajfel, Henri 541
Talmon, Shemaryahu 338–39
Taussig, Hal 531
Taylor, Charles 2, 87, 429, 437, 440
Taylor, Miriam 522
Taylor, Vincent 248–49, 410
Telfer, William 458
Thackeray, Henry St. John 397
Thatcher, Tom 556, 564
Thiselton, Anthony C. 382–83, 468
Thomas, Samuel I. 537
Tidwell, Neville L. A. 278

INDEX OF MODERN AUTHORS

Tomson, Peter J.   10, 24, 40, 87, 139, 166, 171–74, 179, 185, 187, 231, 240–41, 437, 533
Tönges, Elke   169
Tuckett, Christopher M.   6–7, 34–35, 38–39, 49, 66–67, 128, 258, 288–89, 291, 366, 375, 387–88, 400, 402, 425, 441, 448, 459, 471, 497, 534
Tuilier, André   2, 34, 37, 65, 103, 139, 151, 157, 159, 165, 191, 194, 371, 444, 446, 482–83
Tulloch, Janet H.   100
Turner, John C.   541
Turner, Nigel   464,
Turner, Victor   194, 212
Uro, Risto   18, 292
VanderKam, James C.   172
Vanni, Ugo   523
Varner, William   6, 9, 34–35, 37–39, 41–51, 53–57, 258–60, 266–69
Verheyden, Joseph   12, 49, 171, 280, 350, 448, 450
Verme, Marcello del   39, 47, 166, 442, 446–49, 460
Vermes, Geza   329
Vielhauer, Philipp   371
Vokes, Frederick E.   1, 387, 400, 459–60, 538
Vööbus, Arthur   75, 219, 259
Wainwright, Geoffrey   490, 586
Walker, Joan Hazelden   30,
Walker, William O., Jr.   260
Wallace, Daniel B.   377
Wanamaker, Charles A.   402
Warfield, Benjamin B.   429
Wehnert, Jürgen   432
Weidemann, Hans-Ulrich   162
Weinfeld, Moshe   346
Weizsäcker, Carl von   434
Welch, John W.   11, 46, 335, 341, 346, 349, 352, 419–21
Wengst, Klaus   45, 51, 60, 88, 140, 148, 157, 165, 213, 368, 379, 384, 387, 446
Werrett, Ian C.   148
Westcott, Brooke Foss   479, 485

Weyde, Karl William   338
Willetts, Ronald F.   247
Williams, Michael A.   457
Willitts, Joel   461, 470
Wire, Antoinette Clark   298
Witherington, Ben III   402
Wohlenberg, Gustav   34
Wright, Benjamin G.   462
Wright, Brian J.   48,
Wright, N. Thomas   389, 392, 394, 403, 405–6, 457
Young, Stephen E.   39, 366, 470
Zangenberg, Jürgen K.   6, 22–23, 335, 512, 536,
Zetterholm, Magnus   28, 461
Zohar, Zvi   347

CPSIA information can be obtained
at www.ICGtesting.com
Printed in the USA
FFOW03n1427220515
13597FF